Get the eBook FREE!

(PDF, ePub, Kindle, and liveBook all included)

We believe that once you buy a book from us, you should be able to read it in any format we have available. To get electronic versions of this book at no additional cost to you, purchase and then register this book at the Manning website.

Go to https://www.manning.com/freebook and follow the instructions to complete your pBook registration.

That's it!
Thanks from Manning!

Cloud Native Spring in Action

Cloud Native Spring in Action

WITH SPRING BOOT AND KUBERNETES

THOMAS VITALE
Foreword by JOSH LONG

MANNING

SHELTER ISLAND

For online information and ordering of this and other Manning books, please visit
www.manning.com. The publisher offers discounts on this book when ordered in quantity.
For more information, please contact

> Special Sales Department
> Manning Publications Co.
> 20 Baldwin Road
> PO Box 761
> Shelter Island, NY 11964
> Email: orders@manning.com

Manning Publications Co.
20 Baldwin Road
PO Box 761
Shelter Island, NY 11964

Development editor:	Jenny Stout
Technical development editor:	Nickie Buckner
Review editor:	Mihaela Batinić
Production editor:	Andy Marinkovich
Copy editor:	Andy Carroll
Proofreader:	Keri Hales
Technical proofreader:	Niek Palm
Typesetter:	Dennis Dalinnik
Cover designer:	Marija Tudor

ISBN: 9781617298424
Printed and bound by CPI Group (UK) Ltd, Croydon, CR0 4YY

To my sister, Alissa. The bravest person I know.

brief contents

contents

foreword

I've written dozens of forewords and prefaces over the years, but this might be the first time I've been annoyed having to write one. Why? I'm a sore loser! I am sore that I didn't write this book. I am sore because I wonder if I even *could* write it.

This book is *fantastic*. Its pages are brimming with valuable ideas couched in evident, profound experience. I have always wanted to see all these concepts put in one place, and I will be pointing people to this book for the foreseeable future.

Building production-worthy applications, where production is mostly Kubernetes these days, *and* building out production itself? That's a hefty lift, just like this book, which clocks in at more than 600 pages! But don't let my prattling about size dissuade you from buying this book. It's a big book for an even bigger topic.

This book covers the usual suspects: how to build services and microservices, how to handle persistence, messaging, instrumenting for observability, configuration, and security. In addition, there are whole chapters dedicated to some of these concepts.

Your Spring Boot application is the crowning jewel of this book's ambitions (a storefront system, 'natch), but it's by no means the only thing on which the book focuses. The book is as deep as it is broad in focus—a stunning achievement! I suppose I should list some specifics, so you can begin to appreciate just how nuanced this book's coverage is. Before I do, remember, you *must* read this book. The following list is by no means exhaustive, but it includes stuff that I found myself stunned to be reading about. It's stuff that should be in a book about Spring Boot and Spring Cloud but, unfortunately, rarely is.

- There's a fantastic treatment of logging with Loki, FluentBit, and Grafana.
- This book takes you well beyond just "up and running" in Kubernetes. By the end of the book, you'll be wielding Kubernetes Deployments with ease. You'll go serverless with Knative and Spring Cloud Function. Next, you'll build pipelines with tools like GitHub Actions, Kustomize, and Kubeval. Finally, you'll develop locally with tools like Tilt and Docker Compose.
- The discussion of security in the context of a single-page application (SPA) could be its own excellent book. It's competent, iterative, quick, and production minded. Do *not* miss this chapter.
- Everything is done with tests in mind. Spring's got complementary test modules for various projects, which are elegantly on display here.
- This book introduces GraalVM's native-image compiler and the Spring Native project. Spring Native is a relatively recent addition to the ecosystem, so nobody would blame Thomas for not including it. But he did. What a legend!
- Thomas introduces much of why we do the things described in this book, in line with the new technical concepts. I particularly enjoyed the treatment of Agile and GitOps.

Spring Boot has changed the world, and Thomas's book is the best map for this brave, "bootiful" new world. Buy it. Read it. Act on it. Build something amazing and enjoy your journey to production!

—Josh Long
Spring Developer Advocate
VMware Tanzu
@starbuxman

preface

I clearly remember the first time I went on a field trip to see how nurses and practitioners used the software developed by the company I work with in their daily jobs. Witnessing how our applications improved the way they take care of their patients was an incredible moment. Software can make a difference. That's why we build it. We solve problems through technology with the goal of delivering value to our users, our customers, and the business itself.

Another moment I can't forget was when I learned about Spring Boot. Until then, I enjoyed working with the core Spring Framework very much. I was particularly fond of the code I wrote to manage aspects like security, data persistence, HTTP communications, and integrations. It was a lot of hard work, but it was worth it, especially considering the alternatives at that time in the Java landscape. Spring Boot changed everything. Suddenly the platform itself was taking care of all those aspects for me. All the code that handled infrastructural concerns and integrations wasn't needed anymore.

But then it occurred to me: all the code that handled infrastructural concerns and integrations wasn't needed anymore! When I started deleting all that code, I realized how much time I had spent on it, compared to the business logic of the application, the part producing value. And I realized how little code was actually part of the business logic, compared to all the boilerplate code. It was a pivotal moment!

After many years, Spring Boot is still the leading platform for building enterprise-grade software products in the Java landscape, and one of the reasons for its popularity is its focus on developer productivity. What makes each application special is its business logic, not how it exposes its data or connects to a database. And it's that business logic that ultimately delivers value to users, customers, and businesses. Leveraging a broad ecosystem of frameworks, libraries, and integrations, Spring Boot enables developers to focus on the business logic while taking care of the plumbing and boilerplate code.

The cloud was another game-changer in our field, as well as Kubernetes, which quickly imposed itself as the "operating system" of the cloud. Leveraging the features of the cloud computing model, we can build cloud native applications and achieve better scalability, resilience, speed, and cost optimizations for our projects. Ultimately, we have an opportunity to increase the value we produce via our software and solve new types of problems in a way that was not possible before.

The idea for this book came from my wish to help software engineers in their journey to deliver value. I'm glad you decided to join me in this adventure from code to production. Spring Boot, and the Spring ecosystem in general, represent the backbone of such a journey. The cloud native principles and patterns will guide us through our implementation of various applications. The continuous delivery practices will support us in delivering high-quality software safely, quickly, and reliably. Kubernetes and its ecosystem will provide a platform for deploying and releasing our applications to their users.

When structuring and writing this book, my guiding principle was to provide relevant, real-world examples that you can immediately apply to your daily job. All the technologies and patterns covered in the book aim to deliver high-quality software in production, within the limits of what can be included in a book with limited space. I hope I succeeded in meeting that goal.

Thanks again for joining me on this cloud native journey from code to production. I wish you an enjoyable and educational experience reading this book, and I hope it will help you deliver more value with your software and make a difference.

acknowledgments

Writing a book is hard, and it wouldn't have been possible without the support of many people who helped me throughout the development process. First, I want to thank my family and friends who continuously encouraged me and supported me along the way. Special thanks to my parents Sabrina and Plinio, my sister Alissa, and my grandfather Antonio for their constant support and for believing in me.

I want to thank my friends and fellow engineers Filippo, Luciano, Luca, and Marco, who were there for me from the initial proposal and always available to provide feedback and advice to improve this book. I want to thank my coworkers and friends from Systematic, who encouraged me throughout this period. I feel lucky to work with you.

I want to thank Professor Giovanni Malnati from the Polytechnic University of Turin for introducing me to the Spring ecosystem in the first place and changing the course of my career. Big thanks to the Spring team for creating such a productive and valuable ecosystem. Special thanks to Josh Long for his incredible work that taught me so much and for writing the foreword to this book. It means a lot to me!

I want to thank the entire Manning team for their huge help in making this book a valuable resource. I especially want to thank Michael Stephens (acquisition editor), Susan Ethridge (development editor), Jennifer Stout (development editor), Nickie Buckner (technical development editor), and Niek Palm (technical proofreader). Their feedback, advice, and encouragement brought great value to this book. Thanks also go to Mihaela Batinić (review editor), Andy Marinkovich (production editor), Andy Carroll (copy editor), Keri Hales (proofreader), and Paul Wells (production manager).

To all the reviewers: Aaron Makin, Alexandros Dallas, Andres Sacco, Conor Redmond, Domingo Sebastian, Eddú Meléndez Gonzales, Fatih Mehmet Ucar, François-David Lessard, George Thomas, Gilberto Taccari, Gustavo Gomes, Harinath Kuntamukkala, Javid Asgarov, João Miguel, Pires Dias, John Guthrie, Kerry E. Koitzsch, Michał Rutka, Mladen Knežić, Mohamed Sanaulla, Najeeb Arif, Nathan B. Crocker, Neil Croll, Özay Duman, Raffaella Ventaglio, Sani Sudhakaran Subhadra, Simeon Leyzerzon, Steve Rogers, Tan Wee, Tony Sweets, Yogesh Shetty, and Zorodzayi Mukuya, your suggestions helped make this a better book.

Finally, I want to thank the Java community and all the fantastic people I met there over the years: open source contributors, fellow speakers, conference organizers, and everyone who contributes to making this community so special.

about this book

Cloud Native Spring in Action was written to help you design, build, and deploy cloud native applications using Spring Boot and Kubernetes. It defines a curated path to production and teaches effective techniques that you can immediately apply to enterprise-grade applications. It also takes you step by step from your first idea through to production, showing how cloud native development can add business value at every stage of the software development lifecycle. As you develop an online bookshop system, you'll learn how to build and test cloud native applications using the powerful libraries available in the Spring and Java ecosystems. Chapter by chapter, you'll work with REST APIs, data persistence, reactive programming, API gateways, functions, event-driven architectures, resilience, security, testing, and observability. The book then expands on how to package applications for the cloud as container images, how to configure deployments for cloud environments like Kubernetes, how to make your applications production-ready, and how to design your path from code to production using continuous delivery and continuous deployment.

This book provides a hands-on, project-driven guide to help you navigate the increasingly complex cloud landscape and learn how to bring patterns and technologies together to build a real cloud native system and bring it to production.

Who should read this book?

This book is aimed at developers and architects who want to learn more about designing, building, and deploying production-ready cloud native applications using Spring Boot and Kubernetes.

To get the most benefit from this book, you'll want to have established Java programming skills, experience building web applications, and basic knowledge of the Spring core features. I'll assume you're familiar with Git, object-oriented programming, distributed systems, databases, and testing. Experience with Docker and Kubernetes is not required.

How this book is organized: A road map

The book has 4 parts that cover 16 chapters. Part 1 sets the stage for your cloud native journey from code to production and helps you better understand the topics covered in the rest of the book and place them correctly in the overall cloud native picture.

- Chapter 1 is an introduction to the cloud native landscape. It defines what cloud native means, the fundamental properties of cloud native applications, and the processes supporting them.
- Chapter 2 covers the principles of cloud native development and guides you through a first hands-on experience building a minimal Spring Boot application and deploying that to Kubernetes as a container.

Part 2 introduces you to the main practices and patterns for building production-ready cloud native applications using Spring Boot and Kubernetes.

- Chapter 3 covers the fundamentals of starting a new cloud native project, including strategies for organizing the codebase, managing dependencies, and defining the commit stage of a deployment pipeline. You'll learn how to implement and test a REST API using Spring MVC and Spring Boot Test.
- Chapter 4 discusses the importance of externalized configuration and covers some options available for Spring Boot applications, including property files, environment variables, and configuration services with Spring Cloud Config.
- Chapter 5 presents the main aspects of data services in the cloud and shows you how to add data persistence to a Spring Boot application using Spring Data JDBC. You'll learn production options for managing data using Flyway and strategies for testing using Testcontainers.
- Chapter 6 is about containers; you'll learn more about Docker and how to package Spring Boot applications as container images using Dockerfiles and Cloud Native Buildpacks.
- Chapter 7 discusses Kubernetes and covers service discovery, load balancing, scalability, and local development workflows. You'll also learn more about how to deploy Spring Boot applications to a Kubernetes cluster.

Part 3 covers the fundamental properties and patterns of distributed systems in the cloud, including resilience, security, scalability, and API gateways. It also describes reactive programming and event-driven architectures.

- Chapter 8 introduces reactive programming and the main features of the Spring reactive stack, including Spring WebFlux and Spring Data R2DBC. It also teaches you how to make an application more resilient using Project Reactor.

- Chapter 9 covers the API gateway pattern and how to build edge services with Spring Cloud Gateway. You'll learn how to build resilient applications with Spring Cloud and Resilience4J, using patterns like retries, timeouts, fallbacks, circuit breakers, and rate limiters.
- Chapter 10 describes event-driven architectures and teaches you how to implement them with Spring Cloud Function, Spring Cloud Stream, and RabbitMQ.
- Chapter 11 is all about security and shows you how to implement authentication in a cloud native system using Spring Security, OAuth2, OpenID Connect, and Keycloak. It also describes how to address security concerns like CORS and CSRF when single-page applications are part of the system.
- Chapter 12 continues the security journey and covers how to use OAuth2 and Spring Security to delegate access within a distributed system, protect APIs and data, and authorize users based on their roles.

Part 4 guides you through the last few steps to make your cloud native applications production-ready, addressing concerns like observability, configuration management, secrets management, and deployment strategies. It also covers serverless and native images.

- Chapter 13 describes how to make your cloud native applications observable using Spring Boot Actuator, OpenTelemetry, and the Grafana observability stack. You'll learn how to configure Spring Boot applications to produce relevant telemetry data, such as logs, health, metrics, traces, and more.
- Chapter 14 covers advanced configuration and secrets management strategies, including Kubernetes-native options like ConfigMaps, Secrets, and Kustomize.
- Chapter 15 guides you through the final steps of your cloud native journey and teaches you how to configure Spring Boot for production. You'll then set up continuous deployment for your applications and deploy them to a Kubernetes cluster in the public cloud, adopting a GitOps strategy.
- Chapter 16 covers serverless architectures and functions with Spring Native and Spring Cloud Function. You'll also learn about Knative and its powerful features that provide a superior developer experience on top of Kubernetes.

In general, I recommend starting with chapter 1 and working through each chapter sequentially. If you prefer reading the chapters in a different order based on your particular interests, make sure you read chapters 1 through 3 first to better understand the terminology, patterns, and strategies used throughout the book. Even so, each chapter builds on the previous one, so some context might be missing if you decide to do that.

About the code

This book provides a hands-on and project-driven experience. Starting from chapter 2, you'll build a system composed of several cloud native applications for a fictitious online bookshop.

You can get executable snippets of code from the liveBook (online) version of this book at https://livebook.manning.com/book/cloud-native-spring-in-action. All the source code for the project developed throughout the book is available on GitHub and licensed under the Apache License 2.0 (https://github.com/ThomasVitale/cloud-native-spring-in-action). For each chapter, you'll find a "begin" and an "end" folder. Each chapter builds on the previous one, but you can always use the "begin" folder for a given chapter as a starting point, even if you haven't followed the previous chapters. The "end" folder contains the final result after completing the steps for that chapter, and you can compare it against your own solution. For example, you can find the source code for chapter 3 in the Chapter03 folder, which contains 03-begin and 03-end folders.

All the applications developed throughout the book are based on Java 17 and Spring Boot 2.7, and they are built with Gradle. The projects can be imported into any IDE with support for Java, Gradle, and Spring Boot, such as Visual Studio Code, IntelliJ IDEA, or Eclipse. You'll also need Docker installed. Chapter 2 and appendix A will provide more information to help you set up your local environment.

The examples have been tested on macOS, Ubuntu, and Windows. On Windows, I recommend using the Windows Subsystem for Linux to complete the deployment and configuration tasks described throughout the book. On macOS, if you use an Apple Silicon computer, you can run all the examples, but you might experience performance issues from some tools that don't provide native support for ARM64 architectures at the time of writing. The chapters will include additional contextual information when relevant.

The GitHub repository mentioned earlier (https://github.com/ThomasVitale/cloud-native-spring-in-action) contains all the source code for this book in the main branch. Besides that, I plan to maintain an sb-2-main branch, where I'll keep the source code up to date with future releases of Spring Boot 2.x, and an sb-3-main branch where I'll evolve the source code based on future releases of Spring Boot 3.x.

This book contains many examples of source code, both in numbered listings and inline with normal text. In both cases, source code is formatted in a fixed-width font like this to separate it from ordinary text. Sometimes code is also in bold to highlight code that has changed from previous steps in the chapter, such as when a new feature adds to an existing line of code.

In many cases, the original source code has been reformatted; we've added line breaks and reworked indentation to accommodate the available page space in the book. In rare cases, even this was not enough, and listings include line-continuation markers (➥). Additionally, comments in the source code have often been removed from the listings when the code is described in the text. Code annotations accompany many of the listings, highlighting important concepts.

liveBook discussion forum

Purchase of *Cloud Native Spring in Action* includes free access to liveBook, Manning's online reading platform. Using liveBook's exclusive discussion features, you can attach comments to the book globally or to specific sections or paragraphs. It's a snap to make notes for yourself, ask and answer technical questions, and receive help from the author and other users. To access the forum, go to https://livebook.manning.com /book/cloud-native-spring-in-action/discussion. You can also learn more about Manning's forums and the rules of conduct at https://livebook.manning.com/discussion.

Manning's commitment to our readers is to provide a venue where a meaningful dialogue between individual readers and between readers and the author can take place. It is not a commitment to any specific amount of participation on the part of the author, whose contribution to the forum remains voluntary (and unpaid). We suggest you try asking the author some challenging questions lest his interest stray! The forum and the archives of previous discussions will be accessible from the publisher's website as long as the book is in print.

Other online resources

You can find me online through Twitter (@vitalethomas), LinkedIn (www.linkedin .com/in/vitalethomas), or my blog at https://thomasvitale.com.

If you'd like to learn more about the Spring ecosystem, I maintain a list of educational resources with books, videos, podcasts, courses, and events at https://github .com/ThomasVitale/awesome-spring.

about the author

Thomas Vitale is a software engineer and architect specialized in building cloud native, resilient, and secure enterprise applications. He designs and develops software solutions at Systematic, Denmark, where he's been working on modernizing platforms and applications for the cloud native world, focusing on developer experience and security.

Some of his main interests and focus areas are Java, Spring Boot, Kubernetes, Knative, and cloud native technologies in general. Thomas supports continuous delivery practices and believes in a collaboration culture aimed at working together to deliver value to users, customers, and businesses. He likes contributing to open source projects like Spring Security and Spring Cloud, and sharing knowledge with the community.

Thomas has an MSc in Computer Engineering, specializing in software from the Polytechnic University of Turin (Italy). He is a CNCF Certified Kubernetes Application Developer, Pivotal Certified Spring Professional, and RedHat Certified Enterprise Application Developer. His speaking engagements include those for SpringOne, Spring I/O, KubeCon+CloudNativeCon, Devoxx, GOTO, JBCNConf, DevTalks, and J4K.

about the cover illustration

The figure on the cover of *Cloud Native Spring in Action* is captioned "Paisan Dequito," or "Peasant from Quito," taken from a collection by Jacques Grasset de Saint-Sauveur, published in 1797. Each illustration is finely drawn and colored by hand.

In those days, it was easy to identify where people lived and what their trade or station in life was just by their dress. Manning celebrates the inventiveness and initiative of the computer business with book covers based on the rich diversity of regional culture centuries ago, brought back to life by pictures from collections such as this one.

Part 1

Cloud native fundamentals

The cloud native landscape is so broad that getting started can be overwhelming. This part of the book will set the stage for your cloud native journey from code to production. Chapter 1 is a theoretical introduction to the cloud native landscape. It defines what cloud native means, the fundamental properties of cloud native applications, and the processes supporting them. In chapter 2, you'll learn about the principles of cloud native development and get a first hands-on experience building a minimal Spring Boot application and deploying it to Kubernetes as a container. All of that will help you better understand the topics covered in the rest of the book and place them correctly in the overall cloud native picture.

Introduction to cloud native

1

This chapter covers

- What the cloud and cloud computing model are
- The definition of cloud native
- Characteristics of cloud native applications
- Culture and practices supporting cloud native
- When and why you might consider the cloud native approach
- Topologies and architectures for cloud native applications

Cloud native applications are highly distributed systems that live in the cloud and are resilient to change. Systems are made up of several services that communicate through a network and are deployed in a dynamic environment where everything keeps changing.

Before diving into the technologies, it's fundamental to define what cloud native is. Like other buzzwords in our field (such as *agile*, *DevOps*, or *microservices*), *cloud native* is sometimes misunderstood and can be a source of confusion because it means different things to different people.

In this chapter, I'll provide you with the conceptual tools you'll need for the rest of the book. I'll start by defining what cloud native means and what it takes for an application to be identified as such. I'll explain the properties of cloud native applications, examine the characteristics of the cloud computing model, and discuss when and why you might want to move to the cloud. I'll also present some fundamental concepts of cloud native topologies and architectures. Figure 1.1 shows an overview of the different elements I'll cover in this chapter as I define and qualify cloud native systems. At the end of this chapter, you'll be ready to start your journey building cloud native applications with Spring and deploying them to Kubernetes.

What defines cloud native?

The cloud	Application properties		Practices
Cloud infrastructures IT infrastructure supporting cloud computing	**Scalability** Dynamically support increasing or decreasing workloads	**Loose coupling** Components have minimal knowledge of each other	**Automation** Reproducible, efficient, and reliable systems
Cloud computing On-demand network access to computing resources	**Resilience** Maintain level of service in face of adversity	**Manageability** Level of control from the outside: update, configure, deploy	**Continuous delivery** Better and faster software deliveries
Cloud services IaaS, CaaS, PaaS, FaaS, SaaS		**Observability** Knowledge about the internal state inferred from the outside	**DevOps** Culture of collaboration between different roles

Topologies	Goals		Architectures
Containers Lightweight and isolated computing contexts	**Speed** Faster and flexible delivery	**Resilience** Availability and stability	**Application services** Loosely coupled, stateless, independently deployable units
Orchestration Container scheduling, cluster management	**Scale** Elasticity and dynamic scaling	**Cost** Efficiency and cost optimization	**Data services** Databases, messaging systems, and other stateful components
Serverless Servers and backing services managed by the cloud platform			**Interactions** Communication between services, such as HTTP, RSocket, gRPC, messaging

Figure 1.1   Cloud native is an approach to application development aiming at leveraging cloud technologies.

1.1   *What is cloud native?*

On May 25, 2010, Paul Fremantle, a veteran of the cloud industry, wrote a post on his blog titled "Cloud Native."[1] He was among the first to use the term *cloud native*. At a

---

[1] P. Fremantle, "Cloud Native," *Paul Fremantle's Blog*, May 28, 2010, http://mng.bz/Vy1G.

time when concepts and technologies like microservices, Docker, DevOps, Kubernetes, and Spring Boot didn't yet exist, Fremantle discussed what it takes for "applications and middleware to work well in a cloud environment"—to be *cloud native*—with his team at WSO2.

The key concept explained by Fremantle is that cloud native applications should be specifically designed for the cloud and have properties that take advantage of the cloud environment and the cloud computing model. You can move a traditional application (designed to run *on the ground*) to the cloud, an approach commonly referred to as "lift and shift," but that doesn't make the application *native* to the cloud. Let's see what does.

1.1.1 The Three Ps of Cloud Native

What does it mean for applications to be designed specifically for the cloud? The Cloud Native Computing Foundation (CNCF) answers that question in its cloud native definition:[2]

> *Cloud native technologies empower organizations to build and run scalable applications in modern, dynamic environments such as public, private, and hybrid clouds. Containers, service meshes, microservices, immutable infrastructure, and declarative APIs exemplify this approach.*
>
> *These techniques enable loosely coupled systems that are resilient, manageable, and observable. Combined with robust automation, they allow engineers to make high-impact changes frequently and predictably with minimal toil.*

From this definition, I identify three points that I like to call *The Three Ps of Cloud Native*:

- *Platforms*—Cloud native applications run on platforms based on dynamic, distributed environments: the clouds (public, private, or hybrid).
- *Properties*—Cloud native applications are designed to be scalable, loosely coupled, resilient, manageable, and observable.
- *Practices*—Practices around cloud native applications—automation, continuous delivery, and DevOps—include robust automation combined with frequent and predictable changes.

What is the Cloud Native Computing Foundation?

The Cloud Native Computing Foundation (CNCF) is part of the Linux Foundation, and it "builds sustainable ecosystems and fosters communities to support the growth

---

[2] Cloud Native Computing Foundation, "CNCF Cloud Native Definition v1.0," http://mng.bz/de1w.

(continued)

and health of cloud native open-source software." The CNCF hosts many cloud native technologies and projects to enable cloud portability without vendor lock-in. If you want to discover the many projects addressing any cloud native aspect, I recommend checking out the CNCF Cloud Native Interactive Landscape.[a]

---

[a] Cloud Native Computing Foundation, "CNCF Cloud Native Interactive Landscape," https://landscape.cncf.io/.

In the following sections I'll examine those concepts further. However, I'd first like you to notice how the definition of cloud native is not tied to any specific implementation detail or technology. The CNCF mentions some in its definition, like containers and microservices, but they are just examples. One of the common misconceptions when starting a migration to the cloud is that you have to adopt a microservices architecture, build containers, and deploy them to Kubernetes. That is not true. Fremantle's post in 2010 is proof of that. He didn't mention any of those because they didn't exist. Yet, the applications he described not only are still considered cloud native, but they also comply with the definition given by the CNCF eight years later.

1.2   *The cloud and the cloud computing model*

Before focusing on the main characters, the cloud native applications, I'd like to set the scene by describing the context in which cloud native applications run: the *cloud* (figure 1.2). In this section, I'll define the cloud and its main characteristics. After all, if cloud native applications are designed to work well in a cloud environment, we should know what kind of environment that is.

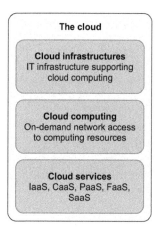

Figure 1.2   **The cloud is an IT infrastructure characterized by different computing models and offered as a service by providers according to the degree of control consumers need.**

The cloud is an IT infrastructure that supports the delivery of computing resources to consumers according to the cloud computing model. The National Institute of Standards and Technology (NIST) defines cloud computing as follows:[3]

> *Cloud computing is a model for enabling ubiquitous, convenient, on-demand network access to a shared pool of configurable computing resources (e.g., networks, servers, storage, applications, and services) that can be rapidly provisioned and released with minimal management effort or service provider interaction.*

Just like you get electricity from a provider rather than generating it on your own, with the cloud you can get computing resources (such as servers, storage, and networks) as a commodity.

The cloud provider manages the underlying cloud infrastructure, so the consumer doesn't need to worry about physical resources like machines or networks. Companies moving to the cloud can get all the computing resources they need via a network (usually the internet) through a set of APIs that allows them to provision and scale resources as they need on an on-demand, self-service basis.

Elasticity is one of the main characteristics of this model: computing resources can be provisioned and released dynamically, depending on the demand.

> *Elasticity is the degree to which a system is able to adapt to workload changes by provisioning and de-provisioning resources in an autonomic manner, such that at each point in time the available resources match the current demand as closely as possible.[4]*

Traditional IT infrastructures weren't able to provide elasticity. Companies had to calculate the maximum computing capabilities needed and set up an infrastructure that would support that, even if most of it was only required sometimes. With the cloud computing model, the usage of computing resources is monitored, and consumers only pay for what they actually use.

There is no strict requirement about where the cloud infrastructure should be or who should manage it. There are several deployment models for delivering cloud services. The main ones are private cloud, public cloud, and hybrid cloud.

- *Private cloud*—Cloud infrastructure provisioned to be used by a single organization. It can be managed by the organization itself or by a third party, and it can be hosted on premises or externally. A private cloud is usually the preferred option for organizations dealing with sensitive data or highly critical systems. It is also a common choice for having complete control over the infrastructure's compliance with specific laws and requirements like the General Data Protection Regulation (GDPR) or the California Consumer Privacy Act (CCPA). For

---

[3] NIST, "The NIST Definition of Cloud Computing," SP 800-145, September 2011, http://mng.bz/rnWy.

[4] N.R. Herbst, S. Kounev, and R. Reussner, "Elasticity in Cloud Computing: What it is, and What it is Not," in *Proceedings of the 10th International Conference on Autonomic Computing (ICAC 2013)*, http://mng.bz/BZm2.

example, banks and healthcare providers are likely to set up their own cloud infrastructure.

- *Public cloud*—Cloud infrastructure provisioned for public use. It is usually owned and managed by an organization, the *cloud provider*, and is hosted on the provider's premises. Examples of public cloud service providers are Amazon Web Services (AWS), Microsoft Azure, Google Cloud, Alibaba Cloud, and DigitalOcean.
- *Hybrid cloud*—Composition of two or more distinct cloud infrastructures belonging to any of the previous types, bound together and offering services as if they were one single environment.

Figure 1.3 describes the five leading cloud computing service models, what is provided by the platform in each model, and which abstractions are provided to the consumer. For example, with the Infrastructure as a Service (IaaS) model, the platform provides and manages computing, storage, and networking resources, whereas the consumer provisions and manages virtual machines. The decision about which service model to choose should be driven by the degree of control the consumer needs over the infrastructure and which type of computing resources they need to manage.

Cloud computing service models

Infrastructure platform	Container platform	Application platform	Serverless platform	Software platform
IaaS	CaaS	PaaS	FaaS	SaaS
Platform: provides computing, storage, and networking resources	**Platform:** provides container engine, orchestrator, and underlying infrastructure	**Platform:** provides development and deployment tools, APIs, and underlying infrastructure	**Platform:** provides the runtime, the whole infrastructure needed to run functions, and autoscaling	**Platform:** provides both the software and the whole infrastructure needed to run it
Consumer: provisions, configures, and manages servers, network, and storage	**Consumer:** builds, deploys, and manages containerized workloads and clusters	**Consumer:** builds, deploys, and manages applications	**Consumer:** builds and deploys functions	**Consumer:** consumes a service via a network

Figure 1.3   The cloud computing service models differ by the level of abstraction they provide and who is responsible for managing which levels (the platform or the consumer).

1.2.1   Infrastructure as a Service (IaaS)

In the *Infrastructure as a Service* (IaaS) model, consumers can directly control and provision resources like servers, storage, and networks. For example, they can provision virtual machines and install software like operating systems and libraries. Even though this model has been used for a while, it was in 2006 that Amazon made it popular and widely accessible with Amazon Web Services (AWS). Examples of IaaS offerings are AWS Elastic Compute Cloud (EC2), Azure Virtual Machines, Google Compute Engine, Alibaba Virtual Machines, and DigitalOcean Droplets.

1.2.2 Container as a Service (CaaS)

Using the *Container as a Service* (CaaS) model, consumers cannot control primitive virtualization resources. Instead, they provision and manage containers. The cloud provider takes care of provisioning the underlying resources that fulfill the needs of those containers, such as by starting new virtual machines and configuring networks to make them accessible through the internet. Docker Swarm, Apache Mesos, and Kubernetes are examples of tools used to build container platforms. All major cloud providers offer a managed Kubernetes service, which has become the de facto technology for CaaS offerings: Amazon Elastic Kubernetes Service (EKS), Azure Kubernetes Service (AKS), Google Kubernetes Engine (GKE), Alibaba Container Service for Kubernetes (ACK), and DigitalOcean Kubernetes.

1.2.3 Platform as a Service (PaaS)

In the *Platform as a Service* (PaaS) model, the platform provides infrastructure, tools, and APIs that developers can use to build and deploy applications. For example, as a developer, you can build a Java application, package it as a Java Archive (JAR) file, and then deploy it to a platform working according to the PaaS model. The platform provides the Java runtime and other required middleware, and it can also offer extra services like databases or messaging systems. Examples of PaaS offerings are Cloud Foundry, Heroku, AWS Elastic Beanstalk, Azure App Service, Google App Engine, Alibaba Web App Service, and DigitalOcean App Platform. In the past few years, vendors have been converging on Kubernetes for building a new PaaS experience for developers and operators. Examples of this new generation of services are VMware Tanzu Application Platform and RedHat OpenShift.

1.2.4 Function as a Service (FaaS)

The *Function as a Service* (FaaS) model relies on serverless computing to let consumers focus on implementing the business logic of their applications (often in the form of functions), whereas the platform takes care of providing servers and the rest of the infrastructure. Serverless applications are triggered by events, such as HTTP requests or messages. For example, you might code a function that analyzes a data set whenever available from a message queue and computes results according to some algorithms. Examples of commercial FaaS offerings are Amazon AWS Lambda, Microsoft Azure Functions, Google Cloud Functions, and Alibaba Functions Compute. Examples of open source FaaS offerings are Knative and Apache OpenWhisk.

1.2.5 Software as a Service (SaaS)

The service with the highest abstraction is *Software as a Service* (SaaS). In this model, consumers access applications as users, while the cloud provider manages the whole stack of software and infrastructure. Many companies build their applications, use a CaaS or PaaS model to run them, and then sell their usage to the end customers as SaaS. The consumers of SaaS applications typically use thin clients like web browsers or mobile devices to access them. Examples of applications available as SaaS are Proton Mail, GitHub, Plausible Analytics, and Microsoft Office 365.

> ### Platform vs. PaaS
> *Platform* is a term that might generate some confusion in a cloud native discussion, so let's clarify. In general, a platform is an operating environment you use to run and manage your applications. Google Kubernetes Engine (GKE) is a platform that offers cloud services according to the CaaS model. Microsoft Azure Functions is a platform that provides cloud services following the FaaS model. At a lower level, if you deploy your applications directly on an Ubuntu machine, that will be your platform. In the rest of the book, whenever I use the term *platform*, I mean the broader concept just explained, unless specified otherwise.

1.3   *Properties of cloud native applications*

The scene is set: you are in the cloud. How should you design applications to take advantage of its characteristics?

The CNCF identifies five main properties that cloud native applications should have: scalability, loose coupling, resilience, observability, and manageability. Cloud native is a methodology for building and running applications that exhibit those properties. Cornelia Davis sums it up by stating that "cloud-native software is defined by how you compute, not about where you compute."[5] In other words, the cloud is about *where*, and cloud native is about *how*.

I have already covered the *where* part: the cloud. Let's go ahead and explore the *how*. For a quick reference, figure 1.4 lists the properties with short descriptions.

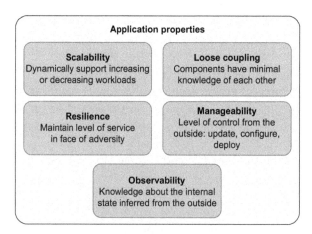

Figure 1.4   The main properties of cloud native applications

---

[5] C. Davis, "Realizing Software Reliability in the Face of Infrastructure Instability," in *IEEE Cloud Computing* 4, 5, pp. 34-40, September/October 2017.

1.3.1   Scalability

Cloud native applications are designed to *scale*, meaning that they can support increasing workloads if provided with additional resources. Depending on the nature of those extra resources, we can distinguish between vertical scalability and horizontal scalability:

- *Vertical scalability*—Scaling vertically, or scaling up or down, means adding hardware resources to or removing them from the computing node, such as CPU or memory. This approach is limited, since it's not possible to keep adding hardware resources. On the other hand, applications don't need to be explicitly designed to be scaled up or down.
- *Horizontal scalability*—Scaling horizontally, or scaling out or in, means adding more computing nodes or containers to, or removing them from, the system. This approach doesn't have the same limits as vertical scalability, but it requires applications to be scalable.

Traditional systems would usually adopt vertical scalability in the event of increasing workloads. Adding CPU and memory was a common approach to enable an application to support more users without redesigning it for scalability. This is still a good option in specific scenarios, but we need something else for the cloud.

In the cloud, where everything is dynamic and in constant change, horizontal scalability is preferred. Thanks to the abstraction levels offered by the cloud computing models, it's straightforward to spin up new instances of your application rather than increasing the computational power of the machines already running. Since the cloud is elastic, we can scale application instances in and out quickly and dynamically. I discussed elasticity as one of the main characteristics of the cloud: computing resources can be provisioned and released proactively, depending on the demand. Scalability is a prerequisite for elasticity.

Figure 1.5 shows the difference between vertical and horizontal scalability. In the first case, we scale by adding more resources to the existing virtual machine. In the second case, we add another virtual machine to help the existing one process the extra workload.

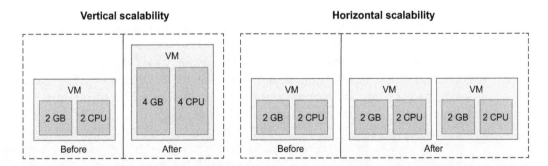

Figure 1.5   When you need to support increasing workloads, the vertical scalability model will add hardware resources to the computing node, while the horizontal scalability model will add more computing nodes.

As you'll see when we discuss Kubernetes, the platform (whether CaaS, PaaS, or something else) takes care of scaling applications in and out dynamically. As developers, it's our responsibility to design applications that can be scaled. The big obstacle to scalability is application state, which essentially is a matter of whether an application is stateful or stateless. Throughout the book, I'll cover techniques for building stateless applications and enabling them to scale without issues. Among other things, I'll show you how to push the application state from Spring to data stores like PostgreSQL and Redis.

1.3.2   Loose coupling

Loose coupling is an essential property of a system where parts have as little knowledge of each other as possible. The goal is to evolve each piece independently so that when one is changed, the others don't need to change accordingly.

Coupling, and its twin concept *cohesion*, have played an essential role in software engineering for decades. It's a good design practice to decompose a system into modules (*modularization*), each of which has minimal dependencies on the other parts (loose coupling) and to encapsulate code that changes together (high cohesion). Depending on the architectural style, a module can model a monolithic component or a standalone service (for example, a microservice). Either way, we should aim at achieving proper modularization with loose coupling and high cohesion.

Parnas identified three benefits of modularization:[6]

- *Managerial*—Since each module is loosely coupled, the team responsible for it should not need to spend much time coordinating and communicating with other teams.
- *Product flexibility*—The overall system should be flexible since each module is evolved independently of the others.
- *Comprehensibility*—People should be able to understand and work with a module without having to study the whole system.

The preceding benefits are usually among those associated with microservices, but the truth is that you don't need microservices to achieve them. In the last few years, many organizations have decided to migrate from monoliths to microservices. Some of them have failed because they lacked proper modularization. A monolith made up of tightly coupled, non-cohesive components, when migrated, produces a tightly coupled, non-cohesive microservice system, which sometimes is referred to as a *distributed monolith.* I don't consider this a good name because it implies that monoliths are made up of tightly coupled, non-cohesive components by definition. That's not true. The architectural style doesn't matter: a bad design is a bad design. Indeed, I like the *modular monolith* term proposed by Simon Brown to increase awareness that monoliths can

---

[6] D.L. Parnas, "On the criteria to be used in decomposing systems into modules," *Communications of the ACM* 15, 12 (December 1972), 1053–1058, http://mng.bz/gwOl.

promote loose coupling and high cohesion, and that both monoliths and microservices can end up being "big balls of mud."

Throughout the book, I'll discuss some techniques for enforcing loose coupling in applications. In particular, we'll adopt a service-based architecture and focus on building services with clear interfaces to communicate with each other, minimal dependencies on other services, and high cohesion.

1.3.3 Resilience

A system is resilient if it provides its services even in the presence of faults or environmental changes. Resilience is "the capability of a hardware-software network to provide and maintain an acceptable level of service in the face of faults and challenges to normal operation."[7]

When building cloud native systems, our goal should be to guarantee that our applications are always available, whether there is a failure in the infrastructure or in our software. Cloud native applications run in a dynamic environment where everything keeps changing, and faults can and will occur. This cannot be prevented. In the past, we used to consider changes and faults as exceptions, but for highly distributed systems like cloud native ones, changes are not exceptions: they are the rule.

When discussing resilience, it's worth defining three essential concepts: fault, error, and failure:[8]

- *Fault*—A fault is a defect that produces an incorrect internal state either in the software or the infrastructure. For example, a method call returns a null value, even if its specification mandates that a non-null value is returned.
- *Error*—An error is a discrepancy between the expected behavior of a system and the actual one. For example, due to the preceding fault, a `NullPointerException` is thrown.
- *Failure*—When a fault is triggered and results in an error, a failure might occur, making the system unresponsive and unable to behave according to its specifications. For example, if the `NullPointerException` is not caught, the error provokes a failure: the system responds to any request with a 500 response.

Faults can become errors, which may provoke failures, so we should design applications to be *fault tolerant*. An essential part of resilience is ensuring that a failure will not cascade to other components of the system but stay isolated while it gets fixed. We also want the system to be *self-repairing* or *self-healing*, and the cloud model can enable that.

Throughout the book, I'll show you some techniques for tolerating faults and preventing their effects from propagating to other parts of the system and spreading the failure. For example, we'll use patterns like circuit breakers, retries, timeouts, and rate limiters.

---

[7] J.E. Blyler, "Heuristics for resilience—A richer metric than reliability," *2016 IEEE International Symposium on Systems Engineering (ISSE)*, 2016, pp. 1–4.

[8] A. Avižienis, J. Laprie, and B. Randell, "Fundamental Concepts of Dependability," 2001, http://mng.bz/e7ez.

1.3.4   *Observability*

Observability is a property that comes from the world of control theory. If you consider a system, observability is a measure of how well you can infer its internal state from its external outputs. In the software engineering context, the system is a single application or a distributed system as a whole. The external outputs can be data like metrics, logs, and traces. Figure 1.6 shows how observability works.

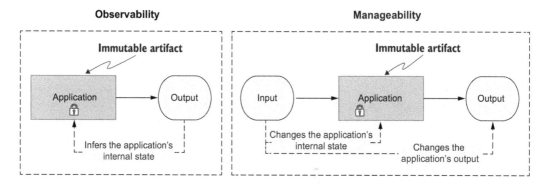

Figure 1.6   Observability is about inferring the internal state of an application from its external outputs. Manageability is about changing the internal state and outputs via external inputs. In both cases, the application artifact is never changed. It's immutable.

The Observability Engineering team at Twitter identifies four pillars of observability:[9]

- *Monitoring*—Monitoring is about measuring specific aspects of an application to get information on its overall health and identify failures. In this book, you'll learn about the useful monitoring features of Spring Boot Actuator and integrate Prometheus with Spring to export relevant metrics about an application.
- *Alerting/visualization*—Collecting data about the state of a system is useful only if it's used to take some action. When a failure is identified while monitoring an application, an alert should be triggered, and some action should be taken to handle it. Specific dashboards are used to visualize the data collected and plot them in relevant graphs to provide a good picture of the system's behavior. This book will show how to use Grafana to visualize data collected from cloud native applications.
- *Distributed systems tracing infrastructure*—In a distributed system, it's not enough to track every single subsystem's behavior. It's essential to trace the data flowing through the different subsystems. In this book, you'll integrate Spring with OpenTelemetry and use Grafana Tempo to collect and visualize the traces.

---

[9] A. Asta, "Observability at Twitter: technical overview, part 1," March 18, 2016, http://mng.bz/pO8G.

- *Log aggregation/analytics*—Keeping track of the main events in an application is critical to infer the software's behavior and debug it if something goes wrong. In a cloud native system, logs should be aggregated and collected to provide a better picture of the system's behavior and ensure the possibility of running analytics to mine information from that data. Throughout the book, I'll talk more about logs. You'll use Fluent Bit, Loki, and Grafana to collect and visualize logs, and you'll learn the best practices for logging in a cloud native context.

1.3.5   Manageability

In control theory, the counterpart of observability is controllability—the ability of external input to change the state or the output of a system in a finite time interval. This concept leads us to the last of the main properties of cloud native: manageability.

Drawing from control theory again, we can say that manageability measures how easily and efficiently an external input can change the state or the output of a system. In less mathematical terms, it's the ability to modify an application's behavior without needing to change its code. This is not to be confused with *maintainability*, which measures how easily and efficiently you can change a system from the inside by changing its code. Figure 1.6 shows how manageability works.

One aspect of manageability is deploying and updating applications while keeping the overall system up and running. Another element is configuration, which I'll address in depth throughout the book. We want to make cloud native applications configurable so we can modify their behavior without changing their code and building a new release. It's common to make configurable settings like data source URLs, service credentials, and certificates. For example, depending on the environment, you may use different data sources: one for development, one for testing, and one for production. Other types of configuration could be feature flags, which determine whether specific features should be enabled at runtime. I'll show you different strategies for configuring applications throughout the book, including using Spring Cloud Config Server, Kubernetes ConfigMaps and Secrets, and Kustomize.

Manageability is not only about particular changes themselves, but also about how easily and efficiently you can apply those changes. Cloud native systems are complex, so it's essential to design applications that can adapt to changing requirements regarding functionality, the environment, and security. Due to this complexity, we should aim at managing as much as possible through automation, which leads us to the last of the Three Ps of Cloud Native: practices.

1.4   Culture and practices supporting cloud native

This section will focus on the last sentence of the definition of cloud native technologies provided by the CNCF: "Combined with robust automation, they allow engineers to make high-impact changes frequently and predictably with minimal toil." I'll discuss three concepts: automation, continuous delivery, and DevOps (figure 1.7).

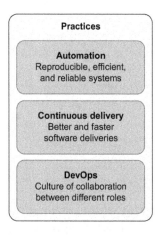

Figure 1.7   Culture and practices
for cloud native development

1.4.1 Automation

Automation is a core tenet of cloud native. The idea is to automate repetitive manual tasks to accelerate the delivery and deployment of cloud native applications. Many tasks can be automated, from building applications to deploying them, from provisioning infrastructure to managing configuration. The most important advantage of automation is that it makes processes and tasks repeatable and overall systems more stable and reliable. Manually executing a task is error-prone and costs money. By automating it, we can get a result that is both more reliable and more efficient.

In the cloud computing model, computing resources are provisioned in an automated, self-service model, and they can be increased or decreased elastically. Two significant categories of automation for the cloud are infrastructure provisioning and configuration management. We call them *infrastructure as code* and *configuration as code.*

Martin Fowler defines *infrastructure as code* as "the approach to defining computing and network infrastructure through source code that can then be treated just like any software system."[10]

Cloud providers offer convenient APIs for creating and provisioning servers, networks, and storage. By automating those tasks with a tool like Terraform, putting the code in source control, and applying the same test and delivery practices used for application development, we get a more reliable and predictable infrastructure, which is reproducible, more efficient, and less risky. A simple example of an automated task could be creating a new virtual machine with 8 CPUs, 64 GB of memory, and Ubuntu 22.04 as the operating system.

After we've provisioned computing resources, we can manage them and automate their configuration. Paraphrasing the previous definition, *configuration as code* is the approach to defining the configuration of computing resources through source code, which can be treated just like any software system.

---

[10] M. Fowler, "Infrastructure As Code," March 1, 2016, http://mng.bz/DD4.

Using tools like Ansible, we can specify how a server or a network should be configured. For example, after provisioning the Ubuntu server from the previous paragraph, we can automate the task of installing the Java Runtime Environment (JRE) 17 and opening the ports 8080 and 8443 from the firewall. Configuration as code applies to application configuration as well.

By automating all the infrastructure provisioning and configuration management tasks, we can avoid unstable, unreliable *snowflake servers*. When each server is provisioned, managed, and configured manually, the result is a *snowflake*: a fragile, unique server that cannot be reproduced and is risky to change. Automation helps avoid snowflakes in favor of *phoenix servers*: all tasks acting on those servers are automated, every change can be tracked in source control, reducing risks, and each setup is reproducible. By taking this concept to its extreme, we achieve the so-called *immutable servers*, also mentioned by the CNCF in its cloud native definition as immutable infrastructure.

> **NOTE** You might have heard the expression "pets vs. cattle" when comparing traditional snowflake infrastructure (requiring a lot of care and attention, like pets) and immutable infrastructure or containers (characterized by being disposable and replaceable, like cattle). I won't use this expression in the book, but it's sometimes used in discussions about this subject, so you should be aware of it.

After their initial provisioning and configuration, immutable servers are not changed: they are immutable. If any change is necessary, it's defined as code and delivered. A new server is then provisioned and configured from the new code while the previous server is destroyed.

For example, you have two options if your current infrastructure consists of Ubuntu 20.04 servers and you want to upgrade to Ubuntu 22.04. The first option is to define the upgrade via code and run the automation scripts to perform the operation on the existing machines (phoenix servers). The second option is to automate the provisioning of new machines running Ubuntu 22.04 and start using those (immutable servers), rather than performing the upgrade on existing machines.

In the next section, I'll talk about automation for building and deploying applications.

1.4.2 *Continuous delivery*

Continuous delivery is "a software development discipline where you build software in such a way that the software can be released to production at any time."[11] With continuous delivery, teams implement features in short cycles, ensuring that the software can be released at any time reliably. Such a discipline is key to "make high-impact changes frequently and predictably with minimal toil," as per the cloud native definition from the CNCF.

---

[11] M. Fowler, "Continuous Delivery," May 30, 2013, http://mng.bz/lRWo.

Continuous integration (CI) is a foundational practice in continuous delivery. Developers commit their changes to the mainline (the main branch) continuously (at least once a day). At each commit, the software is automatically compiled, tested, and packaged as executable artifacts (such as JAR files or container images). The idea is to get fast feedback about the software's status after each new change. If an error is detected, it should be immediately fixed to ensure the mainline keeps being a stable foundation for further development.

Continuous delivery (CD) builds on CI and focuses on keeping the mainline always healthy and in a releasable state. After an executable artifact is produced as part of the integration with the mainline, the software is deployed to a production-like environment. It goes through additional tests to assess its *releasability*, such as user acceptance tests, performance tests, security tests, compliance tests, and any other tests that might increase the confidence that the software can be released. If the mainline is always in a releasable state, releasing a new version of the software becomes a business decision instead of a technical one.

Continuous delivery encourages the automation of the whole process via a *deployment pipeline* (also called a *continuous delivery pipeline*), as described in the foundational book *Continuous Delivery* by Jez Humble and David Farley (Addison-Wesley Professional, 2010). A deployment pipeline goes from code commit to a releasable outcome, and it's the only way to production. Throughout the book, we'll build a deployment pipeline to keep the main branch of our applications always in a releasable state. In the end, we'll use it to deploy applications automatically to a Kubernetes cluster in production.

Sometimes continuous delivery is confused with *continuous deployment*. The former approach makes sure that after every change, the software is in a state in which it can be deployed to production. When that's actually done is a business decision. With continuous deployment we add one last step to the deployment pipeline to automatically deploy a new release in production after every change.

Continuous delivery is not about tools. It's a discipline that involves cultural and structural changes in your organization. Setting up an automated pipeline to test and deliver your applications doesn't mean that you're doing continuous delivery. Similarly, using a CI server to automate builds doesn't mean you're doing continuous integration.[12] That leads us to the next topic, which is also commonly mistaken as being about tools.

---

[12] M. Fowler, "Continuous Integration Certification," January 18, 2017, http://mng.bz/xM4X.

> ## Continuous delivery vs. CI/CD
>
> Since continuous integration is a foundational practice of continuous delivery, the combination is often referred to as CI/CD. As a consequence, deployment pipelines are often called CI/CD pipelines. I have some reservations about the term, because continuous integration is not the only practice included in the continuous delivery discipline. For example, test-driven development (TDD), automated configuration management, acceptance testing, and continuous learning are equally important.
>
> The *CI/CD* term is not used by Jez Humble and Dave Farley in their *Continuous Delivery* book, nor in any other book they have written on the subject. Also, it can be confusing. Does *CD* stand for *continuous delivery* or *continuous deployment*? In this book, I will refer to the holistic approach of delivering "better software faster"[a] as *continuous delivery* rather than CI/CD.
>
> ──────────────
>
> [a] D. Farley, *Continuous Delivery Pipelines*, 2021.

1.4.3 DevOps

DevOps is another of those buzzwords that are pretty popular these days but too often misunderstood. When shifting to cloud native, DevOps is an important concept to grasp.

The origins of DevOps are peculiar. One of the curious aspects is that the creators of this concept didn't initially provide a definition. The result was that several people used their own interpretations and, of course, we ended up using DevOps to mean different things.

> **NOTE** If you're interested in knowing more about the origins of DevOps, I suggest watching the Ken Mugrage talks available on YouTube: "DevOps and DevOpsDays—Where it started, where it is, where it's going" (http://mng.bz/Ooln).

Among all the definitions of DevOps, I find the one proposed by Ken Mugrage (principal technologist at ThoughtWorks) to be particularly informative and interesting. He highlights what I believe is the true meaning of DevOps.

> *A culture where people, regardless of title or background, work together to imagine, develop, deploy, and operate a system.*[13]

So DevOps is a culture, and it's all about working together toward a common goal. Developers, testers, operators, security experts, and other people, regardless of title or background, work together to bring ideas to production and produce value.

It means the end of *silos*—no more walls between feature teams, QA teams, and operations teams. DevOps is often considered a natural continuation of agile, which is

──────────────

[13] K. Mugrage, "My definition of DevOps," December 8, 2020, http://mng.bz/AVox.

an enabler for DevOps with the concept of small teams delivering value to customers frequently. A concise way to describe DevOps is with a famous sentence that Werner Vogels, Amazon CTO, pronounced in 2006 when DevOps was not even a thing yet: "You build it, you run it."[14]

Having defined what DevOps is, I'll briefly mention what it isn't:

- *DevOps doesn't mean NoOps.* It's a common mistake to think that developers take care of operations and that the operator's role disappears. Instead, it's a collaboration. A team will include both roles, contributing to the overall team's skills required to bring a product from the original idea to production.
- *DevOps is not a tool.* Tools like Docker, Ansible, Kubernetes, and Prometheus are usually referred to as DevOps tools, but that's wrong. DevOps is a culture. You don't turn into a DevOps organization by using particular tools. In other words, DevOps is not a product, but tools are relevant enablers.
- *DevOps is not automation.* Even if automation is an essential part of DevOps, automation is not its definition. DevOps is about developers and operators working together from the original idea to production while possibly automating some of their processes, such as continuous delivery.
- *DevOps is not a role.* If we consider DevOps to be a culture or a mindset, it's hard to make sense of a DevOps role. And yet, there is an increasing request for DevOps engineers. Usually when recruiters search for DevOps engineers, they are looking for skills like proficiency with automation tools, scripting, and IT systems.
- *DevOps is not a team.* Organizations not fully understanding the preceding points risk keeping the same silos as before, with one change: replacing the Ops silo with a DevOps silo, or, even worse, simply adding a new DevOps silo.

The collaboration between developers and operators is paramount when going cloud native. As you may have noticed, designing and building cloud native applications requires that you always keep in mind where you're going to deploy those applications: the cloud. Working together with operators allows developers to design and build higher-quality products.

It's called DevOps, but remember that the definition doesn't apply only to developers and operators. Instead, it generically refers to people, regardless of title or background. It means that collaboration also involves other roles like testers and security experts (though we probably don't need new terms like DevSecOps, DevTestOps, DevSecTestOps, or DevBizSecTestOps). Together they are all responsible for the entire product life cycle and are key to achieving the goals of continuous delivery.

---

[14] J. Barr, "ACM Queue: Interview with Amazon's Werner Vogels," *AWS News Blog*, May 16, 2006, http://mng .bz/ZpqA.

1.5 Is the cloud your best option?

One of the biggest mistakes in our industry is deciding to adopt a technology or approach just because it's new and everyone is talking about it. There are endless stories about companies migrating their monoliths to microservices and ending up with disastrous failures. I have already explained the properties of the cloud and of cloud native applications. Those should provide you with some guidance. If your system doesn't need those properties because it doesn't have the problems they are trying to solve, chances are that "going cloud native" is not the best option for your project.

As technologists, it's easy for us to get caught up in the latest, trendiest, shiniest technology. The point is to figure out whether a specific technology or approach can solve *your* problems. We turn ideas into software that we deliver to our customers and that provides them with some value. That's our end goal. If a technology or approach helps you provide more value to your customers, you should consider it. If it's not worthy, and you decide to go with it anyway, you'll likely end up having higher costs and many problems.

When is moving to the cloud a good idea? Why are companies adopting the cloud native approach? The main reasons for going cloud native, illustrated in figure 1.8, are speed, scale, resilience, and cost. If your business vision includes those goals and faces the same problems that cloud technologies try to solve, then it's good to consider moving to the cloud and adopting a cloud native approach. Otherwise, it might be better to stay on the ground. For example, if your company is providing services through a monolithic application in its maintenance phase that will not be further expanded with new features, and that has performed well in the last decade, there might be no good reason to migrate it to the cloud, let alone to turn it into a cloud native application.

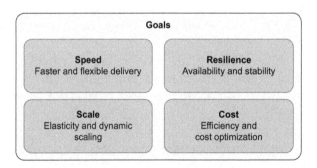

Figure 1.8 Going cloud native can help you meet several goals related to speed, resilience, scale, and cost optimization.

1.5.1 Speed

Being able to deliver software faster is an important goal for enterprises nowadays. Bringing ideas into production as quickly as possible, therefore reducing the time to market, is a critical competitive advantage. Going to production with the right idea at the right time might make the difference between success and failure.

Customers expect to have more and more features implemented or bugs fixed, and they want them now. They will not be happy to wait six months for the next release of your software. Their expectations keep increasing, and you need a way to keep up with them. In the end, it's all about providing value to customers and ensuring they are satisfied with the results. Otherwise, your business will not survive the fierce competition out there.

Delivering faster and frequently is not only about competition and customer deadlines. It's also about making the feedback cycle shorter. Frequent and small releases mean that you can get feedback from customers sooner. A shorter feedback loop, in turn, decreases the risk associated with the new functionality you're releasing. Instead of spending months trying to implement the perfect feature, you can get it out there sooner, get feedback from customers, and adjust it to align with their expectations. Also, smaller releases contain fewer changes, thus reducing the number of parts that could fail.

Flexibility is also needed, since customers expect the continuous evolution of your software. For example, it should be flexible enough to support new types of clients. Nowadays, more and more objects in our daily lives have been connected to the internet, such as all kinds of mobile and IoT systems. You'll want to be open to any future extensions and client types so you can provide business services in new ways.

The traditional software development approach does not support this goal. Too often it is characterized by massive releases, little flexibility, and extended release cycles. The cloud native approach, combined with automated tasks, continuous delivery workflows, and DevOps practices, helps businesses go faster and reduce the time to market.

1.5.2 Resilience

Everything changes, and failures happen all the time. Gone are the times when we tried to predict failures and treat them as exceptions. As I mentioned before, changes are not exceptions. They are the rule.

Customers want software to be available 24/7 and to be upgraded as soon as a new feature is released. Downtime or failures can cause a direct loss of money and customer dissatisfaction. They may even affect one's reputation, damaging the organization's future market opportunities.

Whether there is a failure in the infrastructure or the software, your goal is to guarantee the availability and reliability of your systems, even if only in a degraded operational mode. To guarantee availability, you need to have something in place to face the failures when they arrive, handle them, and ensure that the overall system can still provide services to its users. Any action required to process the failure or tasks like upgrades should require zero downtime. Customers expect that.

We want cloud native applications to be resilient, and cloud technologies provide strategies for implementing resilient infrastructure. If being always available, safe, and resilient is a requirement for your business, the cloud native approach is a good option for you. The resilience of a software system, in turn, enables speed: the more stable the system, the more frequently you can safely release new features.

1.5.3 Scale

Elasticity is about being able to scale your software depending on the load. You can scale an elastic system to ensure an adequate service level for all your customers. If there is a higher load than usual, you'll need to spin up more instances of your services to support that extra traffic. Or perhaps something terrible happened and some services failed—you'll need to be able to spin up new instances to replace them.

Foreseeing what will happen is hard, if not impossible. It's not enough to build scalable applications—you need them to scale dynamically. Whenever there is a high load, your system should scale out dynamically, quickly, and painlessly. When the high peak is over, it should scale in again.

If your business needs to adapt quickly and efficiently to new customers or requires the flexibility to support new types of clients (which increase the workload on the servers), the cloud's very nature can provide you with all the elasticity you need, in combination with cloud native applications that are scalable by definition.

1.5.4 Cost

As a software developer, you might not deal directly with money, but it's your responsibility to take cost into account when designing a solution. The cloud computing model helps optimize IT infrastructure costs with its elasticity and on-demand pay-per-use policies. No more always-on infrastructure: you provision resources when you need them, pay for the actual usage, and then destroy them when you don't need them anymore.

On top of that, adopting the cloud native approach leads to further cost optimizations. Cloud native applications are designed to be scalable so they can take advantage of the cloud's elasticity. They are resilient, so the costs related to downtime and hard failures in production are lower. Being loosely coupled, they enable teams to go faster and speed up the time to market, with notable competitive advantages. And the list goes on.

> ### The hidden costs of moving to the cloud
> Before deciding to migrate to the cloud, it's essential also to consider other types of costs. On the one hand, you can optimize costs by paying for only what you use. But on the other hand, you should consider the cost of migrating and its consequences.
>
> Migrating to the cloud requires specific competencies that employees might not have yet. This may mean investing in their education to acquire the necessary skills and perhaps hiring professionals as consultants to help with the migration to the cloud. Depending on the chosen solution, the organization may need to take over some extra responsibilities, such as handling security in the cloud, which in turn requires specific skills. There are also other considerations, like business interruptions during the migration, retraining end users, and updating documentation and support materials.

1.6   *Cloud native topologies*

My explanation of cloud native didn't involve specific technologies or architectures. The CNCF mentions some in its definition, like containers and microservices, but those are just examples. You don't have to use Docker containers for your applications to be cloud native. Think about serverless or PaaS solutions. Writing functions for the AWS Lambda platform or deploying applications to Heroku doesn't require you to build containers. Still, they are categorized as cloud native.

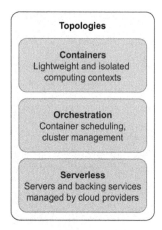

In this section, I'll describe some common cloud native topologies (see figure 1.9). First, I'll introduce the concepts of containers and orchestration, which will be further explored later when I discuss Docker and Kubernetes. Then I'll present the topic of serverless technologies and functions (FaaS). I will not focus much on the FaaS model in this book, but I will cover the basics of how to build serverless applications using Spring Native and Spring Cloud Function.

Figure 1.9   The main cloud native computing models are containers (managed by orchestrators) and serverless.

1.6.1   *Containers*

Imagine you join a team and start working on an application. The first thing you do is follow a guide to set up your local development environment that's similar to the ones used by your colleagues. You develop a new feature and then test it in a quality assurance (QA) environment. Once it's verified, the application can be deployed to staging for some extra testing and finally to production. The application is built to run in an environment with specific characteristics, so it's essential to have all the different environments as similar as possible. How would you do that? That's where containers enter the scene.

Before containers, you would rely on virtual machines to guarantee the reproducibility of the environment, isolation, and configurability. Virtualization works by leveraging a hypervisor component that abstracts the hardware, making it possible to run multiple operating systems on the same machine in an isolated fashion. The hypervisor would run directly on the machine hardware (type 1) or on the host operating system (type 2).

On the other hand, an *OS container* is a lightweight executable package that includes everything needed to run the application. Containers share the same kernel as the host: there's no need to bootstrap full operating systems to add new isolated contexts. On Linux, that is possible by leveraging a couple of features offered by the Linux kernel:

- *namespaces* for partitioning resources among processes so that each process (or group of processes) can only see a subset of the resources available on the machine

- *cgroups* for controlling and limiting the resource usage for a process (or group of processes)

NOTE When using virtualization only, the hardware is shared, whereas containers also share the same operating system kernel. Both provide computing environments for running software in isolation, even if the degree of isolation is not the same.

Figure 1.10 shows the difference between virtualization and container technologies.

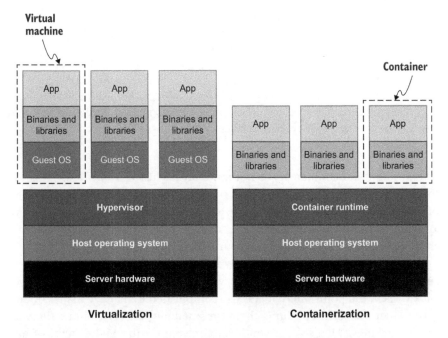

Figure 1.10 Virtualization and container technologies differ in what is shared across isolated contexts. Virtual machines share the hardware only. Containers share the operating system kernel as well. Containers are more lightweight and portable.

Why are containers so popular for cloud native applications? Traditionally, you would have to install and maintain the Java Runtime Environment (JRE) and middleware on a virtual machine to make your application run. Instead, a container can run reliably in almost any computing environment, independent of the application, its dependencies, or middleware. It doesn't matter which kind of application it is, in which language it's written, or which libraries it uses. All containers have a similar shape from the outside, just like the containers used for shipping.

Therefore, containers enable agility, portability across different environments, and deployment repeatability. Being lightweight and less resource-demanding, they are perfect for running in the cloud, where applications are disposable and scaled dynamically and quickly. In comparison, building and destroying virtual machines is much more expensive and time-consuming.

Containers! Containers everywhere!

Container is one of those words that can mean different things. Sometimes this ambiguity can generate confusion, so let's see what it means in specific contexts.

- *OS*—An OS container is a method for running one or more processes in an environment isolated from the rest of the system. This book will focus on *Linux containers*, but note that Windows containers also exist.
- *Docker*—A Docker container is an implementation of a Linux container.
- *OCI*—An OCI container is a standardization of the Docker container implementation by the Open Container Initiative (OCI).
- *Spring*—A Spring container is the application context where objects, properties, and other application resources are managed and executed.
- *Servlet*—A Servlet container provides a runtime for web applications leveraging the Java Servlet API. The Catalina component from the Tomcat server is an example of a Servlet container.

Virtualization and containers are not mutually exclusive. You can use them both in a cloud native context, having an infrastructure made up of virtual machines on which you run containers. The Infrastructure as a Service (IaaS) model provides a virtualization layer that you can use to bootstrap new virtual machines. On top of that, you can install a container runtime and run your containers.

An application is usually made up of different containers that can be run on the same machine during development or while performing early testing. But you would quickly reach the point where it gets too complicated to manage many containers, primarily when you start replicating them for scalability and distributing them across different machines. That's when you'll start relying on the higher level of abstraction provided by the Container as a Service (CaaS) model, which offers functionality to deploy and manage containers in clusters of machines. Note that, behind the scenes, there is still a virtualization layer.

Containers are involved even when you're using PaaS platforms like Heroku or Cloud Foundry. You deploy your applications on those platforms by providing just the JAR artifact, since they take care of the JRE, the middleware, the OS, and any needed dependencies. Behind the scenes they build a container out of all those components and finally run it. The difference is that it's no longer you who is responsible for building a container—the platform does it for you. On the one hand, that's convenient, in terms of fewer responsibilities for developers. On the other hand, you are giving up control over the runtime and middleware, and you might face vendor lock-in.

In this book, you'll learn how to use Cloud Native Buildpacks (a CNCF project) to containerize Spring applications, and you'll use Docker to run them in your local environment.

1.6.2   *Orchestration*

So you have decided to use containers, great! You can rely on their portability to deploy them to any infrastructure providing a container runtime. You can achieve reproducibility, so there are no bad surprises when moving containers from development to staging to production. You can scale them quickly, since they're so lightweight, and get high availability for your applications. You're ready to adopt them for your next cloud native system. Or are you?

Provisioning and managing containers on a single machine is pretty straightforward. But when you start dealing with tens or hundreds of containers scaled and deployed on several machines, you need something else.

When you move from virtual servers (the IaaS model) to container clusters (the CaaS model), you're also switching your point of view.[15] In IaaS you focus on single computing nodes, which are virtual servers. In CaaS the underlying infrastructure is abstracted, and you're focusing on clusters of nodes.

With the new perspective offered by CaaS solutions, the deployment target will not be a machine anymore but rather a cluster of machines. CaaS platforms, such as those based on Kubernetes, provide many features to address all the significant concerns we look for in a cloud native environment, *orchestrating* containers across machines. The two different topologies are shown in figure 1.11.

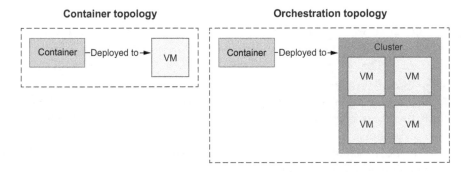

Figure 1.11   The deployment target of containers is a machine, whereas for orchestrators, it's a cluster.

Container orchestration helps you automate many different tasks:

- Managing clusters, bringing up and down machines when necessary
- Scheduling and deploying containers within a cluster to a machine that meets the container requirements for CPU and memory

---

[15] N. Kratzke and R. Peinl, "ClouNS—a Cloud-Native Application Reference Model for Enterprise Architects," *2016 IEEE 20th International Enterprise Distributed Object Computing Workshop (EDOCW),* 2016, pp. 1–10, doi: 10.1109/EDOCW.2016.7584353.

- Dynamically scaling containers for high availability and resilience, leveraging health monitoring
- Setting up networks for containers to communicate with each other, defining routing, service discovery, and load balancing
- Exposing services to the internet, establishing ports and networks
- Allocating resources to containers according to specific criteria
- Configuring the applications running within the containers
- Ensuring security and enforcing access control policies

Orchestration tools are instructed declaratively, such as through YAML files. Following the format and language defined by the specific tool, you usually describe the state you'd like to achieve; for example, you would like to have three replicas of your web application container deployed in a cluster, exposing its services to the internet.

Examples of container orchestrators are Kubernetes (a CNCF project), Docker Swarm, and Apache Mesos. In this book, you'll learn how to use Kubernetes to orchestrate the containers for your Spring applications.

1.6.3 *Serverless*

After moving from virtual machines to containers, we can abstract the infrastructure even more: that's where serverless technologies are placed. The serverless computing model enables developers to focus on implementing the business logic for their applications.

The name *serverless* might be misleading. Of course there is a server. The difference is that you do not need to manage it or orchestrate the application's deployment on it. That's a platform responsibility now. When you use an orchestrator like Kubernetes, you must still consider infrastructure provisioning, capacity planning, and scaling. In contrast, a serverless platform takes care of setting up the underlying infrastructure needed by the applications, including virtual machines, containers, and dynamic scaling.

Serverless architectures are usually associated with functions, but they comprise two main models that are often used together:

- *Backend as a Service* (BaaS)—In this model, applications rely heavily on third-party services offered by cloud providers, such as databases, authentication services, and message queues. The focus is on reducing development and operational costs related to backend services. Developers can implement frontend applications (such as single-page applications or mobile applications) while offloading most or all of the backend functionality to BaaS vendors. For example, they could use Okta to authenticate users, Google Firebase for persisting data, and Amazon API Gateway to publish and manage REST APIs.
- *Function as a Service* (FaaS)—In this model, applications are stateless, triggered by events, and fully managed by the platform. The focus is on reducing deployment and operations costs related to orchestrating and scaling applications.

Developers can implement the business logic for their applications, and the platform takes care of the rest. Serverless applications don't have to be implemented with functions to be categorized as such. There are two main FaaS offerings. One option is to go with vendor-specific FaaS platforms, such as AWS Lambda, Azure Functions, or Google Cloud Functions. Another option is to choose a serverless platform based on open source projects, which can run either in a public cloud or on premises, addressing concerns like vendor lock-in and lack of control. Examples of such projects are Knative and Apache Open-Whisk. Knative provides a serverless runtime environment on top of Kubernetes, as you'll see in chapter 16. It's used as the foundation for enterprise serverless platforms like VMware Tanzu Application Platform, RedHat OpenShift Serverless, and Google Cloud Run.

Serverless applications are typically event-driven and run only when there is an event to handle, such as an HTTP request or a message. The event can be external or be produced by another function. For example, a function might be triggered whenever a message is added to a queue, process it, and then exit the execution.

When there is nothing to process, the serverless platform shuts down all the resources involved with the function, so you can really pay for the actual usage. In the other cloud native topologies like CaaS or PaaS, there is always a server running 24/7. Compared to traditional systems, they offer the advantage of dynamic scalability, reducing the number of resources provisioned at any given time. Still, there is always something up and running, and it has a cost. In the serverless model, resources are provisioned only when necessary. If there is nothing to process, everything is shut down. That's what we call *scaling to zero*, and it's one of the main features offered by serverless platforms.

Besides cost optimization, serverless technologies also move some extra responsibility from the application to the platform. That might be an advantage, since it allows developers to focus exclusively on the business logic. But it's also essential to consider what degree of control you would like to have and how you will deal with vendor lock-in. Each FaaS, and in general serverless, platform has its own features and APIs. Once you start writing functions for a specific platform, you can't move them easily to another, as you would do with containers. With FaaS, you might compromise more than with any other approach—prioritizing responsibility and scope at the cost of control and portability. That's why Knative became popular quickly: it is built on Kubernetes, which means that you can easily move your serverless workloads between platforms and vendors. In the end, it's a matter of tradeoffs.

1.7 Architectures for cloud native applications

We have reached the last step of our journey to define cloud native, and I've introduced the primary characteristics we'll rely on throughout the book. In the previous section, you got familiar with the main cloud native topologies, particularly containers, which are our computation units. Now let's look at what's inside and explore some high-level principles involved in architecting and designing cloud native applications. Figure 1.12 shows the main concepts covered in this section.

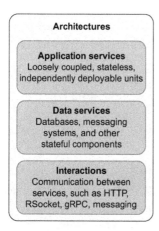

Figure 1.12   Cloud native architectural elements

1.7.1   *From multi-tiered to microservices architectures and beyond*

IT infrastructures have always affected the way software applications are architected and designed. In the beginning, monolithic applications were deployed on huge mainframes as single components. When the internet and PCs became popular, we started designing applications according to the client/server paradigm. A multi-tiered architecture, relying on that paradigm, was widely used for desktop and web applications, decomposing the code into presentation, business, and data layers.

With the increase in application complexity and the need for agility, new ways of further decomposing the code have been explored, and a new architectural style entered the stage: microservices. In the last few years, this architectural style has become more and more popular, and many companies decided to refactor their applications according to this new style. Microservices are usually compared to monolithic applications, as shown in figure 1.13.

The main difference lies in how the application has been decomposed. A monolithic application is associated with using three large layers. A microservice-based application, in contrast, is associated with many components, each implementing only one piece of functionality. Many patterns have been proposed to decompose a monolith into microservices and to handle the complexity created by having many components instead of one.

NOTE   This book is not about microservices, so I won't go into detail about them. If you are interested in the topic, you can check out *Building Microservices*, second ed., by Sam Newman (O'Reilly, 2021) and *Microservices Patterns* by Chris Richardson (Manning, 2018). For a more Spring-oriented analysis, you can find *Spring Microservices in Action*, second ed., by John Carnell and Illary Huaylupo Sanchez (Manning, 2021) in the Manning catalog. If you are

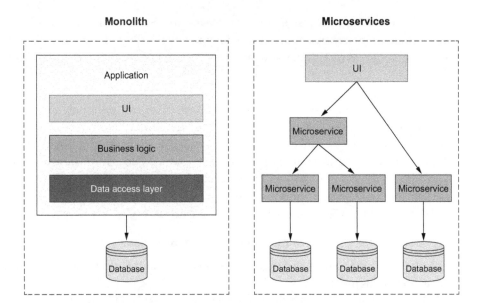

Figure 1.13 Monolithic applications vs. microservices. Monolithic architectures are often multitiered. Microservices are made up of different components that can be deployed independently.

not familiar with microservices, don't worry. That knowledge is not required to follow along with this book.

After many years of fame and failed migrations, intense discussions about the future of this popular architectural style have arisen in the developer community. Some engineers started talking about *macroservices* to reduce the number of components and, therefore, the complexity of managing them. The term "macroservices" was suggested sardonically by Cindy Sridharan, but it has been adopted in the industry and used by companies like Dropbox and Airbnb to describe their new architectures.[16] Others proposed a *citadel* architectural style, consisting of a central monolith surrounded by microservices. Still others are advocating a return to monolithic applications in the form of modular monoliths.

In the end, the important thing is to choose an architecture that can deliver value to our customers and our businesses. That's why we develop applications in the first place. Each architectural style has its use cases. There is no such thing as a silver bullet or one-size-fits-all solution. Most of the negative experiences related to microservices were caused by other issues, such as bad code modularization or unfitting organization structure. There shouldn't be a battle between monoliths and microservices.

In this book, I'm interested in showing you how to build cloud native applications with Spring and deploy them to Kubernetes as containers. Cloud native applications

---

[16] C. Sridharan, May 15, 2022, http://mng.bz/YG5N.

are distributed systems, just like microservices are. Some topics usually discussed in the context of microservices actually belong to any distributed system, such as routing and service discovery. Cloud native applications are loosely coupled by definition, and that is also a feature of microservices.

Even if they have some similar aspects, it's essential to understand that cloud native applications and microservices are not the same. You can definitely use a microservices style for cloud native applications. Many developers do, but it's not a requirement. In this book, I will use an architectural style that we might call *service-based*. Perhaps it's not a catchy name or a fancy one, but it's enough for our purpose. We'll deal with services. They can be of any size, and they can encapsulate logic according to different principles. That doesn't matter. What we want is to design services to fit our development, organizational, and business needs.

1.7.2 *Service-based architecture for cloud native applications*

Throughout this book, we'll design and build cloud native applications according to a service-based architecture.

Our central unit of work will be a service that can interact with other services in different ways. Using the distinction proposed by Cornelia Davis in her book *Cloud Native Patterns* (Manning, 2019), we can identify two elements of the architecture: services and interactions.

- *Service*—A component that provides any kind of service to another component
- *Interaction*—The communication of services with each other to accomplish the system's requirements

Services are quite generic components—they might be anything. We can classify them according to whether they store any kind of state, distinguishing between *application services* (stateless) and *data services* (stateful).

Figure 1.14 shows the elements of a cloud native architecture. An application used to manage the inventory for a book library would be an application service. A PostgreSQL database used to store information about the books would be a data service.

APPLICATION SERVICES

Application services are stateless and are responsible for implementing any kind of logic. They don't have to obey specific rules like those for microservices, as long as they expose all the cloud native properties you learned about earlier in this chapter.

It's paramount that you design each service with loose coupling and high cohesion in mind. Services should be as independent as possible. Distributed systems are complex, so you should be extra careful during the design phase. Increasing the number of services leads to an increased number of problems.

You'll probably develop and maintain most of the application services in your system by yourself, but you can also use some offered by cloud providers, such as authentication or payment services.

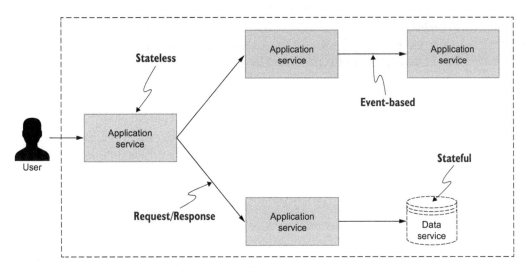

Figure 1.14 Service-based architecture for cloud native applications. The main elements are services (application or data) that interact with each other in different ways.

DATA SERVICES

Data services are stateful and are responsible for storing any kind of state. The *state* is everything that should be preserved when shutting down a service or spinning up a new instance.

Data services can be relational databases like PostgreSQL, key/value stores like Redis, or message brokers like RabbitMQ. You can manage these services by yourself. Doing so is more challenging than managing cloud native applications due to the storage required to save the state, but you will gain more control over your own data. Another option is to use the data services offered by a cloud provider, in which case the provider will be responsible for managing all the concerns related to storage, resilience, scalability, and performance. In this case, you can take advantage of the many data services explicitly built for the cloud, such as Amazon DynamoDB, Azure Cosmos DB, and Google BigQuery.

Cloud native data services are a fascinating topic, but we will mainly deal with applications in this book. Data-related concerns like clustering, replication, consistency, and distributed transactions will not be detailed too much in the book. I would love to, but they deserve their own book to be adequately covered.

INTERACTIONS

Cloud native services communicate with each other to fulfill the requirements of the system. How that communication happens will affect the overall properties of the system. For example, choosing a request/response pattern (synchronous HTTP call) over an event-based approach (messages streamed through RabbitMQ) will result in different levels of resilience for the application. In this book, we'll use different types of interactions, learn the differences between them, and see when to use each approach.

Summary

- Cloud native applications are highly distributed systems that are specifically designed for and live in the cloud.
- The cloud is an IT infrastructure provided as a commodity in terms of computing, storage, and networking resources.
- In the cloud, users pay only for the actual resources they use.
- Cloud platforms deliver their services at different levels of abstraction: infrastructure (IaaS), container (CaaS), platform (PaaS), functions (FaaS), or software (SaaS).
- Cloud native applications are horizontally scalable, loosely coupled, highly cohesive, resilient to faults, manageable, and observable.
- Cloud native development is supported by automation, continuous delivery, and DevOps.
- Continuous delivery is a holistic engineering practice for delivering high-quality software quickly, reliably, and safely.
- DevOps is a culture enabling collaboration among different roles to deliver business value together.
- Modern businesses go cloud native to produce software that can be delivered quickly, can be scaled dynamically depending on demand, and is always available and resilient to failures while optimizing costs.
- Containers (such as Docker containers) can be used as computational units when designing cloud native systems. They are more lightweight than virtual machines and provide portability, immutability, and flexibility.
- Dedicated platforms (such as Kubernetes) offer services to manage containers without directly handling the underlying layers. They provide container orchestration, cluster management, network services, and scheduling.
- Serverless computing is a model where the platform (such as Knative) manages servers and the underlying infrastructure, and the developer only focuses on the business logic. The backend functionality is enabled on a pay-per-use basis for cost optimization.
- A microservices architecture can be used to build cloud native applications, but it's not a requirement.
- To design cloud native applications, we'll use a service-based style characterized by services and their interactions.
- Cloud native services can be classified into application services (stateless) and data services (stateful).

Cloud native patterns
and technologies

This chapter covers

- Understanding development principles for cloud native applications
- Building cloud native applications with Spring Boot
- Containerizing applications with Docker and Buildpacks
- Deploying applications to the cloud with Kubernetes
- Introducing patterns and technologies used in the book

The way we design applications for the cloud is different from traditional approaches. The 12-Factor methodology, consisting of best practices and development patterns, is a good starting point for building applications that can be considered cloud native. I'll explain the methodology in the first part of this chapter, and I'll expand on it throughout the book.

Later in this chapter, we'll build a simple Spring Boot application and run it with Java, Docker, and Kubernetes, as shown in figure 2.1. Throughout the book I'll

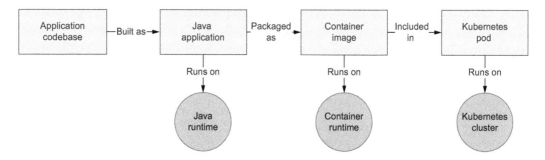

Figure 2.1   The journey of a Spring application from Java to container to Kubernetes

go deeper into each of those topics, so don't worry if something is not entirely clear. This chapter aims to provide you with a mental map of the journey we'll undertake from code to production in a cloud environment, while familiarizing you with patterns and technologies that we'll use in the rest of the book.

Finally, I'll introduce you to the cloud native project we'll build throughout this book using Spring and Kubernetes. We'll employ all the properties and patterns for cloud native applications introduced in this first part of the book.

2.1   *Cloud native development principles: 12 Factors and beyond*

The engineers working at the Heroku cloud platform have proposed the 12-Factor methodology as a collection of development principles for designing and building cloud native applications.[1] They have distilled their experience into best practices for building web applications with the following characteristics:

- Suitable to be deployed on cloud platforms
- Scalable by design
- Portable across systems
- Enablers of continuous deployment and agility

The goal was to help developers build applications for the cloud, highlighting the significant factors that should be considered to achieve the best results.

Later, the methodology was revised and expanded by Kevin Hoffman in his book *Beyond the Twelve-Factor App*, refreshing the contents of the original factors and adding three extra ones.[2] From now on, I will refer to this expanded set of principles as the *15-Factor methodology*.

---

[1] A. Wiggins, "The Twelve-Factor App," https://12factor.net.
[2] K. Hoffman, *Beyond the Twelve-Factor App* (O'Reilly, 2016).

These 15 factors will guide you throughout the book since they are a good starting point for developing cloud native applications. If you are building a new application from scratch or migrating a traditional system to the cloud, these principles can help you on your journey. I will elaborate more on them when relevant, and I'll illustrate how to apply them to Spring applications. It's essential that you become familiar with them.

Let's dig into each of these factors.

2.1.1   One codebase, one application

The 15-Factor methodology establishes a one-to-one mapping between an application and its codebase, so there's one codebase for each application. Any shared code should be tracked in its own codebase as a library that can be included as a dependency or service that can be run in standalone mode, acting as a backing service for other applications. Each codebase can optionally be tracked in its own repository.

A *deployment* is a running instance of the application. Many deployments are possible in different environments, all sharing the same application artifact. There is no need to rebuild the codebase to deploy an application to a specific environment: any aspect that changes between deployments (such as configuration) should be outside the application codebase.

2.1.2   API first

A cloud native system is usually made up of different services that communicate through APIs. Using an *API first* approach while designing a cloud native application encourages you to think about fitting it into a distributed system and favors the distribution of the work across different teams. By designing the API first, another team using that application as a backing service could create their solution against that API. By designing the contract up front, integration with other systems will be more robust and testable as part of the deployment pipeline. Internally, the API implementation can be changed without affecting other applications (and teams) depending on it.

2.1.3   Dependency management

All application dependencies should be declared explicitly in a manifest and be available for the dependency manager to download from a central repository. In the context of Java applications, we are usually well-equipped to follow this principle using tools like Maven or Gradle. The only implicit dependencies an application can have on the surrounding environment are the language runtime and the dependency manager tool. This means that private dependencies should be resolved via the dependency manager.

2.1.4   Design, build, release, run

A codebase goes through different stages in its journey from design to deployment in production:

- *Design stage*—Technologies, dependencies, and tools needed by a specific application feature are decided.
- *Build stage*—The codebase is compiled and packaged together with its dependencies as an immutable artifact called a *build*. The build artifact must be uniquely identified.
- *Release stage*—The build is combined with a specific configuration for the deployment. Each release is immutable and should be uniquely identifiable, such as by using semantic versioning (for example, `3.9.4`) or a timestamp (for example, `2022-07-07_17:21`). Releases should be stored in a central repository for easy access, like when a rollback to a previous version is required.
- *Run stage*—The application runs in the execution environment from a specific release.

The 15-Factor methodology requires a strict separation of these stages and doesn't allow changes to the code at runtime, since that would result in a mismatch with the build stage. The build and the release artifacts should be immutable and labeled with a unique identifier to guarantee reproducibility.

2.1.5   Configuration, credentials, and code

The 15-Factor methodology defines configuration as everything likely to change between deployments. Whenever you need to change the configuration for an application, you should be able to do so without any changes in the code, and without building the application again.

The configuration might include resource handles to backing services like a database or a messaging system, credentials to access third-party APIs, and feature flags. Ask yourself if any credential or environment-specific information would be compromised should your codebase suddenly become public. That will tell you whether you have correctly externalized the configuration.

To be compliant with this factor, the configuration can't be included in the code or tracked in the same codebase. The only exception is the default configuration, which can be packaged with the application codebase. You can still use configuration files for any other type of configuration, but you should store them in a separate repository.

The methodology recommends storing configuration as environment variables. By doing so, you can have the same application deployed in different environments but with different behaviors depending on the environment's configuration.

2.1.6   Logs

A cloud native application isn't concerned with routing and storage of logs. Applications should log to the standard output, treating logs as events emitted in a sequence ordered by time. Log storage and rotation are not application responsibilities anymore. An external tool (a *log aggregator*) will fetch, collect, and make logs available for inspection.

2.1.7 Disposability

In a traditional environment, you would take much care of your applications, ensuring they stay up and running and never terminate. In a cloud environment, you don't need to care that much: applications are ephemeral. If a failure happens and the application doesn't respond anymore, you terminate it and start a new instance. If you have a high-load peak, you can spin up more instances of your applications to sustain the increased workload. We say that an application is disposable if it can be started or stopped at any time.

To handle application instances in such a dynamic way, you should design them to start up quickly whenever you need a new instance and gracefully shut down when you don't need them anymore. A fast startup enables the elasticity of the system, ensuring robustness and resilience. Without a fast startup, you will have performance and availability issues.

A *graceful shutdown* is when an application, on receiving a signal to terminate, stops accepting new requests, completes the ones already in progress, and finally exits. In the case of web processes, that is straightforward. In other cases, such as with worker processes, the jobs they were responsible for must be returned to the work queue, and only afterward can they exit.

2.1.8 Backing services

Backing services can be defined as external resources that an application uses to deliver its functionality. Examples of backing services are databases, message brokers, caching systems, SMTP servers, FTP servers, or RESTful web services. Treating them as attached resources means that you can easily change them without modifying the application code.

Consider how you use databases throughout the software development life cycle. Chances are that you'll use a different database depending on the stage: development, testing, or production. If you treat the database as an attached resource, you can use a different service depending on the environment. The attachment is done through resource binding. For example, resource binding for a database could consist of a URL, a username, and a password.

2.1.9 Environment parity

Environment parity is about keeping all your environments as similar as possible. In reality, there are three gaps that this factor tries to address:

- *Time gap*—The period between a code change and its deployment can be quite large. The methodology strives to promote automation and continuous deployment to reduce the period between when a developer writes code to when it's deployed in production.

- *People gap*—Developers build applications, and operators manage their deployment in production. This gap can be resolved by embracing a DevOps culture, improving collaboration between developers and operators, and embracing the "you build it, you run it" philosophy.
- *Tools gap*—One of the main differences between environments is how backing services are handled. For example, developers might use the H2 database in their local environment but PostgreSQL in production. In general, the same type and version of backing services should be used in all environments.

2.1.10 Administrative processes

Some management tasks are usually needed to support applications. Tasks like database migrations, batch jobs, or maintenance jobs should be treated as one-off processes. Just like application processes, the code for administrative tasks should be tracked in revision control, delivered with the application they support, and executed in the same environment as the application.

It's usually a good idea to frame administrative tasks as small standalone services that run once and then are thrown away or as functions configured in a stateless platform to be triggered when certain events happen, or you can embed them in the application itself, activating them by calling a specific endpoint.

2.1.11 Port binding

Applications following the 15-Factor methodology should be self-contained and export their services via port binding. In production, there might be some routing services that translate requests from public endpoints to the internal port-bound services.

An application is self-contained if it doesn't depend on an external server in the execution environment. A Java web application would probably run inside a server container like Tomcat, Jetty, or Undertow. A cloud native application, in contrast, would not require the environment to have a Tomcat server available; it would manage it itself as any other dependency. Spring Boot, for example, lets you use an embedded server: the application will contain the server rather than depending on one being available in the execution environment. One of the consequences of this approach is that there is always a one-to-one mapping between application and server, unlike the traditional method where multiple applications are deployed to the same server.

The services provided by the application are then exported via port binding. A web application would bind HTTP services to a specific port and potentially become a backing service for another application. That's what usually happens in a cloud native system.

2.1.12 Stateless processes

In the previous chapter, you saw that high scalability is one reason why we move to the cloud. To ensure scalability, we design applications as stateless processes and adopt a *share-nothing architecture*: no state should be shared among different application instances. Ask yourself if any data would be lost should an instance of your application be destroyed and recreated. If the answer is affirmative, then your application is not stateless.

No matter what, we will always need to save some state, or our applications will be useless in most cases. As a result, we design applications to be stateless and then only handle the state in specific stateful services like data stores. In other words, a stateless application delegates the state management and storage to a backing service.

2.1.13 Concurrency

Creating stateless applications is not enough to ensure scalability. If you need to scale, that means you need to serve more users. Therefore, your applications should allow concurrent processing to serve many users at the same time.

The 15-Factor methodology defines processes as first-class citizens. Those processes should be horizontally scalable, distributing the workload across many processes on different machines, and this concurrent processing is only possible if the applications are stateless. In JVM applications, we handle concurrency through multiple threads, available from thread pools.

Processes can be classified according to their types. For example, you might have web processes that handle HTTP requests and worker processes that execute scheduled jobs in the background.

2.1.14 Telemetry

Observability is one of the properties of cloud native applications. Managing a distributed system in the cloud is complex, and the only way to manage such complexity is by ensuring that every system component provides the correct data to monitor the system's behavior remotely. Examples of telemetry data are logs, metrics, traces, health status, and events. Hoffman uses a very catchy image to stress the importance of telemetry: treat your applications like space probes. What kind of telemetry would you need to monitor and control your applications remotely?

2.1.15 Authentication and authorization

Security is one of the essential qualities of a software system, but it often doesn't get the necessary attention. Following a *zero-trust* approach, we must secure any interaction within the system at any architectural and infrastructural levels. There is undoubtedly more to security than just authentication and authorization, but those are a good starting point.

With authentication, we can keep track of who is using the application. Knowing that, we can then check the user permissions to verify whether the user is allowed to perform specific actions. A few standards are available for implementing identity and access management, including OAuth 2.1 and OpenID Connect, which we will use in this book.

2.2 Building cloud native applications with Spring

It's time to get more concrete now and start talking about technologies. So far, you have learned about the cloud native approach and the main development practices we'll follow. Now let's have a look at Spring. If you are reading this book, you have probably had some previous experience with Spring, and you'd like to learn how to use it to build cloud native applications.

The Spring ecosystem provides features for handling almost any requirement your applications might have, including those of cloud native applications. Spring is by far the most used Java framework. It's been around for many years, and it's robust and reliable. The community behind Spring is fantastic and willing to move it forward and make it consistently better. Technologies and development practices evolve continuously, and Spring is very good at keeping up with them. Therefore, using Spring for your next cloud native project is an excellent choice.

This section will highlight some interesting features of the Spring landscape. Then we will start to create a Spring Boot application.

2.2.1 Overview of the Spring landscape

Spring comprises several projects that address many different aspects of software development: web applications, security, data access, integration, batch processing, configuration, messaging, big data, and many more. The beauty of the Spring platform is that it's designed to be modular, so you can use and combine just the projects you need. It doesn't matter which type of application you need to build. Chances are that Spring can help you with it.

Spring Framework is the core of the Spring platform, the project that started it all. It supports dependency injection, transaction management, data access, messaging, web applications, and more. The framework establishes the "plumbing" of enterprise applications so you can focus on the business logic.

Spring Framework provides an execution context (called *Spring context* or *container*), where beans, properties, and resources are managed throughout the entire application life cycle. I'll assume you are already familiar with the framework's core features, so I will not spend too much time on it. In particular, you should be aware of the Spring context's role and be comfortable working with Spring beans, annotation-based configuration, and dependency injection. We will rely on those features, so you should have them sorted out.

Based on the framework, *Spring Boot* makes it possible to build standalone, production-ready applications quickly. Spring Boot takes an opinionated view of Spring and third-party libraries, and it comes bundled with a sensible default configuration that lets developers get started with minimal up-front work while still providing full customization possibilities.

Throughout this book, you'll have a chance to use several Spring projects to implement patterns and best practices for cloud native applications, including Spring Boot, Spring Cloud, Spring Data, Spring Security, Spring Session, and Spring Native.

> **NOTE** If you are interested in learning more about the core Spring features, you can find a few books on the subject in the Manning catalog, including *Spring Start Here* by Laurenţiu Spilcă (Manning, 2021) and *Spring in Action*, sixth edition, by Craig Walls (Manning, 2022). You can also refer to *Spring Boot: Up & Running* by Mark Heckler (O'Reilly, 2021).

2.2.2 Building a Spring Boot application

Imagine that you have been hired to build a Polar Bookshop application for Polarsophia. This organization manages a specialized bookshop and wants to sell its books about the North Pole and the Arctic online. A cloud native approach is being considered.

As a pilot project, your boss has assigned you to demonstrate to your colleagues how to go from implementation to production in the cloud. The web application you are asked to build is Catalog Service, and for now it will only have one responsibility: welcoming users to the book catalog. This pilot project will be the foundation for actual products built as cloud native applications, should it be successful and well-received.

Considering the task's goal, you might decide to implement the application as a RESTful service with a single HTTP endpoint responsible for returning a welcome message. Surprisingly enough, you choose to adopt Spring as the primary technology stack for the one service (Catalog Service) composing the application. The architecture of the system is shown in figure 2.2, and you'll be trying your hand at building and deploying the application in the upcoming sections.

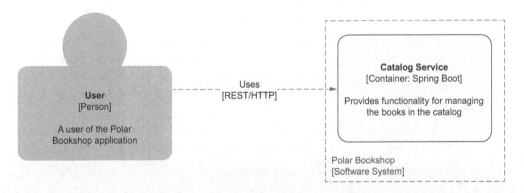

Figure 2.2   Architecture diagram for the Polar Bookshop application, following the C4 model

In figure 2.2, you can see the notation that I'll use to represent architectural diagrams throughout the book, following the C4 model created by Simon Brown (https://c4model.com). To describe the architecture for the Polar Bookshop project, I'm relying on three abstractions from the model:

- *Person*—This represents one of the human users of the software system. In our example, it's a customer of the bookshop.
- *System*—This represents the overall application you will build to deliver value to its users. In our example, it's the Polar Bookshop system.
- *Container*—This represents a service, either application or data. It's not to be confused with Docker. In our example, it's the Catalog Service.

For this task we'll use the Spring Framework and Spring Boot to do the following:

- Declare the dependencies needed to implement the application.
- Bootstrap the application with Spring Boot.
- Implement a controller to expose an HTTP endpoint for returning a welcome message.
- Run and try the application.

All the examples in this book are based on Java 17, the latest long-term release of Java at the time of writing. Before moving on, follow the instructions in section A.1 of appendix A to install an OpenJDK 17 distribution. Then ensure you have an IDE with support for Java, Gradle, and Spring. I'll be using IntelliJ IDEA, but feel free to choose another one, such as Visual Studio Code. Finally, create a free account on GitHub if you don't have one yet (https://github.com). You'll use it to store your code and define continuous delivery pipelines.

INITIALIZING THE PROJECT

Throughout the book, we'll build several cloud native applications. I recommend you define a Git repository for each of them and use GitHub to store them. In the next chapter, I'll talk more about managing codebases. For now, go ahead and create a `catalog-service` Git repository.

Next, you can generate the project from Spring Initializr (https://start.spring.io) and store it in the `catalog-service` Git repository you just created. Spring Initializr is a convenient service you can use from a browser or through its REST API to generate JVM-based projects. It's even integrated into popular IDEs such as IntelliJ IDEA and Visual Studio Code. The initialization parameters for Catalog Service are shown in figure 2.3.

During the initialization, you can provide a few details about the application you want to build, as shown in table 2.1.

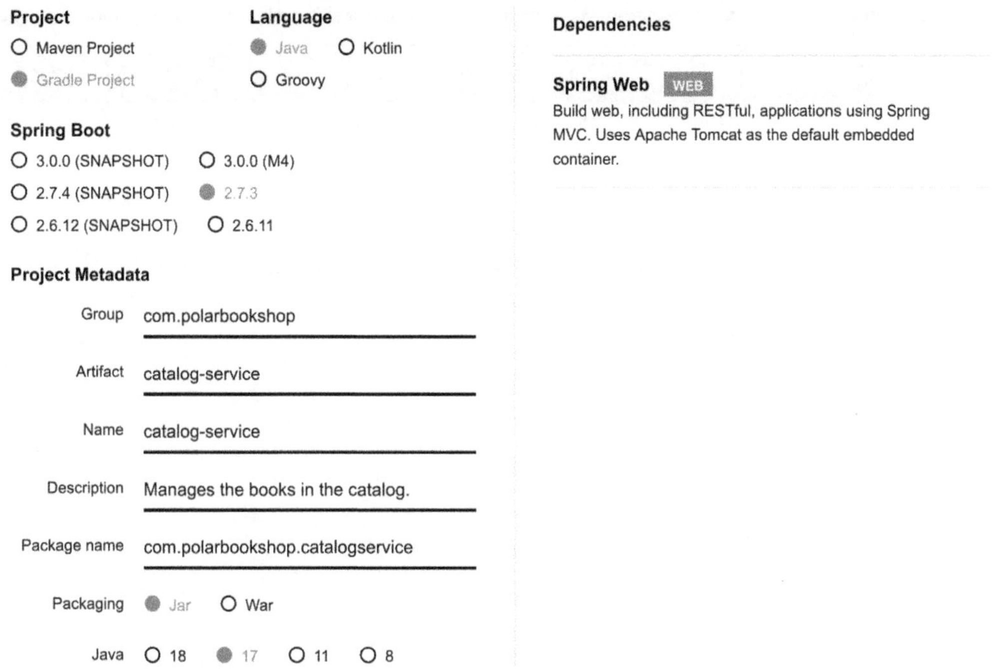

Project
O Maven Project
● Gradle Project

Language
● Java   O Kotlin
O Groovy

Dependencies

Spring Web `WEB`
Build web, including RESTful, applications using Spring
MVC. Uses Apache Tomcat as the default embedded
container.

Spring Boot
O 3.0.0 (SNAPSHOT)   O 3.0.0 (M4)
O 2.7.4 (SNAPSHOT)   ● 2.7.3
O 2.6.12 (SNAPSHOT)   O 2.6.11

Project Metadata

Group   com.polarbookshop

Artifact   catalog-service

Name   catalog-service

Description   Manages the books in the catalog.

Package name com.polarbookshop.catalogservice

Packaging   ● Jar   O War

Java   O 18   ● 17   O 11   O 8

Figure 2.3   The parameters for initializing the Catalog Service project from Spring Initializr

Table 2.1   The main parameters you can configure to generate a project from Spring Initializr

Parameter	Description	Value for Catalog Service
Project	You can decide whether you want to use Gradle or Maven as the build tool for your project. All the examples in this book will use Gradle.	Gradle
Language	Spring supports the three main JVM languages: Java, Kotlin, and Groovy. All the examples in this book will use Java.	Java
Spring Boot	You can choose which version of Spring Boot you want to use. All the examples in this book will use Spring Boot 2.7.3, but any subsequent patch should be fine.	Spring Boot 2.7.3
Group	The group ID for the project, as used in a Maven repository.	`com.polarbookshop`
Artifact	The artifact ID for the project, as used in a Maven repository.	`catalog-service`
Name	The project name.	`catalog-service`
Package name	The base Java package for the project.	`com.polarbookshop` `.catalogservice`
Packaging	How to package the project: WAR (for deployment on application servers) or JAR (for standalone applications). Cloud native applications should be packaged as JARs, so all the examples in this book will use that option.	JAR

Table 2.1   The main parameters you can configure to generate a project from Spring Initializr *(continued)*

Parameter	Description	Value for Catalog Service
Java	The Java version you want to use to build the project. All the examples in this book will use Java 17.	17
Dependencies	Which dependencies to include in the project.	Spring Web

The structure of the newly generated project is shown in figure 2.4. I'll guide you through it in the upcoming sections.

Figure 2.4   The structure of a new Spring Boot project generated from Spring Initializr

In the code repository accompanying this book (https://github.com/ThomasVitale/cloud-native-spring-in-action), you can find "begin" and "end" folders for each chapter, so that you can always start with the same setup as me and check the final result. For example, you are currently reading chapter 2, so you will find the related code in Chapter02/02-begin and Chapter02/02-end.

> **TIP**   In the "begin" folder for this chapter, you'll find a `curl` command that you can run in a Terminal window to download a zip file containing all the code you need to get started, without going through the manual project generation on the Spring Initializr website.

Gradle or Maven?

I'm using Gradle in this book, but feel free to use Maven instead. In the code repository accompanying this book, you can find a table mapping the Gradle commands to Maven so that you can easily follow along, should you use the second option (https://github.com/ThomasVitale/cloud-native-spring-in-action). Each project has different needs that might lead you to choose one build tool over another.

My choice of using Gradle is a personal preference and is due to two main reasons. Building and testing a Java project with Gradle takes less time than Maven, thanks to its incremental and parallel builds and caching system. Also, I find the Gradle build language (Gradle DSL) to be more readable, expressive, and maintainable than Maven XML. In the Spring ecosystem, you can find projects using Gradle and others using Maven. They're both good choices. I recommend you try them both and pick the tool that makes you more productive.

EXPLORING THE BUILD CONFIGURATION

Open the project you have just initialized in your favorite IDE, and look at the Gradle build configuration for the Catalog Service application, defined in the build.gradle file. You can find there all the information you provided to Spring Initializr.

Listing 2.1 The build configuration for Catalog Service

Provides Java support in Gradle, setting up tasks
to compile, build, and test the application

```
plugins {
    id 'org.springframework.boot' version '2.7.3'        ⟵  Provides Spring Boot support
    id 'io.spring.dependency-management'                     in Gradle and declares which
                                                             version to use
    version '1.0.13.RELEASE'        ⟵  Provides dependency
    id 'java'                          management features for Spring
}

group = 'com.polarbookshop'        ⟵  The group ID for the
version = '0.0.1-SNAPSHOT'            Catalog Service project
sourceCompatibility = '17'         ⟵  The version of the application.
                                      By default, it's 0.0.1-SNAPSHOT.

repositories {                     The Java version used
    mavenCentral()                 to build the project
}

dependencies {                     The dependencies used
    implementation 'org.springframework.boot:spring-boot-starter-web'
    testImplementation 'org.springframework.boot:spring-boot-starter-test'
}

tasks.named('test') {
    useJUnitPlatform()        ⟵  Enables testing with the
}                                JUnit Platform provided
                                 by JUnit 5
```

Artifact repositories to
search for dependencies

The project contains the following main dependencies:

- *Spring Web* (`org.springframework.boot:spring-boot-starter-web`) provides the necessary libraries for building web applications with Spring MVC and includes Tomcat as the default embedded server.
- *Spring Boot Test* (`org.springframework.boot:spring-boot-starter-test`) provides several libraries and utilities for testing applications, including Spring Test, JUnit, AssertJ, and Mockito. It's automatically included in every Spring Boot project.

NOTE   Spring Boot offers convenient starter dependencies that bundle together all the libraries necessary for a specific use case, taking care to choose versions that are compatible with each other. This feature significantly simplifies your build configuration.

The name of the project is defined in a second file called settings.gradle:

```
rootProject.name = 'catalog-service'
```

BOOTSTRAPPING THE APPLICATION

In a previous section, you initialized the Catalog Service project and chose the JAR packaging option. Any Java application packaged as a JAR must have a `public static void main(String[] args)` method that is executed at startup, and Spring Boot is no different. In Catalog Service, a `CatalogServiceApplication` class was autogenerated during the initialization; that's where the `main()` method is defined, and it's how the Spring Boot application is run.

Listing 2.2   The bootstrap class for Catalog Service

```
package com.polarbookshop.catalogservice;

import org.springframework.boot.SpringApplication;
import org.springframework.boot.autoconfigure.SpringBootApplication;

@SpringBootApplication
public class CatalogServiceApplication {
  public static void main(String[] args) {
    SpringApplication.run(CatalogServiceApplication.class, args);
  }
}
```

Defines a Spring configuration class and triggers component scanning and Spring Boot auto-configuration

The method used to launch the application. It registers the current class to be run during the application's bootstrap phase.

The `@SpringBootApplication` annotation is a shortcut that includes three different annotations:

- `@Configuration` marks the class as a source of beans definitions.
- `@ComponentScan` enables component scanning to find and register beans in the Spring context automatically.

- `@EnableAutoConfiguration` enables the auto-configuration capabilities offered by Spring Boot.

Spring Boot auto-configuration is triggered by several conditions, such as the presence of certain classes in the classpath, the existence of specific beans, or the values of some properties. Since the Catalog Service project depends on `spring-boot-starter-web`, Spring Boot will initialize an embedded Tomcat server instance and apply the minimal configuration required to get a web application up and running in almost zero time.

That's it for the application setup. Let's go ahead and expose an HTTP endpoint from Catalog Service.

IMPLEMENTING THE CONTROLLER

So far, we have looked at the project as generated by Spring Initializr. It's time to implement the business logic for the application.

Catalog Service will expose an HTTP GET endpoint to return a friendly greeting to the user to welcome them to the book catalog. You can define a handler for it in a controller class. Figure 2.5 shows the interaction flow.

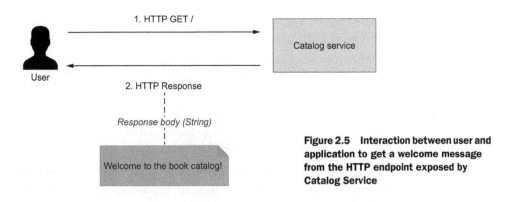

Figure 2.5 Interaction between user and application to get a welcome message from the HTTP endpoint exposed by Catalog Service

In the Catalog Service project, create a new `HomeController` class, and implement a method responsible for handling GET requests to the root endpoint (/).

Listing 2.3 Defining an HTTP endpoint to return a welcome message

```
package com.polarbookshop.catalogservice;

import org.springframework.web.bind.annotation.GetMapping;
import org.springframework.web.bind.annotation.RestController;

@RestController                              ◁── Identifies a class defining handlers
public class HomeController {                     for REST/HTTP endpoints

    @GetMapping("/")                         ◁── Handles GET requests
    public String getGreeting() {                 to the root endpoint
```

```
    return "Welcome to the book catalog!";
  }
}
```

The @RestController annotation identifies a class as a controller handling incoming HTTP requests. Using the @GetMapping annotation, you can mark the getGreeting() method as a handler for GET requests arriving at the root endpoint (/). Any GET request to that endpoint will be processed by this method. In the next chapter, I'll cover how to build RESTful services with Spring in more detail.

TESTING THE APPLICATION

A basic test setup is included when you create a Spring project from Spring Initializr. In the build.gradle file you automatically get the dependencies needed for testing a Spring application. Furthermore, a test class is automatically generated. Let's look at what the CatalogServiceApplicationTests class might look like after you initialize the project.

> **Listing 2.4   The auto-generated test class verifying the Spring context**

```
package com.polarbookshop.catalogservice;

import org.junit.jupiter.api.Test;
import org.springframework.boot.test.context.SpringBootTest;

@SpringBootTest                                        ⟵  Provides a setup for testing
class CatalogServiceApplicationTests {                     Spring Boot applications

  @Test
  void contextLoads() {                       ⟵  Empty test used to verify
  }                                               that the application context
}                                                 is loaded correctly
```

Identifies a test case — @SpringBootTest, class CatalogServiceApplicationTests {, @Test, void contextLoads() {

The default test class is identified by the @SpringBootTest annotation, which provides many helpful features for testing Spring Boot applications. I'll present them in more detail throughout the book. For now, it's enough to know that it loads a full Spring application context for the tests to be run in. There is currently only one test case, which is empty: it's used to verify that the Spring context is loaded correctly.

Open a Terminal window, navigate to the application root folder (catalog-service), and run the test Gradle task to execute the application's tests.

```
$ ./gradlew test
```

The task should be successful and the test green, meaning that the Spring application can start up without errors. What about the HTTP endpoint? Let's find out.

RUNNING THE APPLICATION

You are done implementing the application, so you can go ahead and run it. There are different ways to do that, and I will show you some of them later. For now, you can use the task provided by the Spring Boot Gradle plugin: bootRun.

From the same Terminal window where you launched the tests, run this command:

```
$ ./gradlew bootRun
```

The application should be up and running in a second and ready to accept requests. In figure 2.6 you can see the logs streamed during the startup phase.

```
  .   ____          _            __ _ _
 /\\ / ___'_ __ _ _(_)_ __  __ _ \ \ \ \
( ( )\___ | '_ | '_| | '_ \/ _` | \ \ \ \
 \\/  ___)| |_)| | | | | || (_| |  ) ) ) )
  '  |____| .__|_| |_|_| |_\__, | / / / /
 =========|_|==============|___/=/_/_/_/
 :: Spring Boot ::              (v2.7.3)

2022-08-28 17:35:36.231  INFO 55496 --- [           main] c.p.c.CatalogServiceApplication          : Starting CatalogServiceApplication using Java 17
2022-08-28 17:35:36.233  INFO 55496 --- [           main] c.p.c.CatalogServiceApplication          : No active profile set, falling back to 1 default profile
2022-08-28 17:35:36.842  INFO 55496 --- [           main] o.s.b.w.embedded.tomcat.TomcatWebServer  : Tomcat initialized with port(s): 8080 (http)
2022-08-28 17:35:36.849  INFO 55496 --- [           main] o.apache.catalina.core.StandardService   : Starting service [Tomcat]
2022-08-28 17:35:36.849  INFO 55496 --- [           main] org.apache.catalina.core.StandardEngine  : Starting Servlet engine: [Apache Tomcat/9.0.65]
2022-08-28 17:35:36.907  INFO 55496 --- [           main] o.a.c.c.C.[Tomcat].[localhost].[/]        : Initializing Spring embedded WebApplicationContext
2022-08-28 17:35:36.907  INFO 55496 --- [           main] w.s.c.ServletWebServerApplicationContext : Root WebApplicationContext: initialization completed in 637 ms
2022-08-28 17:35:37.162  INFO 55496 --- [           main] o.s.b.w.embedded.tomcat.TomcatWebServer  : Tomcat started on port(s): 8080 (http) with context path ''
2022-08-28 17:35:37.171  INFO 55496 --- [           main] c.p.c.CatalogServiceApplication          : Started CatalogServiceApplication in 1.222 seconds
```

Figure 2.6 The startup logs from the Catalog Service application

From the logs in figure 2.6, you'll notice that the startup phase is composed of two main steps:

- Initialization and running of the embedded Tomcat server (which, by default, listens to port 8080 over HTTP)
- Initialization and running of the Spring application context

At this point, you can finally verify whether your HTTP endpoint is working as intended. Open a browser window, navigate to http://localhost:8080/, and be ready to be welcomed to the Polar Bookshop's book catalog.

```
Welcome to the book catalog!
```

The development part of the Polar Bookshop application is done: you have a Catalog Service application welcoming users to the book catalog. Remember to terminate the bootRun process (Ctrl-C) to stop the application execution before moving on.

The next step is deploying the application to the cloud. To make it portable on any cloud infrastructure, you should containerize it first. Enter Docker.

2.3 Containerizing applications with Docker

The Catalog Service application is working. Before deploying it to the cloud, however, you should containerize it. Why? Containers provide isolation from the surrounding environment, and they're equipped with all the dependencies required by the application to run.

In our case, most of the dependencies are managed by Gradle and are packaged together with the application (JAR artifact). But the Java runtime is not included.

Without a container, you would have to install the Java runtime on any machine where you want to deploy the application. Containerizing the application means it will be self-contained and portable across any cloud environment. With containers you can manage all applications in a standard way, no matter the language or framework used to implement them.

The *Open Container Initiative* (OCI), a Linux Foundation project, defines industry standards for working with containers (https://opencontainers.org). In particular, the OCI Image Specification defines how to build container images, the OCI Runtime Specification defines how to run those container images, and the OCI Distribution Specification defines how to distribute them. The tool we'll use to work with containers is Docker (www.docker.com), which is compliant with the OCI specifications.

Docker is an open source platform that "provides the ability to package and run an application in a loosely isolated environment called a container" (https://docs.docker .com). *Docker* is also the name of the company behind this technology, which is a founding member of the OCI. The same term is used in several of their commercial products, too. Whenever I write *Docker*, unless specified otherwise, I am referring to the open source platform we'll use to build and run containers.

Before moving on, follow the instructions in section A.2 of appendix A to install and configure Docker in your development environment.

2.3.1 *Introducing Docker: Images and containers*

When you install the Docker platform on your machine, you get the Docker Engine package characterized by a client/server architecture. The *Docker server* contains the *Docker daemon*, a background process responsible for creating and managing Docker objects like images, containers, volumes, and networks. The machine where the Docker server runs is called the *Docker host*. Each machine where you want to run containers should be a Docker host, so it should have a Docker daemon running. The portability of containers is made possible by the daemon process itself.

The Docker daemon exposes an API you can use to send instructions, such as to run a container or create a volume. The *Docker client* talks to the daemon through that API. The client is command-line based and can be used to interact with the Docker daemon either through scripting (for example, Docker Compose) or through the Docker CLI directly.

Besides the client and server components characterizing the Docker Engine, another essential element of the platform is a *container registry*, which has a similar function to a Maven repository. While Maven repositories are used to host and distribute Java libraries, container registries do the same for container images, and they follow the OCI Distribution Specification. We distinguish between public and private registries. The Docker company provides a public registry called Docker Hub (https:// hub.docker.com), which is configured by default with your local Docker installation and hosts images for many popular open source projects, like Ubuntu, PostgreSQL, and OpenJDK.

Based on the architecture description included in the Docker documentation (https://docs.docker.com), figure 2.7 shows how the Docker client, Docker server, and container registry interact.

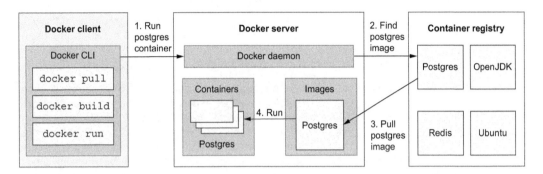

Figure 2.7   The Docker Engine has a client/server architecture, and it interacts with a registry.

The Docker daemon manages different objects. For now we'll focus on images and containers.

A *container image* (or, simply, an *image*) is a lightweight executable package that includes everything needed to run the application inside. The *Docker image* format is the most used one for creating container images, and it has been standardized by the OCI project (in the OCI Image Specification). OCI images can be created from scratch by defining instructions in a Dockerfile, a text-based file containing all the steps to generate the image. Usually, images are created based on another image. For example, you might build an image based on the OpenJDK one, on top of which you can add a Java application. After it's created, the image can be pushed to a container registry like Docker Hub. A base name and a tag identify each image, where the tag is usually the version number. For example, the Ubuntu image for version 22.04 is called ubuntu:22.04. A colon separates the base name and version.

A *container* is a runnable instance of a container image. You can manage the container life cycle from the Docker CLI or Docker Compose: you can start, stop, update, and delete containers. Containers are defined by the image on which they are based and the configuration provided at startup time (for example, environment variables used to customize the container). By default, containers are isolated from each other and the host machine, but you can make them expose services to the outside world through specific ports with a process called *port forwarding* or *port mapping*. Containers can have any name. If you don't specify one, the Docker server will assign a random one, like bazinga_schrodinger. To run OCI images as containers, you'll need Docker or any other container runtime compatible with the OCI specifications.

When you want to run a new container, you can use the Docker CLI to interact with the Docker daemon, which checks whether the specified image is already present on the local server. If not, it will find the image on a registry, download it, and then use it to run a container. The workflow, again, is shown in figure 2.7.

Docker on macOS and Windows. How does it work?

In the previous chapter, you learned that containers share the same operating system kernel and rely on Linux features such as namespaces and cgroups. We'll use Docker to run Spring Boot applications in Linux containers, but how is Docker supposed to work on a macOS or Windows machine?

When you install Docker on a Linux operating system, you get the full Docker Engine on your Linux host. However, if you install either *Docker Desktop for Mac* or *Docker Desktop for Windows*, only the Docker client is installed on your macOS/Windows host. Under the hood, a lightweight virtual machine is configured with Linux, and the Docker server component is installed on that machine. As a user, you will get almost the same experience as on a Linux machine; you will hardly notice any difference. But in reality, whenever you use the Docker CLI to perform operations, you are actually interacting with a Docker server on a different machine (the virtual machine running Linux).

You can verify this yourself by starting Docker and running the docker version command. You'll notice that the Docker client is running on a darwin/amd64 architecture (on macOS) or on windows/amd64 (on Windows), while the Docker server is running on linux/amd64.

```
$ docker version
Client:
 Cloud integration: v1.0.24
 Version:           20.10.14
 API version:       1.41
 Go version:        go1.16.15
 Git commit:        a224086
 Built:             Thu Mar 24 01:49:20 2022
 OS/Arch:           darwin/amd64
 Context:           default
 Experimental:      true

Server:
 Engine:
  Version:          20.10.14
  API version:      1.41 (minimum version 1.12)
  Go version:       go1.16.15
  Git commit:       87a90dc
  Built:            Thu Mar 24 01:45:44 2022
  OS/Arch:          linux/amd64
  Experimental:     false
```

Docker provides support for architectures other than AMD64. For example, if you use a MacBook with Apple Silicon (ARM-based chips), you'll find your Docker client running on a darwin/arm64 architecture and the Docker server on linux/arm64.

2.3.2 *Running a Spring application as a container*

Let's go back to Catalog Service and see how you can run it as a container. There are different ways to achieve that, but here you will use the out-of-the-box integration of Spring Boot with Cloud Native Buildpacks (https://buildpacks.io), a project initiated by Heroku and Pivotal and now hosted by the CNCF. It provides a high-level abstraction for automatically transforming application source code into container images instead of using a low-level `Dockerfile`.

The Paketo Buildpacks (an implementation of the Cloud Native Buildpacks specification) are fully integrated with the Spring Boot Plugin, both for Gradle and Maven. This means that you can containerize your Spring Boot applications without downloading any additional tools, providing any extra dependencies, or writing a Dockerfile.

Chapter 6 will describe how the Cloud Native Buildpacks project works and how you can configure it to containerize your Spring Boot applications. For now, I'll give you a little preview of its features.

Open a Terminal window, navigate to the root folder of your Catalog Service project (`catalog-service`), and run the `bootBuildImage` Gradle task. That's all you need to do to package your application as a container image, using Cloud Native Buildpacks under the hood.

```
$ ./gradlew bootBuildImage
```

> **WARNING** As I write this, the Paketo project is working on adding support for ARM64 images. You can follow the feature's progress on the Paketo Buildpacks project on GitHub: https://github.com/paketo-buildpacks/stacks/issues/51. Until that's complete, you can still use Buildpacks to build containers and run them via Docker Desktop on Apple Silicon computers, but the build process and the application startup phase will be slower than usual. Until official support is added, you can alternatively use the following command, which points to an experimental version of Paketo Buildpacks with ARM64 support: `./gradlew bootBuildImage --builder ghcr.io/thomasvitale/java-builder-arm64`. Be aware that it's experimental and not ready for production. For more information, you can refer to the documentation on GitHub: https://github.com/ThomasVitale/paketo-arm64.

The first time you run the task, it will take a minute to download the packages used by Buildpacks to create the container image. The second time it will take only a few seconds. The resulting image will be named `catalog-service:0.0.1-SNAPSHOT` by default (`<project_name>:<version>`). You can run the following command to get the details of the newly created image:

```
$ docker images catalog-service:0.0.1-SNAPSHOT
REPOSITORY          TAG              IMAGE ID       CREATED        SIZE
catalog-service     0.0.1-SNAPSHOT   f0247a113eff   42 years ago   275MB
```

NOTE   You might have noticed in the previous command's output that it looks like the image was created 42 years ago. That's a convention used by Cloud Native Buildpacks to achieve reproducible builds. Subsequent execution of the build command should give the same output if nothing is changed in the input. Using an accurate creation timestamp would make that impossible, so Cloud Native Buildpacks uses a conventional timestamp (January 1, 1980).

The last thing to do is run the image and verify that the containerized application is working correctly. Open a Terminal window and run the following command:

```
$ docker run --rm --name catalog-service -p 8080:8080 \
    catalog-service:0.0.1-SNAPSHOT
```

WARNING   If you're running the container on an Apple Silicon computer, the previous command might return a message like "WARNING: The requested image's platform (linux/amd64) does not match the detected host platform (linux/arm64/v8) and no specific platform was requested." In that case, you'll need to include an additional argument to the preceding command (before the image name) until support for ARM64 is added to Paketo Build-packs: `--platform linux/amd64`.

You can refer to figure 2.8 for a description of the command.

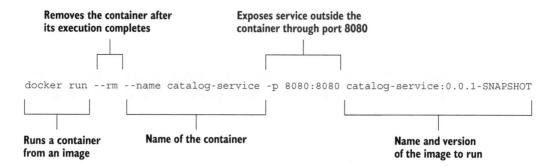

Figure 2.8   The Docker command to start a containerized application from an image

Open a browser window, navigate to `http://localhost:8080/`, and verify that you still get the same greeting you got earlier.

```
Welcome to the book catalog!
```

When you are done, stop the container with Ctrl-C.

In chapter 6, you'll learn more about how Docker works, how container images are built from a Spring Boot application, and how to use a container registry. I'll also show you how to use Docker Compose to manage containers instead of using the Docker CLI.

2.4 Managing containers with Kubernetes

So far, you have built a web application with Spring Boot (Catalog Service), container-ized it with Cloud Native Buildpacks, and run it with Docker. To complete the pilot project for Polar Bookshop, you must perform one last step: deploy the application to a cloud environment. To do that, you will use Kubernetes, which has become the de facto standard for container orchestration. I will provide more details about Kuber-netes in later chapters, but I want you to have a first taste of how it works and how you can use it to deploy a web application.

Kubernetes (often shortened as *K8s*) is an open source system for automating the deployment, scaling, and management of containerized applications (https:// kubernetes.io). When you are working with containers in Docker, your deployment target is a machine. In the example from the previous section, it was your computer. In other scenarios it might be a virtual machine (VM). In any case, it's about deploy-ing containers to a specific machine. However, when it comes to deploying containers without downtime, scaling them by leveraging the cloud's elasticity, or connecting them across different hosts, you'll need something more than a container engine. Instead of deploying to a specific machine, you are deploying to a cluster of machines, and Kubernetes, among other things, manages a cluster of machines for you. I cov-ered this distinction in the previous chapter in the context of topologies. Figure 2.9 will remind you of the different deployment targets in a container topology and an orchestration topology.

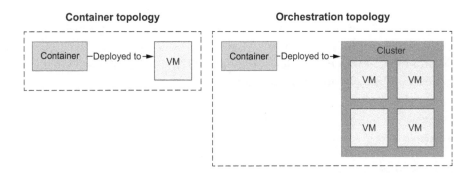

Figure 2.9 The deployment target of containers is a machine, whereas for orchestrators it's a cluster.

Before moving on, follow the instructions in section A.3 of appendix A to install mini-kube and set up a Kubernetes cluster in your local development environment. Once you are done with the installation procedure, you can start a local Kubernetes cluster with the following command:

```
$ minikube start
```

2.4.1   Introducing Kubernetes: Deployments, Pods, and Services

Kubernetes is an open source container orchestrator hosted by the CNCF. In just a few years, it has become the most used solution for container orchestration, and all the major cloud providers have offerings for Kubernetes as a service. Kubernetes can run on a desktop, on a data center on premises, in the cloud, and even on an IoT device.

When using a container topology, you need a machine with a container runtime. With Kubernetes, however, you switch to an orchestration topology, meaning that you need a cluster. A Kubernetes *cluster* is a set of worker machines (*nodes*) that run containerized applications. Every cluster has at least one worker node. With minikube. you can easily create a single-node cluster on your local machine. In production, you'll use a cluster managed by a cloud provider.

A Kubernetes cluster comprises machines called *worker nodes* on which your containerized applications are deployed. They provide capacity such as CPU, memory, network, and storage so that the containers can run and connect to a network.

The *control plane* is the container orchestration layer that manages the worker nodes. It exposes the API and interfaces to define, deploy, and manage the life cycle of containers. It offers all the essential elements that implement the typical features of an orchestrator, like cluster management, scheduling, and health monitoring.

> **NOTE** In the context of container orchestration, *scheduling* means matching a container instance with a node where it will be run. The matching is based on a set of criteria, including the availability of enough computational resources to run the container on the node.

You can interact with Kubernetes through a CLI client, kubectl, which communicates with the control plane to perform some operations on the worker nodes. A client doesn't interact with the worker nodes directly. Figure 2.10 shows the high-level components of the Kubernetes architecture.

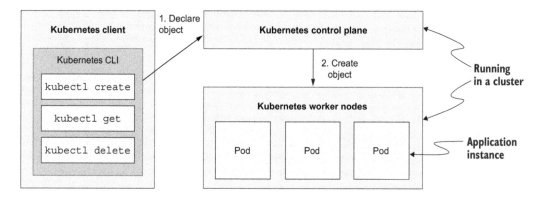

Figure 2.10 Kubernetes' main components are the API, the control plane, and the worker nodes.

Kubernetes can manage many different objects, either built-in or custom. In this section, you will use Pods, Deployments, and Services.

- *Pod*—The smallest deployable unit, which can include one or more containers. A Pod usually contains only one of your applications. It might also include extra containers supporting the primary application (such as containers providing additional functionality like logging or administrative tasks to run during the initialization step). Kubernetes manages Pods rather than containers directly.
- *Deployment*—A Deployment informs Kubernetes about the desired deployment state for your application. For each instance, it creates a Pod and keeps it healthy. Among other things, a Deployment allows you to manage Pods as a set.
- *Service*—A Deployment (a set of Pods) can be exposed to other nodes in the cluster or outside by defining a Service that also takes care of balancing the load between Pod instances.

NOTE Throughout the book, I will write Kubernetes resources with capital letters to distinguish them from when the same terms are used with different meanings. For example, I'll use *service* when referring to an application, whereas I'll write *Service* when I mean the Kubernetes object.

When you want to run a new application, you can define a *resource manifest*, a file that describes the desired state for the application. For example, you might specify that it should be replicated five times and exposed to the outside world through port 8080. Resource manifests are usually written using YAML. You can then use the kubectl client to ask the control plane to create the resources described by the manifest. In the end, the control plane processes the request using its internal components and creates the resources in the worker nodes. The control plane still relies on a container registry to fetch the image defined in the resource manifest. The workflow, again, is shown in figure 2.10.

2.4.2 *Running a Spring application on Kubernetes*

Let's go back to the Polar Bookshop project. In the previous section, you containerized the Catalog Service application. Now it's time to deploy it to a cluster using Kubernetes. You already have a cluster up and running in your local environment. What you need is a resource manifest.

The standard way to interact with Kubernetes is through declarative instructions that you can define in a YAML or JSON file. I will show you how to write resource manifests in chapter 7. Until then, you can use the Kubernetes CLI as you did with Docker earlier.

First you need to tell Kubernetes to deploy Catalog Service from a container image. You built one previously (`catalog-service:0.0.1-SNAPSHOT`). By default, minikube uses the Docker Hub registry to pull images, and it doesn't have access to your local ones. Therefore, it will not find the image you built for the Catalog Service application. But don't worry: you can manually import it into your local cluster.

Open a Terminal window, and run the following command:

```
$ minikube image load catalog-service:0.0.1-SNAPSHOT
```

The deployment unit will be a Pod, but you will not manage Pods directly. Instead, you'll want to let Kubernetes handle that. Pods are application instances, and as such they are ephemeral. To achieve the cloud native goals, you want the platform to take care of instantiating Pods so that if one goes down, it can be replaced by another one. What you need is a *Deployment* resource that will make Kubernetes create application instances as *Pod* resources.

From a Terminal window, run the following command:

```
$ kubectl create deployment catalog-service \
    --image=catalog-service:0.0.1-SNAPSHOT
```

You can refer to figure 2.11 for a description of the command.

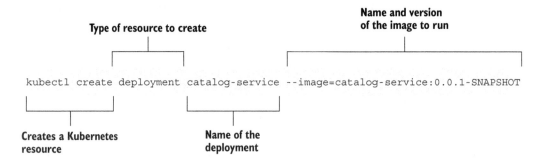

Figure 2.11   The Kubernetes command to create a Deployment from a container image. Kubernetes will take care of creating Pods for the application.

You can verify the creation of the Deployment object as follows:

```
$ kubectl get deployment
NAME             READY   UP-TO-DATE   AVAILABLE   AGE
catalog-service  1/1     1            1           7s
```

Behind the scenes, Kubernetes created a Pod for the application defined in the Deployment resource. You can verify the creation of the Pod object as follows:

```
$ kubectl get pod
NAME                              READY   STATUS    RESTARTS   AGE
catalog-service-5b9c996675-nzbhd  1/1     Running   0          21s
```

> **TIP**   You can check the application logs by running `kubectl logs deployment/catalog-service`.

By default, applications running in Kubernetes are not accessible. Let's fix that. First, you can expose Catalog Service to the cluster through a Service resource by running the following command:

```
$ kubectl expose deployment catalog-service \
    --name=catalog-service \
    --port=8080
```

Figure 2.12 provides a description of the command.

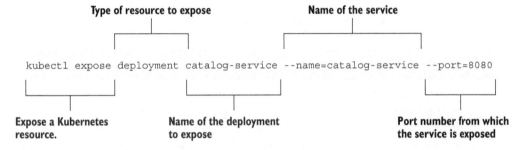

Figure 2.12   The Kubernetes command to expose a Deployment as a Service. The Catalog Service application will be exposed to the cluster network through port 8080.

The Service object exposes the application to other components inside the cluster. You can verify that it's been created correctly with the following command:

```
$ kubectl get service catalog-service
NAME                TYPE        CLUSTER-IP       EXTERNAL-IP   PORT(S)    AGE
catalog-service     ClusterIP   10.96.141.159    <none>        8080/TCP   7s
```

You can then forward the traffic from a local port on your computer (for example, 8000) to the port exposed by the Service inside the cluster (8080). Remember the port mapping in Docker? This works in a similar way. The output of the command will tell you if the port forwarding is configured correctly:

```
$ kubectl port-forward service/catalog-service 8000:8080
Forwarding from 127.0.0.1:8000 -> 8080
Forwarding from [::1]:8000 -> 8080
```

You can refer to figure 2.13 for a description of the command.

Now whenever you access port 8000 on your localhost, you will be forwarded to the Service inside the Kubernetes cluster responsible for exposing the Catalog Service application. Open a browser window, navigate to http://localhost:8000/ (make sure you use 8000 and not 8080), and verify that you still get the same greeting as before.

```
Welcome to the book catalog!
```

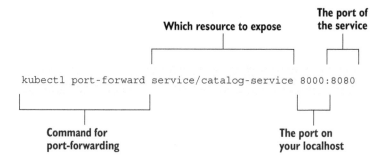

Figure 2.13   **The Kubernetes command for forwarding a port from your localhost to a Service inside the cluster. The Catalog Service application will be exposed to your localhost through port 8000.**

Well done! You started with a Java application implemented using Spring Boot. Then you containerized it with Cloud Native Buildpacks and ran it on Docker. Finally, you used Kubernetes to get the application deployed to a cluster. Sure, it was a local cluster, but it could have been a remote one in the cloud. The beauty of this process is that it works the same way regardless of the environment. You could use the exact same approach to deploy Catalog Service to a cluster in a public cloud infrastructure. Isn't it great?

In chapter 7, you will work more with Kubernetes. For now, terminate the port-forwarding process with Ctrl-C, delete the Service with `kubectl delete service catalog -service`, and delete the Deployment with `kubectl delete deployment catalog -service`. Finally, you can stop the Kubernetes cluster with `minikube stop`.

2.5   *Polar Bookshop: A cloud native application*

In this book, I aim to provide real-world code examples as often as possible. Now that you have explored some of the key concepts and have tried your hand at building, containerizing, and deploying a Spring application, let's take on a slightly more complicated project: an online bookshop. In the rest of the book, I'll guide you through developing a complete cloud native system based on Spring applications, containerizing it, and deploying it with Kubernetes in a public cloud.

For each concept we cover in the following chapters, I'll show you how to apply it to a real-world cloud native scenario for a complete hands-on learning experience. Remember that all the code used in this book is available on the book's GitHub repository.

This section will define the requirements for the cloud native project we'll build, and it will describe its architecture. Then I'll outline the main technologies and patterns we'll use to implement it.

2.5.1   *Understanding the requirements of the system*

Polar Bookshop is a specialized bookshop whose mission is to spread knowledge and information about the North Pole and the Arctic, where the bookshop is located: the

Arctic's history, geography, animals, and so on. The organization managing the bookshop, Polarsophia, has decided to start selling its books online to spread them worldwide, but that is only the beginning. The project is very ambitious, and the vision includes a suite of software products to fulfill the Polarsophia mission. After the successful pilot project earlier in this chapter, the organization has decided to embark on a cloud native journey.

Throughout the book, you'll build the core part of a system with endless possibilities in terms of functionality and integration. The management plans to deliver new features in short iterations, reducing the time to market and getting early feedback from users. Their goal is to bring the bookshop close to everyone, everywhere, so the application should be highly scalable. With a worldwide audience, such a system needs to be highly available, so resilience is essential.

Polarsophia is a small organization, and they need to optimize costs, especially those regarding infrastructure. They can't afford to build their own data center, so they have decided to rent IT hardware from a third party.

By now, you can probably recognize some of the reasons why companies move to the cloud. That's what we'll do for the Polar Bookshop application. Of course, it will be a cloud native application.

Books will be available for sale through the application. When a customer purchases a book, they should be able to check on the status of their order. Two categories of people will use the Polar Bookshop application:

- Customers can browse books in the catalog, buy some, and check their orders.
- Employees can manage books, update existing ones, and add new items to the catalog.

Figure 2.14 describes the architecture of the Polar Bookshop cloud native system. As you can see, it's made up of several services. Some will implement the business logic of the system to provide the functionality already mentioned. Other services will implement shared concerns like centralized configuration. For clarity, the figure doesn't show the services responsible for the security and observability concerns. You'll learn about them later in the book.

In the following chapters, I'll guide you through figure 2.14 in more detail, adding more information about specific services and adopting different points of view to visualize the system in its deployment stage. For now, let's look at the patterns and technologies we'll use in the project.

2.5.2   *Exploring patterns and technologies used in the project*

I'll show you how to apply specific technologies or patterns to the Polar Bookshop project when I introduce each new topic in the book. Here I'll give you an overview of the main concerns we will address and the technologies and patterns we'll use to accomplish them.

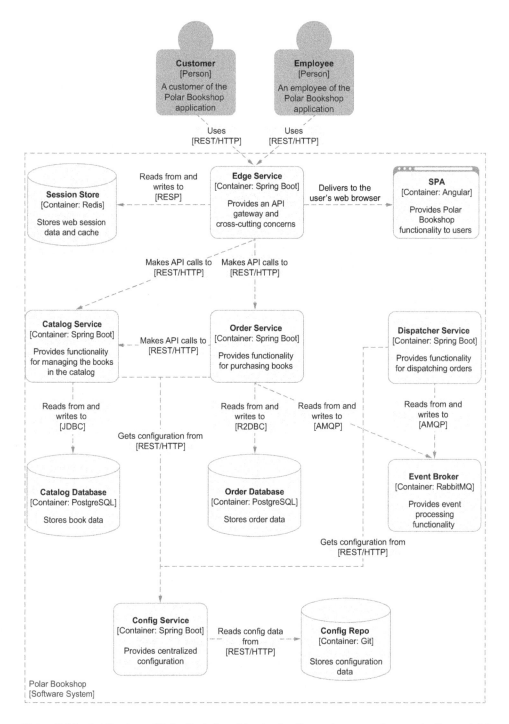

Figure 2.14 Architecture of Polar Bookshop. The cloud native system comprises application and data services with different responsibilities. For clarity, the security and observability services are not shown.

WEB AND INTERACTIONS

Polar Bookshop comprises several services that will have to communicate with each other to provide their functionality. You'll build RESTful services that interact synchronously over HTTP, both in a blocking way (using traditional servlets) and non-blocking ways (using reactive programming). Spring MVC and Spring WebFlux (on top of Project Reactor) will be your main tools for accomplishing such a result.

When building cloud native applications, you should design loosely coupled services and consider how you can keep data consistent in a distributed system context. Synchronous communications can generate problems when multiple services are involved in accomplishing a function. That's why event-driven programming is getting very popular in the cloud: it allows you to overcome the issues of synchronous communications.

I'll show you how to use events and messaging systems to decouple services and ensure data consistency. You'll use Spring Cloud Stream to implement data streams between services and Spring Cloud Function to define message handlers as functions. The latter approach could naturally evolve in serverless applications deployed to platforms like Azure Functions, AWS Lambda, or Knative.

DATA

Data is a crucial part of software systems. In Polar Bookshop you'll use the PostgreSQL relational database to permanently store the data processed by the application. I'll show you how to integrate an application with a data source using Spring Data JDBC (imperative) and Spring Data R2DBC (reactive). You'll then learn how to evolve a data source and manage schema migrations with Flyway.

Cloud native applications should be stateless, but the state needs to be stored somewhere. In Polar Bookshop you'll use Redis to externalize the session storage to a data store and keep applications stateless and scalable. Spring Session makes it easy to implement clustered user sessions. In particular, I'll show you how to use Spring Session Data Redis to integrate the application session management with Redis.

Besides persisted data and session data, you'll also deal with messages to implement event-driven programming patterns. Spring AMQP and RabbitMQ will be the technologies you'll use to do so.

Locally, you'll run these data services in Docker containers. In production, you'll rely on the managed services offered by a cloud provider like DigitalOcean or Azure, which take care of critical concerns like high availability, clustering, storage, and data replication.

CONFIGURATION

Throughout the book I'll show you how to configure the services in Polar Bookshop in different ways. I'll start by exploring the options offered by Spring Boot properties and profiles, and when to use them. You'll then learn how to apply external configuration by using environment variables when running a Spring application as a JAR and as a container. Then you'll see how to centralize the configuration management through a configuration server with Spring Cloud Config. Finally, I'll teach you how to use ConfigMaps and Secrets in Kubernetes.

ROUTING

Polar Bookshop, being a distributed system, will need some routing configuration. Kubernetes has a built-in service discovery feature that can help you decouple services from their physical addresses and hostnames. Cloud native applications are scalable, so any interactions between them should take that into account: which instance should you call? Once again, Kubernetes offers you a load-balancing feature natively, so you don't need to implement anything in your application.

Using Spring Cloud Gateway, I'll guide you through implementing a service that will act as an API gateway to shield the outside from any internal API changes. It will also be an edge service that you'll use to address cross-cutting concerns, like security and resilience, in one place. Such a service will be the entry point to Polar Bookshop, and it will have to be highly available, performant, and fault-tolerant.

OBSERVABILITY

The services in the Polar Bookshop system should be observable to be defined as cloud native. I'll show you how to use Spring Boot Actuator to set up health and info endpoints and expose metrics with Micrometer to be fetched and processed by Prometheus. You'll then use Grafana to visualize the most critical metrics in informative dashboards.

Requests can be handled by more than one service, so you'll need distributed tracing functionality to follow the request flow from one service to another. You'll set that up with OpenTelemetry. Then Grafana Tempo will fetch, process, and visualize the traces to give you a complete picture of how the system accomplishes its functions.

Finally you'll need a logging strategy in place. We should handle logs as event streams, so you'll make your Spring applications stream log events to the standard output without considering how they are processed or stored. Fluent Bit will take care of collecting logs from all services, Loki will store and process them, and Grafana will let you browse them.

RESILIENCE

Cloud native applications should be resilient. For the Polar Bookshop project, I'll show you various techniques for making an application resilient using Project Reactor, Spring Cloud Circuit Breaker, and Resilience4J to implement circuit breakers, retries, timeouts, and other patterns.

SECURITY

Security is a vast subject that I won't be able to cover deeply in this book. Still, I recommend exploring the topic, since it's one of the most critical software concerns nowadays. It's a pervasive concern that should be addressed continuously from the very beginning of the project.

For Polar Bookshop, I'll show you how to add authentication and authorization functionality to cloud native applications. You'll see how to secure communications between services, and between users and applications. OAuth 2.1 and OpenID Connect will be the standards you'll rely on to implement such functionality. Spring Security supports those standards and integrates seamlessly with external services to provide authentication and authorization. You'll use Keycloak for identity and access control management.

Also, I'll introduce the concepts of secrets management and encryption. I won't be able to go too deep into those topics, but I'll show you how to manage secrets to configure Spring Boot applications.

TESTING

Automated testing is paramount for the success of a cloud native application. A few levels of automated tests will cover the Polar Bookshop application. I'll show you how to use JUnit5 to write unit tests. Spring Boot adds many convenient utilities that improve integration testing, and you will use them to ensure the quality of your services. You'll write tests for the various features used in Polar Bookshop, including REST endpoints, messaging streams, data integrations, and security.

Keeping parity across environments is essential to ensure the quality of your applications. This is especially true when it comes to backing services. In production, you will use services such as PostgreSQL and Redis. During testing, you should use similar services rather than mocks or test-specific tools like the H2 in-memory database. The Testcontainers framework will help you use real services as containers in your automated tests.

BUILD AND DEPLOYMENT

Polar Bookshop's primary services will use Spring. You'll see how to package a Spring application, run it as a JAR file, containerize it with Cloud Native Buildpacks, run it with Docker, and finally deploy containers with Kubernetes. You'll also see how to compile Spring applications to native images using Spring Native and GraalVM, and use them in serverless architectures, taking advantage of their instant startup time, instant peak performance, reduced memory consumption, and reduced image size. Then you'll deploy them on a serverless platform built on top of Kubernetes with Knative.

I'll show you how to automate the build stage by setting up a deployment pipeline with GitHub Actions. The pipeline will build the application at every commit, run the tests, and package it ready for deployment. Such automation will support a continuous delivery culture to bring value to customers quickly and reliably. In the end, you'll also automate the deployment of Polar Bookshop to the production Kubernetes cluster using GitOps practices and Argo CD.

UI

This book is focused on backend technologies, so I won't teach you any frontend subjects. Of course, your application will need a frontend for the users to interact with. In the case of Polar Bookshop, you'll rely on a client application using the Angular framework. I won't show you the UI application code in this book because it's out of scope, but I've included it in the code repository accompanying the book.

Summary

- The 15-Factor methodology identifies development principles for building applications that offer maximum portability across execution environments, are suitable to be deployed on cloud platforms, can be scaled, guarantee environment parity between development and production, and enable continuous delivery.

- Spring is a suite of projects that provide all of the most common functionality for building modern applications in Java.

- Spring Framework provides an application context in which beans and properties are managed throughout the entire life cycle.

- Spring Boot lays the foundation for cloud native development by speeding up the building of production-ready applications, including embedded servers, auto-configuration, monitoring, and containerization features.

- Container images are lightweight executable packages that include everything needed to run the applications inside.

- Docker is an OCI-compliant platform for building and running containers.

- A Spring Boot application can be packaged as a container image with Cloud Native Buildpacks, a CNCF project that specifies how to convert application source code into production-ready container images.

- When dealing with several containers, as is usually the case in a cloud native system, you need to manage this complex system. Kubernetes provides functionality to orchestrate, schedule, and manage containers.

- Kubernetes Pods are the minimum deployment units.

- Kubernetes Deployments describe how to create application instances as Pods, starting from container images.

- Kubernetes Services allow you to expose application endpoints outside the cluster.

Part 2

Cloud native development

Part 1 defined the main features of cloud native applications, and you got a first taste of the journey from code to deployment. Part 2 will introduce you to the main practices and patterns for building production-ready cloud native applications using Spring Boot and Kubernetes.

Chapter 3 covers the fundamentals of starting a new cloud native project, including strategies for organizing the codebase, managing dependencies, and defining the commit stage of a deployment pipeline. You'll learn how to implement and test a REST API using Spring MVC and Spring Boot Test. Chapter 4 discusses the importance of externalized configuration and covers some options available for Spring Boot applications, including property files, environment variables, and configuration services with Spring Cloud Config. Chapter 5 presents the main aspects of data services in the cloud and shows how to add data persistence to a Spring Boot application using Spring Data JDBC. You'll learn production options for managing data using Flyway and testing strategies using Testcontainers. Chapter 6 is about containers; you'll learn more about Docker and how to package Spring Boot applications as container images using Dockerfiles and Cloud Native Buildpacks. Finally, chapter 7 discusses Kubernetes and covers service discovery, load balancing, scalability, and local development workflows. You'll also learn more about how to deploy Spring Boot applications to a Kubernetes cluster.

Getting started with cloud native development

This chapter covers
- Bootstrapping a cloud native project
- Working with embedded servers and Tomcat
- Building a RESTful application with Spring MVC
- Testing a RESTful application with Spring Test
- Automating the build and tests with GitHub Actions

The cloud native landscape is so broad that getting started can be overwhelming. In part 1 of this book, you got a theoretical introduction to cloud native applications and the processes supporting them, and you had a first hands-on experience building a minimal Spring Boot application and deploying it to Kubernetes as a container. All of that will help you better understand the overall cloud native picture and correctly place the topics I'll be covering in the rest of the book.

The cloud opened up endless possibilities for what we can achieve with many types of applications. In this chapter, I'll start with one of the most common types: a web application that exposes its functionality over HTTP through a REST API. I'll guide you through the development process you'll follow in all the subsequent chapters, addressing the significant differences between traditional and cloud native web applications, consolidating some necessary aspects of Spring Boot and Spring MVC, and highlighting essential testing and production considerations. I'll also explain some of the guidelines recommended by the 15-Factor methodology, including dependency management, concurrency, and API first.

Along the way, you'll implement the Catalog Service application you initialized in the previous chapter. It will be responsible for managing the catalog of books in the Polar Bookshop system.

NOTE The source code for the examples in this chapter is available in the Chapter03/03-begin and Chapter03/03-end folders, which contain the initial and final states of the project (https://github.com/ThomasVitale/cloud-native-spring-in-action).

3.1 *Bootstrapping a cloud native project*

Starting a new development project is always exciting. The 15-Factor methodology contains some practical guidelines for bootstrapping a cloud native application.

- *One codebase, one application*—Cloud native applications should consist of a single codebase tracked in a version control system.
- *Dependency management*—Cloud native applications should use a tool that manages dependencies explicitly and shouldn't rely on implicit dependencies from the environment where they are deployed.

In this section, I'll provide a few more details about those two principles and explain how to apply them to Catalog Service, the first cloud native application in the Polar Bookshop system.

3.1.1 *One codebase, one application*

A cloud native application should consist of a single codebase tracked in a version control system like Git. Each codebase must produce immutable artifacts, called *builds*, that can be deployed to multiple environments. Figure 3.1 shows the relationship between codebase, build, and deployments.

As you'll see in the next chapter, anything environment-specific like configuration must be outside of the application codebase. In case of code that's needed by more than one application, you should either turn it into an independent service or into a library that you can import into the project as a dependency. You should carefully evaluate the latter option to prevent the system from becoming a *distributed monolith*.

NOTE Thinking about how your code is organized into codebases and repositories can help you focus more on the system architecture and identify those parts that might actually stand on their own as independent services. If this is done correctly, the codebase's organization can favor modularity and loose coupling.

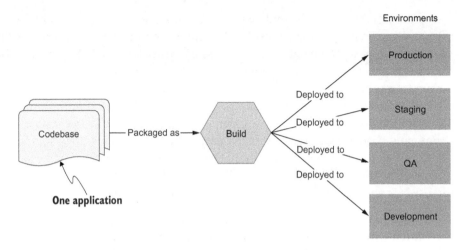

Figure 3.1 Each application has its codebase, from which immutable builds are produced and then deployed to the appropriate environments without changes to the code.

According to the 15-Factor methodology, each codebase should be mapped to an application, but nothing is said about repositories. You can decide to track each codebase in a separate repository or in the same one. Both options are used in the cloud native business. Throughout the book, you'll build several applications, and I recommend you track each codebase in its own Git repository because it'll improve maintainability and deployability.

In the previous chapter, you initialized the first application in the Polar Bookshop system, Catalog Service, and placed it in a `catalog-service` Git repository. I recommend you use GitHub for storing your repositories because later we're going to use GitHub Actions as the workflow engine to define deployment pipelines in support of continuous delivery.

3.1.2 *Dependency management with Gradle and Maven*

How you manage dependencies for your applications is relevant because it affects their reliability and portability. In the Java ecosystem, the two most used tools for dependency management are Gradle and Maven. Both provide the functionality to declare dependencies in a manifest and download them from a central repository. The reason for listing all the dependencies your project needs is to ensure that you do not depend on any implicit library leaking from the surrounding environment.

> **NOTE** Apart from dependency management, Gradle and Maven offer additional features for building, testing, and configuring a Java project, which are fundamental for application development. All the examples in the book will use Gradle, but feel free to use Maven instead.

Even though you have a dependency manifest in place, you'll still need to provide the dependency manager itself. Both Gradle and Maven offer a feature to run the tool from a *wrapper script* named `gradlew` or `mvnw` that you can include in your codebase. For example, rather than running a Gradle command like `gradle build` (which assumes you have Gradle installed on your machine), you can run `./gradlew build`. The script invokes the specific version of the build tool defined in the project. If the build tool is not present yet, the wrapper script will download it first and then run the command. Using the wrapper, you can ensure that all team members and automated tools building the project use the same Gradle or Maven version. When you're generating a new project from Spring Initializr, you'll also get a wrapper script that's ready to use, so you don't need to download or configure anything.

> **NOTE**   No matter what, you'll usually have at least one external dependency: the runtime. In our case, that's the Java Runtime Environment (JRE). If you package your application as a container image, the Java runtime will be included in the image itself, granting you more control over it. On the other hand, the final application artifact will depend on the container runtime required to run the image. You'll learn more about the containerization process in chapter 6.

Now, on to the code. The Polar Bookshop system has a Catalog Service application that's responsible for managing the books available in the catalog. In the previous chapter, we initialized the project. The architecture of the system is shown again in figure 3.2.

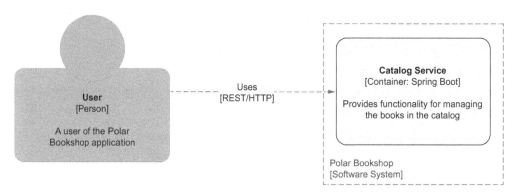

Figure 3.2   The architecture of the Polar Bookshop system, currently consisting of only one application service

All the dependencies required by the application are listed in the autogenerated build.gradle file (catalog-service/build.gradle).

```
dependencies {
  implementation 'org.springframework.boot:spring-boot-starter-web'
  testImplementation 'org.springframework.boot:spring-boot-starter-test'
}
```

These are the main dependencies:

- Spring Web (`org.springframework.boot:spring-boot-starter-web`) provides the necessary libraries for building web applications with Spring MVC and includes Tomcat as the default embedded server.
- Spring Boot Test (`org.springframework.boot:spring-boot-starter-test`) provides several libraries and utilities for testing applications, including Spring Test, JUnit, AssertJ, and Mockito. It's automatically included in every Spring Boot project.

One of the great features of Spring Boot is the way it handles dependency management. Starter dependencies like `spring-boot-starter-web` relieve you of managing many more dependencies and verifying that the particular versions you import are compatible with each other. It's yet another Spring Boot feature that will get you started in a simple and productive way.

In the next section, you'll learn more about how the server embedded in Spring Boot works and how to configure it.

3.2   *Working with embedded servers*

With Spring Boot, you can build different types of applications (e.g., web, event-driven, serverless, batch, and task applications) characterized by various use cases and patterns. In a cloud native context, they all share some common aspects:

- They are entirely self-contained, with no external dependencies other than the runtime.
- They are packaged as standard, executable artifacts.

Consider a web application. Traditionally, you would package it as a WAR or EAR file (archive formats used to package Java applications) and deploy it to a web server like Tomcat or an application server like WildFly. The external dependency on a server would limit the portability and evolution of the application itself and increase the maintenance costs.

In this section, you'll see how to solve those problems in a cloud native web application with Spring Boot, Spring MVC, and an embedded server, but similar principles apply to other types of applications as well. You'll learn the differences between traditional and cloud native applications, how an embedded server like Tomcat works, and how you can configure it. I'll also elaborate on a few guidelines from the 15-Factor methodology regarding servers, port binding, and concurrency:

- *Port binding*—Unlike traditional applications that depend on an external server being available in the execution environment, cloud native applications are self-contained and export their services by binding to a port that can be configured depending on the environment.
- *Concurrency*—In JVM applications, we handle concurrency through multiple threads available as thread pools. When the concurrency limit is hit, we favor horizontal over vertical scaling. Instead of adding more computational resources

to the application, we prefer to deploy more instances and distribute the workload among them.

Following those principles, we'll continue working on Catalog Service to ensure it's self-contained and packaged as an executable JAR.

Servers! Servers everywhere!

So far I've used the terms *application servers* and *web servers*. Later, I will also mention *Servlet containers*. What's the difference?

- *Web server*—A server that handles HTTP requests coming from a client and replies with HTTP responses, such as Apache HTTPD.
- *Servlet container*—A component, part of a web server, that provides an execution context for web applications using the Java Servlet API (like Spring MVC apps). Tomcat (Catalina) is one example.
- *Application server*—A server that provides a complete execution environment (like Jakarta EE) for different types of applications and supports several protocols, such as WildFly.

3.2.1 *Executable JARs and embedded servers*

One of the differences between a traditional approach and a cloud native one is how you package and deploy applications. Traditionally, we used to have application servers or standalone web servers. They were expensive to set up and maintain in production, so they were used to deploy several applications, packaged as EAR or WAR artifacts for the sake of efficiency. Such a scenario created coupling among the applications. If any of them wanted to change something at the server level, the change would have to be coordinated with other teams and applied to all the applications, limiting agility and application evolution. Besides that, the deployment of an application depended on a server being available on the machine, limiting the application's portability across different environments.

When you go cloud native, things are different. Cloud native applications should be self-contained and not dependent on a server being available in the execution environment. Instead, the necessary server capabilities are included in the application itself. Spring Boot offers built-in server functionality that helps you remove the external dependency and make the application standalone. Spring Boot comes bundled with a preconfigured Tomcat server, but it's possible to replace it with Undertow, Jetty, or Netty.

Having solved the server dependency problem, we need to change how we package the application accordingly. In the JVM ecosystem, cloud native applications are packaged as JAR artifacts. Since they are self-contained, they can run as standalone Java applications with no external dependency apart from the JVM. Spring Boot is flexible enough to allow both JAR and WAR types of packaging. Still, for cloud native applications, you'll want to use self-contained JARs, also called *fat-JARs* or *uber-JARs*, since they contain the application itself, the dependencies, and the embedded server. Figure 3.3 compares the traditional and cloud native ways of packaging and running web applications.

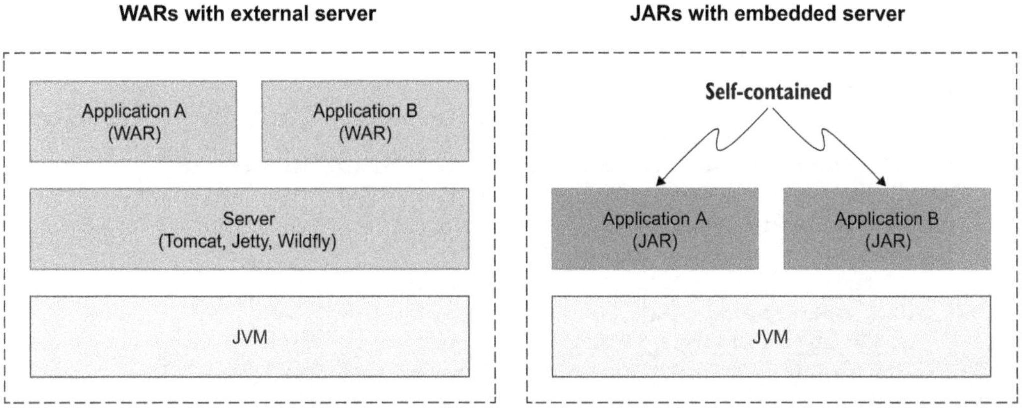

WARs with external server   **JARs with embedded server**

Figure 3.3   Traditionally, applications are packaged as WARs and require a server to be available in the execution environment to run. Cloud native applications are packaged as JARs, are self-contained, and use an embedded server.

The embedded servers used for cloud native applications usually comprise a web server component and an execution context to make a Java web application interact with the web server. For example, Tomcat contains a web server component (Coyote) and an execution context based on the Java Servlet API, usually called the Servlet container (Catalina). I will use *web server* and *Servlet container* interchangeably. On the other hand, application servers are not recommended for cloud native applications.

In the previous chapter, when generating the Catalog Service project, we chose the JAR packaging option. We then ran the application using the bootRun Gradle task. That is a convenient way to build a project and run it as a standalone application during development. But now that you know more about the embedded server and JAR packaging, I'll show you another way.

First, let's package the application as a JAR file. Open a Terminal window, navigate to the root folder of the Catalog Service project (catalog-service), and run the following command.

```
$ ./gradlew bootJar
```

The bootJar Gradle task compiles the code and packages the application as a JAR file. By default, the JAR is generated in the build/libs folder. You should get an executable JAR file named catalog-service-0.0.1-SNAPSHOT.jar. Once you get the JAR artifact, you can go ahead and run it like any standard Java application.

```
$ java -jar build/libs/catalog-service-0.0.1-SNAPSHOT.jar
```

NOTE   Another practical Gradle task is `build`, which combines the operations of the `bootJar` and `test` tasks.

Since the project contains the `spring-boot-starter-web` dependency, Spring Boot automatically configures an embedded Tomcat server. By looking at the logs in figure 3.4, you can see that one of the first execution steps is initializing a Tomcat server instance embedded in the application itself.

```
...Starting CatalogServiceApplication using Java 17
...No active profile set, falling back to 1 default profile: "default"
...Tomcat initialized with port(s): 9001 (http)
...Starting service [Tomcat]
...Starting Servlet engine: [Apache Tomcat/9.0.65]
...Initializing Spring embedded WebApplicationContext
...Root WebApplicationContext: initialization completed in 276 ms
...Tomcat started on port(s): 9001 (http) with context path ''
...Started CatalogServiceApplication in 0.529 seconds (JVM running for 0.735)
```

Figure 3.4   The startup logs from the Catalog Service application

In the next section, you'll learn more about how the embedded server works in Spring Boot. Before moving on, though, you can stop the application with Ctrl-C.

3.2.2   *Understanding the thread-per-request model*

Let's consider the request/response pattern commonly used in web applications to establish synchronous interactions over HTTP. A client sends an HTTP request to a server that performs some computation, and it then replies with an HTTP response.

In web applications running in a Servlet container like Tomcat, requests are processed based on a model called *thread-per-request*. For each request, the application dedicates a thread exclusively to handling that specific request; the thread will not be used for anything else until a response is returned to the client. When the request-handling involves intensive operations like I/O, the thread will block until the operations are completed. For example, if a database read is required, the thread will wait until data is returned from the database. That's why we say that this type of processing is *synchronous* and *blocking*.

Tomcat is initialized with a thread pool that's used to manage all incoming HTTP requests. New requests will be queued when all threads are in use, waiting for a thread to become free. In other words, the number of threads in Tomcat defines an upper limit to how many requests are supported concurrently. This is very useful to remember when debugging performance issues. If the thread concurrency limit is hit continuously, you can always tune the thread pool configuration to accept more workload. With traditional applications we would add more computational resources to a specific instance. For cloud native applications, we rely on horizontal scaling and deploying more replicas.

NOTE In some applications that have to respond to high demands, the thread-per-request model might not be ideal, because it doesn't use the available computational resources in the most efficient way due to the blocking. In chapter 8, I'll introduce an *asynchronous* and *non-blocking* alternative with Spring WebFlux and Project Reactor, adopting the reactive programming paradigm.

Spring MVC is the library included in the Spring Framework to implement web applications, either full MVC or REST-based. Either way, the functionality is based on a server like Tomcat that provides a Servlet container compliant with the Java Servlet API. Figure 3.5 shows how the REST-based request/response interaction works in a Spring web application.

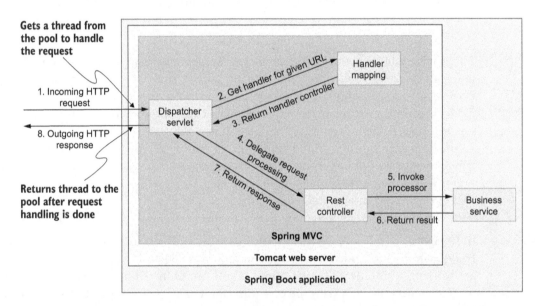

Figure 3.5 The `DispatcherServlet` component is the entry point to the Servlet container (Tomcat). It delegates the actual HTTP request processing to a controller identified by `HandlerMapping` as the one responsible for a given endpoint.

The `DispatcherServlet` component provides a central entry point for request processing. When a client sends a new HTTP request for a specific URL pattern, `Dispatcher-Servlet` asks the `HandlerMapping` component for the controller responsible for that endpoint, and it finally delegates the actual processing of the request to the specified controller. The controller processes the request, possibly by calling some other services, and then returns a response to `DispatcherServlet`, which finally replies to the client with an HTTP response.

Notice how the Tomcat server is embedded in the Spring Boot application. Spring MVC relies on the web server to accomplish its functionality. The same is true for any web server implementing the Servlet API, but since we are explicitly using Tomcat, let's go ahead and explore some options for configuring it.

3.2.3 Configuring the embedded Tomcat

Tomcat is the default server that comes preconfigured with any Spring Boot web application. Sometimes the default configuration might be enough, but for applications in production, you'll likely need to customize its behavior to meet the specific requirements.

> **NOTE** In a traditional Spring application, you would configure a server like Tomcat in dedicated files such as server.xml and context.xml. With Spring Boot, you can configure an embedded web server in two ways: through properties or in a `WebServerFactoryCustomizer` bean.

This section will show you how to configure Tomcat through properties. You'll learn more about configuring applications in the next chapter. For now, it's enough to know that you can define properties in an application.properties or application.yml file located in the src/main/resources folder of your project. You're free to choose which format to use: .properties files rely on key/value pairs while .yml files use the YAML format. In this book, I'll define properties using YAML. Spring Initializr generates an empty application.properties file by default, so remember to change its extension from .properties to .yml before moving on.

Let's go ahead and configure the embedded server for the Catalog Service application (catalog-service). All the configuration properties will go in the application.yml file.

HTTP PORT

By default, the embedded server is listening on port 8080. That is fine as long as you are working with only one application. If you run more Spring applications during development, which is usually the case with cloud native systems, you'll want to specify a different port number for each application using the `server.port` property.

Listing 3.1   Configuring the web server port

```
server:
  port: 9001
```

CONNECTION TIMEOUT

The `server.tomcat.connection-timeout` property defines a limit for how much time Tomcat should wait between accepting a TCP connection from a client and actually receiving the HTTP request. It helps prevent denial-of-service (DoS) attacks where a connection is established, Tomcat reserves a thread to handle the request, and the request never comes. The same timeout is used to limit the time spent reading the HTTP request body when there is one.

The default value is 20s (20 seconds), which is probably too much for a standard cloud native application. In the context of highly distributed systems in the cloud, we probably don't want to wait more than a couple of seconds and risk a cascading failure due to a Tomcat instance hanging for too long. Something like 2s would be better. You can also use the `server.tomcat.keep-alive-timeout` property to configure how long to keep a connection open while waiting for new HTTP requests.

Listing 3.2 Configuring timeouts for Tomcat

```
server:
  port: 9001
  tomcat:
    connection-timeout: 2s
    keep-alive-timeout: 15s
```

THREAD POOL

Tomcat has a pool of threads that process requests, following the thread-per-request model. The number of available threads will determine how many requests can be handled simultaneously. You can configure the maximum number of request processing threads through the `server.tomcat.threads.max` property. You can also define the minimum number of threads that should always be kept running (`server.tomcat.threads.min-spare`), which is also how many threads are created at startup.

Determining the best configuration for a thread pool is complicated, and there's no magic formula for computing it. Resource analysis, monitoring, and many trials are usually necessary to find a suitable configuration. The default thread pool can grow up to 200 threads and has 10 worker threads always running, which are good starting values in production. In your local environment, you might want to lower those values to optimize resource consumption, since it increases linearly with the number of threads.

Listing 3.3 Configuring the Tomcat thread pool

```
server:
  port: 9001
  tomcat:
    connection-timeout: 2s
    keep-alive-timeout: 15s
    threads:
      max: 50
      min-spare: 5
```

So far, you've seen that cloud native applications with Spring Boot are packaged as JAR files and rely on an embedded server to remove extra dependencies on the execution environment and enable agility. You learned how the thread-per-request model works, familiarized yourself with the request processing flow with Tomcat and Spring MVC, and configured Tomcat. In the next section, we'll move on to the business logic of Catalog Service and the implementation of a REST API with Spring MVC.

3.3   Building a RESTful application with Spring MVC

If you're building cloud native applications, chances are that you are working on a distributed system composed of several services, such as microservices, interacting with each other to accomplish the overall functionality of the product. Your application might be consumed by a service developed by another team in your organization, or you might be exposing its functionality to third parties. Either way, there's an essential element in any inter-service communication: the API.

The 15-Factor methodology promotes the *API first* pattern. It encourages you to establish the service interface first and work on the implementation later. The API represents a public contract between your application and its consumers, and it's in your best interests to define it first thing.

Suppose you agree on a contract and define the API first. In that case, other teams can start working on their solutions and develop against your API to implement their integration with your application. If you don't develop the API first, there will be a bottleneck, and other teams will have to wait until you're done with your application. Discussing the API up front also enables productive discussions with stakeholders, which can lead to you clarifying the scope of the application and even defining user stories to implement.

In the cloud, any application can be a backing service for another one. Adopting an API first mentality will help you evolve your applications and adapt them to future requirements.

This section will guide you by defining a contract for Catalog Service as a REST API, the most used service interface model for cloud native applications. You'll use Spring MVC to implement the REST API, validate it, and test it. I'll also outline some considerations for evolving an API for future requirements, a common issue in highly distributed systems like cloud native applications.

3.3.1   REST API first, business logic later

Designing the API first assumes you have already defined the requirements, so let's start with those. Catalog Service will be responsible for supporting the following use cases:

- View the list of books in the catalog.
- Search books by their International Standard Book Number (ISBN).
- Add a new book to the catalog.
- Edit information for an existing book.
- Remove a book from the catalog.

In other words, we can say the application should provide an API to perform CRUD operations on books. The format will follow the REST style applied to HTTP. There are several ways to design an API to fulfill those use cases. In this chapter, we'll use the approach described in table 3.1.

Table 3.1 Specifications for the REST API that will be exposed by Catalog Service

Endpoint	HTTP method	Request body	Status	Response body	Description
/books	GET		200	Book[]	Get all the books in the catalog.
/books	POST	Book	201	Book	Add a new book to the catalog.
			422		A book with the same ISBN already exists.
/books/{isbn}	GET		200	Book	Get the book with the given ISBN.
			404		No book with the given ISBN exists.
/books/{isbn}	PUT	Book	200	Book	Update the book with the given ISBN.
			201	Book	Create a book with the given ISBN.
/books/{isbn}	DELETE		204		Delete the book with the given ISBN.

Documenting APIs

Documenting APIs is an essential task when you're following the API-first approach. In the Spring ecosystem, there are two main options:

- Spring provides a Spring REST Docs project (https://spring.io/projects/spring -restdocs) that helps you document REST APIs via test-driven development (TDD), resulting in high-quality and maintainable documentation. The resulting documentation is aimed at people, relying on formats like Asciidoc or Markdown. If you'd like to obtain an OpenAPI representation as well, you can check the restdocs-api-spec community-driven project to add OpenAPI support to Spring REST Docs (https://github.com/ePages-de/restdocs-api-spec).
- The springdoc-openapi community-driven project helps automate the generation of API documentation according to the OpenAPI 3 format (https:// springdoc.org).

The contract is established through the REST API, so let's move on and look at the business logic. The solution is centered around three concepts:

- *Entity*—An entity represents the noun in a domain, such as "book."
- *Service*—A service defines the use cases for the domain. For example, "adding a book to the catalog."

■ *Repository*—A repository is an abstraction to let the domain layer access data independently from its source.

Let's start with the domain entity.

DEFINING THE DOMAIN ENTITY

The REST API defined in table 3.1 should make it possible to operate on books. That's the *domain entity*. In the Catalog Service project, create a new com.polarbook-shop.catalogservice.domain package for the business logic, and create a Book Java record to represent the domain entity.

Listing 3.4   Using the `Book` **record to define a domain entity for the application**

```
package com.polarbookshop.catalogservice.domain;

public record Book (
  String isbn,
  String title,
  String author,
  Double price
){}
```

The domain model is implemented as a record, an immutable object.

Uniquely identifies a book

IMPLEMENTING THE USE CASES

The use cases enumerated by the application requirements can be implemented in a @Service class. In the com.polarbookshop.catalogservice.domain package, create a BookService class, as shown in the following listing. The service relies on some classes that you'll create in a minute.

Listing 3.5   Implementing the use cases for the application

```
package com.polarbookshop.catalogservice.domain;

import org.springframework.stereotype.Service;

@Service
public class BookService {
  private final BookRepository bookRepository;

  public BookService(BookRepository bookRepository) {
    this.bookRepository = bookRepository;
  }

  public Iterable<Book> viewBookList() {
    return bookRepository.findAll();
  }

  public Book viewBookDetails(String isbn) {
    return bookRepository.findByIsbn(isbn)
      .orElseThrow(() -> new BookNotFoundException(isbn));
  }
```

Stereotype annotation that marks a class to be a service managed by Spring

BookRepository is provided through constructor autowiring.

When trying to view a book that doesn't exist, a dedicated exception is thrown.

```
public Book addBookToCatalog(Book book) {
  if (bookRepository.existsByIsbn(book.isbn())) {       ◄────┐   When adding the
    throw new BookAlreadyExistsException(book.isbn());            same book to the
  }                                                               catalog multiple
  return bookRepository.save(book);                               times, a dedicated
}                                                                 exception is thrown.

public void removeBookFromCatalog(String isbn) {
  bookRepository.deleteByIsbn(isbn);
}

public Book editBookDetails(String isbn, Book book) {
  return bookRepository.findByIsbn(isbn)
    .map(existingBook -> {
      var bookToUpdate = new Book(        ◄────┐   When editing the book, all
        existingBook.isbn(),                        the Book fields can be updated
        book.title(),                               except the ISBN code, because
        book.author(),                              it's the entity identifier.
        book.price());
      return bookRepository.save(bookToUpdate);
    })
    .orElseGet(() -> addBookToCatalog(book));   ◄────┐   When changing the details
}                                                         for a book not in the catalog
}                                                         yet, create a new book.
```

NOTE The Spring Framework provides two flavors of dependency injection: *constructor-based* and *setter-based.* We'll use constructor-based dependency injection in any production code, as advocated by the Spring team, because it ensures that the required dependencies are always returned fully initialized and never null. Furthermore, it encourages building immutable objects and improves their testability. For more information, refer to the Spring Framework documentation (https://spring.io/projects/spring-framework).

USING THE REPOSITORY ABSTRACTION FOR DATA ACCESS

The BookService class relies on a BookRepository object to retrieve and save books. The domain layer should be unaware of how data is persisted, so BookRepository should be an interface to decouple the abstraction from the actual implementation. Create a BookRepository interface in the com.polarbookshop.catalogservice.domain package to define the abstraction for accessing book data.

Listing 3.6 The abstraction used by the domain layer to access data

```
package com.polarbookshop.catalogservice.domain;

import java.util.Optional;

public interface BookRepository {
  Iterable<Book> findAll();
  Optional<Book> findByIsbn(String isbn);
  boolean existsByIsbn(String isbn);
  Book save(Book book);
```

```
    void deleteByIsbn(String isbn);
}
```

While the repository interface belongs to the domain, its implementation is part of
the persistence layer. We'll add a data persistence layer using a relational database in
chapter 5. For now, it's enough to add a simple in-memory map to retrieve and save
books. You can define the implementation in an InMemoryBookRepository class,
located in a new com.polarbookshop.catalogservice.persistence package.

> **Listing 3.7   In-memory implementation of the BookRepository interface**

```
package com.polarbookshop.catalogservice.persistence;

import java.util.Map;
import java.util.Optional;
import java.util.concurrent.ConcurrentHashMap;
import com.polarbookshop.catalogservice.domain.Book;
import com.polarbookshop.catalogservice.domain.BookRepository;
import org.springframework.stereotype.Repository;

@Repository
public class InMemoryBookRepository implements BookRepository {
  private static final Map<String, Book> books =
    new ConcurrentHashMap<>();

  @Override
  public Iterable<Book> findAll() {
    return books.values();
  }

  @Override
  public Optional<Book> findByIsbn(String isbn) {
    return existsByIsbn(isbn) ? Optional.of(books.get(isbn)) :
      Optional.empty();
  }

  @Override
  public boolean existsByIsbn(String isbn) {
    return books.get(isbn) != null;
  }

  @Override
  public Book save(Book book) {
    books.put(book.isbn(), book);
    return book;
  }

  @Override
  public void deleteByIsbn(String isbn) {
    books.remove(isbn);
  }
}
```

Stereotype annotation that marks a class to be a repository managed by Spring

In-memory map to store books for testing purposes

USING EXCEPTIONS TO SIGNAL ERRORS IN THE DOMAIN

Let's complete the business logic for Catalog Service by implementing the two exceptions we used in listing 3.5.

BookAlreadyExistsException is a runtime exception thrown when we try to add a book to the catalog that is already there. It prevents duplicate entries in the catalog.

> **Listing 3.8 Exception thrown when adding a book that already exists**

```
package com.polarbookshop.catalogservice.domain;

public class BookAlreadyExistsException extends RuntimeException {
  public BookAlreadyExistsException(String isbn) {
    super("A book with ISBN " + isbn + " already exists.");
  }
}
```

BookNotFoundException is a runtime exception thrown when we try to fetch a book that is not in the catalog.

> **Listing 3.9 Exception thrown when a book cannot be found**

```
package com.polarbookshop.catalogservice.domain;

public class BookNotFoundException extends RuntimeException {
  public BookNotFoundException(String isbn) {
    super("The book with ISBN " + isbn + " was not found.");
  }
}
```

That completes the business logic for the Catalog Service. It's relatively simple, but it's recommended not to be influenced by how data is persisted or exchanged with clients. The business logic should be independent of anything else, including the API. If you're interested in this topic, I suggest exploring the concepts of *domain-driven design* and *hexagonal architecture.*

3.3.2 Implementing a REST API with Spring MVC

After implementing the business logic, we can expose the use cases through a REST API. Spring MVC provides @RestController classes to define methods that handle incoming HTTP requests for specific HTTP methods and resource endpoints.

As you saw in the previous section, the DispatcherServlet component will invoke the right controller for each request. Figure 3.6 shows the scenario where a client sends an HTTP GET request to view the details of a specific book.

We want to implement a method handler for each use case defined in the application requirements, since we want to make all of them available to clients. Create a package for the web layer (com.polarbookshop.catalogservice.web) and add a BookController class responsible for handling HTTP requests sent to the /books base endpoint.

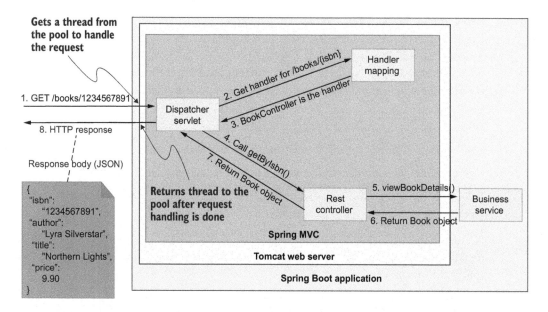

Figure 3.6   The processing flow for an HTTP GET request arriving at the /books/<isbn> endpoint

---

Listing 3.10   Defining handlers for REST endpoints

```
package com.polarbookshop.catalogservice.web;

import com.polarbookshop.catalogservice.domain.Book;
import com.polarbookshop.catalogservice.domain.BookService;
import org.springframework.http.HttpStatus;
import org.springframework.web.bind.annotation.*;

@RestController
@RequestMapping("books")
public class BookController {
  private final BookService bookService;

  public BookController(BookService bookService) {
    this.bookService = bookService;
  }

  @GetMapping
  public Iterable<Book> get() {
    return bookService.viewBookList();
  }

  @GetMapping("{isbn}")
  public Book getByIsbn(@PathVariable String isbn) {
    return bookService.viewBookDetails(isbn);
  }
}
```

Stereotype annotation marking a class as a Spring component and a source of handlers for REST endpoints

Identifies the root path mapping URI for which the class provides handlers ("/books")

Maps HTTP GET requests to the specific handler method

A URI template variable appended to the root path mapping URI ("/books/{isbn}")

@PathVariable binds a method parameter to a URI template variable ({isbn}).

```
@PostMapping
@ResponseStatus(HttpStatus.CREATED)
public Book post(@RequestBody Book book) {
    return bookService.addBookToCatalog(book);
}

@DeleteMapping("{isbn}")
@ResponseStatus(HttpStatus.NO_CONTENT)
public void delete(@PathVariable String isbn) {
    bookService.removeBookFromCatalog(isbn);
}

@PutMapping("{isbn}")
public Book put(@PathVariable String isbn, @RequestBody Book book) {
    return bookService.editBookDetails(isbn, book);
}
}
```

Returns a 201 status if the book is created successfully

@RequestBody binds a method parameter to the body of a web request.

Returns a 204 status if the book is deleted successfully

Maps HTTP PUT requests to the specific handler method

Maps HTTP DELETE requests to the specific handler method

Maps HTTP POST requests to the specific handler method

Go ahead and run the application (./gradlew bootRun). When verifying HTTP interactions with an application, you can either use a command-line tool like curl or software with a graphical user interface like Insomnia. I'm going to use a convenient command-line tool called HTTPie (https://httpie.org). You can find information about how to install it in section A.4 of appendix A.

Open a Terminal window and perform an HTTP POST request to add a book to the catalog:

```
$ http POST :9001/books author="Lyra Silverstar" \
    title="Northern Lights" isbn="1234567891" price=9.90
```

The result should be an HTTP response with the 201 code, meaning that the book has been created successfully. Let's double-check by submitting an HTTP GET request to fetch the book with the ISBN code we used on creation.

```
$ http :9001/books/1234567891

HTTP/1.1 200
Content-Type: application/json

{
  "author": "Lyra Silverstar",
  "isbn": "1234567891",
  "price": 9.9,
  "title": "Northern Lights"
}
```

When you're done trying the application, stop its execution with Ctrl-C.

About content negotiation

All handler methods in `BookController` work on `Book` Java objects. And yet, when you perform a request, you get back a JSON object. How is that possible?

Spring MVC relies on an `HttpMessageConverter` bean to convert the returned object into a specific representation the client supports. The decision about the content type is driven by a process called *content negotiation*, during which the client and the server agree on a representation that both can understand. The client can inform the server about which content types it supports through the `Accept` header in the HTTP request.

By default, Spring Boot configures a set of `HttpMessageConverter` beans to return objects represented as JSON, and the HTTPie tool is configured to accept any content type by default. The result is that both client and server support the JSON content type, so they agree on using that to communicate

---

The application we have implemented so far is still not complete. For example, nothing prevents you from posting a new book with an ISBN in the wrong format or without specifying a title. We need to validate the input.

3.3.3   *Data validation and error handling*

As a general rule, before saving any data, you should always validate the content, both for data consistency and security reasons. A book with no title will be of no use in our application, and it would probably make it fail.

For the `Book` class, we might think of using these validation constraints:

- The ISBN must be defined and in the correct format (ISBN-10 or ISBN-13).
- The title must be defined.
- The author must be defined.
- The price must be defined and be greater than zero.

Java Bean Validation is a popular specification for expressing constraints and validation rules on Java objects via annotations. Spring Boot provides a convenient starter dependency containing the Java Bean Validation API and its implementation. Add the new dependency in the build.gradle file for your Catalog Service project. Remember to refresh or reimport the Gradle dependencies after the new addition.

Listing 3.11   Adding dependency for Spring Boot Validation

```
dependencies {
  ...
  implementation 'org.springframework.boot:spring-boot-starter-validation'
}
```

You can now use the Java Bean Validation API to define validation constraints as annotations directly on the `Book` record fields.

Listing 3.12   Validation constraints defined for each field

```
package com.polarbookshop.catalogservice.domain;

import javax.validation.constraints.NotBlank;
import javax.validation.constraints.NotNull;
import javax.validation.constraints.Pattern;
import javax.validation.constraints.Positive;

public record Book (

  @NotBlank(message = "The book ISBN must be defined.")
  @Pattern(
    regexp = "^([0-9]{10}|[0-9]{13})$",
    message = "The ISBN format must be valid."
  )
  String isbn,

  @NotBlank(
    message = "The book title must be defined."
  )
  String title,

  @NotBlank(message = "The book author must be defined.")
  String author,

  @NotNull(message = "The book price must be defined.")
  @Positive(
    message = "The book price must be greater than zero."
  )
  Double price
){}
```

The annotated element must match the specified regular expression (standard ISBN format).

The annotated element must not be null and must contain at least one non-whitespace character.

The annotated element must not be null and must be greater than zero.

NOTE   Books are uniquely identified by their ISBN (International Standard Book Number). ISBNs used to be composed of 10 digits, but they now consist of 13. For simplicity, we'll limit ourselves to checking for their length and whether all the elements are digits by using a regular expression.

The annotations from the Java Bean Validation API define the constraints, but they are not enforced yet. We can instruct Spring to validate the Book object in the Book-Controller class by using the @Valid annotation whenever a @RequestBody is specified as a method argument. In this way, whenever we create or update a book, Spring will run the validation and throw an error if any constraint is violated. We can update the post() and put() methods in the BookController class as follows.

Listing 3.13   Validating books passed in a request body

```
...
@PostMapping
@ResponseStatus(HttpStatus.CREATED)
public Book post(@Valid @RequestBody Book book) {
  return bookService.addBookToCatalog(book);
}
```

```
@PutMapping("{isbn}")
public Book put(@PathVariable String isbn, @Valid @RequestBody Book book) {
  return bookService.editBookDetails(isbn, book);
}
...
```

Spring lets you handle error messages in different ways. When building an API, it's good to consider which types of errors it can throw, since they are just as important as the domain data. When it's a REST API, you want to ensure that the HTTP response uses a status code that best fits the purpose and includes a meaningful message to help the client identify the problem.

When the validation constraints we have just defined are not met, a `MethodArgument-NotValidException` is thrown. What if we try to fetch a book that doesn't exist? The business logic we previously implemented throws dedicated exceptions (`BookAlready-ExistsException` and `BookNotFoundException`). All those exceptions should be handled in the REST API context to return the error codes defined in the original specification.

To handle errors for a REST API, we can use the standard Java exceptions and rely on a `@RestControllerAdvice` class to define what to do when a given exception is thrown. It's a centralized approach that allows us to decouple the exception handling from the code throwing the exception. In the `com.polarbookshop.catalogservice.web` package, create a `BookControllerAdvice` class as follows.

> **Listing 3.14   The advice class defining how to handle exceptions**

```
package com.polarbookshop.catalogservice.web;

import java.util.HashMap;
import java.util.Map;
import com.polarbookshop.catalogservice.domain.BookAlreadyExistsException;
import com.polarbookshop.catalogservice.domain.BookNotFoundException;
import org.springframework.http.HttpStatus;
import org.springframework.validation.FieldError;
import org.springframework.web.bind.MethodArgumentNotValidException;
import org.springframework.web.bind.annotation.ExceptionHandler;
import org.springframework.web.bind.annotation.ResponseStatus;
import org.springframework.web.bind.annotation.RestControllerAdvice;

@RestControllerAdvice                              ◁──┐  Marks the class as a
public class BookControllerAdvice {                   │  centralized exception handler

  @ExceptionHandler(BookNotFoundException.class)    ◁────  Defines the exception
  @ResponseStatus(HttpStatus.NOT_FOUND)                    for which the handler
  String bookNotFoundHandler(BookNotFoundException ex) {   must be executed
    return ex.getMessage();    ◁──┐  The message that will
  }                               │  be included in the HTTP
                                     response body
```

```
@ExceptionHandler(BookAlreadyExistsException.class)
@ResponseStatus(HttpStatus.UNPROCESSABLE_ENTITY)          <──────────────┐
String bookAlreadyExistsHandler(BookAlreadyExistsException ex) {         │
  return ex.getMessage();                                          Defines the status
}                                                                  code for the HTTP
                                                                   response created
                                                                   when the exception
@ExceptionHandler(MethodArgumentNotValidException.class)           is thrown
@ResponseStatus(HttpStatus.BAD_REQUEST)
public Map<String, String> handleValidationExceptions(
 MethodArgumentNotValidException ex                      <───────┐ Handles the
) {                                                               exception thrown
  var errors = new HashMap<String, String>();                     when the Book
  ex.getBindingResult().getAllErrors().forEach(error -> {         validation fails
    String fieldName = ((FieldError) error).getField();
    String errorMessage = error.getDefaultMessage();
    errors.put(fieldName, errorMessage);         <───┐ Collects meaningful error
  });                                                 messages about which Book
  return errors;                                      fields were invalid instead of
}                                                     returning an empty message
}
```

The mapping provided in the `@RestControllerAdvice` class makes it possible to obtain an HTTP response with status 422 (unprocessable entity) when we try to create a book that already exists in the catalog, a response with status 404 (not found) when we try to read a book that doesn't exist, and a response with status 400 (bad request) when one or more fields in a `Book` object are invalid. Each response will contain a meaningful message that we defined as part of the validation constraint or custom exception.

Build and rerun the application (`./gradlew bootRun`): if you now try to create a book without a title and with a wrongly formatted ISBN, the request will fail.

```
$ http POST :9001/books author="Jon Snow" title="" isbn="123ABC456Z" \
    price=9.90
```

The result will be an error message with a "400 Bad Request" status, meaning that the server couldn't process the HTTP request because it was incorrect. The response body contains a detailed message about which part of the request was incorrect and how to fix it, just as we defined in listing 3.12.

```
HTTP/1.1 400
Content-Type: application/json

{
  "isbn": "The ISBN format must be valid.",
  "title": "The book title must be defined."
}
```

When you're done trying the application, stop its execution with Ctrl-C.

That concludes our implementation of the REST API that exposes the Catalog Service's book-management functionality. Next I'll discuss a few aspects of how we can evolve APIs to adapt to new requirements.

3.3.4   Evolving APIs for future requirements

In a distributed system, we need a plan to evolve APIs so we don't break the functionality of other applications. This is a challenging task because we want independent applications, but they probably exist to provide services to other applications, so we are somewhat limited in the number of changes we can make independently of the clients.

The best approach is to make backward-compatible changes to the API. For example, we can add an optional field to the Book object without affecting the clients of the Catalog Service application.

Sometimes, breaking changes are necessary. In this situation, you can use *API versioning*. For example, should you decide to make a breaking change to the REST API for the Catalog Service application, you might introduce a versioning system for the endpoints. The version might be part of the endpoint itself, like /v2/books. Or it might be specified as an HTTP header. This system helps prevent existing clients from breaking, but they will have to update their interface to match the new API version sooner or later, meaning that coordination is needed.

A different approach focuses on making the REST API client as resilient to API changes as possible. The solution is to use the *hypermedia* aspect of the REST architecture, as described by Dr. Roy Fielding in his doctorate dissertation, "Architectural Styles and the Design of Network-based Software Architectures" (www.ics.uci.edu/~fielding/pubs/dissertation/top.htm). REST APIs can return the object requested along with information about *where* to go next and *links* to perform related operations. The beauty of this feature is that the links are only shown when it makes sense to follow them, providing information about *when* to go.

This hypermedia aspect is also called *HATEOAS* (Hypermedia as the Engine of Application State), and it represents the highest level of API maturity according to Richardson's Maturity Model. Spring provides the Spring HATEOAS project to add hypermedia support to a REST API. I will not use it in this book, but I encourage you to check the project's online documentation at https://spring.io/projects/spring-hateoas.

These considerations conclude our discussion of building a RESTful application with Spring. In the next section you'll see how to write automated tests to verify the behavior of your application.

3.4   Testing a RESTful application with Spring

Automated tests are paramount to producing high-quality software. One of the goals for adopting a cloud native approach is speed. It's impossible to move quickly if the code is not adequately tested in an automated fashion, let alone to implement a continuous delivery process.

As a developer, you'll usually implement a feature, deliver it, and then move on to a new one, possibly refactoring the existing code. Refactoring code is risky, since you might break some existing functionality. Automated tests reduce the risk and encourage refactoring, because you know that a test will fail, should you break something.

You'll probably also want to reduce the feedback cycle so you'll know if you made any mistakes as soon as possible. That will lead you to design tests in a way that maximizes their usefulness and efficiency. You shouldn't aim to reach maximum test coverage but rather to write meaningful tests. For example, writing tests for standard getters and setters doesn't make sense.

An essential practice of continuous delivery is *test-driven development* (TDD), which helps achieve the goal of delivering software quickly, reliably, and safely. The idea is to drive software development by writing tests before implementing the production code. I recommend adopting TDD in real-world scenarios. However, it's not very suitable when teaching new technologies and frameworks in a book, so I won't follow its principles here.

Automated tests assert that new features work as intended and that you haven't broken any existing functionality. This means that automated tests work as *regression tests*. You should write tests to protect your colleagues and yourself from making mistakes. What to test and how in-depth to test is driven by the risk associated with a specific piece of code. Writing tests is also a learning experience and will improve your skills, especially if you're beginning your software development journey.

One way of classifying software tests is defined by the Agile Testing Quadrants model originally introduced by Brian Marick, and later described and expanded on by Lisa Crispin and Janet Gregory in their books *Agile Testing* (Addison-Wesley Professional, 2008), *More Agile Testing* (Addison-Wesley Professional, 2014), and *Agile Testing Condensed* (Library and Archives Canada, 2019). Their model was also embraced by Jez Humble and Dave Farley in *Continuous Delivery* (Addison-Wesley Professional, 2010). The quadrants classify software tests based on whether they are technology or business-facing and whether they support development teams or are used to critique the product. Figure 3.7 shows some examples of testing types I'll mention throughout the book, based on the model presented in *Agile Testing Condensed*.

Agile testing quadrants

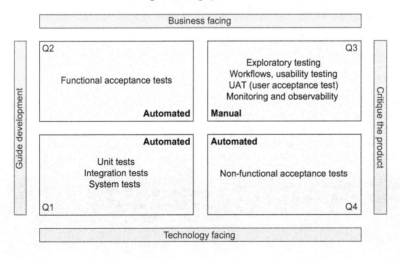

Figure 3.7 The Agile Testing Quadrants model is helpful in planning a software testing strategy.

Following continuous delivery practices, we should aim at achieving fully automated tests in three out of four quadrants, as shown in figure 3.7. Throughout the book, we'll mainly focus on the bottom-left quadrant. In this section, we'll work with unit tests and integration tests (sometimes called *component tests*). We write *unit tests* to verify the behavior of single application components in isolation, whereas *integration tests* assert the overall functioning of different parts of an application interacting with each other.

In a Gradle or Maven project, test classes are usually placed in a src/test/java folder. In Spring, unit tests aren't required to load the Spring application context, and they don't rely on any Spring library. On the other hand, integration tests need a Spring application context to run. This section will show you how to test a RESTful application like Catalog Service with unit and integration tests.

3.4.1   *Unit tests with JUnit 5*

Unit tests are not aware of Spring and don't rely on any Spring library. They are intended to test the behavior of single components as isolated units. Any dependency at the edge of the unit is mocked to keep the test shielded from external components.

Writing unit tests for Spring applications is no different from writing them for any other Java application, so I won't go into detail about them. By default, any Spring project created from Spring Initializr contains the `spring-boot-starter-test` dependency, which imports testing libraries like JUnit 5, Mockito, and AssertJ into the project. So we're all set for writing unit tests.

The business logic of an application is usually a sensible area to cover with unit tests. In the Catalog Service application, a good candidate for unit testing might be the validation logic for the `Book` class. The validation constraints are defined using the Java Validation API annotations, and we are interested in testing that they are applied correctly to the `Book` class. We can check that in a new `BookValidationTests` class, as shown in the following listing.

> **Listing 3.15   Unit tests to verify book validation constraints**

```
package com.polarbookshop.catalogservice.domain;

import java.util.Set;
import javax.validation.ConstraintViolation;
import javax.validation.Validation;
import javax.validation.Validator;
import javax.validation.ValidatorFactory;
import org.junit.jupiter.api.BeforeAll;
import org.junit.jupiter.api.Test;
import static org.assertj.core.api.Assertions.assertThat;

class BookValidationTests {
    private static Validator validator;                    Identifies a block of
                                                           code executed before
    @BeforeAll                              ◄────────────  all tests in the class
    static void setUp() {
```

```
                    ValidatorFactory factory = Validation.buildDefaultValidatorFactory();
                    validator = factory.getValidator();
                }
```

Creates a book with a valid ISBN

```
                @Test                ◄──────────────┐  Identifies a test case
                void whenAllFieldsCorrectThenValidationSucceeds() {
              ▷   var book =
                    new Book("1234567890", "Title", "Author", 9.90);
                  Set<ConstraintViolation<Book>> violations = validator.validate(book);
                  assertThat(violations).isEmpty();        ◄──┐  Asserts that there is
                }                                             │  no validation error
```

Creates a book with a non-valid ISBN code

```
                @Test
                void whenIsbnDefinedButIncorrectThenValidationFails() {
              ▷   var book =
                    new Book("a234567890", "Title", "Author", 9.90);
                  Set<ConstraintViolation<Book>> violations = validator.validate(book);
                  assertThat(violations).hasSize(1);
                  assertThat(violations.iterator().next().getMessage())
                    .isEqualTo("The ISBN format must be valid.");  ◄──┐  Asserts that the violated
                }                                                     │  validation constraint is
              }                                                       │  about the incorrect ISBN
```

Then we can run the tests with the following command:

```
$ ./gradlew test --tests BookValidationTests
```

3.4.2 Integration tests with @SpringBootTest

Integration tests cover the interactions among software components, and in Spring they require an application context to be defined. The spring-boot-starter-test dependency also imports the test utilities from Spring Framework and Spring Boot.

Spring Boot offers a powerful @SpringBootTest annotation that you can use on a test class to bootstrap an application context automatically when running tests. The configuration used to create the context can be customized if needed. Otherwise, the class annotated with @SpringBootApplication will become the configuration source for component scanning and properties, including the usual auto-configuration provided by Spring Boot.

When working with web applications, you can run tests on a mock web environment or a running server. You can configure that by defining a value for the webEnvironment attribute that the @SpringBootTest annotation provides, as shown in table 3.2.

When using a mock web environment, you can rely on the MockMvc object to send HTTP requests to the application and check their results. For environments with a running server, the TestRestTemplate utility lets you perform REST calls to an application running on an actual server. By inspecting the HTTP responses, you can verify that the API works as intended.

Table 3.2   A Spring Boot integration test can be initialized with a mock web environment or a running server.

Web environment option	Description
MOCK	Creates a web application context with a mock Servlet container. This is the default option.
RANDOM_PORT	Creates a web application context with a Servlet container listening on a random port.
DEFINED_PORT	Creates a web application context with a Servlet container listening on the port defined through the `server.port` property.
NONE	Creates an application context without a Servlet container.

Recent versions of Spring Framework and Spring Boot have extended the features for testing web applications. You can now use the `WebTestClient` class to test REST APIs both on mock environments and running servers. Compared to `MockMvc` and `TestRestTemplate`, `WebTestClient` provides a modern and fluent API and additional features. Furthermore, you can use it for both imperative (e.g., Catalog Service) and reactive applications, optimizing learning and productivity.

Since `WebTestClient` is part of the Spring WebFlux project, you'll need to add a new dependency in your Catalog Service project (`build.gradle`). Remember to refresh or reimport the Gradle dependencies after the new addition.

Listing 3.16   Adding test dependency for Spring Reactive Web

```
dependencies {
  ...
  testImplementation 'org.springframework.boot:spring-boot-starter-webflux'
}
```

Chapter 8 will cover Spring WebFlux and reactive applications. For now we're only interested in using the `WebTestClient` object to test the API exposed by Catalog Service.

In the previous chapter you saw that Spring Initializr generated an empty `Catalog-ServiceApplicationTests` class. Let's populate it with integration tests. For this setup, we'll use the `@SpringBootTest` annotation configured to provide a full Spring application context, including a running server that exposes its services through a random port (because it doesn't matter which one).

Listing 3.17   Integration tests for Catalog Service

```
package com.polarbookshop.catalogservice;

import com.polarbookshop.catalogservice.domain.Book;
import org.junit.jupiter.api.Test;
import org.springframework.beans.factory.annotation.Autowired;
import org.springframework.boot.test.context.SpringBootTest;
```

```
import org.springframework.test.web.reactive.server.WebTestClient;
import static org.assertj.core.api.Assertions.assertThat;

@SpringBootTest(
  webEnvironment = SpringBootTest.WebEnvironment.RANDOM_PORT
)
class CatalogServiceApplicationTests {

  @Autowired
  private WebTestClient webTestClient;

  @Test
  void whenPostRequestThenBookCreated() {
    var expectedBook = new Book("1231231231", "Title", "Author", 9.90);

    webTestClient
      .post()
      .uri("/books")
      .bodyValue(expectedBook)
      .exchange()
      .expectStatus().isCreated()
      .expectBody(Book.class).value(actualBook -> {
        assertThat(actualBook).isNotNull();
        assertThat(actualBook.isbn())
          .isEqualTo(expectedBook.isbn());
      });
  }
}
```

Utility to perform REST calls for testing

Loads a full Spring web application context and a Servlet container listening on a random port

Sends the request to the "/books" endpoint

Sends an HTTP POST request

Adds the book in the request body

Sends the request

Verifies that the HTTP response has status "201 Created"

Verifies that the HTTP response has a non-null body

Verifies that the created object is as expected

NOTE   You might be wondering why I didn't use constructor-based dependency injection in listing 3.17, considering that I previously stated that's the recommended option. Using field-based dependency injection in production code has been deprecated and is strongly discouraged, but it's still acceptable to autowire dependencies in a test class. In every other scenario, I recommend sticking with constructor-based dependency injection for the reasons I explained earlier. For more information, you can refer to the official Spring Framework documentation (https://spring.io/projects/spring-framework).

Then you can run the tests with the following command:

```
$ ./gradlew test --tests CatalogServiceApplicationTests
```

Depending on the application's size, loading a full application context with auto-configuration for all integration tests might be too much. Spring Boot has a convenient feature (enabled by default) to cache the context, so that it's re-used in all test classes that are annotated with @SpringBootTest and the same configuration. Sometimes that's not enough.

Test execution time matters, so Spring Boot is fully equipped to run integration tests by loading only the parts of the application that are needed. Let's see how that works.

3.4.3 *Testing REST controllers with @WebMvcTest*

Some integration tests might not need a fully initialized application context. For example, there's no need to load the web components when you're testing the data persistence layer. If you're testing the web components, you don't need to load the data persistence layer.

Spring Boot allows you to use contexts initialized only with a subgroup of components (beans), targeting a specific application slice. *Slice tests* don't use the @Spring-BootTest annotation, but one of a set of annotations dedicated to particular parts of an application: Web MVC, Web Flux, REST client, JDBC, JPA, Mongo, Redis, JSON, and others. Each of those annotations initializes an application context, filtering out all the beans outside that slice.

We can test that Spring MVC controllers work as intended by using the @WebMvc-Test annotation, which loads a Spring application context in a mock web environment (no running server), configures the Spring MVC infrastructure, and includes only the beans used by the MVC layer, like @RestController and @RestController-Advice. It's also a good idea to limit the context to the beans used by the specific controller under test. We can do so by providing the controller class as an argument to the @WebMvcTest annotation in a new BookControllerMvcTests class.

> Listing 3.18 Integration tests for the web MVC slice

```
package com.polarbookshop.catalogservice.web;

import com.polarbookshop.catalogservice.domain.BookNotFoundException;
import com.polarbookshop.catalogservice.domain.BookService;
import org.junit.jupiter.api.Test;
import org.springframework.beans.factory.annotation.Autowired;
import org.springframework.boot.test.autoconfigure.web.servlet.WebMvcTest;
import org.springframework.boot.test.mock.mockito.MockBean;
import org.springframework.test.web.servlet.MockMvc;
import static org.mockito.BDDMockito.given;
import static org.springframework.test.web.servlet.request
➥.MockMvcRequestBuilders.get;
import static org.springframework.test.web.servlet.result
➥.MockMvcResultMatchers.status;

@WebMvcTest(BookController.class)        ⟵─┤ Identifies a test class that focuses on
class BookControllerMvcTests {             │ Spring MVC components, explicitly
                                           │ targeting BookController

  @Autowired                               │ Utility class to test the web
  private MockMvc mockMvc;        ⟵─┤ layer in a mock environment

  @MockBean                       ⟵──┐
  private BookService bookService;   │ Adds a mock of
                                     │ BookService to the Spring
                                     │ application context

  @Test
  void whenGetBookNotExistingThenShouldReturn404() throws Exception {
    String isbn = "73737313940";
    given(bookService.viewBookDetails(isbn))
```

```
        .willThrow(BookNotFoundException.class);  ◁
    mockMvc
        .perform(get("/books/" + isbn))  ◁
        .andExpect(status().isNotFound());  ◁
    }
}
```

Defines the expected
behavior for the
BookService mock bean

**MockMvc is used to perform
an HTTP GET request and
verify the result.**

**Expects the response to have
a "404 Not Found" status**

> **WARNING** If you use IntelliJ IDEA, you might get a warning that `MockMvc` cannot be autowired. Don't worry. It's a false positive. You can get rid of the warning by annotating the field with `@SuppressWarnings("SpringJavaInjection-PointsAutowiringInspection")`.

Then you can run the tests with the following command:

```
$ ./gradlew test --tests BookControllerMvcTests
```

`MockMvc` is a utility class that lets you test web endpoints without loading a server like Tomcat. Such a test is naturally lighter than the one we wrote in the previous section, where an embedded server was needed to run the test.

Slice tests run against an application context containing only the parts of the configuration requested by that application slice. In the case of collaborating beans outside the slice, such as the `BookService` class, we use mocks.

Mocks created with the `@MockBean` annotation are different from standard mocks (for example, those created with Mockito) since the class is not only mocked, but the mock is also included in the application context. Whenever the context is asked to autowire that bean, it automatically injects the mock rather than the actual implementation.

3.4.4 Testing the JSON serialization with @JsonTest

The `Book` objects returned by the methods in `BookController` are parsed into JSON objects. By default, Spring Boot automatically configures the Jackson library to parse Java objects into JSON (*serialization*) and vice versa (*deserialization*).

Using the `@JsonTest` annotation, you can test JSON serialization and deserialization for your domain objects. `@JsonTest` loads a Spring application context and autoconfigures the JSON mappers for the specific library in use (by default, it's Jackson). Furthermore, it configures the `JacksonTester` utility, which you can use to check that the JSON mapping works as expected, relying on the JsonPath and JSONAssert libraries.

> **NOTE** JsonPath provides expressions you can use to navigate a JSON object and extract data from it. For example, if I wanted to get the `isbn` field from the `Book` object's JSON representation, I could use the following JsonPath expression: `@.isbn`. For more information on the JsonPath library, you can refer to the project documentation: https://github.com/json-path/JsonPath.

The following listing shows an example of both serialization and deserialization tests implemented in a new `BookJsonTests` class.

Listing 3.19   Integration tests for the JSON slice

```
package com.polarbookshop.catalogservice.web;

import com.polarbookshop.catalogservice.domain.Book;
import org.junit.jupiter.api.Test;
import org.springframework.beans.factory.annotation.Autowired;
import org.springframework.boot.test.autoconfigure.json.JsonTest;
import org.springframework.boot.test.json.JacksonTester;
import static org.assertj.core.api.Assertions.assertThat;

@JsonTest                                    ◁─── Identifies a test class
class BookJsonTests {                             that focuses on JSON
                                                  serialization          Utility class to assert
  @Autowired                                                             JSON serialization and
  private JacksonTester<Book> json;           ◁───                       deserialization

  @Test
  void testSerialize() throws Exception {
    var book = new Book("1234567890", "Title", "Author", 9.90);
    var jsonContent = json.write(book);       ◁────────────────────
    assertThat(jsonContent).extractingJsonPathStringValue("@.isbn")
      .isEqualTo(book.isbn());
    assertThat(jsonContent).extractingJsonPathStringValue("@.title")
      .isEqualTo(book.title());
    assertThat(jsonContent).extractingJsonPathStringValue("@.author")
      .isEqualTo(book.author());
    assertThat(jsonContent).extractingJsonPathNumberValue("@.price")
      .isEqualTo(book.price());
  }                                             Verifying the parsing
                                                from Java to JSON, using
  @Test                                         the JsonPath format to
  void testDeserialize() throws Exception {     navigate the JSON object
    var content = """                  ◁───┐
      {                                      Defines a JSON object
        "isbn": "1234567890",                using the Java text
        "title": "Title",                    block feature
        "author": "Author",
        "price": 9.90
      }
      """;                                      Verifies the
    assertThat(json.parse(content))             parsing from
      .usingRecursiveComparison()        ◁───┘ JSON to Java
      .isEqualTo(new Book("1234567890", "Title", "Author", 9.90));
  }
}
```

WARNING If you use IntelliJ IDEA, you might get a warning that Jackson-Tester cannot be autowired. Don't worry. It's a false positive. You can get rid of the warning by annotating the field with `@SuppressWarnings("Spring-JavaInjectionPointsAutowiringInspection")`.

You can run the tests with the following command:

```
$ ./gradlew test --tests BookJsonTests
```

In the code repository accompanying the book, you can find more examples of unit and integration tests for the Catalog Service project.

After automating the tests for your application, it's time to automate its execution whenever a new feature or bug fix is delivered. The following section will introduce the key pattern of continuous delivery: the deployment pipeline.

3.5 Deployment pipeline: Build and test

Continuous delivery is a holistic approach for quickly, reliably, and safely delivering high-quality software, as I explained in chapter 1. The primary pattern for adopting such an approach is the deployment pipeline, which goes from code commit to releasable software. It should be automated as much as possible, and it should represent the only path to production.

Based on the concepts described by Jez Humble and Dave Farley in their *Continuous Delivery* book (Addison-Wesley Professional, 2010) and by Dave Farley in his *Continuous Delivery Pipelines* book (2021), we can identify a few key stages in a deployment pipeline:

- *Commit stage*—After a developer commits new code to the mainline, this stage goes through build, unit tests, integration tests, static code analysis, and packaging. At the end of this stage, an executable application artifact is published to an artifact repository. It is a *release candidate*. For example, it can be a JAR artifact published to a Maven repository or a container image published to a container registry. This stage supports the continuous integration practice. It's supposed to be fast, possibly under five minutes, to provide developers with fast feedback about their changes and allow them to move on to the next task.
- *Acceptance stage*—The publication of a new release candidate to the artifact repository triggers this stage, which consists of deploying the application to production-like environments and running additional tests to increase the confidence about its releasability. The tests that run in the acceptance stage are usually slow, but we should strive to keep the whole deployment pipeline execution to under one hour. Examples of tests included in this stage are functional acceptance tests and non-functional acceptance tests, such as performance tests, security tests, and compliance tests. If necessary, this stage can also include manual tasks like exploratory and usability tests. At the end of this stage, the release candidate is ready to be deployed to production at any time. If we are still not confident about it, this stage is missing some tests.
- *Production stage*—After a release candidate has gone through the commit and acceptance stages, we are confident enough to deploy it to production. This stage is triggered manually or automatically, depending on whether the organization has decided to adopt a continuous deployment practice. The new release candidate is deployed to a production environment using the same deployment

scripts employed (and tested) in the acceptance stage. Optionally, some final automated tests can be run to verify that the deployment was successful.

This section will guide you through bootstrapping a deployment pipeline for Catalog Service and defining the first steps in the commit stage. Then I'll show you how to automate those steps using GitHub Actions.

3.5.1 Understanding the commit stage of the deployment pipeline

Continuous integration is a foundational practice of continuous delivery. When adopted successfully, developers work in small steps and commit to the mainline (the main branch) multiple times a day. After each code commit, the commit stage of the deployment pipeline takes care of building and testing the application with the new changes.

This stage should be fast, because a developer will wait until it completes successfully before moving on to their next task. That's a critical point. If the commit stage fails, the developer responsible for it should immediately deliver a fix or revert their changes so as not to leave the mainline in a broken state and prevent all other developers from integrating their code.

Let's start designing a deployment pipeline for a cloud native application like Catalog Service. For now, we'll focus on the first few steps in the commit stage (figure 3.8).

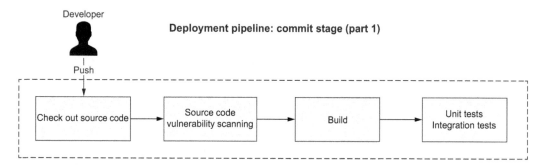

Figure 3.8   The first part of the commit stage in a deployment pipeline

After a developer pushes new code to the mainline, the commit stage starts by checking out the source code from the repository. The starting point is always a commit to the main branch. Following continuous integration practices, we'll aim to work in small steps and integrate our changes with the main branch multiple times a day (*continuously*).

Next, the pipeline can perform several types of static code analysis. For this example, we'll focus on vulnerability scanning. In a real-world project, you would probably want to include additional steps, such as running static code analysis to identify security issues and check compliance with specific coding standards (*code linting*).

Finally, the pipeline builds the application and runs automated tests. In the commit stage, we include technically focused tests that don't require deploying the entire application. These are unit tests and often integration tests. If the integration tests take too long, it's better to move them to the acceptance stage to keep the commit stage fast.

The vulnerability scanner we'll use in the Polar Bookshop project is `grype` (https://github.com/anchore/grype), a powerful open source tool that's increasingly used in the cloud native world. For example, it's part of the supply chain security solution provided by the VMware Tanzu Application Platform. You can find instructions on how to install it in section A.4 of appendix A.

Let's see how grype works. Open a Terminal window, navigate to the root folder of your Catalog Service project (catalog-service), and build the application with `./gradlew build`. Then use `grype` to scan your Java codebase for vulnerabilities. The tool will download a list of known vulnerabilities (a *vulnerability database*) and scan your project against them. The scanning happens locally on your machine, which means none of your files or artifacts is sent to an external service. That makes it a good fit for more regulated environments or air-gapped scenarios.

```
$ grype .
✓ Vulnerability DB          [updated]
✓ Indexed .
✓ Cataloged packages        [35 packages]
✓ Scanned image             [0 vulnerabilities]

No vulnerabilities found
```

> **NOTE** Remember that security is not a static property of a system. At the time of writing, the dependencies used by Catalog Service have no known vulnerabilities, but that doesn't mean this will be true forever. You should scan your projects continuously and apply security patches as soon as they are released, to fix newly discovered vulnerabilities.

Chapters 6 and 7 will cover the remaining steps in the commit stage. For now, let's see how we can automate a deployment pipeline with GitHub Actions. That's the subject of the following section.

3.5.2 Implementing the commit stage with GitHub Actions

When it comes to automating deployment pipelines, there are many solutions from which you can choose. In this book, I'm going to use GitHub Actions (https://github.com/features/actions). It's a managed solution, it provides all the features we need for our project, and it's conveniently already configured for all GitHub repositories. I'm introducing this topic early in this book so that you can use the deployment pipeline to verify your changes while working on the project throughout the book.

> **NOTE** In the cloud native ecosystem, Tekton (https://tekton.dev) is a popular choice for defining deployment pipelines and other software workflows.

It's an open source and Kubernetes-native solution hosted at the Continuous Delivery Foundation (https://cd.foundation). It runs directly on a cluster and lets you declare pipelines and tasks as Kubernetes custom resources.

GitHub Actions is a platform built into GitHub that lets you automate software workflows directly from your code repositories. A *workflow* is an automated process. We'll use workflows to model the commit stage of our deployment pipeline. Each workflow listens to specific *events* that trigger its execution.

Workflows should be defined in a .github/workflows folder in a GitHub repository root, and they should be described following the YAML format provided by GitHub Actions. In your Catalog Service project (catalog-service), create a commit-stage.yml file under a new .github/workflows folder. This workflow will be triggered whenever new code is pushed to the repository.

Listing 3.20   Defining a workflow name and trigger

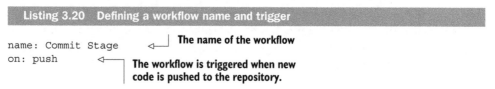

Each workflow is organized into *jobs* that run in parallel. For now, we'll define a single job to collect the steps described previously in figure 3.8. Each job is executed on a *runner* instance, which is a server provided by GitHub. You can choose between Ubuntu, Windows, and macOS. For Catalog Service, we'll run everything on Ubuntu runners provided by GitHub. We'll also want to be specific regarding which *permissions* each job should have. The "Build and Test" job will need read access to the Git repository and write access to the security events when submitting a vulnerability report to GitHub.

Listing 3.21   Configuring a job for building and testing the application

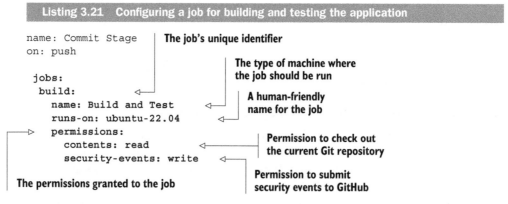

Each job is composed of *steps*, which are executed sequentially. A step could be either a shell command or an *action*. Actions are custom applications used to perform complex tasks in a more structured and reproducible way. For example, you could have actions for packaging an application into an executable, running tests, creating a container image, or pushing an image to a container registry. The GitHub organization provides a basic set of actions, but there's also a marketplace with many more actions developed by the community.

WARNING When using actions from the GitHub marketplace, handle them like any other third-party application and manage the security risks accordingly. Prefer using trusted actions provided by GitHub or verified organizations over other third-party options.

Let's complete this first part of the commit stage by describing what steps the "Build and Test" job should run. The final result is shown in the following listing.

Listing 3.22 Implementing the steps to build and test the application

```
name: Commit Stage
on: push

jobs:
  build:
    name: Build and Test
    runs-on: ubuntu-22.04
    permissions:
      contents: read
      security-events: write
    steps:
      - name: Checkout source code
        uses: actions/checkout@v3
      - name: Set up JDK
        uses: actions/setup-java@v3
        with:
          distribution: temurin
          java-version: 17
          cache: gradle
      - name: Code vulnerability scanning
        uses: anchore/scan-action@v3
        id: scan
        with:
          path: "${{ github.workspace }}"
          fail-build: false
          severity-cutoff: high
          acs-report-enable: true
      - name: Upload vulnerability report
        uses: github/codeql-action/upload-sarif@v2
        if: success() || failure()
        with:
          sarif_file: ${{ steps.scan.outputs.sarif }}
      - name: Build, unit tests and integration tests
        run: |
          chmod +x gradlew
          ./gradlew build
```

Checks out the current Git repository (catalog-service)

Installs and configures a Java runtime

Scans the codebase for vulnerabilities using grype

Defines which version, distribution, and cache type to use

Assigns an identifier to the current step so that it can be referenced from subsequent steps

The minimum security category to be considered as an error (low, medium, high, critical)

The path to the checked-out repository

Whether to enable the generation of a report after the scan is completed

Whether to fail the build in the event of security vulnerabilities

Uploads the security vulnerability report to GitHub (SARIF format)

Uploads the report even if the previous step fails

Fetches the report from the output of the previous step

Ensures the Gradle wrapper is executable, solving Windows incompatibilities

Runs the Gradle build task, which compiles the codebase and runs unit and integration tests

WARNING   The action that uploads the vulnerability report requires the GitHub repository to be public. It works for private repositories only if you have an enterprise subscription. If you prefer keeping your repository private, you'll need to skip the "Upload vulnerability report" step. Throughout the book, I'll assume all the repositories we create on GitHub for the Polar Bookshop project are public.

After completing the declaration of the initial commit stage for the deployment pipeline, commit your changes and push them to the remote GitHub repository. The newly created workflow will be immediately triggered. You can see the execution results on your GitHub repository page on the Actions tab. Figure 3.9 shows an example of the results after running the workflow in listing 3.22. By keeping the result of the commit stage green, you can be quite sure that you haven't broken anything or introduced new regressions (assuming that you have proper tests in place).

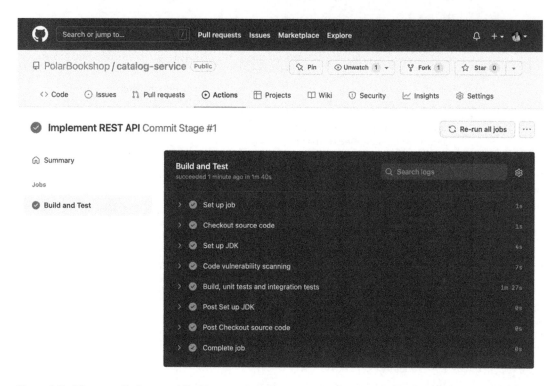

Figure 3.9   The commit stage workflow is executed after you push new changes to the remote repository.

The step for running the vulnerability scan is based on an action provided by Anchore, the company behind grype. In listing 3.22, we do not fail the workflow if serious vulnerabilities are discovered. However, you can find the scanning results in the Security section of your catalog-service GitHub repository.

At the time of writing, there is no high or critical vulnerability in the Catalog Service project, but things might be different in the future. If that's the case, consider using the latest available security patches for the affected dependencies. For the sake of the example, and because I don't want to disrupt your learning journey, I decided not to make the build fail on finding vulnerabilities. In a real-world scenario, however, I recommend you configure and tune grype carefully and according to your company policies regarding supply chain security, and make the workflow fail if the result is not compliant (setting the `fail-build` property to `true`). For more information, refer to the official grype documentation (https://github.com/anchore/grype).

After scanning the Java project for vulnerabilities, we also included a step to fetch the security report generated by grype and upload it to GitHub, independently of whether the build succeeds or not. If any security vulnerability is found, you can see the results in the Security tab of your GitHub repository page (figure 3.10).

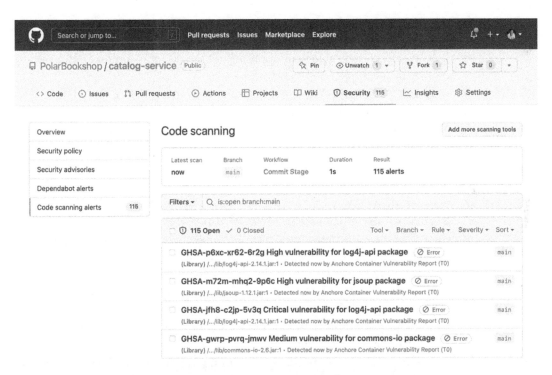

Figure 3.10 A security vulnerability report generated by grype and published to GitHub

NOTE At the time of writing, grype doesn't find any vulnerabilities in the codebase provided with this book. To show you an example of a vulnerability report, figure 3.10 shows the results of grype scanning a different version of the project, purposely full of known vulnerabilities.

That's it for this chapter. Next, I'll cover one of the main cloud native development practices: externalized configuration.

Summary

- Each cloud native application should be tracked in its own codebase, and all its dependencies should be declared in a manifest using tools like Gradle or Maven.
- Cloud native applications don't depend on servers being injected into the environment. Instead, they use an embedded server and are self-contained.
- Tomcat is the default embedded server for Spring Boot applications, and it can be configured through properties to customize the ports it listens on, connections, timeouts, and threads.
- The request/response interaction provided by a Servlet container like Tomcat is both synchronous and blocking. Each thread handles an HTTP request until a response is returned.
- The API first principle recommends designing the API before implementing the business logic to establish a contract. In this way, other teams can develop their services to consume your application based on the contract itself, without waiting for the application to be finished.
- In Spring MVC, REST APIs are implemented in `@RestController` classes.
- Each REST controller method handles an incoming request with a specific method (`GET`, `POST`, `PUT`, `DELETE`) and endpoint (e.g., /books).
- Controller methods can declare which endpoints and operations they handle through the annotations `@GetMapping`, `@PostMapping`, `@PutMapping`, `@DeleteMapping`, and `@RequestMapping`.
- Methods of a `@RestController` class can validate the HTTP request body before the processing happens by applying the `@Valid` annotation.
- The validation constraints for a given Java object are defined using annotations from the Java Bean Validation API on the fields (for example, `@NotBlank`, `@Pattern`, `@Positive`).
- Java exceptions thrown during the processing of an HTTP request can be mapped to an HTTP status code and body in a centralized `@RestControllerAdvice` class, decoupling the exception handling for the REST API from the code throwing the exception.
- Unit tests are not aware of the Spring configuration but can be written as standard Java tests using familiar tools like JUnit, Mockito, and AssertJ.
- Integration tests need a Spring application context to run. A full application context, including an optional embedded server, can be initialized for testing using the `@SpringBootTest` annotation.
- When tests are focused only on a "slice" of the application and only need a part of the configuration, Spring Boot provides several annotations for more targeted integration tests. When you use those annotations, a Spring application context

is initialized, but only the components and configuration parts used by the specific functionality slice are loaded.

- `@WebMvcTest` is for testing Spring MVC components.
- `@JsonTest` is for testing JSON serialization and deserialization.
- GitHub Actions is a tool provided by GitHub to declare pipelines (or workflows) for automating tasks. It can be used to build a deployment pipeline.

Externalized configuration management

This chapter covers

- Configuring Spring with properties and profiles
- Applying external configuration with Spring Boot
- Implementing a configuration server with Spring Cloud Config Server
- Configuring applications with Spring Cloud Config Client

In the previous chapter, we built a RESTful application for managing a catalog of books. As part of the implementation, we defined some data to configure certain aspects of the application (in an application.yml file), such as the Tomcat thread pool and connection timeout. The next step might be to deploy the application to different environments: first in a test environment, then staging, and finally in production. What if you needed a different Tomcat configuration for each of these environments? How would you achieve that?

Traditional applications were usually packaged as a bundle, including the source code and a series of configuration files containing data for different environments, with the appropriate configuration being selected through a flag at runtime. The implication was that you had to make a new application build every time you needed to update the configuration data for a specific environment. A variant

112

of this process was to create a different build for each environment, meaning that you had no guarantee whether what you ran in a staging environment would work the same way in production because they were different artifacts.

Configuration is defined as everything likely to change between deployments (as per the 15-Factor methodology), like credentials, resource handles, and URLs to backing services. An application deployed in multiple locations will likely have different needs in each location and require different configurations. A key aspect of cloud native applications is that the application artifact will stay immutable across environments. No matter which environment you deploy it to, the application build will not be changed.

Each release you deploy is a combination of build and configuration. The same build can be deployed to different environments with different configuration data, as shown in figure 4.1.

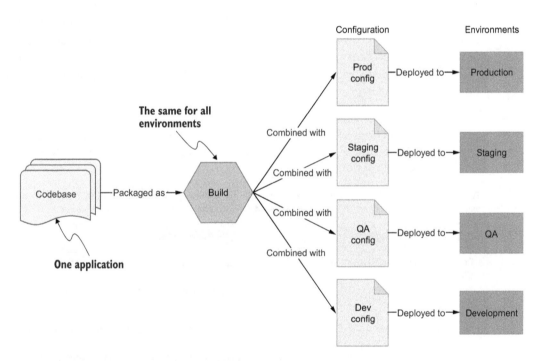

Figure 4.1 Each release you deploy is a combination of build and configuration, which is different for each environment.

Anything that might need to change across deployments should be configurable. For example, you'll probably want to change feature flags, credentials for accessing backing services, resource handles for databases, or URLs to external APIs, all depending on the environment to which you're deploying the application. Cloud native applications favor externalized configuration so that you can replace it without having to rebuild your code. Regarding credentials, it's even more critical not to store them with your application code. There have been countless data breaches because of companies including credentials in a repository that went public by accident. Make sure you won't be one of them.

In Spring, configuration data is abstracted as properties (key/value pairs) defined in different sources, such as property files, JVM system properties, and system environment variables. This chapter covers various aspects of configuring Spring applications that are relevant in a cloud native context. I'll first present the main concepts behind how Spring handles configuration, including properties and profiles, and how you can apply externalized configuration with Spring Boot. Then I'll show you how to set up a configuration server with Spring Cloud Config Server, using a Git repository as the backend for storing your configuration data. Finally, you'll learn how to use the config server to configure a Spring Boot application by relying on Spring Cloud Config Client.

By the end of this chapter, you'll be able to configure your cloud native Spring applications in different ways, depending on your needs and the type of configuration data you have. Table 4.1 summarizes the three main strategies for defining configuration data for cloud native applications covered in this chapter. Chapter 14 will further extend the subjects covered here, including secrets management and how to use ConfigMaps and Secrets in Kubernetes.

NOTE The source code for the examples in this chapter is available in the `Chapter04/04-begin` and `Chapter04/04-end` folders, which contain the initial and final states of the project (https://github.com/ThomasVitale/cloud -native-spring-in-action).

Table 4.1 Cloud native applications can be configured according to different strategies. You will likely use them all, depending on the type of configuration data and the application requirements.

Configuration strategy	Characteristics
Property files packaged with the application	■ These files can act as specifications of what configuration data the application supports. ■ These are useful for defining sensible default values, mainly oriented to the development environment.
Environment variables	■ Environment variables are supported by any operating system, so they are great for portability. ■ Most programming languages allow you access to the environment variables. In Java you can access them with the `System.getenv()` method. In Spring you can also rely on the `Environment` abstraction. ■ These are useful for defining configuration data that depends on the infrastructure and platform where the application is deployed, such as active profiles, hostnames, service names, and port numbers.
Configuration service	■ Provides configuration data persistence, auditing, and accountability. ■ Allows secrets management by using encryption or dedicated secret vaults. ■ This is useful for defining configuration data specific to the application, such as connection pools, credentials, feature flags, thread pools, and URLs to third-party services.

4.1   Configuration in Spring: Properties and profiles

The term *configuration* can have different meanings depending on the context. When discussing the Spring Framework's core features and its `ApplicationContext`, configuration refers to which beans (Java objects registered in Spring) have been defined to be managed by the Spring container and are injected where needed. For example, you can define beans in an XML file (XML configuration), in a `@Configuration` class (Java configuration), or by relying on annotations like `@Component` (annotation-driven configuration).

In this book, unless specified otherwise, whenever I mention *configuration*, I don't mean the previous concept, but rather everything that's likely to change between deployments, as defined by the 15-Factor methodology.

Spring provides you with a convenient `Environment` abstraction that gives you access to any configuration data, no matter its source. The two key aspects of a Spring application environment are *properties* and *profiles*. You have already worked with properties in the previous chapter. Profiles are a tool for labeling logical groups of beans or configuration data that should be loaded at runtime only if a given profile is enabled. Figure 4.2 shows the main aspects of a Spring application environment.

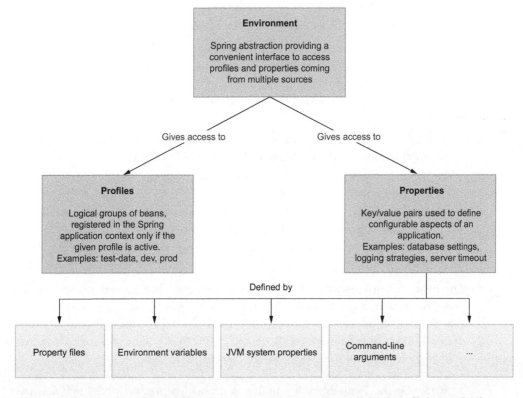

Figure 4.2   The `Environment` interface gives access to the two key aspects of any Spring application configuration: properties and profiles.

This section will cover the fundamental aspects of properties and profiles for cloud native applications, including how to define custom properties and when to use profiles.

4.1.1 Properties: Key/value pairs for configuration

Properties are key/value pairs supported in Java as first-class citizens with `java.util.Properties`. They play an essential role in many applications for storing configuration parameters outside of the compiled Java code. Spring Boot automatically loads them from different sources. When the same property is defined in multiple sources, there are rules that determine which one takes precedence. For example, if you specify a value for the `server.port` property both in a property file and a command-line argument, the latter takes precedence over the former. The following is a prioritized list of some of the most common property sources, starting with the highest priority:

1 `@TestPropertySource` annotations on test classes
2 Command-line arguments
3 JVM System properties from `System.getProperties()`
4 OS environment variables from `System.getenv()`
5 Configuration data files
6 `@PropertySource` annotations on `@Configuration` classes
7 Default properties from `SpringApplication.setDefaultProperties`

For the complete list, you can refer to the Spring Boot documentation (https://spring.io/projects/spring-boot).

Configuration data files can be further prioritized, starting with the highest priority:

1 Profile-specific application properties from application-{profile}.properties and application-{profile}.yml files packaged outside your JAR
2 Application properties from application.properties and application.yml files packaged outside your JAR
3 Profile-specific application properties from application-{profile}.properties and application-{profile}.yml files packaged inside your JAR
4 Application properties from application.properties and application.yml files packaged inside your JAR

The beauty of property handling in Spring is that you don't need to know the specific property source to get a value: the `Environment` abstraction lets you access any property defined in any source through a unified interface. And if the same property is defined in multiple sources, it returns the one with the highest priority. You can even add your own custom sources and assign a priority to them.

> **NOTE** Spring Framework has built-in support for properties defined according to the `Properties` format. On top of that, Spring Boot adds support for

defining properties using the YAML format. YAML is a superset of JSON that provides more flexibility than the simpler `Properties` format. The official website describes YAML as "a human-friendly data serialization language for all programming languages" (https://yaml.org). Feel free to choose either approach in your applications. All the examples in the book will use YAML.

USING APPLICATION PROPERTIES

There are a few ways to access properties from a Java class, as shown in figure 4.3. The most generic approach is based on the `Environment` interface, which you can autowire wherever you need access to an application property. For example, you can use it to access the value for the `server.port` property as follows:

```
@Autowired
private Environment environment;

public String getServerPort() {
  return environment.getProperty("server.port");
}
```

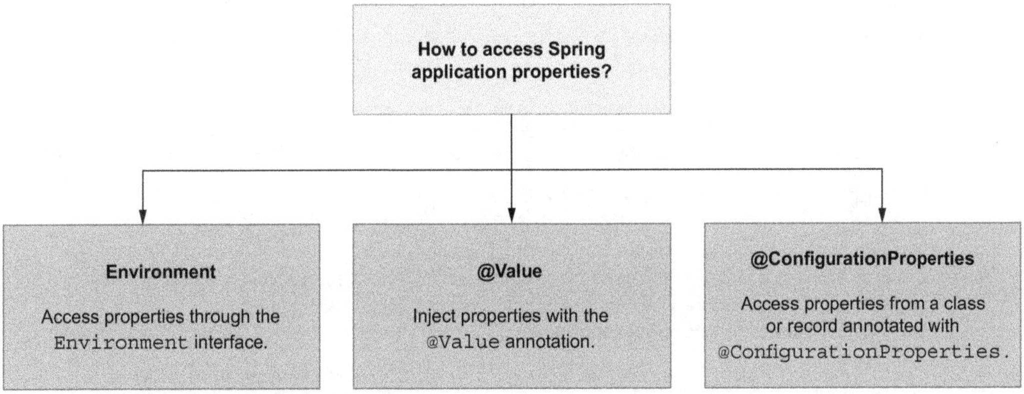

Figure 4.3   You can access Spring properties in different ways.

Properties can also be injected without explicitly invoking the `Environment` object. Just like you use the `@Autowired` annotation for injecting Spring beans, you can apply the `@Value` annotation to inject property values:

```
@Value("${server.port}")
private String serverPort;

public String getServerPort() {
  return serverPort;
}
```

You can configure the application using properties without hardcoding values inside the code, which is one of our goals. But when using the Environment object or the @Value annotation, you still have a hardcoded value that can become difficult to manage: the property key. A more robust and maintainable option, which is also the one recommended by the Spring team, is to use special beans marked with the @ConfigurationProperties annotation to hold configuration data. We'll explore this feature in the next section while you learn how to define custom properties.

DEFINING CUSTOM PROPERTIES

Spring Boot comes bundled with tons of properties for configuring any aspect of your application, depending on which starter dependency you import into your project. Sooner or later, though, you'll find you need to define your own properties.

Let's consider the Catalog Service application we have been working on. In chapter 2, we defined an HTTP endpoint that returned a welcome message to users. We now have a new requirement to implement: the welcome message should be configurable. This is probably not the most useful functionality, but it will help me illustrate the different configuration options.

The first thing to do is tell Spring Boot to scan the application context for configuration data beans. We can do so by adding the @ConfigurationPropertiesScan annotation to the CatalogServiceApplication class in your Catalog Service project (catalog-service).

Listing 4.1   Enabling scanning of configuration data beans

```
package com.polarbookshop.catalogservice;

import org.springframework.boot.SpringApplication;
import org.springframework.boot.autoconfigure.SpringBootApplication;
import org.springframework.boot.context.properties
    .ConfigurationPropertiesScan;

@SpringBootApplication
@ConfigurationPropertiesScan          ⟵——  Loads configuration data
public class CatalogServiceApplication {          beans in the Spring context
  public static void main(String[] args) {
    SpringApplication.run(CatalogServiceApplication.class, args);
  }
}
```

NOTE   Instead of making Spring scan the application context, searching for configuration data beans, you can directly specify which ones Spring should consider by using the @EnableConfigurationProperties annotation.

Next, you can define a new com.polarbookshop.catalogservice.config package, and create a PolarProperties class annotated with @ConfigurationProperties to mark it as a holder of configuration data. The @ConfigurationProperties annotation takes a prefix argument, combined with a field name, to produce the final property key. Spring Boot will try to map all properties with that prefix to fields in the class. In this case, there's only one property mapped to the bean: polar.greeting. Optionally, you can add a description for each property using JavaDoc comments that can be converted into metadata, as I'll show you in a minute.

Listing 4.2   Defining custom properties in a Spring bean

```
package com.polarbookshop.catalogservice.config;

import org.springframework.boot.context.properties.ConfigurationProperties;

@ConfigurationProperties(prefix = "polar")          Marks the class as a source for
public class PolarProperties {                      configuration properties starting
  /**                                                with the prefix "polar"
   * A message to welcome users.
   */
  private String greeting;              Field for the custom polar.greeting
                                        (prefix + field name) property,
  public String getGreeting() {         parsed as String
    return greeting;
  }

  public void setGreeting(String greeting) {
    this.greeting = greeting;
  }
}
```

Optionally, you can add a new dependency on the Spring Boot Configuration Processor in your build.gradle file. That will automatically generate metadata for the new properties and store them in META-INF/spring-configuration-metadata.json when building the project. The IDE can pick them up, show you the description message for each property, and help you with autocompletion and type checks. Remember to refresh or reimport the Gradle dependencies after the new addition.

Listing 4.3   Adding dependency for the Spring Boot Configuration Processor

```
configurations {                              Configures Gradle to use the
  compileOnly {                               Configuration Processor when
    extendsFrom annotationProcessor           building the project
  }
}

dependencies {
  ...
  annotationProcessor
  ➥ 'org.springframework.boot:spring-boot-configuration-processor'
}
```

Now you can trigger the metadata generation by building your project (./gradlew clean build). At this point you can go ahead and define a default value for the polar.greeting property in the application.yml file. While you are inserting the new property, your IDE should provide you with an autocompletion option and type check, as shown in figure 4.4.

Listing 4.4   Defining a value for a custom property in Catalog Service

```
polar:
  greeting: Welcome to the local book catalog!
```

```
polar:
  greeting: Welcome to the local book catalog!
    polar.greeting
    String

    A message to welcome users.

    ·catalog-service.main                    ⋮
```

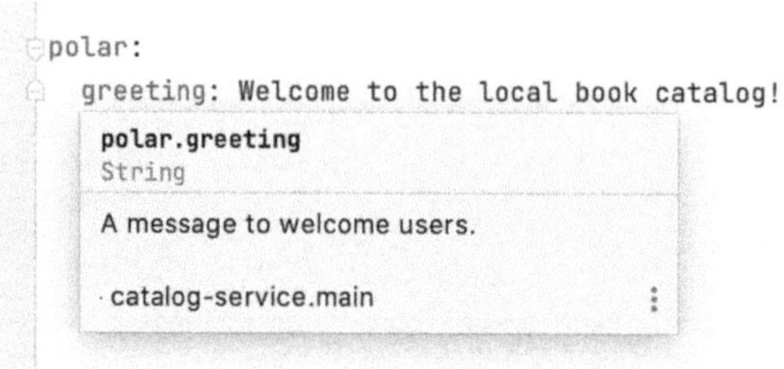

Figure 4.4   Using the Spring Boot Configuration Processor, the JavaDoc comment from your custom property bean is converted into metadata that's used by your IDE to provide useful information, autocompletion, and a type check.

In listing 4.2, the greeting field will be mapped to the polar.greeting property, for which you have just defined a value in application.yml.

USING CUSTOM PROPERTIES

Classes or records annotated with @ConfigurationProperties are standard Spring beans, so you can inject them wherever you need them. Spring Boot initializes all the configuration beans at startup and populates them with the data provided through any of the supported configuration data sources. In the case of Catalog Service, the data will be populated from the application.yml file.

The new requirement for Catalog Service is to make the welcome message returned by the root endpoint configurable via the polar.greeting property. Open the HomeController class and update the handler method to get the message from the custom property instead of using a fixed value.

Listing 4.5   Using custom properties from a configuration properties bean

```
package com.polarbookshop.catalogservice;

import com.polarbookshop.catalogservice.config.PolarProperties;
import org.springframework.web.bind.annotation.GetMapping;
import org.springframework.web.bind.annotation.RestController;

@RestController
public class HomeController {
  private final PolarProperties polarProperties;         ⟵── Bean to access the custom
                                                            properties injected via
                                                            constructor autowiring
  public HomeController(PolarProperties polarProperties) {
    this.polarProperties = polarProperties;
  }
```

```
@GetMapping("/")
public String getGreeting() {
  return polarProperties.getGreeting();   ◁─┐
}                                            │
}
```

> Uses the welcome message
> from the configuration
> data bean

You can now build and run the application to verify that it works as intended (./gradlew bootRun). Then open a Terminal window, and send a GET request to the root endpoint exposed by Catalog Service. The result should be the message you configured in application.yml for the polar.greeting property:

```
$ http :9001/
Welcome to the local book catalog!
```

> **NOTE**   Property files packaged with your application code are useful for defining sensible default values for your configuration data. They can also act as specifications for what configuration properties your application supports.

The following section will cover the other key aspect modeled by the Spring Environment abstraction: profiles, and how to use them for cloud native applications. Before moving on, you can stop the application with Ctrl-C.

4.1.2   *Profiles: Feature flags and configuration groups*

Sometimes you might want to load a bean into the Spring context only under specific conditions. For example, you might want to define a bean responsible for generating test data only when you're working locally or testing the application. Profiles are logical groups of beans that are loaded into the Spring context only if the specified profile is active. Spring Boot also extends this concept to property files, allowing you to define groups of configuration data that are loaded only if a specific profile is active.

You can activate zero, one, or more profiles at a time. All beans not assigned to a profile will always be activated. Beans assigned to the default profile are only activated when no other profile is active.

This section presents Spring profiles in the context of two different use cases: feature flags and configuration groups.

USING PROFILES AS FEATURE FLAGS

The first use case for profiles is for loading groups of beans only if a specified profile is active. The deployment environment shouldn't influence the reasoning behind the groupings too much. A common mistake is using profiles like dev or prod to load beans conditionally. If you do that, the application will be coupled to the environment, which is usually not what we want for a cloud native application.

Consider the case where you deploy applications to three different environments (development, test, and production) and define three profiles to load certain beans conditionally (dev, test, and prod). At some point you decide to add a staging environment, where you also want to enable the beans marked with the prod profile. What do you do? You have two options. Either you activate the prod profile in the staging environment (which doesn't make much sense), or you update the source code to add a staging profile, and assign it to the beans marked as prod (which prevents your application from being immutable and deployable to any environment without any change to the source code). Instead, I recommend using profiles as feature flags when they're associated with groups of beans to be loaded conditionally. Consider what functionality a profile provides, and name it accordingly, rather than thinking about where it will be enabled.

You might still have cases where a bean that handles infrastructural concerns is required in specific platforms. For example, you might have certain beans that should only be loaded when the application is deployed to a Kubernetes environment (no matter whether it is for staging or production). In that case, you could define a kubernetes profile.

In chapter 3 we built the Catalog Service application to manage books. Whenever you run it locally, there are no books in the catalog yet, and you need to add some explicitly if you want to work with the application. A better option would be to let the application generate some test data at startup, but only when it's needed (for example, in a development or test environment). Loading test data can be modeled as a feature that you enable or disable through configuration. You could define a testdata profile to toggle the loading of this test data. In that way, you'll keep the profiles independent from the deployment environment, and you can use them as feature flags with no constraint on the deployment environment whatsoever. Let's do that.

First, add a new com.polarbookshop.catalogservice.demo package to your Catalog Service project, and create a BookDataLoader class. You can instruct Spring to load this class only when the testdata profile is active by applying the @Profile annotation. Then you can use the BookRepository we implemented in chapter 3 to save the data. Finally, the @EventListener(ApplicationReadyEvent.class) annotation will trigger the test data generation after the application has completed the startup phase.

> **Listing 4.6   Loading book test data when the testdata profile is active**

```
package com.polarbookshop.catalogservice.demo;

import com.polarbookshop.catalogservice.domain.Book;
import com.polarbookshop.catalogservice.domain.BookRepository;
import org.springframework.boot.context.event.ApplicationReadyEvent;
import org.springframework.context.annotation.Profile;
import org.springframework.context.event.EventListener;
import org.springframework.stereotype.Component;

@Component
@Profile("testdata")          ⟵——————————  Assigns the class to the testdata
public class BookDataLoader {                 profile. It will be registered only
  private final BookRepository bookRepository;  when the testdata profile is active.
```

```
public BookDataLoader(BookRepository bookRepository) {
  this.bookRepository = bookRepository;
}

@EventListener(ApplicationReadyEvent.class)          ◁─────────
public void loadBookTestData() {
  var book1 = new Book("1234567891", "Northern Lights",
    "Lyra Silverstar", 9.90);
  var book2 = new Book("1234567892", "Polar Journey",
    "Iorek Polarson", 12.90);
  bookRepository.save(book1);
  bookRepository.save(book2);
}
}
```

The test data generation is triggered when an ApplicationReadyEvent is sent—that is when the application startup phase is completed.

In your development environment, you can use the spring.profiles.active property to set the testdata profile as active. You could set it in the application.yml file for the Catalog Service project, but it's not ideal to have the test data feature enabled by default. What if you forget to overwrite it in production? A better option is configuring it specifically for the local development environment when running the boot-Run task. You can achieve that by adding the following code to the build.gradle file.

Listing 4.7   Defining the active profiles for the development environment

```
bootRun {
  systemProperty 'spring.profiles.active', 'testdata'
}
```

Let's verify that it works. Build and run the application (./gradlew bootRun). You'll see a message in the application logs listing all the active profiles (in this case, it's just testdata, but there can be more), as shown in figure 4.5.

```
...Starting CatalogServiceApplication using Java 17
...|The following 1 profile is active: "testdata"|
...Tomcat initialized with port(s): 9001 (http)
...Starting service [Tomcat]
...Starting Servlet engine: [Apache Tomcat/9.0.65]
...Initializing Spring embedded WebApplicationContext
...Root WebApplicationContext: initialization completed in 276 ms
...Tomcat started on port(s): 9001 (http) with context path ''
...Started CatalogServiceApplication in 0.529 seconds (JVM running for 0.735)
```

Figure 4.5   The logs for Catalog Service when the "testdata" profile is active

Then you can send a request to the application to fetch all the books in the catalog:

```
$ http :9001/books
```

It should return the test data we created in listing 4.6. When you're done, stop the application with Ctrl-C.

> **NOTE**   Instead of using profiles as feature flags, a more scalable and structured approach is defining custom properties to configure functionality, and relying on annotations such as `@ConditionalOnProperty` and `@Conditional-OnCloudPlatform` to control when certain beans should be loaded into the Spring application context. That's one of the foundations of Spring Boot autoconfiguration. For example, you could define a `polar.testdata.enabled` custom property and use the `@ConditionalOnProperty(name = "polar.testdata.enabled", havingValue = "true")` annotation on the `BookDataLoader` class.

Next, I'll show you how to use profiles to group configuration data.

USING PROFILES AS CONFIGURATION GROUPS

The Spring Framework's profile functionality allows you to register some beans only if a given profile is active. Likewise, Spring Boot lets you define configuration data that is loaded only when a specific profile is active. A common way to do that is inside a property file named with the profile as a suffix. In the case of the Catalog Service, you could create a new application-dev.yml file and define a value for the `polar.greeting` property, which would be used by Spring Boot only if the dev profile was active. Profile-specific property files take precedence over the non-specific property files, so the value defined in application-dev.yml would take precedence over the one in application.yml.

In the context of property files, profiles are used to group configuration data, and they can be mapped to deployment environments without facing the same issues we analyzed in the previous section when using profiles as feature flags. But that applies only as long as you don't package the profile-specific property files with the application. The 15-Factor methodology recommends not batching configuration values into groups named after environments and bundled with the application source code because it wouldn't scale. As a project grows, new environments might be created for different stages; developers might create their own custom environments to try out new functionality. You can quickly end up with way too many configuration groups, implemented like Spring profiles and requiring new builds. Instead, you'll want to keep them outside the application, such as in a dedicated repository served by a configuration server, as you'll see later in this chapter. The only exception is for defaults and development-oriented configuration.

The following section will cover how Spring Boot addresses externalized configuration. You'll learn how to use command-line arguments, JVM system properties, and environment variables to provide configuration data from the outside while using the same application build.

4.2   Externalized configuration: One build, multiple configurations

Property files bundled with the application source code are useful for defining some sensible defaults. Still, if you need to provide different values depending on the environment, you'll need something else. Externalized configuration allows you to configure your application depending on where it's deployed while consistently using the same immutable build for your application code. The critical aspect is that you don't change your application after you build and package it. If any configuration change is needed (for example, different credentials or database handles), it's done from the outside.

The 15-Factor methodology promotes storing configuration in the environment, and Spring Boot provides several ways to achieve that. You can use one of the higher priority property sources to override the default values, depending on where the application is deployed. In this section you'll see how to use command-line arguments, JVM properties, and environment variables to configure a cloud native application without rebuilding it. Figure 4.6 illustrates how the precedence rules work for overriding a Spring property.

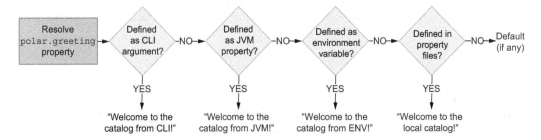

Figure 4.6   Spring Boot evaluates all property sources according to a precedence list. In the end, each property will have the value defined from the source with the highest precedence.

Let's consider the Catalog Service application. First, you need to package the application as a JAR artifact. You can do so from a Terminal window, navigating to the project's root folder and running the following command:

```
$ ./gradlew bootJar
```

We're not relying on Gradle to run the application this time because I want to demonstrate how you can change the application configuration while using the same immutable JAR artifact (that is, changing the configuration without rebuilding the application). You can run it as a standard Java application:

```
$ java -jar build/libs/catalog-service-0.0.1-SNAPSHOT.jar
```

You haven't overridden any properties yet, so the root endpoint will return the `polar.greeting` value defined in the application.yml file:

```
$ http :9001/
Welcome to the local book catalog!
```

In the following sections you'll see how to provide a different value for the `polar.greeting` property. Remember to terminate the Java process (Ctrl-C) before moving on to new examples.

4.2.1   *Configuring an application through command-line arguments*

By default, Spring Boot converts any command-line argument to a property key/value pair and includes it in the `Environment` object. In a production application, that is the property source with the highest precedence. Using the same JAR you built earlier, you can specify a command-line argument to customize the application configuration:

```
$ java -jar build/libs/catalog-service-0.0.1-SNAPSHOT.jar \
    --polar.greeting="Welcome to the catalog from CLI"
```

The command-line argument has the same name as the Spring property, prefixed with the familiar `--` for CLI arguments. This time the application will use the message defined in the command-line argument, since it takes precedence over property files:

```
$ http :9001/
Welcome to the catalog from CLI
```

4.2.2   *Configuring an application through JVM system properties*

JVM system properties can override Spring properties much like command-line arguments, but they have a lower priority. It's all part of externalizing the configuration, so you don't need to build a new JAR artifact—you can still use the one packaged earlier. Terminate the Java process from the previous example (Ctrl-C) and run the following command:

```
$ java -Dpolar.greeting="Welcome to the catalog from JVM" \
    -jar build/libs/catalog-service-0.0.1-SNAPSHOT.jar
```

The JVM system property has the same name as the Spring property, prefixed with the usual `-D` for JVM arguments. This time the application will use the message defined as a JVM system property, since it takes precedence over property files:

```
$ http :9001/
Welcome to the catalog from JVM
```

What if you specify both a JVM system property and a CLI argument? The precedence rules will ensure Spring uses the value specified as a command-line argument, since it takes precedence over JVM properties.

Once again, terminate the previous Java process (Ctrl-C) and run the following command:

```
$ java -Dpolar.greeting="Welcome to the catalog from JVM" \
    -jar build/libs/catalog-service-0.0.1-SNAPSHOT.jar \
    --polar.greeting="Welcome to the catalog from CLI"
```

The result, as you can imagine, will be the following:

```
$ http :9001/
Welcome to the catalog from CLI
```

Both CLI arguments and JVM properties let you externalize the configuration and keep the application build immutable. However, they require different commands to run the application, which might result in errors at deployment time. A better approach is using environment variables, as recommended by the 15-Factor methodology. Before moving on to the next section, terminate the current Java process (Ctrl-C).

4.2.3   Configuring an application through environment variables

Environment variables defined in the operating system are commonly used for externalized configuration, and they are the recommended option according to the 15-Factor methodology. One of the advantages of environment variables is that every operating system supports them, making them portable across any environment. Furthermore, most programming languages provide features for accessing environment variables. For example, in Java, you can do that by calling the `System.getenv()` method.

In Spring, you are not required to read environment variables from the surrounding system explicitly. Spring automatically reads them during the startup phase and adds them to the Spring `Environment` object, making them accessible, just like any other property. For example, if you run a Spring application in an environment where the `MY_ENV_VAR` variable is defined, you can access its value either from the `Environment` interface or using the `@Value` annotation.

On top of that, Spring Boot extends the Spring Framework functionality by allowing you to use environment variables to override Spring properties automatically. For command-line arguments and JVM system properties, you used the same naming convention as the Spring property. However, environment variables have some naming constraints dictated by the operating system. For example, on Linux, the common syntax consists of having all capital letters and words separated by an underscore.

You can turn a Spring property key into an environment variable by making all the letters uppercase and replacing any dot or dash with an underscore. Spring Boot will map it correctly to the internal syntax. For example, a `POLAR_GREETING` environment variable is recognized as the `polar.greeting` property. This feature is called *relaxed binding*.

In the Catalog Service application, you can override the `polar.greeting` property with the following command:

```
$ POLAR_GREETING="Welcome to the catalog from ENV" \
    java -jar build/libs/catalog-service-0.0.1-SNAPSHOT.jar
```

> **TIP** On Windows, you can achieve the same result by running `$env:POLAR_GREETING="Welcome to the catalog from ENV"; java -jar build/libs/catalog-service-0.0.1-SNAPSHOT.jar` from a PowerShell console.

During the startup phase of Catalog Service, Spring Boot will read the variables defined in the surrounding environment, recognize that `POLAR_GREETING` can be mapped to the `polar.greeting` property, and store its value in the Spring `Environment` object, overriding the value defined in application.yml. The result will be the following:

```
$ http :9001/
Welcome to the catalog from ENV
```

After testing the application, stop the process with Ctrl-C. If you ran the application from Windows PowerShell, remember to unset the environment variable with `Remove-Item Env:\POLAR_GREETING`.

When you use environment variables for storing configuration data, you don't have to change the command to run your application (as you did for CLI arguments and JVM properties). Spring will automatically read environment variables from the context where it's deployed. This approach is less error-prone and fragile than using CLI arguments or JVM system properties.

> **NOTE** You can use environment variables to define configuration values that depend on the infrastructure or platform where the application is deployed, such as profiles, port numbers, IP addresses, and URLs.

Environment variables work seamlessly on virtual machines, OCI containers, and Kubernetes clusters. However, they might not be enough. In the next section, I'll go through some of the issues affecting environment variables and how Spring Cloud Config can help address them.

4.3   *Centralized configuration management with Spring Cloud Config Server*

With environment variables, you can externalize your application's configuration and follow the 15-Factor methodology. However, there are some issues they cannot handle:

- Configuration data is as important as the application code, so it should be handled with the same care and attention, starting from its persistence. Where should you store configuration data?

- Environment variables don't provide granular access control features. How can you control access to configuration data?
- Configuration data will evolve and require changes, just like application code. How should you keep track of the revisions to configuration data? How should you audit the configuration used in a release?
- After changing your configuration data, how can you make your application read it at runtime without requiring a full restart?
- When the number of application instances increases, it can be challenging to handle configuration in a distributed fashion for each instance. How can you overcome such challenges?
- Neither Spring Boot properties nor environment variables support configuration encryption, so you can't safely store passwords. How should you manage secrets?

The Spring ecosystem offers many options to address those issues. We can categorize them into three groups.

- *Configuration services*—The Spring Cloud project provides modules you can use to run your own configuration services and configure your Spring Boot applications.
  - Spring Cloud Alibaba provides a configuration service using Alibaba Nacos as the data store.
  - Spring Cloud Config provides a configuration service backed by a pluggable data source, such as a Git repository, a data store, or HashiCorp Vault.
  - Spring Cloud Consul provides a configuration service using HashiCorp Consul as the data store.
  - Spring Cloud Vault provides a configuration service using HashiCorp Vault as the data store.
  - Spring Cloud Zookeeper provides a configuration service using Apache Zookeeper as the data store.
- *Cloud vendor services*—If you run your applications on a platform provided by a cloud vendor, you might consider using one of their configuration services. Spring Cloud provides integration with the main cloud vendor configuration services that you can use to configure your Spring Boot applications.
  - Spring Cloud AWS provides integration with AWS Parameter Store and AWS Secrets Manager.
  - Spring Cloud Azure provides integration with Azure Key Vault.
  - Spring Cloud GCP provides integration with GCP Secret Manager.
- *Cloud platform services*—When running your applications on a Kubernetes platform, you can seamlessly use ConfigMaps and Secrets to configure Spring Boot.

This section will show you how to set up a centralized configuration server with Spring Cloud Config that's responsible for delivering configuration data stored in a Git repository to all applications. Chapter 14 will cover more advanced configuration topics, including secrets management and Kubernetes features like ConfigMaps and Secrets. Many of the features and patterns you'll use with Spring Cloud Config are easily applicable to the other solutions involving configuration services and cloud vendor services.

> **NOTE** Your choice of configuration service will depend on your infrastructure and requirements. For example, suppose you're running your workloads on Azure already, and you need a GUI to manage configuration data. In that case, it might make sense to use Azure Key Vault rather than running a configuration service yourself. If you want to version-control your configuration data with Git, Spring Cloud Config or Kubernetes ConfigMaps and Secrets would be a better choice. You might even compromise and use a managed Spring Cloud Config service offered by vendors like Azure or VMware Tanzu.

The idea of centralized configuration is built around two main components:

- A data store for configuration data, providing persistence, versioning, and possibly access control
- A server sitting on top of the data store to manage configuration data and serve it to multiple applications

Imagine having many applications deployed in different environments. A configuration server could manage configuration data for all of them from a centralized place, and that configuration data might be stored in different ways. For example, you could use a dedicated Git repository for storing non-sensitive data and use HashiCorp Vault to store your secrets. No matter how the data is stored, a configuration server will deliver it to different applications through a unified interface. Figure 4.7 shows how centralized configuration works.

It's clear from figure 4.7 that the configuration server becomes a backing service for all the applications, which means it's at risk of being a single point of failure. If it's suddenly unavailable, all the applications will probably fail to start up. This risk can be easily mitigated by scaling the config server, as you would with other applications requiring high availability. When using a configuration server, it's fundamental to deploy at least two replicas.

> **NOTE** You can use a centralized configuration server for configuration data that doesn't depend on the specific infrastructure or deployment platform, such as credentials, feature flags, URLs to third-party services, thread pools, and timeouts.

We'll use Spring Cloud Config Server to set up a centralized configuration server for the Polar Bookshop system. The project also provides a client library (Spring Cloud Config Client) that you can use to integrate Spring Boot applications with the config server.

Let's start by defining a repository for storing configuration data.

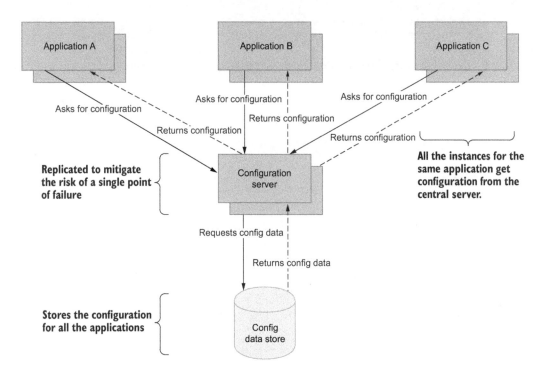

Figure 4.7   A centralized configuration server manages external properties for many applications across all environments.

4.3.1   *Using Git to store your configuration data*

The config server will be responsible for providing configuration data to Spring applications. Before setting that up, though, we need a way to store and keep track of that data. Spring Cloud Config Server integrates with many different backend solutions to store configuration data. One of the most common choices is a Git repository.

First, create a new config-repo Git repository (for the final result, you can refer to Chapter04/04-end/config-repo). The repository can be local or remote, but for this example I recommend initializing a remote one on GitHub, just like you did for the application repositories. I'm using main as the default branch name.

Inside the config repo, you can store properties directly in Spring format as *.properties or *.yml files.

Continuing with the Catalog Service example, let's define an external property for the welcome message. Navigate to the config-repo folder and create a catalog-service.yml file. Then define a value for the polar.greeting property used by the Catalog Service.

Listing 4.8   Defining a new message for when the config server is used

```
polar:
  greeting: "Welcome to the catalog from the config server"
```

Next, create a catalog-service-prod.yml file, and define a different value for the `polar.greeting` property to be used only when the `prod` profile is active.

Listing 4.9   Defining a new message for when the `prod` profile is active

```
polar:
  greeting: "Welcome to the production catalog from the config server"
```

Finally, commit and push your changes to the remote repository.

How does Spring Cloud Config resolve the correct configuration data for each application? How should you organize the repository to host properties for multiple applications? The library relies on three parameters to identify which property file to use to configure a specific application:

- {application}—The name of the application as defined by the `spring .application.name` property.
- {profile}—One of the active profiles defined by the `spring.profiles.active` property.
- {label}—A discriminator defined by the specific configuration data repository. In the case of Git, it can be a tag, a branch name, or a commit ID. It's useful for identifying a versioned set of config files.

Depending on your needs, you can organize the folder structure using different combinations, such as these:

```
/{application}/application-{profile}.yml
/{application}/application.yml
/{application}-{profile}.yml
/{application}.yml
/application-{profile}.yml
/application.yml
```

For each application, you can either use property files named after the application itself and placed in the root folder (e.g., /catalog-service.yml or /catalog-service-prod.yml) or use the default naming and put them in a subfolder named after the application (e.g., /catalog-service/application.yml or /catalog-service/application-prod.yml).

You can also put application.yml or application-{profile}.yml files in the root folder to define default values for all applications. They can be used as a fallback whenever there is no more specific property source. Spring Cloud Config Server will always return the properties from the most specific path, using the application name, active profiles, and Git labels.

The *label* concept is particularly interesting when using Git as the backend for the config server. For example, you could create long-lived branches of your config repo for different environments or short-lived branches while testing specific features. Spring Cloud Config Server can use the label information to return the correct configuration data from the right Git branch, tag, or commit ID.

Now that you have a Git repository in place for your configuration data, it's time to set up a config server to manage them.

4.3.2   Setting up a configuration server

Spring Cloud Config Server is a project that lets you set up a configuration server with minimal effort. It's a standard Spring Boot application with specific properties that enable the configuration server functionality and the Git repository as the configuration data backend. The Polar Bookshop system will use this server to provide configuration to the Catalog Service application. Figure 4.8 illustrates the architecture of the solution.

Now, on to the code.

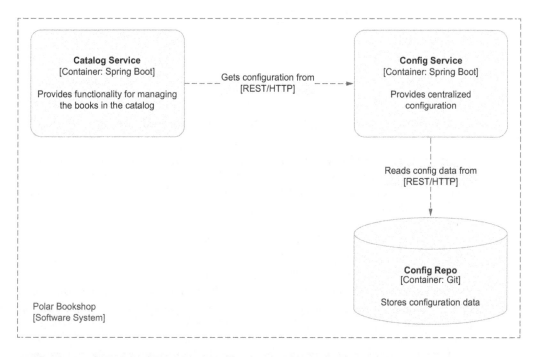

Figure 4.8   A centralized configuration server, backed by a Git repository, provides configuration to the Catalog Service application.

BOOTSTRAPPING THE PROJECT

The Polar Bookshop system needs a Config Service application to provide centralized configuration. You can initialize the project from Spring Initializr (https://start.spring.io/)

and store the result in a new `config-service` Git repository. The parameters for the initialization are shown in figure 4.9.

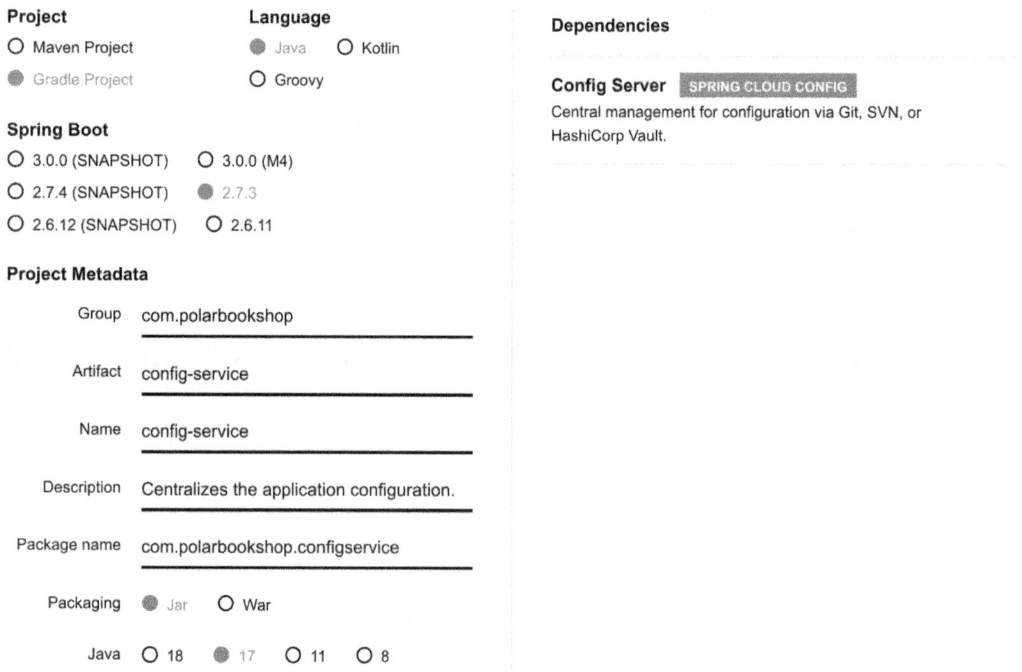

Project
O Maven Project
⦿ Gradle Project

Language
⦿ Java   O Kotlin
O Groovy

Spring Boot
O 3.0.0 (SNAPSHOT)   O 3.0.0 (M4)
O 2.7.4 (SNAPSHOT)   ⦿ 2.7.3
O 2.6.12 (SNAPSHOT)   O 2.6.11

Project Metadata

Group	com.polarbookshop
Artifact	config-service
Name	config-service
Description	Centralizes the application configuration.
Package name	com.polarbookshop.configservice
Packaging	⦿ Jar O War
Java	O 18 ⦿ 17 O 11 O 8

Dependencies

Config Server `SPRING CLOUD CONFIG`
Central management for configuration via Git, SVN, or HashiCorp Vault.

Figure 4.9   The parameters for initializing the Config Service project from Spring Initializr

> **TIP** You may prefer to avoid manually generating the project through the Spring Initializr website. In the `begin` folder for this chapter, you can find a `curl` command that you can run in a Terminal window to download a zip file containing all the code you need to get started.

In the generated build.gradle file, you can see how the management of Spring Cloud dependencies works differently than for Spring Boot. All Spring Cloud projects follow an independent release train that relies on a bill of materials (BOM) to manage all the dependencies. Spring Cloud release trains are named after a year (for example, 2021.0.3) rather than adopting a semantic version strategy (for example, the Spring Boot version is 2.7.3).

Listing 4.10   The Gradle configuration for Config Service

```
plugins {
    id 'org.springframework.boot' version '2.7.3'
    id 'io.spring.dependency-management' version '1.0.13.RELEASE'
    id 'java'
}
```

```
group = 'com.polarbookshop'
version = '0.0.1-SNAPSHOT'
sourceCompatibility = '17'

repositories {
  mavenCentral()
}

ext {
  set('springCloudVersion', "2021.0.3")          ◁─┐  Defines the Spring
}                                                      Cloud version to use

dependencies {
  implementation 'org.springframework.cloud:spring-cloud-config-server'
  testImplementation 'org.springframework.boot:spring-boot-starter-test'
}

dependencyManagement {
  imports {
    mavenBom "org.springframework.cloud:
⇒ spring-cloud-dependencies:${springCloudVersion}"   ◁─┐  BOM for Spring
  }                                                        Cloud dependency
}                                                          management

tasks.named('test') {
  useJUnitPlatform()
}
```

These are the main dependencies:

- *Spring Cloud Config Server* (`org.springframework.cloud:spring-cloud-config-server`)—Provides libraries and utilities to build a configuration server on top of Spring Web.
- *Spring Boot Test* (`org.springframework.boot:spring-boot-starter-test`)—Provides several libraries and utilities to test applications, including Spring Test, JUnit, AssertJ, and Mockito. It's automatically included in every Spring Boot project.

ENABLING THE CONFIGURATION SERVER

Turning the project you initialized earlier into a functioning configuration server doesn't require too many steps. The only thing you need to do in Java is add the `@EnableConfigServer` annotation on a configuration class, such as `ConfigService-Application`.

Listing 4.11 Enabling configuration server in Spring Boot

```
package com.polarbookshop.configservice;

import org.springframework.boot.SpringApplication;
import org.springframework.boot.autoconfigure.SpringBootApplication;
import org.springframework.cloud.config.server.EnableConfigServer;
```

```
@SpringBootApplication
@EnableConfigServer                    ◁─────    Activates the configuration
public class ConfigServiceApplication {          server implementation in the
  public static void main(String[] args) {       Spring Boot application
    SpringApplication.run(ConfigServiceApplication.class, args);
  }
}
```

That was it on the Java side.

CONFIGURING THE CONFIGURATION SERVER

The next step is configuring the behavior of the config server. Yes, that's right. Even a configuration server needs configuration! First of all, Spring Cloud Config Server runs on an embedded Tomcat server, so you can configure connection timeouts and thread pools as you did for Catalog Service.

You previously initialized a Git repository to host configuration data, so you should now instruct Spring Cloud Config Server where to find it. You can do so in an application.yml file located in the src/main/resources path of your Config Service project (rename the autogenerated application.properties file as application.yml).

The spring.cloud.config.server.git.uri property should point to where you defined the config repo. If you followed along with what I did, it will be on GitHub, and the default branch will be called main. You can configure which branch the config server should consider by default by setting the spring.cloud.config.server.git .default-label property. Remember that, when using Git repositories, the label concept is an abstraction over Git branches, tags, or commit IDs.

Listing 4.12   Configuring integration between config server and config repo

```
server:
  port: 8888                  ◁─────┐   The port that the
  tomcat:                            │   Config Service
    connection-timeout: 2s           │   application will
    keep-alive-timeout: 15s          │   listen on
    threads:
      max: 50
      min-spare: 5

spring:                            A name for
  application:                     the current
    name: config-service   ◁───┘   application
  cloud:
    config:
      server:
        git:                                          The URL to the remote Git
          uri: <your-config-repo-github-url>   ◁──┐   repository to use as the
          default-label: main    ◁───┐             configuration data backend. For
                                      │             example, https://github.com/
                 By default, the server will       PolarBookshop/config-repo.
                 return configuration data
                 from the "main" branch.
```

WARNING The configuration I used for Config Service assumes the config repo is publicly available on GitHub. When you use private repositories (which is often true for real-world applications), you need to specify how to authenticate with the code repository provider by using additional configuration properties. For more information, refer to the official Spring Cloud Config documentation (https://spring.io/projects/spring-cloud-config). I'll further discuss handling credentials in chapter 14.

4.3.3 Making the configuration server resilient

The Config Service might become a single point of failure in your system. If all the applications rely on it to fetch configuration data, you need to ensure it's highly available. The first step toward that goal is deploying multiple instances of Config Service in a production environment. If one of them stops working for some reason, another replica can provide the required configuration. In chapter 7, you'll learn more about scaling applications and how to make that work in Kubernetes.

However, scaling the Config Service is not enough. Since it's using a remote Git repository as the configuration data backend, you'll need to make that interaction more resilient too. First, you can define a timeout to prevent the config server from waiting too long to establish a connection with the remote repository. You can do so with the `spring.cloud.config.server.git.timeout` property.

Spring Cloud Config is implemented to clone the remote repository locally upon the first request for configuration data. I recommend using the `spring.cloud.config` `.server.git.clone-on-start` property so that the repo clone happens at startup. Even though it makes the startup phase a bit slower, it makes your deployment fail faster if there's any difficulty communicating with the remote repository, rather than waiting for the first request to find out that something is wrong. Also, it makes the first request from a client faster.

The local copy of the repository improves the config server's fault tolerance because it ensures it can return configuration data to the client applications even if the communication with the remote repository is temporarily failing (for example, if GitHub is down or there's a problem with the network). However, if the config server hasn't cloned the repository locally yet, there's no fallback in place. That's why it's better to fail fast at startup and investigate the issue right away.

When a local copy of the repository is created successfully, there's a chance the local repo may get changed independently of the remote repo. You can ensure your config server always uses the same data that's defined in the remote repository by setting the `spring.cloud.config.server.git.force-pull` property so that a fresh copy is pulled whenever the local copy is corrupted, and any local changes are discarded. By default, the local repository is cloned in a folder with a random name. If needed, you can control where it is cloned through the `spring.cloud.config.server.git` `.basedir` property. For Config Service, we'll rely on the default behavior.

You can update the application.yml file for the Config Service application as follows and make it more resilient to faults affecting interactions with the code repository service (in this case, GitHub).

Listing 4.13   Making Config Service more resilient

```
spring:
  application:
    name: config-service
  cloud:
    config:
      server:
        git:
          uri: <your-config-repo-github-url>
          default-label: main
          timeout: 5              ◄──────────
          clone-on-start: true   ◄──
          force-pull: true       ◄──┐
```

Time limit to establish
a connection with the
remote repository

Clones the remote repository
locally on startup

Forces pulling the remote repository
and discarding any local changes

In the next section we'll verify that Config Service is working correctly.

4.3.4   *Understanding the configuration server REST API*

Spring Cloud Config Server works seamlessly with Spring Boot applications, providing properties in their native formats through a REST API. You can try it out fairly easily. Build and run Config Service (./gradlew bootRun), open a Terminal window, and make an HTTP GET request to /catalog-service/default:

```
$ http :8888/catalog-service/default
```

The result is the configuration that's returned when no Spring profile is active. You can try fetching the configuration for the scenario where the prod profile is active as follows:

```
$ http :8888/catalog-service/prod
```

As shown in figure 4.10, the result is the configuration defined for the Catalog Service application in catalog-service.yml and catalog-service-prod.yml, where the latter takes precedence over the former because the prod profile is specified.

When you are done testing the application, stop its execution with Ctrl-C.

Spring Cloud Config Server exposes properties through a series of endpoints using different combinations of the {application}, {profile}, and {label} parameters:

```
/{application}/{profile}[/{label}]
/{application}-{profile}.yml
/{label}/{application}-{profile}.yml
/{application}-{profile}.properties
/{label}/{application}-{profile}.properties
```

Figure 4.10   The configuration server exposes a REST API to fetch configuration data based on the application name, profile, and label. This image shows the result for the `/catalog-service/prod` **endpoint.**

You won't need to call these endpoints from your application when using Spring Cloud Config Client (it does that for you), but it's useful to know how the server exposes configuration data. A configuration server built with Spring Cloud Config Server exposes a standard REST API that any application can access over a network. You can use the same server for applications built with other languages and frameworks and use the REST API directly.

In chapter 14, I'll address more aspects of how to handle configuration. For example, Spring Cloud Config has a few features for encrypting properties containing secrets before storing them in a Git repository. Also, multiple backend solutions can be used as configuration data repositories, meaning that you could save all the non-sensitive properties in Git and use HashiCorp Vault to store secrets. Furthermore, the REST API itself should be protected, and I'll talk about that as well. I will address all those critical aspects from a security point of view—considering these issues is necessary before deploying to production.

For now, let's complete our solution and update Catalog Service to integrate with the Config Service application.

4.4   Using a configuration server with Spring Cloud Config Client

The Config Service application built in the previous section is a server that exposes configuration through a REST API. In general, applications would interact with this API, but you can use Spring Cloud Config Client for Spring applications.

This section will teach you how to use Spring Cloud Config Client and integrate Catalog Service with the config server. You'll see how to make the interaction more robust and how to refresh the client's configuration when new changes are pushed to the config repo.

4.4.1   Setting up a configuration client

The first thing you'll need to do to integrate a Spring Boot application with a config server is add a new dependency to Spring Cloud Config Client. Update the build.gradle file for the Catalog Service project (catalog-service) as follows. Remember to refresh or reimport the Gradle dependencies after the new addition.

Listing 4.14   Adding dependency for Spring Cloud Config Client

```
ext {
  set('springCloudVersion', "2021.0.3")
}

dependencies {
  ...
  implementation 'org.springframework.cloud:spring-cloud-starter-config'
}

dependencyManagement {
  imports {
    mavenBom "org.springframework.cloud:
      spring-cloud-dependencies:${springCloudVersion}"
  }
}
```

We now need to instruct Catalog Service to fetch its configuration from the Config Service. You can do that via the `spring.config.import` property by passing `config-server:` as the property value. You probably don't want the config server running in your local environment when working with client applications like Catalog Service, and in that case you can make the interaction optional with the `optional:` prefix (`optional:configserver:`). If the config server is not running when you start Catalog Service, the application will log a warning, but it won't stop working. Be careful not to make this optional in production, or you'll risk using the wrong configuration.

Next, Catalog Service needs to know the URL to contact the Config Service. You have two options. Either you can add it to the `spring.config.import` property (`optional:configserver:http://localhost:8888`) or rely on the more specific `spring.cloud.config.uri` property. We'll use the second option so we only need to change the URL value when deploying the application in different environments.

Since the config server uses the application name to return the correct configuration data, you'll also need to set the `spring.application.name` property to `catalog-service`. Remember the {application} parameter? That's where the `spring.application.name` value is used.

Open the application.yml file for your Catalog Service project and apply the following configuration.

Listing 4.15 Instructing Catalog Service to get config from Config Service

```
spring:
  application:
    name: catalog-service          ←─┐  The name of the application, used by the
  config:                               config server to filter the configuration
    import: "optional:configserver:"  ←─┤  Imports configuration data from
  cloud:                                   a config server when available
    config:
      uri: http://localhost:8888   ←──  The URL of the configuration server
```

Let's go ahead and verify that it works correctly. The Catalog Service application contains a `polar.greeting` property with the value "Welcome to the local book catalog!" When using a configuration server, the centralized properties take precedence over the local ones, so the value you defined in the `config-repo` repository will be used instead.

First, run Config Service (`./gradlew bootRun`). Then package Catalog Service as a JAR artifact (`./gradlew bootJar`) and run it as follows:

```
$ java -jar build/libs/catalog-service-0.0.1-SNAPSHOT.jar
```

Then, in another Terminal window, send a GET request to the root endpoint:

```
$ http :9001/
Welcome to the catalog from the config server!
```

As expected, the welcome message returned by the application is the one defined in the `config-repo` repository, specifically in the catalog-service.yml file.

You can also try running the application with the `prod` profile enabled. Stop Catalog Service with Ctrl-C, and then start the application again with `prod` as an active profile:

```
$ java -jar build/libs/catalog-service-0.0.1-SNAPSHOT.jar \
    --spring.profiles.active=prod
```

The expected result is now the message defined in the catalog-service-prod.yml file in the `config-repo` repository:

```
$ http :9001/
Welcome to the production catalog from the config server
```

Once again, stop the previous application's execution with Ctrl-C.

The following section will cover how you can make the interaction between application and config server more fault-tolerant.

4.4.2 *Making the configuration client resilient*

When the integration with the config server is not optional, the application fails to start up if it cannot contact a config server. If the server is up and running, you could still experience issues due to the distributed nature of the interaction. Therefore it's a good idea to define some timeouts to make the application fail faster. You can use the `spring.cloud.config.request-connect-timeout` property to control the time limit for establishing a connection with the config server. The `spring.cloud.config.request-read-timeout` property lets you limit the time spent reading configuration data from the server.

Open the application.yml file for your Catalog Service project and apply the following configuration to make the interaction with Config Service more resilient. Once again, there's no universal rule for setting up timeouts. Depending on your architecture and infrastructure characteristics, you might need to adjust these values.

Listing 4.16 Making Spring Cloud Config Client more resilient

```
spring:
  application:
    name: catalog-service
  config:
    import: "optional:configserver:"
  cloud:
    config:
      uri: http://localhost:8888
      request-connect-timeout: 5000    ⊲─┐ Timeout on waiting
      request-read-timeout: 5000    ⊲──┐   to connect to the
                                        │   config server (ms)
             Timeout on waiting to read configuration
             data from the config server (ms)
```

Even if Config Service is replicated, there's still a chance it will be temporarily unavailable when a client application like Catalog Service starts up. In that scenario, you can leverage the *retry* pattern and configure the application to try again to connect with the config server before giving up and failing. The retry implementation for Spring Cloud Config Client is based on Spring Retry, so you'll need to add a new dependency to the build.gradle file for your Catalog Service project. Remember to refresh or reimport the Gradle dependencies after the new addition.

Listing 4.17 Adding dependency for Spring Retry in Catalog Service

```
dependencies {
  ...
  implementation 'org.springframework.retry:spring-retry'
}
```

In chapter 8, I'll explain the retry pattern in detail. For now, I'll show you how to configure Catalog Service so that it retries connecting to Config Service a few times before failing (`spring.cloud.config.retry.max-attempts`). Each connection attempt is delayed according to an exponential backoff strategy, computed as the current delay multiplied by the value of the `spring.cloud.config.retry.multiplier` property. The initial delay is configured by `spring.cloud.config.retry.initial-interval`, and each delay cannot exceed the value of `spring.cloud.config.retry.max-interval`.

You can add the retry configuration to the application.yml file in the Catalog Service project.

> **Listing 4.18 Applying retry pattern to Spring Cloud Config Client**

```yaml
spring:
  application:
    name: catalog-service
  config:
    import: "optional:configserver:"
  cloud:
    config:
      uri: http://localhost:8888
      request-connect-timeout: 5000
      request-read-timeout: 5000
      fail-fast: true              ⟵  Makes a failure to connect
      retry:                            to the config server fatal
        max-attempts: 6
        initial-interval: 1000     ⟵  Initial retry interval
        max-interval: 2000              for backoff (ms)
        multiplier: 1.1            ⟵  Multiplier to compute
                                        the next interval
```

Maximum number of attempts → `max-attempts: 6`

Maximum retry interval for backoff (ms) → `max-interval: 2000`

The retry behavior is enabled only when the `spring.cloud.config.fail-fast` property is set to `true`. You probably don't want to retry in your local environment if the config server is down, especially considering we made it an optional backing service. Feel free to test the application's behavior when retrying the connection with the config server down, but remember to set the `fail-fast` property back to `false` if you want to keep it optional in your local environment. In production you can set it to `true` using one of the strategies covered in this chapter. When you're done testing the applications, stop both of them with Ctrl-C.

You are now ready to use the Config Service to configure any application you want. However, there's still an aspect I haven't covered yet. How can we change the configuration at runtime?

4.4.3 Refreshing configuration at runtime

What happens when new changes are pushed to the Git repository that's backing the Config Service? For a standard Spring Boot application, you would have to restart it when you change a property (either in a property file or an environment variable). However, Spring Cloud Config gives you the possibility to refresh configuration in client applications at runtime. Whenever a new change is pushed to the configuration repository, you can signal all the applications integrated with the config server, and they will reload the parts affected by the configuration change. Spring Cloud Config offers different options for doing that.

In this section, I'll show you a simple refresh option consisting of sending a special POST request to a running Catalog Service instance to trigger the reloading of the configuration data that has changed (*hot reload*). Figure 4.11 shows how it works.

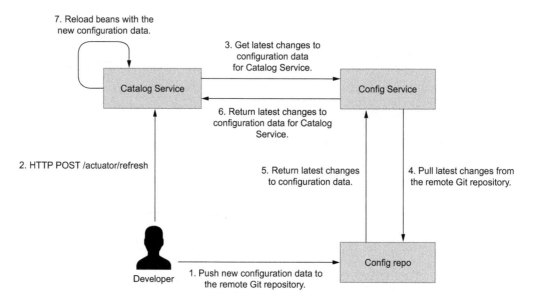

Figure 4.11   **After changing the configuration in the Git repository backing the Config Service, a signal is sent to Catalog Service to refresh the parts of the application using the configuration.**

This functionality is one of those *administrative processes* described by the 15-Factor methodology introduced in chapter 2. In this case, the strategy adopted for managing the process was to embed it in the applications themselves, with the ability to activate it by calling a specific HTTP endpoint.

> **NOTE**   In production, you'll probably want a more automated and efficient way of refreshing configuration than explicitly triggering each application instance. When a remote Git repository backs your config server, you can configure a webhook that notifies the config server automatically whenever new changes are pushed to the repository. In turn, the config server can notify all client applications through a message broker like RabbitMQ, using Spring Cloud Bus. Chapter 14 will cover more scenarios for refreshing configuration in production.

ENABLING CONFIGURATION REFRESH

After committing and pushing the new configuration changes to the remote Git repository, you can send a POST request to a client application through a specific endpoint that will trigger a RefreshScopeRefreshedEvent inside the application context. You can rely on the Spring Boot Actuator project to expose the refresh endpoint by adding a new dependency in the build.gradle file for the Catalog Service project. Remember to refresh or reimport the Gradle dependencies after the new addition.

Listing 4.19   Adding dependency for Spring Boot Actuator in Catalog Service

```
dependencies {
  ...
  implementation 'org.springframework.boot:spring-boot-starter-actuator'
}
```

The Spring Boot Actuator library configures an /actuator/refresh endpoint that triggers a refresh event. By default, the endpoint is not exposed, so you have to enable it explicitly in the application.yml file of your Catalog Service project (catalog-service).

Listing 4.20   Making Spring Boot Actuator expose the refresh endpoint

```
management:
  endpoints:
    web:
      exposure:
        include: refresh   ⊲──┘  Exposes the /actuator/refresh
                                 endpoint through HTTP
```

NOTE   I will discuss Spring Boot Actuator extensively in chapter 13, so don't worry if you don't fully understand the preceding configuration. For now, it's enough to know that Spring Boot Actuator provides many useful endpoints for monitoring and managing applications in production.

The refresh event, RefreshScopeRefreshedEvent, will have no effect if there is no component listening. You can use the @RefreshScope annotation on any bean you'd like to be reloaded whenever a refresh is triggered. Here's the nice part: since you defined your custom properties through a @ConfigurationProperties bean, it is already listening to RefreshScopeRefreshedEvent by default, so you don't need to make any changes to your code. When a refresh is triggered, the PolarProperties bean will be reloaded with the latest configuration available. Let's see if it works.

CHANGING CONFIGURATION AT RUNTIME

In this final section, I'll show you how to change configuration at runtime. First, make sure you have both the Config Service and Catalog Service up and running (./gradlew bootRun). Then open the config-repo repository hosting the configuration data and change the value of the polar.greeting property in the config-repo/catalog-service.yml file.

Listing 4.21   Updating the welcome message value in the config repo

```
polar:
  greeting: "Welcome to the catalog from a fresh config server"
```

Next, commit and push the changes.

Config Service will now return the new property value. You can check that by running the `http :8888/catalog-service/default` command. However, no signal has been sent yet to Catalog Service. If you try running the `http :9001/` command, you will still get the old "Welcome to the catalog from the config server" message. Let's trigger a refresh.

Go ahead and send a `POST` request to the Catalog Service application at the `/actuator/refresh` endpoint:

```
$ http POST :9001/actuator/refresh
```

This request will trigger a `RefreshScopeRefreshedEvent` event. The `PolarProperties` bean, because it's annotated with `@ConfigurationProperties`, will react to the event and read the new configuration data. Let's verify that:

```
$ http :9001/
Welcome to the catalog from a fresh config server
```

Finally, stop the execution of both applications with Ctrl-C.

Good job! You have just updated the configuration of an application at runtime without restarting it, without rebuilding the application, and ensuring the traceability of changes. It's perfect for the cloud. In chapter 14, you'll learn more advanced techniques for managing configuration that you'll need in production, including secrets management, ConfigMaps, and Secrets.

Summary

- The Spring `Environment` abstraction provides a unified interface for accessing properties and profiles.
- Properties are key/value pairs used to store configuration.
- Profiles are logical groups of beans registered only when a specific profile is active.
- Spring Boot collects properties from different sources according to precedence rules. From the highest to the lowest precedence, properties can be defined in command-line arguments, JVM system variables, OS environment variables, profile-specific property files, and generic property files.
- Spring beans can access properties from the `Environment` object by injecting the value with the `@Value` annotation, or from a bean mapped to a set of properties with the `@ConfigurationProperties` annotation.
- The active profiles can be defined with the `spring.profiles.active` property.

- The `@Profile` annotation marks beans or configuration classes to be considered only when the specified profile is active.
- Properties, as managed in Spring Boot, provide externalized configuration as defined by the 15-Factor methodology, but that's not enough.
- A configuration server handles aspects like secret encryption, configuration traceability, versioning, and context refreshing at runtime with no restart.
- A configuration server can be set up with the Spring Cloud Config Server library.
- The configuration itself can be stored according to different strategies, such as in a dedicated Git repository.
- The config server uses the application name, active profiles, and Git-specific labels to identify which configuration should be provided to which application.
- A Spring Boot application can be configured through a config server using the Spring Cloud Config Client library.
- `@ConfigurationProperties` beans are configured to listen to `RefreshScope-RefreshedEvent` events.
- `RefreshScopeRefreshedEvent` events can be triggered after a new change is pushed to the configuration repository, so that the client application reloads the context using the latest configuration data.
- Spring Boot Actuator defines an `/actuator/refresh` endpoint that you can use to trigger the event manually.

Persisting and
managing data
in the cloud

This chapter covers

- Understanding databases in a cloud native system
- Implementing data persistence with Spring Data JDBC
- Testing data persistence with Spring Boot and Testcontainers
- Managing databases in production with Flyway

In chapter 1, I distinguished between application services and data services in a cloud native system. So far, we have worked with application services, which should be stateless to play well in a cloud environment. However, most applications are useless if they don't store any state or data somewhere. For example, the Catalog Service application we built in chapter 3 has no persistent storage mechanism, so you can't really use it to manage a catalog of books. Once you shut it down, all the books you added to the catalog are gone. As a consequence of being stateful, you can't even scale the application horizontally.

The *state* is everything that should be preserved when you shut down a service and spin up a new instance. Data services are the stateful components of a system.

For example, they can be data stores like PostgreSQL, Cassandra, and Redis, or they can be messaging systems like RabbitMQ and Apache Kafka.

This chapter will introduce databases for cloud native systems and the main aspects of persisting data in the cloud. We'll rely on Docker to run PostgreSQL in the local environment, but in production we're going to replace it with a managed service offered by a cloud platform. Then we'll add a data persistence layer to Catalog Service using Spring Data JDBC. Finally, I'll cover some common concerns about managing and evolving databases in production with Flyway.

> **NOTE** The source code for the examples in this chapter is available in the Chapter05/05-begin, Chapter05/05-intermediate, and Chapter05/05-end folders on GitHub, containing the initial, intermediate, and final states of the project (https://github.com/ThomasVitale/cloud-native-spring-in-action).

5.1 Databases for cloud native systems

Data can be stored in many ways. Traditionally you would probably use a single massive database server to save as much as possible, since getting a new one would be expensive and time-consuming. Depending on your organization's processes, a task like that could take from a few days to several months. Not in the cloud.

The cloud offers elastic, self-service, and on-demand provisioning features—strong motivators for migrating your data services there. For each cloud native application you design, you should consider the most suitable storage type for the data it will produce. Then your cloud platform should let you provision it through an API or a graphical user interface. A task that used to be very time-consuming now requires only a few minutes. For example, deploying an instance of a PostgreSQL database server on Azure is as simple as running the `az postgres server create` command.

Cloud native applications are designed to be stateless because of the nature of the cloud itself. It's a dynamic infrastructure where the computing nodes can spread across different clusters, geographical regions, and clouds. The problem of applications storing state is evident. How could the state survive such a distributed and dynamic environment? That's why we want to keep applications stateless.

Yet, we need to achieve statefulness in the cloud. This section will present the challenges of data services and persistence management in the cloud and describe your options, depending on whether you want to manage a data service yourself or rely on one of the offerings from a cloud provider. Then I'll guide you through setting up a PostgreSQL database instance as a container for your local environment.

5.1.1 Data services in the cloud

Data services are the components of a cloud native architecture designed to be stateful. By designing applications to be stateless, you can limit cloud storage challenges to those few components.

Traditionally, storage was handled by operations engineers and database administrators. But the cloud and DevOps practices enable developers to pick the data service that best fits the application's requirements and deploy it with the same approach used for cloud native applications. Specialists like database administrators are consulted to make the most of the technology that developers have picked, addressing aspects like performance, security, and efficiency. However, the goal is to provide storage and data services on demand, just like you would for cloud native applications, and configure them in a self-service manner.

The difference between application and data services can also be visualized in terms of the three basic building blocks of cloud infrastructure: compute, storage, and network. As shown in figure 5.1, application services use computing and networking resources because they are stateless. On the other hand, data services are stateful and require storage to persist the state.

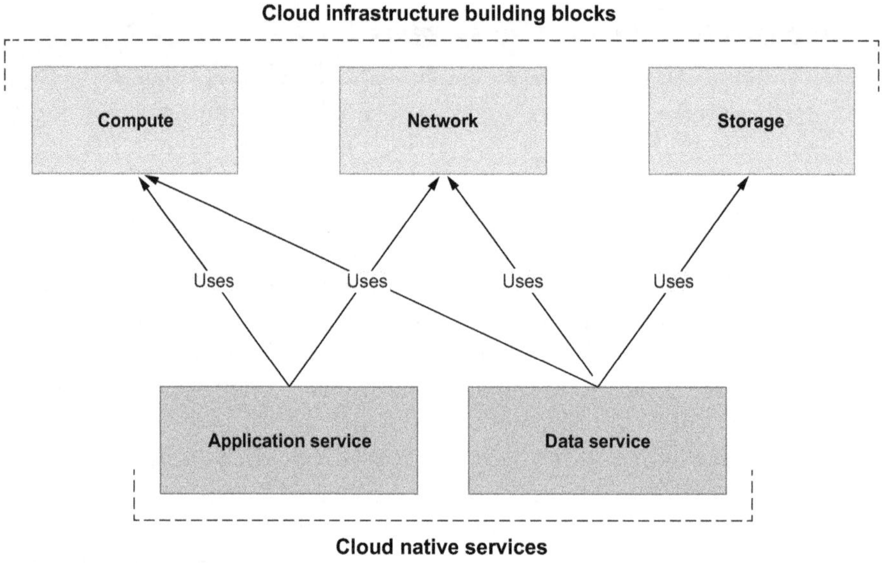

Figure 5.1   Application services (stateless) only use computing and networking resources in a cloud infrastructure. Data services (stateful) also need storage.

Let's look at the challenges of data services in a cloud environment. We'll also explore the main categories of data services, from which you can choose the most suitable solution for your applications.

CHALLENGES WITH DATA SERVICES

Data services in a cloud native system are generally off-the-shelf components like databases and message brokers. There are a few properties you should consider to ensure you choose the most suitable technology.

- *Scalability*—Cloud native applications can scale in and out dynamically. Data services are no different: they should scale to adapt to increasing or decreasing workloads. The new challenge is scaling while ensuring safe access to the data storage. The amount of data flying through a system in the cloud is larger than ever, and there can be sudden increments, so data services should support the likelihood of increasing workloads and be resilient.

- *Resilience*—Much like cloud native applications, data services should be resilient to failures. The new aspect here is that the data persisted using a specific storage technology should also be resilient. One of the key strategies for ensuring your data is resilient and preventing data loss is duplication. Replicating data across different clusters and geographical zones makes it even more resilient, but this comes at a cost. Data services like relational databases allow replication while ensuring data consistency. Others, like some non-relational databases, provide a high level of resilience but can't always guarantee data consistency (they offer what is referred to as *eventual consistency*).

- *Performance*—The way data is duplicated can affect performance, which is also limited by the I/O access latency of the specific storage technology and the network latency. Where the storage is located compared to the data services relying on it becomes important—this is a concern that we haven't encountered with cloud native applications.

- *Compliance*—You might face compliance challenges with data services more than with cloud native applications. Persisted data is usually critical for businesses and often contains information protected by specific laws, regulations, or customer agreements regarding how it's managed. For example, when dealing with personal and sensitive information, it's vital that you manage data in accordance with privacy laws. In Europe, that would mean following the General Data Protection Regulation (GDPR). In California, there is the California Consumer Privacy Act (CCPA). In other domains, further laws apply. For example, health data in the United States should be handled in compliance with the Health Insurance Portability and Accountability Act (HIPAA). Both the cloud native storage and cloud provider should comply with whatever laws or agreements you are required to respect. Because of this challenge, some organizations dealing with very sensitive data, like health care providers and banks, prefer to use a type of cloud native storage on their premises so they have more control over data management and can ensure compliance with the applicable regulations.

CATEGORIES OF DATA SERVICES

Data services can be categorized based on who is responsible for them: the cloud provider or you. Cloud providers have multiple offerings for data services, addressing all the main challenges of cloud native storage.

You can find industry-standard services like PostgreSQL, Redis, and MariaDB. Some cloud providers even offer enhancements on top of them, optimized for scalability, availability, performance, and security. For example, should you need a relational database, you could use Amazon Relational Database Service (RDS), Azure Database, or Google Cloud SQL.

Cloud providers also offer new types of data services specifically built for the cloud and exposing their own unique APIs. For instance, Google BigQuery is a serverless data warehouse solution with a particular focus on high scalability. Another example is the extremely fast, non-relational database Cosmos DB offered by Azure.

The other option is to manage data services yourself, increasing the complexity for you, but giving you more control over the solution. You can choose to use a more traditional setup based on virtual machines, or you could use containers and take advantage of the lessons you've learned managing cloud native applications. Using containers will allow you to manage all the services in your system through a unified interface, such as Kubernetes, handling both compute and storage resources and reducing costs. Figure 5.2 illustrates these categories of data services for the cloud.

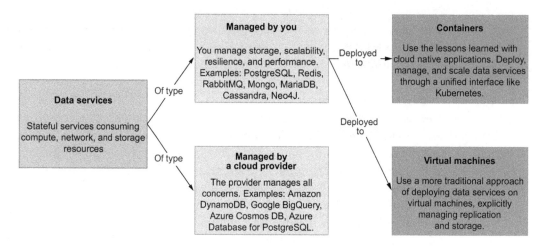

Figure 5.2   Data services can be managed by you (as containers or on virtual machines) or by the cloud provider. In the first case you can use more traditional services, and in the second, you can also access multiple services built specifically for the cloud by the provider.

> **NOTE**   When choosing to run and manage a data service by yourself (whether a virtual machine or a container on Kubernetes), another essential decision is what type of storage you'll use. Local persistence storage? Remote persistence storage? The subject of cloud native storage is fascinating, but it's out of scope for this book. If you'd like to learn more, I recommend checking out the Cloud Native Storage section in the CNCF Cloud Native Interactive Landscape (https://landscape.cncf.io).

The following section will focus on relational databases and will guide you through setting up a PostgreSQL container for your local environment.

5.1.2 Running PostgreSQL as a container

For the Catalog Service application, we'll use a relational database, PostgreSQL, to store the data about the books in the catalog (www.postgresql.org). PostgreSQL is a popular open source database with strong reliability, robustness, and performance, supporting both relational and non-relational data. Most cloud providers offer PostgreSQL as a managed service, freeing you from dealing with issues like high availability, resilience, and persistent storage on your own. Examples are Azure Database for PostgreSQL, Amazon RDS for PostgreSQL, Google Cloud SQL for PostgreSQL, Alibaba Cloud ApsaraDB RDS for PostgreSQL, and DigitalOcean PostgreSQL.

Later in the book, we'll deploy the Polar Bookshop system to a Kubernetes cluster managed by a cloud provider, and I'll show you how to use their offerings for managed PostgreSQL. You'll want to ensure environment parity, as recommended by the 15-Factor methodology, so you'll use PostgreSQL in development as well. Docker makes running databases locally easier than ever, so I'll show you how to run PostgreSQL as a container on your local machine.

In chapter 2, you gave Docker a first try with the Catalog Service application. Running PostgreSQL as a container is no different. Make sure your Docker Engine is up and running, open a Terminal window, and execute the following command:

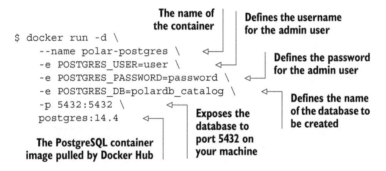

Compared to how you ran the Catalog Service container, you'll notice a few new elements. First, the Docker image from which you run a container (`postgres:14.4`) is not created by you—it's pulled from the Docker Hub container registry (configured by default when you install Docker).

The second new thing is passing environment variables as arguments to the container. PostgreSQL accepts a few environment variables that are used during the container's creation to configure a database.

> **NOTE** In this book, I won't cover how to configure storage in Docker (*volumes*). This means that all the data saved in your local PostgreSQL container will be lost once you remove the container. It might seem counterintuitive given the topic of this chapter, but any storage-related concern will be handled by the cloud provider in production, so you won't have to deal with it yourself. If you need to add persistent storage to your local containers, though,

you can read how to use volumes in the official Docker documentation (https://docs.docker.com).

In the next section, you'll see how to add data persistence to a Spring Boot application using Spring Data JDBC and PostgreSQL.

> **NOTE** If you need to, you can stop the container with `docker stop polar-postgres` and start it again with `docker start polar-postgres`. If you want to start over, you can remove the container with `docker rm -fv polar-postgres` and create it again with the previous `docker run` command.

5.2   *Data persistence with Spring Data JDBC*

Spring supports a wide variety of data persistence technologies through the Spring Data project, which contains specific modules dedicated to relational (JDBC, JPA, R2DBC) and non-relational databases (Cassandra, Redis, Neo4J, MongoDB, and so on). Spring Data provides common abstractions and patterns, making it straightforward to navigate the different modules. This section focuses on relational databases, but the key points of the interaction between an application using Spring Data and a database (shown in figure 5.3) apply to all of them.

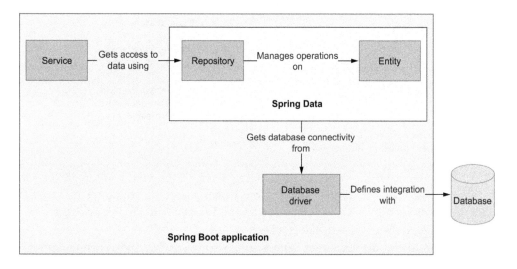

Figure 5.3   A driver configures the connection between the application and the database. Entities represent domain objects and can be stored and retrieved through a repository.

The main elements in the interaction shown in figure 5.3 are database drivers, entities, and repositories:

- *Database drivers*—Components that provide integration with a specific database (through *connection factories*). For relational databases, you can use a JDBC driver

(Java Database Connectivity API) in imperative/blocking applications or an R2DBC driver in reactive/non-blocking applications. For non-relational databases, each vendor has its own dedicated solution.

- *Entities*—Domain objects that are persisted in a database. They must contain a field to uniquely identify each instance (a *primary key*) and can use dedicated annotations to configure the mapping between Java objects and database entries.
- *Repositories*—The abstractions used for data storage and retrieval. Spring Data provides basic implementations, which are further extended by each module to provide features specific to the database in use.

This section will show you how to use Spring Data JDBC to add data persistence to a Spring Boot application like Catalog Service. You'll configure a connection pool to interact with a PostgreSQL database through the JDBC driver, define entities to be persisted, use repositories to access data, and work with transactions. Figure 5.4 shows how the Polar Bookshop architecture will look by the end of this chapter.

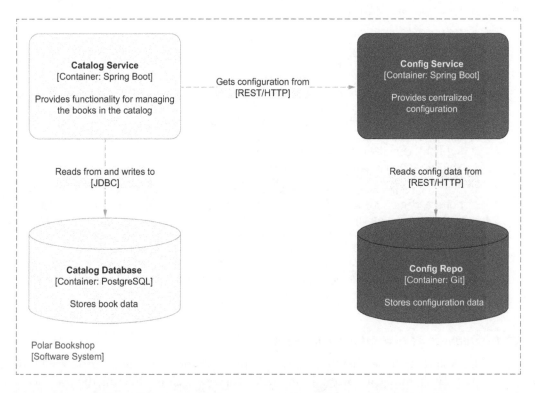

Figure 5.4   The Catalog Service application uses a PostgreSQL database to persist book data.

Spring Data JDBC or Spring Data JPA?

Spring Data offers two main options for integrating applications with a relational database over the JDBC driver: Spring Data JDBC and Spring Data JPA. How to choose between the two? As always, the answer is that it depends on your requirements and specific context.

Spring Data JPA (https://spring.io/projects/spring-data-jpa) is the most-used module in the Spring Data project. It's based on the Java Persistence API (JPA), a standard specification included in Jakarta EE (previously known as Java EE). Hibernate is the most popular implementation. It's a robust and battle-tested object-relational mapping (ORM) framework for managing data persistence in Java applications. Hibernate provides many useful features, but it's also a complex framework. If you're not aware of aspects like persistence context, lazy loading, dirty checking, or sessions, you might face issues that will be hard to debug without a sound familiarity with JPA and Hibernate. Once you know the framework better, you'll appreciate how much Spring Data JPA simplifies things and boosts your productivity. To learn more about JPA and Hibernate, you can check out *High-Performance Java Persistence and SQL* by Vlad Mihalcea (https://vladmihalcea.com) and *Java Persistence with Spring Data and Hibernate* by Cătălin Tudose (Manning, 2022).

Spring Data JDBC (https://spring.io/projects/spring-data-jdbc) is a more recent addition to the Spring Data family. It integrates with relational databases following the domain-driven design (DDD) concepts like aggregates, aggregate roots, and repositories. It's lightweight, simpler, and an excellent choice for microservices where domains are usually defined as bounded contexts (another DDD concept). It gives developers more control over SQL queries and allows the use of immutable entities. Being a simpler alternative to Spring Data JPA, it's not a drop-in replacement for every scenario, since it doesn't provide all the features offered by JPA. I recommend learning both, considering your requirements, and then deciding which module suits the specific scenario better.

I've chosen to cover Spring Data JDBC here for its good fit with cloud native applications and its simplicity. Thanks to the Spring Data common abstractions and patterns, you can easily convert a project from Spring Data JDBC to Spring Data JPA. In the following sections, I'll point out the main differences between the two to give you enough information in case you want to try implementing the same requirements using Spring Data JPA. In the code repository accompanying the book, you'll also find a JPA version of Catalog Service you can use as a reference (Chapter05/05-end/catalog-service-jpa).

5.2.1   Connecting to a database with JDBC

Let's start implementing the data persistence layer for the Catalog Service application. As a minimum, you'll need to import the Spring Data module for the specific database you want to use and, if required, also the database driver. Since Spring Data JDBC supports different relational databases, you'll need to explicitly declare a dependency on the specific database driver you want to use.

You can add the two new dependencies to the build.gradle file for the Catalog Service project (catalog-service). Remember to refresh or reimport the Gradle dependencies after the new addition.

> **Listing 5.1 Adding dependency for Spring Data JDBC in Catalog Service**

```
dependencies {
    ...
    implementation 'org.springframework.boot:spring-boot-starter-data-jdbc'
    runtimeOnly 'org.postgresql:postgresql'
}
```

These are the main dependencies:

- *Spring Data JDBC* (`org.springframework.boot:spring-boot-starter-data-jdbc`)—Provides the necessary libraries to persist data in relational databases using Spring Data and JDBC.
- *PostgreSQL* (`org.postgresql:postgresql`)—Provides a JDBC driver that allows the application to connect to a PostgreSQL database.

The PostgreSQL database is a backing service to the Catalog Service application. As such, it should be handled as an attached resource according to the 15-factor methodology. The attachment is done through resource binding, which in the case of PostgreSQL, consists of the following:

- A URL to define which driver to use, where to find the database server, and which database to connect the application to
- Username and password to establish a connection with the specified database

Thanks to Spring Boot, you can provide those values as configuration properties. This means you can easily replace the attached database by changing the values for the resource binding.

Open the application.yml file for the Catalog Service project, and add the properties for configuring the connection with PostgreSQL. Those values are the ones you defined earlier as environment variables when creating the PostgreSQL container.

> **Listing 5.2 Configuring the connection to a database using JDBC**

```
spring:                              The credentials for a user with privileges to access
  datasource:          ◀────         the given database and a JDBC URL to identify with
    username: user                   which database you want to establish a connection
    password: password
    url: jdbc:postgresql://localhost:5432/polardb_catalog
```

Opening and closing database connections are relatively expensive operations, so you don't want to do that every time your application accesses data. The solution is *connection pooling*: the application establishes several connections with the database and reuses them, rather than creating new ones for each data access operation. This is a considerable performance optimization.

Spring Boot uses HikariCP for connection pooling, and you can configure it from the application.yml file. You want to configure at least a connection timeout (`spring.datasource.hikari.connection-timeout`) and a maximum number of connections in the pool (`spring.datasource.hikari.maximum-pool-size`), because these both affect application resilience and performance. As you saw for the Tomcat thread pool, multiple factors influence which values you should use. As a starting point, you can refer to the HikariCP analysis of pool sizing (https://github.com/brettwooldridge/HikariCP/wiki/About-Pool-Sizing).

Listing 5.3   Configuring the connection pool to interact with the database

```
spring:
  datasource:
    username: user
    password: password
    url: jdbc:postgresql://localhost:5432/polardb_catalog
    hikari:
      connection-timeout: 2000        ◁         The maximum time
      maximum-pool-size: 5            ◁─┐        (ms) to spend waiting
                                        │        to get a connection
          The maximum number of        │        from the pool
          connections HikariCP will    │
          keep in the pool             ┘
```

Now that you have connected a Spring Boot application to a PostgreSQL database, you can go ahead and define what data you want to persist.

5.2.2   *Defining persistent entities with Spring Data*

In Catalog Service, you already have a `Book` record representing a domain entity for the application. Depending on the business domain and its complexity, you might want to distinguish the domain entity from the persistent entity, making the domain layer utterly independent of the persistence layer. If you'd like to explore how to model that scenario, I recommend referring to domain-driven design and hexagonal architecture principles.

In this case, the business domain is quite simple, so we'll update the `Book` record to also be a persistent entity.

MAKING A DOMAIN CLASS PERSISTENT

Spring Data JDBC encourages working with immutable entities. Using Java records to model entities is an excellent choice, since they're immutable by design and expose an all-args constructor that the framework can use to populate objects.

A persistent entity must have a field that acts as the identifier for the object, which will translate to the primary key in the database. You can mark a field as an identifier with the `@Id` annotation (from the `org.springframework.data.annotation` package). The database is responsible for generating a unique identifier for each created object automatically.

NOTE Books are uniquely identified by an ISBN, which we can call a *natural key* (or *business key*) for the domain entity. We could decide to use it also as the primary key or introduce a *technical key* (or *surrogate key*). There are pros and cons to both approaches. I chose to use a technical key to make it easier to manage and to decouple domain concerns from persistence implementation details.

That is enough to create and persist a Book in the database. It's also OK when a single user updates an existing Book object in isolation. But what happens if the same entity is updated by multiple users concurrently? Spring Data JDBC supports *optimistic locking* to address that concern. Users can read data concurrently. When a user attempts an update operation, the application checks if there has been any change since the last read. If there was, the operation is not performed, and an exception is thrown. The check is based on a numeric field that starts counting from 0 and automatically increases at every update operation. You can mark such a field with the @Version annotation (from the org.springframework.data.annotation package).

When the @Id field is null and the @Version field is 0, Spring Data JDBC assumes it's a new object. Consequently, it relies on the database to generate an identifier when inserting the new row in the table. When values are provided, it expects to find the object in the database already and to update it.

Let's go ahead and add two new fields to the Book record for the identifier and the version number. Since both fields are populated and handled by Spring Data JDBC under the hood, using the all-args constructor might be too verbose for situations such as generating test data. For convenience, let's add a static factory method to the Book record for building an object by passing only the business fields.

Listing 5.4 Defining identifier and version for Book objects

```
package com.polarbookshop.catalogservice.domain;

public record Book (

    @Id                 ⟵————  Identifies the field
    Long id,                    as the primary key
                                for the entity

    @NotBlank(message = "The book ISBN must be defined.")
    @Pattern(
        regexp = "^([0-9]{10}|[0-9]{13})$",
        message = "The ISBN format must be valid."
    )
    String isbn,

    @NotBlank(message = "The book title must be defined.")
    String title,

    @NotBlank(message = "The book author must be defined.")
    String author,
```

```
@NotNull(message = "The book price must be defined.")
@Positive(message = "The book price must be greater than zero.")
Double price,

@Version                ◁─┐  The entity version number,
int version               │  which is used for optimistic
                          │  locking
){
  public static Book of(
    String isbn, String title, String author, Double price
  ) {
    return new Book(
      null, isbn, title, author, price, 0    ◁─┐  An entity is considered
    );                                          │  new when the ID is null
  }                                             │  and the version is 0.
}
```

NOTE Spring Data JPA works with mutating objects, so you can't use Java records. JPA entity classes must be marked with the `@Entity` annotation and expose a no-args constructor. JPA identifiers are annotated with `@Id` and `@Version` from the `javax.persistence` package instead of `org.spring-framework.data.annotation`.

After adding the new fields, we need to update a few classes using the `Book` constructor, which now requires passing values for `id` and `version`.

The `BookService` class contains the logic for updating books. Open it and change the `editBookDetails()` method to ensure the book identifiers and versions are correctly passed along when calling the data layer.

Listing 5.5   Including existing identifier and version on book updates

```
package com.polarbookshop.catalogservice.domain;

@Service
public class BookService {

  ...

  public Book editBookDetails(String isbn, Book book) {
    return bookRepository.findByIsbn(isbn)
      .map(existingBook -> {
        var bookToUpdate = new Book(   ┐  Uses the identifier
          existingBook.id(),        ◁──┘  of the existing book
          existingBook.isbn(),
          book.title(),
          book.author(),                    ┐  Uses the version of the existing book,
          book.price(),                     │  which will be increased automatically
          existingBook.version());  ◁───────┘  if the update operation succeeds
        return bookRepository.save(bookToUpdate);
      })
      .orElseGet(() -> addBookToCatalog(book));
  }
}
```

In BookDataLoader, we can use the new static factory method for building Book objects. The framework will take care of handling the id and version fields.

Listing 5.6 Using the static factory method when creating a book

```
package com.polarbookshop.catalogservice.demo;

@Component
@Profile("testdata")
public class BookDataLoader {

  ...

  @EventListener(ApplicationReadyEvent.class)
  public void loadBookTestData() {
    var book1 = Book.of("1234567891", "Northern Lights",
      "Lyra Silverstar", 9.90);
    var book2 = Book.of("1234567892", "Polar Journey",
      "Iorek Polarson", 12.90);
    bookRepository.save(book1);
    bookRepository.save(book2);
  }
}
```

> The framework takes care of assigning a value for the identifier and the version under the hood.

I'll leave it to you to update the autotests similarly. You can also extend the tests in the BookJsonTests class to verify the serialization and deserialization of the new fields. As a reference, you can check Chapter05/05-intermediate/catalog-service in the code repository accompanying this book.

As a persistent entity, the Book record will be automatically mapped to relational resources. Class and field names are transformed into lowercase, and the camel case is translated into words joined by underscores. The Book record will result in the book table, the title field will result in the title column, the price field will result in the price column, and so on. Figure 5.5 shows the mapping between the Java object and the relational table.

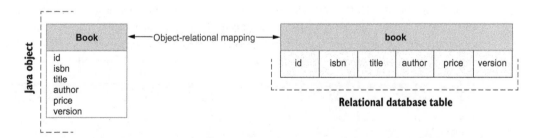

Figure 5.5   Java classes marked as persistent entities are automatically mapped by Spring Data JDBC to relational resources in the database.

CREATING THE DATABASE SCHEMA

The database must have a table defined (as shown in figure 5.5) for the mapping to work. Spring Data offers a feature to initialize a data source at startup time. By default, you can use a schema.sql file to create a schema and a data.sql file to insert data in the newly created tables. Such files should be placed in the src/main/resources folder.

That is a convenient feature, and it's useful for demos and experiments. However, it's too limited for use in production. As you'll see later in the chapter, it's better to create and evolve relational resources with a more sophisticated tool, like Flyway or Liquibase, which will let you version-control your database. For now we'll use the built-in database initialization mechanism so that we can focus on the data layer implementation first.

> **NOTE**   Hibernate, the foundation for Spring Data JPA, offers an interesting feature for automatically generating schemas from the entities defined in Java. Once again, this is convenient for demos and experiments, but please think twice before using it in production.

In your Catalog Service project, add a new schema.sql file in the src/main/resources folder. Then write the SQL instructions to create the book table, which will be mapped to the Book record in Java.

Listing 5.7   Defining the SQL instructions to create the `book` table

Drops the book table if it already exists

The primary key for the table. The database will generate it as a sequence of numbers (bigserial type).

The UNIQUE constraint ensures that a particular ISBN is assigned only to one book.

```
DROP TABLE IF EXISTS book;
CREATE TABLE book (
    id              BIGSERIAL PRIMARY KEY NOT NULL,
    author          varchar(255) NOT NULL,
    isbn            varchar(255) UNIQUE NOT NULL,
    price           float8 NOT NULL,
    title           varchar(255) NOT NULL,
    version         integer NOT NULL
);
```

The entity version number, stored as an integer

The NOT NULL constraint ensures the related column is assigned a value.

By default, Spring Data loads the schema.sql file only when using an embedded, in-memory database. Since we're using PostgreSQL, we need to enable the functionality explicitly. In the application.yml file for your Catalog Service project, add the following configuration to initialize the database schema from the schema.sql file.

Listing 5.8   Initializing the database schema from an SQL script

```yaml
spring:
  sql:
    init:
      mode: always
```

At startup, Spring Data will read the file and execute the SQL instructions in the PostgreSQL database to create a new book table and make it possible to start inserting data.

In the next section, you'll make it possible to capture audit events related to the persistent entities and keep track of when each row has been inserted into the table and modified most recently.

5.2.3   Enabling and configuring JDBC auditing

When persisting data, it's useful to know the creation date for each row in a table and the date when it was updated last. After securing an application with authentication and authorization, you can even register who created each entity and recently updated it. All of that is called *database auditing*.

With Spring Data JDBC, you can enable auditing for all the persistent entities using the `@EnableJdbcAuditing` annotation on a configuration class. In the `com .polarbookshop.catalogservice.config` package, add a `DataConfig` class to gather JDBC-related configuration.

> **Listing 5.9   Enabling JDBC auditing via annotation configuration**

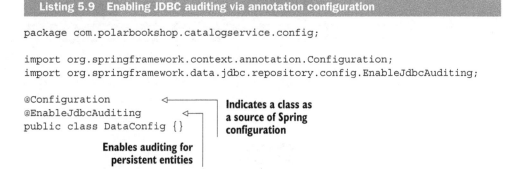

```
package com.polarbookshop.catalogservice.config;

import org.springframework.context.annotation.Configuration;
import org.springframework.data.jdbc.repository.config.EnableJdbcAuditing;

@Configuration
@EnableJdbcAuditing
public class DataConfig {}
```

Indicates a class as a source of Spring configuration

Enables auditing for persistent entities

> **NOTE**   In Spring Data JPA, you would use the `@EnableJpaAuditing` annotation to enable JPA auditing, and you would annotate the entity class with `@EntityListeners(AuditingEntityListener.class)` to make it listen to audit events, which doesn't happen automatically as in Spring Data JDBC.

When this feature is enabled, audit events are generated whenever data is created, updated, or deleted. Spring Data provides convenient annotations (listed in table 5.1) that we can use on dedicated fields to capture the information from such events (*audit metadata*) and store it in the database as part of the entity.

Table 5.1   When database auditing is enabled, these annotations can be used on entity fields to capture audit metadata.

Annotation	What it does on an entity field
`@CreatedBy`	Identifies the field representing the user that created the entity. It's defined on creation and never changed.
`@CreatedDate`	Identifies the field representing when the entity was created. It's defined on creation and never changed.

Table 5.1 *(continued)*   **When database auditing is enabled, these annotations can be used on entity fields to capture audit metadata.**

Annotation	What it does on an entity field
@LastModifiedBy	Identifies the field representing the user that most recently modified the entity. It's updated at every create or update operation.
@LastModifiedDate	Identifies the field representing when the entity was most recently modified. It's updated at every create or update operation.

In Catalog Service we can add the createdDate and lastModifiedDate fields to the Book record. In chapter 12, after introducing Spring Security, we'll extend this object to also capture who created or updated the entity.

Open the Book record, add the two new fields, and update the static factory method accordingly. They can be null when instantiating a new object because they will be populated by Spring Data under the hood.

Listing 5.10   Adding fields to store audit metadata in a persistent entity

```
package com.polarbookshop.catalogservice.domain;

public record Book (

  @Id
  Long id,

  ...

  @CreatedDate              ◄─┐  When the
  Instant createdDate,         │  entity was
                               └  created

  @LastModifiedDate         ◄─┐  When the
  Instant lastModifiedDate,    │  entity was
                               │  last modified
  @Version
  int version

){
  public static Book of(
    String isbn, String title, String author, Double price
  ) {
    return new Book(null, isbn, title, author, price, null, null, 0);
  }
}
```

After extending the Book record, the BookService class needs to be updated one more time. Open it and change the editBookDetails() method to ensure the audit metadata is correctly passed along when calling the data layer.

Listing 5.11   Including the existing audit metadata when updating a book

```
package com.polarbookshop.catalogservice.domain;

@Service
public class BookService {

  ...

  public Book editBookDetails(String isbn, Book book) {
    return bookRepository.findByIsbn(isbn)
      .map(existingBook -> {
        var bookToUpdate = new Book(
          existingBook.id(),
          existingBook.isbn(),
          book.title(),
          book.author(),
          book.price(),
          existingBook.createdDate(),
          existingBook.lastModifiedDate(),
          existingBook.version());
        return bookRepository.save(bookToUpdate);
      })
      .orElseGet(() -> addBookToCatalog(book));
  }
}
```

> **Uses the creation date of the existing book record**

> **Uses the last modified date of the existing book record. It will be updated automatically by Spring Data if the operation succeeds.**

Next, let's update the schema.sql file to add the columns for the new fields to the book table.

Listing 5.12   Adding columns for audit metadata to the book table

```
DROP TABLE IF EXISTS book;
CREATE TABLE book (
  id                    BIGSERIAL PRIMARY KEY NOT NULL,
  author                varchar(255) NOT NULL,
  isbn                  varchar(255) UNIQUE NOT NULL,
  price                 float8 NOT NULL,
  title                 varchar(255) NOT NULL,
  created_date          timestamp NOT NULL,
  last_modified_date    timestamp NOT NULL,
  version               integer NOT NULL
);
```

> **When the entity was created (stored as a timestamp)**

> **When the entity was last modified (stored as a timestamp)**

I'll leave it to you to update the autotests accordingly, when necessary. You can also extend the tests in BookJsonTests to verify the serialization and deserialization of the new fields. As a reference, you can check Chapter05/05-intermediate/catalog-service in the code repository accompanying this book.

So far, you have got everything in place to map your Java objects to relational objects in a database, including audit metadata. You still need a way to access data from the database, though. That's the subject of the next section.

5.2.4   *Data repositories with Spring Data*

The *repository* pattern provides an abstraction for accessing data independently of its source. The BookRepository interface used by BookService is an example of a repository. The domain layer, which contains the business logic, doesn't need to know where the data comes from, as long as it gets access. In chapter 3, we added an implementation of the repository interface to store data in memory. Now that we're building the persistence layer, we'll need a different implementation to access data from PostgreSQL.

The good news is that we can use Spring Data repositories, a technical solution that provides access to data from a data store independently of the specific persistence technology used. It's one of the most valuable features of Spring Data, because we can use the same repository abstraction in any persistence scenario, whether relational or non-relational.

USING A DATA REPOSITORY

When using Spring Data repositories, your responsibility is limited to defining an interface. At startup time, Spring Data will generate an implementation for your interface. At the Catalog Service project (catalog-service), go ahead and delete the InMemoryBookRepository class.

Let's now see how we can refactor the BookRepository interface from the Catalog Service project. First, it should extend one of the available Repository interfaces provided by Spring Data. Most Spring Data modules add Repository implementations specific to the data source supported. The Catalog Service application requires standard CRUD operations on Book objects, so you can make the BookRepository interface extend from CrudRepository.

CrudRepository provides methods to perform CRUD operations, including save() and findAll(), so you can remove their explicit declarations from your interface. The default methods defined by CrudRepository for Book objects are based on their @Id-annotated fields. Since the application needs to access books based on the ISBN, we must explicitly declare those operations.

Listing 5.13   Repository interface for accessing books

```
package com.polarbookshop.catalogservice.domain;

import java.util.Optional;
import org.springframework.data.jdbc.repository.query.Modifying;
import org.springframework.data.jdbc.repository.query.Query;
import org.springframework.data.repository.CrudRepository;

public interface BookRepository
    extends CrudRepository<Book,Long> {          ◁──── Extends a repository providing
                                                        CRUD operations, specifying the
  Optional<Book> findByIsbn(String isbn);    ◁───      type of managed entity (Book)
  boolean existsByIsbn(String isbn);                   and its primary key type (Long)

        Methods implemented by Spring Data at runtime
```

```
@Modifying
@Query("delete from Book where isbn = :isbn")
void deleteByIsbn(String isbn);
}
```

Identifies an operation that will modify the database state

Declares the query that Spring Data will use to implement the method

At startup time, Spring Data will provide an implementation for `BookRepository` with all the most common CRUD operations and the methods you declared in the interface. There are two main options for defining custom queries in Spring Data:

- Using the `@Query` annotation to provide an SQL-like statement that will be executed by the method.
- Defining query methods following a specific naming convention, as described in the official documentation (https://spring.io/projects/spring-data). Generally, you can build a method name by combining multiple pieces, as described in table 5.2. At the time of writing, Spring Data JDBC supports this option only for read operations. On the other hand, Spring Data JPA provides full support for it.

Table 5.2   You can add custom queries to a repository and have Spring Data generate implementations for you by following a specific naming convention comprising these building blocks.

Repository method building block	Examples
Action	`find, exists, delete, count`
Limit	`One, All, First10`
-	`By`
Property expression	`findByIsbn, findByTitleAndAuthor, findByAuthorOrPrice`
Comparison	`findByTitleContaining, findByIsbnEndingWith, findByPriceLessThan`
Ordering operator	`orderByTitleAsc, orderByTitleDesc`

Using some of the methods provided by the `CrudRepository` interface and inherited by `BookRepository`, we can improve the `BookDataLoader` class so that we start with an empty database during development and create books with a single command.

Listing 5.14   Using Spring Data methods to delete and save books

```
package com.polarbookshop.catalogservice.demo;

@Component
@Profile("testdata")
public class BookDataLoader {
  private final BookRepository bookRepository;
```

```
public BookDataLoader(BookRepository bookRepository) {
  this.bookRepository = bookRepository;
}

@EventListener(ApplicationReadyEvent.class)
public void loadBookTestData() {
  bookRepository.deleteAll();
  var book1 = Book.of("1234567891", "Northern Lights",
    "Lyra Silverstar", 9.90);
  var book2 = Book.of("1234567892", "Polar Journey",
    "Iorek Polarson", 12.90);
  bookRepository.saveAll(List.of(book1, book2));
}
}
```

`bookRepository.deleteAll();` ← **Deletes all existing books, if any, to start from an empty database**

`bookRepository.saveAll(List.of(book1, book2));` ← **Saves multiple objects at once**

DEFINING TRANSACTIONAL CONTEXTS

The repositories provided by Spring Data come configured with transactional contexts for all the operations. For example, all methods in CrudRepository are transactional. That means you can safely call the saveAll() method, knowing that it will be executed in a transaction.

When you add your own query methods, as you did for BookRepository, it's up to you to define which ones should be part of a transaction. You can rely on the declarative transaction management provided by the Spring Framework and use the @Transactional annotation (from the org.springframework.transaction .annotation package) on classes or methods to ensure they are executed as part of a single *unit of work.*

Among the custom methods you defined in BookRepository, deleteByIsbn() is a good candidate for being transactional, since it modifies the database state. You can ensure it runs in a transaction by applying the @Transactional annotation.

Listing 5.15   Defining transactional operations

```
package com.polarbookshop.catalogservice.domain;

import java.util.Optional;
import org.springframework.data.jdbc.repository.query.Modifying;
import org.springframework.data.jdbc.repository.query.Query;
import org.springframework.data.repository.CrudRepository;
import org.springframework.transaction.annotation.Transactional;

public interface BookRepository extends CrudRepository<Book,Long> {

  Optional<Book> findByIsbn(String isbn);
  boolean existsByIsbn(String isbn);

  @Modifying
  @Transactional
  @Query("delete from Book where isbn = :isbn")
  void deleteByIsbn(String isbn);
}
```

`@Transactional` ← **Identifies the method to be executed in a transaction**

NOTE For more information about the declarative transaction management provided by Spring Framework, you can refer to the official documentation (https://spring.io/projects/spring-framework).

Great job! You successfully added data persistence capabilities to the Catalog Service application. Let's verify that it works correctly. First of all, make sure the PostgreSQL container is still running. If not, run it as described at the beginning of this chapter. Then start the application (`./gradlew bootRun`), send HTTP requests to each REST endpoint, and ensure it works as expected. When you're done, remove the database container (`docker rm -fv polar-postgres`) and stop the application (Ctrl-C).

TIP In the repository accompanying the book, you will find useful commands for querying the PostgreSQL database directly and verifying schemas and data generated by the application (Chapter05/05-intermediate/catalog-service/README.md).

Manual verification of data persistence is fine, but automated verification is better. That's what the next section is all about.

5.3 *Testing data persistence with Spring and Testcontainers*

In the previous sections, we added data persistence functionality to an application by developing against a PostgreSQL database in a container, which is the same technology used in production. That was a good step toward the environment parity recommended by the 15-Factor methodology. Keeping all environments as similar as possible improves the quality of the project.

Data sources are one of the primary causes of differences across environments. It's common practice to use an in-memory database while developing locally—something like H2 or HSQL. But that affects the predictability and robustness of your applications. Even if all relational databases speak the SQL language and Spring Data JDBC provides generic abstractions, each vendor has its own dialect and unique features that make it essential to use the same database in production that you use in development and testing. Otherwise, you may not catch errors that might happen only in production.

"What about testing?" you might ask. That is an excellent question. Another reason for using in-memory databases is to make integration tests more accessible. However, integration tests are also supposed to test the integration with your application's external services. Using something like H2 makes those tests less reliable. Each commit should be a candidate for release when adopting a continuous delivery approach. Suppose the autotests run by the deployment pipeline are not using the same backing services used in production. In that case, you'll need to do extra manual testing before deploying the application safely in production because you can't be sure it will work correctly. Therefore, it's essential to reduce the gap between environments.

Docker makes it easier to set up and develop applications with an actual database locally, as you experienced with PostgreSQL. In a similar way, Testcontainers (a Java library for testing) makes it easy to use backing services as containers in the context of integration tests.

This section will show you how to write slice tests for the data persistence layer using the @DataJdbcTest annotation and include a database in integration tests using the @SpringBootTest annotation. In both cases, you'll rely on Testcontainers to run the autotests against an actual PostgreSQL database.

5.3.1 Configuring Testcontainers for PostgreSQL

Testcontainers (https://testcontainers.org) is a Java library for testing. It supports JUnit and provides lightweight, throwaway containers such as databases, message brokers, and web servers. It's perfect for implementing integration tests with the actual backing services used in production. The result is more reliable and stable tests, which lead to higher-quality applications and favor continuous delivery practices.

You can configure a lightweight PostgreSQL container with Testcontainers and use it in your autotests involving a data persistence layer. Let's see how it works.

First, you need to add a dependency on the Testcontainers module for PostgreSQL in the build.gradle file of your Catalog Service project. Remember to refresh or reimport the Gradle dependencies after the new addition.

Listing 5.16   Adding dependency on Testcontainers in Catalog Service

```
ext {
    ...                                      Defines the
    set('testcontainersVersion', "1.17.3")  ◁── Testcontainers
}                                               version to use

dependencies {
    ...                                                    Provides container
    testImplementation 'org.testcontainers:postgresql' ◁──┘ management features for
}                                                          PostgreSQL databases

dependencyManagement {
    imports {
        ...                                              BOM (bill of materials)
        mavenBom "org.testcontainers:                    for Testcontainers
        ⇨ testcontainers-bom:${testcontainersVersion}" ◁─┘ dependency
    }                                                       management
}
```

When running tests, we want the application to use a PostgreSQL instance provided by Testcontainers rather than the one we configured earlier via the spring.datasource .url property. We can overwrite that value in a new application-integration.yml file created under src/test/resources. Any property defined in this file will take precedence over the main one when the integration profile is enabled. In this case, we'll overwrite the value for spring.datasource.url following a format defined by Testcontainers.

Create a new application-integration.yml file in src/test/resources, and add the following configuration.

Listing 5.17 Using a PostgreSQL data source provided by Testcontainers

```
spring:
  datasource:
    url: jdbc:tc:postgresql:14.4:///
```
◁─┐ **Identifies the PostgreSQL module in Testcontainers. "14.4" is the version of PostgreSQL to use.**

That's all we need to configure Testcontainers. When the integration profile is enabled, Spring Boot will use the PostgreSQL container instantiated by Testcontainers. We're now ready to write autotests to verify the data persistence layer.

5.3.2 Testing data persistence with @DataJdbcTest and Testcontainers

As you might recall from chapter 3, Spring Boot allows you to run integration tests by loading only the Spring components used by a specific application slice (*slice tests*). In Catalog Service, we created tests for the MVC and the JSON slices. Now I'll show you how to write tests for the data slice.

Create a BookRepositoryJdbcTests class, and mark it with the @DataJdbcTest annotation. That will trigger Spring Boot to include all Spring Data JDBC entities and repositories in the application context. It will also auto-configure JdbcAggregate-Template, a lower-level object we can use to set up the context for each test case instead of using the repository (the object under testing).

Listing 5.18 Integration tests for the Data JDBC slice

```
package com.polarbookshop.catalogservice.domain;

import java.util.Optional;
import com.polarbookshop.catalogservice.config.DataConfig;
import org.junit.jupiter.api.Test;
import org.springframework.beans.factory.annotation.Autowired;
import org.springframework.boot.test.autoconfigure.data.jdbc.DataJdbcTest;
import org.springframework.boot.test.autoconfigure.jdbc
    .AutoConfigureTestDatabase;
import org.springframework.context.annotation.Import;
import org.springframework.data.jdbc.core.JdbcAggregateTemplate;
import org.springframework.test.context.ActiveProfiles;
import static org.assertj.core.api.Assertions.assertThat;

@DataJdbcTest
@Import(DataConfig.class)
@AutoConfigureTestDatabase(
    replace = AutoConfigureTestDatabase.Replace.NONE
)
@ActiveProfiles("integration")
class BookRepositoryJdbcTests {

    @Autowired
    private BookRepository bookRepository;
```

Imports the data configuration (needed to enable auditing)

Disables the default behavior of relying on an embedded test database since we want to use Testcontainers

Enables the "integration" profile to load configuration from application-integration.yml

Identifies a test class that focuses on Spring Data JDBC components

```
@Autowired
private JdbcAggregateTemplate jdbcAggregateTemplate;          ◁──┐  A lower-level object
                                                                 │  to interact with the
@Test                                                            │  database
void findBookByIsbnWhenExisting() {
  var bookIsbn = "1234561237";
  var book = Book.of(bookIsbn, "Title", "Author", 12.90);
  jdbcAggregateTemplate.insert(book);                            ◁──┐
  Optional<Book> actualBook = bookRepository.findByIsbn(bookIsbn);  │

  assertThat(actualBook).isPresent();
  assertThat(actualBook.get().isbn()).isEqualTo(book.isbn());
  }                                                JdbcAggregateTemplate is used to
}                                                prepare the data targeted by the test.
```

The @DataJdbcTest annotation encapsulates handy features. For example, it makes each test method run in a transaction and rolls it back at its end, keeping the database clean. After running the test method in listing 5.18, the database will not contain the book created in findBookByIsbnWhenExisting() because the transaction is rolled back at the end of the method's execution.

Let's verify that the Testcontainers configuration works. First, make sure the Docker Engine is running in your local environment. Then open a Terminal window, navigate to the root folder of your Catalog Service project, and run the following command to ensure the tests are successful. Under the hood, Testcontainers will create a PostgreSQL container before the test's execution and remove it at the end.

```
$ ./gradlew test --tests BookRepositoryJdbcTests
```

In the code repository accompanying the book, you can find more examples of unit and integration tests for the Catalog Service project. The following section will cover how to run full integration tests with Testcontainers.

5.3.3   *Integration tests with @SpringBootTest and Testcontainers*

In the Catalog Service application, we already have a CatalogServiceApplication-Tests class annotated with @SpringBootTest and containing full integration tests. The Testcontainers configuration we defined earlier applies to all autotests for which the integration profile is enabled, so we need to add the profile configuration to the CatalogServiceApplicationTests class.

> Listing 5.19   Enabling integration profile for the integration tests

```
package com.polarbookshop.catalogservice;

@SpringBootTest(webEnvironment = SpringBootTest.WebEnvironment.RANDOM_PORT)
@ActiveProfiles("integration")           ◁──┐  Enables the "integration" profile
class CatalogServiceApplicationTests {       │  to load configuration from
  ...                                        │  application-integration.yml
}
```

Open a Terminal window, navigate to the root folder of your Catalog Service project, and run the following command to ensure the tests are successful. Under the hood, Testcontainers will create a PostgreSQL container before the test's execution and remove it at the end.

```
$ ./gradlew test --tests CatalogServiceApplicationTests
```

Good job! You have added data persistence to a Spring Boot application and written tests while ensuring environment parity. Let's move on and complete this chapter by discussing how to manage schemas and data in production.

5.4 *Managing databases in production with Flyway*

It's good practice to register any database changes, just like you do for your application source code through version control. You'll need a deterministic and automated way to infer the database's state, whether specific changes have already been applied, how to recreate a database from scratch, and how to migrate it in a controlled, repeatable, and reliable way. The continuous delivery approach encourages automating as much as possible, including database management.

In the Java ecosystem, the two most-used tools for tracking, versioning, and deploying database changes are Flyway (https://flywaydb.org) and Liquibase (https://liquibase.org). Both of them are fully integrated with Spring Boot. This section will show you how to use Flyway.

5.4.1 *Understanding Flyway: Version control for your database*

Flyway is a tool that provides version control for your database. It offers a single source of truth for the version of your database's state and keeps track of any changes incrementally. It automates changes and lets you reproduce or roll back the state of a database. Flyway is highly reliable, safe to use in cluster environments, and supports several relational databases, including the cloud ones like Amazon RDS, Azure Database, and Google Cloud SQL.

> **NOTE** In this section, I will introduce some features offered by Flyway, but I recommend you check the official documentation to discover all the powerful possibilities provided by this tool (https://flywaydb.org).

At its core, Flyway manages database changes. Any database change is called a *migration*, and migrations can be either *versioned* or *repeatable*. Versioned migrations are identified by a unique version number and are applied in order exactly once. For each *regular* versioned migration, you can also provide an optional *undo* migration to revert its effects (in case something goes wrong). They can be used to create, alter, or drop relational objects like schemas, tables, columns, and sequences or to correct data. On the other hand, repeatable migrations are applied every time their checksum changes. They can be used for creating or updating views, procedures, and packages.

Both types of migration can be defined in standard SQL scripts (useful for DDL changes) or Java classes (useful for DML changes, like data migrations). Flyway keeps track of which migrations have already been applied through a `flyway_schema_history` table automatically created in the database the first time it runs. You can picture migrations as commits in a Git repository and the schema history table as the repository log containing the list of all the commits applied over time (figure 5.6).

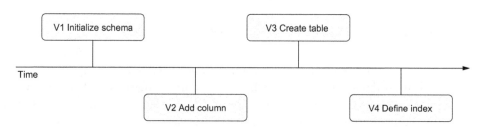

Figure 5.6   Flyway migrations represent database changes that can be pictured as commits in a Git repository.

> **NOTE**   A prerequisite for using Flyway is that both the database you want to manage and a user with the correct access privileges exist. Once you have a database and a user, Flyway can manage database changes for you. You shouldn't use Flyway to manage users.

You can use Flyway in standalone mode or embedded in a Java application. Spring Boot provides auto-configuration for it, making it very convenient to include Flyway in your applications. When integrated with Spring Boot, Flyway will search for SQL migrations in the src/main/resources/db/migration folder and Java migrations in src/main/java/db/migration.

Running schema and data migrations is one of those administrative processes described by the 15-Factor methodology introduced in chapter 2. In this case, the strategy adopted for managing such a process was to embed it in the application itself. By default, it's activated during the application startup phase. Let's see how we can implement it for Catalog Service.

Open your Catalog Service project (catalog-service) and add a dependency on Flyway in the build.gradle file. Remember to refresh or reimport the Gradle dependencies after the addition.

Listing 5.20   Adding a dependency on Flyway in Catalog Service

```
dependencies {
    ...
    implementation 'org.flywaydb:flyway-core'
}
```

In the next section, you'll learn how to create your first migration to initialize the database schema.

5.4.2 Initializing a database schema with Flyway

The first database change you'll apply is usually to initialize the schema. So far we've been relying on the built-in data source initialization capabilities offered by Spring Boot and providing a schema.sql file with the SQL statements to run. Now we can initialize the schema using an SQL Flyway migration.

First, delete the schema.sql file and remove the `spring.sql.init.mode` property from the application.yml file in your Catalog Service project.

Next, create a src/main/resources/db/migration folder. That's where Flyway will look for SQL migrations by default. Inside the folder, create a V1__Initial_schema.sql file, which will contain the SQL statement for initializing the database schema required by the Catalog Service application. Ensure you type two underscores after the version number.

Flyway expects SQL migration files to comply with a specific naming pattern. Regular versioned migrations should follow this structure:

- *Prefix*—V for versioned migrations
- *Version*—Version number using dots or underscores to separate it into multiple parts (e.g., 2.0.1)
- *Separator*—Two underscores: __
- *Description*—Words separated by underscores
- *Suffix*—.sql

In the V1__Initial_schema.sql migration script, you can include the SQL instructions to create a book table that Spring Boot JDBC will map to the Book persistent entity.

Listing 5.21 Flyway migration script for schema initialization

```
CREATE TABLE book (
    id                    BIGSERIAL PRIMARY KEY NOT NULL,
    author                varchar(255) NOT NULL,
    isbn                  varchar(255) UNIQUE NOT NULL,
    price                 float8 NOT NULL,
    title                 varchar(255) NOT NULL,
    created_date          timestamp NOT NULL,
    last_modified_date    timestamp NOT NULL,
    version               integer NOT NULL
);
```

Definition of the book table — annotation for `CREATE TABLE book (`

Declares the id field as the primary key — annotation for the `id` line

Constrains the isbn field to be unique — annotation for the `isbn` line

When you let Flyway manage changes to the database schema, you gain all the benefits of version control. You can now start a new PostgreSQL container following the instructions provided in section 5.1.2 (if you still have the previous one running, remove it with `docker rm -fv polar-postgres`), run the application (`./gradlew bootRun`), and verify that everything works correctly.

NOTE In the repository accompanying the book, you can find useful commands to query the PostgreSQL database directly and verify the schemas and data generated by Flyway (Chapter05/05-end/catalog-service/README.md).

Your autotests will also use Flyway. Go ahead and run them; they should all succeed. Once you're done, push your changes to your remote Git repository, and check the commit stage results from GitHub Actions. They should be successful as well. Finally, stop the application execution (Ctrl-C) and the PostgreSQL container (`docker rm -fv polar-postgres`).

In the final section, you'll learn how to use Flyway migrations to evolve a database.

5.4.3   *Evolving a database with Flyway*

Imagine that you completed the Catalog Service application and deployed it to production. Employees of the bookshop have started adding books to the catalog and gathered feedback about the application. The result is a new requirement for the catalog's functionality: it should provide information about the book publisher. How can you do that?

Since the application is already in production and some data has already been created, you can use Flyway to apply a new database change, altering the `book` table to add a new `publisher` column. Create a new V2__Add_publisher_column.sql file in the src/main/resources/db/migration folder of your Catalog Service project, and add the following SQL instruction to add the new column.

Listing 5.22   **Flyway migration script for updating a table schema**

```
ALTER TABLE book
ADD COLUMN publisher varchar(255);
```

Then update the `Book` Java record accordingly. The change should take into account that, in production, there are already books saved in the database without the publisher information, so it must be an optional field or the existing data will become invalid. You should also update the static factory method accordingly.

Listing 5.23   **Adding a new optional field to an existing data entity**

```
package com.polarbookshop.catalogservice.domain;

public record Book (
  @Id
  Long id,

  ...                              A new,
                                   optional
                                   field
  String publisher,      ⟵────

  @CreatedDate
  Instant createdDate,
```

```
   @LastModifiedDate
   Instant lastModifiedDate,

   @Version
   int version

){
  public static Book of(
    String isbn, String title, String author, Double price, String publisher
  ) {
    return new Book(
      null, isbn, title, author, price, publisher, null, null, 0
    );
  }
}
```

> **NOTE** After making this change, you must update the classes that call the static factory method and the `Book()` constructor to include a value for the `publisher` field. You can use either `null` (since it's optional) or a string value like `Polarsophia`. Check the source code (Chapter05/05-end/catalog-service) to see the final result. In the end, check that both the autotests and the application run correctly.

When this new version of Catalog Service is deployed to production, Flyway will skip the V1__Initial_schema.sql migration because it's already been applied, but it will execute the change described in V2__Add_publisher_column.sql. At this point, bookshop employees can start including the publisher name when adding new books to the catalog, and all the existing data will still be valid.

What if you need to make the `publisher` field mandatory? You can do that in a third version of Catalog Service, using an SQL migration to enforce the `publisher` column to be NON NULL and implementing a Java migration that adds a publisher to all the existing books in the database that don't have one already.

This two-step approach is very common to ensure backward compatibility during an upgrade. As you'll learn in a later chapter, there are usually multiple instances of the same application running. Deploying a new version is generally done through a *rolling upgrade* procedure consisting of updating one (or a few) instances at a time to ensure zero downtime. There will be both old and new versions of the application running during the upgrade, so it's paramount that the old instances can still run correctly even after the database changes introduced in the latest version have been applied.

Summary

- The state is everything that should be preserved when shutting down a service and spinning up a new instance.
- Data services are the stateful components of a cloud native architecture, requiring storage technologies to persist the state.
- Using data services in the cloud is challenging because it's a dynamic environment.

- Some issues to consider when choosing a data service are scalability, resilience, performance, and compliance with specific regulations and laws.
- You can use data services that are offered and managed by your cloud provider or manage your own, either relying on virtual machines or containers.
- Spring Data provides common abstractions and patterns for accessing data, making it straightforward to navigate the different modules dedicated to relational and non-relational databases.
- The main elements in Spring Data are database drivers, entities, and repositories.
- Spring Data JDBC is a framework that supports integrating Spring applications with relational databases relying on a JDBC driver.
- Entities represent domain objects and can be managed by Spring Data JDBC as immutable objects. They must have the field hosting the primary key annotated with `@Id`.
- Spring Data lets you capture audit metadata whenever an entity is created or updated. You can enable this feature with `@EnableJdbcAuditing`.
- Data repositories grant access to entities from the database. You need to define an interface, and then Spring Data will generate the implementation for you.
- Depending on your requirements, you can extend one of the available `Repository` interfaces provided by Spring Data, such as `CrudRepository`.
- In Spring Data JDBC, all mutating custom operations (create, update, delete) should run in transactions.
- Use the `@Transactional` annotation to run operations in a single unit of work.
- You can run integration tests for the Spring Data JDBC slice using the `@DataJdbcTest` annotation.
- Environment parity is essential for the quality and reliability of your tests and deployment pipeline.
- You can test the integration between your application and backing services defined as containers by using the Testcontainers library. It lets you use lightweight, throwaway containers in your integration tests.
- Database schemas are critical for applications. In production, you should use a tool like Flyway, which provides version control for your database.
- Flyway should manage any database changes to ensure reproducibility, traceability, and reliability.

Containerizing Spring Boot

6

This chapter covers

- Working with container images on Docker
- Packaging Spring Boot applications as container images
- Managing Spring Boot containers with Docker Compose
- Automating image build and push with GitHub Actions

So far, we have developed a Catalog Service application that exposes a REST API and persists data through a PostgreSQL database running inside a container. We're getting closer to deploying the first components of the Polar Bookshop system to a Kubernetes cluster. Before doing that, however, you need to learn how to package Spring Boot applications as container images and manage their life cycles.

This chapter will teach you the essential characteristics of container images and how to build one. We'll use Docker to work with containers, but you can do the same with any other container runtime compatible with the Open Container Initiative (OCI) standards (https://opencontainers.org). In the remainder of the book, whenever I refer to a *container image* or *Docker image*, I mean an image compatible with the OCI Image Specification.

Along the way, I'll share with you several considerations regarding building container images for production, such as security and performance. We'll explore two possibilities: Dockerfiles and Cloud Native Buildpacks.

When we start working with more than one container, the Docker CLI is not very efficient. Instead, we'll use Docker Compose to manage several containers and their life cycles.

Finally, we'll continue work on the deployment pipeline we started in chapter 3. I'll show you how to add new steps to the commit stage for packaging and publishing container images automatically to GitHub Container Registry.

> **NOTE**   The source code for the examples in this chapter is available in the Chapter06/06-begin and Chapter06/06-end folders, which contain the initial and final states of the project (https://github.com/ThomasVitale/cloud-native -spring-in-action).

6.1   *Working with container images on Docker*

In chapter 2, I introduced the main components of the Docker platform. The Docker Engine has a client/server architecture. The Docker CLI is the client you use to interact with the Docker server. The latter is responsible for managing all Docker resources (for example, images, containers, and networks) through the Docker daemon. The server can also interact with container registries to upload and download images. For your convenience, figure 6.1 shows the interaction flow among those components again.

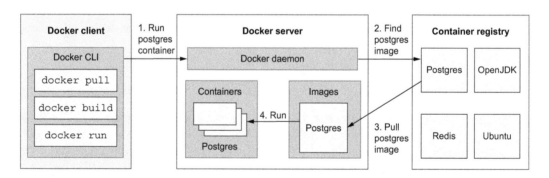

Figure 6.1   The Docker Engine has a client/server architecture and interacts with a container registry.

This section will continue from where we left off in chapter 2 and elaborate more on container images, which are lightweight executable packages that include everything needed to run the application that's inside. You'll learn the main characteristics of a container image, how to create one, and finally how to publish it to a container registry. Before moving on, make sure the Docker Engine on your computer is up and running by executing the `docker version` command from a Terminal window.

6.1.1 Understanding container images

Container images are the product of executing an ordered sequence of instructions, each resulting in a *layer*. Each image is made up of several layers, and each layer represents a modification produced by the corresponding instruction. The final artifact, an image, can be run as a container.

Images can be created from scratch or starting from a base image. The latter is the most common approach. For example, you can start from an Ubuntu image and apply a series of modifications on top of it. The sequence of instructions would be as follows:

1 Use Ubuntu as the base image.
2 Install the Java Runtime Environment.
3 Run the `java --version` command.

Each of these instructions will generate a layer, producing the final container image shown in figure 6.2.

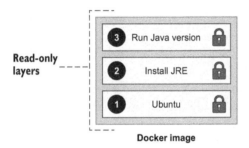

Read-only layers

Docker image

Figure 6.2 Container images are composed of an ordered sequence of read-only layers. The first one represents the base image; the others represent modifications applied on top of it.

All layers in a container image are read-only. Once they are applied, you can't modify them anymore. If you need to change something, you can do so by applying a new layer on top of it (by executing a new instruction). Changes applied to the upper layers will not affect the lower ones. This approach is called *copy-on-write*: a copy of the original item is created in the upper layer, and changes are applied to the copy rather than to the original item.

When an image is *run* as a container, one last layer is automatically applied on top of all the existing ones: the *container layer*. It is the only writable layer, and it's used to store data created during the execution of the container itself. At runtime, this layer might be used to generate files required by the application to run or maybe to store temporary data. Even though it's writable, remember that it's volatile: once you delete your container, everything stored in that layer is gone. Figure 6.3 compares the layers in a running container and those in the corresponding image.

NOTE The fact that all the layers in a container image are read-only has some security implications. You should never store secrets or sensitive information in the lower layers because they will always be accessible, even if the upper

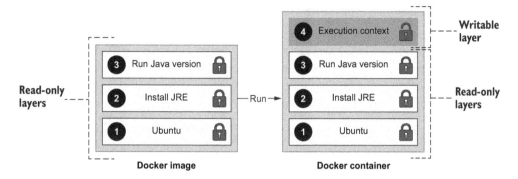

Figure 6.3   Running containers have an extra layer on top of the image layers. That is the only writable layer, but remember that it's volatile.

layers delete them. For example, you shouldn't package passwords or encryption keys within a container image.

So far you have learned how container images are composed, but you haven't yet seen how to create one. That's coming up next.

6.1.2   *Creating images with Dockerfiles*

Following the OCI format, you can define a container image by listing the sequence of instructions in a particular file called a *Dockerfile*. It's a script that acts as a recipe containing all the steps to *build* the desired image.

In a Dockerfile, each instruction starts with a command from the Docker-specific syntax. Then you can pass familiar shell commands as arguments to the instructions, depending on which Linux distribution you're using as your base image. The format is as follows:

```
INSTRUCTION arguments
```

> **NOTE** Docker supports Linux containers on machines with AMD64 and ARM64 architectures. It also supports working with Windows containers (runnable only on Windows systems), but we will exclusively use Linux containers in this book.

Let's put that into practice by defining a Dockerfile to build the container image mentioned in the previous section, composed of the following main instructions:

1 Use Ubuntu as the base image.
2 Install the Java Runtime Environment.
3 Run the `java --version` command.

Create a my-java-image folder and an empty file inside it named Dockerfile, with no extension (Chapter06/06-end/my-java-image). You might name it differently, but in this case let's go with the default convention.

Listing 6.1   A Dockerfile with the instructions to build an OCI image

```
FROM ubuntu:22.04
```
← **Bases the new image on the official image for Ubuntu, version 22.04**

Installs the JRE using familiar bash commands

```
RUN apt-get update && apt-get install -y default-jre
```
←

```
ENTRYPOINT ["java", "--version"]
```
← **Defines the execution entry point for the running container**

By default, Docker is configured to use Docker Hub to find and download images. That's where the ubuntu:22.04 image comes from. Docker Hub is a registry that you can use for free (within specific rate limits), and it's automatically configured when you install Docker.

The java --version command is the *entry point* of the executing container. If you don't specify any entry point, the container will not run as an executable. Unlike virtual machines, containers are meant to run tasks, not operating systems. Indeed, when running an Ubuntu container with docker run ubuntu, the container will exit right away because no task has been defined as the entry point, only the operating system.

The most common instructions defined in a Dockerfile are listed in table 6.1.

Table 6.1   The most common instructions used in a Dockerfile for building container images

Instruction	Description	Example
FROM	Defines the base image for the subsequent instructions. It must be the first instruction in a Dockerfile.	FROM ubuntu:22.04
LABEL	Adds metadata to the image, following a key/value format. Multiple LABEL instructions can be defined.	LABEL version="1.2.1"
ARG	Defines a variable that users can pass at build time. Multiple ARG instructions can be defined.	ARG JAR_FILE
RUN	Executes the commands passed as arguments in a new layer on top of the existing ones. Multiple RUN instructions can be defined.	RUN apt-get update && apt-get install -y default-jre
COPY	Copies files or directories from the host filesystem to the one inside the container.	COPY app-0.0.1-SNAPSHOT.jar app.jar
USER	Defines the user that will run all the subsequent instructions and the image itself (as a container).	USER sheldon
ENTRYPOINT	Defines the program to execute when the image is run as a container. Only the last ENTRYPOINT instruction in a Dockerfile is considered.	ENTRYPOINT ["/bin/bash"]
CMD	Specifies defaults for an executing container. If the ENTRYPOINT instruction is defined, they are passed as arguments. If not, it should also contain an executable. Only the last CMD instruction in a Dockerfile is considered.	CMD ["sleep", "10"]

Once you have the specifications for creating a container image declared in a Docker-file, you can use the `docker build` command to run all the instructions one by one, producing a new layer for each of them. The whole process from Dockerfile to image to container is illustrated in figure 6.4. Notice how the first instruction in a Dockerfile produces the lowest layer of the image.

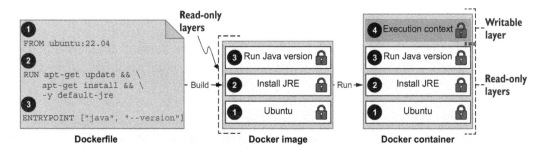

Figure 6.4   Images are built starting from Dockerfiles. Each instruction in a Dockerfile results in an ordered sequence of layers in the image.

Now open a Terminal window, navigate to the my-java-image folder where your Dock-erfile is located, and run the following command (don't forget the final dot).

```
$ docker build -t my-java-image:1.0.0 .
```

The command syntax is explained in figure 6.5.

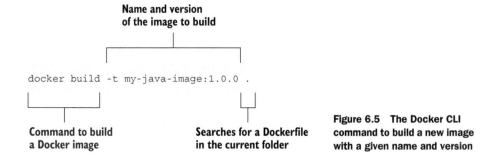

Figure 6.5   The Docker CLI command to build a new image with a given name and version

When it's done, you can get some details about your newly created image using the `docker images` command:

```
$ docker images my-java-image
REPOSITORY      TAG      IMAGE ID      CREATED         SIZE
my-java-image   1.0.0    96d1f58857aa  6 seconds ago   549MB
```

The layered approach makes the image build very performant. Each image layer is a delta from the previous one, and Docker caches all of them. If you make changes to only one of them and build the image again, only that layer and the subsequent ones are recreated. If you run a container from a new version of an image stored in a registry, only the new layers will be downloaded, improving performance at runtime.

For that reason, it's recommended that you order layers based on their likelihood to change, optimizing the image build process. Place the instructions that change more often toward the end of the Dockerfile.

A container image can be run with the `docker run` command, which starts a container and executes the process described in the Dockerfile as the entry point:

```
$ docker run --rm my-java-image:1.0.0

openjdk 11.0.15 2022-04-19
OpenJDK Runtime Environment (build 11.0.15+10-Ubuntu-0ubuntu0.22.04.1)
OpenJDK 64-Bit Server VM (build 11.0.15+10-Ubuntu-0ubuntu0.22.04.1, mixed mode)
```

After completing the execution, the container will stop. Since you used the `--rm` argument, the container will be removed automatically after the execution ends.

> **NOTE**   When you run the previous command, you'll see that the default OpenJDK in Ubuntu 22.04 is Java 11 instead of the 17 version we are working with throughout the book.

Let's now see how to publish the image to a container registry.

6.1.3   *Publishing images on GitHub Container Registry*

So far you have learned how to define, build, and run a container image. In this section, I'll complete the picture by expanding on container registries.

A container registry is to images what a Maven repository is to Java libraries. Many cloud providers offer their own registry solutions with extra services, like image scanning for vulnerabilities and certified images. By default, a Docker installation is configured to use the container registry provided by the Docker company (Docker Hub), which hosts images for many popular open source projects, like PostgreSQL, RabbitMQ, and Redis. We'll keep using it to pull images for third parties, as you did for Ubuntu in the previous section.

How about publishing your own images? You can certainly use Docker Hub or one of the registries offered by cloud providers like Azure Container Registry. For the specific project we are working on throughout the book, I chose to rely on the GitHub Container Registry (https://docs.github.com/en/packages) for a few reasons:

- It is available for use with all personal GitHub accounts, and it's free for public repositories. You can also use it with private repositories, but with some limitations.
- It allows you to access public container images anonymously without rate limiting, even with a free account.
- It is fully integrated into the GitHub ecosystem making it possible to navigate from images to related source code seamlessly.

- It lets you generate multiple tokens to access the registry even with a free account. It's recommended that you issue a different access token for each use case, and GitHub lets you do that via the personal access token (PAT) feature without limitations on the number of tokens. Furthermore, if you access GitHub Container Registry from GitHub Actions, you don't need to configure a PAT—you get a token auto-configured by GitHub out of the box, and it's provided securely to the automated pipeline without further configuration.

Publishing images to the GitHub Container Registry requires you to be authenticated, and for that you'll need a personal access token (PAT). Go to your GitHub account, navigate to Settings > Developer Settings > Personal access tokens, and choose Generate New Token. Input a meaningful name, and assign it the `write:packages` scope to give the token permissions to publish images to the container registry (figure 6.6). Finally, generate the token and copy its value. GitHub will show you the token value only once. Make sure you save it, because you'll need it soon.

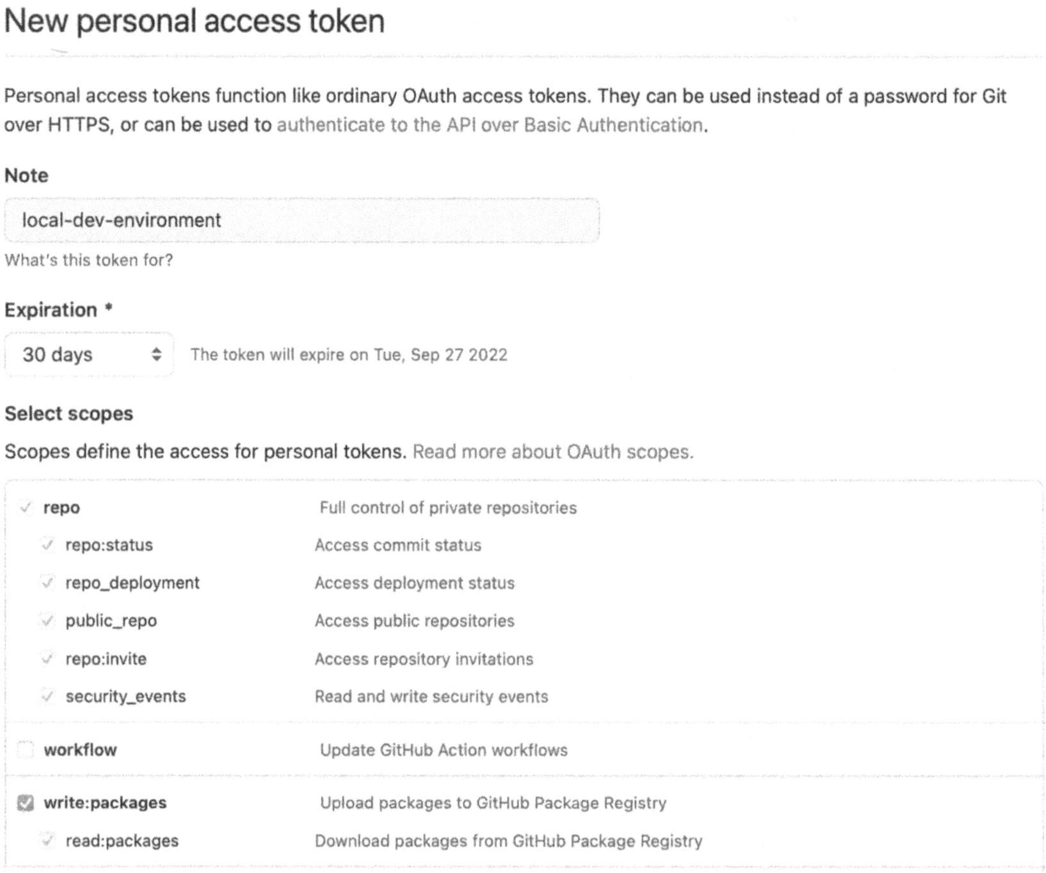

New personal access token

Personal access tokens function like ordinary OAuth access tokens. They can be used instead of a password for Git over HTTPS, or can be used to authenticate to the API over Basic Authentication.

Note

local-dev-environment

What's this token for?

Expiration *

| 30 days   ⇕ | The token will expire on Tue, Sep 27 2022

Select scopes

Scopes define the access for personal tokens. Read more about OAuth scopes.

☑ **repo**	Full control of private repositories
☑ repo:status	Access commit status
☑ repo_deployment	Access deployment status
☑ public_repo	Access public repositories
☑ repo:invite	Access repository invitations
☑ security_events	Read and write security events
☐ workflow	Update GitHub Action workflows
☑ **write:packages**	Upload packages to GitHub Package Registry
☑ read:packages	Download packages from GitHub Package Registry

Figure 6.6   A personal access token granting write access to the GitHub Container Registry

Next, open a Terminal window and authenticate with GitHub Container Registry (make sure your Docker Engine is running). When asked, insert username (your GitHub username) and password (your GitHub PAT):

```
$ docker login ghcr.io
```

If you followed along, you should have your custom `my-java-image` Docker image on your machine. If not, make sure you performed the operations described in the previous section.

Container images follow common naming conventions, which are adopted by OCI-compliant container registries: `<container_registry>/<namespace>/<name>[:<tag>]`:

- *Container registry*—The hostname for the container registry where the image is stored. When using Docker Hub, the hostname is `docker.io` and it's usually omitted. The Docker Engine will implicitly prepend the image name with `docker.io` if you don't specify a registry. When using GitHub Container Registry, the hostname is `ghcr.io` and must be explicit.
- *Namespace*—When using Docker Hub or GitHub Container Registry, the namespace will be your Docker/GitHub username written all in lowercase. In other registries, it might be the path to the repository.
- *Name and tag*—The image name represents the repository (or *package*) that contains all the versions of your image. It's optionally followed by a tag for selecting a specific version. If no tag is defined, the `latest` tag will be used by default.

Official images like `ubuntu` or `postgresql` can be downloaded by specifying the name only, which is implicitly converted to fully qualified names like `docker.io/library/ubuntu` or `docker.io/library/postgres`.

When uploading your images to GitHub Container Registry, you are required to use fully qualified names, according to the `ghcr.io/<your_github_username>/<image_name>` format. For example, my GitHub username is `ThomasVitale`, and all my personal images are named `ghcr.io/thomasvitale/<image_name>` (notice how the username is converted to lowercase).

Since you previously built an image with the name `my-java-image:1.0.0`, you have to assign it a fully qualified name before publishing it to a container registry (that is, you need to *tag* the image). You can do so with the `docker tag` command:

```
$ docker tag my-java-image:1.0.0 \
    ghcr.io/<your_github_username>/my-java-image:1.0.0
```

Then you can finally *push* it to GitHub Container Registry:

```
$ docker push ghcr.io/<your_github_username>/my-java-image:1.0.0
```

Go to your GitHub account, navigate to your profile page, and enter the Packages section. You should see a new `my-java-image` entry. If you click on it, you'll find the `ghcr.io/<your_github_username>/my-java-image:1.0.0` image you just published (figure 6.7). By default, the repository hosting your new image will be private.

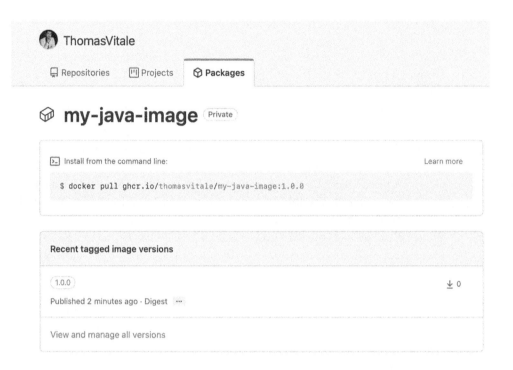

Figure 6.7   GitHub Container Registry is a public registry that you can use to publish your container images. You can see your images in the Packages section of your GitHub profile.

> **TIP**   From the same Packages page, you can also delete the published image or the entire image repository (called a *package* in GitHub) by going to the Package Settings via the link in the sidebar.

That concludes this section. Now that you know the main features of container images, how to create them, and how to publish them, let's dive deeper into packaging Spring Boot applications as images.

6.2   *Packaging Spring Boot applications as container images*

In the previous chapters, we built the Catalog Service application, featuring a REST API and database integration. In this section, as an intermediate step before deploying it to Kubernetes, we'll build an image to run Catalog Service as a container on Docker.

First I'll review some aspects you should consider when packaging a Spring Boot application as a container image. Then I'll show you how to do that with a Dockerfile and with Cloud Native Buildpacks.

6.2.1   Preparing Spring Boot for containerization

Packaging a Spring Boot application as a container image means that the application will run in an isolated context, including computational resources and network. Two main questions may arise from this isolation:

- How can you reach the application through the network?
- How can you make it interact with other containers?

We'll look at those two issues next.

EXPOSING APPLICATION SERVICES THROUGH PORT FORWARDING

In chapter 2, when you ran Catalog Service as a container, you mapped port 8080, on which the application exposed its services, to port 8080 on your local machine. After doing that, you could use the application by visiting http://localhost:8080. What you did there is called *port forwarding* or *port mapping* or *port publishing*, and it's used to make your containerized application accessible from the outside world.

By default, containers join an isolated network inside the Docker host. If you want to access any container from your local network, you must explicitly configure the port mapping. For example, when you ran the Catalog Service application, you specified the mapping as an argument to the docker run command: -p 8080:8080 (where the first is the external port and the second is the container port). Figure 6.8 illustrates how this works.

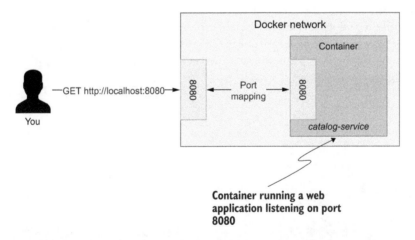

Figure 6.8   Port mapping lets you access the services exposed by a containerized application by forwarding the traffic from the container network to the outside world.

USING DOCKER'S BUILT-IN DNS SERVER FOR SERVICE DISCOVERY

Thanks to port forwarding, the Catalog Service application in the previous chapter could access the PostgreSQL database server through the URL jdbc:postgresql://localhost:5432, even if it was running inside a container. The interaction is shown in figure 6.9. When running Catalog Service as a container, however, you will not be able to do that anymore, since `localhost` would represent the inside of your container and not your local machine. How can you solve this problem?

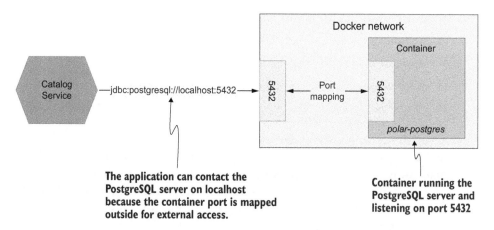

The application can contact the PostgreSQL server on localhost because the container port is mapped outside for external access.

Container running the PostgreSQL server and listening on port 5432

Figure 6.9   The Catalog Service application can interact with the PostgreSQL container thanks to the port mapping, making the database accessible from the outside world.

Docker has a built-in DNS server that can enable containers in the same network to find each other using the container name rather than a hostname or an IP address. For example, Catalog Service will be able to call the PostgreSQL server through the URL `jdbc:postgresql://polar-postgres:5432`, where `polar-postgres` is the container name. Figure 6.10 shows how it works. Later in the chapter you'll see how to achieve this result in code.

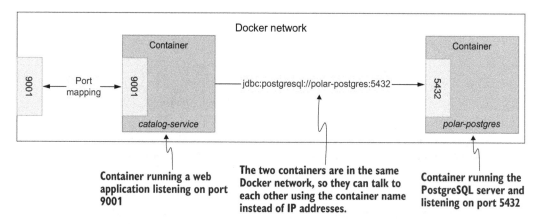

Container running a web application listening on port 9001

The two containers are in the same Docker network, so they can talk to each other using the container name instead of IP addresses.

Container running the PostgreSQL server and listening on port 5432

Figure 6.10   The Catalog Service container can directly interact with the PostgreSQL container because they are both on the same Docker network.

So before moving on, let's create a network inside which Catalog Service and Post-greSQL can talk to each other using the container name instead of an IP address or a hostname. You can run this command from any Terminal window:

```
$ docker network create catalog-network
```

Next, verify that the network has been successfully created:

```
$ docker network ls
NETWORK ID      NAME                DRIVER    SCOPE
178c7a048fa9    catalog-network     bridge    local
...
```

You can then start a PostgreSQL container, specifying that it should be part of the catalog-network you just created. Using the `--net` argument ensures the container will join the specified network and rely on the Docker built-in DNS server:

```
$ docker run -d \
    --name polar-postgres \
    --net catalog-network \
    -e POSTGRES_USER=user \
    -e POSTGRES_PASSWORD=password \
    -e POSTGRES_DB=polardb_catalog \
    -p 5432:5432 \
    postgres:14.4
```

If the command fails, you might have the PostgreSQL container from chapter 5 still running. Remove it with `docker rm -fv polar-postgres` and run the previous command again.

6.2.2   Containerizing Spring Boot with Dockerfiles

Cloud native applications are self-contained. Spring Boot lets you package your applications as standalone JARs, including everything they need to run except the runtime environment. That makes the containerization very straightforward, since all you need in a container image besides the JAR artifact is an operating system and a JRE. This section will show you how to containerize the Catalog Service application using a Dockerfile.

First, you need to identify which image you want to base yours on. You could choose an Ubuntu image, as we did before, and then explicitly install the JRE, or you could choose a base image that provides a JRE already, which is more convenient. All the major OpenJDK distributions have a related image available on Docker Hub. Feel free to choose the one you prefer. In this example I'll be using Eclipse Temurin 17, which is the same OpenJDK distribution I've been using locally so far. Then you need to copy the JAR file of Catalog Service into the image itself. Finally, declare that the entry point for the container execution is the command to run the application on the JRE.

Open your Catalog Service project (catalog-service), and create an empty file called Dockerfile (with no extension) in the root folder. That file will contain the recipe for containerizing your application.

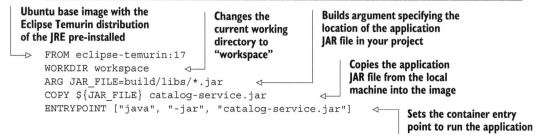

Listing 6.2   Dockerfile for describing the Catalog Service image

Ubuntu base image with the Eclipse Temurin distribution of the JRE pre-installed

Changes the current working directory to "workspace"

Builds argument specifying the location of the application JAR file in your project

Copies the application JAR file from the local machine into the image

```
FROM eclipse-temurin:17
WORKDIR workspace
ARG JAR_FILE=build/libs/*.jar
COPY ${JAR_FILE} catalog-service.jar
ENTRYPOINT ["java", "-jar", "catalog-service.jar"]
```

Sets the container entry point to run the application

This Dockerfile declares a `JAR_FILE` argument that can be specified when creating the image with the `docker build` command.

Before moving on, you need to build the JAR artifact for the Catalog Service application. Open a Terminal window and navigate to the Catalog Service project's root folder. First, build the JAR artifact:

```
$ ./gradlew clean bootJar
```

By default, the Dockerfile script will copy the application's JAR file from the location path used by Gradle: `build/libs/`. So if you're using Gradle, you can build the container image by running this command:

```
$ docker build -t catalog-service .
```

If you're using Maven, you can specify the location used by Maven as a build argument with the following command (don't forget the final dot):

```
$ docker build --build-arg JAR_FILE=target/*.jar -t catalog-service .
```

In either case, you'll end up with your Catalog Service application packaged as a container image. Since we haven't specified any version, the image will be tagged as `latest` automatically. Let's verify that it works.

Remember the two aspects I covered in the previous section: port forwarding and using the Docker built-in DNS server. You can handle them by adding two arguments to the `docker run` command:

- `-p 9001:9001` will map port 9001 inside the container (where the Catalog Service is exposing its services) to port 9001 on your localhost.
- `--net catalog-network` will connect the Catalog Service container to the catalog-network you previously created so that it can contact the PostgreSQL container.

That is still not enough. In the previous chapter, we set the `spring.datasource.url` property for Catalog Service to `jdbc:postgresql://localhost:5432/polardb_catalog`.

Since it points to `localhost`, it will not work from within a container. You already know how to configure a Spring Boot application from the outside without having to recompile it, right? An environment variable will do. We need to overwrite the `spring.datasource.url` property and specify the same URL, replacing `localhost` with the PostgreSQL container name: `polar-postgres`. Using another environment variable, we can also enable the `testdata` Spring profile to trigger the creation of test data in the catalog:

```
$ docker run -d \
    --name catalog-service \
    --net catalog-network \
    -p 9001:9001 \
    -e SPRING_DATASOURCE_URL=
➥jdbc:postgresql://polar-postgres:5432/polardb_catalog \
    -e SPRING_PROFILES_ACTIVE=testdata \
    catalog-service
```

That's quite a long command, isn't it? You won't use the Docker CLI for long, though, I promise. Later in the chapter I'll introduce Docker Compose.

Open a Terminal window, call the application, and verify that it works correctly, as it did in chapter 5:

```
$ http :9001/books
```

When you're done, remember to delete both containers:

```
$ docker rm -f catalog-service polar-postgres
```

The approach you've just followed is perfectly fine for experimenting with Docker in your development environment and understanding how images work, but you'll need to consider several aspects before achieving a production-grade image. That's the topic of the next section.

6.2.3 Building container images for production

Getting started with Dockerfiles might not be that difficult at the beginning, but building production-grade images can be challenging. In this section, you'll see how to improve the image you built in the previous section.

You'll use the layered-JAR feature provided by Spring Boot to build more efficient images. Then you'll consider essential security aspects related to container images. Finally, I'll discuss some factors to consider when choosing between Dockerfiles and Cloud Native Buildpacks for containerizing applications.

PERFORMANCE

When building container images, you should consider performance at build time and at run time. The layered architecture characterizing OCI images enables the caching and reusing of unchanged layers when building an image. Container registries store images by layers, so that when you pull a new version, only the changed layers are downloaded. That is quite an advantage in a cloud environment, considering the time and bandwidth you'll save for all your application instances.

In the previous section, you copied the Catalog Service standalone JAR file into a layer in the image. As a result, whenever you change something in your application, the whole layer must be rebuilt. Consider the scenario where you just add a new REST endpoint to your application. Even if all the Spring libraries and dependencies are unchanged, and the only difference is in your own code, you must rebuild the whole layer, since everything is together. We can do better. And Spring Boot can help us.

Putting uber-JARs inside a container image has never been efficient. A JAR artifact is a compressed archive containing all the dependencies, classes, and resources used by the application. All those files are organized in folders and subfolders within the JAR. We could expand standard JAR artifacts and put each folder on a different container image level. Starting with version 2.3, Spring Boot made that even more efficient by introducing a new way of packaging applications as JAR artifacts: the layered-JAR mode. And since Spring Boot 2.4, that's been the default mode, so you don't need any extra configuration to use the new functionality.

Applications packaged using the *layered-JAR mode* are made up of layers, similar to how container images work. This new feature is excellent for building more efficient images. When using the new JAR packaging, we can expand the JAR artifact and then create a different image layer for each JAR layer. The goal is to have your own classes (which change more frequently) on a separate layer from the project dependencies (which change less frequently).

By default, Spring Boot applications are packaged as JAR artifacts made up of the following layers, starting from the lowest:

- `dependencies`—For all the main dependencies added to the project
- `spring-boot-loader`—For the classes used by the Spring Boot loader component
- `snapshot-dependencies`—For all the snapshot dependencies
- `application`—For your application classes and resources

If you consider the previous scenario where you added a new REST endpoint to an existing application, only the `application` layer must be built when you containerize it. Moreover, when you upgrade the application in production, only that new layer must be downloaded to the nodes where the container is running, making the upgrade faster and cheaper (especially on cloud platforms, which bill for the bandwidth used).

Let's update the previous Dockerfile to containerize Catalog Service more efficiently using the layered-JAR mode. Using this new strategy means doing some preparation work to copy the JAR file into the image and expand it into the four layers described previously. We don't want to keep the original JAR file inside the image, or our optimization plan will not work. Docker provides a solution for that: *multi-stage builds*.

We'll divide the work into two stages. In the first stage we extract the layers from the JAR file. The second stage is where we place each JAR layer into a separate image layer. In the end, the result of the first stage is discarded (including the original JAR file), while the second stage will produce the final container image.

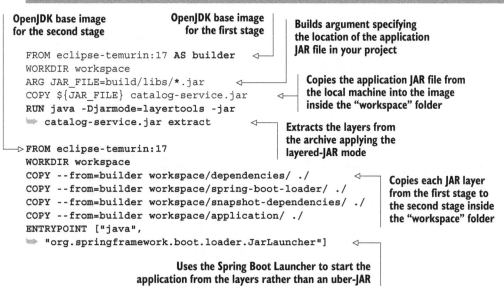

Listing 6.3   More efficient Dockerfile to build a Catalog Service image

```
FROM eclipse-temurin:17 AS builder
WORKDIR workspace
ARG JAR_FILE=build/libs/*.jar
COPY ${JAR_FILE} catalog-service.jar
RUN java -Djarmode=layertools -jar
    catalog-service.jar extract

FROM eclipse-temurin:17
WORKDIR workspace
COPY --from=builder workspace/dependencies/ ./
COPY --from=builder workspace/spring-boot-loader/ ./
COPY --from=builder workspace/snapshot-dependencies/ ./
COPY --from=builder workspace/application/ ./
ENTRYPOINT ["java",
    "org.springframework.boot.loader.JarLauncher"]
```

OpenJDK base image for the second stage

OpenJDK base image for the first stage

Builds argument specifying the location of the application JAR file in your project

Copies the application JAR file from the local machine into the image inside the "workspace" folder

Extracts the layers from the archive applying the layered-JAR mode

Copies each JAR layer from the first stage to the second stage inside the "workspace" folder

Uses the Spring Boot Launcher to start the application from the layers rather than an uber-JAR

NOTE   What if you want to change the configuration for the layers in the JAR file? As always, Spring Boot provides sensible defaults, but you can customize it and adapt it to your needs. Perhaps your project has internal shared dependencies you might want to place in a separate layer, since they change more often than third-party dependencies. You can do that through the Spring Boot Gradle or Maven plugin. For more information, refer to the Spring Boot documentation at https://spring.io/projects/spring-boot.

The process for building and running the container is the same as before, but now the image is more efficient and is optimized at build and execution time. However, it's still not ready for production. What about security? That's the topic of the next section.

SECURITY

Security is a critical aspect that is too often underestimated by people getting started with Docker and containerization. You should be aware that containers run using the root user by default, potentially letting them get root access to the Docker host. You can mitigate the risk by creating a non-privileged user and using it to run the entrypoint process defined in the Dockerfile, following the principle of least privilege.

Consider the Dockerfile you wrote for Catalog Service. You can improve it by adding new steps to create a new non-root user that will run the application.

Listing 6.4   More secure Dockerfile to build a Catalog Service image

```
FROM eclipse-temurin:17 AS builder
WORKDIR workspace
ARG JAR_FILE=build/libs/*.jar
COPY ${JAR_FILE} catalog-service.jar
RUN java -Djarmode=layertools -jar catalog-service.jar extract

FROM eclipse-temurin:17           Creates a          Configures
RUN useradd spring         ◁──    "spring" user      "spring" as the
USER spring                       ◁─────────────     current user
WORKDIR workspace
COPY --from=builder workspace/dependencies/ ./
COPY --from=builder workspace/spring-boot-loader/ ./
COPY --from=builder workspace/snapshot-dependencies/ ./
COPY --from=builder workspace/application/ ./
ENTRYPOINT ["java", "org.springframework.boot.loader.JarLauncher"]
```

As previously noted, you should never store secrets like passwords or keys in a container image. Even if they are removed in an upper layer, they will remain intact in the original layer and be easily accessible.

Finally, it's also critical to use up-to-date base images and libraries in your Dockerfile. Scanning your container images for vulnerabilities is a best practice that should be embraced and automated in your deployment pipeline. In chapter 3, you learned how to use grype to scan codebases for vulnerabilities. Now we'll also use it to scan a container image.

Using the updated Dockerfile, build a new container image for Catalog Service. Open a Terminal window, navigate to the Catalog Service root folder, and run this command (don't forget the final dot):

```
$ docker build -t catalog-service .
```

Next, use grype to check if the newly created image contains any vulnerabilities:

```
$ grype catalog-service
```

Have you found any high-severity vulnerabilities? Discussing supply chain security and related risk management is out of scope for this book. I want to show you how to perform and automate vulnerability scanning for application artifacts, but I'll leave it up to you to follow up on the scan results. I can't stress enough how important it is to define a security strategy in your organization and automate, as much as possible, its compliance verification throughout the whole value stream.

In this section, I mentioned a few essential aspects you should consider when building production-grade container images, but there's even more to cover. Is there another way to build production-grade container images? The following section introduces a different option.

DOCKERFILES OR BUILDPACKS

Dockerfiles are very powerful, and they give you complete fine-grained control over the result. However, they require extra care and maintenance and can lead to several challenges in your value stream.

As a developer, you might not want to deal with all the performance and security concerns we've discussed. You might prefer to focus on the application code instead. After all, one reason to move to the cloud is to deliver value to customers faster. Adding the Dockerfile step and considering all those issues might not be for you.

As an operator, it might be challenging to control and secure the supply chain within the organization when container images are built from a Dockerfile. It's pretty common to invest some time in scripting the *perfect* Dockerfile and to copy that into multiple repositories for different applications. But it's hard to keep all teams on the same page, verify adherence to the approved Dockerfile, synchronize any changes throughout the organization, and understand who is responsible for what.

Cloud Native Buildpacks provide a different approach, focusing on consistency, security, performance, and governance. As a developer, you get a tool that automatically builds a production-ready OCI image from your application source code without having to write a Dockerfile. As an operator, you get a tool that defines, controls, and secures application artifacts within the entire organization.

Ultimately, the decision to use a Dockerfile or a tool like Buildpacks depends on your organization and requirements. Both approaches are valid and are used in production. In general, my recommendation is to use Buildpacks unless it makes sense not to.

> **NOTE** Another option for packaging Java applications as container images without writing a Dockerfile is using Jib, a Gradle and Maven plugin developed by Google (https://github.com/GoogleContainerTools/jib).

In the next section and the rest of the book, we'll use Cloud Native Buildpacks rather than Dockerfiles. It was important for me to show you how a Dockerfile works, because it makes understanding the container image features and layers easier. Furthermore, I wanted to show you how to write a basic Dockerfile for containerizing a Spring Boot application to highlight what's needed and illustrate the execution of the application JAR from within the container. Finally, it will be easier for you to debug containers when something goes wrong, even if they're automatically generated by Buildpacks, because you now know how to build images from scratch. If you'd like to learn more about Dockerfiles for Spring Boot applications, I recommend you look at the official documentation (https://spring.io/projects/spring-boot).

6.2.4 *Containerizing Spring Boot with Cloud Native Buildpacks*

Cloud Native Buildpacks (https://buildpacks.io) is a project hosted by the CNCF to "transform your application source code into images that can run on any cloud." When introducing containers in chapter 1, I underlined how PaaS platforms like

Heroku and Cloud Foundry are actually using containers behind the scenes, converting your application source code into containers before running them. Buildpacks is the tool they use to accomplish that.

Cloud Native Buildpacks has been developed and advanced based on Heroku and Pivotal's many years of experience running cloud native applications as containers on their PaaS platforms. It's a mature project, and since Spring Boot 2.3, it has been integrated natively in the Spring Boot Plugin for both Gradle and Maven, so you're not required to install the dedicated Buildpacks CLI (`pack`).

These are some of its features:

- It auto-detects the type of application and packages it without requiring a Dockerfile.
- It supports multiple languages and platforms.
- It's highly performant through caching and layering.
- It guarantees reproducible builds.
- It relies on best practices in terms of security.
- It produces production-grade images.
- It supports building native images using GraalVM.

NOTE   If you'd like to know more about Cloud Native Buildpacks, I recommend watching "Cloud Native Buildpacks with Emily Casey" (http://mng.bz/M0xB). Emily Casey is a member of the Buildpacks core team.

The container generation process is orchestrated by a *builder* image containing the complete information on how to containerize your application. Such information is provided as a sequence of *buildpacks*, each dedicated to a specific aspect of the application (such as the operating system, OpenJDK, and JVM configuration). The Spring Boot Plugin adopts the Paketo Buildpacks builder, an implementation of the Cloud Native Buildpacks specification that provides support for many types of applications, including Java and Spring Boot ones (https://paketo.io).

The Paketo builder component relies on a series of default buildpacks for the actual build operation. This structure is highly modular and customizable. You can add new buildpacks to the sequence (for example, to add a monitoring agent to the application), replace existing ones (for example, to replace the default Bellsoft Liberica OpenJDK with Microsoft OpenJDK), or even use a different builder image entirely.

NOTE   The Cloud Native Buildpacks project manages a registry where you can discover and analyze buildpacks you can use to containerize your applications, including all the buildpacks from the Paketo implementation (https://registry.buildpacks.io).

The Buildpacks integration provided by the Spring Boot Plugin can be configured in the build.gradle file located in your Catalog Service project. Let's configure the image name and define which Java version to use through an environment variable.

Listing 6.5   Configuration for containerizing Catalog Service

**The Spring Boot Plugin task
to build an OCI image
using Buildpacks**

**The name of the OCI image to build. The
name is the same one defined in the Gradle
configuration for the project. We rely on
the implicit "latest" tag when working
locally rather than a version number.**

```
bootBuildImage {            ◁───┘
  imageName = "${project.name}"    ◁──────┘
  environment = ["BP_JVM_VERSION" : "17.*"]    ◁──────┐
}
```

**The JVM version to be installed
in the image. It uses the latest
Java 17 version.**

Go ahead and build the image by running the following command:

```
$ ./gradlew bootBuildImage
```

> **WARNING** At the time of writing, the Paketo project is working on adding
> support for ARM64 images. You can follow the feature's progress on the
> Paketo Buildpacks project on GitHub: https://github.com/paketo-buildpacks/
> stacks/issues/51. Until it's complete, you can still use Buildpacks to build
> containers and run them via Docker Desktop on Apple Silicon computers.
> However, the build process and the application startup phase will be slower
> than usual. Until official support is added, you can alternatively use the fol-
> lowing command, pointing to an experimental version of Paketo Buildpacks
> with ARM64 support: ./gradlew bootBuildImage --builder ghcr.io/
> thomasvitale/java-builder-arm64. Be aware that it's experimental and not
> ready for production. For more information, you can refer to the documenta-
> tion on GitHub: https://github.com/ThomasVitale/paketo-arm64.

The first time you run the task, it will take a minute to download the packages used by
Buildpacks to create the container image. The second time, it will take only a few seconds. If you look closely at the output of the command, you can see all the steps performed by Buildpacks to generate the image. These steps include adding a JRE and
using the layered JAR built by Spring Boot. The plugin accepts more properties to
customize its behavior, such as providing your own builder component instead of
Paketo's. Check the official documentation for the complete list of configuration
options (https://spring.io/projects/spring-boot).

Let's try running Catalog Service as a container once again, but this time we'll use
the image generated by Buildpacks. Remember to start the PostgreSQL container
first, following the instructions in section 6.2.1:

```
$ docker run -d \
    --name catalog-service \
    --net catalog-network \
    -p 9001:9001 \
    -e SPRING_DATASOURCE_URL=
⇒jdbc:postgresql://polar-postgres:5432/polardb_catalog \
    -e SPRING_PROFILES_ACTIVE=testdata \
    catalog-service
```

WARNING   If you're running the container on an Apple Silicon computer, the previous command might return a message like "WARNING: The requested image's platform (linux/amd64) does not match the detected host platform (linux/arm64/v8) and no specific platform was requested." In that case, you'll need to include this additional argument to the previous command (before the image name) until support for ARM64 is added to Paketo Build-packs: `--platform linux/amd64`.

Open a browser window, call the application on http://localhost:9001/books, and verify that it works correctly. When you're done, remember to delete both the Post-greSQL and Catalog Service containers:

```
$ docker rm -f catalog-service polar-postgres
```

Finally, you can remove the network you used to make Catalog Service communicate with PostgreSQL. You won't need it anymore, after I introduce Docker Compose in the next section:

```
$ docker network rm catalog-network
```

Since Spring Boot 2.4, you can also configure the Spring Boot plugin to publish the image directly to a container registry. To do so, you first need to add configuration for authenticating with the specific container registry in the build.gradle file.

Listing 6.6   Configuration for containerizing Catalog Service

```
bootBuildImage {
  imageName = "${project.name}"
  environment = ["BP_JVM_VERSION" : "17.*"]        Section to configure
                                                    the connection with
  docker {                                          a container registry
    publishRegistry {
      username = project.findProperty("registryUsername")
      password = project.findProperty("registryToken")
      url = project.findProperty("registryUrl")
    }
  }
}
```

Section to configure authentication to the publishing container registry. The values are passed as Gradle properties.

The details on how to authenticate with the container registry are externalized as Gradle properties both for flexibility (you can publish the image to different registries without changing the Gradle build) and for security (the token, in particular, should never be included in version control).

Remember this golden rule of credentials: you should never give your password away. Never! If you need to delegate some service to access a resource on your behalf, you should rely on an access token. The Spring Boot plugin lets you use a password to authenticate with the registry, but you should use a token instead. In section 6.1.3, you generated a personal access token in GitHub to let you push images to the GitHub Container Registry from your local environment. If you don't know its value anymore, feel free to generate a new one following the procedure I explained earlier in the chapter.

Finally, you can build and publish the image by running the `bootBuildImage` task. With the `--imageName` argument, you can define a fully qualified image name as container registries require. With the `--publishImage` argument, you can instruct the Spring Boot plugin to push the image to the container registry directly. Also, remember to pass values for the container registry via the Gradle properties:

```
$ ./gradlew bootBuildImage \
    --imageName ghcr.io/<your_github_username>/catalog-service \
    --publishImage \
    -PregistryUrl=ghcr.io \
    -PregistryUsername=<your_github_username> \
    -PregistryToken=<your_github_token>
```

> **TIP** If you're working on ARM64 machines (such as Apple Silicon computers), you can add the `--builder ghcr.io/thomasvitale/java-builder-arm64` argument to the previous command to use an experimental version of Paketo Buildpacks with ARM64 support. Be aware that it's experimental and not ready for production. For more information, you can refer to the documentation on GitHub: https://github.com/ThomasVitale/paketo-arm64. Without this workaround, until official support is added (https://github.com/paketo-buildpacks/stacks/issues/51), you can still use Buildpacks to build containers and run them via Docker Desktop on Apple Silicon computers, but the build process and application startup phase will be slower than usual.

Once the command completes successfully, go to your GitHub account, navigate to your profile page, and enter the Packages section. You should see a new `catalog -service` entry (by default, packages hosting container images are private), similar to what you saw with the `my-java-image` you published in section 6.1.3. If you click on the `catalog-service` entry, you'll find the `ghcr.io/<your_github_username>/catalog-service:latest` image you just published (figure 6.11).

However, the `catalog-service` package is not linked to your `catalog-service` source code repository yet. Later, I'll show you how to automate building and publishing your images with GitHub Actions, which makes it possible to publish images in the context of the source code repository from which they are built.

For now, let's remove the `catalog-service` package that was created when you published the image so that it won't cause any conflicts once you start using GitHub Actions to publish images. From the `catalog-service` package page (figure 6.11), click Package Settings in the sidebar menu, scroll to the bottom of the settings page, and click Delete This Package (figure 6.12).

> **NOTE** So far, we've been using the implicit `latest` tag for naming container images. That's not recommended for production scenarios. In chapter 15, you'll see how to handle versions when releasing your applications. Until then, we'll rely on the implicit `latest` tag.

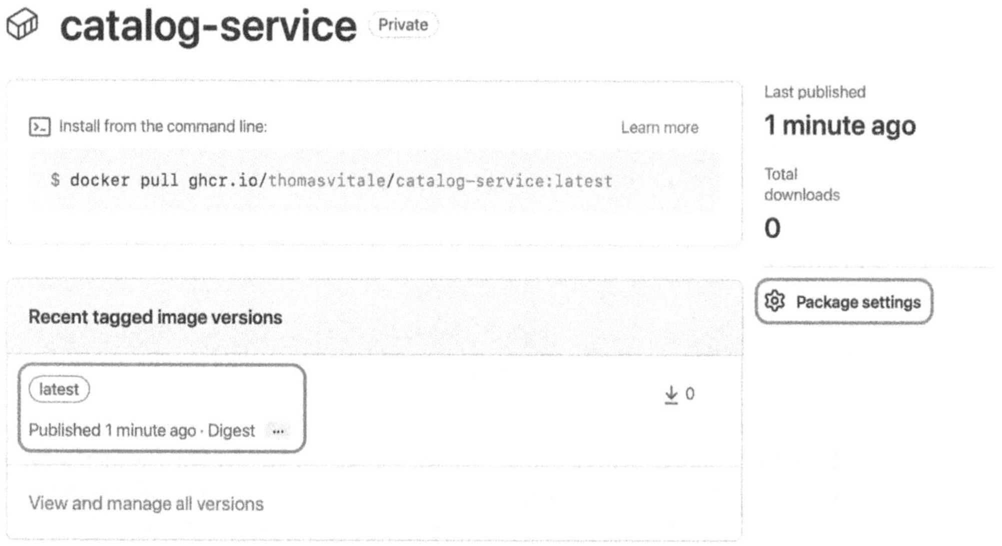

🗇 catalog-service (Private)

Install from the command line: Learn more

```
$ docker pull ghcr.io/thomasvitale/catalog-service:latest
```

Last published
1 minute ago

Total
downloads

0

Recent tagged image versions

⚙ Package settings

(latest)

Published 1 minute ago · Digest ...

⬇ 0

View and manage all versions

Figure 6.11 **Images published to the GitHub Container Registry are organized as "packages."**

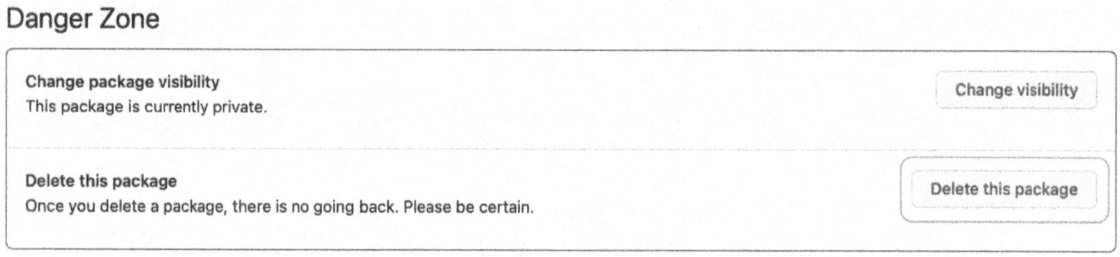

Danger Zone

Change package visibility
This package is currently private.

Change visibility

Delete this package
Once you delete a package, there is no going back. Please be certain.

Delete this package

Figure 6.12 **Delete the** `catalog-service` **package created manually.**

6.3   *Managing Spring Boot containers with Docker Compose*

Cloud Native Buildpacks lets you containerize Spring Boot applications quickly and efficiently without writing a Dockerfile yourself. But when it comes to running multiple containers, the Docker CLI can be a bit cumbersome. Writing commands in a Terminal window can be error-prone, hard to read, and challenging when it comes to applying version control.

Docker Compose provides a better experience than the Docker CLI. Instead of a command line, you work with YAML files that describe which containers you want to run and their characteristics. With Docker Compose, you can define all the applications and services composing your system in one place, and you can manage their life cycles together.

In this section, you'll configure the execution of the Catalog Service and Post-greSQL containers using Docker Compose. Then you'll learn how to debug a Spring Boot application running within a container.

If you have installed Docker Desktop for Mac or Docker Desktop for Windows, you already have Docker Compose installed. If you're on Linux, visit the Docker Compose installation page at www.docker.com and follow the instructions for your distribution. In any case, you can verify that Docker Compose is correctly installed by running the command `docker-compose --version`.

6.3.1   Using Docker Compose to manage the container life cycle

The Docker Compose syntax is very intuitive and self-explanatory. Often, it can be mapped one-to-one to Docker CLI arguments. The two root sections of a docker-compose.yml file are `version`, where you specify which syntax of Docker Compose you want to use, and `services`, containing the specifications for all the containers you want to run. Other optional root-level sections you may add are `volumes` and `networks`.

> **NOTE**   If you don't add any network configuration, Docker Compose will automatically create one for you and make all the containers in the file join it. That means they can interact with each other through their container names, relying on Docker's built-in DNS server.

It's good practice to gather all deployment-related scripts in a separate codebase and, possibly, in a separate repository. Go ahead and create a new `polar-deployment` repository on GitHub. It'll contain all the Docker and Kubernetes scripts needed to run the applications composing the Polar Bookshop system. Inside the repository, create a "docker" folder to host the Docker Compose configuration for Polar Bookshop. In the source code accompanying the book, you can refer to Chapter06/06-end/polar-deployment for the final result.

In the polar-deployment/docker folder, create a docker-compose.yml file, and define the services to run as follows.

Listing 6.7   Docker Compose file describing the catalog services

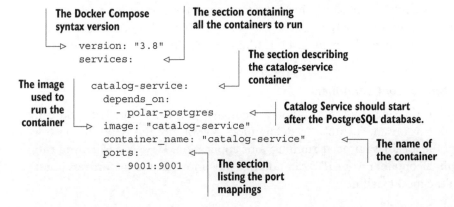

The section listing the environment variables

```
environment:
  - BPL_JVM_THREAD_COUNT=50
  - SPRING_DATASOURCE_URL=
jdbc:postgresql://polar-postgres:5432/polardb_catalog
  - SPRING_PROFILES_ACTIVE=testdata

polar-postgres:
  image: "postgres:14.4"
  container_name: "polar-postgres"
  ports:
    - 5432:5432
  environment:
    - POSTGRES_USER=user
    - POSTGRES_PASSWORD=password
    - POSTGRES_DB=polardb_catalog
```

A Paketo Buildpacks environment variable to configure the number of threads for memory calculation

Enables the "testdata" Spring profile

The section describing the polar-postgres container

You might have noticed the presence of an additional environment variable for the Catalog Service container. In chapter 15, you'll learn about the Java memory calculator provided by Paketo Buildpacks and how to configure CPU and memory for Spring Boot applications. For now, it's enough to know that the BPL_JVM_THREAD_COUNT environment variable is used to configure the number of threads memory should be allocated for in the JVM stack. The default value for Servlet-based applications is 250. In chapter 3, we used a low value for the Tomcat thread pool, and it's good to do the same for the JVM memory configuration to keep the container's memory usage low locally. You're going to deploy many containers throughout the book (both applications and backing services), and such configuration helps make that possible without overloading your computer.

Docker Compose configures both containers on the same network by default, so you don't need to specify one explicitly, as you did previously.

Let's see now how to spin them up. Open a Terminal window, navigate to the folder containing the file, and run the following command to start the containers in detached mode:

```
$ docker-compose up -d
```

When the command is done, try calling the Catalog Service application at http://localhost:9001/books and verify that it works correctly. Then keep your containers running and move on to the next section, where you'll debug the Catalog Service application.

6.3.2   *Debugging Spring Boot containers*

When running a Spring Boot application as standard Java from your IDE, you can specify whether you want to run it in debug mode. If you do, the IDE will attach a debugger to the local Java process running your application. However, when you run it from within a container, your IDE can't do that anymore because the process is not running on the local machine.

Fortunately, Spring Boot applications running in a container can be debugged almost as easily as when running locally. First you need to instruct the JVM inside the container to listen for debug connections on a specific port. The container image produced by Paketo Buildpacks supports dedicated environment variables for running the application in debug mode (`BPL_DEBUG_ENABLED` and `BPL_DEBUG_PORT`). Then you need to expose the debug port outside the container so that your IDE can reach it. Figure 6.13 illustrates how it works.

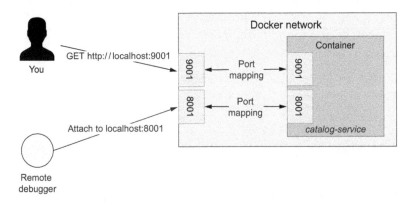

Figure 6.13   From a container, you can expose as many ports as you want. For Catalog Service, expose both the server port and the debug port.

Next, update your docker-compose.yml file to configure the Catalog Service application for debugging.

Listing 6.8   Configuring Catalog Service to run in debug mode

```
version: "3.8"
services:

  catalog-service:
    depends_on:
      - polar-postgres
    image: "catalog-service"
    container_name: "catalog-service"
    ports:
      - 9001:9001
      - 8001:8001
    environment:
      - BPL_JVM_THREAD_COUNT=50
      - BPL_DEBUG_ENABLED=true
      - BPL_DEBUG_PORT=8001
      - SPRING_DATASOURCE_URL=
jdbc:postgresql://polar-postgres:5432/polardb_catalog
      - SPRING_PROFILES_ACTIVE=testdata
  ...
```

The port where the JVM will listen for debug connections

Activates the JVM configuration for accepting debug connections (provided by Buildpacks)

Debug connections are accepted via a socket on port 8001 (provided by Buildpacks).

From a Terminal window, navigate to the folder where the docker-compose.yml file is located, and rerun the following command:

```
$ docker-compose up -d
```

You'll notice that Docker Compose is smart enough to know that the PostgreSQL container configuration is unchanged, and it will do nothing about it. Instead, it will reload the Catalog Service container with the new configuration.

Then, in your IDE of choice, you need to configure a remote debugger and point it to port 8001. Refer to your IDE's documentation to find the instructions on how to do that. Figure 6.14 shows how to configure a remote debugger in IntelliJ IDEA.

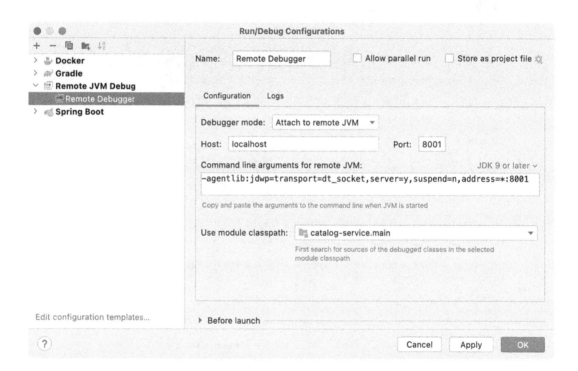

Figure 6.14   Configuration to debug a containerized Java application from IntelliJ IDEA

Once you run the Catalog Service, you can debug it as though it were running locally.

That's it for this section. You can stop and remove both containers with the following command from the same folder where you keep your docker-compose.yml file:

```
$ docker-compose down
```

> **NOTE** In this book I'm only covering those Docker topics needed in your journey to successfully deploy Spring Boot applications in production with

Kubernetes. If you're interested in learning more about Docker images, networks, volumes, security, and architecture, refer to the official documentation on https://docs.docker.com. Also, Manning has a few books in its catalog on the subject, such as *Learn Docker in a Month of Lunches* by Elton Stoneman (Manning, 2020) and *Docker in Practice*, second edition, by Ian Miell and Aidan Hobson Sayers (Manning, 2019).

When you make changes to an application, you don't want to build and publish a new image manually. That's a job for an automated workflow engine like GitHub Actions. The following section will show you how to complete the commit stage of the deployment pipeline we started in chapter 3.

6.4 Deployment pipeline: Package and publish

In chapter 3, we started implementing a deployment pipeline to support continuous delivery for the Polar Bookshop project. Continuous delivery is a holistic engineering approach for quickly, reliably, and safely delivering high-quality software. The deployment pipeline is the primary pattern for automating the entire journey from code commit to releasable software. We identified three main stages for the deployment pipeline: commit stage, acceptance stage, and production stage.

We'll continue focusing on the commit stage. After a developer commits new code to the mainline, this stage goes through build, unit tests, integration tests, static code analysis, and packaging. At the end of this stage, an executable application artifact is published to an artifact repository. That is a *release candidate*. Chapter 3 covered all the main steps except for the final packaging and publishing of a release candidate. That's what you'll see in this section.

6.4.1 Building release candidates in the commit stage

After running static code analysis, compilation, unit tests, and integration tests, it's time to package the application as an executable artifact and publish it. In our case, the executable artifact is a container image that we'll publish to a container registry.

An essential idea in continuous delivery, also present in the 15-Factor methodology, is that you should build artifacts only once. At the end of the commit stage, we'll produce a container image that we can reuse in any following stage in the deployment pipeline up to production. If the pipeline proves something is wrong (a test fails) at any point, the release candidate is rejected. If the release candidate goes through all subsequent stages successfully, it's proven to be ready for deployment in production.

After we build an executable artifact, we can perform additional operations before publishing it. For example, we could scan it for vulnerabilities. That's what we're going to do with grype, much as we did for the codebase. A container image includes application libraries but also system libraries that were not included in the previous security analysis. That's why we need to scan both the codebase and the artifact for vulnerabilities. Figure 6.15 illustrates the new steps we will add to the commit stage for building and publishing a release candidate.

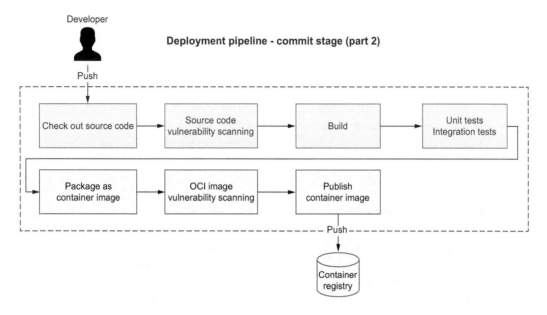

Figure 6.15   At the end of the commit stage, a release candidate is published to an artifact repository. In this case, a container image is published to a container registry.

Once a release candidate is published, several parties can download it and use it, including the next stages in the deployment pipeline. How can we ensure that all interested parties use a legitimate container image from the Polar Bookshop project, and not one that has been compromised? We can achieve that by signing the image. After the publishing step, we could add a new step for signing the release candidate. For example, we could use Sigstore (www.sigstore.dev), a non-profit service that provides open source tools for signing, verifying, and protecting software integrity. If you're interested in this subject, I recommend visiting the project's website.

In the following section, I'll show you how to implement the new steps in the commit stage of our deployment pipeline.

6.4.2   *Publishing container images with GitHub Actions*

GitHub Actions is an engine that you can use to automate software workflows directly from your GitHub repositories. Workflow definitions are conventionally stored in a .github/workflows directory placed in the root of a repository on GitHub.

In chapter 3, we started developing a workflow to implement the commit stage of the deployment pipeline for Catalog Service. Let's now continue the implementation by adding further steps to package and publish the application.

From your Catalog Service project (catalog-service), open the workflow definition for the commit stage (.github/workflows/commit-stage.yml) and define a few environment variables to store some essential facts you'll need when building a container image for the application. By using environment variables, you can easily change which container registry you use or the version for the release artifact. Remember to add your GitHub username, all in lowercase, instead of the placeholder in the following listing. Chapter 15 will cover software release strategies, but until then we're going to tag every image with `latest` instead of a version number.

Listing 6.9   Configuring facts about the release candidate

```
name: Commit Stage
on: push

env:
  REGISTRY: ghcr.io            ◁── Uses the GitHub
  IMAGE_NAME: <your_github_username>/catalog-service        Container Registry
  VERSION: latest       ◁──

jobs:
  ...
```

The name of the image. Remember to add your GitHub username, all in lowercase.

For the moment, any new image will be tagged as "latest".

Next let's add a new "Package and Publish" job to the workflow. If the "Build and Test" job completes successfully, and the workflow runs on the `main` branch, the new job will be executed. We'll use the same strategy we used locally to package Catalog Service as a container image, relying on the Buildpacks integration provided by the Spring Boot Gradle plugin. Notice that we are not pushing the image directly. That's because we first want to scan the image for vulnerabilities, which we'll do in a moment. For now, update the commit-stage.yml file as follows.

Listing 6.10   Packaging the application as an OCI image using Buildpacks

```
name: Commit Stage
on: push

env:
  REGISTRY: ghcr.io
  IMAGE_NAME: <your_github_username>/catalog-service
  VERSION: latest

jobs:
  build:
    ...
  package:
    name: Package and Publish
    if: ${{ github.ref == 'refs/heads/main' }}
    needs: [ build ]
    runs-on: ubuntu-22.04
    permissions:
      contents: read
      packages: write
      security-events: write
    steps:
      - name: Checkout source code
```

Runs the job only if the "build" job completes successfully

Runs the job on an Ubuntu 22.04 machine

Permission to check out the current Git repository

The job's unique identifier

Runs the job only on the main branch

Permission to upload images to GitHub Container Registry

Permission to submit security events to GitHub

```
      uses: actions/checkout@v3          ◁────┐   Checks out the
    - name: Set up JDK                         │   current Git repository
      uses: actions/setup-java@v3      ◁───┐   │   (catalog-service)
      with:                                │   │
        distribution: temurin            Installs and configures
        java-version: 17                 a Java runtime
        cache: gradle
    - name: Build container image
      run: |                             Relies on the Buildpacks integration in
        chmod +x gradlew                 Spring Boot to build a container image and
        ./gradlew bootBuildImage \   ◁── defines the name for the release candidate
          --imageName
          ⇨ ${{ env.REGISTRY }}/${{ env.IMAGE_NAME }}:${{ env.VERSION }}
```

After packaging the application as a container image, let's update the commit-stage.yml file to use grype to scan the image for vulnerabilities and publish a report to GitHub, similar to what we did in chapter 3. Finally, we can authenticate with the container registry and push the image representing our release candidate.

Listing 6.11   Scanning the image for vulnerabilities and publishing it

```
name: Commit Stage
on: push

env:
  REGISTRY: ghcr.io
  IMAGE_NAME: polarbookshop/catalog-service
  VERSION: latest

jobs:
  build:
    ...
  package:
    ...
    steps:
      - name: Checkout source code
        ...
      - name: Set up JDK
        ...
      - name: Build container image
        ...
      - name: OCI image vulnerability scanning
        uses: anchore/scan-action@v3
        id: scan
        with:                       ◁───┐  The image to scan is
          image:                         │  the release candidate.
            ⇨ ${{ env.REGISTRY }}/${{ env.IMAGE_NAME }}:${{ env.VERSION }}
          fail-build: false
          severity-cutoff: high    ◁───┐
          acs-report-enable: true       It won't fail the build if vulnerabilities
      - name: Upload vulnerability report   are found in the image.
        uses: github/codeql-action/upload-sarif@v2  ◁──  Uploads the security vulnerability
        if: success() || failure()              report to GitHub (SARIF format)
```

Scans the release candidate image for vulnerabilities using grype

Authenticates with GitHub Container Registry

```
    with:
      sarif_file: ${{ steps.scan.outputs.sarif }}
    - name: Log into container registry
      uses: docker/login-action@v2
      with:
        registry: ${{ env.REGISTRY }}
        username: ${{ github.actor }}
        password: ${{ secrets.GITHUB_TOKEN }}
    - name: Publish container image
      run: docker push
        ${{ env.REGISTRY }}/${{ env.IMAGE_NAME }}:${{ env.VERSION }}
```

The registry value as defined in the environment variable earlier

The GitHub username of the current user, provided by GitHub Actions

Pushes the release candidate to the registry

The token needed to authenticate with the registry, provided by GitHub Actions

In listing 6.11 we do not fail the workflow if serious vulnerabilities are discovered. However, you can find the scanning results in the Security section of your catalog-service GitHub repository. At the time of writing, no high or critical vulnerabilities are found in the Catalog Service project, but things might be different in the future. As already mentioned in chapter 3, in a real-world scenario, I recommend that you configure and tune grype carefully and according to your company's policies regarding supply chain security, and make the workflow fail if the result is not compliant (setting the fail-build property to true). For more information, refer to the official grype documentation (https://github.com/anchore/grype).

After completing the commit stage of the deployment pipeline, make sure your catalog-service GitHub repository is public. Then push your changes to the main branch of your remote repository, and see the workflow execution results in the Actions tab.

> **WARNING** The action of uploading the vulnerability report requires the GitHub repository to be public. It works for private repositories only if you have an enterprise subscription. If you prefer to keep your repository private, you'll need to skip the "Upload vulnerability report" step. Throughout the book, I'll assume all the repositories you create on GitHub for the Polar Bookshop project are public.

Images published from GitHub Actions and named after a repository are automatically associated. After the workflow completes its execution, you'll find a Packages section in the sidebar of your GitHub catalog-service repository's main page, with a "catalog-service" item (figure 6.16). Click on that item, and you'll be directed to the container image repository for Catalog Service.

> **NOTE** Images published to GitHub Container Registry will have the same visibility as the related GitHub code repository. If no repository is associated with the image, it's private by default. Throughout the book I'll assume that all the images you build for Polar Bookshop are publicly accessible via the GitHub Container Registry. If that's not the case, you can go to the package's

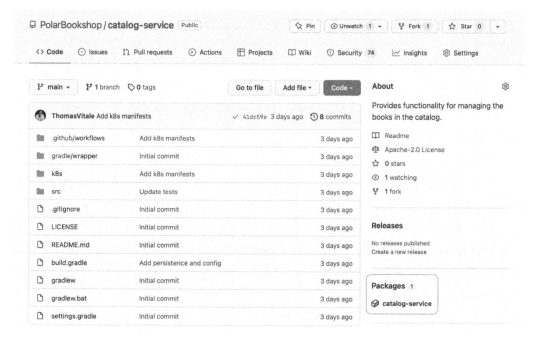

Figure 6.16   When using the GitHub Container Registry, you can store container images next to the source code.

main page, select Package Settings from the sidebar menu, scroll to the bottom of the settings page, and make the package public by clicking the Change Visibility button.

Great job! So far you've built a Spring Boot application that exposes a REST API and interacts with a relational database; you wrote unit and integration tests for the application; you handled the database schema with Flyway so it was production-ready; and you ran everything within containers and dealt with image generation, Docker, Cloud Native Buildpacks, and vulnerability scanning. The next chapter will complete the first part of this cloud native journey toward production by diving deep into Kubernetes. But before moving on, take a break, congratulate yourself on what you have achieved so far, and perhaps celebrate with a beverage of your choice.

Polar Labs

Feel free to apply what you've learned in this chapter to Config Service.

1 Configure the Cloud Native Buildpacks integration and package the application as a container.

2 Update your Docker Compose file to run Config Service as a container.

3 Configure Catalog Service with the Config Service URL via the `SPRING_CLOUD_CONFIG_URI` environment variable, relying on the Docker built-in DNS.

4 Bootstrap a deployment pipeline for Config Service by implementing the workflow for the commit stage using GitHub Actions.

You can refer to the Chapter06/06-end folder in the code repository accompanying the book to see the final result (https://github.com/ThomasVitale/cloud-native-spring-in-action).

Summary

- Container images are lightweight executable packages that include everything needed to run the application inside.
- Each image is made up of several layers, and each layer represents a modification produced by the corresponding instruction. The final artifact can be run as a container.
- When you run a container, an additional writable layer is added on top of the image layers.
- The standard way to define a container image is by listing the sequence of instructions in a particular file called a Dockerfile.
- A Dockerfile acts as a recipe containing all the steps to build the desired image.
- Performance and security are important concerns when building container images. For example, you shouldn't store secrets in any image layer, and never run the container with a root user.
- A container registry is to OCI images what a Maven repository is to Java libraries. Examples of container registries are Docker Hub and GitHub Container Registry.
- You can package Spring Boot applications as container images in different ways.
- Dockerfiles give you maximum flexibility but make it your responsibility to configure everything you need.
- Cloud Native Buildpacks (integrated with the Spring Boot Plugin) let you build OCI images directly from the source code, optimizing security, performance, and storage for you.
- When you run Spring Boot applications as containers, you should consider which ports you want to make available to the outside world (such as 8080) and whether containers should communicate with each other. If yes, you can use the Docker DNS server to contact containers in the same network by container name instead of IP or hostname.
- If you want to debug an application running as a container, remember to expose the debug port.

- Docker Compose is a client for interacting with the Docker server, and it provides a better user experience than Docker CLI. From a YAML file, you can manage all your containers.
- You can use GitHub Actions to automate the process of packaging an application as a container image, scanning it for vulnerabilities, and publishing it to a container registry. That's part of the commit stage of a deployment pipeline.
- The outcome of the commit stage of a deployment pipeline is a release candidate.

Kubernetes fundamentals for Spring Boot

This chapter covers

- Moving from Docker to Kubernetes
- Deploying Spring Boot applications on Kubernetes
- Understanding service discovery and load balancing
- Building scalable and disposable applications
- Establishing a local Kubernetes development workflow
- Validating Kubernetes manifests with GitHub Actions

In the previous chapter, you learned about Docker and the main characteristics of images and containers. With Buildpacks and Spring Boot, you can build a production-ready image in one command, without even having to write your own Dockerfile or install additional tools. With Docker Compose, you can simultaneously control multiple applications, which is convenient for architectures like microservices. But what if a container stops working? What if the machine where your containers are running (the Docker host) crashes? What if you want to scale your applications?

This chapter will introduce Kubernetes into your workflow to address issues that Docker alone cannot.

As a developer, it's not your job to configure and manage a Kubernetes cluster. You would probably use either a managed service offered by a cloud provider such as Amazon, Microsoft, or Google, or a service managed on premises by a specialized team in your organization (commonly known as the *platform team*). For now you'll use a local Kubernetes cluster provisioned with *minikube*. Later in the book you'll use a managed Kubernetes service offered by a cloud provider.

In our daily job as developers, we don't want to spend too much time on infrastructural concerns, but it's critical to know the basics. Kubernetes has become the de facto orchestration tool and the common language for talking about containerized deployments. Cloud vendors have been building platforms on top of Kubernetes to provide a better experience for developers. Once you know how Kubernetes works, it'll be straightforward to use those platforms, because you'll be familiar with the language and the abstractions.

This chapter will walk you through the main features of Kubernetes and teach you how to create and manage Pods, Deployments, and Services for your Spring Boot applications. Along the way you'll enable graceful shutdown for your applications, learn how to scale them, and learn how to use the service discovery and load balancing features provided by Kubernetes. You'll also learn to automate your local development workflow with Tilt, visualize your workloads with Octant, and validate your Kubernetes manifests.

> **NOTE**   The source code for the examples in this chapter is available in the Chapter07/07-begin and Chapter07/07-end folders, which contain the initial and final states of the project (https://github.com/ThomasVitale/cloud-native -spring-in-action).

7.1   *Moving from Docker to Kubernetes*

With Docker Compose, you can manage the deployment of several containers at once, including the configuration of networks and storage. That is extremely powerful, but it's limited to one machine.

Using Docker CLI and Docker Compose, the interaction happens with a single Docker daemon that manages Docker resources on a single machine, called the Docker host. Furthermore, it's not possible to scale a container. All of this is limiting when you need cloud native properties like scalability and resilience for your system. Figure 7.1 shows how you target a single machine when using Docker.

You learned in chapter 2 that we change our point of view when we move from a container runtime like Docker to an orchestration platform like Kubernetes. With Docker, we deploy containers to an individual machine. With Kubernetes, we deploy containers to a cluster of machines, enabling scalability and resilience.

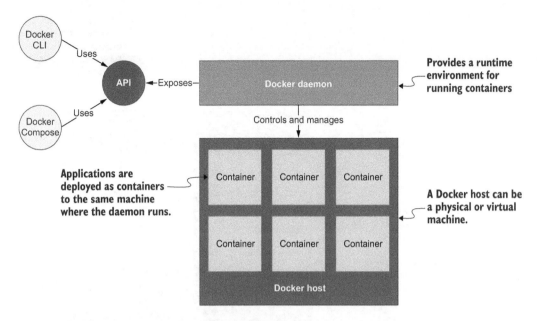

Figure 7.1 Docker clients interact with a Docker daemon that can only manage resources on the machine where it is installed, called the Docker host. Applications are deployed as containers to the Docker host.

Kubernetes clients use an API to interact with the Kubernetes Control Plane, which is responsible for creating and managing objects in a Kubernetes cluster. In this new scenario, we still send commands to a single entity, but it acts on several machines rather than only one. Figure 7.2 shows the logical infrastructure when we use Kubernetes.

These are the main components shown in figure 7.2:

- *Cluster*—A set of nodes running containerized applications. It hosts the Control Plane and comprises one or more worker nodes.
- *Control Plane*—The cluster component exposing the API and interfaces to define, deploy, and manage the life cycle of Pods. It comprises all the essential elements that implement the typical features of an orchestrator, like cluster management, scheduling, and health monitoring.
- *Worker nodes*—Physical or virtual machines providing capacity such as CPU, memory, network, and storage so that containers can run and connect to a network.
- *Pod*—The smallest deployable unit wrapping an application container.

Now that you have a good understanding of the Kubernetes infrastructure, let's see how you can create and manage a Kubernetes cluster on your local machine.

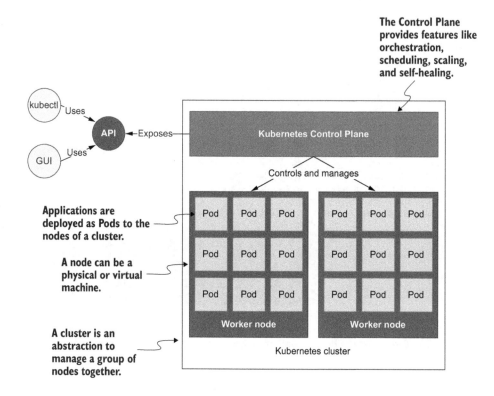

Figure 7.2   Kubernetes clients interact with the Control Plane, which manages containerized applications in a cluster consisting of one or more nodes. Applications are deployed as Pods to the nodes of a cluster.

7.1.1   *Working with a local Kubernetes cluster*

In chapter 2, we worked with *minikube* (https://minikube.sigs.k8s.io), a tool for running Kubernetes clusters on local environments. We used the minikube CLI to create a local Kubernetes cluster relying on the default configuration. In this section, you'll see how to define a custom configuration for minikube that you can use when initializing a new local Kubernetes cluster for deploying Polar Bookshop.

> **NOTE**   If you haven't installed minikube yet, refer to the instructions in section A.3 of appendix A.

Since we run minikube on top of Docker, remember to start the Docker Engine first. Then make sure the default cluster is not running by executing the minikube stop command. From now on, we won't use the default cluster. Instead, we'll create a custom one for working with Polar Bookshop. With minikube you can create and control multiple clusters identified via *profiles*. When no profile is specified, minikube falls back on the default cluster.

> **WARNING** Running the examples on a local Kubernetes cluster requires Docker to have at least 2 CPUs and 4 GB of memory. If you are using Docker Desktop for Mac or for Windows, and you need to increase the resources assigned to the Docker Engine, refer to the product documentation for instructions on how to do that for your specific operating system (https://docs .docker.com/desktop).

Let's create a new Kubernetes cluster named `polar` on top of Docker. This time, we also want to declare the resource limits for CPU and memory:

```
$ minikube start --cpus 2 --memory 4g --driver docker --profile polar
```

You can get a list of all the nodes in the cluster with the following command:

```
$ kubectl get nodes

NAME     STATUS   ROLES                 AGE   VERSION
polar    Ready    control-plane,master  21s   v1.24.3
```

The cluster we have just created is composed of a single node, which hosts the Control Plane and acts as a worker node for deploying containerized workloads.

You can use the same Kubernetes client (`kubectl`) to interact with different local or remote clusters. The following command will list all the available *contexts* with which you can interact:

```
$ kubectl config get-contexts

CURRENT   NAME    CLUSTER   AUTHINFO
*         polar   polar     polar
```

If you have more than one context, make sure `kubectl` is configured to use `polar`. You can verify which is the current context by running this command:

```
$ kubectl config current-context
polar
```

If the result is different from `polar`, you can change the current context as follows:

```
$ kubectl config use-context polar
Switched to context "polar".
```

For the rest of the chapter, I will assume you have this local cluster up and running. At any time, you can stop the cluster with `minikube stop --profile polar` and start it again with `minikube start --profile polar`. If you ever want to delete it and start over, you can run the `minikube delete --profile polar` command.

In the next section, you'll complete the setup for your local Kubernetes cluster by deploying a PostgreSQL database.

7.1.2   *Managing data services in a local cluster*

As you learned in chapter 5, data services are the stateful components of a system and require special care in a cloud environment due to the challenges of handling their storage. Managing persistence and storage in Kubernetes is a complex topic, and it's not usually the responsibility of developers.

When you deploy the Polar Bookshop system in production, you'll rely on the managed data services offered by the cloud provider, so I have prepared the configuration for deploying PostgreSQL in your local Kubernetes cluster. Check the source code repository accompanying this book (Chapter07/07-end) and copy the content of the polar-deployment/kubernetes/platform/development folder into the same path in your `polar-deployment` repository. The folder contains basic Kubernetes manifests to run a PostgreSQL database.

Open a Terminal window, navigate to the kubernetes/platform/development folder located in your `polar-deployment` repository, and run the following command to deploy PostgreSQL in your local cluster:

```
$ kubectl apply -f services
```

> **NOTE**   The preceding command creates the resources defined in the manifests within the services folder. In the next section, you'll learn more about the `kubectl apply` command and Kubernetes manifests.

The result will be a Pod running a PostgreSQL container in your local Kubernetes cluster. You can check it out with the following command:

```
$ kubectl get pod

NAME                              READY   STATUS    RESTARTS   AGE
polar-postgres-677b76bfc5-1kkqn   1/1     Running   0          48s
```

> **TIP**   You can check the database logs by running `kubectl logs deployment/polar-postgres`.

Running Kubernetes services with Helm

A popular way of running third-party services in a Kubernetes cluster is through Helm (https://helm.sh). Think of it as a package manager. To install software on your computer, you can use one of the operating system package managers, like Apt (Ubuntu), Homebrew (macOS), or Chocolatey (Windows); in Kubernetes, you can similarly use Helm, but we call them *charts* instead of *packages*.

At this stage in our cloud native journey, using Helm would be a bit premature and perhaps confusing. To fully understand how it works, it's essential to acquire more familiarity with Kubernetes first.

For the rest of the chapter, I'll assume you have a PostgreSQL instance running in your local cluster. If at any point you need to undeploy the database, you can run the `kubectl delete -f services` command from the same folder.

The following section will present the main Kubernetes concepts and guide you through deploying Spring Boot applications on your local cluster.

7.2 Kubernetes Deployments for Spring Boot

This section will walk you through the main Kubernetes objects you'll be working with as a developer and the vocabulary necessary to communicate efficiently with a platform team and deploy your applications to a cluster.

You have already gone through the containerization of a Spring Boot application. A Spring Boot application on Kubernetes is still packaged as a container, but it runs in a Pod controlled by a Deployment object.

Pods and Deployments are core concepts you need to understand when working with Kubernetes. Let's start by looking at some of their main characteristics, after which you'll practice declaring and creating Kubernetes resources to deploy the Catalog Service application.

7.2.1 From containers to Pods

As we discussed in the previous section, Pods are the smallest deployable units in Kubernetes. When moving from Docker to Kubernetes, we switch from managing containers to managing Pods.

A *Pod* is the smallest Kubernetes object, and it "represents a set of running containers" in a cluster. It's usually set up to run a single primary container (your application), but it can also run optional helper containers with additional features like logging, monitoring, or security (https://kubernetes.io/docs/reference/glossary).

A Pod is usually comprised of one container: the application instance. When that happens, it's not much different from working with containers directly. However, there are some scenarios where your application container needs to be deployed together with some *helper* containers that perhaps perform initialization tasks required by the application or add extra functionality such as logging. For example, Linkerd (a *service mesh*) adds its own container (a *sidecar*) to Pods to perform operations such as intercepting HTTP traffic and encrypting it to guarantee secure communication between all Pods via mTLS (mutual Transport Layer Security). Figure 7.3 illustrates single-container and multi-container Pods.

In this book, you'll work with single-container Pods, where the container is the application. Compared to containers, Pods allow you to manage related containers as a single entity. But that's not enough. Directly creating and managing Pods would not be much different than working with plain Docker containers. We need something at a higher level of abstraction to define how we want to deploy and scale our applications. That's where the Deployment objects come into play.

Single-container Pod   **Multi-container Pod**

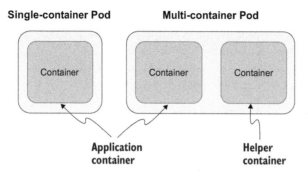

Figure 7.3 **Pods are the smallest deployable units in Kubernetes. They run at least one primary container (the application) and might run optional helper containers for additional features like logging, monitoring, or security.**

7.2.2 *Controlling Pods with Deployments*

How can you scale an application to have five replicas running? How can you ensure there are always five replicas up and running even when failures occur? How can you deploy a new version of the application without downtime? With *Deployments*.

A *Deployment* is an object that manages the life cycle of a stateless, replicated application. Each replica is represented by a Pod. The replicas are distributed among the nodes of a cluster for better resilience (https://kubernetes.io/docs/reference/glossary).

In Docker you manage your application instances directly by creating and removing containers. In Kubernetes you don't manage Pods. You let a Deployment do that for you. Deployment objects have several important and valuable characteristics. You can use them to deploy your applications, roll out upgrades without downtime, roll back to a previous version in case of errors, and pause and resume upgrades.

Deployments also let you manage replication. They make use of an object named *ReplicaSet* to ensure there's always the desired number of Pods up and running in your cluster. If one of them crashes, a new one is created automatically to replace it. Furthermore, replicas are deployed across different nodes in your cluster to ensure even higher availability if one node crashes. Figure 7.4 shows the relationship between containers, Pods, ReplicaSets, and Deployments.

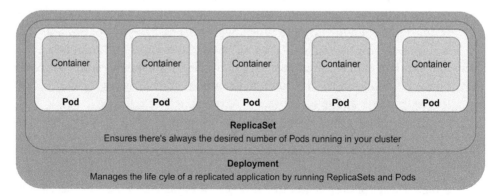

Figure 7.4 **A Deployment manages replicated applications with ReplicaSets and Pods in your cluster. A ReplicaSet ensures the desired number of Pods is always up and running. A Pod runs a containerized application.**

Deployments provide a convenient abstraction for us to declare what we want to achieve (the *desired state*), and we can let Kubernetes make it happen. You don't need to worry about how to achieve a specific result. Unlike imperative tools such as Ansible or Puppet, you can just tell Kubernetes what you want, and the orchestrator will figure out how to achieve the desired result and keep it consistent. That's what we call *declarative configuration*.

Kubernetes uses controllers that watch the system and compare the desired state with the actual state. When there is any difference between the two, it acts to make them match again. Deployments and ReplicaSets are controller objects, handling rollout, replication, and self-healing. For example, suppose you declare that you want three replicas of your Spring Boot application deployed. If one crashes, the associated ReplicaSet notices it and creates a new Pod to align the actual state with the desired one.

After packaging a Spring Boot application as an OCI image, all you need to do to run it in a Kubernetes cluster is define a Deployment object. You'll learn how in the next section.

7.2.3 Creating a Deployment for a Spring Boot application

There are a few options for creating and managing Kubernetes objects in a cluster. In chapter 2 we used the kubectl client directly, but that approach lacks version control and reproducibility. It's the same reason why we prefer Docker Compose over the Docker CLI.

In Kubernetes, the recommended approach is to describe an object's desired state in a *manifest* file, typically specified in YAML format. We use *declarative configuration*: we declare what we want instead of how to achieve it. In chapter 2 we *imperatively* used kubectl to create and delete objects, but when we work with manifests, we *apply* them to the cluster. Then Kubernetes will automatically reconcile the actual state in the cluster with the desired state in the manifest.

A Kubernetes manifest usually comprises four main sections, as shown in figure 7.5:

- `apiVersion` defines the versioned schema of the specific object representation. Core resources such as Pods or Services follow a versioned schema composed of only a version number (such as v1). Other resources like Deployments or ReplicaSet follow a versioned schema consisting of a group and a version number (for example, apps/v1). If in doubt about which version to use, you can refer to the Kubernetes documentation (https://kubernetes.io/docs) or use the `kubectl explain <object_name>` command to get more information about the object, including the API version to use.
- `kind` is the type of Kubernetes object you want to create, such as Pod, ReplicaSet, Deployment, or Service. You can use the `kubectl api-resources` command to list all the objects supported by the cluster.
- `metadata` provides details about the object you want to create, including the name and a set of labels (key/value pairs) used for categorization. For example,

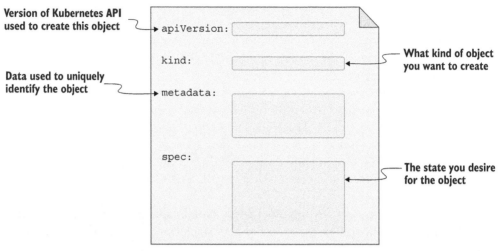

Figure 7.5   A Kubernetes manifest is typically composed of four main sections: `apiVersion`, `kind`, `metadata`, **and** `spec`.

you can instruct Kubernetes to replicate all the objects with a specific label attached.

- `spec` is a section specific to each object type and is used to declare the desired configuration.

Now that you're familiar with the main sections of a Kubernetes manifest, let's define one for a Deployment object that will run a Spring Boot application.

DEFINING A DEPLOYMENT MANIFEST WITH YAML

There are different strategies for organizing Kubernetes manifests. For the Catalog Service application, create a "k8s" folder in the project root (catalog-service). We will use it to store the manifests for the application.

> **NOTE**   If you haven't followed along with the examples implemented in the previous chapters, you can refer to the repository accompanying the book (https://github.com/ThomasVitale/cloud-native-spring-in-action) and use the project in Chapter07/07-begin/catalog-service as a starting point.

Let's start by creating a deployment.yml file inside the catalog-service/k8s folder. As you saw in figure 7.5, the first sections you need to include are `apiVersion`, `kind`, and `metadata`.

Listing 7.1 Initializing a Deployment manifest for Catalog Service

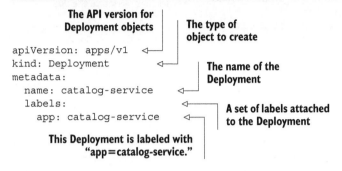

The API version for Deployment objects

The type of object to create

The name of the Deployment

A set of labels attached to the Deployment

This Deployment is labeled with "app=catalog-service."

```
apiVersion: apps/v1
kind: Deployment
metadata:
  name: catalog-service
  labels:
    app: catalog-service
```

NOTE The Kubernetes API can change over time. Make sure you always use the API supported by the version of Kubernetes you're running. If you have followed along so far, you shouldn't have this problem. But if it happens, kubectl will return a very descriptive error message telling you exactly what's wrong and how to fix it. You can also use the `kubectl explain <object_name>` command to check the API version supported by your Kubernetes installation for a given object.

The `spec` section of a Deployment manifest contains a `selector` part to define a strategy for identifying which objects should be scaled by a ReplicaSet (more on this later) and a `template` part describing the specifications for creating the desired Pod and containers.

Listing 7.2 The desired state for the Catalog Service deployment

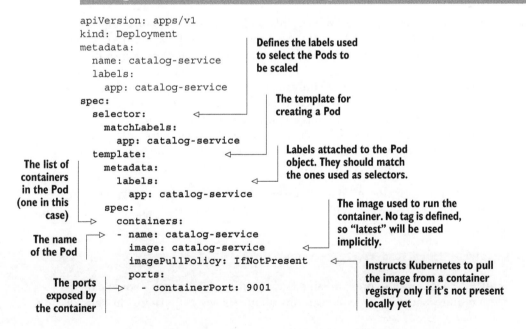

Defines the labels used to select the Pods to be scaled

The template for creating a Pod

Labels attached to the Pod object. They should match the ones used as selectors.

The list of containers in the Pod (one in this case)

The name of the Pod

The image used to run the container. No tag is defined, so "latest" will be used implicitly.

The ports exposed by the container

Instructs Kubernetes to pull the image from a container registry only if it's not present locally yet

```
apiVersion: apps/v1
kind: Deployment
metadata:
  name: catalog-service
  labels:
    app: catalog-service
spec:
  selector:
    matchLabels:
      app: catalog-service
  template:
    metadata:
      labels:
        app: catalog-service
    spec:
      containers:
        - name: catalog-service
          image: catalog-service
          imagePullPolicy: IfNotPresent
          ports:
            - containerPort: 9001
```

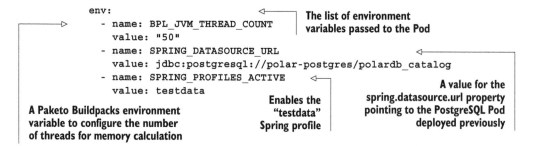

```
env:
  - name: BPL_JVM_THREAD_COUNT
    value: "50"
  - name: SPRING_DATASOURCE_URL
    value: jdbc:postgresql://polar-postgres/polardb_catalog
  - name: SPRING_PROFILES_ACTIVE
    value: testdata
```

The list of environment variables passed to the Pod

A value for the spring.datasource.url property pointing to the PostgreSQL Pod deployed previously

Enables the "testdata" Spring profile

A Paketo Buildpacks environment variable to configure the number of threads for memory calculation

The `containers` part should look familiar, since it resembles how you defined containers in the `services` section of a Docker Compose file. Like you did with Docker, you can use an environment variable to define the URL for the PostgreSQL instance the application should use. The hostname part of the URL (`polar-postgres`) is the name of the Service object that was used to expose the database and was created previously from the kubernetes/platform/development folder. You'll learn more about Services later in the chapter. For now, it's enough to know that `polar-postgres` is the name through which other objects in the cluster can communicate with the PostgreSQL instance.

In a production scenario, the image would be fetched from a container registry. During development, it's more convenient to work with local images. Let's build one for Catalog Service, as you learned in the previous chapter.

Open a Terminal window, navigate to the Catalog Service root folder (catalog-service), and build a new container image as follows:

```
$ ./gradlew bootBuildImage
```

> **TIP** If you're working on ARM64 machines (such as Apple Silicon computers), you can add the `--builder ghcr.io/thomasvitale/java-builder-arm64` argument to the previous command to use an experimental version of Paketo Buildpacks with ARM64 support. Be aware that it's experimental and not ready for production. For more information, you can refer to the documentation on GitHub: https://github.com/ThomasVitale/paketo-arm64. Without this workaround, until official support is added (https://github.com/paketo -buildpacks/stacks/issues/51), you can still use Buildpacks to build containers and run them via Docker Desktop on Apple Silicon computers, but the build process and application startup phase will be slower than usual.

By default, minikube doesn't have access to your local container images, so it will not find the image you have just built for Catalog Service. But don't worry: you can manually import it into your local cluster:

```
$ minikube image load catalog-service --profile polar
```

> **NOTE** YAML is an expressive language, but it can make your coding experience quite bad due to its constraints about spaces or perhaps the lack of

support from your editor. When a `kubectl` command involving a YAML file fails, verify that spaces and indentation are used correctly. For Kubernetes, you can install a plugin in your editor to support you while writing YAML manifests, ensuring that you always use the correct syntax, spaces, and indentation. You can find a few plugin options in the README.md file in the repository accompanying this book: https://github.com/ThomasVitale/cloud-native -spring-in-action.

Now that you have a Deployment manifest, let's move on and see how to apply it to your local Kubernetes cluster.

CREATING A DEPLOYMENT OBJECT FROM A MANIFEST

You can apply Kubernetes manifests to a cluster using the kubectl client. Open a Terminal window, navigate to your Catalog Service root folder (catalog-service), and run the following command:

```
$ kubectl apply -f k8s/deployment.yml
```

The command is processed by the Kubernetes Control Plane, which will create and maintain all the related objects in the cluster. You can verify which objects have been created with the following command:

```
$ kubectl get all -l app=catalog-service
```

```
NAME                                  READY   STATUS      RESTARTS   AGE
pod/catalog-service-68bc5659b8-k6dpb  1/1     Running     0          42s

NAME                                  READY   UP-TO-DATE  AVAILABLE  AGE
deployment.apps/catalog-service       1/1     1           1          42s

NAME                                            DESIRED  CURRENT  READY  AGE
replicaset.apps/catalog-service-68bc5659b8      1        1        1      42s
```

Since you used labels consistently in your Deployment manifest, you can use the label `app=catalog-service` to fetch all the Kubernetes objects related to the Catalog Service deployment. As you can see, the declaration in deployment.yml resulted in the creation of a Deployment, a ReplicaSet, and a Pod.

To verify that Catalog Service started up correctly, you can check the logs from its Deployment as follows:

```
$ kubectl logs deployment/catalog-service
```

NOTE You can monitor whether Pods have been created successfully by inspecting the STATUS column when you run `kubectl get pods`. Should a Pod fail to be deployed, check that column. Common error statuses are `ErrImagePull` or `ImagePullBackOff`. They happen when Kubernetes can't pull the image used by the Pod from the configured container registry. We're currently working with local images, so make sure you built and loaded a Catalog

Service container image into minikube. You can use the `kubectl describe pod <pod_name>` command to get more information about the error and `kubectl logs <pod_name>` to get the application logs from a specific Pod instance.

When deploying containers in a cloud environment like a Kubernetes cluster, you'll want to be sure it has enough resources to operate. In chapter 15, you'll learn how to assign CPU and memory resources to a container running in Kubernetes and how to configure memory for the JVM by applying the Java memory calculator provided by Cloud Native Buildpacks. For now, we'll rely on the default resource configuration.

So far, you have created a Deployment for a Spring Boot application and run it in your local Kubernetes cluster. But it's not possible to use it yet, since it's isolated inside the cluster. In the next section you'll learn how to expose your application to the outside world and how to use the service-discovery and load-balancing functionality provided by Kubernetes.

7.3   Service discovery and load balancing

We've talked about Pods and Deployments, so let's dig into Services a bit. You've got the Catalog Service application running as a Pod in your local Kubernetes cluster, but there are still unanswered questions. How can it interact with the PostgreSQL Pod running in the cluster? How does it know where to find it? How can you expose a Spring Boot application to be used by other Pods in the cluster? How can you expose it outside the cluster?

This section will answer those questions by introducing two important aspects of cloud native systems: service discovery and load balancing. I'll present the two main patterns available to implement them when working with Spring applications: client-side and server-side. Then you'll apply the latter approach, which is conveniently offered natively by Kubernetes through Service objects, meaning you don't have to change anything in your code to support it (unlike the client-side option). Finally, you'll learn how the communication between the Catalog Service Pod and the PostgreSQL Pod happens, and you'll expose the Catalog Service application as a network service.

7.3.1   Understanding service discovery and load balancing

When one service needs to communicate with another, it must be provided with information about where to find it, such as an IP address or a DNS name. Let's consider two applications: Alpha App and Beta App. Figure 7.6 shows how the communication between the two would happen if there were only one Beta App instance.

In the scenario illustrated in figure 7.6, we say that Alpha App is *upstream* and Beta App is *downstream*. Furthermore, Beta App is a *backing service* with respect to Alpha App. There's only one instance of Beta App running, so the DNS name gets resolved to its IP address.

Interprocess communication: no service discovery or load balancing

Figure 7.6   If there were only one Beta App instance, the interprocess communication between Alpha App and Beta App would be based on a DNS name resolving to the IP address of Beta App.

In the cloud, you'll probably want to have multiple instances of a service running, and each service instance will have its own IP address. Unlike physical machines or long-running virtual machines, a service instance will not live long in the cloud. Application instances are disposable—they can be removed or replaced for different reasons, such as when they are not responsive anymore. You can even enable the auto-scaling feature to automatically scale your application in and out, depending on the workload. Using IP addresses for interprocess communication in the cloud is not an option.

To overcome that issue, you might consider using DNS records, relying on a round-robin name resolution pointing to one of the IP addresses assigned to the replicas. Knowing the hostname, you can reach the backing service even if one of the IP addresses changes because the DNS server would be updated with the new ones. However, this approach is not the best fit for cloud environments because the topology changes too often. Some DNS implementations cache the results of name lookups even after they should have expired. Similarly, some applications cache DNS lookup responses for too long. Either way, there's a high chance of using a hostname/IP address resolution that is no longer valid.

Service discovery in cloud environments requires a different solution. First, we need to keep track of all the service instances running and store that information in a *service registry*. Whenever a new instance is created, an entry should be added to the registry. When it's shut down, it should be removed accordingly. The registry recognizes that multiple instances of the same application can be up and running. When an application needs to call a backing service, it performs a *lookup* in the registry to determine which IP address to contact. If multiple instances are available, a *load-balancing* strategy is applied to distribute the workload across them.

We distinguish between client-side and server-side service discovery, depending on where the problem is solved. Let's take a look at both options.

7.3.2   *Client-side service discovery and load balancing*

Client-side service discovery requires applications to register themselves with a service registry upon startup and unregister when shutting down. Whenever they need to call a backing service, they ask the service registry for an IP address. If multiple instances are available, the registry will return the list of IP addresses. The application will choose one of them, depending on a load-balancing strategy defined by the application itself. Figure 7.7 shows how that works.

Client-side service discovery and load balancing: model

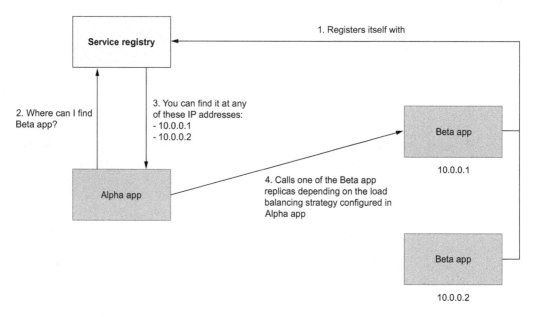

Figure 7.7   The interprocess communication between Alpha App and Beta App is based on the IP address of the specific instance to call, chosen from a list of IP addresses returned upon lookup in the service registry.

The Spring Cloud project offers a few options for adding client-side service discovery to your Spring applications. One of the popular choices is Spring Cloud Netflix Eureka, which wraps the Eureka service registry developed by Netflix. Alternatives are Spring Cloud Consul, Spring Cloud Zookeeper Discovery, and Spring Cloud Alibaba Nacos.

Besides managing a service registry explicitly, you'll also need to add the correct integration to all your applications. For each of the previously mentioned options, Spring Cloud provides a client library you can add to your Spring application so it can use the service registry with minimal effort. Finally, Spring Cloud Load Balancer can be used for client-side load balancing, which is the preferred choice over Spring Cloud Netflix Ribbon (no longer maintained).

All those libraries offered by Spring Cloud contributed to making it an excellent choice for building cloud native applications and implementing microservices architectures. A benefit of such a solution is that your applications have complete control over the load-balancing strategy. Suppose you need to implement patterns like *hedging*.

sending the same request to multiple instances to increase the chance one responds correctly within a specific time limit. Client service discovery can help you with that.

A drawback is that client service discovery assigns more responsibility to developers. If your system includes applications built using different languages and frameworks, you'll need to handle the client part of each of them in different ways. Also, it results in one more service to deploy and maintain (the service registry), unless you use PaaS solutions like Azure Spring Apps or VMware Tanzu Application Service, which provide it for you. Server-side discovery solutions solve these issues at the expense of fine-grained control in the application. Let's see how.

7.3.3   Server-side service discovery and load balancing

Server-side service discovery solutions move a lot of responsibility to the deployment platform, so that developers can focus on the business logic and rely on the platform to provide all the necessary functionality for service discovery and load balancing. Such solutions automatically register and deregister application instances and rely on a load-balancer component to route any incoming requests to one of the available instances according to a specific strategy. In this case, the application doesn't need to interact with the service registry, which is updated and managed by the platform. Figure 7.8 shows how that works.

Server-side service discovery and load balancing: model

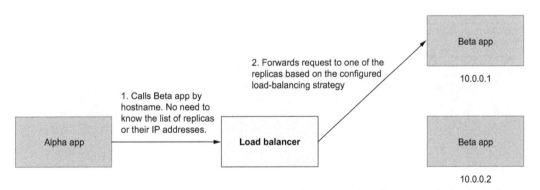

Figure 7.8   The interprocess communication between Alpha App and Beta App is based on a DNS name that gets resolved to one of the instance IP addresses by a load-balancer component. The service registration process is handled by the platform transparently.

The Kubernetes implementation of this service discovery pattern is based on Service objects. A *Service* is "an abstract way to expose an application running on a set of Pods as a network service" (https://kubernetes.io/docs/reference/glossary).

A Service object is an abstraction targeting a set of Pods (typically using labels) and defining the access policy. When an application needs to contact a Pod exposed by a

Service object, it can use the Service name instead of calling the Pod directly. That's what you did to let the Catalog Service application interact with the PostgreSQL instance (polar-postgres was the name of the Service exposing the PostgreSQL Pod). The Service name is then resolved to the IP address of the Service itself by a local DNS server running in the Kubernetes Control Plane.

> **NOTE** The IP address assigned to a Service is fixed for its lifetime. Therefore, the DNS resolution of a Service name doesn't change as often as it would with application instances.

After resolving the Service name to its IP address, Kubernetes relies on a proxy (called *kube-proxy*), which intercepts the connection to the Service object and forwards the request to one of the Pods targeted by the Service. The proxy knows all the replicas available and adopts a load-balancing strategy depending on the type of Service and the proxy configuration. There is no DNS resolution involved in this step, solving the problems I mentioned earlier. The service discovery implementation adopted by Kubernetes is shown in figure 7.9.

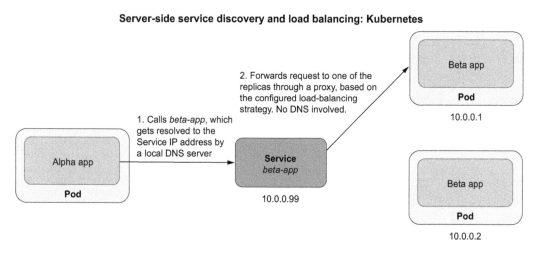

Figure 7.9 In Kubernetes, the interprocess communication between Alpha App and Beta App happens through a Service object. Any request arriving at the Service is intercepted by a proxy that forwards it to one of the replicas targeted by the Service based on a specific load-balancing strategy.

This solution is transparent to your Spring Boot applications. Unlike options like Spring Cloud Netflix Eureka, you get service discovery and load balancing out of the box in Kubernetes, without requiring any change to your code. That's why it's the preferred option when you use a Kubernetes-based platform to deploy your applications.

Service discovery and Spring Cloud Kubernetes

If you need to migrate existing applications that use one of the client-side service discovery options I mentioned in the previous section, you can use Spring Cloud Kubernetes to make the transition smoother. You can keep your existing service discovery and load-balancing logic in your application. However, instead of solutions like Spring Cloud Netflix Eureka, you can use the *Spring Cloud Kubernetes Discovery Server* for service registry. This can be a convenient way to migrate applications to Kubernetes without changing too much in your application code. For more information, refer to the project documentation: https://spring.io/projects/spring-cloud-kubernetes.

Unless what you're doing requires specific handling of service instances and load balancing in your applications, my recommendation is to migrate over time to using the native service discovery functionality offered by Kubernetes, aiming at removing infrastructural concerns from your applications.

With this general understanding of how service discovery and load balancing are implemented in Kubernetes, let's look at how we can define a Service to expose a Spring Boot application.

7.3.4 *Exposing Spring Boot applications with Kubernetes Services*

As you learned in the previous section, Kubernetes Services let you expose a set of Pods via an interface that other applications can call without knowing the details about the individual Pod instances. This model provides applications with transparent service-discovery and load-balancing functionality.

First of all, there are different types of Services, depending on which access policy you want to enforce for the application. The default and most common type is called *ClusterIP*, and it exposes a set of Pods to the cluster. This is what makes it possible for Pods to communicate with each other (for example, Catalog Service and PostgreSQL).

Four pieces of information characterize a ClusterIP Service:

- The `selector` label used to match all the Pods that should be targeted and exposed by the Service
- The network `protocol` used by the Service
- The `port` on which the Service is listening (we're going to use port 80 for all our application Services)
- The `targetPort`, which is the port exposed by the targeted Pods to which the Service will forward requests

Figure 7.10 shows the relationship between a ClusterIP Service and a set of target Pods running applications exposed on port 8080. The name of the Service must be a valid DNS name, since it will be used by other Pods as a hostname to access the targeted Pods.

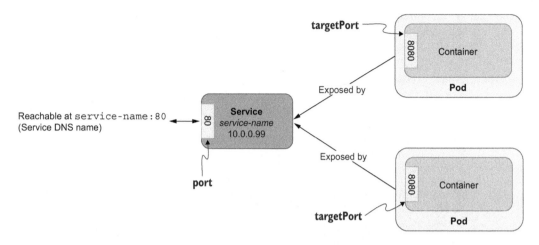

Figure 7.10   A ClusterIP service exposes a set of Pods to the network inside the cluster.

DEFINING A SERVICE MANIFEST WITH YAML

Let's see how we can define a manifest for a Service object to expose the Catalog Service application through the DNS name `catalog-service` and port `80`. Open the catalog-service/k8s folder you created earlier and add a new service.yml file.

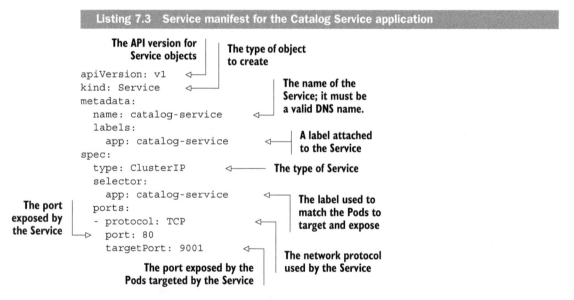

Listing 7.3   Service manifest for the Catalog Service application

CREATING A SERVICE OBJECT FROM A MANIFEST

You can apply a Service manifest as you did for Deployments. Open a Terminal window, navigate to your Catalog Service root folder (catalog-service), and run the following command:

```
$ kubectl apply -f k8s/service.yml
```

The command will be processed by the Kubernetes Control Plane, which will create and maintain the Service object in the cluster. You can verify the result with the following command:

```
$ kubectl get svc -l app=catalog-service

NAME              TYPE        CLUSTER-IP       EXTERNAL-IP   PORT(S)   AGE
catalog-service   ClusterIP   10.102.29.119    <none>        80/TCP    42s
```

Since it's of type ClusterIP, the Service makes it possible for other Pods within the cluster to communicate with the Catalog Service application, either using its IP address (called the cluster IP) or through its name. That will be useful for the applications you'll build in the next chapters, but what about us? How can we expose the application outside the cluster to test it?

For now, we'll rely on the port-forwarding feature offered by Kubernetes to expose an object (in this case, a Service) to a local machine. You did that already in chapter 2, so the command should look familiar:

```
$ kubectl port-forward service/catalog-service 9001:80
Forwarding from 127.0.0.1:9001 -> 9001
Forwarding from [::1]:9001 -> 9001
```

You can finally call the application from localhost on port 9001, and all requests will be forwarded to the Service object and ultimately to the Catalog Service Pod. Try visiting http://localhost:9001 from your browser to see the welcome message, or http://localhost:9001/books to browse the books available in the catalog.

> **TIP** The process started by the kubectl port-forward command will keep running until you explicitly stop it with Ctrl-C. Until then, you'll need to open another Terminal window if you want to run CLI commands.

Figure 7.11 illustrates how the communication works between your computer, Catalog Service, and PostgreSQL.

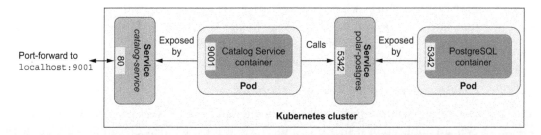

Figure 7.11 The Catalog Service application is exposed to your local machine through port forwarding. Both Catalog Service and PostgreSQL are exposed to the inside of the cluster through the cluster-local hostname, IP address, and port assigned to the Service objects.

So far we've been working with only one instance of Catalog Service, but we can take advantage of Kubernetes and scale it out. The following section will cover how to scale Spring Boot applications and address aspects such as fast startup and graceful shutdown, which are essential for cloud native applications.

> **NOTE** Imagine running all those commands every time you change something in your application, and you want to test it locally. It doesn't look very appealing, does it? Don't worry! In section 7.5 I'll show you how to set up a local Kubernetes development workflow to automate all those operations.

7.4 Scalability and disposability

Deploying multiple instances of the same application helps in achieving high availability. When the workload is high, it can be distributed across different replicas. When an instance enters a faulty state and can't process requests anymore, it can be deleted and a new one created. This continuous and dynamic scaling of application instances requires stateless and disposable applications, as per the 15-Factor methodology.

This section will show you what it means for an application to be disposable, how to enable graceful shutdown, and how to scale an application in Kubernetes.

7.4.1 Ensuring disposability: Fast startup

Traditional applications deployed on application servers take quite some time to start. It's not rare for them to take several minutes before they're ready to accept connections. On the other hand, cloud native applications should be optimized for starting quickly, taking a few seconds rather than minutes to become ready. Spring Boot is already optimized for fast startup, and each new version is shipped with more improvements.

Fast startup is relevant in a cloud environment because applications are disposable and are frequently created, destroyed, and scaled. The quicker the startup, the sooner a new application instance is ready to accept connections.

Standard applications, like microservices, are good with a startup time in the range of a few seconds. On the other hand, serverless applications usually require a faster startup phase in the range of milliseconds rather than seconds. Spring Boot covers both needs, but the second use case might require a bit of additional configuration.

In chapter 16, you'll learn about serverless applications with Spring Cloud Function, and I'll show you how to package them as native images using Spring Native and GraalVM. The result will be an application with almost instant startup time, reduced resource consumption, and reduced image size.

7.4.2 Ensuring disposability: Graceful shutdown

Having applications start quickly is not enough to address our scalability needs. Whenever an application instance is shut down, it must happen gracefully without clients experiencing downtime or errors. Gracefully shutting down means the application stops accepting new requests, completes all those still in progress, and closes any open resources, like database connections.

All the embedded servers available in Spring Boot support a graceful shutdown mode, but in slightly different ways. Tomcat, Jetty, and Netty stop accepting new requests entirely when the shutdown signal is received. On the other hand, Undertow keeps accepting new requests but immediately replies with an HTTP 503 response.

By default, Spring Boot stops the server immediately after receiving a termination signal (SIGTERM). You can switch to a graceful mode by configuring the server.shut-down property. You can also configure the *grace period*, which is how long the application can spend processing all the pending requests. After the grace period expires, the application is terminated even if there are still pending requests. By default, the grace period is 30 seconds. You can change it through the spring.lifecycle.time-out-per-shutdown-phase property.

Let's configure graceful shutdown for Catalog Service. We could do that via environment variables or set it as a default configuration. We'll go with the second option. Open the application.yml file located in the catalog-service/src/main/resources folder, and update the configuration as follows:

```
server:
  port: 9001
  shutdown: graceful          ◁──┐  Enable graceful
  tomcat:                         │  shutdown
    connection-timeout: 2s
    keep-alive-timeout: 15s
    threads:
      max: 50
      min-spare: 5

spring:
  application:
    name: catalog-service
  lifecycle:                                        ┐ Defines a 15 s
    timeout-per-shutdown-phase: 15s   ◁──┘  grace period
...
```

Since we've modified the application source code, we need to build a new container image and load it into minikube. That's not very efficient, is it? Later in the chapter, I'll show you a better way. For now, follow the procedure I described earlier to package Catalog Service as a container image (./gradlew bootBuildImage) and load it into the Kubernetes cluster we are using for Polar Bookshop (minikube image load catalog -service --profile polar).

After enabling application support for graceful shutdown, you need to update the Deployment manifest accordingly. When a Pod has to be terminated (for example, during a downscaling process or as part of an upgrade), Kubernetes sends a SIGTERM signal to it. Spring Boot will intercept that signal and start shutting down gracefully. By default, Kubernetes waits for a grace period of 30 seconds. If the Pod is not terminated after that period, Kubernetes sends a SIGKILL signal to force the Pod's termination. Since the Spring Boot grace period is lower than the Kubernetes one, the application is in control of when it will terminate.

When it sends the SIGTERM signal to a Pod, Kubernetes will also inform its own components to stop forwarding requests to the terminating Pod. Since Kubernetes is a distributed system, and the two actions happen in parallel, there is a short time window when the terminating Pod might still receive requests, even if it has already started the graceful shutdown procedure. When that happens, those new requests will be rejected, resulting in errors in the clients. Our goal was to make the shutdown procedure transparent to the clients, so that scenario is unacceptable.

The recommended solution is to delay sending the SIGTERM signal to the Pod so that Kubernetes has enough time to spread the news across the cluster. By doing so, all Kubernetes components will already know not to send new requests to the Pod when it starts the graceful shutdown procedure. Technically, the delay can be configured through a preStop hook. Let's see how we can update the Deployment manifest for Catalog Service to support a transparent and graceful shutdown.

Open the deployment.yml file located in catalog-service/k8s, and add a preStop hook to delay the SIGTERM signal by 5 seconds.

Listing 7.4   Configuring a delay in Kubernetes before the shutdown starts

```yaml
apiVersion: apps/v1
kind: Deployment
metadata:
  name: catalog-service
  labels:
    app: catalog-service
spec:
  ...
  template:
    metadata:
      labels:
        app: catalog-service
    spec:
      containers:
        - name: catalog-service
          image: catalog-service
          imagePullPolicy: IfNotPresent        ┐ Makes Kubernetes wait 5
          lifecycle:                            │ seconds before sending the
            preStop:            ◀───────────────┘ SIGTERM signal to the Pod
              exec:
                command: [ "sh", "-c", "sleep 5" ]
        ...
```

Finally, apply the updated version of the Deployment object with `kubectl apply -f k8s/deployment.yml`. Kubernetes will reconcile the new desired state and replace the existing Pod with a new one for which graceful shutdown is fully configured.

NOTE   When a Pod contains multiple containers, the SIGTERM signal is sent to all of them in parallel. Kubernetes will wait up to 30 seconds. If any of the containers in the Pod are not terminated yet, it will shut them down forcefully.

Now that we've configured the graceful shutdown behavior for Catalog Service, let's look at how to scale it in a Kubernetes cluster.

7.4.3 Scaling Spring Boot applications

Scalability is one of the main properties of a cloud native application, as you learned in chapter 1. To be scalable, applications should be disposable and stateless, as per the 15-Factor methodology.

We handled disposability in the previous section, and Catalog Service is already a stateless application. It has no state but relies on a stateful service (the PostgreSQL database) to permanently store the data about books. We scale applications in and out, and if they weren't stateless, we would lose the state every time an instance is shut down. The general idea is to keep the applications stateless and rely on data services for storing the state, just like we do in Catalog Service.

In Kubernetes, replication is handled at the Pod level by a ReplicaSet object. As you saw earlier, Deployment objects are already configured to use ReplicaSets. All you need to do is specify how many replicas you want to be deployed. You can do that in the Deployment manifest.

Open the deployment.yml file located in catalog-service/k8s, and define how many replicas of the Pod running Catalog Service you want. Let's go with two.

> **Listing 7.5 Configuring number of replicas for the Catalog Service Pod**

```
apiVersion: apps/v1
kind: Deployment
metadata:
  name: catalog-service
  labels:
    app: catalog-service        ┐ How many Pod
spec:                            │ replicas should
  replicas: 2      ◁─────────────┘ be deployed
  selector:
    matchLabels:
      app: catalog-service
  ...
```

The replication is controlled using labels. In listing 7.5, the configuration instructs Kubernetes to manage all Pods with the label `app=catalog-service` so that there are always two replicas running.

Let's check it out. Open a Terminal window, navigate to the catalog-service folder, and apply the updated version of the Deployment resource:

```
$ kubectl apply -f k8s/deployment.yml
```

Kubernetes will realize that the actual state (one replica) and the desired state (two replicas) don't match, and it will immediately deploy a new replica of Catalog Service. You can verify the result with the following command:

```
$ kubectl get pods -l app=catalog-service

NAME                                  READY   STATUS     RESTARTS    AGE
catalog-service-68bc5659b8-fkpcv      1/1     Running    0           2s
catalog-service-68bc5659b8-kmwm5      1/1     Running    0           3m94s
```

In the "age" column, you can tell which Pod is the one that has just been deployed to achieve a state with two replicas.

What happens if one of them terminates? Let's find out. Pick one of the two Pod replicas and copy its name. For example, I might use the Pod named `catalog-service-68bc5659b8-kmwm5`. Then, from a Terminal window, delete that Pod with the following command:

```
$ kubectl delete pod <pod-name>
```

The Deployment manifest declares two replicas as the desired state. Since there is now only one, Kubernetes will immediately step up to ensure the actual state and the desired state are aligned. If you inspect the Pods again with `kubectl get pods -l app=catalog-service`, you will still see two Pods, but one of them has just been created to replace the deleted Pod. You can identify it by checking its age:

```
$ kubectl get pods -l app=catalog-service

NAME                                  READY   STATUS     RESTARTS    AGE
catalog-service-68bc5659b8-fkpcv      1/1     Running    0           42s
catalog-service-68bc5659b8-wqchr      1/1     Running    0           3s
```

Under the hood, a ReplicaSet object keeps checking the number of replicas deployed and ensures they are always in the desired state. That's the basic functionality on top of which you can configure an autoscaler to dynamically increase or decrease the number of Pods, depending on the workload and without having to update the manifest every time.

Before moving on to the next section, make sure you change the number of replicas back to one and clean up your cluster by removing all the resources you have created so far. First, open a Terminal window, navigate to the catalog-service folder where you defined the Kubernetes manifests, and delete all the objects created for Catalog Service:

```
$ kubectl delete -f k8s
```

Finally, go to your `polar-deployment` repository, navigate to the kubernetes/platform/development folder, and delete the PostgreSQL installation:

```
$ kubectl delete -f services
```

7.5 Local Kubernetes development with Tilt

In the previous sections, you learned about the basic Kubernetes concepts and worked with the fundamental objects used to deploy applications to a cluster: Pods, Replica-Sets, Deployments, and Services. After defining the Deployment and Service manifests, you probably don't want to keep rebuilding container images manually and using the kubectl client to update the Pods whenever you make a change. Luckily for you, you don't have to.

This section will show you how to set up a local Kubernetes development workflow to automate steps like building images and applying manifests to a Kubernetes cluster. It's part of implementing the *inner development loop* of working with a Kubernetes platform. Tilt takes care of many infrastructural concerns and lets you focus more on the business logic of your applications. I'll also introduce Octant, which will help you visualize and manage your Kubernetes objects through a convenient GUI.

7.5.1 Inner development loop with Tilt

Tilt (https://tilt.dev) aims at providing a good developer experience when working on Kubernetes. It's an open source tool that offers features for building, deploying, and managing containerized workloads in your local environment. We'll use some of its basic features to automate a development workflow for a specific application, but Tilt can also help you orchestrate the deployment of multiple applications and services in a centralized way. You can find information about how to install it in section A.4 of appendix A.

Our goal will be to design a workflow that will automate the following steps:

- Package a Spring Boot application as a container image using Cloud Native Buildpacks.
- Upload the image to a Kubernetes cluster (in our case, the one created with minikube).
- Apply all the Kubernetes objects declared in the YAML manifests.
- Enable the port-forwarding functionality to access applications from your local computer.
- Give you easy access to the logs from the applications running on the cluster.

Before configuring Tilt, make sure you have a PostgreSQL instance up and running in your local Kubernetes cluster. Open a Terminal window, navigate to the kubernetes/platform/development folder in your `polar-deployment` repository, and run the following command to deploy PostgreSQL:

```
$ kubectl apply -f services
```

Let's now see how to configure Tilt to establish that automated development workflow.

Tilt can be configured via a *Tiltfile*, an extensible configuration file written in Starlark (a simplified Python dialect). Go to your Catalog Service project (`catalog-service`) and create a file named "Tiltfile" (with no extension) in the root folder. The file will contain three main configurations:

- How to build a container image (Cloud Native Buildpacks)
- How to deploy the application (Kubernetes YAML manifests)
- How to access the application (port forwarding)

Listing 7.6   Tilt configuration for Catalog Service (Tiltfile)

```
# Build
custom_build(
    # Name of the container image
    ref = 'catalog-service',
    # Command to build the container image
    command = './gradlew bootBuildImage --imageName $EXPECTED_REF',
    # Files to watch that trigger a new build
    deps = ['build.gradle', 'src']
)

# Deploy
k8s_yaml(['k8s/deployment.yml', 'k8s/service.yml'])

# Manage
k8s_resource('catalog-service', port_forwards=['9001'])
```

> **TIP** If you're working on ARM64 machines (such as Apple Silicon computers), you can add the `--builder ghcr.io/thomasvitale/java-builder-arm64` argument to the `./gradlew bootBuildImage --imageName $EXPECTED_REF` command to use an experimental version of Paketo Buildpacks with ARM64 support. Be aware that it's experimental and not ready for production. For more information, you can refer to the documentation on GitHub: https://github.com/ThomasVitale/paketo-arm64.

The Tiltfile configures Tilt to use the same approach we used throughout the chapter for building, loading, deploying, and publishing applications on the local Kubernetes cluster. The main difference? It's all automated now! Let's give it a try.

Open a Terminal window, navigate to the root folder of your Catalog Service project, and run the following command to start Tilt:

```
$ tilt up
Tilt started on http://localhost:10350/
```

The process started by the `tilt up` command will keep running until you explicitly stop it with Ctrl-C. One of the useful features provided by Tilt is a convenient GUI where you can keep track of the services managed by Tilt, check application logs, and trigger updates manually. Go to the URL where Tilt started its services (by default, it should be http://localhost:10350), and monitor the process that Tilt follows to build and deploy Catalog Service (figure 7.12). The first time it can take one or two minutes

Figure 7.12 Tilt provides a convenient GUI where you can monitor and manage applications.

because the Buildpacks libraries need to be downloaded. The subsequent times it will be much faster.

Besides building and deploying the application, Tilt has also activated port forwarding to your local machine on port `9001`. Go ahead and verify that the application is working correctly:

```
$ http :9001/books
```

Tilt will keep the application in sync with the source code. Whenever you make any change to the application, Tilt will trigger an *update* operation to build and deploy a new container image. All of that happens automatically and continuously.

> **NOTE** Rebuilding the whole container image every time you change something in your code is not very efficient. You can configure Tilt to synchronize only the changed files and upload them into the current image. To achieve that, you can rely on the features offered by Spring Boot DevTools (https://mng.bz/nY8v) and Paketo Buildpacks (https://mng.bz/vo5x).

When you're done testing the application, stop the Tilt process in the Catalog Service project and run the following command to undeploy the application:

```
$ tilt down
```

7.5.2   *Visualizing your Kubernetes workloads with Octant*

When you start deploying multiple applications to a Kubernetes cluster, it can become challenging to manage all the related Kubernetes objects or investigate failures when they happen. There are different solutions for visualizing and managing Kubernetes workloads. This section will cover Octant (https://octant.dev), an "open source developer-centric web interface for Kubernetes that lets you inspect a Kubernetes cluster and its applications." You can find information about how to install it in section A.4 of appendix A.

I expect you still have the local Kubernetes cluster you used in the previous section up and running and PostgreSQL deployed. You can also deploy Catalog Service by going into the project's root folder and running tilt up. Then, open a new Terminal window and run the following command:

```
$ octant
```

This command will open the Octant Dashboard in your browser (usually at http:// localhost:7777). Figure 7.13 shows the Dashboard. The Overview page provides a picture of all the Kubernetes objects running in the cluster. If you followed along, you should have PostgreSQL and Catalog Service running in the cluster.

Figure 7.13   Octant offers a web interface for inspecting a Kubernetes cluster and its workloads.

From the Overview page you can expand the objects to get more details. For example, if you click the item corresponding to the Catalog Service Pod, you'll get access to information about the object, as shown in figure 7.14. You can also perform several

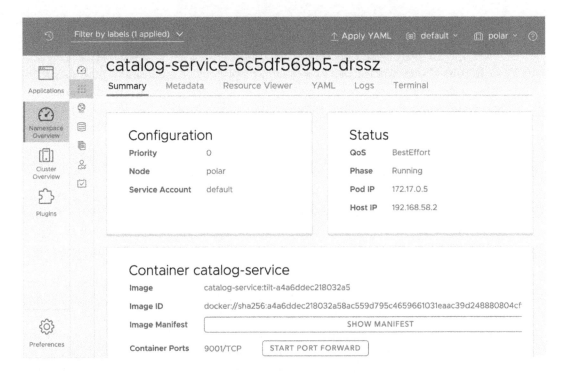

Figure 7.14   Octant lets you access Pod information easily, check their logs, and enable a port forward.

operations like enabling port forwarding, reading the logs, modifying the Pod's manifest, and investigating failures.

Take your time exploring the many features provided by Octant. It's a convenient tool that you can use to inspect and troubleshoot a local Kubernetes cluster or a remote one. We'll also use Octant to examine the remote production cluster where we'll deploy the Polar Bookshop application. For now, close Octant by stopping its process with Ctrl-C.

When you're done, you can stop the Tilt process in the Catalog Service project and run `tilt down` to undeploy the application. Then go to your `polar-deployment` repository, navigate to the kubernetes/platform/development folder, and delete the PostgreSQL installation with `kubectl delete -f services`. Finally, stop the cluster as follows:

```
$ minikube stop --profile polar
```

7.6   *Deployment pipeline: Validate Kubernetes manifests*

Chapter 3 introduced the concept of a deployment pipeline and its importance in the continuous delivery approach for delivering software quickly, reliably, and safely. So far we've automated the first part of a deployment pipeline: the commit stage. After a developer commits new code to the mainline, this stage goes through build, unit tests, integration tests, static code analysis, and packaging. At the end of this stage, an executable application artifact is published to an artifact repository. That is a *release candidate*.

In this chapter, you learned how to deploy Spring Boot applications on Kubernetes using a declarative approach based on *resource manifests*. They are fundamental to a successful deployment of the release candidate on Kubernetes, so we should guarantee their correctness. This section will show you how to validate Kubernetes manifests as part of the commit stage.

7.6.1   *Validating Kubernetes manifests in the commit stage*

Throughout this chapter, we've worked with resource manifests for creating Deployments and Services in a Kubernetes cluster. A *manifest* is "a specification of a Kubernetes API object in JSON or YAML format." It specifies "the desired state of an object that Kubernetes will maintain when you apply the manifest" (https://kubernetes.io/docs/reference/glossary).

Since a manifest specifies the desired state of an object, we should ensure that our specification complies with the API exposed by Kubernetes. It's a good idea to automate this validation in the commit stage of a deployment pipeline to get fast feedback in case of errors (rather than waiting until the acceptance stage, where we need to use those manifests to deploy the application in a Kubernetes cluster). Figure 7.15 illustrates the main steps of the commit stage after including the validation of Kubernetes manifests.

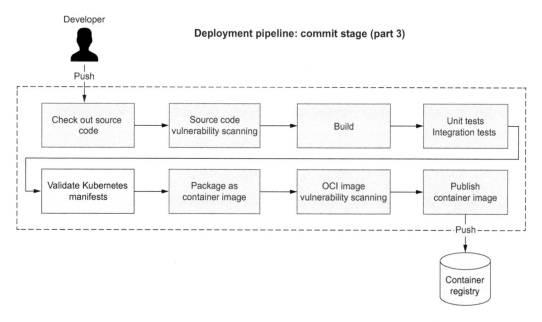

Figure 7.15   When Kubernetes manifests are included in the application repository, a new step in the commit stage is included to validate them.

There are several ways of validating Kubernetes manifests against the Kubernetes API. We'll use Kubeval (www.kubeval.com), an open source tool. You can find information about how to install it in section A.4 of appendix A.

Let's see how it works. Open a Terminal window and navigate to the root folder of your Catalog Service project (catalog-service). Then use the `kubeval` command to validate the Kubernetes manifests within the k8s directory (`-d k8s`). The `--strict` flag disallows adding additional properties not defined in the object schema:

```
$ kubeval --strict -d k8s

PASS - k8s/deployment.yml contains a valid Deployment (catalog-service)
PASS - k8s/service.yml contains a valid Service (catalog-service)
```

In the next section, you'll see how to use Kubeval in the commit stage workflow we implemented with GitHub Actions.

7.6.2 Automating Kubernetes manifests validation with GitHub Actions

GitHub Actions is the workflow engine we used to implement the commit stage for the Catalog Service's deployment pipeline. Let's extend it to include the Kubernetes manifest validation step, as illustrated in figure 7.15.

Go to your Catalog Service project (catalog-service), and open the commit-stage.yml file within the .github/workflows folder. To implement the validation step, we'll rely on an action built by Stefan Prodan. He's the maintainer of FluxCD, a CNCF-incubating project providing a continuous deployment solution on Kubernetes based on the GitOps principles. The action lets you install specific versions of useful Kubernetes-related tools. We'll configure the action to install kubectl and Kubeval.

> **Listing 7.7 Validating the Kubernetes manifests for Catalog Service**

```
name: Commit Stage
on: push
...

jobs:
  build:
    name: Build and Test
    ...
    steps:
      ...
      - name: Validate Kubernetes manifests       ◁── An action capable of
        uses: stefanprodan/kube-tools@v1                installing useful tools to
        with:                                           work with Kubernetes
          kubectl: 1.24.3          ◁── Includes the Kubernetes
          kubeval: 0.16.1              CLI in the installation
          command: |
            kubeval --strict -d k8s   ◁── Uses Kubeval to validate
      package:                            the Kubernetes manifests
      ...                                 in the k8s folder
```

Includes Kubeval in the installation

After updating the commit-stage.yml file with the additional validation step, you can commit and push your changes to your `catalog-service` repository on GitHub and verify that the commit stage workflow completes successfully, meaning what you included in the manifests is compliant with the Kubernetes API.

Polar Labs

Feel free to apply what you learned in this chapter to Config Service and prepare the application for deployment.

1 Configure graceful shutdown and a grace period for the application.

2 Write the Deployment and Service manifests for deploying Config Service to a Kubernetes cluster.

3 Update the commit stage of the deployment pipeline for Config Service to validate the Kubernetes manifests.

4 Configure the Catalog Service Deployment with the Config Service URL via the `SPRING_CLOUD_CONFIG_URI` environment variable, relying on the Kubernetes native service discovery feature.

5 Configure Tilt to automate the Config Service deployment to your local Kubernetes cluster bootstrapped with minikube.

When you're done, try deploying all the components of the Polar Bookshop system we've built so far, and check their status in Octant. You can refer to the Chapter07/07-end folder in the code repository accompanying the book to check the final result (https://github.com/ThomasVitale/cloud-native-spring-in-action).

Congratulations!

Summary

- Docker works fine when running single-instance containers on a single machine. When your system needs properties like scalability and resilience, you can use Kubernetes.

- Kubernetes provides all the features for scaling containers across a cluster of machines, ensuring resilience both when a container fails and when a machine goes down.

- Pods are the smallest deployable units in Kubernetes.

- Rather than creating Pods directly, you can use a Deployment object to declare the desired state for your applications, and Kubernetes will ensure it matches the actual state. That includes having the desired number of replicas up and running at any time.

- The cloud is a dynamic environment, and the topology keeps changing. Service discovery and load balancing let you dynamically establish interactions between services, managed either on the client side (for example, using Spring Cloud Netflix Eureka) or on the server side (for example, using Kubernetes).

- Kubernetes provides a native service-discovery and load-balancing feature that you can use through the Service objects.
- Each Service name can be used as a DNS name. Kubernetes will resolve the name to the Service IP address and, ultimately, forward the request to one of the instances available.
- You can deploy Spring Boot applications to a Kubernetes cluster by defining two YAML manifests: one for the Deployment object and one for the Service object.
- The kubectl client lets you create objects from a file with the command `kubectl apply -f <your-file.yml>`.
- Cloud native applications should be disposable (fast startup and graceful shutdown) and stateless (rely on data services for storing the state).
- Graceful shutdown is supported both by Spring Boot and Kubernetes and is an essential aspect of scalable applications.
- Kubernetes uses ReplicaSet controllers to replicate your application Pods and keep them running.
- Tilt is a tool that automates your local development workflow with Kubernetes: you work on the application while Tilt takes care of building the image, deploying it to your local Kubernetes cluster, and keeping it up-to-date whenever you change something in the code.
- You can start Tilt for your project with `tilt up`.
- The Octant dashboard lets you visualize your Kubernetes workloads.
- Octant is a convenient tool that you can use not only for inspecting and troubleshooting a local Kubernetes cluster but also for a remote one.
- Kubeval is a convenient tool you can use to validate Kubernetes manifests. It's particularly useful when it's included in your deployment pipeline.

Part 3

Cloud native distributed systems

Cloud native applications are highly distributed and scalable systems by definition. So far, we have worked with a single application. It's time to broaden our horizons and address patterns, challenges, and technologies for building distributed systems in the cloud. Part 3 covers fundamental properties of cloud native systems, such as resilience, scalability, and security. It also describes reactive programming and event-driven architectures.

Chapter 8 introduces reactive programming and the main features of the Spring reactive stack, including Project Reactor, Spring WebFlux, and Spring Data R2DBC. Chapter 9 covers the API gateway pattern and how to build edge services with Spring Cloud Gateway. You'll learn how to build resilient applications with Reactor, Spring Cloud, and Resilience4J, using patterns like retries, timeouts, fallbacks, circuit breakers, and rate limiters. Chapter 10 describes event-driven architectures and teaches you how to implement them with Spring Cloud Function, Spring Cloud Stream, and RabbitMQ. Security is a critical concern for all cloud native applications, and chapters 11 and 12 are all about security. You'll learn how to implement authentication and authorization using Spring Security, OAuth2, and OpenID Connect. You'll also see a few techniques for protecting APIs and data, including when single-page applications are part of the system.

Reactive Spring: Resilience and scalability

This chapter covers

- Understanding reactive programming with Reactor and Spring
- Building reactive servers with Spring WebFlux and Spring Data R2DBC
- Building reactive clients with WebClient
- Improving resilience for applications with Reactor
- Testing reactive applications with Spring and Testcontainers

Polarsophia, the organization behind the Polar Bookshop business, is very happy with the progress of its new software product. Its mission is to spread knowledge and awareness about the North Pole and the Arctic, and making its book catalog available worldwide is an essential part of this.

The Catalog Service application you built so far is a good starting point. It fulfills the requirements of browsing and managing books, and it does that while following cloud native patterns and practices. It's self-contained and stateless. It uses a database as a backing service to store the state. It can be configured externally through environment variables or a configuration server. It respects environment parity. It's verified through the automated execution of tests as part of a deployment pipeline, following continuous delivery practices. For maximum portability, it's also containerized and can be deployed to a Kubernetes cluster using native functionality like service discovery, load balancing, and replication.

Another essential feature of the system is the possibility of purchasing books. In this chapter, you will start working on the Order Service application. This new component will interact not only with a database but also with Catalog Service. When you have applications extensively relying on I/O operations such as database calls or interactions with other services like HTTP request/response communications, the thread-per-request model used in Catalog Service begins to expose its technical limits.

In the thread-per-request model, each request is bound to a thread exclusively allocated to its processing. If database or service calls are part of the processing, the thread will send out a request and then block, waiting for a response. During idle time, the resources allocated for that thread are wasted, since they cannot be used for anything else. The reactive programming paradigm solves this problem and improves scalability, resilience, and cost-effectiveness for all I/O-bound applications.

Reactive applications operate asynchronously and in a non-blocking way, meaning that computational resources are used more effectively. That's a huge advantage in the cloud, since you pay for what you use. When a thread sends a call to a backing service, it will not wait idle, but it will move on to executing other operations. This eliminates the linear dependency between the number of threads and the number of concurrent requests, leading to more scalable applications. With the same amount of computational resources, reactive applications can serve more users than their non-reactive counterparts.

Cloud native applications are highly distributed systems deployed in a dynamic environment where change is a constant and failures can and will happen. What if the service is not available? What happens if the request gets lost on its way to the target service? What if the response gets lost on its way back to the caller? Can we guarantee high availability in this context?

Resilience is one of the goals for moving to the cloud and one of the properties characterizing cloud native applications. Our systems should be resilient to failures and stable enough to ensure a certain service level to their users. The integration points between services over a network are among the most critical areas for achieving a stable and resilient system for production. It's so important that Michael T. Nygard spends a large part of his book *Release It! Design and Deploy Production-Ready Software* (Pragmatic Bookshelf, 2018) on the subject.

This chapter will focus on building resilient, scalable, and efficient applications for the cloud using the reactive paradigm. First I'll introduce the event loop model and the main features of Reactive Streams, Project Reactor, and the Spring reactive stack. Then you'll build a reactive Order Service application using Spring WebFlux and Spring Data R2DBC.

Order Service will interact with Catalog Service to check the availability of books and their details, so you'll see how to implement a reactive REST client using Spring

WebClient. The integration point between the two services is a critical area that needs extra care to achieve robustness and fault tolerance. Relying on the Reactor project, you'll adopt stability patterns like retries, timeouts, and failovers. Finally, you'll write autotests to verify the behavior of a reactive application using Spring Boot and Testcontainers.

> **NOTE** The source code for the examples in this chapter is available in the Chapter08/08-begin and Chapter08/08-end folders, containing the initial and final states of the project (https://github.com/ThomasVitale/cloud-native -spring-in-action).

8.1 Asynchronous and non-blocking architectures with Reactor and Spring

The *Reactive Manifesto* (www.reactivemanifesto.org) describes a reactive system as responsive, resilient, elastic, and message-driven. Its mission to build loosely coupled, scalable, resilient, and cost-effective applications is fully compatible with our definition of cloud native. The new part is achieving that goal by using an asynchronous and non-blocking communication paradigm based on message-passing.

Before diving into building reactive applications in Spring, we'll explore the basics of reactive programming, why it matters for cloud native applications, and how it differs from imperative programming. I'll introduce the event loop model, which overcomes the thread-per-request model's shortcomings. Then you'll learn the essential concepts of the Reactive Streams specification implemented by Project Reactor and the Spring reactive stack.

8.1.1 From thread-per-request to event loop

As you saw in chapter 3, non-reactive applications allocate a thread per request. Until a response is returned, the thread will not be used for anything. That is the *thread-per-request* model. When the request handling involves intensive operations like I/O, the thread will block until those operations are completed. For example, if a database read is required, the thread will wait until data is returned from the database. During the waiting time, the resources allocated to the handling thread are not used efficiently. If you want to support more concurrent users, you'll have to ensure you have enough threads and resources available. In the end, this paradigm sets constraints on the application's scalability and doesn't use computational resources in the most efficient way possible. Figure 8.1 shows how it works.

Reactive applications are more scalable and efficient by design. Handling requests in a reactive application doesn't involve allocating a given thread exclusively—requests are fulfilled asynchronously based on events. For example, if a database read is required, the thread handling that part of the flow will not wait until data is returned from the database. Instead, a callback is registered, and whenever the information is ready, a notification is sent, and one of the available threads will execute the callback. During

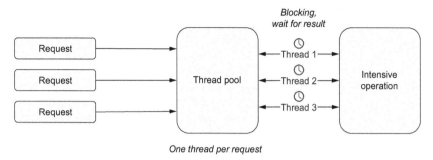

The thread-per-request model

Figure 8.1   **In the thread-per-request model, each request is handled by a thread dedicated exclusively to its handling.**

that time, the thread that requested the data can be used to process other requests rather than waiting idle.

This paradigm, called *event loop*, doesn't set hard constraints on the application's scalability. It actually makes it easier to scale, since an increase in the number of concurrent requests does not strictly depend on the number of threads. As a matter of fact, a default configuration for reactive applications in Spring is to use only one thread per CPU core. With the non-blocking I/O capability and a communication paradigm based on events, reactive applications allow for more efficient utilization of computational resources. Figure 8.2 shows how it works.

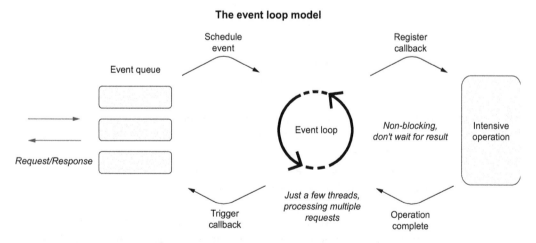

The event loop model

Figure 8.2   **In the event loop model, requests are handled by threads that don't block while waiting for an intensive operation, allowing them to process other requests in the meantime.**

I wanted to briefly mention the difference between those two paradigms because it helps explain the reasoning behind reactive programming. However, you don't need to know the details of these paradigms' inner mechanics since we won't have to work at such a low level or implement an event loop. Instead, we're going to rely on convenient higher-level abstractions that will let us focus on the business logic of our applications rather than spending time handling the processing at the thread level.

Scale and cost optimization are two critical reasons for moving to the cloud, so the reactive paradigm perfectly fits cloud native applications. Scaling applications to support a workload increase becomes less demanding. By using resources more efficiently, you can save money on the computational resources offered by a cloud provider. Another reason for moving to the cloud is resilience, and reactive applications also help with that.

One of the essential features of reactive applications is that they provide non-blocking backpressure (also called *control flow*). This means that consumers can control the amount of data they receive, which lowers the risk of producers sending more data than consumers can handle, which can cause a DoS attack, slowing the application, cascading the failure, or even leading to a total crash.

The reactive paradigm is a solution to the problem of blocking I/O operations that require more threads to handle high concurrency and which may lead to slow or entirely unresponsive applications. Sometimes the paradigm is mistaken as a way to increase the speed of an application. Reactive is about improving scalability and resilience, not speed.

With great powers come great troubles, though. Going reactive is an excellent choice when you expect high traffic and concurrency with fewer computational resources or in streaming scenarios. However, you should also be aware of the additional complexity introduced by such a paradigm. Besides requiring a mindset shift to think in an event-driven way, reactive applications are more challenging to debug and troubleshoot because of the asynchronous I/O. Before rushing to rewrite all your applications to make them reactive, think twice about whether that's necessary, and consider both the benefits and drawbacks.

Reactive programming is not a new concept. It's been used for years. The reason for the recent success of the paradigm in the Java ecosystem is due to the Reactive Streams specification and its implementations, like Project Reactor, RxJava, and Vert.x, which provided developers with convenient and high-level interfaces for building asynchronous and non-blocking applications without dealing with the underlying details of designing a message-driven flow. The following section will introduce Project Reactor, the reactive framework used by Spring.

8.1.2   *Project Reactor: Reactive streams with Mono and Flux*

Reactive Spring is based on Project Reactor, a framework for building asynchronous, non-blocking applications on the JVM. Reactor is an implementation of the *Reactive Streams* specification, and it aims to provide "a standard for asynchronous stream processing with non-blocking back pressure" (www.reactive-streams.org).

Conceptually, reactive streams resemble the Java `Stream` API in the way we use them to build data pipelines. One of the key differences is that a Java stream is pull-based:

consumers process data in an imperative and synchronous fashion. Instead, reactive streams are push-based: consumers are notified by the producers when new data is available, so the processing happens asynchronously.

Reactive streams work according to a producer/consumer paradigm. Producers are called *publishers*. They produce data that might be eventually available. Reactor provides two central APIs implementing the `Producer<T>` interface for objects of type `<T>`, and they are used to compose asynchronous, observable data streams: `Mono<T>` and `Flux<T>`:

- `Mono<T>`—Represents a single asynchronous value or empty result (0..1)
- `Flux<T>`—Represents an asynchronous sequence of zero or more items (0..N)

In a Java stream, you would process objects like `Optional<Customer>` or `Collection <Customer>`. In a reactive stream, you would have `Mono<Customer>` or `Flux<Customer>`. The possible outcomes of a reactive stream are an empty result, a value, or an error. All of them are handled as data. When the publisher returns all the data, we say that the reactive stream has been *completed* successfully.

Consumers are called *subscribers* because they subscribe to a publisher and are notified whenever new data is available. As part of the *subscription*, consumers can also define backpressure by informing the publisher that they can process only a certain amount of data at a time. That is a powerful feature that puts consumers in control of how much data is received, preventing them from being overwhelmed and becoming unresponsive. Reactive streams are only activated if there's a subscriber.

You can build reactive streams that combine data from different sources and manipulate it using Reactor's vast collection of *operators*. In a Java stream, you can use a fluent API to process data through operators like `map`, `flatMap`, or `filter`, each of which builds a new `Stream` object that keeps the previous step immutable. Similarly, you can build reactive streams using a fluent API and operators to process the data received asynchronously.

Besides the standard operators available to Java streams, you can use more powerful ones to apply backpressure, handle errors, and increase application resilience. For example, you'll see how to use the `retryWhen()` and `timeout()` operators to make the interaction between Order Service and Catalog Service more robust. Operators can perform actions on a publisher and return a new publisher without modifying the original one, so you can build functional and immutable data streams with ease.

Project Reactor is the foundation of the Spring reactive stack, which lets you implement your business logic in terms of `Mono<T>` and `Flux<T>`. In the next section, you'll learn more about which options you have for building reactive applications with Spring.

8.1.3 *Understanding the Spring reactive stack*

When you build applications with Spring, you can choose between a servlet stack and a reactive stack. The servlet stack relies on synchronous, blocking I/O and uses the thread-per-request model to handle requests. On the other hand, the reactive stack relies on asynchronous, non-blocking I/O and uses the event loop model to handle requests.

The servlet stack is based on the Servlet API and a Servlet container (such as Tomcat). In contrast, the reactive model is based on the Reactive Streams API (implemented by Project Reactor) and either Netty or a Servlet container (version 3.1 as a minimum). Both stacks let you build RESTful applications using either classes annotated as @Rest-Controller (which you used in chapter 3) or functional endpoints called router functions (which you'll learn about in chapter 9). The servlet stack uses Spring MVC, while the reactive stack uses Spring WebFlux. Figure 8.3 compares the two stacks. (For a broader overview, you can refer to https://spring.io/reactive.)

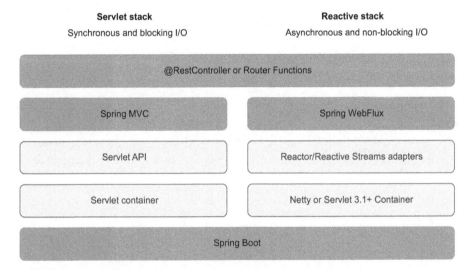

Figure 8.3   The servlet stack is based on the Servlet API and supports synchronous and blocking operations. The reactive stack is based on Project Reactor and supports asynchronous and non-blocking operations.

Tomcat is the default choice for servlet-based applications like Catalog Service. Netty is the preferred choice for reactive applications, providing the best performance.

All the major frameworks in the Spring ecosystem offer both non-reactive and a reactive options, including Spring Security, Spring Data, and Spring Cloud. Overall, the Spring reactive stack provides a higher-level interface for building reactive applications, relying on the familiar Spring projects without being concerned with the underlying implementation of the reactive streams.

8.2   Reactive servers with Spring WebFlux and Spring Data R2DBC

So far we have worked on Catalog Service, a non-reactive (or *imperative*) application, using Spring MVC and Spring Data JDBC. This section will teach you how to build a reactive web application (Order Service) using Spring WebFlux and Spring Data R2DBC.

Order Service will provide functionality for purchasing books. Like Catalog Service, it will expose a REST API and store data in a PostgreSQL database. Unlike Catalog Service, it will use the reactive programming paradigm to improve scalability, resilience, and cost-effectiveness.

You'll see that the principles and patterns you learned in the previous chapters also apply to reactive applications. The main difference is that we'll shift from implementing the business logic in an imperative way to building reactive streams that are processed asynchronously.

Order Service will also interact with Catalog Service through its REST API to fetch details about books and check their availability. That will be the focus of section 8.3. Figure 8.4 shows the new components of the system.

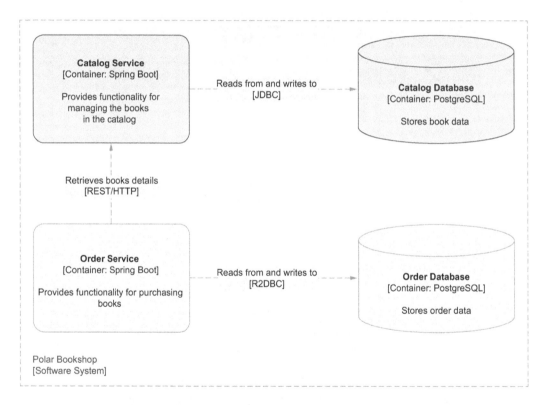

Figure 8.4   The Order Service application exposes an API to submit and retrieve book orders, uses a PostgreSQL database to store data, and communicates with Book Service to fetch book details.

As you learned in chapter 3, we should start with the API first. Order Service will expose a REST API to retrieve existing book orders and submit new ones. Each order can be related to one book only, and up to five copies. The API is described in table 8.1.

Table 8.1 Specifications for the REST API that Order Service will expose

Endpoint	HTTP method	Request body	Status	Response body	Description
/orders	POST	OrderRequest	200	Order	Submits a new order for a given book in a given quantity
/orders	GET		200	Order[]	Retrieves all the orders

Now, on to the code.

NOTE If you haven't followed along with the examples implemented in the previous chapters, you can refer to the repository accompanying the book and use the project in the Chapter08/08-begin folder as a starting point (https://github.com/ThomasVitale/cloud-native-spring-in-action).

8.2.1 Bootstrapping a reactive application with Spring Boot

You can initialize the Order Service project from Spring Initializr (https://start.spring.io), store the result in a new `order-service` Git repository, and push it to GitHub. The parameters for the initialization are shown in figure 8.5.

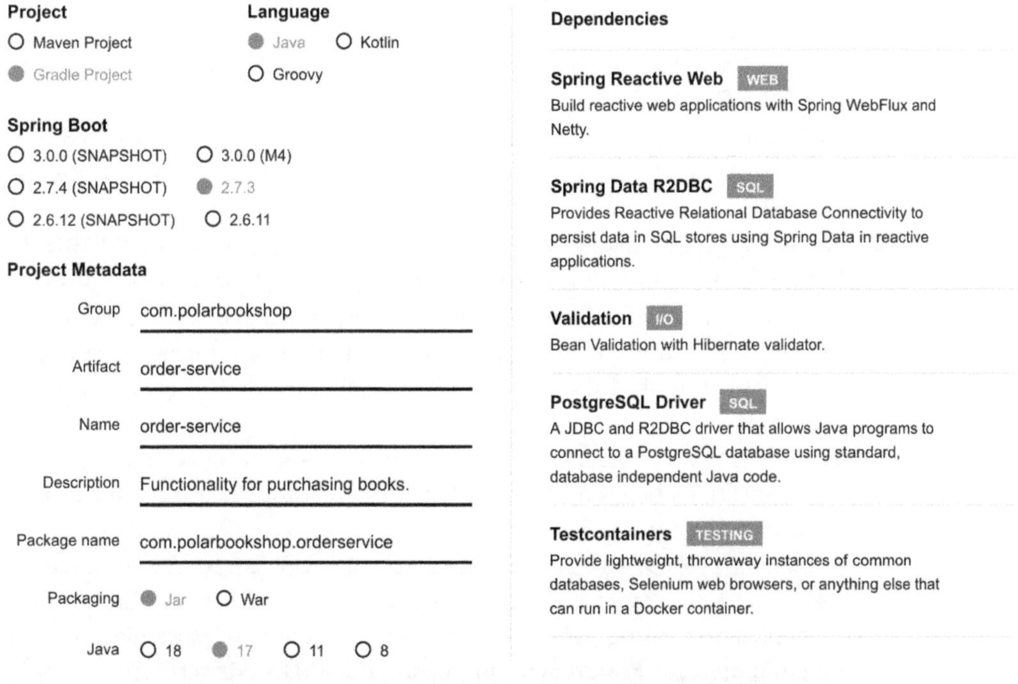

Project
- ○ Maven Project
- ● Gradle Project

Language
- ● Java   ○ Kotlin
- ○ Groovy

Spring Boot
- ○ 3.0.0 (SNAPSHOT)   ○ 3.0.0 (M4)
- ○ 2.7.4 (SNAPSHOT)   ● 2.7.3
- ○ 2.6.12 (SNAPSHOT)   ○ 2.6.11

Project Metadata

Group	com.polarbookshop
Artifact	order-service
Name	order-service
Description	Functionality for purchasing books.
Package name	com.polarbookshop.orderservice
Packaging	● Jar ○ War
Java	○ 18 ● 17 ○ 11 ○ 8

Dependencies

Spring Reactive Web `WEB`
Build reactive web applications with Spring WebFlux and Netty.

Spring Data R2DBC `SQL`
Provides Reactive Relational Database Connectivity to persist data in SQL stores using Spring Data in reactive applications.

Validation `I/O`
Bean Validation with Hibernate validator.

PostgreSQL Driver `SQL`
A JDBC and R2DBC driver that allows Java programs to connect to a PostgreSQL database using standard, database independent Java code.

Testcontainers `TESTING`
Provide lightweight, throwaway instances of common databases, Selenium web browsers, or anything else that can run in a Docker container.

Figure 8.5 The parameters for initializing the Order Service project from Spring Initializr

TIP If you don't want to go through the manual generation on the Spring Initializr website, you'll find a `curl` command in the begin folder for this chapter that you can run in a Terminal window to download a zip file. It contains all the code you'll need to get started.

The `dependencies` section of the autogenerated build.gradle file is shown here:

```
dependencies {
  implementation 'org.springframework.boot:spring-boot-starter-data-r2dbc'
  implementation 'org.springframework.boot:spring-boot-starter-validation'
  implementation 'org.springframework.boot:spring-boot-starter-webflux'

  runtimeOnly 'org.postgresql:r2dbc-postgresql'

  testImplementation 'org.springframework.boot:spring-boot-starter-test'
  testImplementation 'io.projectreactor:reactor-test'
  testImplementation 'org.testcontainers:junit-jupiter'
  testImplementation 'org.testcontainers:postgresql'
  testImplementation 'org.testcontainers:r2dbc'
}
```

These are the main dependencies:

- *Spring Reactive Web* (`org.springframework.boot:spring-boot-starter-webflux`)—Provides the necessary libraries for building reactive web applications with Spring WebFlux and includes Netty as the default embedded server.
- *Spring Data R2DBC* (`org.springframework.boot:spring-boot-starter-data-r2dbc`)—Provides the necessary libraries to persist data in relational databases with R2DBC using Spring Data in reactive applications.
- *Validation* (`org.springframework.boot:spring-boot-starter-validation`)—Provides the necessary libraries for object validation using the Java Bean Validation API.
- *PostgreSQL* (`org.postgresql:r2dbc-postgresql`)—Provides an R2DBC driver that allows the application to connect to a PostgreSQL database reactively.
- *Spring Boot Test* (`org.springframework.boot:spring-boot-starter-test`)—Provides several libraries and utilities to test applications, including Spring Test, JUnit, AssertJ, and Mockito. It's automatically included in every Spring Boot project.
- *Reactor Test* (`io.projectreactor:reactor-test`)—Provides utilities to test reactive applications based on Project Reactor. It's automatically included in every reactive Spring Boot project.
- *Testcontainers* (`org.testcontainers:junit-jupiter`, `org.testcontainers:postgresql`, `org.testcontainers:r2dbc`)—Provides the necessary libraries for testing applications using lightweight Docker containers. In particular, it provides test containers for PostgreSQL supporting the R2DBC driver.

The default and recommended embedded server for reactive applications in Spring Boot is Reactor Netty, which is built on top of Netty to provide reactive capabilities within Project Reactor. You can configure it either through properties or by defining a

WebServerFactoryCustomizer<NettyReactiveWebServerFactory> component. Let's use the first approach.

First of all, rename the application.properties file generated by Spring Initializr to application.yml, and define the application name using the spring.application.name property. Like you did for Tomcat, you can define the server port through the server.port property, configure the graceful shutdown through server.shutdown, and set the grace period with spring.lifecycle.timeout-per-shutdown-phase. Using the specific Netty properties, you can further customize the server's behavior. For example, you can define connection and idle timeouts for Netty with the server.netty .connection-timeout and server.netty.idle-timeout properties.

Listing 8.1 Configuring Netty server and graceful shutdown

Enables graceful shutdown

```
server:
  port: 9002        ◁──┐ The port where the server
  shutdown: graceful     will accept connections
  netty:
    connection-timeout: 2s   ◁── How long to wait for a TCP connection
    idle-timeout: 15s   ◁──       to be established with the server
                              How long to wait before closing a TCP
spring:                       connection if no data is transferred
  application:
    name: order-service
  lifecycle:                         Defines a 15 s
    timeout-per-shutdown-phase: 15s  ◁── grace period
```

With this basic setup in place, we can now define the domain entity and its persistence.

8.2.2 Persisting data reactively with Spring Data R2DBC

In chapter 5, you learned that interactions between a Spring Boot application and a database involve database drivers, entities, and repositories. The same concepts you learned in the context of Spring Data JDBC also apply to Spring Data R2DBC. Spring Data provides common abstractions and patterns, making it straightforward to navigate the different modules.

The main difference for Order Service, compared to Catalog Service, is the type of database driver. JDBC is the most common driver used by Java applications to communicate with a relational database, but it doesn't support reactive programming. There have been a few attempts to provide reactive access to a relational database. One project that stood out and that is widely supported is Reactive Relational Database Connectivity (R2DBC) initiated by Pivotal (now VMware Tanzu). R2DBC drivers are available for all the major databases (such as PostgreSQL, MariaDB, MySQL, SQL Server, and Oracle DB), and there are clients for several projects, including Spring Boot with Spring Data R2DBC and Testcontainers.

This section will guide you through defining a domain entity and a persistence layer for Order Service using Spring Data R2DBC and PostgreSQL. Let's get started.

RUN A POSTGRESQL DATABASE FOR ORDER SERVICE

First of all, we need a database. We'll adopt a *database-per-service* approach to keep our applications loosely coupled. Having decided that Catalog Service and Order Service will have a database each, we have two options for the actual storage. We could either use the same database server for both databases or two different ones. For convenience, we'll use the same PostgreSQL server we set up in chapter 5 to host both the `polardb_catalog` database used by Catalog Service and the new `polardb_order` database used by Order Service.

Go to your `polar-deployment` repository, and create a new docker/postgresql folder. Then add a new init.sql file in the folder. Add the following code to the init.sql file; it is the initialization script that PostgreSQL should run during the startup phase.

Listing 8.2 Initializing the PostgreSQL server with two databases

```
CREATE DATABASE polardb_catalog;
CREATE DATABASE polardb_order;
```

Next, open the docker-compose.yml file and update the PostgreSQL container definition to load the initialization script. Remember to remove the value for the `POSTGRES_DB` environment variable, since we'll now delegate the database creation to the script. In the book's source code, refer to Chapter08/08-end/polar-deployment/docker to check the final result.

Listing 8.3 Initializing the PostgreSQL server from an SQL script

```
version: "3.8"
services:
  ...
  polar-postgres:
    image: "postgres:14.4"
    container_name: "polar-postgres"
    ports:
      - 5432:5432                    No value is defined for
    environment:          ◄───────  POSTGRES_DB anymore.
      - POSTGRES_USER=user
      - POSTGRES_PASSWORD=password   Mounts the initialization SQL script
    volumes:              ◄───────   to the container as a volume
      - ./postgresql/init.sql:/docker-entrypoint-initdb.d/init.sql
```

Finally, start a new PostgreSQL container based on the new configuration. Open a Terminal window, navigate to the folder where you defined the docker-compose.yml file, and run the following command:

```
$ docker-compose up -d polar-postgres
```

For the rest of the chapter, I will assume you have the database up and running.

CONNECTING TO A DATABASE WITH **R2DBC**

Spring Boot lets you configure the integration of a reactive application with a relational database through the `spring.r2dbc` properties. Open the application.yml file for the Order Service project, and configure the connection with PostgreSQL. Connection pooling is enabled by default, and you can further configure it by defining connection timeout and sizes, just like you did for JDBC in chapter 5. Since it's a reactive application, the connection pool will probably be smaller than when using JDBC. You can tune the values after monitoring your applications running under normal conditions.

Listing 8.4   Configuring the database integration over R2DBC

A user with privileges to
access the given database

```
spring:
  r2dbc:
    username: user
    password: password
    url: r2dbc:postgresql://localhost:5432/polardb_order
    pool:
      max-create-connection-time: 2s
      initial-size: 5
      max-size: 10
```

The password for
the given user

The R2DBC URL
identifying the
database you
want to establish
a connection with

The initial size of
the connection pool

The maximum time to wait
to get a connection from
the pool

The maximum number of
connections kept in the pool

Now that you have connected a reactive Spring Boot application to a PostgreSQL database through an R2DBC driver, you can go ahead and define the data you want to persist.

DEFINING PERSISTENT ENTITIES

The Order Service application provides functionality for submitting and retrieving orders. That's the *domain entity*. Add a new `com.polarbookshop.orderservice.order` `.domain` package for the business logic, and create an `Order` Java record to represent the domain entity, much like you defined `Book` in Catalog Service.

Following the same approach used in chapter 5, use the `@Id` annotation to mark the field representing the primary key in the database, and use `@Version` to provide a version number, which is essential for handling concurrent updates and using optimistic locking. You can also add the necessary fields to hold audit metadata using the `@CreatedDate` and `@LastModifiedDate` annotations.

The default strategy for mapping an entity to a relational table is to transform the Java object name into lowercase. In this example, Spring Data would try to map the `Order` record to an `order` table. The problem is that `order` is a reserved word in SQL. It's not recommended that you use it as a table name because it would require special handling. You can overcome that issue by naming the table `orders` and configuring the object-relational mapping through the `@Table` annotation (from the `org.spring-framework.data.relational.core.mapping` package).

Listing 8.5   The `Order` record defines the domain and persistent entity

```
package com.polarbookshop.orderservice.order.domain;

import java.time.Instant;
import org.springframework.data.annotation.CreatedDate;
import org.springframework.data.annotation.Id;
import org.springframework.data.annotation.LastModifiedDate;
import org.springframework.data.annotation.Version;
import org.springframework.data.relational.core.mapping.Table;

@Table("orders")            ◁──────   Configures the mapping
public record Order (                  between the "Order" object
                                       and the "orders" table
  @Id
  Long id,          ◁──────   The primary key
                             of the entity
  String bookIsbn,
  String bookName,
  Double bookPrice,
  Integer quantity,
  OrderStatus status,

  @CreatedDate                   When the entity
  Instant createdDate,     ◁──   was created

  @LastModifiedDate              When the entity was
  Instant lastModifiedDate,  ◁── modified the last time

  @Version             The entity's
  int version     ◁──  version number
){
  public static Order of(
    String bookIsbn, String bookName, Double bookPrice,
    Integer quantity, OrderStatus status
  ) {
    return new Order(
      null, bookIsbn, bookName, bookPrice, quantity, status, null, null, 0
    );
  }
}
```

Orders can go through different phases. If the requested book is available in the catalog, then the order is *accepted*. If not, it's *rejected*. Once the order is accepted, it can be *dispatched*, as you'll see in chapter 10. You can define these three statuses in an `Order-Status` enum in the `com.polarbookshop.orderservice.order.domain` package.

Listing 8.6   Enum describing the statuses for the orders

```
package com.polarbookshop.orderservice.order.domain;

public enum OrderStatus {
  ACCEPTED,
  REJECTED,
```

```
DISPATCHED
}
```

The R2DBC auditing functionality can be enabled in a configuration class using the `@EnableR2dbcAuditing` annotation. Create a `DataConfig` class in a new `com.polar-bookshop.orderservice.config` package, and enable auditing there.

Listing 8.7   Enabling R2DBC auditing via annotation configuration

```
package com.polarbookshop.orderservice.config;

import org.springframework.context.annotation.Configuration;
import org.springframework.data.r2dbc.config.EnableR2dbcAuditing;

@Configuration            ◁──────────┐  Indicates a class as a source
@EnableR2dbcAuditing       ◁──────┐  │  of Spring configuration
public class DataConfig {}          │  
                                    Enables R2DBC auditing
                                    for persistent entities
```

Having defined the data you want to persist, you can go ahead and explore how to access it.

USING REACTIVE REPOSITORIES

Spring Data provides the *repository* abstraction for all the modules in the project, including R2DBC. The only difference between this and what you did in chapter 5 is that you're going to use a reactive repository.

In the `com.polarbookshop.orderservice.order.domain` package, create a new `OrderRepository` interface and make it extend `ReactiveCrudRepository`, specifying the type of data handled (`Order`) and the data type of the `@Id`-annotated field (`Long`).

Listing 8.8   Repository interface for accessing orders

```
package com.polarbookshop.orderservice.order.domain;

import org.springframework.data.repository.reactive.ReactiveCrudRepository;

public interface OrderRepository
  extends ReactiveCrudRepository<Order,Long> {}    ◁──┐

       Extends a reactive repository providing CRUD operations, specifies
       the type of managed entity (Order), and its primary key type (Long)
```

The CRUD operations provided by `ReactiveCrudRepository` are enough for the use cases of the Order Service application, so you won't need to add any custom methods. However, we're still missing the `orders` table in the database. Let's define it using Flyway.

MANAGING DATABASE SCHEMAS WITH FLYWAY

Spring Data R2DBC supports initializing data sources through schema.sql and data.sql files, just like Spring Data JDBC. As you learned in chapter 5, that functionality is convenient for demos and experiments, but it's better to manage schemas explicitly for production use cases.

For Catalog Service we used Flyway to create and evolve its database schemas. We can do the same for Order Service. However, Flyway doesn't support R2DBC yet, so we need to provide a JDBC driver to communicate with the database. The Flyway migration tasks are only run at application startup and in a single thread, so using a nonreactive communication approach for this one case doesn't impact the overall application's scalability and efficiency.

In the build.gradle file for your Order Service project, add new dependencies to Flyway, the PostgreSQL JDBC driver, and Spring JDBC. Remember to refresh or reimport the Gradle dependencies after the new addition.

> **Listing 8.9   Adding a dependency for Flyway and JDBC in Order Service**

```
dependencies {
    ...
    runtimeOnly 'org.flywaydb:flyway-core'
    runtimeOnly 'org.postgresql:postgresql'
    runtimeOnly 'org.springframework:spring-jdbc'
}
```

Provides functionality to version-control your database through migrations

Provides a JDBC driver that allows the application to connect to a PostgreSQL database

Provides Spring integration with the JDBC API. It's part of the Spring Framework, not to be confused with Spring Data JDBC.

Then you can write the SQL script for creating the orders table in a V1__Initial_schema.sql file under src/main/resources/db/migration. Ensure you type two underscores after the version number.

> **Listing 8.10   Flyway migration script for schema initialization**

```
CREATE TABLE orders (
    id                  BIGSERIAL PRIMARY KEY NOT NULL,
    book_isbn           varchar(255) NOT NULL,
    book_name           varchar(255),
    book_price          float8,
    quantity            int NOT NULL,
    status              varchar(255) NOT NULL,
    created_date        timestamp NOT NULL,
    last_modified_date  timestamp NOT NULL,
    version             integer NOT NULL
);
```

Definition of the orders table

Declares the id field as the primary key

Finally, open the application.yml file, and configure Flyway to use the same database managed with Spring Data R2DBC but using the JDBC driver.

> **Listing 8.11   Configuring the Flyway integration over JDBC**

```
spring:
  r2dbc:
    username: user
    password: password
    url: r2dbc:postgresql://localhost:5432/polardb_order
```

```
pool:
    max-create-connection-time: 2s
    initial-size: 5
    max-size: 10
flyway:
    user: ${spring.r2dbc.username}
    password: ${spring.r2dbc.password}
    url: jdbc:postgresql://localhost:5432/polardb_order
```

Gets the value from the username configured for R2DBC

Gets the value from the password configured for R2DBC

The same database configured for R2DBC but using the JDBC driver

As you probably noticed, defining domain objects and adding a persistence layer in a reactive application is similar to what you would do with imperative applications. The main differences you encountered in this session are using the R2DBC driver instead of JDBC and having a separate Flyway configuration (at least until R2DBC support is added to the Flyway project: https://github.com/flyway/flyway/issues/2502).

In the next section you'll learn how to use Mono and Flux in your business logic.

8.2.3   Implementing the business logic with reactive streams

The Spring reactive stack makes it straightforward to build asynchronous, non-blocking applications. In the previous section, we used Spring Data R2DBC and didn't have to deal with any underlying reactive concerns. That's generally true for all the reactive modules in Spring. As a developer, you can rely on a familiar, simple, and productive approach for building reactive applications while the framework takes care of all the heavy lifting.

By default, Spring WebFlux assumes that everything is reactive. This assumption means that you're expected to interact with the framework by exchanging Publisher<T> objects like Mono<T> and Flux<T>. For example, the OrderRepository we created earlier will give access to orders as Mono<Order> and Flux<Order> objects instead of returning Optional<Order> and Collection<Order> like it would do in a non-reactive context. Let's see that in action.

In the com.polarbookshop.orderservice.order.domain package, create a new OrderService class. For starters, let's implement the logic to read orders through the repository. When multiple orders are involved, you can use a Flux<Order> object, representing an asynchronous sequence of zero or more orders.

Listing 8.12   Fetching orders via a reactive stream

```java
package com.polarbookshop.orderservice.order.domain;

import reactor.core.publisher.Flux;
import org.springframework.stereotype.Service;

@Service
public class OrderService {
    private final OrderRepository orderRepository;

    public OrderService(OrderRepository orderRepository) {
        this.orderRepository = orderRepository;
    }
```

Stereotype annotation that marks a class to be a service managed by Spring

```
public Flux<Order> getAllOrders() {          ◁——  A Flux is used to publish
    return orderRepository.findAll();               multiple orders (0..N)
  }
}
```

Next, we need a method to submit orders. Until we have the integration with Catalog Service in place, we can always default to rejecting submitted orders. OrderRepository exposes a save() method provided by ReactiveCrudRepository. You can build a reactive stream to pass an object of type Mono<Order> to OrderRepository that will save the order in the database.

Given an ISBN identifying a book and the number of copies to order, you can build a Mono object with Mono.just() in the same way you would build a Java Stream object with Stream.of(). The difference is in the reactive behavior.

You can use the Mono object to start a reactive stream and then rely on the flat-Map() operator to pass the data to OrderRepository. Add the following code to the OrderService class, and complete the business logic implementation.

Listing 8.13   Persisting rejected orders upon submitting order requests

Saves the Order object produced asynchronously by the
previous step of the reactive stream into the database

```
  ...
  public Mono<Order> submitOrder(String isbn, int quantity) {          ┐ Creates a "Mono"
    return Mono.just(buildRejectedOrder(isbn, quantity))              │ out of an "Order"
 ┌———▷  .flatMap(orderRepository::save);          ◁——                 ┘ object
  }

  public static Order buildRejectedOrder(              ┐ When an order is rejected, we only
    String bookIsbn, int quantity                      │ specify ISBN, quantity, and status.
  ) {                                                  │ Spring Data takes care of adding
    return Order.of(bookIsbn, null, null, quantity, OrderStatus.REJECTED);
  }                          ◁——————————————┘ identifier, version, and audit metadata.
  ...
```

---

map VS. flatMap

When using Reactor, choosing between the map() and flatMap() operators is usually a source of confusion. Both operators return a reactive stream (either Mono<T> or Flux<T>), but while map() maps between two standard Java types, flatMap() maps from a Java type to another reactive stream.

In listing 8.13, we map from an object of type Order to a Mono<Order> (which is returned by OrderRepository). Since the map() operator expects the target type not to be a reactive stream, it will wrap it in one nevertheless and return a Mono<Mono<Order>> object. On the other hand, the flatMap() operator expects the target type to be a reactive stream, so it knows how to handle the publisher produced by OrderRepository and returns a Mono<Order> object correctly.

In the next section, you'll complete the basic implementation of Order Service by exposing an API to fetch and submit orders.

8.2.4   *Exposing a REST API with Spring WebFlux*

There are two options for defining RESTful endpoints in a Spring WebFlux application: @RestController classes or functional beans (router functions). For the Order Service application, we'll use the first option. Unlike what we did in chapter 3, the method handlers will return reactive objects.

For the GET endpoint, we can use the Order domain entity we defined earlier and return a Flux<Order> object. When submitting an order, the user must provide the ISBN of the desired book and the number of copies they would like to purchase. We can model that information in an OrderRequest record that will act as a data transfer object (DTO). It's also good practice to validate the input, as you learned in chapter 3.

Create a new com.polarbookshop.orderservice.order.web package, and define an OrderRequest record to hold the submitted order information.

Listing 8.14   The OrderRequest DTO class with validation constraints

```
package com.polarbookshop.orderservice.order.web;

import javax.validation.constraints.*;

public record OrderRequest (

  @NotBlank(message = "The book ISBN must be defined.")
  String isbn,

  @NotNull(message = "The book quantity must be defined.")
  @Min(value = 1, message = "You must order at least 1 item.")
  @Max(value = 5, message = "You cannot order more than 5 items.")
  Integer quantity
){}
```

Must not be null and must contain at least one non-whitespace character

Must not be null and must contain a value from 1 to 5

In the same package, create an OrderController class to define the two RESTful endpoints exposed by the Order Service application. Since you defined validation constraints for the OrderRequest object, you also need to use the familiar @Valid annotation to trigger the validation when the method is called.

Listing 8.15   Defining handlers to process REST requests

```
package com.polarbookshop.orderservice.order.web;

import javax.validation.Valid;
import com.polarbookshop.orderservice.order.domain.Order;
import com.polarbookshop.orderservice.order.domain.OrderService;
import reactor.core.publisher.Flux;
import reactor.core.publisher.Mono;
import org.springframework.web.bind.annotation.*;

@RestController
@RequestMapping("orders")
public class OrderController {
  private final OrderService orderService;
```

Stereotype annotation marking a class as a Spring component and a source of handlers for REST endpoints

Identifies the root path mapping URI for which the class provides handlers (/orders)

```
public OrderController(OrderService orderService) {
  this.orderService = orderService;
}

@GetMapping
public Flux<Order> getAllOrders() {          ◁——┐  A Flux is used to publish
  return orderService.getAllOrders();                multiple orders (0..N).
}

@PostMapping
public Mono<Order> submitOrder(
  @RequestBody @Valid OrderRequest orderRequest    ◁——┐
) {
  return orderService.submitOrder(
   orderRequest.isbn(), orderRequest.quantity()
  );
}
}
```

Accepts an OrderRequest
object, validated and used to
create an order. The created
order is returned as a Mono.

This REST controller completes our basic implementation of the Order Service application. Let's see it in action. First, make sure the PostgreSQL container you created earlier is still running. Then open a Terminal window, navigate to the Order Service project's root folder, and run the application:

```
$ ./gradlew bootRun
```

You can try out the API by submitting an order. The application will save the order as rejected and return a 200 response to the client:

```
$ http POST :9002/orders isbn=1234567890 quantity=3

HTTP/1.1 200 OK
{
  "bookIsbn": "1234567890",
  "bookName": null,
  "bookPrice": null,
  "createdDate": "2022-06-06T09:40:58.374348Z",
  "id": 1,
  "lastModifiedDate": "2022-06-06T09:40:58.374348Z",
  "quantity": 3,
  "status": "REJECTED",
  "version": 1
}
```

To make it possible to submit orders successfully, we'll need to make Order Service call Catalog Service to check the book's availability and fetch the necessary information for processing the order. That's the focus of the next section. Before moving on, stop the application with Ctrl-C.

8.3 Reactive clients with Spring WebClient

In a cloud native system, applications can interact in different ways. This section focuses on the request/response interactions over HTTP that you'll establish between Order Service and Catalog Service. In this kind of interaction, the client making the request expects to receive a response. In an imperative application, that would translate into a thread blocking until a response is returned. Instead, in a reactive application, we can use resources more efficiently so that no thread will wait for a response, freeing up resources to deal with other processing.

The Spring Framework comes bundled with two clients that perform HTTP requests: `RestTemplate` and `WebClient`. `RestTemplate` is the original Spring REST client that allows blocking HTTP request/response interactions based on a template method API. Since Spring Framework 5.0, it's in maintenance mode and practically deprecated. It's still widely used, but it will not get any new functionality in future releases.

`WebClient` is the modern alternative to `RestTemplate`. It provides blocking and non-blocking I/O, making it the perfect candidate for both imperative and reactive applications. It can be operated through a functional-style, fluent API that lets you configure any aspect of the HTTP interaction.

This section will teach you how to use `WebClient` to establish non-blocking request/response interactions. I will also explain how to make your application more resilient by adopting patterns like timeouts, retries, and failovers using the Reactor operators `timeout()`, `retryWhen()`, and `onError()`.

8.3.1 Service-to-service communication in Spring

As per the 15-Factor methodology, any backing service should be attached to an application through resource binding. For databases, you relied on the configuration properties provided by Spring Boot to specify credentials and the URL. When a backing service is another application, you need to provide its URL in a similar way. Following the externalized configuration principle, the URL should be configurable, not hardcoded. In Spring, you can achieve that through a `@ConfigurationProperties` bean, as you learned in chapter 4.

In the Order Service project, add a `ClientProperties` record in the `com.polar-bookshop.orderservice.config` package. There, define your custom `polar.catalog-service-uri` property to configure the URI for calling the Catalog Service.

Listing 8.16 Defining a custom property for the Catalog Service URI

```
package com.polarbookshop.orderservice.config;

import java.net.URI;
import javax.validation.constraints.NotNull;
import org.springframework.boot.context.properties.ConfigurationProperties;

@ConfigurationProperties(prefix = "polar")        ◁─┤  The prefix for the
public record ClientProperties(                        custom properties
```

```
  @NotNull
  URI catalogServiceUri          ◄──┤  The property for specifying the
){}                                   Catalog Service URI. It cannot be null.
```

NOTE To get autocompletion and type-validation checks from your IDE, you need to add a dependency on org.springframework.boot:spring-boot-configuration-processor with scope annotationProcessor in the build .gradle file, like you did in chapter 4. You can refer to the Chapter08/08-end/order-service/build.gradle file in the code repository accompanying the book to check the final result (https://github.com/ThomasVitale/cloud-native -spring-in-action).

Then, enable the custom configuration properties in your OrderServiceApplication class using the @ConfigurationPropertiesScan annotation.

Listing 8.17 Enabling custom configuration properties

```
package com.polarbookshop.orderservice;

import org.springframework.boot.SpringApplication;
import org.springframework.boot.autoconfigure.SpringBootApplication;
import org.springframework.boot.context.properties
    .ConfigurationPropertiesScan;

@SpringBootApplication                           Loads configuration data
@ConfigurationPropertiesScan    ◄──┘             beans in the Spring context
public class OrderServiceApplication {
  public static void main(String[] args) {
    SpringApplication.run(OrderServiceApplication.class, args);
  }
}
```

Finally, add a value for the new property to your application.yml file. As a default, you can use the URI for the Catalog Service instance running in your local environment.

Listing 8.18 Configuring the URI for Catalog Service (application.yml)

```
...
polar:
  catalog-service-uri: "http://localhost:9001"
```

NOTE When deploying the system with Docker Compose or Kubernetes, you can override the property value via an environment variable, taking advantage of the service discovery features offered by the two platforms.

In the next section, you'll use the value configured through this property to call the Catalog Service from Order Service.

8.3.2 Understanding how to exchange data

Whenever a user submits an order for a specific book, Order Service needs to call Catalog Service to check the requested book's availability and fetch its details, like the title, author, and price. The interaction (HTTP request/response) is illustrated in figure 8.6.

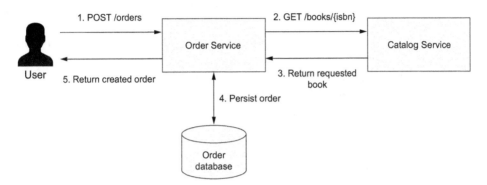

Figure 8.6 When an order is submitted, Order Service calls Catalog Service over HTTP to check the book's availability and fetch its details.

Each order request is submitted for a specific ISBN. Order Service needs to know the book's ISBN, title, author, and price to process an order correctly. Currently, Catalog Service exposes a /books/{bookIsbn} endpoint that returns all the available information about a book. In a real scenario, you might expose a different endpoint that returns an object containing only the required information (a DTO). For the sake of this example, we'll reuse the existing endpoint, since our focus right now is on building reactive clients.

Having established which endpoint to call, how should you model the exchange between the two applications? You've just reached a crossroad:

- *Create a shared library*—One option is to create a shared library with the classes used by both applications, and import it as a dependency into both projects. As per the 15-factor methodology, such a library would be tracked in its own codebase. Doing so would ensure that the model used by both applications is consistent and never out of sync. However, it would mean adding implementation coupling.
- *Duplicate the class*—The other option is to replicate the class into the upstream application. By doing so, you wouldn't have implementation coupling, but you would have to take care of evolving the replicated model as the original one changes in the downstream application. There are a few techniques like consumer-driven contracts that can identify, through automated tests, when the called API changes. Besides checking the data model, those tests would also verify other aspects of the exposed API, like HTTP methods, response statuses, headers, variables, and so on. I will not cover this subject here, but I recommend checking the Spring Cloud Contract project if you're interested (https://spring.io/projects/spring-cloud-contract).

Both are viable options. Which strategy you adopt is up to your project requirements and your organization's structure. For the Polar Bookshop project, we will use the second option.

In a new `com.polarbookshop.orderservice.book` package, create a `Book` record to be used as a DTO, and include only the fields used by the order processing logic. As I pointed out earlier, in a real scenario I would expose a new endpoint in Catalog Service, returning book objects modeled as this DTO. For simplicity, we'll use the existing `/books/{bookIsbn}` endpoint, so any information that doesn't map to any of the fields in this class will be discarded when deserializing the JSON received into the Java object. Make sure the fields you do define have the same names as in the `Book` object defined in Catalog Service, or else the parsing will fail. That is something that consumer-driven contract tests can verify for you automatically.

> **Listing 8.19 The `Book` record is a DTO for storing book information**

```
package com.polarbookshop.orderservice.book;

public record Book(
  String isbn,
  String title,
  String author,
  Double price
){}
```

Now that you have a DTO in Order Service ready to hold book information, let's see how you can retrieve it from Catalog Service.

8.3.3   *Implementing REST clients with WebClient*

The modern and reactive choice for REST clients in Spring is `WebClient`. The framework provides several ways of instantiating a `WebClient` object—in this example we'll use `WebClient.Builder`. Refer to the official documentation to explore the other options (https://spring.io/projects/spring-framework).

In the `com.polarbookshop.orderservice.config` package, create a `ClientConfig` class to configure a `WebClient` bean with the base URL provided by `ClientProperties`.

> **Listing 8.20 Configuring a `WebClient` bean to call Catalog Service**

```
package com.polarbookshop.orderservice.config;

import org.springframework.context.annotation.Bean;
import org.springframework.context.annotation.Configuration;
import org.springframework.web.reactive.function.client.WebClient;

@Configuration
public class ClientConfig {

  @Bean
  WebClient webClient(
```

```
    ClientProperties clientProperties,
    WebClient.Builder webClientBuilder        ◄──┐  An object auto-configured by Spring
) {                                                   Boot to build WebClient beans
    return webClientBuilder                   ◄──────────────────────────────┐
      .baseUrl(clientProperties.catalogServiceUri().toString())             │
      .build();                                                              │
}                                                    Configures the WebClient base
}                                                    URL to the Catalog Service URL
                                                     defined as a custom property
```

WARNING   If you use IntelliJ IDEA, you might get a warning that `WebClient`
`.Builder` cannot be autowired. Don't worry. It's a false positive. You can get
rid of the warning by annotating the field with `@SuppressWarnings("Spring-`
`JavaInjectionPointsAutowiringInspection")`.

Next, create a `BookClient` class in the `com.polarbookshop.orderservice.book`
package. That is where you are going to use the `WebClient` bean to send HTTP
calls to the `GET /books/{bookIsbn}` endpoint exposed by Catalog Service through
its fluent API. The `WebClient` will ultimately return a `Book` object wrapped in a
`Mono` publisher.

Listing 8.21   Defining a reactive REST client using `WebClient`

```
package com.polarbookshop.orderservice.book;

import reactor.core.publisher.Mono;
import org.springframework.stereotype.Component;
import org.springframework.web.reactive.function.client.WebClient;

@Component
public class BookClient {
  private static final String BOOKS_ROOT_API = "/books/";
  private final WebClient webClient;

  public BookClient(WebClient webClient) {        A WebClient bean as
    this.webClient = webClient;              ◄──  configured previously
  }

  public Mono<Book> getBookByIsbn(String isbn) {  The request should use
    return webClient                              the GET method.
      .get()                              ◄──────  The target URI of the
      .uri(BOOKS_ROOT_API + isbn)         ◄──────  request is /books/{isbn}.
      .retrieve()                         ◄──────  Sends the request
      .bodyToMono(Book.class);            ◄──────  and retrieves the
  }                                                response
}                    Returns the retrieved
                     object as Mono<Book>
```

`WebClient` is a reactive HTTP client. You've just seen how it can return data as reactive
publishers. In particular, the result of calling Catalog Service to fetch details about a
specific book is a `Mono<Book>` object. Let's see how you can include that in the order-
processing logic implemented in `OrderService`.

The submitOrder() method in the OrderService class is currently rejecting orders all the time. But not for long. You can now autowire a BookClient instance and use the underlying WebClient to start a reactive stream to process the book information and create an order. The map() operator lets you map a Book to an accepted Order. If BookClient returns an empty result, you can define a rejected Order with the defaultIfEmpty() operator. Finally, the stream is ended by calling OrderRepository to save the order (either as accepted or rejected).

Listing 8.22   Calling `BookClient` to get the book info when ordered

```
package com.polarbookshop.orderservice.order.domain;

import com.polarbookshop.orderservice.book.Book;
import com.polarbookshop.orderservice.book.BookClient;
import reactor.core.publisher.Flux;
import reactor.core.publisher.Mono;
import org.springframework.stereotype.Service;

@Service
public class OrderService {
  private final BookClient bookClient;
  private final OrderRepository orderRepository;

  public OrderService(
   BookClient bookClient, OrderRepository orderRepository
  ) {
    this.bookClient = bookClient;
    this.orderRepository = orderRepository;
  }

  ...

  public Mono<Order> submitOrder(String isbn, int quantity) {
    return bookClient.getBookByIsbn(isbn)
      .map(book -> buildAcceptedOrder(book, quantity))
      .defaultIfEmpty(
        buildRejectedOrder(isbn, quantity)
      )
      .flatMap(orderRepository::save);
  }

  public static Order buildAcceptedOrder(Book book, int quantity) {
    return Order.of(book.isbn(), book.title() + " - " + book.author(),
      book.price(), quantity, OrderStatus.ACCEPTED);
  }

  public static Order buildRejectedOrder(String bookIsbn, int quantity) {
    return Order.of(bookIsbn, null, null, quantity, OrderStatus.REJECTED);
  }
}
```

If the book is available, it accepts the order.

Calls the Catalog Service to check the book's availability

If the book is not available, it rejects the order.

Saves the order (either as accepted or rejected)

When an order is accepted, we specify ISBN, book name (title + author), quantity, and status. Spring Data takes care of adding the identifier, version, and audit metadata.

Let's try that out. First, ensure the PostgreSQL container is up and running by executing the following command from the folder where you keep your Docker Compose configuration (polar-deployment/docker):

```
$ docker-compose up -d polar-postgres
```

Then build and run both Catalog Service and Order Service (`./gradlew bootRun`).

> **WARNING** If you're using an Apple Silicon computer, the application logs from Order Service might include some warnings related to DNS resolutions in Netty. In this specific case, the application should still work correctly. If you experience issues, you can add the following additional dependency to the Order Service project as `runtimeOnly` to fix the problem: `io.netty:netty-resolver-dns-native-macos:4.1.79.Final:osx-aarch_64`.

Finally, send an order for one of the books created in Catalog Service at startup time. If the book exists, the order should be accepted:

```
$ http POST :9002/orders isbn=1234567891 quantity=3

HTTP/1.1 200 OK
{
  "bookIsbn": "1234567891",
  "bookName": "Northern Lights - Lyra Silverstar",
  "bookPrice": 9.9,
  "createdDate": "2022-06-06T09:59:32.961420Z",
  "id": 2,
  "lastModifiedDate": "2022-06-06T09:59:32.961420Z",
  "quantity": 3,
  "status": "ACCEPTED",
  "version": 1
}
```

When you are done verifying the interaction, stop the applications with Ctrl-C and the container with `docker-compose down`.

That concludes our implementation of the order-creation logic. If the book exists in the catalog, the order will be accepted. If an empty result is returned, it's rejected. But what if Catalog Service takes too much time to reply? What if it's momentarily unavailable and can't process any new requests? What if it replies with an error? The following section will answer and handle all these questions.

8.4 Resilient applications with Reactive Spring

Resilience is about keeping a system available and delivering its services, even when failures happen. Since failures will happen, and there's no way to prevent them all, it is critical to design fault-tolerant applications. The goal is to keep the system available without the user noticing any failures. In the worst-case scenario, the system may have degraded functionality (*graceful degradation*), but it should still be available.

The critical point in achieving resilience (or fault-tolerance) is keeping the faulty component isolated until the fault is fixed. By doing that, you'll prevent what Michael T. Nygard calls *crack propagation*. Think about Polar Bookshop. If Catalog Service enters a faulty state and becomes unresponsive, you don't want Order Service to be affected as well. Integration points between application services should be carefully guarded and made resilient to failures affecting the other party.

There are several patterns for building resilient applications. In the Java ecosystem, a popular library for implementing such patterns was Hystrix, developed by Netflix, but as of 2018 it entered maintenance mode and will not be developed further. Resilience4J gained a lot of popularity, filling the void left by Hystrix. Project Reactor, the Reactive Spring stack foundation, also provides some useful features for resilience.

In this section, you'll make the integration point between Order Service and Catalog Service more robust, using Reactive Spring to configure timeouts, retries, and fallbacks. In the next chapter, you'll learn more about building resilient applications with Resilience4J and Spring Cloud Circuit Breaker.

8.4.1   Timeouts

Whenever your application calls a remote service, you don't know if and when a response will be received. Timeouts (also called *time limiters*) are a simple, yet effective, tool for preserving the responsiveness of your application in case a response is not received within a reasonable time period.

There are two main reasons for setting up timeouts:

- If you don't limit the time your client waits, you risk your computational resources being blocked for too long (for imperative applications). In the worst-case scenario, your application will be completely unresponsive because all the available threads are blocked, waiting for responses from a remote service, and there are no threads available to handle new requests.
- If you can't meet your Service Level Agreements (SLAs), there's no reason to keep waiting for an answer. It's better to fail the request.

Here are some examples of timeouts:

- *Connection timeout*—This is the time limit for establishing a communication channel with a remote resource. Earlier you configured the `server.netty`
  `.connection-timeout` property to limit the time Netty waits for a TCP connection to be established.
- *Connection pool timeout*—This is the time limit for a client to get a connection from a pool. In chapter 5, you configured a timeout for the Hikari connection pool through the `spring.datasource.hikari.connection-timeout` property.
- *Read timeout*—This is the time limit for reading from a remote resource after establishing the initial connection. In the following sections, you'll define a read timeout for the call to the Catalog Service performed by the `BookClient` class.

In this section, you'll define a timeout for `BookClient` so that if it expires, the Order Service application will throw an exception. You can also specify a failover instead of throwing the exception to the user. Figure 8.7 details how the request/response interaction will work when timeouts and failovers are defined.

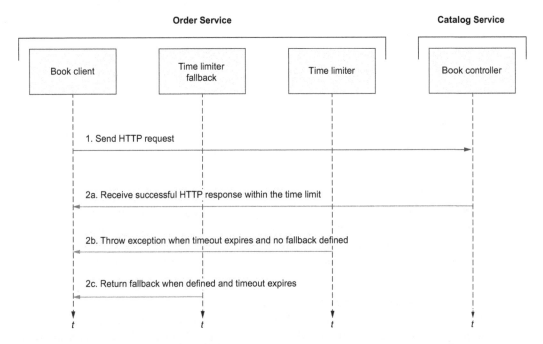

Figure 8.7   When a response is received from the remote service within the time limit, the request is successful. If the timeout expires and no response is received, then a fallback behavior is executed, if any. Otherwise, an exception is thrown.

DEFINING A TIMEOUT FOR WEBCLIENT

Project Reactor provides a `timeout()` operator you can use to define a time limit for completing an operation. You can chain it with the result of the `WebClient` call to continue the reactive stream. Update the `getBookByIsbn()` method in the `BookClient` class as follows to define a timeout of 3 seconds.

Listing 8.23   Defining a timeout for the HTTP interaction

```
...
public Mono<Book> getBookByIsbn(String isbn) {
  return webClient
    .get()
    .uri(BOOKS_ROOT_API + isbn)
    .retrieve()
    .bodyToMono(Book.class)
    .timeout(Duration.ofSeconds(3));      ⟵  Sets a 3-second timeout
}                                             for the GET request
...
```

Instead of throwing an exception when the timeout expires, you have the chance to provide a fallback behavior. Considering that Order Service can't accept an order if the book's availability is not verified, you might consider returning an empty result so that the order will be rejected. You can define a reactive empty result using `Mono.empty()`. Update the `getBookByIsbn()` method in the `BookClient` class as follows.

Listing 8.24   Defining timeout and fallback for the HTTP interaction

```
...
public Mono<Book> getBookByIsbn(String isbn) {
  return webClient
    .get()
    .uri(BOOKS_ROOT_API + isbn)
    .retrieve()
    .bodyToMono(Book.class)
    .timeout(Duration.ofSeconds(3), Mono.empty())    ◁── The fallback
}                                                         returns an empty
...                                                       Mono object.
```

> **NOTE**   In a real production scenario, you might want to externalize the timeout configuration by adding a new field to the `ClientProperties`. In that way, you can change its value depending on the environment without having to rebuild the application. It's also essential to monitor any timeout and tune its value if necessary.

UNDERSTANDING HOW TO USE TIMEOUTS EFFECTIVELY

Timeouts improve application resilience and follow the principle of failing fast. But setting a good value for the timeout can be tricky. You should consider your system architecture as a whole. In the previous example, you defined a 3-second timeout. This means that a response should get from Catalog Service to Order Service within that time limit. Otherwise, either a failure or a fallback occurs. Catalog Service, in turn, sends a request to the PostgreSQL database to fetch the data about the specific book and waits for a response. A connection timeout guards that interaction. You should carefully design a time-limiting strategy for all the integration points in your system to meet your software's SLAs and guarantee a good user experience.

If Catalog Service were available, but a response couldn't get to Order Service within the time limit, the request would likely still be processed by Catalog Service. That is a critical point to consider when configuring timeouts. It doesn't matter much for read or query operations because they are idempotent. For write or command operations, you want to ensure proper handling when a timeout expires, including providing the user with the correct status about the operation's outcome.

When Catalog Service is overloaded, it can take several seconds to get a JDBC connection from the pool, fetch data from the database, and send a response back to Order Service. In that case, you could think of retrying the request rather than falling back on a default behavior or throwing an exception.

8.4.2 Retries

When a service downstream doesn't respond within a specific time limit or replies with a server error related to its momentary inability to process the request, you can configure your client to try again. When a service doesn't respond correctly, it's likely because it's going through some issues, and it's unlikely that it will manage to recover immediately. Starting a sequence of retry attempts, one after the other, risks making the system even more unstable. You don't want to launch a DoS attack on your own applications!

A better approach is using an *exponential backoff* strategy to perform each retry attempt with a growing delay. By waiting for more and more time between one attempt and the next, you're more likely to give the backing service time to recover and become responsive again. The strategy for computing the delay can be configured.

In this section, you'll configure retries for `BookClient`. Figure 8.8 details how the request/response interaction will work when retries are configured with exponential backoff. For example, the figure shows a scenario where each retry attempt's delay is computed as the number of attempts multiplied by 100 ms (the initial backoff value).

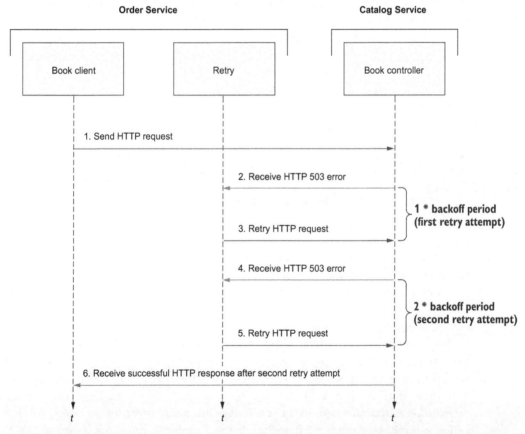

Figure 8.8 When Catalog Service doesn't respond successfully, Order Service will try at most three more times with a growing delay.

DEFINING RETRIES FOR WEBCLIENT

Project Reactor provides a `retryWhen()` operator to retry an operation when it fails. The position where you apply it to the reactive stream matters.

- Placing the `retryWhen()` operator after `timeout()` means that the timeout is applied to each retry attempt.
- Placing the `retryWhen()` operator before `timeout()` means that the timeout is applied to the overall operation (that is, the whole sequence of the initial request and retries has to happen within the given time limit).

In `BookClient`, we want the timeout to apply to each retry attempt, so we'll use the first option. The time limiter is applied first. If the timeout expires, the `retryWhen()` operator kicks in and tries the request again.

Update the `getBookByIsbn()` method in the `BookClient` class to configure a retry strategy. You can define the number of attempts and the minimum duration for the first backoff. The delay is computed for each retry as the current attempt number multiplied by the minimum backoff period. A jitter factor can be used to add randomness to the exponential of each backoff. By default, a jitter of at most 50% of the computed delay is used. When you have multiple instances of Order Service running, the jitter factor ensures that the replicas will not retry requests simultaneously.

Listing 8.25 Defining retries with exponential backoff for the HTTP call

```
public Mono<Book> getBookByIsbn(String isbn) {
  return webClient
    .get()
    .uri(BOOKS_ROOT_API + isbn)
    .retrieve()
    .bodyToMono(Book.class)
    .timeout(Duration.ofSeconds(3), Mono.empty())
    .retryWhen(
      Retry.backoff(3, Duration.ofMillis(100))
    );
}
```

Exponential backoff is used as the retry strategy. Three attempts are allowed with a 100 ms initial backoff.

UNDERSTANDING HOW TO USE RETRIES EFFECTIVELY

Retries increase the chance of getting a response back from a remote service when it's momentarily overloaded or unresponsive. Use them wisely. In the context of timeouts, I highlighted the need for handling read and write operations differently. When it comes to retries, this is even more critical.

Idempotent requests like read operations can be retried without harm. Even some write requests can be idempotent. For example, a request to change the author of a book with a given ISBN from "S.L. Cooper" to "Sheldon Lee Cooper" is idempotent. You could perform it a few times, but the outcome will not change. You shouldn't retry non-idempotent requests, or you'll risk generating inconsistent states. When you order a book, you don't want to be charged multiple times just because the first attempt failed due to the response being lost in the network and never received.

When retries are configured in a flow where the user is involved, remember to balance resilience and user experience. You don't want users to wait too long while retrying the request behind the scenes. If you can't avoid that, make sure you inform the users and give them feedback about the status of the request.

Retries are a helpful pattern whenever the service downstream is momentarily unavailable or slow due to overloading, but it's likely to heal soon. In this case, you should limit the number of retries and use exponential backoff to prevent adding extra load on an already overloaded service. On the other hand, you shouldn't retry the request if the service fails with a recurrent error, such as if it's entirely down or returns an acceptable error like 404. The following section will show you how to define fallbacks when specific errors happen.

8.4.3 Fallbacks and error handling

A system is resilient if it keeps providing its services in the face of faults without the user noticing. Sometimes that's not possible, so the least you can do is ensure a graceful degradation of the service level. Specifying a fallback behavior can help you limit the fault to a small area while preventing the rest of the system from misbehaving or entering a faulty state.

In the previous discussion of timeouts, you already provided a fallback behavior if no response is received within the time limit. You'll want to include fallbacks in your general strategy to make your system resilient, and not just in a specific case like timeouts. A fallback function can be triggered when some errors or exceptions occur, but they're not all the same.

Some errors are acceptable and semantically meaningful in the context of your business logic. When Order Service calls Catalog Service to fetch information about a specific book, a 404 response might be returned. That's an acceptable response that should be addressed to inform the user that the order cannot be submitted because the book is not available in the catalog.

The retry strategy you defined in the previous section is not limited: it will retry the request as long as an error response is received, including acceptable ones like 404. However, in that case, you don't want to retry the request. Project Reactor provides an `onErrorResume()` operator to define a fallback when a specific error occurs. You can add it to the reactive stream after the `timeout()` operator and before the `retryWhen()` so that if a 404 response is received (`WebClientResponseException.NotFound` exception), the retry operator is not triggered. Then you can use the same operator again at the end of the stream to catch any other exception and fall back to an empty `Mono`. Update the `getBookByIsbn()` method in the `BookClient` class as follows.

> **Listing 8.26 Defining exception handling and fallbacks for the HTTP call**

```
public Mono<Book> getBookByIsbn(String isbn) {
  return webClient
    .get()
    .uri(BOOKS_ROOT_API + isbn)
```

```
    .retrieve()
    .bodyToMono(Book.class)
    .timeout(Duration.ofSeconds(3), Mono.empty())
    .onErrorResume(WebClientResponseException.NotFound.class,
      exception -> Mono.empty())
    .retryWhen(Retry.backoff(3, Duration.ofMillis(100)))
    .onErrorResume(Exception.class,
      exception -> Mono.empty());
}
```

Returns an empty object when a 404 response is received

If any error happens after the 3 retry attempts, catch the exception and return an empty object.

NOTE   In a real-world scenario, you would probably want to return some contextual information depending on the type of error, instead of always returning an empty object. For example, you could add a `reason` field to the `Order` object to describe why it's been rejected. Was it because the book is unavailable in the catalog or because of network problems? In the second case, you could inform the user that the order cannot be processed because it's momentarily unable to check the book's availability. A better option would be to save the order in a pending state, queue the order submission request, and try it again later, using one of the strategies I'll cover in chapter 10.

The key goal is designing a resilient system that, in the best-case scenario, can provide its services without the user noticing that there has been a failure. In contrast, in the worst-case scenario, it should still work but with graceful degradation.

NOTE   Spring WebFlux and Project Reactor are exciting subjects in the Spring landscape. If you want to learn more about how reactive Spring works, I recommend looking at *Reactive Spring* by Josh Long (https://reactivespring.io). In the Manning catalog, see part 3 of *Spring in Action*, sixth edition, by Craig Walls (Manning, 2022).

In the next section, you'll write automated tests to verify the different aspects of the Order Service application.

8.5   *Testing reactive applications with Spring, Reactor, and Testcontainers*

When an application depends on a service downstream, you should test the interaction against the API specification of the latter. In this section, you'll first try the `BookClient` class against a mock web server acting as the Catalog Service to ensure the correctness of the client. Then you'll test the data persistence layer with sliced tests using the `@DataR2dbcTest` annotation and Testcontainers, much as you did in chapter 5 with `@DataJdbcTest`. Finally, you'll write sliced tests for the web layer using the `@WebFluxTest` annotation, which works in the same way as `@WebMvcTest` but for reactive applications.

You already have the necessary dependencies on the Spring Boot test libraries and Testcontainers. What is missing is a dependency on `com.squareup.okhttp3:mockweb-server`, which will provide utilities to run a mock web server. Open the build.gradle file of the Order Service project and add the missing dependency.

Listing 8.27 Adding test dependency for OkHttp `MockWebServer`

```
dependencies {
  ...
  testImplementation 'com.squareup.okhttp3:mockwebserver'
}
```

Let's start by testing the `BookClient` class.

8.5.1 Testing REST clients with a mock web server

The OkHttp project provides a mock web server that you can use to test HTTP-based request/response interactions with a service downstream. `BookClient` returns a `Mono<Book>` object, so you can use the convenient utilities provided by Project Reactor for testing reactive applications. The `StepVerifier` object lets you process reactive streams and write assertions in steps through a fluent API.

First, let's set up the mock web server and configure `WebClient` to use it in a new `BookClientTests` class.

Listing 8.28 Preparing the test setup with a mock web server

```
package com.polarbookshop.orderservice.book;

import java.io.IOException;
import okhttp3.mockwebserver.MockWebServer;
import org.junit.jupiter.api.*;
import org.springframework.web.reactive.function.client.WebClient;

class BookClientTests {
  private MockWebServer mockWebServer;
  private BookClient bookClient;

  @BeforeEach
  void setup() throws IOException {
    this.mockWebServer = new MockWebServer();       │ Starts the mock server
    this.mockWebServer.start();             ◄───────┘ before running a test case
    var webClient = WebClient.builder()                  ◄─┐ Uses the mock server
      .baseUrl(mockWebServer.url("/").uri().toString())     │ URL as the base URL
      .build();                                             │ for WebClient
    this.bookClient = new BookClient(webClient);
  }

  @AfterEach
  void clean() throws IOException {
    this.mockWebServer.shutdown();        ◄──┐ Shuts the mock server down
  }                                          │ after completing a test case
}
```

Next, in the `BookClientTests` class, you can define some test cases to validate the client's functionality in Order Service.

Listing 8.29   Testing the interaction with the Catalog Service application

```java
package com.polarbookshop.orderservice.book;

...
import okhttp3.mockwebserver.MockResponse;
import reactor.core.publisher.Mono;
import reactor.test.StepVerifier;
import org.springframework.http.HttpHeaders;
import org.springframework.http.MediaType;

class BookClientTests {
  private MockWebServer mockWebServer;
  private BookClient bookClient;

  ...

  @Test
  void whenBookExistsThenReturnBook() {
    var bookIsbn = "1234567890";

    var mockResponse = new MockResponse()            ◁─┐ Defines the response
      .addHeader(HttpHeaders.CONTENT_TYPE, MediaType.APPLICATION_JSON_VALUE)  to be returned by
      .setBody("""                                        the mock server
        {
          "isbn": %s,
          "title": "Title",
          "author": "Author",
          "price": 9.90,
          "publisher": "Polarsophia"
        }
        """.formatted(bookIsbn));              Adds a mock response
                                               to the queue processed
    mockWebServer.enqueue(mockResponse);    ◁─ by the mock server

    Mono<Book> book = bookClient.getBookByIsbn(bookIsbn);

    StepVerifier.create(book)           ◁──────────┐  Initializes a
      .expectNextMatches(                              StepVerifier object
        b -> b.isbn().equals(bookIsbn))  ◁──┐          with the object
      .verifyComplete();                       │        returned by
  }                                    Asserts that the  BookClient
}                                      Book returned has
                                       the ISBN requested
```

Verifies that the reactive stream completed successfully

Let's run the tests and ensure they succeed. Open a Terminal window, navigate to the root folder of your Order Service project, and run the following command:

```
$ ./gradlew test --tests BookClientTests
```

NOTE When using mocks, there might be situations where the test results depend on the order in which test cases are executed, which tend to be the same on the same operating system. To prevent unwanted execution dependencies, you can annotate the test class with `@TestMethodOrder(Method-Orderer.Random.class)` to ensure that a pseudo-random order is used at each execution.

After testing the REST client part, you can move on and verify the data persistence layer for Order Service.

8.5.2 Testing data persistence with @DataR2dbcTest and Testcontainers

As you might recall from the previous chapters, Spring Boot allows you to run integration tests by loading only the Spring components used by a specific application slice. For the REST API, you will create tests for the WebFlux slice. Here I'll show you how to write tests for the R2DBC slice using the `@DataR2dbcTest` annotation.

The approach is the same you used in chapter 5 for testing the data layer in Catalog Service, but there are two main differences. First, you will use the `StepVerifier` utility to test the `OrderRepository` behavior reactively. Second, you will define a PostgreSQL test container instance explicitly.

For the Catalog Service application, we relied on the test container auto-configuration. In this case, we'll define a test container in the test class and mark it as `@Container`. Then the `@Testcontainers` annotation on the class will activate the automatic startup and cleanup of the test container. Finally, we'll use the `@DynamicProperties` annotation provided by Spring Boot to pass the test database's credentials and URL to the application. This approach of defining test containers and overwriting properties is generic and can be applied to other scenarios.

Now, on to the code. Create an `OrderRepositoryR2dbcTests` class and implement autotests to verify the data persistence layer of the application.

Listing 8.30   Integration tests for the Data R2DBC slice

```
package com.polarbookshop.orderservice.order.domain;

import com.polarbookshop.orderservice.config.DataConfig;
import org.junit.jupiter.api.Test;
import org.testcontainers.containers.PostgreSQLContainer;
import org.testcontainers.junit.jupiter.Container;
import org.testcontainers.junit.jupiter.Testcontainers;
import org.testcontainers.utility.DockerImageName;
import reactor.test.StepVerifier;
import org.springframework.beans.factory.annotation.Autowired;
import org.springframework.boot.test.autoconfigure.data.r2dbc.DataR2dbcTest;
import org.springframework.context.annotation.Import;
import org.springframework.test.context.DynamicPropertyRegistry;
import org.springframework.test.context.DynamicPropertySource;
```

```
@DataR2dbcTest                                    ◄───────────    Identifies a test class that
@Import(DataConfig.class)          ◄──────────────────────┐      focuses on R2DBC components
@Testcontainers                            ◄──────────┐    │
class OrderRepositoryR2dbcTests {    Activates automatic│   Imports R2DBC configuration
                                     startup and cleanup │   needed to enable auditing
                                     of test containers  │
    @Container                                           │
    static PostgreSQLContainer<?> postgresql =
        new PostgreSQLContainer<>(DockerImageName.parse("postgres:14.4"));

    @Autowired
    private OrderRepository orderRepository;          Overwrites R2DBC and Flyway
                                                      configuration to point to the test
                                                      PostgreSQL instance
    @DynamicPropertySource
    static void postgresqlProperties(DynamicPropertyRegistry registry) {
        registry.add("spring.r2dbc.url", OrderRepositoryR2dbcTests::r2dbcUrl);
        registry.add("spring.r2dbc.username", postgresql::getUsername);
        registry.add("spring.r2dbc.password", postgresql::getPassword);
        registry.add("spring.flyway.url", postgresql::getJdbcUrl);
    }
                                                      Builds an R2DBC connection
    private static String r2dbcUrl() {           ◄──  string, because Testcontainers
        return String.format("r2dbc:postgresql://%s:%s/%s",  doesn't provide one out of the
            postgresql.getContainerIpAddress(),             box as it does for JDBC
            postgresql.getMappedPort(PostgreSQLContainer.POSTGRESQL_PORT),
            postgresql.getDatabaseName());
    }

    @Test
    void createRejectedOrder() {
        var rejectedOrder = OrderService.buildRejectedOrder("1234567890", 3);
        StepVerifier
            .create(orderRepository.save(rejectedOrder))    ◄──    Initializes a
            .expectNextMatches(                                    StepVerifier object
                order -> order.status().equals(OrderStatus.REJECTED))  with the object
            .verifyComplete();        ◄──                           returned by
    }                               Verifies that the              OrderRepository
}                                   reactive stream
                                    completed
                                    successfully
```

Identifies a PostgreSQL container for testing (left margin annotation)

Asserts that the Order returned has the correct status (left margin annotation)

Since those slice tests are based on Testcontainers, ensure the Docker Engine is running in your local environment. Then run the tests:

```
$ ./gradlew test --tests OrderRepositoryR2dbcTests
```

In the next section, you'll write tests for the web slice.

8.5.3   *Testing REST controllers with @WebFluxTest*

The WebFlux slice can be tested similarly to how you tested the MVC layer in chapter 3 and using the same WebTestClient utility you used for the integration tests. It's an enhanced version of the standard `WebClient` object, containing extra features to simplify tests.

Create an `OrderControllerWebFluxTests` class, and annotate it with `@WebFlux-Test(OrderController.class)` to collect the slice tests for `OrderController`. As you learned in chapter 3, you can use the `@MockBean` Spring annotation to mock the `OrderService` class and have Spring add it to the Spring context used in the test. That's what makes it injectable.

Listing 8.31   Integration tests for the WebFlux slice

```
package com.polarbookshop.orderservice.order.web;

import com.polarbookshop.orderservice.order.domain.Order;
import com.polarbookshop.orderservice.order.domain.OrderService;
import com.polarbookshop.orderservice.order.domain.OrderStatus;
import org.junit.jupiter.api.Test;
import reactor.core.publisher.Mono;
import org.springframework.beans.factory.annotation.Autowired;
import org.springframework.boot.test.autoconfigure.web.reactive.WebFluxTest;
import org.springframework.boot.test.mock.mockito.MockBean;
import org.springframework.test.web.reactive.server.WebTestClient;
import static org.assertj.core.api.Assertions.assertThat;
import static org.mockito.BDDMockito.given;

@WebFluxTest(OrderController.class)          ◄─  Identifies a test class that focuses
class OrderControllerWebFluxTests {              on Spring WebFlux components,
                                                 targeting OrderController

  @Autowired                                     A WebClient variant with
  private WebTestClient webClient;        ◄─     extra features to make testing
                                                 RESTful services easier

  @MockBean                             ◄─
  private OrderService orderService;      Adds a mock of OrderService to
                                          the Spring application context
  @Test
  void whenBookNotAvailableThenRejectOrder() {
    var orderRequest = new OrderRequest("1234567890", 3);
    var expectedOrder = OrderService.buildRejectedOrder(
     orderRequest.isbn(), orderRequest.quantity());
    given(orderService.submitOrder(                  Defines the expected
     orderRequest.isbn(), orderRequest.quantity())   behavior for the
    ).willReturn(Mono.just(expectedOrder));   ◄─     OrderService
                                                     mock bean
    webClient
      .post()
      .uri("/orders/")
      .bodyValue(orderRequest)
      .exchange()                                Expects the order is
      .expectStatus().is2xxSuccessful()   ◄─     created successfully
      .expectBody(Order.class).value(actualOrder -> {
        assertThat(actualOrder).isNotNull();
        assertThat(actualOrder.status()).isEqualTo(OrderStatus.REJECTED);
      });
  }
}
```

Next, run the slice tests for the web layer to ensure they pass:

```
$ ./gradlew test --tests OrderControllerWebFluxTests
```

Great job! You successfully built and tested a reactive application, maximizing scalability, resilience, and cost-effectiveness. In the source code accompanying the book, you can find more test examples, including full integration tests using the `@Spring-BootTest` annotation and slice tests for the JSON layer using `@JsonTest`, as you learned in chapter 3.

Polar Labs

Feel free to apply what you learned in the previous chapters and prepare the Order Service application for deployment.

1. Add Spring Cloud Config Client to Order Service to make it fetch configuration data from Config Service.
2. Configure the Cloud Native Buildpacks integration, containerize the application, and define the commit stage of the deployment pipeline.
3. Write the Deployment and Service manifests for deploying Order Service to a Kubernetes cluster.
4. Configure Tilt to automate the Order Service deployment to your local Kubernetes cluster initialized with minikube.

You can refer to the Chapter08/08-end folder in the code repository accompanying the book to check the final result (https://github.com/ThomasVitale/cloud-native-spring-in-action). You can deploy the backing services from the manifests available in the Chapter08/08-end/polar-deployment/kubernetes/platform/development folder with `kubectl apply -f services`.

The next chapter will continue our discussion of resilience and introduce more patterns, like circuit breakers and rate limiters, using Spring Cloud Gateway, Spring Cloud Circuit Breaker, and Resilience4J.

Summary

- When you expect high traffic and concurrency with fewer computational resources, the reactive paradigm can improve the application's scalability, resilience, and cost-effectiveness at the expense of a steeper initial learning curve.
- Choose between a non-reactive and a reactive stack according to your requirements.
- Spring WebFlux is based on Project Reactor and is the core of the reactive stack in Spring. It supports asynchronous, non-blocking I/O.
- Reactive RESTful services can be implemented through `@RestController` classes or router functions.
- The Spring WebFlux slice can be tested through the `@WebFluxTest` annotation.

- Spring Data R2DBC provides support for reactive data persistence using the R2DBC driver. The approach is the same as for any Spring Data project: database drivers, entities, and repositories.
- Database schemas can be managed with Flyway.
- The persistence slice of a reactive application can be tested using the `@DataR2-dbcTest` annotation and Testcontainers.
- A system is resilient if it keeps providing its services in the face of faults without the user noticing it. Sometimes that's not possible, so the least you can do is ensure a graceful degradation of the services.
- WebClient is based on Project Reactor and works with `Mono` and `Flux` publishers.
- You can use the Reactor operators to configure timeouts, retries, fallbacks, and error handling to make the interaction more resilient to any failure in the service downstream or due to the network.

API gateway
and circuit breakers

This chapter covers

- Implementing edge services with Spring Cloud Gateway and Reactive Spring

- Configuring circuit breakers with Spring Cloud Circuit Breaker and Resilience4J

- Defining rate limiters with Spring Cloud Gateway and Redis

- Managing distributed sessions with Spring Session Data Redis

- Routing application traffic with Kubernetes Ingress

In the previous chapter, you learned several aspects of building resilient, scalable, and cost-effective applications using the reactive paradigm. In this chapter, the Spring reactive stack will be the foundation for implementing an API gateway for the Polar Bookshop system. An API gateway is a common pattern in distributed architectures, like microservices, used to decouple the internal APIs from the clients. When establishing such an entry point to your system, you can also use it to handle cross-cutting concerns, such as security, monitoring, and resilience.

This chapter will teach you how to use Spring Cloud Gateway to build an Edge Service application and implement an API gateway and some of those cross-cutting concerns. You'll improve the resilience of the system by configuring circuit breakers with Spring Cloud Circuit Breaker, defining rate limiters with Spring Data Redis Reactive, and using retries and timeouts just like you learned in the previous chapter.

Next, I'll discuss how to design stateless applications. Some states will need to be saved for the applications to be useful—you have already used relational databases. This chapter will teach you how to store web session state using Spring Session Data Redis, a NoSQL in-memory data store.

Finally, you'll see how to manage external access to the applications running in a Kubernetes cluster by relying on the Kubernetes Ingress API.

Figure 9.1 shows what the Polar Bookshop system will look like after completing this chapter.

NOTE The source code for the examples in this chapter is available in the Chapter09/09-begin and Chapter09/09-end folders, containing the initial and final states of the project (https://github.com/ThomasVitale/cloud-native -spring-in-action).

9.1   Edge servers and Spring Cloud Gateway

Spring Cloud Gateway is a project built on top of Spring WebFlux and Project Reactor to provide an API gateway and a central place to handle cross-cutting concerns like security, resilience, and monitoring. It's built for developers, and it's a good fit in Spring architectures and heterogeneous environments.

An API gateway provides an entry point to your system. In distributed systems like microservices, that's a convenient way to decouple the clients from any changes to the internal services' APIs. You're free to change how your system is decomposed into services and their APIs, relying on the fact that the gateway can translate from a more stable, client-friendly, public API to the internal one.

Suppose you're in the process of moving from a monolith to microservices. In that case, an API gateway can be used as a *monolith strangler* and can wrap your legacy applications until they are migrated to the new architecture, keeping the process transparent to clients. In case of different client types (single-page applications, mobile applications, desktop applications, IoT devices), an API gateway gives you the option to provide a better-crafted API to each of them depending on their needs (also called the *backend-for-frontend* pattern). Sometimes a gateway can also implement the *API composition* pattern, letting you query and join data from different services before returning the result to a client (for example, using the new Spring for GraphQL project).

Calls are forwarded to downstream services from the gateway according to specified routing rules, similar to a reverse proxy. This way the client doesn't need to keep track of the different services involved in a transaction, simplifying the client's logic and reducing the number of calls it has to make.

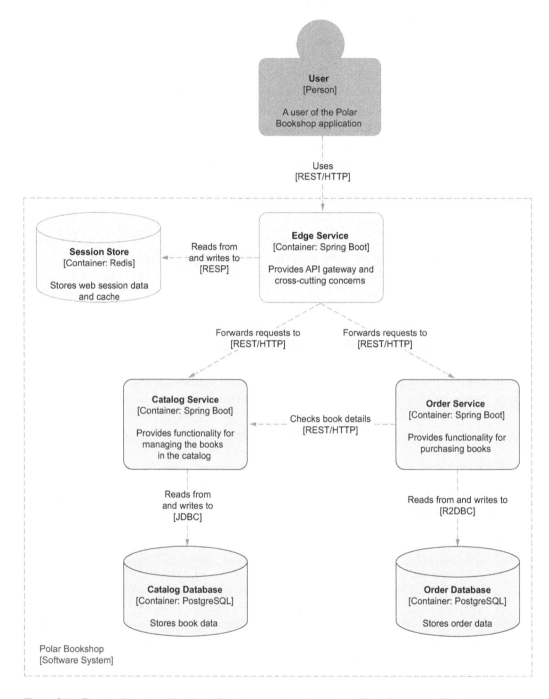

Figure 9.1   The architecture of the Polar Bookshop system after adding Edge Service and Redis

Since the API gateway is the entry point to your system, it can also be an excellent place to handle cross-cutting concerns like security, monitoring, and resilience. *Edge servers* are applications at the edge of a system that implement aspects like API gateways and cross-cutting concerns. You can configure circuit breakers to prevent cascading failures when invoking the services downstream. You can define retries and timeouts for all the calls to internal services. You can control the ingress traffic and enforce quota policies to limit the use of your system depending on some criteria (such as the membership level of your users: basic, premium, pro). You can also implement authentication and authorization at the edge and pass tokens to downstream services (as you'll see in chapters 11 and 12).

However, it's important to remember that an edge server adds complexity to the system. It's another component to build, deploy, and manage in production. It also adds a new network hop to the system, so the response time will increase. That's usually an insignificant cost, but you should keep it in mind. Since the edge server is the entry point to the system, it's at risk of becoming a single point of failure. As a basic mitigation strategy, you should deploy at least two replicas of an edge server following the same approach we discussed for configuration servers in chapter 4.

Spring Cloud Gateway greatly simplifies building edge services, focusing on simplicity and productivity. Furthermore, since it's based on a reactive stack, it can scale efficiently to handle the high workload naturally happening at the edge of a system.

The following section will teach you how to set up an edge server with Spring Cloud Gateway. You'll learn about routes, predicates, and filters, which are the building blocks of the gateway. And you'll apply the retry and timeout patterns you learned in the previous chapter to the interactions between the gateway and the downstream services.

> **NOTE** If you haven't followed along with the examples implemented in the previous chapters, you can refer to the repository accompanying the book and use the project in Chapter09/09-begin as a starting point (https://github .com/ThomasVitale/cloud-native-spring-in-action).

9.1.1 Bootstrapping an edge server with Spring Cloud Gateway

The Polar Bookshop system needs an edge server to route traffic to the internal APIs and address several cross-cutting concerns. You can initialize our new Edge Service project from Spring Initializr (https://start.spring.io), store the result in a new edge-service Git repository, and push it to GitHub. The parameters for the initialization are shown in figure 9.2.

> **TIP** In the begin folder for this chapter, you'll find a `curl` command you can run in a Terminal window. It downloads a zip file containing all the code you need to get started, without going through the manual generation on the Spring Initializr website.

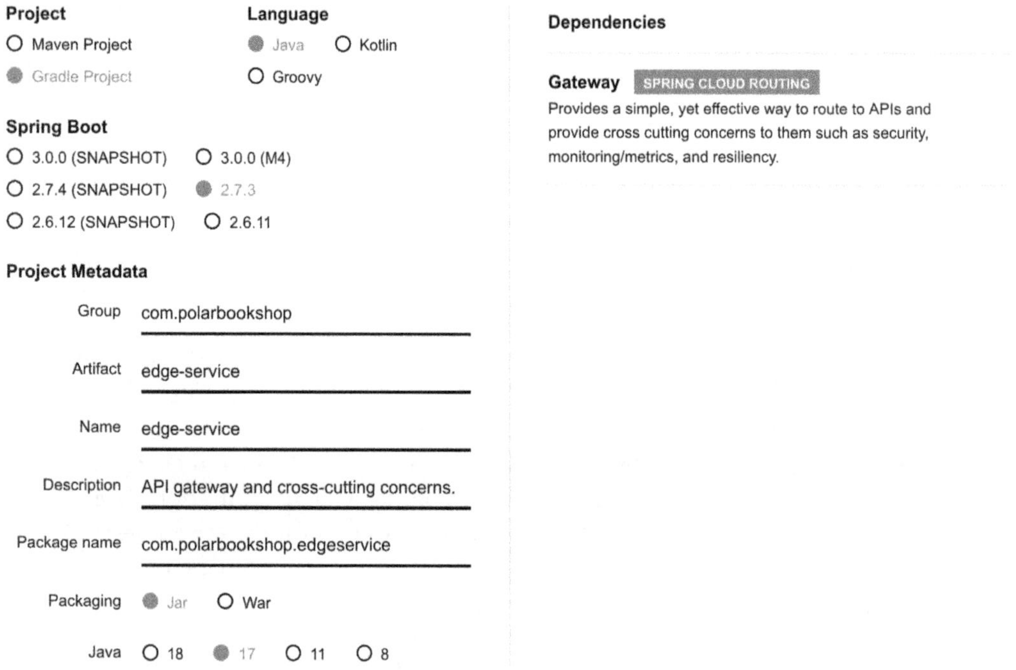

Project

○ Maven Project
● Gradle Project

Spring Boot

○ 3.0.0 (SNAPSHOT)   ○ 3.0.0 (M4)
○ 2.7.4 (SNAPSHOT)   ● 2.7.3
○ 2.6.12 (SNAPSHOT)   ○ 2.6.11

Language

● Java   ○ Kotlin
○ Groovy

Dependencies

Gateway SPRING CLOUD ROUTING
Provides a simple, yet effective way to route to APIs and
provide cross cutting concerns to them such as security,
monitoring/metrics, and resiliency.

Project Metadata

Group   com.polarbookshop

Artifact   edge-service

Name   edge-service

Description API gateway and cross-cutting concerns.

Package name com.polarbookshop.edgeservice

Packaging   ● Jar   ○ War

Java   ○ 18   ● 17   ○ 11   ○ 8

Figure 9.2   The parameters for initializing the Edge Service project

The dependencies section of the autogenerated build.gradle file looks like this:

```
dependencies {
  implementation 'org.springframework.cloud:spring-cloud-starter-gateway'
  testImplementation 'org.springframework.boot:spring-boot-starter-test'
}
```

These are the main dependencies:

- *Spring Cloud Gateway* (org.springframework.cloud:spring-cloud-starter-gateway)—Provides utilities to route requests to APIs and cross-cutting concerns like resilience, security, and monitoring. It's built on top of the Spring reactive stack.
- *Spring Boot Test* (org.springframework.boot:spring-boot-starter-test)—Provides several libraries and utilities for testing applications, including Spring Test, JUnit, AssertJ, and Mockito. It's automatically included in every Spring Boot project.

At its core, Spring Cloud Gateway is a Spring Boot application. It provides all the convenient features we've been using in the previous chapters, such as auto-configuration, embedded servers, test utilities, externalized configuration, and so on. It's also built on the Spring reactive stack, so you can use the tools and patterns you learned in the previous chapter regarding Spring WebFlux and Reactor. Let's start by configuring the embedded Netty server.

First, rename the application.properties file generated by Spring Initializr (edge-service/src/main/resources) to application.yml. Then open the file and configure the Netty server as you learned in the previous chapter.

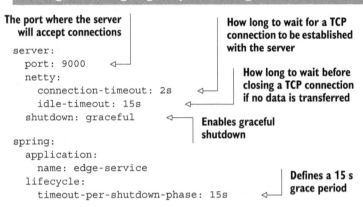

Listing 9.1   Configuring Netty server and graceful shutdown

The port where the server will accept connections

How long to wait for a TCP connection to be established with the server

```
server:
  port: 9000
  netty:
    connection-timeout: 2s
    idle-timeout: 15s
  shutdown: graceful
spring:
  application:
    name: edge-service
  lifecycle:
    timeout-per-shutdown-phase: 15s
```

How long to wait before closing a TCP connection if no data is transferred

Enables graceful shutdown

Defines a 15 s grace period

The application is set up, so you can move on and start exploring the features of Spring Cloud Gateway.

9.1.2   *Defining routes and predicates*

Spring Cloud Gateway provides three main building blocks:

- *Route*—This is identified by a unique ID, a collection of predicates for deciding whether to follow the route, a URI for forwarding the request if the predicates allow, and a collection of filters that are applied either before or after forwarding the request downstream.
- *Predicate*—This matches anything from the HTTP request, including path, host, headers, query parameters, cookies, and body.
- *Filter*—This modifies an HTTP request or response before or after forwarding the request to the downstream service.

Suppose a client sends a request to Spring Cloud Gateway. If the request matches a route through its predicates, the Gateway HandlerMapping will send the request to the Gateway WebHandler, which in turn will run the request through a chain of filters. There are two filter chains. One chain contains the filters to be run before the request is sent to the downstream service. The other chain is run after sending the request downstream and before forwarding the response. You'll learn about the different types of filters in the next section. Figure 9.3 shows how the routing works in Spring Cloud Gateway.

In the Polar Bookshop system, we have built two applications with APIs that are meant to be accessible from the outside world (public APIs): Catalog Service and Order Service. We can use Edge Service to hide them behind an API gateway. For starters, we need to define the routes.

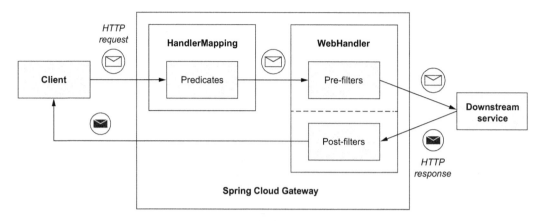

Figure 9.3   Requests are matched against predicates, filtered, and finally forwarded to the downstream service, which replies with a response that goes through another set of filters before being returned to the client.

A minimal route must be configured with a unique ID, a URI where the request should be forwarded, and at least one predicate. Open the application.yml file for the Edge Service project, and configure two routes to Catalog Service and Order Service.

Listing 9.2   Configuring routes to downstream services

```
spring:
  cloud:
    gateway:
      routes:              ◁─── A list of route
        - id: catalog-route      definitions
          uri: ${CATALOG_SERVICE_URL:http://localhost:9001}/books   ◁─── The route ID
          predicates:
            - Path=/books/**    ◁─── The predicate is
        - id: order-route          a path to match
          uri:
⇒ ${ORDER_SERVICE_URL:http://localhost:9002}/orders   ◁─── The URI value comes from
          predicates:                                       an environment variable,
            - Path=/orders/**                               or else from the default.
```

Both the routes for Catalog Service and Order Service are matched based on a `Path` predicate. All the incoming requests with a path starting with /books will be forwarded to Catalog Service. If the path starts with /orders, then Order Service will receive the request. The URIs are computed using the value from an environment variable (`CATALOG_SERVICE_URL` and `ORDER_SERVICE_URL`). If they are not defined, the default value written after the first colon (:) symbol will be used. It's an alternative approach compared to how we defined URLs in the previous chapter, based on custom properties; I wanted to show you both options.

The project comes with many different predicates built-in, which you can use in your route configuration to match against any aspect of an HTTP request, including `Cookie`, `Header`, `Host`, `Method`, `Path`, `Query`, and `RemoteAddr`. You can also combine them to form *AND* conditionals. In the previous example, we used the `Path` predicate. Refer to the official documentation for an extensive list of predicates available in Spring Cloud Gateway: https://spring.io/projects/spring-cloud-gateway.

Defining routes with the Java/Kotlin DSL

Spring Cloud Gateway is a very flexible project that lets you configure routes the way that best suits your needs. Here you have configured routes in a property file (application.yml or application.properties), but there's also a DSL available for configuring routes programmatically in Java or Kotlin. Future versions of the project will also implement a feature to fetch the route configuration from a data source using Spring Data.

How you use it is up to you. Putting routes in configuration properties gives you the chance to customize them easily depending on the environment and to update them at runtime without the need to rebuild and redeploy the application. For example, you would get those benefits when using Spring Cloud Config Server. On the other hand, the DSL for Java and Kotlin lets you define more complex routes. Configuration properties allow you to combine different predicates with an *AND* logical operator only. The DSL also enables you to use other logical operators like *OR* and *NOT*.

Let's verify that it works as intended. We'll use Docker to run the downstream services and PostgreSQL, whereas we'll run Edge Service locally on the JVM to make it more efficient to work with, since we are actively implementing the application.

First, we need both Catalog Service and Order Service up and running. From each project's root folder, run `./gradlew bootBuildImage` to package them as container images. Then start them via Docker Compose. Open a Terminal window, navigate to the folder where your docker-compose.yml file is located (polar-deployment/docker), and run the following command:

```
$ docker-compose up -d catalog-service order-service
```

Since both applications depend on PostgreSQL, Docker Compose will also run the PostgreSQL container.

When the downstream services are all up and running, it's time to start Edge Service. From a Terminal window, navigate to the project's root folder (edge-service), and run the following command:

```
$ ./gradlew bootRun
```

The Edge Service application will start accepting requests on port 9000. For the final test, try executing operations on books and orders, but this time through the API gateway (that is, using port 9000 rather than the individual ports to which Catalog Service and Order Service are listening). They should return a 200 OK response:

```
$ http :9000/books
$ http :9000/orders
```

The result is the same as if you called Catalog Service and Order Service directly, but you only need to know one hostname and port this time. When you are done testing the application, stop its execution with Ctrl-C. Then terminate all the containers with Docker Compose:

```
$ docker-compose down
```

Under the hood, Edge Service uses Netty's HTTP client to forward requests to downstream services. As extensively discussed in the previous chapter, whenever an application calls an external service, it's essential to configure a timeout to make it resilient to interprocess communication failures. Spring Cloud Gateway provides dedicated properties to configure the HTTP client timeouts.

Open the Edge Service application.yml file once again, and define values for the connection timeout (the time limit for a connection to be established with the downstream service) and for the response timeout (the time limit for receiving a response).

Listing 9.3   Configuring timeouts for the gateway HTTP client

```
spring:
  cloud:
    gateway:                  Configuration         Time limit for a connection
      httpclient:             properties for        to be established (in ms)
                              the HTTP client
        connect-timeout: 2000                        Time limit for a response
        response-timeout: 5s                         to be received (Duration)
```

By default, the Netty HTTP client used by Spring Cloud Gateway is configured with an *elastic* connection pool to increase the number of concurrent connections dynamically as the workload increases. Depending on the number of requests your system receives simultaneously, you might want to switch to a *fixed* connection pool so you have more control over the number of connections. You can configure the Netty connection pool in Spring Cloud Gateway through the `spring.cloud.gateway.httpclient.pool` property group in the application.yml file.

Listing 9.4   Configuring the connection pool for the gateway HTTP client

```
spring:                         Type of connection pool
  cloud:                        (elastic, fixed, or disabled)
    gateway:
      httpclient:                 Idle time after which the
        connect-timeout: 5000     communication channel
        response-timeout: 5s      will be closed
        pool:
          type: elastic           Time after which the
          max-idle-time: 15s      communication channel
          max-life-time: 60s      will be closed
```

You can refer to the official Reactor Netty documentation for more details about how the connection pool works, what configurations are available, and tips on what values to use based on specific scenarios (https://projectreactor.io/docs).

In the next section, we'll start implementing something more interesting than merely forwarding requests—we'll look at the power of Spring Cloud Gateway filters.

9.1.3 Processing requests and responses through filters

Routes and predicates alone make the application act as a proxy, but it's filters that make Spring Cloud Gateway really powerful.

Filters can run before forwarding incoming requests to a downstream application (*pre-filters*). They can be used for:

- Manipulating the request headers
- Applying rate limiting and circuit breaking
- Defining retries and timeouts for the proxied request
- Triggering an authentication flow with OAuth2 and OpenID Connect

Other filters can apply to outgoing responses after they are received from the downstream application and before sending them back to the client (*post-filters*). They can be used for:

- Setting security headers
- Manipulating the response body to remove sensitive information

Spring Cloud Gateway comes bundled with many filters that you can use to perform different actions, including adding headers to a request, configuring a circuit breaker, saving the web session, retrying the request on failure, or activating a rate limiter.

In the previous chapter, you learned how to use the retry pattern to improve application resilience. You'll now learn how to apply it as a default filter for all `GET` requests going through the routes defined in the gateway.

USING THE RETRY FILTER

You can define default filters in the application.yml file located under src/main/resources. One of the filters provided by Spring Cloud Gateway is the `Retry` filter. The configuration is similar to what we did in chapter 8.

Let's define a maximum of three retry attempts for all `GET` requests whenever the error is in the 5xx range (`SERVER_ERROR`). We don't want to retry requests when the error is in the 4xx range. For example, if the result is a `404` response, it doesn't make sense to retry the request. We can also list the exceptions for which a retry should be attempted, such as `IOException` and `TimeoutException`.

By now, you know that you shouldn't keep retrying requests one after the other. You should use a backoff strategy instead. By default, the delay is computed using the formula `firstBackoff * (factor ^ n)`. If you set the `basedOnPreviousValue` parameter to `true`, the formula will be `prevBackoff * factor`.

Listing 9.5 Applying the retry filter to all routes

```
spring:
  cloud:
    gateway:
```

A list of default filters ⟶

Retries only GET requests ⟶

```
default-filters:
  - name: Retry
    args:
      retries: 3
      methods: GET
      series: SERVER_ERROR
      exceptions: java.io.IOException,
      ↳ java.util.concurrent.TimeoutException
      backoff:
        firstBackoff: 50ms
        maxBackOff: 500ms
        factor: 2
        basedOnPreviousValue: false
```

The name of the filter

Maximum of 3 retry attempts

Retries only when 5XX errors

Retries only when the given exceptions are thrown

Retries with a delay computed as "firstBackoff * (factor ^ n)"

The retry pattern is useful when a downstream service is momentarily unavailable. But what if it stays down for more than a few instants? At that point we could stop forwarding requests to it until we're sure that it's back. Continuing to send requests won't be beneficial for the caller or the callee. In that scenario, the circuit breaker pattern comes in handy. That's the topic of the next section.

9.2 Fault tolerance with Spring Cloud Circuit Breaker and Resilience4J

As you know, resilience is a critical property of cloud native applications. One of the principles for achieving resilience is blocking a failure from cascading and affecting other components. Consider a distributed system where application X depends on application Y. If application Y fails, will application X fail, too? A circuit breaker can block a failure in one component from propagating to the others depending on it, protecting the rest of the system. That is accomplished by temporarily stopping communication with the faulty component until it recovers. This pattern comes from electrical systems, for which the circuit is physically opened to break the electrical connection and avoid destroying the entire house when a part of the system fails due to current overload.

In the world of distributed systems, you can establish circuit breakers at the integration points between components. Think about Edge Service and Catalog Service. In a typical scenario, the circuit is *closed*, meaning that the two services can interact over the network. For each server error response returned by Catalog Service, the circuit breaker in Edge Service would register the failure. When the number of failures exceeds a certain threshold, the circuit breaker trips, and the circuit transitions to *open*.

While the circuit is open, communications between Edge Service and Catalog Service are not allowed. Any request that should be forwarded to Catalog Service will fail right away. In this state, either an error is returned to the client, or fallback logic is executed. After an appropriate amount of time to permit the system to recover, the circuit breaker transitions to a *half-open* state, allowing the next call to Catalog Service to go through. That is an exploratory phase to check if there are still issues in contacting the downstream service. If the call succeeds, the circuit breaker is reset and transitions to *closed*. Otherwise it goes back to being *open*. Figure 9.4 shows how a circuit breaker changes state.

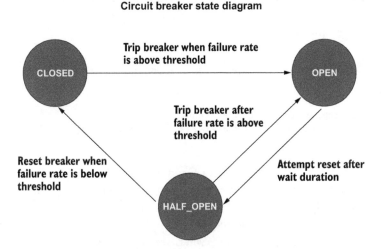

Circuit breaker state diagram

Figure 9.4 A circuit breaker ensures fault tolerance when a downstream service exceeds the maximum number of failures allowed by blocking any communication between upstream and downstream services. The logic is based on three states: closed, open, and half-open.

Unlike with retries, when the circuit breaker trips, no calls to the downstream service are allowed anymore. Like with retries, the circuit breaker's behavior depends on a threshold and a timeout, and it lets you define a fallback method to call. The goal of resilience is to keep the system available to users, even in the face of failures. In the worst-case scenario, like when a circuit breaker trips, you should guarantee a graceful degradation. You can adopt different strategies for the fallback method. For example, you might decide to return a default value or the last available value from a cache, in case of a GET request.

The Spring Cloud Circuit Breaker project provides an abstraction for defining circuit breakers in a Spring application. You can choose between reactive and nonreactive implementations based on Resilience4J (https://resilience4j.readme.io). Netflix Hystrix was the popular choice for microservices architectures, but it entered maintenance mode back in 2018. After that, Resilience4J became the preferred choice because it provides the same features offered by Hystrix and more.

Spring Cloud Gateway integrates natively with Spring Cloud Circuit Breaker, providing you with a CircuitBreaker gateway filter that you can use to protect the interactions with all downstream services. In the following sections, you'll configure a circuit breaker for the routes to Catalog Service and Order Service from Edge Service.

9.2.1 *Introducing circuit breakers with Spring Cloud Circuit Breaker*

To use Spring Cloud Circuit Breaker in Spring Cloud Gateway, you need to add a dependency to the specific implementation you'd like to use. In this case, we'll use the Resilience4J reactive version. Go ahead and add the new dependency in the build.gradle file for the Edge Service project (edge-service). Remember to refresh or reimport the Gradle dependencies after the new addition.

Listing 9.6   Adding dependency for Spring Cloud Circuit Breaker

```
dependencies {
  ...
  implementation 'org.springframework.cloud:
  ➥ spring-cloud-starter-circuitbreaker-reactor-resilience4j'
}
```

The `CircuitBreaker` filter in Spring Cloud Gateway relies on Spring Cloud Circuit Breaker to wrap a route. As with the `Retry` filter, you can choose to apply it to specific routes or define it as a default filter. Let's go with the first option. You can also specify an optional fallback URI to handle the request when the circuit is in an open state. In this example (application.yml), both routes will be configured with a `CircuitBreaker` filter, but only `catalog-route` will have a `fallbackUri` value so that I can show you both scenarios.

Listing 9.7   Configuring circuit breakers for the gateway routes

```
spring:
  cloud:
    gateway:
      routes:
        - id: catalog-route
          uri: ${CATALOG_SERVICE_URL:http://localhost:9001}/books
          predicates:
            - Path=/books/**
          filters:                                   Name of the
            - name: CircuitBreaker                   circuit breaker
              args:
                name: catalogCircuitBreaker          ◁──
                fallbackUri: forward:/catalog-fallback  ◁──
        - id: order-route
          uri: ${ORDER_SERVICE_URL:http://localhost:9002}/orders
          predicates:
            - Path=/orders/**
          filters:
            - name: CircuitBreaker     ◁──
              args:
                name: orderCircuitBreaker
```

Name of the filter → (pointing to `- name: CircuitBreaker`)

Forwards request to this URI when the circuit is open (pointing to `fallbackUri: forward:/catalog-fallback`)

No fallback defined for this circuit breaker. (pointing to `- name: CircuitBreaker`)

The next step is configuring the circuit breaker.

9.2.2 Configuring a circuit breaker with Resilience4J

After defining which routes you want to apply the `CircuitBreaker` filter to, you need to configure the circuit breakers themselves. As often in Spring Boot, you have two main choices. You can configure circuit breakers through the properties provided by Resilience4J or via a `Customizer` bean. Since we're using the reactive version of Resilience4J, the specific configuration bean would be of type `Customizer<ReactiveResilience4JCircuitBreakerFactory>`.

Either way, you can choose to define a specific configuration for each circuit breaker you used in your application.yml file (`catalogCircuitBreaker` and `orderCircuitBreaker` in our case) or declare some defaults that will be applied to all of them.

For the current example, we can define circuit breakers to consider a window of 20 calls (`slidingWindowSize`). Each new call will make the window move, dropping the oldest registered call. When at least 50% of the calls in the window have produced an error (`failureRateThreshold`), the circuit breaker will trip, and the circuit will enter the open state. After 15 seconds (`waitDurationInOpenState`), the circuit will be allowed to transition to a half-open state in which 5 calls are permitted (`permittedNumberOfCallsInHalfOpenState`). If at least 50% of them result in an error, the circuit will go back to the open state. Otherwise, the circuit breaker will trip to the closed state.

On to the code. In the Edge Service project (edge-service), at the end of the application.yml file, define a default configuration for all Resilience4J circuit breakers.

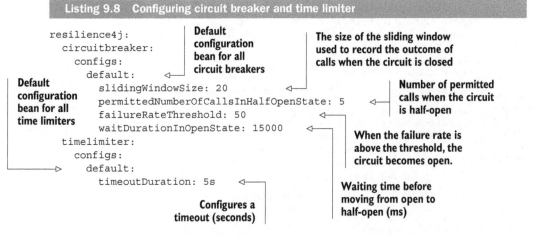

Listing 9.8 Configuring circuit breaker and time limiter

```
resilience4j:
  circuitbreaker:
    configs:
      default:
        slidingWindowSize: 20
        permittedNumberOfCallsInHalfOpenState: 5
        failureRateThreshold: 50
        waitDurationInOpenState: 15000
  timelimiter:
    configs:
      default:
        timeoutDuration: 5s
```

Default configuration bean for all circuit breakers

The size of the sliding window used to record the outcome of calls when the circuit is closed

Default configuration bean for all time limiters

Number of permitted calls when the circuit is half-open

When the failure rate is above the threshold, the circuit becomes open.

Waiting time before moving from open to half-open (ms)

Configures a timeout (seconds)

We configure both the circuit breaker and a time limiter, a required component when using the Resilience4J implementation of Spring Cloud Circuit Breaker. The timeout configured via Resilience4J will take precedence over the response timeout we defined in the previous section for the Netty HTTP client (`spring.cloud.gateway.httpclient.response-timeout`).

When a circuit breaker switches to the open state, we'll want at least to degrade the service level gracefully and make the user experience as pleasant as possible. I'll show you how to do that in the next section.

9.2.3 Defining fallback REST APIs with Spring WebFlux

When we added the `CircuitBreaker` filter to `catalog-route`, we defined a value for the `fallbackUri` property to forward the requests to the `/catalog-fallback` endpoint when the circuit is in an open state. Since the `Retry` filter is also applied to that route, the fallback endpoint will be invoked even when all retry attempts fail for a given request. It's time to define that endpoint.

As I mentioned in previous chapters, Spring supports defining REST endpoints either using `@RestController` classes or router functions. Let's use the functional way of declaring the fallback endpoints.

In a new `com.polarbookshop.edgeservice.web` package in the Edge Service project, create a new `WebEndpoints` class. Functional endpoints in Spring WebFlux are defined as routes in a `RouterFunction<ServerResponse>` bean, using the fluent API provided by `RouterFunctions`. For each route, you need to define the endpoint URL, a method, and a handler.

Listing 9.9   Fallback endpoints for when the Catalog Service is down

```
package com.polarbookshop.edgeservice.web;

import reactor.core.publisher.Mono;
import org.springframework.context.annotation.Bean;
import org.springframework.context.annotation.Configuration;
import org.springframework.http.HttpStatus;
import org.springframework.web.reactive.function.server.RouterFunction;
import org.springframework.web.reactive.function.server.RouterFunctions;
import org.springframework.web.reactive.function.server.ServerResponse;

@Configuration
public class WebEndpoints {          ◁── Functional REST endpoints are defined in a bean.

    @Bean
    public RouterFunction<ServerResponse> routerFunction() {    ◁── Offers a fluent API to build routes
        return RouterFunctions.route()
            .GET("/catalog-fallback", request ->               ◁── Fallback response used to handle the GET endpoint
                ServerResponse.ok().body(Mono.just(""), String.class))
            .POST("/catalog-fallback", request ->              ◁── Fallback response used to handle the POST endpoint
                ServerResponse.status(HttpStatus.SERVICE_UNAVAILABLE).build())
            .build();        ◁── Builds the functional endpoints
    }
}
```

For simplicity, the fallback for `GET` requests returns an empty string, whereas the fallback for `POST` requests returns an HTTP 503 error. In a real scenario, you might want to adopt different fallback strategies depending on the context, including throwing a custom exception to be handled from the client or returning the last value saved in the cache for the original request.

So far, we have used retries, timeouts, circuit breakers, and failovers (fallbacks). In the next section, I'll expand on how we can work with all those resilience patterns together.

9.2.4 *Combining circuit breakers, retries, and time limiters*

When you combine multiple resilience patterns, the sequence in which they are applied is fundamental. Spring Cloud Gateway takes care of applying the `TimeLimiter` first (or the timeout on the HTTP client), then the `CircuitBreaker` filter, and finally `Retry`. Figure 9.5 shows how these patterns work together to increase the application's resilience.

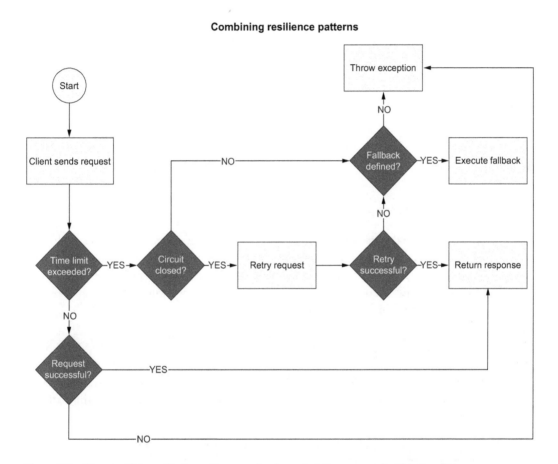

Figure 9.5 When multiple resilience patterns are implemented, they are applied in a specific sequence.

You can verify the result of applying these patterns to Edge Service by using a tool like Apache Benchmark (https://httpd.apache.org/docs/2.4/programs/ab.html). If you're using macOS or Linux, you might have this tool already installed. Otherwise, you can follow the instructions on the official website and install it.

Make sure both Catalog Service and Order Service are not running so that you can test circuit breakers in a failure scenario. Then enable debug logging for Resilience4J so you can follow the state transitions of the circuit breaker. At the end of the application.yml file in your Edge Service project, add the following configuration.

> **Listing 9.10   Enabling debug logging for Resilience4J**

```
logging:
  level:
    io.github.resilience4j: DEBUG
```

Next, build and run Edge Service (./gradlew bootRun). Since no downstream services are running (if they are, you should stop them), all the requests sent to them from Edge Service will result in errors. Let's see what happens if we run 21 sequential POST requests (-n 21 -c 1 -m POST) to the /orders endpoint. Remember that POST requests have no retry configuration, and order-route has no fallback, so the result will only be affected by the timeout and circuit breaker:

```
$ ab -n 21 -c 1 -m POST http://localhost:9000/orders
```

From the ab output, you can see that all the requests returned an error:

```
Complete requests: 21
Non-2xx responses: 21
```

The circuit breaker is configured to trip to the open state when at least 50% of the calls in a 20-sized time window fails. Since you have just started the application, the circuit will transition to the open state after 20 requests. In the application logs, you can analyze how the requests have been handled. All the requests failed, so the circuit breaker registers an ERROR event for each of them:

```
Event ERROR published: CircuitBreaker 'orderCircuitBreaker'
  recorded an error.
```

At the 20th request, a FAILURE_RATE_EXCEEDED event is recorded because it exceeded the failure threshold. That will result in a STATE_TRANSITION event that will open the circuit:

```
Event ERROR published: CircuitBreaker 'orderCircuitBreaker'
  recorded an error.
Event FAILURE_RATE_EXCEEDED published: CircuitBreaker 'orderCircuitBreaker'
  exceeded failure rate threshold.
Event STATE_TRANSITION published: CircuitBreaker 'orderCircuitBreaker'
  changed state from CLOSED to OPEN
```

The 21st request will not even try contacting Order Service: the circuit is open, so it cannot go through. A NOT_PERMITTED event is registered to signal why the request failed:

```
Event NOT_PERMITTED published: CircuitBreaker 'orderCircuitBreaker'
  recorded a call which was not permitted.
```

NOTE   Monitoring the status of circuit breakers in production is a critical task. In chapter 13, I'll show you how to export that information as Prometheus metrics that you can visualize in a Grafana dashboard instead of checking the logs. In the meantime, for a more visual explanation, feel free to watch my "Spring Cloud Gateway: Resilience, Security, and Observability" session on circuit breakers at Spring I/O, 2022 (http://mng.bz/z55A).

Now let's see what happens when we call a GET endpoint for which both retries and fallback have been configured. Before proceeding, rerun the application so you can start with a clear circuit breaker state (./gradlew bootRun). Then run the following command:

```
$ ab -n 21 -c 1 -m GET http://localhost:9000/books
```

If you check the application logs, you'll see how the circuit breaker behaves precisely like before: 20 allowed requests (closed circuit), followed by a non-permitted request (open circuit). However, the result of the previous command shows 21 requests completed with no errors:

```
Complete requests: 21
Failed requests: 0
```

This time, all requests have been forwarded to the fallback endpoint, so the client didn't experience any errors.

We configured the Retry filter to be triggered when an IOException or Timeout-Exception occurs. In this case, since the downstream service is not running, the exception thrown is of type ConnectException, so the request is conveniently not retried, which allowed me to show you the combined behavior of circuit breakers and fallbacks without retries.

So far we have looked at patterns that make the interactions between Edge Service and the downstream applications more resilient. What about the entry point of the system? The next section will introduce rate limiters, which will control the request flow coming into the system through the Edge Service application. Before proceeding, stop the application's execution with Ctrl-C.

9.3   Request rate limiting with Spring Cloud Gateway and Redis

Rate limiting is a pattern used to control the rate of traffic sent to or received from an application, helping to make your system more resilient and robust. In the context of HTTP interactions, you can apply this pattern to control outgoing or incoming network traffic using client-side and server-side rate limiters, respectively.

Client-side rate limiters are for constraining the number of requests sent to a downstream service in a given period. It's a useful pattern to adopt when third-party organizations like cloud providers manage and offer the downstream service. You'll want to avoid incurring extra costs for having sent more requests than are allowed by your subscription. In the case of pay-per-use services, this helps prevent unexpected expenses.

If the downstream service belongs to your system, you might use a rate limiter to avoid causing DoS problems for yourself. In this case, though, a *bulkhead* pattern (or *concurrent request limiter*) would be a better fit, setting constraints on how many concurrent requests are allowed and queuing up the blocked ones. Even better is an adaptive bulkhead, for which the concurrency limits are dynamically updated by an algorithm to better adapt to the elasticity of cloud infrastructure.

Server-side rate limiters are for constraining the number of requests received by an upstream service (or client) in a given period. This pattern is handy when implemented in an API gateway to protect the whole system from overloading or from DoS attacks. When the number of users increases, the system should scale in a resilient way, ensuring an acceptable quality of service for all users. Sudden increases in user traffic are expected, and they are usually initially addressed by adding more resources to the infrastructure or more application instances. Over time, though, they can become a problem and even lead to service outages. Server-side rate limiters help with that.

When a user has exceeded the number of allowed requests in a specific time window, all the extra requests are rejected with an `HTTP 429 - Too Many Requests` status. The limit is applied according to a given strategy. For example, you can limit requests per session, per IP address, per user, or per tenant. The overall goal is to keep the system available for all users in case of adversity. That is the definition of resilience. This pattern is also handy for offering services to users depending on their subscription tiers. For example, you might define different rate limits for basic, premium, and enterprise users.

Resilience4J supports the client-side rate limiter and bulkhead patterns for both reactive and non-reactive applications. Spring Cloud Gateway supports the server-side rate limiter pattern, and this section will show you how to use it for Edge Service by using Spring Cloud Gateway and Spring Data Redis Reactive. Let's start with setting up a Redis container.

9.3.1 Running Redis as a container

Imagine you want to limit access to your API so that each user can only perform 10 requests per second. Implementing such a requirement would require a storage mechanism to track the number of requests each user performs every second. When the limit is reached, the following requests should be rejected. When the second is over, each user can perform 10 more requests within the next second. The data used by the rate-limiting algorithm is small and temporary, so you might think of saving it in memory inside the application itself.

However, that would make the application stateful and lead to errors, since each application instance would limit requests based on a partial data set. It would mean letting users perform 10 requests per second per instance rather than overall, because each instance would only keep track of its own incoming requests. The solution is to use a dedicated data service to store the rate-limiting state and make it available to all the application replicas. Enter Redis.

Redis (https://redis.com) is an in-memory store that is commonly used as a cache, message broker, or database. In Edge Service, we'll use it as the data service backing the request rate limiter implementation provided by Spring Cloud Gateway. The Spring Data Redis Reactive project provides the integration between a Spring Boot application and Redis.

Let's first define a Redis container. Open the docker-compose.yml file you created in your `polar-deployment` repository. (If you haven't followed along with the examples, you can use Chapter09/09-begin/polar-deployment/docker/docker-compose.yml from the source code accompanying the book as a starting point.) Then add a new service definition using the Redis official image, and expose it through port 6379.

Listing 9.11 Defining a Redis container

```
version: "3.8"
services:
  ...
  polar-redis:
    image: "redis:7.0"          ◁─── Uses Redis 7.0
    container_name: "polar-redis"
    ports:
      - 6379:6379               ◁─── Exposes Redis
                                     through port 6379
```

Next, open a Terminal window, navigate to the folder where your docker-compose.yml file is located, and run the following command to start a Redis container:

```
$ docker-compose up -d polar-redis
```

In the following section, you'll configure the Redis integration with Edge Service.

9.3.2 Integrating Spring with Redis

The Spring Data project has modules supporting several database options. In the previous chapters, we worked with Spring Data JDBC and Spring Data R2DBC to use relational databases. Now we'll use Spring Data Redis, which provides support for this in-memory, non-relational data store. Both imperative and reactive applications are supported.

First we need to add a new dependency on Spring Data Redis Reactive in the build.gradle file of the Edge Service project (edge-service). Remember to refresh or reimport the Gradle dependencies after the new addition.

Listing 9.12 Adding dependency for Spring Data Redis Reactive

```
dependencies {
  ...
  implementation
  ⟿ 'org.springframework.boot:spring-boot-starter-data-redis-reactive'
}
```

Then, in the application.yml file, configure the Redis integration through the properties provided by Spring Boot. Besides `spring.redis.host` and `spring.redis.port` for defining where to reach Redis, you can also specify connection and read timeouts using `spring.redis.connect-timeout` and `spring.redis.timeout` respectively.

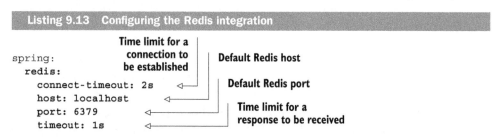

Listing 9.13   Configuring the Redis integration

In the next section, you'll see how to use Redis to back the `RequestRateLimiter` gateway filter that provides server-side rate limiting support.

9.3.3   *Configuring a request rate limiter*

Depending on the requirements, you can configure the `RequestRateLimiter` filter for specific routes or as a default filter. In this case we'll configure it as a default filter so that it's applied to all routes, current and future.

The implementation of `RequestRateLimiter` on Redis is based on the *token bucket algorithm*. Each user is assigned a bucket inside which tokens are dripped over time at a specific rate (the *replenish rate*). Each bucket has a maximum capacity (the *burst capacity*). When a user makes a request, a token is removed from its bucket. When there are no more tokens left, the request is not permitted, and the user will have to wait until more tokens are dripped into its bucket.

> **NOTE**   If you want to know more about the token bucket algorithm, I recommend reading Paul Tarjan's "Scaling your API with Rate Limiters" article about how they use it to implement rate limiters at Stripe (https://stripe.com/blog/rate-limiters).

For this example, let's configure the algorithm so that each request costs 1 token (`redis-rate-limiter.requestedTokens`). Tokens are dripped in the bucket following the configured replenish rate (`redis-rate-limiter.replenishRate`), which we'll set as 10 tokens per second. Sometimes there might be spikes, resulting in a larger number of requests than usual. You can allow temporary bursts by defining a larger capacity for the bucket (`redis-rate-limiter.burstCapacity`), such as 20. This means that when a spike occurs, up to 20 requests are allowed per second. Since the replenish rate is lower than the burst capacity, subsequent bursts are not allowed. If two spikes happen sequentially, only the first one will succeed, while the second will result in some requests being dropped with an `HTTP 429 - Too Many Requests` response. The resulting configuration in the application.yml file is shown in the following listing.

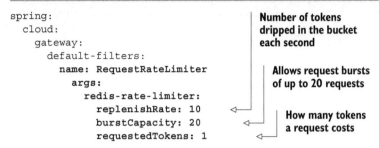

Listing 9.14 Configuring a request rate limiter as a gateway filter

```yaml
spring:
  cloud:
    gateway:
      default-filters:
        name: RequestRateLimiter
         args:
           redis-rate-limiter:
             replenishRate: 10
             burstCapacity: 20
             requestedTokens: 1
```

Number of tokens dripped in the bucket each second

Allows request bursts of up to 20 requests

How many tokens a request costs

There's no general rule to follow in coming up with good numbers for the request rate limiter. You should start with your application requirements and go with a trial and error approach: analyze your production traffic, tune the configuration, and do this all over again until you achieve a setup that keeps your system available while not affecting the user experience badly. Even after that, you should keep monitoring the status of your rate limiters, since things can change in the future.

Spring Cloud Gateway relies on Redis to keep track of the number of requests happening each second. By default, each user is assigned a bucket. However, we haven't introduced an authentication mechanism yet, so we'll use a single bucket for all requests until we address the security concerns in chapters 11 and 12.

> **NOTE** What happens if Redis becomes unavailable? Spring Cloud Gateway has been built with resilience in mind, so it will keep its service level, but the rate limiters would be disabled until Redis is up and running again.

The `RequestRateLimiter` filter relies on a `KeyResolver` bean to determine which bucket to use for each request. By default, it uses the currently authenticated user in Spring Security. Until we add security to Edge Service, we'll define a custom `Key-Resolver` bean and make it return a constant value (for example, `anonymous`) so that all requests will be mapped to the same bucket.

In your Edge Service project, create a `RateLimiterConfig` class in a new `com.polarbookshop.edgeservice.config` package, and declare a `KeyResolver` bean, implementing a strategy to return a constant key.

Listing 9.15 Defining a strategy to resolve the bucket to use per request

```java
package com.polarbookshop.edgeservice.config;

import reactor.core.publisher.Mono;
import org.springframework.cloud.gateway.filter.ratelimit.KeyResolver;
import org.springframework.context.annotation.Bean;
import org.springframework.context.annotation.Configuration;

@Configuration
public class RateLimiterConfig {
```

```
@Bean
public KeyResolver keyResolver() {
    return exchange -> Mono.just("anonymous");    ⟵⎯  Rate limiting is
}                                                       applied to requests
}                                                       using a constant key.
```

Spring Cloud Gateway is configured to append headers with details about rate-limiting to each HTTP response, which we can use to verify its behavior. Rebuild and run Edge Service (./gradlew bootRun), and then try calling one of the endpoints.

```
$ http :9000/books
```

The response body depends on whether Catalog Service is running or not, but that doesn't matter in this example. The interesting aspect to notice is the HTTP headers of the response. They show the rate limiter's configuration and the number of remaining requests allowed within the time window (1 second):

```
HTTP/1.1 200 OK
Content-Type: application/json
X-RateLimit-Burst-Capacity: 20
X-RateLimit-Remaining: 19
X-RateLimit-Replenish-Rate: 10
X-RateLimit-Requested-Tokens: 1
```

You might not want to expose this information to clients in cases where the information could help bad actors craft attacks against your system. Or you might need different header names. Either way, you can use the spring.cloud.gateway.redis-rate-limiter property group to configure that behavior. When you're done testing the application, stop it with Ctrl-C.

> **NOTE** When the rate limiter pattern is combined with other patterns like time limiters, circuit breakers, and retries, the rate limiter is applied first. If a user's request exceeds the rate limit, it is rejected right away.

Redis is an efficient data store ensuring fast data access, high availability, and resilience. In this section, we used it to provide storage for the rate limiters, and the next section will show you how to use it in another common scenario: session management.

9.4   *Distributed session management with Redis*

In the previous chapters, I often highlighted how cloud native applications should be stateless. We scale them in and out, and if they weren't stateless, we would lose the state every time an instance is shut down. Some state needs to be saved, or the applications would probably be useless. For example, Catalog Service and Order Service are stateless, but they rely on a stateful service (the PostgreSQL database) to permanently store the data about books and orders. Even if the applications are shut down, the data will survive and be available to all the application instances.

Edge Service is not dealing with any business entities it needs to store, but it still needs a stateful service (Redis) to store the state related to the RequestRateLimiter filter. When Edge Service is replicated, it's important to keep track of how many requests are left before exceeding the threshold. Using Redis, the rate limiter functionality is guaranteed consistently and safely.

Furthermore, in chapter 11 you'll expand Edge Service to add authentication and authorization. Since it's the entry point to the Polar Bookshop system, it makes sense to authenticate the user there. Data about the authenticated session will have to be saved outside the application for the same reason as the rate limiter information is. If it wasn't, the user might have to authenticate themselves every time a request hits a different Edge Service instance.

The general idea is to keep the applications stateless and use data services for storing the state. As you learned in chapter 5, data services need to guarantee high availability, replication, and durability. In your local environment, you can ignore that aspect, but in production you'll rely on the data services offered by cloud providers, both for PostgreSQL and Redis.

The following section will cover how you can work with Spring Session Data Redis to establish distributed session management.

9.4.1 Handling sessions with Spring Session Data Redis

Spring provides session management features with the Spring Session project. By default, session data is stored in memory, but that's not feasible in a cloud native application. You want to keep it in an external service so that the data survives the application shutdown. Another fundamental reason for using a distributed session store is that you usually have multiple instances of a given application. You'll want them to access the same session data to provide a seamless experience to the user.

Redis is a popular option for session management, and it's supported by Spring Session Data Redis. Furthermore, you have already set it up for the rate limiters. You can add it to Edge Service with minimal configuration.

First you need to add a new dependency on Spring Session Data Redis to the build.gradle file for the Edge Service project. You can also add the Testcontainers library so you can use a lightweight Redis container when writing integration tests. Remember to refresh and reimport the Gradle dependencies after the new addition.

Listing 9.16 Adding dependency for Spring Session and Testcontainers

```
ext {
  ...
  set('testcontainersVersion', "1.17.3")
}

dependencies {
  ...
  implementation 'org.springframework.session:spring-session-data-redis'
```

```
    testImplementation 'org.testcontainers:junit-jupiter'
}

dependencyManagement {
  imports {
    ...
    mavenBom
    ➥ "org.testcontainers:testcontainers-bom:${testcontainersVersion}"
  }
}
```

Next, you need to instruct Spring Boot to use Redis for session management (`spring.session.store-type`) and define a unique namespace to prefix all session data coming from Edge Service (`spring.session.redis.namespace`). You can also define a timeout for the session (`spring.session.timeout`). If you don't specify a timeout, the default is 30 minutes.

Configure Spring Session in the application.yml file as follows.

Listing 9.17 Configuring Spring Session to store data in Redis

```
spring:
  session:
    store-type: redis
    timeout: 10m
    redis:
      namespace: polar:edge
```

Managing web sessions in a gateway requires some additional care to ensure you save the right state at the right time. In this example, we want the session to be saved in Redis before forwarding a request downstream. How can we do that? If you were thinking about whether there's a gateway filter for it, you would be right!

In the application.yml file for the Edge Service project, add `SaveSession` as a default filter to instruct Spring Cloud Gateway to always save the web session before forwarding requests downstream.

Listing 9.18 Configuring the gateway to save the session data

```
spring:
  cloud:
    gateway:                        Ensures the session data is
      default-filters:              saved before forwarding a
        - SaveSession    ◁——┘       request downstream
```

That's a critical point when Spring Session is combined with Spring Security. Chapters 11 and 12 will cover more details about session management. For now, let's set up an integration test to verify the Spring context in Edge Service loads correctly, including the integration with Redis.

The approach we'll use is similar to the one we used to define PostgreSQL test containers in the previous chapter. Let's extend the existing `EdgeServiceApplicationTests` class generated by Spring Initializr and configure a Redis test container. For this example, it's enough to verify that the Spring context loads correctly when Redis is used for storing web session–related data.

> **Listing 9.19 Using a Redis container to test the Spring context loading**

```
package com.polarbookshop.edgeservice;

import org.junit.jupiter.api.Test;
import org.testcontainers.containers.GenericContainer;
import org.testcontainers.junit.jupiter.Container;
import org.testcontainers.junit.jupiter.Testcontainers;
import org.testcontainers.utility.DockerImageName;
import org.springframework.boot.test.context.SpringBootTest;
import org.springframework.test.context.DynamicPropertyRegistry;
import org.springframework.test.context.DynamicPropertySource;

@SpringBootTest(
  webEnvironment = SpringBootTest.WebEnvironment.RANDOM_PORT
)
@Testcontainers
class EdgeServiceApplicationTests {

    private static final int REDIS_PORT = 6379;

    @Container
    static GenericContainer<?> redis =
      new GenericContainer<>(DockerImageName.parse("redis:7.0"))
        .withExposedPorts(REDIS_PORT);

    @DynamicPropertySource
    static void redisProperties(DynamicPropertyRegistry registry) {
      registry.add("spring.redis.host",
          () -> redis.getHost());
      registry.add("spring.redis.port",
          () -> redis.getMappedPort(REDIS_PORT));
    }

    @Test
    void verifyThatSpringContextLoads() {
    }

}
```

Loads a full Spring web application context and a web environment listening on a random port

Activates automatic startup and cleanup of test containers

Defines a Redis container for testing

Overwrites the Redis configuration to point to the test Redis instance

An empty test used to verify that the application context is loaded correctly and that a connection with Redis has been established successfully

Finally, run the integration tests as follows:

```
$ ./gradlew test --tests EdgeServiceApplicationTests
```

Should you want to disable the session management through Redis in some of your tests, you can do so by setting the spring.session.store-type property to none in a specific test class using the @TestPropertySource annotation, or in a property file if you want to make it apply to all test classes.

Polar Labs

Feel free to apply what you learned in the previous chapters and prepare the Edge Service application for deployment.

1   Add Spring Cloud Config Client to Edge Service to make it fetch configuration data from Config Service.
2   Configure the Cloud Native Buildpacks integration, containerize the application, and define the commit stage of the deployment pipeline, as you learned in chapters 3 and 6.
3   Write the Deployment and Service manifests for deploying Edge Service to a Kubernetes cluster.
4   Configure Tilt to automate the Edge Service deployment to your local Kubernetes cluster initialized with minikube.

You can refer to the Chapter09/09-end folder in the code repository accompanying the book to check the final result (https://github.com/ThomasVitale/cloud-native-spring-in-action). You can also deploy the backing services from the manifests available in the Chapter09/09-end/polar-deployment/kubernetes/platform/development folder with `kubectl apply -f services`.

9.5 *Managing external access with Kubernetes Ingress*

Spring Cloud Gateway helps you define an edge service where you can implement several patterns and cross-cutting concerns at the ingress point of a system. In the previous sections, you saw how to use it as an API gateway, implement resilience patterns like rate limiting and circuit breakers, and define distributed sessions. In chapters 11 and 12, we'll also add authentication and authorization features to Edge Service.

Edge Service represents the entry point to the Polar Bookshop system. However, when it's deployed in a Kubernetes cluster, it's only accessible from within the cluster itself. In chapter 7, we used the *port-forward* feature to expose a Kubernetes Service defined in a minikube cluster to your local computer. That's a useful strategy during development, but it's not suitable for production.

This section will cover how you can manage external access to applications running in a Kubernetes cluster using the Ingress API.

NOTE   This section assumes you have gone through the tasks listed in the previous "Polar Labs" sidebar and prepared Edge Service for deployment on Kubernetes.

9.5.1 *Understanding Ingress API and Ingress Controller*

When it comes to exposing applications inside a Kubernetes cluster, we can use a Service object of type `ClusterIP`. That's what we've done so far to make it possible for Pods to interact with each other within the cluster. For example, that's how Catalog Service Pods can communicate with the PostgreSQL Pod.

A Service object can also be of type `LoadBalancer`, which relies on an external load balancer provisioned by a cloud provider to expose an application to the internet. We could define a `LoadBalancer` Service for Edge Service instead of the `ClusterIP` one. When running the system in a public cloud, the vendor would provision a load balancer, assign a public IP address, and all the traffic coming from that load balancer would be directed to the Edge Service Pods. It's a flexible approach that lets you expose a service directly to the internet, and it works with different types of traffic.

The `LoadBalancer` Service approach involves assigning a different IP address to each service we decide to expose to the internet. Since services are directly exposed, we don't have the chance to apply any further network configuration, such as TLS termination. We could configure HTTPS in Edge Service, route all traffic directed to the cluster through the gateway (even platform services that don't belong to Polar Bookshop), and apply further network configuration there. The Spring ecosystem provides everything we need to address those concerns, and it's probably what we would do in many scenarios. However, since we want to run our system on Kubernetes, we can manage those infrastructural concerns at the platform level and keep our applications simpler and more maintainable. That's where the Ingress API comes in handy.

An *Ingress* is an object that "manages external access to the services in a cluster, typically HTTP. Ingress may provide load balancing, SSL termination and name-based virtual hosting" (https://kubernetes.io/docs). An Ingress object acts as an entry point into a Kubernetes cluster and is capable of routing traffic from a single external IP address to multiple services running inside the cluster. We can use an Ingress object to perform load balancing, accept external traffic directed to a specific URL, and manage the TLS termination to expose the application services via HTTPS.

Ingress objects don't accomplish anything by themselves. We use an Ingress object to declare the *desired state* in terms of routing and TLS termination. The actual component that enforces those rules and routes traffic from outside the cluster to the applications inside is the *ingress controller*. Since multiple implementations are available, there's no default ingress controller included in the core Kubernetes distribution— it's up to you to install one. Ingress controllers are applications that are usually built using reverse proxies like NGINX, HAProxy, or Envoy. Some examples are Ambassador Emissary, Contour, and Ingress NGINX.

In production, the cloud platform or dedicated tools would be used to configure an ingress controller. In our local environment, we'll need some additional configuration to make the routing work. For the Polar Bookshop example, we'll use Ingress NGINX (https://github.com/kubernetes/ingress-nginx) in both environments.

NOTE There are two popular ingress controllers based on NGINX. The Ingress NGINX project (https://github.com/kubernetes/ingress-nginx) is developed, supported, and maintained in the Kubernetes project itself. It's open source, and it's what we'll use in this book. The NGINX Controller (www.nginx.com/products/nginx-controller) is a product developed and maintained by the F5 NGINX company, and it comes with free and commercial options.

Let's see how we can use Ingress NGINX on our local Kubernetes cluster. An ingress controller is a workload just like any other application running on Kubernetes, and it can be deployed in different ways. The simplest option would be using kubectl to apply its deployment manifests to the cluster. Since we use minikube to manage a local Kubernetes cluster, we can rely on a built-in add-on to enable the Ingress functionality based on Ingress NGINX.

First, let's start the `polar` local cluster we introduced in chapter 7. Since we configured minikube to run on Docker, make sure your Docker Engine is up and running:

```
$ minikube start --cpus 2 --memory 4g --driver docker --profile polar
```

Next we can enable the `ingress` add-on, which will make sure that Ingress NGINX is deployed to our local cluster:

```
$ minikube addons enable ingress --profile polar
```

In the end, you can get information about the different components deployed with Ingress NGINX as follows:

```
$ kubectl get all -n ingress-nginx
```

The preceding command contains an argument we haven't encountered yet: `-n ingress-nginx`. It means that we want to fetch all objects created in the `ingress-nginx` *namespace*.

A *namespace* is "an abstraction used by Kubernetes to support isolation of groups of resources within a single cluster. Namespaces are used to organize objects in a cluster and provide a way to divide cluster resources" (https://kubernetes.io/docs/reference/glossary).

We use namespaces to keep our clusters organized and define network policies to keep certain resources isolated for security reasons. So far, we've been working with the `default` namespace, and we'll keep doing that for all our Polar Bookshop applications. However, when it comes to platform services such as Ingress NGINX, we'll rely on dedicated namespaces to keep those resources isolated.

Now that Ingress NGINX is installed, let's go ahead and deploy the backing services used by our Polar Bookshop applications. Check the source code repository accompanying this book (Chapter09/09-end) and copy the content of the polar-deployment/kubernetes/platform/development folder into the same path in your `polar-deployment` repository, overwriting any existing file we used in previous chapters. The folder contains basic Kubernetes manifests to run PostgreSQL and Redis.

Open a Terminal window, navigate to the kubernetes/platform/development folder located in your `polar-deployment` repository, and run the following command to deploy PostgreSQL and Redis in your local cluster:

```
$ kubectl apply -f services
```

You can verify the results with the following command:

```
$ kubectl get deployment
NAME             READY   UP-TO-DATE   AVAILABLE   AGE
polar-postgres   1/1     1            1           73s
polar-redis      1/1     1            1           73s
```

TIP For your convenience, I prepared a script that performs all the previous operations with a single command. You can run it to create a local Kubernetes cluster with minikube, enable the Ingress NGINX add-on, and deploy the backing services used by Polar Bookshop. You'll find the create-cluster.sh and destroy-cluster.sh files in the kubernetes/platform/development folder that you have just copied over to your `polar-deployment` repository. On macOS and Linux, you might need to make the scripts executable via the `chmod +x create-cluster.sh` command.

Let's conclude this section by packaging Edge Service as a container image and loading the artifact to the local Kubernetes cluster. Open a Terminal window, navigate to the Edge Service root folder (edge-service), and run the following commands:

```
$ ./gradlew bootBuildImage
$ minikube image load edge-service --profile polar
```

In the next section, you'll define an Ingress object and configure it to manage external access to the Polar Bookshop system running in a Kubernetes cluster.

9.5.2 Working with Ingress objects

Edge Service takes care of application routing, but it should not be concerned with the underlying infrastructure and network configuration. Using an Ingress resource, we can decouple the two responsibilities. Developers would maintain Edge Service, while the platform team would manage the ingress controller and the network configuration (perhaps relying on a service mesh like Linkerd or Istio). Figure 9.6 shows the deployment architecture of Polar Bookshop after introducing an Ingress.

Let's define an Ingress to route all HTTP traffic coming from outside the cluster to Edge Service. It's common to define Ingress routes and configurations based on the DNS name used to send the HTTP request. Since we are working locally, and assuming we don't have a DNS name, we can call the external IP address provisioned for the Ingress to be accessible from outside the cluster. On Linux, you can use the IP address

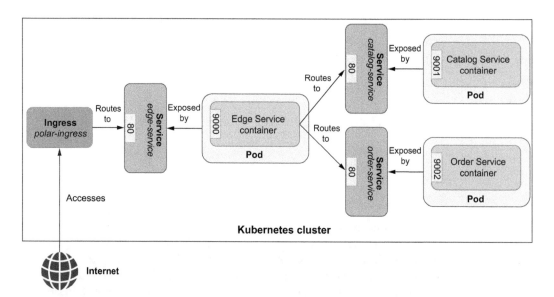

Figure 9.6   The deployment architecture of the Polar Bookshop system after introducing an Ingress to manage external access to the cluster

assigned to the minikube cluster. You can retrieve that value by running the following command:

```
$ minikube ip --profile polar
192.168.49.2
```

On macOS and Windows, the `ingress` add-on doesn't yet support using the minikube cluster's IP address when running on Docker. Instead, we need to use the `minikube tunnel --profile polar` command to expose the cluster to the local environment, and then use the `127.0.0.1` IP address to call the cluster. This is similar to the `kubectl port-forward` command, but it applies to the whole cluster instead of a specific service.

After identifying the IP address to use, let's define the Ingress object for Polar Bookshop. In the Edge Service project, create a new ingress.yml file in the k8s folder.

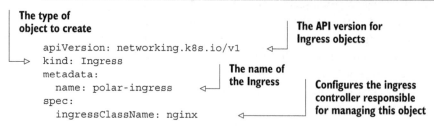

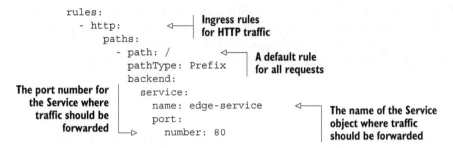

```
rules:
  - http:
      paths:
        - path: /
          pathType: Prefix
          backend:
            service:
              name: edge-service
              port:
                number: 80
```

Ingress rules for HTTP traffic

A default rule for all requests

The port number for the Service where traffic should be forwarded

The name of the Service object where traffic should be forwarded

At this point we are ready to deploy Edge Service and the Ingress to the local Kubernetes cluster. Open a Terminal window, navigate to the Edge Service root folder (edge-service), and run the following command:

```
$ kubectl apply -f k8s
```

Let's verify that the Ingress object has been created correctly with the following command:

```
$ kubectl get ingress

NAME            CLASS    HOSTS   PORTS   AGE
polar-ingress   nginx    *       80      21s
```

It's time to test that Edge Service is correctly available through the Ingress. If you're on Linux, you don't need any further preparation steps. If you're on macOS or Windows, open a new Terminal window and run the following command to expose your minikube cluster to your localhost. The command will continue running for the tunnel to be accessible, so make sure you keep the Terminal window open. The first time you run this command, you might be asked to input your machine's password to authorize the tunneling to the cluster:

```
$ minikube tunnel --profile polar
```

Finally, open a new Terminal window and run the following command to test the application (on Linux, use the minikube's IP address instead of 127.0.0.1):

```
$ http 127.0.0.1/books
```

Since Catalog Service is not running, Edge Service will execute the fallback behavior we configured earlier and return a 200 OK response with an empty body. That's what we expected, and it proves that the Ingress configuration works.

When you are done trying out the deployment, you can stop and delete the local Kubernetes cluster with the following commands:

```
$ minikube stop --profile polar
$ minikube delete --profile polar
```

TIP For your convenience, you can also use the destroy-cluster.sh script (available in the kubernetes/platform/development folder of your `polar-deployment` repository) that you copied earlier from the book's source code. On macOS and Linux, you might need to make the script executable via the `chmod +x destroy-cluster.sh` command.

Good job! We're now ready to make Edge Service even better by adding authentication and authorization. Before configuring security, though, we still need to complete the Polar Bookshop business logic for dispatching orders. In the next chapter, you'll do that while learning event-driven architectures, Spring Cloud Function, and Spring Cloud Stream with RabbitMQ.

Summary

- An API gateway provides several benefits in a distributed architecture, including decoupling the internal services from the external API and offering a central, convenient place for handling cross-cutting concerns like security, monitoring, and resilience.
- Spring Cloud Gateway is based on the Spring reactive stack. It provides an API gateway implementation, and it integrates with the other Spring projects to add cross-cutting concerns to the application, including Spring Security, Spring Cloud Circuit Breaker, and Spring Session.
- Routes are the core of Spring Cloud Gateway. They are identified by a unique ID, a collection of predicates determining whether to follow the route, a URI for forwarding the request if the predicates allow, and a collection of filters that are applied before or after forwarding the request downstream.
- The `Retry` filter is for configuring retry attempts for specific routes.
- The `RequestRateLimiter` filter, integrated with Spring Data Redis Reactive, limits the number of requests that can be accepted within a specific time window.
- The `CircuitBreaker` filter, based on Spring Cloud Circuit Breaker and Resilience4J, defines circuit breakers, time limiters, and fallbacks to specific routes.
- Cloud native applications should be stateless. Data services should be used for storing the state. For example, PostgreSQL is used for persistence storage and Redis for cache and session data.
- A Kubernetes Ingress resource allows you to manage external access to applications running inside the Kubernetes cluster.
- The routing rules are enforced by an ingress controller, which is an application that also runs in the cluster.

Event-driven
applications
and functions

This chapter covers
- Understanding event-driven architectures
- Using RabbitMQ as a message broker
- Implementing functions with Spring Cloud Function
- Processing events with Spring Cloud Stream
- Producing and consuming events with Spring Cloud Stream

In the previous chapters, we worked on a system of distributed applications that interact according to the request/response pattern, a type of synchronous communication. You saw how to design the interaction both in an imperative and a reactive way. In the first case, processing threads would block, waiting for a response from an I/O operation. In the second case, threads would not wait. A response would be processed by any available thread asynchronously once it was received.

Even if the reactive programming paradigm lets you subscribe to producers and process the incoming data asynchronously, the interaction between the two applications is synchronous. The first application (the client) sends a request to the second one (the server) and expects a response to arrive in a short time. How the client processes the response (imperative or reactive) is an implementation detail that doesn't affect the interaction itself. No matter what, a response is expected to arrive.

Cloud native applications should be loosely coupled. The microservices expert Sam Newman identifies a few different types of coupling, including *implementation, deployment,* and *temporal* coupling.[1] Let's consider the Polar Bookshop system we've been working on so far.

We can change the implementation of any of the applications without having to change the others. For example, we can re-implement Catalog Service using the reactive paradigm without affecting Order Service. Using a service interface like a REST API, we hide the implementation details, improving loose coupling. All the applications can be deployed independently. They're not coupled, reducing risks and increasing agility.

However, if you think about how the applications we built so far interact, you'll notice that they need other components of the system to be available. Order Service needs Catalog Service to ensure that a user can order a book successfully. We know that failures happen all the time, so we adopted several strategies to ensure resilience even in the face of adversity, or at least ensuring a graceful degradation of functionality. That's a consequence of *temporal coupling*: Order Service and Catalog Service need to be available at the same time to fulfill the system requirements.

Event-driven architectures describe distributed systems that interact by *producing* and *consuming* events. The interaction is asynchronous, solving the problem of temporal coupling. This chapter will cover the basics of event-driven architectures and event brokers. You'll then learn how to implement business logic using the functional programming paradigm and Spring Cloud Function. Finally, you'll use Spring Cloud Stream to expose the functions as message channels via RabbitMQ, building event-driven applications through the publisher/subscriber (pub/sub) model.

> **NOTE** The source code for the examples in this chapter is available in the Chapter10/10-begin, Chapter10/10-intermediate, and Chapter10/10-end folders, containing the initial, intermediate, and final state of the project (https://github.com/ThomasVitale/cloud-native-spring-in-action).

10.1 Event-driven architectures

An event is an occurrence. It's something relevant that happened in a system, like a state change, and there can be many sources of events. This chapter will focus on applications, but events can very well be happening in IoT devices, sensors, or networks. When an event occurs, interested parties can be notified. Event notification is usually done through messages, which are data representations of events.

In an event-driven architecture, we identify *event producers* and *event consumers*. A producer is a component that detects the event and sends a notification. A consumer is a component that is notified when a specific event occurs. Producers and consumers don't know each other and work independently. A producer sends an event notification

---

[1] See Sam Newman, *Monolith to Microservices* (O'Reilly, 2019).

by publishing a message to a channel operated by an event broker that's responsible for collecting and routing messages to consumers. A consumer is notified by the broker when an event occurs and can act upon it.

Producers and consumers have minimal coupling when using a broker that takes the processing and distribution of events on itself. In particular, they are temporally decoupled, because the interaction is asynchronous. Consumers can fetch and process messages at any time without affecting the producers whatsoever.

In this section, you'll learn the fundamentals of event-driven models and how they can help build more resilient and loosely coupled applications in the cloud.

10.1.1 Understanding the event-driven models

Event-driven architectures can be based on two main models:

- *Publisher/subscriber (pub/sub)*—This model is based on subscriptions. Producers publish events that are sent to all subscribers to be consumed. Events cannot be replayed after being received, so new consumers joining will not be able to get the past events.
- *Event streaming*—In this model, events are written to a log. Producers publish events as they occur, and they are all stored in an ordered fashion. Consumers don't subscribe to them, but they can read from any part of the event stream. In this model, events can be replayed. Clients can join at any time and receive all the past events.

In a basic scenario, consumers receive and process events as they arrive. For specific use cases like pattern matching, they can also process a series of events over a time window. In the event streaming model, consumers have the additional possibility of processing event streams. At the core of event-driven architectures are platforms that can process and route events. For example, RabbitMQ is a common choice to use with the pub/sub model. Apache Kafka is a powerful platform for event stream processing.

The event streaming model is fascinating and growing in popularity, thanks to the many technologies developed in the last few years, allowing you to build real-time data pipelines. It's a complex model, though, that deserves its own book to be taught effectively. In this chapter, I will cover the pub/sub model.

Before we analyze this model in more detail, I'll define some requirements for the Polar Bookshop system, and we'll use them as a means to explore event-driven architectures with the pub/sub model.

10.1.2 Using the pub/sub model

In the Polar Bookshop system, we need to implement an event-driven solution to allow different applications communicate with each other asynchronously while reducing their coupling. These are the requirements:

- When an order is accepted:
  - Order Service should notify interested consumers of the event.
  - Dispatcher Service should execute some logic to dispatch the order.

- When an order is dispatched:
  - Dispatcher Service should notify consumers interested in such an event.
  - Order Service should update the order status in the database.

If you paid attention, you probably noticed that the requirements don't specify which applications Order Service should notify upon order creation. In our example, only the new Dispatcher Service application will be interested in those events. Still, more applications might subscribe to the order creation events in the future. The beauty of this design is that you can evolve a software system and add more applications without affecting the existing ones at all. For example, you could add a Mail Service that sends an email to users whenever an order they made has been accepted, and Order Service wouldn't even be aware of it.

This type of interaction should be asynchronous and can be modeled with the pub/sub model. Figure 10.1 illustrates the interaction and describes three flows for accepting, dispatching, and updating an order. They are temporally decoupled and executed asynchronously. You will probably notice that the operations for persisting data into a database and for producing events have the same numbered step. That's because they belong to the same unit of work (a *transaction*), as I'll explain later in the chapter.

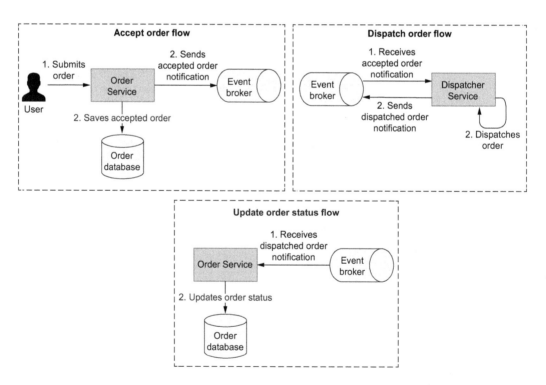

Figure 10.1   Order Service and Dispatcher Service communicate asynchronously and indirectly by producing and consuming events that are collected and distributed by an event broker (RabbitMQ).

In the rest of the chapter, you'll learn a few technologies and patterns you can use to implement this event-driven design for Polar Bookshop. RabbitMQ will be the event-processing platform responsible for collecting, routing, and distributing messages to consumers. Figure 10.2 highlights the event-driven part of the Polar Bookshop system after we introduce the Dispatcher Service application and RabbitMQ.

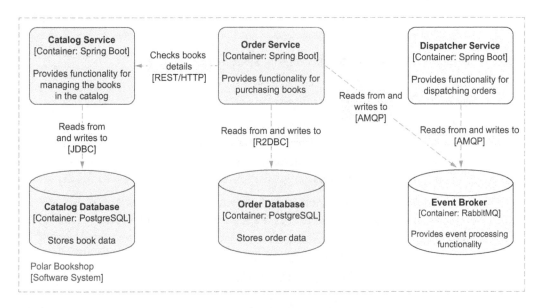

Figure 10.2   In the Polar Bookshop system, Order Service and Dispatcher Service communicate asynchronously based on events distributed by RabbitMQ.

The following section will introduce the basic concepts of RabbitMQ, its protocol, and how to run it in your local environment.

10.2   Message brokers with RabbitMQ

A messaging system requires two main things: a message broker and a protocol. The Advanced Message Queuing Protocol (AMQP) ensures interoperability across platforms and reliable message delivery. It has become widely used in modern architectures, and it's a good fit in the cloud, where we need resilience, loose coupling, and scalability. RabbitMQ is a popular open source message broker that relies on AMQP and provides flexible asynchronous messaging, distributed deployment, and monitoring. Recent RabbitMQ versions have also introduced event streaming features.

Spring provides broad support for the most-used messaging solutions. The Spring Framework itself has built-in support for the Java Message Service (JMS) API. The Spring AMQP project (https://spring.io/projects/spring-amqp) adds support for this messaging protocol and provides integration with RabbitMQ. Apache Kafka is another technology that has become increasingly used in the last few years, such as to implement the event sourcing pattern or real-time stream processing. The Spring for Apache Kafka project (https://spring.io/projects/spring-kafka) provides that integration.

This section will cover the fundamental aspects of the AMQP protocol and RabbitMQ, which is the message broker we'll use to implement messaging in the Polar Bookshop system. On the application side, we'll use Spring Cloud Stream, which offers convenient and robust integration with RabbitMQ by relying on the Spring AMQP project.

10.2.1 Understanding AMQP for messaging systems

When using an AMQP-based solution like RabbitMQ, the actors involved in the interaction can be categorized as follows:

- *Producer*—The entity sending messages (publisher)
- *Consumer*—The entity receiving messages (subscriber)
- *Message broker*—The middleware accepting messages from producers and routing them to consumers

Figure 10.3 illustrates the interaction between the actors. From the protocol point of view, we can also say that the broker is the *server*, while producers and consumers are the *clients*.

The AMQP actors

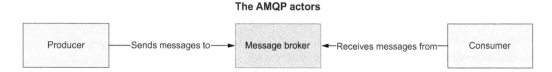

Figure 10.3   In AMQP, a broker accepts messages from producers and routes them to consumers.

> **NOTE** RabbitMQ was initially developed to support AMQP, but it also supports other protocols, including STOMP, MQTT, and even WebSockets for delivering messages over HTTP. Since version 3.9, it also supports event streaming.

The AMQP messaging model is based on *exchanges* and *queues,* as illustrated in figure 10.4. Producers send messages to an exchange. RabbitMQ computes which queues should receive a copy of the message according to a given routing rule. Consumers read messages from a queue.

The protocol establishes that a message comprises attributes and a payload, as shown in figure 10.5. AMQP defines some attributes, but you can add your own to pass the information that's needed to route the message correctly. The payload must be of a binary type and has no constraints besides that.

Now that you know the basics of AMQP, let's get RabbitMQ up and running.

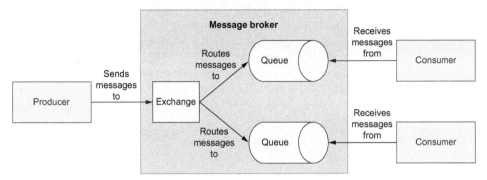

Figure 10.4 Producers publish messages to an exchange. Consumers subscribe to queues. Exchanges route messages to queues according to a routing algorithm.

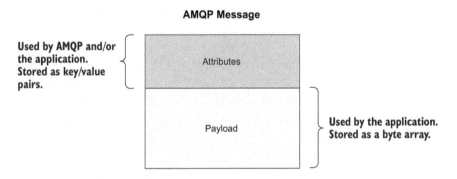

Figure 10.5 An AMQP Message is composed of attributes and a payload.

10.2.2 Using RabbitMQ for publish/subscribe communications

RabbitMQ, on top of AMQP, provides a simple yet effective solution for implementing a publish/subscribe interaction that is precisely the one we want to establish between Order Service and Dispatcher Service. Besides the functionality itself, it's essential to look for those properties I addressed in previous chapters for cloud systems and data services, including resilience, high availability, and data replication. RabbitMQ offers all of that. For example, it provides delivery acknowledgment, clustering, monitoring, queue durability, and replication. Furthermore, several cloud providers offer integrations with managed RabbitMQ services.

For now, you'll run RabbitMQ as a container on your local machine. First, make sure your Docker Engine is running. Then open the docker-compose.yml file located in your `polar-deployment` repository.

NOTE   If you haven't followed along with the examples, you can use Chapter10/ 10-begin/polar-deployment/docker/docker-compose.yml from the source code accompanying the book as a starting point.

In your docker-compose.yml file, add a new service definition using the RabbitMQ official image (including the management plugin) and expose it through port 5672 (for AMQP) and 15672 (for the management console). The RabbitMQ management plugin is convenient for inspecting exchanges and queues from a browser-based UI.

Listing 10.1   Defining a container for RabbitMQ

```
version: "3.8"
services:
  ...
  polar-rabbitmq:
    image: rabbitmq:3.10-management
    container_name: polar-rabbitmq
    ports:
      - 5672:5672
      - 15672:15672
    volumes:
      - ./rabbitmq/rabbitmq.conf:/etc/rabbitmq/rabbitmq.conf
```

Annotations:
- The official RabbitMQ image with the management plugin enabled
- The port where RabbitMQ listens for AMQP requests
- The port that exposes the management GUI
- Configuration file mounted as a volume

The configuration is based on a file mounted as a volume, similar to how we configured PostgreSQL. Create a docker/rabbitmq folder within your `polar-deployment` repository, and add a new rabbitmq.conf file to configure the default account.

Listing 10.2   Configuring RabbitMQ default account

```
default_user = user
default_pass = password
```

Next, open a Terminal window, navigate to the folder where your docker-compose.yml file is located, and run the following command to start RabbitMQ:

```
$ docker-compose up -d polar-rabbitmq
```

Finally, open a browser window and navigate to http://localhost:15672 to access the RabbitMQ management console. Log in using the credentials we defined in the configuration file (user/password) and have a look around. In the following sections you'll be able to follow the message flows between Order Service and Dispatcher Service in the Exchanges and Queues areas of the management console.

When you're done exploring the RabbitMQ management console, you can shut it down as follows:

```
$ docker-compose down
```

Spring Cloud Stream helps integrate applications with event brokers like RabbitMQ seamlessly. But before we get to it, we need to define the logic that will process messages.

In the next section, you'll learn about Spring Cloud Function and how to implement the business logic of the new order flow in terms of suppliers, functions, and consumers.

10.3 Functions with Spring Cloud Function

Oleg Zhurakousky, project lead for Spring Cloud Function and Spring Cloud Stream, often asks conference audiences this question: Is there any business feature that you cannot define in terms of suppliers, functions, and consumers? It's an interesting and challenging question. Can you think of anything? Most software requirements can be expressed with functions.

Why use functions in the first place? They are a simple, uniform, and portable programming model that is a perfect fit for event-driven architectures, inherently based on these concepts.

Spring Cloud Function promotes the implementation of business logic via functions based on the standard interfaces introduced by Java 8: `Supplier`, `Function`, and `Consumer`.

- *Supplier*—A supplier is a function with only output, no input. It's also known as a *producer, publisher,* or *source*.
- *Function*—A function has both input and output. It's also known as a *processor*.
- *Consumer*—A consumer is a function with input but no output. It's also known as a *subscriber* or *sink*.

In this section, you'll learn how Spring Cloud Function works and how to implement business logic via functions.

10.3.1 Using the functional paradigm in Spring Cloud Function

Let's get started with functions by considering the business requirements I listed earlier for the Dispatcher Service application. Whenever an order is accepted, Dispatcher Service should be responsible for packing and labeling the order, and for notifying interested parties (in this case, the Order Service) once the order has been dispatched. For simplicity, let's assume that both the *pack* and *label* actions are performed by the application itself, and we'll consider how to implement the business logic via functions before even thinking about frameworks.

The two actions to be performed as part of dispatching an order could be represented as functions:

- The *pack* function takes the identifier of an accepted order as input, packs the order (in the example, the processing is represented by a log message), and returns the order identifier as output, ready to be labeled.
- The *label* function takes the identifier of a packed order as input, labels the order (in the example, the processing is represented by a log message), and returns the order identifier as output, completing the dispatch.

The composition of these two functions in sequence gives the full implementation of the business logic for Dispatcher Service, as shown in figure 10.6.

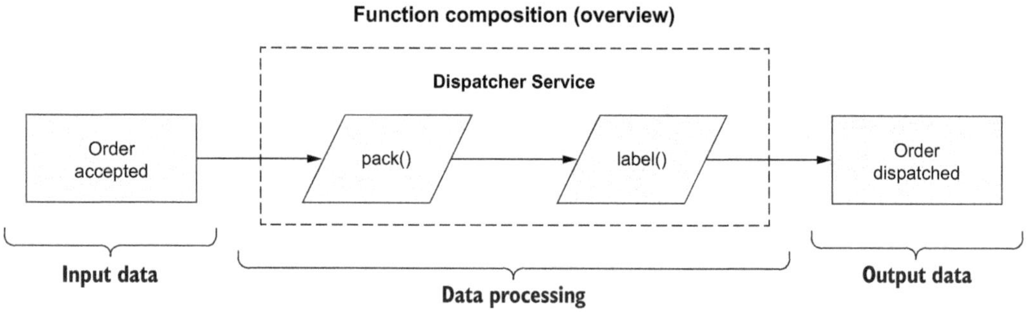

Function composition (overview)

Figure 10.6   The business logic for Dispatcher Service is implemented as a composition of two functions: pack and label.

Let's see how we can implement these functions and what Spring Cloud Function brings to the table.

INITIALIZING A SPRING CLOUD FUNCTION PROJECT

You can initialize the Dispatcher Service project from Spring Initializr (https://start .spring.io) and store the result in a new `dispatcher-service` Git repository. The parameters for the initialization are shown in figure 10.7.

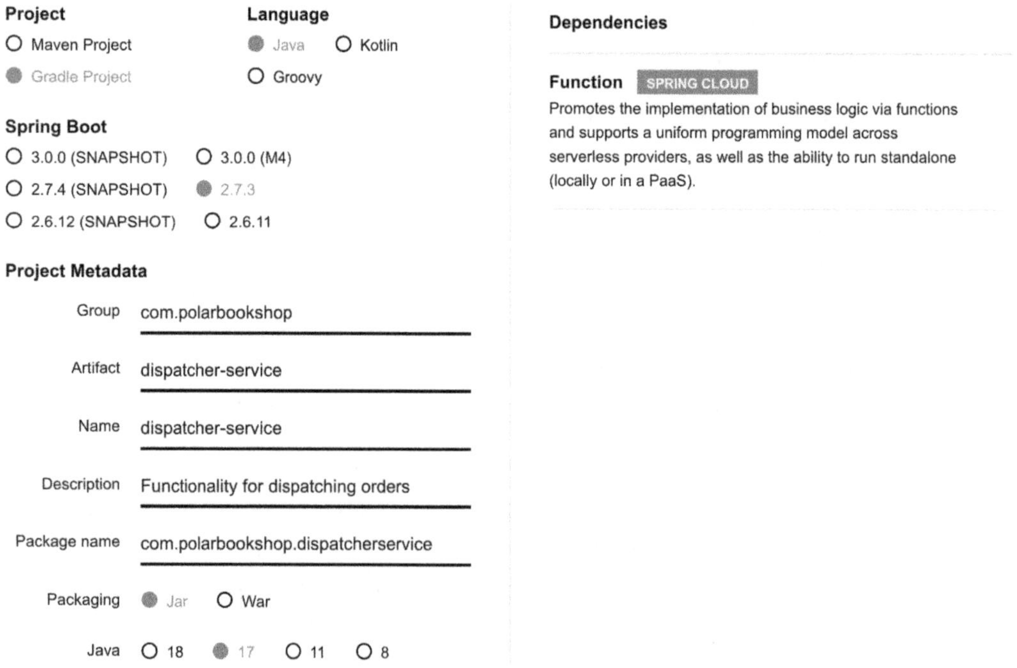

Project
- O Maven Project
- ● Gradle Project

Language
- ● Java   O Kotlin
- O Groovy

Spring Boot
- O 3.0.0 (SNAPSHOT)   O 3.0.0 (M4)
- O 2.7.4 (SNAPSHOT)   ● 2.7.3
- O 2.6.12 (SNAPSHOT)   O 2.6.11

Project Metadata

Group	com.polarbookshop
Artifact	dispatcher-service
Name	dispatcher-service
Description	Functionality for dispatching orders
Package name	com.polarbookshop.dispatcherservice
Packaging	● Jar O War
Java	O 18 ● 17 O 11 O 8

Dependencies

Function `SPRING CLOUD`
Promotes the implementation of business logic via functions and supports a uniform programming model across serverless providers, as well as the ability to run standalone (locally or in a PaaS).

Figure 10.7   The parameters for initializing the Dispatcher Service project

TIP In the `begin` folder for this chapter, you can find a `curl` command that you can run in a Terminal window. It downloads a zip file containing all the code you need to get started, without going through the manual generation on the Spring Initializr website.

The resulting `dependencies` section of the build.gradle file looks like this:

```
dependencies {
  implementation 'org.springframework.boot:spring-boot-starter'
  implementation 'org.springframework.cloud:spring-cloud-function-context'
  testImplementation 'org.springframework.boot:spring-boot-starter-test'
}
```

The main dependencies are

- *Spring Boot* (`org.springframework.boot:spring-boot-starter`)—Provides basic Spring Boot libraries and auto-configuration.
- *Spring Cloud Function* (`org.springframework.cloud:spring-cloud-function-context`)—Provides the Spring Cloud Function libraries that promote and support business logic implementation via functions.
- *Spring Boot Test* (`org.springframework.boot:spring-boot-starter-test`)—Provides several libraries and utilities for testing applications, including Spring Test, JUnit, AssertJ, and Mockito. It's automatically included in every Spring Boot project.

Next, rename the autogenerated application.properties file to application.yml, and configure the server port and application name. At present, the application doesn't contain a web server. Nevertheless, we'll configure the server port number because it will be used when we add monitoring capabilities to the application in chapter 13.

Listing 10.3 Configuring server and application name

```
server:
  port: 9003          ◁──┤  The port that will be used by
spring:                     the embedded web server
  application:
    name: dispatcher-service   ◁──┘  The name of the application
```

Next, let's see how we can implement the business logic using functions.

IMPLEMENTING THE BUSINESS LOGIC VIA FUNCTIONS

The business logic can be implemented in a standard way by using the Java `Function` interface. No Spring needed.

Let's first consider the *pack* function. The input of the function should provide the identifier of an order that has previously been accepted. We can model this data via a simple DTO.

In the `com.polarbookshop.dispatcherservice` package, create an `OrderAccepted-Message` record to hold the order identifier.

Listing 10.4   A DTO representing the event about orders being accepted

```
package com.polarbookshop.dispatcherservice;

public record OrderAcceptedMessage (
  Long orderId
){}
```

DTO containing the order identifier as a Long field

NOTE Modeling events is a fascinating topic that goes beyond Spring and would require a few chapters to cover properly. If you'd like to learn more about this subject, I recommend reading these articles by Martin Fowler: "Focusing on Events" (https://martinfowler.com/eaaDev/EventNarrative.html); "Domain Event" (https://martinfowler.com/eaaDev/DomainEvent.html); and "What do you mean by 'Event-Driven'?" (https://martinfowler.com/articles/201701-event-driven.html), all on his MartinFowler.com blog.

The output of the function can be the simple identifier of the packed order represented as a Long object.

Now that input and output are clear, it's time to define the function. Create a new DispatchingFunctions class, and add a pack() method to implement order packing as a function.

Listing 10.5   Implementing the "pack" action as a function

```
package com.polarbookshop.dispatcherservice;

import java.util.function.Function;
import org.slf4j.Logger;
import org.slf4j.LoggerFactory;

public class DispatchingFunctions {
  private static final Logger log =
    LoggerFactory.getLogger(DispatchingFunctions.class);

  public Function<OrderAcceptedMessage, Long> pack() {
    return orderAcceptedMessage -> {
      log.info("The order with id {} is packed.",
        orderAcceptedMessage.orderId());
      return orderAcceptedMessage.orderId();
    };
  }
}
```

Function implementing the order-packing business logic

It takes an OrderAcceptedMessage object as input.

Returns an order identifier (Long) as output

You can see how there's only standard Java code in this listing. I strive to provide real-world examples in this book, so you might wonder what's happening here. In this case, I decided to focus on the essential aspects of using the functional programming paradigm in the context of an event-driven application. Inside the function, you can add any processing logic you like. What matters here is the contract provided by the function, its signature: inputs and outputs. After defining that, you're free to implement the function as needed. I could have provided a more real-world implementation of this function, but it would have added nothing valuable considering the goal of this chapter. It doesn't even have to be Spring-based code. And in this example, it's not: it's plain Java code.

Spring Cloud Function is capable of managing functions defined in different ways, as long as they adhere to the standard Java interfaces `Function`, `Supplier`, and `Consumer`. You can make Spring Cloud Function aware of your functions by registering them as beans. Go ahead and do that for the `pack()` function by annotating the `DispatchingFunctions` class as `@Configuration` and the method as `@Bean`.

Listing 10.6 Configuring the function as a bean

```
@Configuration                                 ◁─────  Functions are defined in
public class DispatchingFunctions {                    a configuration class.
  private static final Logger log =
    LoggerFactory.getLogger(DispatchingFunctions.class);

  @Bean
  public Function<OrderAcceptedMessage, Long> pack() {   ◁───  Functions defined
    return orderAcceptedMessage -> {                            as beans can be
      log.info("The order with id {} is packed.",              discovered and
        orderAcceptedMessage.orderId());                        managed by
      return orderAcceptedMessage.orderId();                    Spring Cloud
    };                                                          Function.
  }
}
```

As you'll see later, functions registered as beans are enhanced with extra features by the Spring Cloud Function framework. The beauty of this is that the business logic itself is not aware of the surrounding framework. You can evolve it independently and test it without being concerned about framework-related issues.

USING IMPERATIVE AND REACTIVE FUNCTIONS

Spring Cloud Function supports both imperative and reactive code, so you're free to implement functions using reactive APIs like `Mono` and `Flux`. You can also mix and match. For the sake of the example, let's implement the *label* function using Project Reactor. The input of the function will be the identifier of an order that has been packed, represented as a `Long` object. The output of the function will be the identifier of the order that has been labeled, resulting in the dispatching process being complete. We can model such data via a simple DTO, just like we did for `OrderAcceptedMessage`.

In the `com.polarbookshop.dispatcherservice` package, create an `Order-DispatchedMessage` record to hold the identifier for a dispatched order.

Listing 10.7 A DTO representing the event about orders being dispatched

```
package com.polarbookshop.dispatcherservice;

public record OrderDispatchedMessage (      ◁───  DTO containing the
  Long orderId                                     order identifier as
){}                                                a Long field
```

Now that the input and output are clear, it's time to define the function. Open the DispatchingFunctions class and add a label() method to implement the order labeling as a function. Since we want it to be reactive, both input and output are wrapped in a Flux publisher.

Listing 10.8   Implementing the "label" action as a function

```
package com.polarbookshop.dispatcherservice;

import java.util.function.Function;
import org.slf4j.Logger;
import org.slf4j.LoggerFactory;
import reactor.core.publisher.Flux;
import org.springframework.context.annotation.Bean;
import org.springframework.context.annotation.Configuration;

@Configuration
public class DispatchingFunctions {
  private static final Logger log =
    LoggerFactory.getLogger(DispatchingFunctions.class);

  ...
  @Bean
  public Function<Flux<Long>, Flux<OrderDispatchedMessage>> label() {
    return orderFlux -> orderFlux.map(orderId -> {
      log.info("The order with id {} is labeled.", orderId);
      return new OrderDispatchedMessage(orderId);
    });
  }
}
```

Function implementing the order-labeling business logic ← `@Bean`

It takes an order identifier (Long) as input.

Returns an OrderDispatchedMessage as output

We have just implemented both functions, so let's see how we can combine and use them.

10.3.2   *Composing and integrating functions: REST, serverless, data streams*

The implementation of the business logic for Dispatcher Service is almost done. We still need a way to compose the two functions. Based upon our requirements, dispatching an order consists of two steps to be executed in sequence: pack() first and label() after.

Java provides features to compose Function objects in sequence using the andThen() or compose() operators. The problem is that you can use them only when the output type of the first function is the same as the second function's input. Spring Cloud Function provides a solution to that problem and lets you compose functions seamlessly through transparent type conversion, even between imperative and reactive functions like those we defined earlier.

Composing functions with Spring Cloud is as simple as defining a property in your application.yml (or application.properties) file. Open the application.yml file in your Dispatcher Service project, and configure Spring Cloud Function to manage and compose the pack() and label() functions as follows.

```
spring:
  cloud:
    function:
      definition: pack|label
```
← **Definition of the function managed by Spring Cloud Function**

The spring.cloud.function.definition property lets you declare which functions you want Spring Cloud Function to manage and integrate, resulting in a specific data flow. In the previous section, we implemented the basic pack() and label() functions. Now we can instruct Spring Cloud Function to use them as building blocks and produce a new function that comes from the composition of those two.

In a serverless application like those meant to be deployed on a FaaS platform (such as AWS Lambda, Azure Functions, Google Cloud Functions, or Knative), you would usually have one function defined per application. The cloud function definition can be mapped one-to-one to a function declared in your application, or you can use the *pipe* (|) operator to compose functions together in a data flow. If you need to define multiple functions, you can use the semicolon (;) character as the separator instead of the pipe (|).

To sum up, you only need to implement standard Java functions, and you can then configure Spring Cloud Function to use them as they are or after combining them. The framework will do the rest, including transparently converting input and output types to make the composition possible. Figure 10.8 illustrates the function composition.

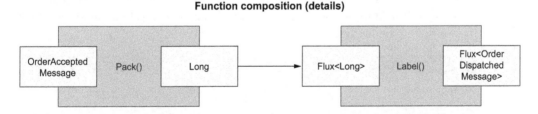

Figure 10.8   You can combine functions with different input and output types and mix imperative and reactive types as well. Spring Cloud Function will transparently handle any type conversion.

At this point you're probably wondering how you can use these functions. That's my favorite part. Once you define the functions, the framework can expose them in different ways depending on your needs. For example, Spring Cloud Function can automatically expose the functions defined in `spring.cloud.function.definition` as REST endpoints. Then you can directly package the application, deploy it on a FaaS platform like Knative, and voilà: you've got your first serverless Spring Boot application. That's what we'll do in chapter 16 when we build serverless applications. Or you can use one of the adapters provided by the framework to package the application and deploy it on AWS Lambda, Azure Functions, or Google Cloud Functions. Or you can combine it with Spring Cloud Stream and bind the function to message channels in an event broker like RabbitMQ or Kafka.

Before we explore the integration with RabbitMQ using Spring Cloud Stream, I want to show you how to test the functions and their composition in isolation. Once the business logic is implemented as functions and tested, we can be sure it will work the same way, whether it's triggered by a REST endpoint or an event notification.

10.3.3 *Writing integration tests with @FunctionalSpringBootTest*

Using the functional programming paradigm, we can implement business logic in standard Java and write unit tests with JUnit without being affected by the framework. At that level there is no Spring code, just plain Java. Once you've ensured that each function works, you'll want to write some integration tests to verify your application's overall behavior when your functions are processed by Spring Cloud Function and exposed the way you configured.

Spring Cloud Function provides a `@FunctionalSpringBootTest` annotation you can use to set up the context for your integration tests. Unlike unit tests, you don't want to invoke the function directly but rather ask the framework to provide that for you. All the functions managed by the framework are available through the `Function-Catalog`, an object that acts as a function registry. When the framework serves the function, it doesn't only contain the implementation you wrote; it's enhanced with extra features offered by Spring Cloud Function, like transparent type conversion and function composition. Let's see how this works.

First, you need to add a test dependency on Reactor Test in the build.gradle file, since part of the business logic is implemented using Reactor. Remember to refresh or reimport the Gradle dependencies after the new addition.

> **Listing 10.10 Adding dependency for Reactor Test in Dispatcher Service**

```
dependencies {
  ...
  testImplementation 'io.projectreactor:reactor-test'
}
```

Then, in the src/test/java folder of your Dispatcher Service project, create a new `DispatchingFunctionsIntegrationTests` class. You can write integration tests for the two functions individually, but it's more interesting verifying the behavior of the composed function, `pack()` + `label()`, as provided by Spring Cloud Function.

Listing 10.11 Integration tests for a function composition

```
package com.polarbookshop.dispatcherservice;

import java.util.function.Function;
import org.junit.jupiter.api.Test;
import reactor.core.publisher.Flux;
import reactor.test.StepVerifier;
import org.springframework.beans.factory.annotation.Autowired;
import org.springframework.cloud.function.context.FunctionCatalog;
import org.springframework.cloud.function.context.test
    .FunctionalSpringBootTest;

@FunctionalSpringBootTest
class DispatchingFunctionsIntegrationTests {

  @Autowired
  private FunctionCatalog catalog;

  @Test
  void packAndLabelOrder() {
    Function<OrderAcceptedMessage, Flux<OrderDispatchedMessage>>
      packAndLabel = catalog.lookup(
        Function.class,
        "pack|label");          ⟵  Gets the composed
    long orderId = 121;             function from the
                                    FunctionCatalog

    StepVerifier.create(packAndLabel.apply(
      new OrderAcceptedMessage(orderId)
    ))
      .expectNextMatches(dispatchedOrder ->
        dispatchedOrder.equals(new OrderDispatchedMessage(orderId)))
      .verifyComplete();
  }
}
```

Gets the composed function from the FunctionCatalog

Defines an OrderAccepted-Message, which is the input to the function

Asserts that the output of the function is the expected OrderDispatchedMessage object

Finally, open a Terminal window, navigate to the Dispatcher Service project root folder, and run the tests:

```
$ ./gradlew test --tests DispatchingFunctionsIntegrationTests
```

This type of integration test ensures the correct behavior of the defined cloud function, independently of how it will be exposed. In the source code accompanying the book, you'll find a broader set of autotests (Chapter10/10-intermediate/dispatcher-service).

Functions are a simple yet effective way to implement business logic and delegate infrastructural concerns to the framework. In the next section you'll learn how to bind functions to message channels on RabbitMQ using Spring Cloud Stream.

10.4 Processing messages with Spring Cloud Stream

The principles that drive the Spring Cloud Function framework can also be found in Spring Cloud Stream. The idea is that you, as a developer, are responsible for the business logic, while the framework handles infrastructural concerns like how to integrate a message broker.

Spring Cloud Stream is a framework for building scalable, event-driven, and streaming applications. It's built on top of Spring Integration, which offers the communication layer with message brokers; Spring Boot, which provides auto-configuration for the middleware integration; and Spring Cloud Function, which produces, processes, and consumes events. Spring Cloud Stream relies on the native features of each message broker, but it also provides an abstraction to ensure a seamless experience independently of the underlying middleware. For example, features like consumer groups and partitions (native in Apache Kafka) are not present in RabbitMQ, but you can still use them thanks to the framework providing them for you.

My favorite Spring Cloud Stream feature is that you can drop a dependency in a project like Dispatcher Service and get functions automatically bound to an external message broker. The best part of it? You don't have to change any code in the application, just the configuration in application.yml or application.properties. In previous versions of the framework, it was necessary to use dedicated annotations to match the business logic with the Spring Cloud Stream components. Now it's completely transparent.

The framework supports integrations with RabbitMQ, Apache Kafka, Kafka Streams, and Amazon Kinesis. There are also integrations maintained by partners for Google PubSub, Solace PubSub+, Azure Event Hubs, and Apache RocketMQ.

This section will cover how to expose the composed function we defined in Dispatcher Service through message channels in RabbitMQ.

10.4.1 Configuring the integration with RabbitMQ

Spring Cloud Stream is based on a few essential concepts:

- *Destination binder*—The component providing the integration with external messaging systems, like RabbitMQ or Kafka
- *Destination binding*—The bridge between the external messaging system entities, like queues and topics, and the application-provided producers and consumers
- *Message*—The data structure used by the application producers and consumers to communicate with the destination binders, and therefore with the external messaging systems

All three of these are handled by the framework itself. The core of your application, the business logic, is not aware of the external messaging system. Destination binders are responsible for letting the application communicate with the external message brokers, including any vendor-specific concerns. The bindings are auto-configured by the framework, but you can still provide your own configuration to adapt them to your needs, as we'll do for Dispatcher Service. Figure 10.9 shows a model of a Spring Boot application using Spring Cloud Stream.

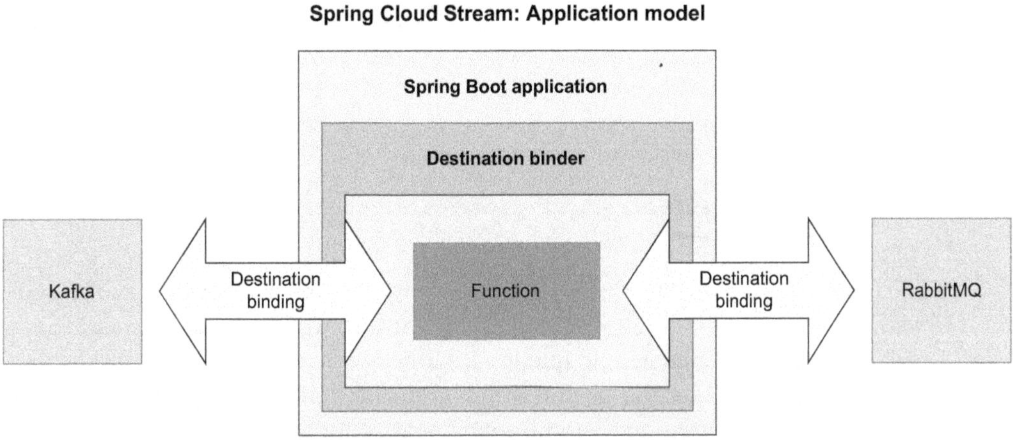

Spring Cloud Stream: Application model

Figure 10.9 In Spring Cloud Stream, a destination binder provides integration with external messaging systems and establishes message channels with them.

Once you have defined the business logic of your application as functions, and you've configured Spring Cloud Function to manage them (like we did for Dispatcher Service), you can expose the functions through a message broker by adding a dependency on the Spring Cloud Stream binder project specific to the broker you want to use. I'll show you how to work with RabbitMQ both for input and output message channels, but you can also bind to multiple messaging systems within the same application.

INTEGRATING RABBITMQ WITH SPRING

First, open the build.gradle file for the Dispatcher Service project (dispatcher-service), and replace the Spring Cloud Function dependency with the RabbitMQ binder for Spring Cloud Stream. Since Spring Cloud Function is already included in Spring Cloud Stream, you don't need to add it explicitly. You can also remove the dependency on Spring Boot Starter, which is also included in the Spring Cloud Stream dependency. Remember to refresh or reimport the Gradle dependencies after the new addition.

Listing 10.12 Updating dependencies in Dispatcher Service

```
dependencies {
  implementation
    'org.springframework.cloud:spring-cloud-stream-binder-rabbit'
  testImplementation 'org.springframework.boot:spring-boot-starter-test'
  testImplementation 'io.projectreactor:reactor-test'
}
```

Next, open the application.yml file and add the following configuration for the RabbitMQ integration. Port, username, and password are the same ones we previously defined in Docker Compose (listings 10.1 and 10.2).

```
spring:
  rabbitmq:
    host: localhost
    port: 5672
    username: user
    password: password
    connection-timeout: 5s
```

That's it. If you run the Dispatcher Service, you'll notice it already works perfectly without further configuration. Spring Cloud Stream will auto-generate and configure the bindings to exchanges and queues in RabbitMQ.

That's great for getting up and running quickly, but you will probably want to add your own configuration to customize the behavior for a production scenario. The following section will show you how to do that, again without changing any code in your business logic. How great is that?

10.4.2 *Binding functions to message channels*

Getting started with Spring Cloud Stream is straightforward, but there's a chance of confusing concepts with similar names. In the context of message brokers and Spring Cloud Stream, the term *binding* and its variations are used a lot and can lead to misunderstandings. Figure 10.10 shows all the entities in place.

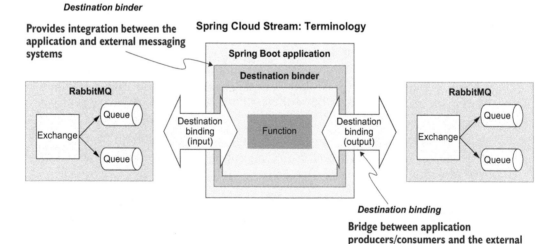

Figure 10.10   **In Spring Cloud Stream, bindings establish message channels between applications and message brokers.**

Spring Cloud Stream provides a Spring Boot application with a *destination binder* that integrates with an external messaging system. The binder is also responsible for establishing communication channels between the application producers and consumers and the messaging system entities (exchanges and queues for RabbitMQ). These communication channels are called *destination bindings*, and they are bridges between applications and brokers.

A *destination binding* can be either an input channel or an output channel. By default, Spring Cloud Stream maps each binding (both input and output) to an exchange in RabbitMQ (a *topic exchange*, to be more precise). Furthermore, for each input binding, it binds a queue to the related exchange. That's the queue from which consumers receive and process events. This setup provides all the plumbing for implementing event-driven architectures based on the pub/sub model.

In the following sections, I'll tell you more about destination bindings in Spring Cloud Stream and how they relate to exchanges and queues in RabbitMQ.

UNDERSTANDING DESTINATION BINDINGS

As you can see in figure 10.10, destination bindings are an abstraction representing a bridge between application and broker. When using the functional programming model, Spring Cloud Stream generates an input binding for each function accepting input data, and an output binding for each function returning output data. Each binding is assigned a logical name following this convention:

- Input binding: `<functionName>` + `-in-` + `<index>`
- Output binding: `<functionName>` + `-out-` + `<index>`

Unless you use partitions (for example, with Kafka), the `<index>` part of the name will always be 0. The `<functionName>` is computed from the value of the `spring.cloud` `.function.definition` property. In case of a single function, there is a one-to-one mapping. For example, if in Dispatcher Service we only had one function called `dispatch`, the related binding would be named `dispatch-in-0` and `dispatch-out-0`. We actually used a composed function (`pack|label`), so the binding names are generated by combining the names of all the functions involved in the composition:

- Input binding: `packlabel-in-0`
- Output binding: `packlabel-out-0`

These names are only relevant for configuring the bindings themselves in the application. They're like unique identifiers that let you reference a specific binding and apply custom configuration. Notice that these names exist only in Spring Cloud Stream—they're logical names. RabbitMQ doesn't know about them.

CONFIGURING DESTINATION BINDINGS

By default, Spring Cloud Stream uses the binding names to generate the names for exchanges and queues in RabbitMQ, but in a production scenario you'd probably want to manage them explicitly for several reasons. For example, it's likely that both exchanges and queues already exist in production. You will also want to control different options for exchanges and queues, like durability or routing algorithms.

For Dispatcher Service, I'll show you how to configure input and output bindings. At startup, Spring Cloud Stream will check if the related exchanges and queues already exist in RabbitMQ. If they don't, it will create them according to your configuration.

Let's start by defining the destination names that will be used to name exchanges and queues in RabbitMQ. In your Dispatcher Service project, update the application.yml file as follows.

Listing 10.14   Configuring Cloud Stream bindings and RabbitMQ destinations

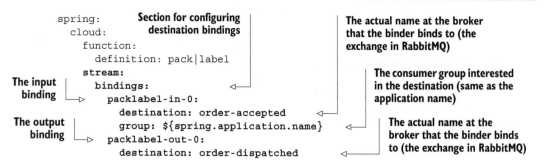

The output binding (`packlabel-out-0`) will be mapped to an `order-dispatched` exchange in RabbitMQ. The input binding (`packlabel-in-0`) will be mapped to an `order-accepted` exchange and an `order-accepted.dispatcher-service` queue in RabbitMQ. If they don't exist already in RabbitMQ, the binder will create them. The queue-naming strategy (`<destination>.<group>`) includes a parameter called *consumer group*.

The idea of *consumer groups* has been borrowed from Kafka and is very useful. In a standard pub/sub model, all consumers receive a copy of the messages sent to the queues they're subscribed to. That is convenient when different applications need to process the messages. But in a cloud native context, where multiple instances of an application are running simultaneously for scaling and resilience, that would be a problem. If you have numerous Dispatcher Service instances, you don't want an order to be dispatched from all of them. That would lead to errors and an inconsistent state.

Consumer groups solve the problem. All consumers in the same group share a single subscription. As a consequence, each message arriving at the queue to which they're subscribed will be processed by one consumer only. Assume we have two applications (Dispatcher Service and Mail Service) interested in receiving events about accepted orders and deployed in a replicated fashion. Using the application name to configure consumer groups, we can ensure that each event is received and processed by a single instance of Dispatcher Service and a single instance of Mail Service, as shown in figure 10.11.

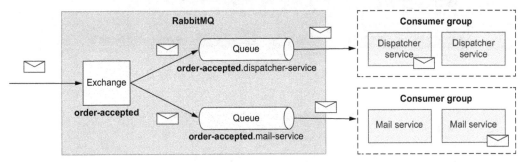

Figure 10.11 Consumer groups ensure that each message is received and processed by only one consumer within the same group.

EXPLORING EXCHANGES AND QUEUES IN RABBITMQ

After configuring the integration with RabbitMQ through Spring Cloud Stream, it's time to try running Dispatcher Service.

First, start a RabbitMQ container. Open a Terminal window, navigate to the folder in your `polar-deployment` repository where you keep your docker-compose.yml file (polar-deployment/docker), and run the following command:

```
$ docker-compose up -d polar-rabbitmq
```

Then open another Terminal window, navigate to the Dispatcher Service project's root folder (dispatcher-service), and run the application as follows:

```
$ ./gradlew bootRun
```

The application logs will already give you a hint of what happened, but for a clearer understanding, let's check the RabbitMQ management console (exposed through port 15672).

Open a browser window and navigate to http://localhost:15672. The credentials are the same that we defined in Docker Compose (`user`/`password`). Then go to the Exchanges section. Figure 10.12 shows a list of default exchanges provided by RabbitMQ and the two exchanges generated by our application: `order-accepted` and `order-dispatched`. Spring Cloud Stream maps them to the `packlabel-in-0` and `packlabel-out-0` bindings respectively. The exchanges are *durable* (denoted by the `D` icon in the management console), meaning that they will survive a broker restart.

Next, let's take a look at the queues. In Dispatcher Service we configured a `packlabel-in-0` binding and a consumer group. That's the only input channel for the application, so it should result in a single queue. Let's verify that. In the RabbitMQ management console, as illustrated in figure 10.13, you can see a durable `order-accepted.dispatcher-service` queue in the Queues section.

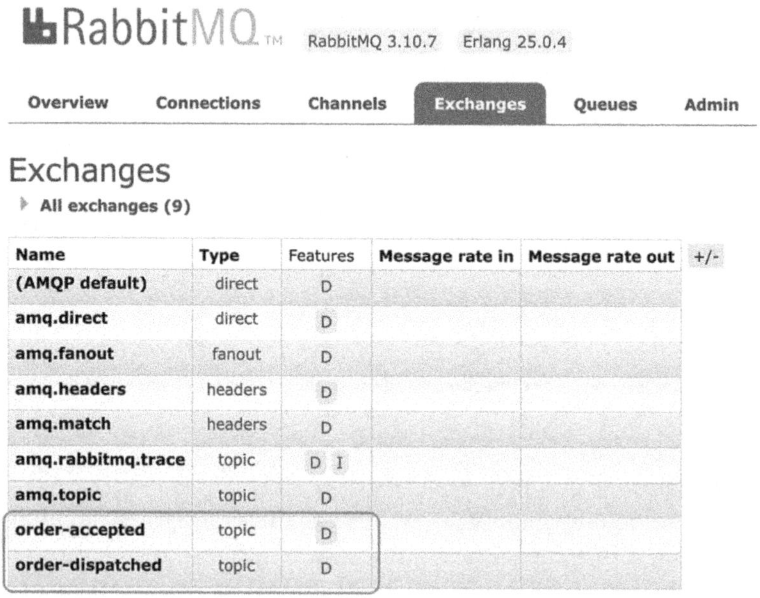

Figure 10.12   Spring Cloud Stream maps the two destination binding to two exchanges in RabbitMQ.

Figure 10.13   Spring Cloud Stream maps each input binding to a queue, named according to the configured consumer group.

> **NOTE**   No queue has been created for the `packlabel-out-0` binding because no consumer subscribed to it. Later you'll see that a queue will be created after configuring Order Service to listen to it.

We can verify that the integration works by manually sending a message to the `order-accepted` exchange. If everything is configured correctly, Dispatcher Service will read the message from the `order-accepted.dispatcher-service` queue, process it through the composed function pack|label, and finally send it to the order-dispatched exchange.

Go to the Exchanges section again, select the order-accepted exchange, and in the Publish Message panel, insert an OrderAcceptedMessage object in JSON format, as shown in figure 10.14. When you're done, click the Publish Message button.

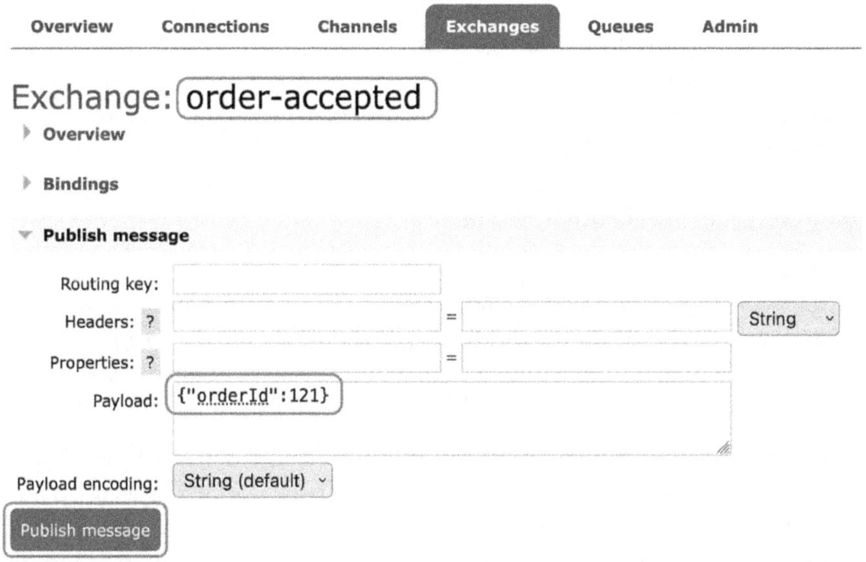

Overview	Connections	Channels	Exchanges	Queues	Admin

Exchange: [order-accepted]

▸ **Overview**

▸ **Bindings**

▾ **Publish message**

Routing key:	
Headers: ?	= [String ∨]
Properties: ?	=
Payload:	{"orderId":121}

Payload encoding: [String (default) ∨]

[Publish message]

Figure 10.14   You can trigger the data flow in Dispatcher Service by sending a message to the order-accepted exchange.

In the application logs, you should see the following messages signaling that the data flow happened correctly:

```
...c.p.d.DispatchingFunctions: The order with id 394 is packed.
...c.p.d.DispatchingFunctions: The order with id 394 is labeled.
```

The output message has been sent to the order-dispatched exchange, but it has not been routed to any queue because no consumer has subscribed. In the final part of this chapter, we'll complete the flow by defining a supplier in Order Service to publish messages to the order-accepted exchange whenever an order is accepted, and a consumer to read messages from the order-dispatched queue whenever an order is dispatched. But first, let's add some tests to verify the integration with the Spring Cloud Stream binder.

Before moving on, stop the application process with Ctrl-C and the RabbitMQ container with docker-compose down.

10.4.3 *Writing integration tests with a test binder*

As I have stressed several times, Spring Cloud Function and Spring Cloud Stream's whole philosophy is about keeping the application's business logic infrastructure—and middleware—neutral. After defining the original pack() and label() functions, all we did was update dependencies in Gradle and modify the configuration in application.yml.

It's a good idea to have unit tests covering the business logic, independent of the framework. But it's worth adding a few integration tests to cover the application's behavior in a Spring Cloud Stream context. You should disable the integration tests you wrote earlier in the DispatchingFunctionsIntegrationTests class, since now you'll want to test the integration with the external messaging system.

The framework provides a binder specifically for implementing integration tests focusing on the business logic rather than the middleware. Let's see how it works, using Dispatcher Service as an example.

> **NOTE** The test binder provided by Spring Cloud Stream is meant to verify the correct configuration and integration with a technology-agnostic destination binder. If you want to test the application against a specific broker (in our case, it would be for RabbitMQ), you can rely on Testcontainers, as you learned in the previous chapter. I'll leave that up to you as an exercise.

First, add a dependency to the test binder in the build.gradle file of your Dispatcher Service project. Unlike the other dependencies we've been working on so far, the test binder requires a more elaborate syntax to be included. For more information, refer to the Spring Cloud Stream documentation (https://spring.io/projects/spring-cloud-stream). Remember to refresh or reimport the Gradle dependencies after the new addition.

Listing 10.15 Adding a dependency for the test binder in Dispatcher Service

```
dependencies {
  ...
  testImplementation("org.springframework.cloud:spring-cloud-stream") {
    artifact {
      name = "spring-cloud-stream"
      extension = "jar"
      type ="test-jar"
      classifier = "test-binder"
    }
  }
}
```

Next, create a new FunctionsStreamIntegrationTests class for testing. The test setup consists of three steps:

1 Import the TestChannelBinderConfiguration class providing configuration for the test binder.

2 Inject an InputDestination bean representing the input binding packlabel-in-0 (by default, since it's the only one).

3 Inject an `OutputDestination` bean representing the output binding `packlabel-out-0` (by default, since it's the only one).

The data flow is based on `Message` objects (from the `org.springframework.messaging` package). The framework handles type conversion for you transparently when running the application. However, in this type of test, you need to provide `Message` objects explicitly. You can use `MessageBuilder` to create the input message, and use the `ObjectMapper` utility to perform the type conversion from the binary format used for storing message payloads in a broker.

Listing 10.16 Testing the integration with external messaging systems

```
package com.polarbookshop.dispatcherservice;

import java.io.IOException;
import com.fasterxml.jackson.databind.ObjectMapper;
import org.junit.jupiter.api.Test;
import org.springframework.beans.factory.annotation.Autowired;
import org.springframework.boot.test.context.SpringBootTest;
import org.springframework.cloud.stream.binder.test.InputDestination;
import org.springframework.cloud.stream.binder.test.OutputDestination;
import org.springframework.cloud.stream.binder.test.
    TestChannelBinderConfiguration;
import org.springframework.context.annotation.Import;
import org.springframework.integration.support.MessageBuilder;
import org.springframework.messaging.Message;
import static org.assertj.core.api.Assertions.assertThat;

@SpringBootTest                                          Configures the
@Import(TestChannelBinderConfiguration.class)    ◁──    test binder
class FunctionsStreamIntegrationTests {
                                          Represents the
    @Autowired                            input binding
    private InputDestination input;   ◁── packlabel-in-0

    @Autowired                            Represents the output
    private OutputDestination output;  ◁── binding packlabel-out-0

    @Autowired                             Uses Jackson to deserialize
    private ObjectMapper objectMapper;  ◁── JSON message payloads to
                                           Java objects
    @Test
    void whenOrderAcceptedThenDispatched() throws IOException {
        long orderId = 121;
        Message<OrderAcceptedMessage> inputMessage = MessageBuilder
            .withPayload(new OrderAcceptedMessage(orderId)).build();
        Message<OrderDispatchedMessage> expectedOutputMessage = MessageBuilder
            .withPayload(new OrderDispatchedMessage(orderId)).build();

        this.input.send(inputMessage);
        assertThat(objectMapper.readValue(output.receive().getPayload(),
            OrderDispatchedMessage.class))
            .isEqualTo(expectedOutputMessage.getPayload());
    }
}
```

Sends a message to the input channel → points to `this.input.send(inputMessage);`

Receives and asserts a message from the output channel → points to `.isEqualTo(expectedOutputMessage.getPayload());`

> **WARNING** If you use IntelliJ IDEA, you might get a warning that `Input-Destination`, `OutputDestination`, and `ObjectMapper` cannot be autowired. Don't worry. It's a false positive. You can get rid of the warning by annotating the field with `@SuppressWarnings("SpringJavaInjectionPointsAutowiring-Inspection")`.

Message brokers like RabbitMQ deal with binary data, so any data flowing through them is mapped to `byte[]` in Java. The conversion between bytes and DTOs is handled by Spring Cloud Stream transparently. But just like for messages, we need to handle that explicitly in this test scenario when asserting the content of the message received from the output channel.

After writing the integration tests, open a Terminal window, navigate to the Dispatcher Service project's root folder, and run the tests:

```
$ ./gradlew test --tests FunctionsStreamIntegrationTests
```

The next section will go through some points to consider regarding resilient integrations with messaging systems.

10.4.4 *Making messaging resilient to failures*

Event-driven architectures solve some issues affecting synchronous request/response interactions. For example, if you remove the temporal coupling between applications, you won't need to adopt patterns like circuit breakers, since the communication will be asynchronous. If the consumer is momentarily unavailable while the producer sends a message, it doesn't matter. The consumer will receive the message once it's up and running again.

In software engineering, there are no silver bullets. Everything comes at a cost. On the one hand, applications that are decoupled can operate more independently. On the other hand, you introduced a new component in your system that needs to be deployed and maintained: the message broker.

Assuming that part is taken care of by the platform, there's still something for you to do as the application developer. When an event happens and your application wants to publish a message, something might go wrong. Retries and timeouts are still helpful, but this time we'll use them to make the interaction between application and broker more resilient. Spring Cloud Stream uses the retry pattern with an exponential backoff strategy by default, relying on the Spring Retry library for imperative consumers and the `retryWhen()` Reactor operator for reactive consumers (the one you learned about in chapter 8). As usual, you can customize it via configuration properties.

Spring Cloud Stream defines several defaults to make the interaction more resilient, including error channels and graceful shutdown. You can configure different aspects of message processing, including dead-letter queues, acknowledgment flows, and republishing messages on error.

RabbitMQ itself has several features in place to improve reliability and resilience. Among other things, it guarantees that each message is delivered at least once. Be aware that consumers in your applications might receive the same message twice, so your business logic should know how to identify and handle duplicates.

I won't go further into the details, since this is an extensive subject that would require several dedicated chapters to cover it adequately. Instead, I encourage you to read the documentation for the different projects involved in your event-driven architecture: RabbitMQ (https://rabbitmq.com), Spring AMQP (https://spring.io/projects/spring-amqp), and Spring Cloud Stream (https://spring.io/projects/spring-cloud-stream). You can also check out the event-driven patterns described in Sam Newman's *Building Microservices* (O'Reilly, 2021) and Chris Richardson's *Microservices Patterns* (Manning, 2018).

In the last part of the chapter, you'll work with suppliers and consumers and complete the order flow for the Polar Bookshop system.

10.5 Producing and consuming messages with Spring Cloud Stream

In previous sections, you learned about the functional programming paradigm and how it fits in the Spring ecosystem, using Spring Cloud Function and Spring Cloud Stream. This last section will guide you through the implementation of producers and consumers.

As you'll see, consumers are not that different from the functions you wrote in Dispatcher Service. On the other hand, producers are slightly different because, unlike functions and consumers, they are not naturally activated. I'll show you how to use them both in Order Service while implementing the last part of the order flow for the Polar Bookshop system.

10.5.1 Implementing event consumers, and the problem of idempotency

The Dispatcher Service application we previously built produces messages when orders are dispatched. The Order Service should be notified when that happens so that it can update the order status in the database.

First, open your Order Service project (order-service), and add the dependencies on Spring Cloud Stream and the test binder in the build.gradle file. Remember to refresh or reimport the Gradle dependencies after the new addition.

Listing 10.17 Adding dependency for Spring Cloud Stream and test binder

```
dependencies {
    ...
    implementation 'org.springframework.cloud:
    ➥ spring-cloud-stream-binder-rabbit'
    testImplementation("org.springframework.cloud:spring-cloud-stream") {
        artifact {
            name = "spring-cloud-stream"
            extension = "jar"
            type ="test-jar"
            classifier = "test-binder"
```

```
          }
        }
    }
```

Next we need to model the event we'd like Order Service to listen to. Create a new com.polarbookshop.orderservice.order.event package, and add an Order-DispatchedMessage class to hold the identifier for a dispatched order.

Listing 10.18   A DTO representing the event about orders being dispatched

```
package com.polarbookshop.orderservice.order.event;

public record OrderDispatchedMessage (
  Long orderId
){}
```

Now we'll implement the business logic using a functional approach. Create an OrderFunctions class (com.polarbookshop.orderservice.order.event package), and implement a function to consume the messages produced by the Dispatcher Service application when an order is dispatched. The function will be a Consumer responsible for listening to the incoming messages and updating the database entities accordingly. Consumer objects are functions with input but no output. To keep the function clean and readable, we'll move the processing of OrderDispatchedMessage objects to the OrderService class (which we'll implement in a minute).

Listing 10.19   Consuming messages from RabbitMQ

```
package com.polarbookshop.orderservice.order.event;

import java.util.function.Consumer;
import com.polarbookshop.orderservice.order.domain.OrderService;
import org.slf4j.Logger;
import org.slf4j.LoggerFactory;
import reactor.core.publisher.Flux;
import org.springframework.context.annotation.Bean;
import org.springframework.context.annotation.Configuration;

@Configuration
public class OrderFunctions {

  private static final Logger log =
    LoggerFactory.getLogger(OrderFunctions.class);

  @Bean
  public Consumer<Flux<OrderDispatchedMessage>> dispatchOrder(
    OrderService orderService
  ) {
    return flux ->
      orderService.consumeOrderDispatchedEvent(flux)
        .doOnNext(order -> log.info("The order with id {} is dispatched",
          order.id()))
```

For each order updated in the database, it logs a message.

For each dispatched message, it updates the related order in the database.

```
          .subscribe();
  }
}
```

Subscribes to the reactive stream in order
to activate it. Without a subscriber, no
data flows through the stream.

Order Service is a reactive application, so the dispatchOrder function will consume
messages as a reactive stream (a Flux of OrderDispatchedMessage). Reactive streams
are *activated* only if there's a subscriber interested in receiving the data. For that reason, it's critical that we end the reactive stream by subscribing to it, or else no data will
ever be processed. In previous examples, the subscription part was handled transparently by the framework (for example, when using reactive streams to return data via a
REST endpoint or to send data to a backing service). In this case, we have to explicitly
do that with the subscribe() clause.

Next, let's implement the consumeOrderDispatchedMessageEvent() method in
the OrderService class to update the status in the database for an existing order after
it's dispatched.

Listing 10.20   Implementing the logic for updating an order as dispatched

Accepts a reactive stream of
OrderDispatchedMessage objects as input

```
@Service
public class OrderService {
  ...

  public Flux<Order> consumeOrderDispatchedEvent(
    Flux<OrderDispatchedMessage> flux
  ) {
    return flux
      .flatMap(message ->
        orderRepository.findById(message.orderId()))
      .map(this::buildDispatchedOrder)
      .flatMap(orderRepository::save);
  }

  private Order buildDispatchedOrder(Order existingOrder) {
    return new Order(
      existingOrder.id(),
      existingOrder.bookIsbn(),
      existingOrder.bookName(),
      existingOrder.bookPrice(),
      existingOrder.quantity(),
      OrderStatus.DISPATCHED,
      existingOrder.createdDate(),
      existingOrder.lastModifiedDate(),
      existingOrder.version()
    );
  }
}
```

For each object
emitted to the stream,
it reads the related
order from the
database.

Updates the
order with the
"dispatched"
status

Saves the updated
order in the database

Given an order, it returns
a new record with the
"dispatched" status.

Consumers are triggered by a message arriving in the queue. RabbitMQ provides an
at-least-one delivered guarantee, so you need to be aware of possible duplicates. The

code we implemented updates the status of the specific order to be DISPATCHED, an operation that can be executed several times with the same result. Since the operation is idempotent, the code is resilient to duplicates. A further optimization would be to check for the status and skip the update operation if it's already dispatched.

Finally, we need to configure Spring Cloud Stream in the application.yml file so that the dispatchOrder-in-0 binding (inferred from the dispatchOrder function name) is mapped to the order-dispatched exchange in RabbitMQ. Also, remember to define dispatchOrder as the function that Spring Cloud Function should manage, and the integration with RabbitMQ.

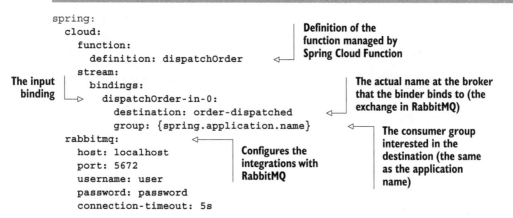

Listing 10.21   Configuring Cloud Stream bindings and RabbitMQ integration

```
spring:
  cloud:
    function:
      definition: dispatchOrder          ◁──  Definition of the
    stream:                                     function managed by
      bindings:                                 Spring Cloud Function
        dispatchOrder-in-0:
          destination: order-dispatched   ◁──  The actual name at the broker
          group: {spring.application.name}      that the binder binds to (the
  rabbitmq:                                      exchange in RabbitMQ)
    host: localhost
    port: 5672                                  The consumer group
    username: user                              interested in the
    password: password                          destination (the same
    connection-timeout: 5s                      as the application
                                                name)
```

The input binding → dispatchOrder-in-0

Configures the integrations with RabbitMQ

As you can see, it works the same way as the functions in Dispatcher Service. The consumers in Order Service will be part of the order-service consumer group, and Spring Cloud Stream will define a message channel between them and an order-dispatched .order-service queue in RabbitMQ.

Next, we'll complete the order flow by defining a supplier responsible for triggering the whole procedure.

10.5.2   *Implementing event producers, and the problem of atomicity*

Suppliers are message sources. They produce messages when an event happens. In Order Service, a supplier should notify the interested parties (in this case, Dispatcher Service) whenever an order has been accepted. Unlike functions and consumers, suppliers need to be activated. They act only upon invocation.

Spring Cloud Stream provides a few ways to define suppliers and cover different scenarios. In our case, the event source is not a message broker, but a REST endpoint. When a user sends a POST request to Order Service for purchasing a book, we want to publish an event signaling whether the order has been accepted.

Let's start by modeling that event as a DTO. It will be the same as the OrderAccepted-Message record we used in Dispatcher Service. Add the record to the com.polarbook-shop.orderservice.order.event package in your Order Service project (order-service).

Listing 10.22   A DTO representing the event about orders being accepted

```
package com.polarbookshop.orderservice.order.event;

public record OrderAcceptedMessage (
  Long orderId
){}
```

We can bridge the REST layer with the stream part of the application using a Stream-Bridge object that allows us to send data to a specific destination imperatively. Let's break this new functionality down. First, we can implement a method that accepts an Order object as input, verifies it's accepted, builds an OrderAcceptedMessage object, and sends it to a RabbitMQ destination using StreamBridge.

Open the OrderService class, autowire a StreamBridge object, and define a new publishOrderAcceptedEvent method.

Listing 10.23   Implementing the logic for publishing events to a destination

```
package com.polarbookshop.orderservice.order.domain;

import com.polarbookshop.orderservice.book.BookClient;
import com.polarbookshop.orderservice.order.event.OrderAcceptedMessage;
import org.slf4j.Logger;
import org.slf4j.LoggerFactory;
import org.springframework.cloud.stream.function.StreamBridge;
import org.springframework.stereotype.Service;
...

@Service
public class OrderService {
  private static final Logger log =
    LoggerFactory.getLogger(OrderService.class);

  private final BookClient bookClient;
  private final OrderRepository orderRepository;
  private final StreamBridge streamBridge;

  public OrderService(BookClient bookClient,
    StreamBridge streamBridge, OrderRepository orderRepository
  ) {
    this.bookClient = bookClient;
    this.orderRepository = orderRepository;
    this.streamBridge = streamBridge;
  }

  ...

  private void publishOrderAcceptedEvent(Order order) {
    if (!order.status().equals(OrderStatus.ACCEPTED)) {
      return;
    }
    var orderAcceptedMessage =
      new OrderAcceptedMessage(order.id());
```

If the order is not accepted, it does nothing.

Builds a message to notify that an order has been accepted

```
log.info("Sending order accepted event with id: {}", order.id());
var result = streamBridge.send("acceptOrder-out-0",
  orderAcceptedMessage);                              ◁─────────┐
log.info("Result of sending data for order with id {}: {}",    │
  order.id(), result);                                          │
  }                                  Explicitly sends a message to the
}                                         acceptOrder-out-0 binding
```

Since the data source is a REST endpoint, there is no `Supplier` bean we can register with Spring Cloud Function, and therefore there is no trigger for the framework to create the necessary bindings with RabbitMQ. Yet, in listing 10.23, `StreamBridge` is used to send data to an `acceptOrder-out-0` binding. Where does it come from? There is no `acceptOrder` function!

At startup time, Spring Cloud Stream will notice that `StreamBridge` wants to publish messages via an `acceptOrder-out-0` binding, and it will create one automatically. Similar to the bindings created from functions, we can configure the destination name in RabbitMQ. Open the application.yml file and configure the binding as follows.

> **Listing 10.24   Configuring Cloud Stream output binding**

```
spring:
  cloud:
    function:
      definition: dispatchOrder               Output binding
    stream:                                    created and managed
      bindings:                                by StreamBridge
        dispatchOrder-in-0:
          destination: order-dispatched
          group: ${spring.application.name}    The actual name at the broker
        acceptOrder-out-0:              ◁──┘   that the binder binds to (the
          destination: order-accepted   ◁───  exchange in RabbitMQ)
```

All that's left now is calling the method whenever a submitted order is accepted. That's a critical point and one of the aspects characterizing the *saga pattern*, a popular alternative to distributed transactions in microservice architectures. To ensure consistency in your system, persisting an order in the database and sending a message about it must be done atomically. Either both operations succeed, or they both must fail. A simple yet effective way to ensure atomicity is by wrapping the two operations in a local transaction. To do that, we can rely on the built-in Spring transaction management functionality.

> **NOTE**   The saga pattern is described extensively in chapter 4 of Chris Richardson's book, *Microservices Patterns* (Manning, 2018; https://livebook.manning.com/book/microservices-patterns/chapter-4). I recommend you check it out if you're interested in designing business transactions that span multiple applications.

In the `OrderService` class, modify the `submitOrder()` method to call the `publishOrderAcceptedEvent` method, and annotate it with `@Transactional`.

Listing 10.25 Defining a saga transaction with database and event broker

```
@Service
public class OrderService {
  ...
                                        Executes the method
                                        in a local transaction
  @Transactional          ◄──┘
  public Mono<Order> submitOrder(String isbn, int quantity) {
    return bookClient.getBookByIsbn(isbn)
      .map(book -> buildAcceptedOrder(book, quantity))      Saves the order
      .defaultIfEmpty(buildRejectedOrder(isbn, quantity))   in the database
      .flatMap(orderRepository::save)          ◄──┘
      .doOnNext(this::publishOrderAcceptedEvent);  ◄──┐
  }                                                      Publishes an
                                                         event if the order
                                                         is accepted
  private void publishOrderAcceptedEvent(Order order) {
    if (!order.status().equals(OrderStatus.ACCEPTED)) {
      return;
    }
    var orderAcceptedMessage = new OrderAcceptedMessage(order.id());
    log.info("Sending order accepted event with id: {}", order.id());
    var result = streamBridge.send("acceptOrder-out-0",
      orderAcceptedMessage);
    log.info("Result of sending data for order with id {}: {}",
      order.id(), result);
  }
}
```

Spring Boot comes preconfigured with transaction management functionality and can handle transactional operations involving relational databases (as you learned in chapter 5). However, the channel established with RabbitMQ for the message producer is not transactional by default. To make the event-publishing operation join the existing transaction, we need to enable RabbitMQ's transactional support for the message producer in the application.yml file.

Listing 10.26 Configuring the output binding to be transactional

```
spring:
  cloud:
    function:
      definition: dispatchOrder
    stream:
      bindings:
        dispatchOrder-in-0:
          destination: order-dispatched
          group: ${spring.application.name}
        acceptOrder-out-0:                      RabbitMQ-specific
          destination: order-accepted           configuration for the Spring
      rabbit:                     ◄──┘           Cloud Stream bindings
        bindings:
          acceptOrder-out-0:              Makes the
            producer:                     acceptOrder-out-0
              transacted: true   ◄──┘     binding transactional
```

Now you can write new integration tests for the supplier and the consumer, like we did for the functions in Dispatcher Service. I'll leave the autotests to you, since you have the necessary tools now. If you need inspiration, check out the source code accompanying this book (Chapter10/10-end/order-service).

You will also need to import the configuration for the test binder (`@Import(Test-ChannelBinderConfiguration.class)`) in the existing `OrderServiceApplication-Tests` class to make it work.

We've had a nice journey through event-driven models, functions, and messaging systems. Before wrapping up, let's look at the order flow in action. First, start RabbitMQ, PostgreSQL (`docker-compose up -d polar-rabbitmq polar-postgres`), and Dispatcher Service (`./gradlew bootRun`). Then run Catalog Service and Order Service (`./gradlew bootRun` or from Docker Compose after building the images first).

Once all those services are up and running, add a new book to the catalog:

```
$ http POST :9001/books author="Jon Snow" \
    title="All I don't know about the Arctic" isbn="1234567897" \
    price=9.90 publisher="Polarsophia"
```

Then order three copies of that book:

```
$ http POST :9002/orders isbn=1234567897 quantity=3
```

If you order a book that exists, the order will be accepted, and Order Service will publish an `OrderAcceptedEvent` message. Dispatcher Service, subscribed to that same event, will process the order and publish an `OrderDispatchedEvent` message. Order Service will be notified and update the order status in the database.

> **TIP** You can follow the message flow by checking the application logs from Order Service and Dispatcher Service.

Now the moment of the truth. Fetch the order from Order Service:

```
$ http :9002/orders
```

The status should be `DISPATCHED`:

```
{
  "bookIsbn": "1234567897",
  "bookName": "All I don't know about the Arctic - Jon Snow",
  "bookPrice": 9.9,
  "createdDate": "2022-06-06T19:40:33.426610Z",
  "id": 1,
  "lastModifiedDate": "2022-06-06T19:40:33.866588Z",
  "quantity": 3,
  "status": "DISPATCHED",
  "version": 2
}
```

And it is. Great job! When you're done testing the system, stop all the applications (Ctrl-C) and Docker containers (`docker-compose down`).

That concludes the main implementation of the business logic for the Polar Bookshop system. The next chapter will cover security for cloud native applications using Spring Security, OAuth 2.1, and OpenID Connect.

Polar Labs

Feel free to apply what you've learned in the previous chapters and prepare the Dispatcher Service application for deployment.

1 Add Spring Cloud Config Client to Dispatcher Service to make it fetch configuration data from Config Service.
2 Configure the Cloud Native Buildpacks integration, containerize the application, and define the commit stage of the deployment pipeline.
3 Write the Deployment and Service manifests for deploying Dispatcher Service to a Kubernetes cluster.
4 Configure Tilt to automate the Dispatcher Service's deployment to your local Kubernetes cluster initialized with minikube.

Then update the Docker Compose specification and the Kubernetes manifests to configure the RabbitMQ integration for Order Service.

You can refer to the Chapter10/10-end folder in the code repository accompanying the book to check on the final result (https://github.com/ThomasVitale/cloud-native-spring-in-action). Deploy the backing services from the manifests, available in the Chapter10/10-end/polar-deployment/kubernetes/platform/development folder, with `kubectl apply -f services`.

Summary

- Event-driven architectures are distributed systems that interact with each other by producing and consuming events.
- An event is something relevant that happened in a system.
- In the pub/sub model, producers publish events, which are sent to all subscribers to be consumed.
- Event processing platforms like RabbitMQ and Kafka are responsible for collecting events from the producers, routing, and distributing them to the interested consumers.
- In the AMQP protocol, producers send messages to an exchange in a broker that forwards them to queues according to specific routing algorithms.
- In the AMQP protocol, consumers receive messages from the queues in the broker.
- In the AMQP protocol, messages are data structures composed of key/value attributes and a binary payload.

- RabbitMQ is a message broker based on the AMQP protocol that you can use to implement event-driven architectures based on the pub/sub model.
- RabbitMQ provides high availability, resilience, and data replication.
- Spring Cloud Function enables you to implement your business logic using the standard Java `Function`, `Supplier`, and `Consumer` interfaces.
- Spring Cloud Function wraps your function and provides several exciting features like transparent type conversion and function composition.
- Functions implemented in the context of Spring Cloud Function can be exposed and integrated with external systems in different ways.
- Functions can be exposed as REST endpoints, packaged, and deployed in a FaaS platform as serverless applications (Knative, AWS Lambda, Azure Function, Google Cloud Functions), or they can be bound to message channels.
- Spring Cloud Stream, built on top of Spring Cloud Function, provides you with all the necessary plumbing to integrate your functions with external messaging systems like RabbitMQ or Kafka.
- Once you implement your functions, you don't have to make any changes to your code. You only need to add a dependency on Spring Cloud Stream and configure it to adapt to your needs.
- In Spring Cloud Stream, destination binders provide integration with external messaging systems.
- In Spring Cloud Stream, destination bindings (input and output) bridge the producers and consumers in your applications with exchanges and queues in a message broker like RabbitMQ.
- Functions and consumers are activated automatically when new messages arrive.
- Suppliers need to be explicitly activated, such as by explicitly sending a message to a destination binding.

Security: Authentication and SPA

Security is one of the most critical aspects of web applications and probably the one with the most catastrophic effects when done wrong. For educational purposes, I'm introducing this topic only now. In a real-world scenario, I recommend considering security from the beginning of each new project or feature and never letting it go until the application is retired.

Access control systems allow users access to resources only when their identity has been proven and they have the required permissions. To accomplish that, we need to follow three pivotal steps: identification, authentication, and authorization.

1 *Identification* happens when a user (human or machine) claims an identity. In the physical world, that's when I introduce myself by stating my name. In the digital world, I would do that by providing my username or email address.

   2 *Authentication* is about verifying the user's claimed identity through factors like a passport, a driver's license, a password, a certificate, or a token. When multiple factors are used to verify the user's identity, we talk about *multi-factor authentication.*

   3 *Authorization* always happens after authentication, and it checks what the user is allowed to do in a given context.

This chapter and the next one will cover implementing access control systems in cloud native applications. You'll see how to add authentication to a system like Polar Bookshop and use a dedicated identity and access management solution like Keycloak. I'll show you how to use Spring Security to secure applications and adopt standards like JWT, OAuth2, and OpenID Connect. In the process, you'll also add an Angular frontend to the system and learn the best practices for security when a single-page application (SPA) is involved.

> **NOTE** The source code for the examples in this chapter is available in the Chapter11/11-begin and Chapter11/11-end folders, which contain the initial and final states of the project (https://github.com/ThomasVitale/cloud-native -spring-in-action).

11.1 *Understanding the Spring Security fundamentals*

Spring Security (https://spring.io/projects/spring-security) is the de facto standard for securing Spring applications, supporting imperative and reactive stacks. It provides authentication and authorization features as well as protection against the most common attacks.

   The framework provides its main functionality by relying on *filters*. Let's consider a possible requirement for adding authentication to a Spring Boot application. Users should be able to authenticate with their username and password through a login form. When we configure Spring Security to enable such a feature, the framework adds a filter that intercepts any incoming HTTP request. If the user is already authenticated, it sends the request through to be processed by a given web handler, such as a @RestController class. If the user is not authenticated, it forwards the user to a login page and prompts for their username and password.

> **NOTE** In imperative Spring applications, a filter is implemented as a Servlet Filter class. In reactive applications, the WebFilter class is used.

Most Spring Security features, when enabled, are handled via filters. The framework establishes a chain of filters that are executed according to a well-defined and sensible order. For instance, the filter that handles authentication runs before the one that checks for authorization because we can't verify a user's authority before knowing who it is.

   Let's start with a basic example to better understand how Spring Security works. We want to add authentication to the Polar Bookshop system. Since Edge Service is the entry point, it makes sense to handle cross-cutting concerns like security there. Users should be able to authenticate with a username and password via a login form.

First, add a new dependency on Spring Security in the build.gradle file for the Edge Service project (edge-service). Remember to refresh or reimport the Gradle dependencies after the new addition.

Listing 11.1 Adding dependency for Spring Security in Edge Service

```
dependencies {
  ...
  implementation 'org.springframework.boot:spring-boot-starter-security'
}
```

The central place for defining and configuring security policies in Spring Security is a SecurityWebFilterChain bean. That object tells the framework which filters should be enabled. You can build a SecurityWebFilterChain bean through the DSL provided by ServerHttpSecurity.

For now, we want to comply with the following requirements:

- All endpoints exposed by Edge Service must require user authentication.
- The authentication must happen via a login form page.

To collect all the configurations related to security, create a SecurityWebFilterChain bean in a new SecurityConfig class (com.polarbookshop.edgeservice.config package):

```
                     The SecurityWebFilterChain bean is
                     used to define and configure security
                     policies for the application.
@Bean        <──┘
SecurityWebFilterChain springSecurityFilterChain(
  ServerHttpSecurity http
) {}
```

The ServerHttpSecurity object, autowired by Spring, provides a convenient DSL for configuring Spring Security and building a SecurityWebFilterChain bean. With authorizeExchange(), you can define access policies for any request (called an *exchange* in reactive Spring). In this case, we want all requests to require authentication (authenticated()):

```
@Bean
SecurityWebFilterChain springSecurityFilterChain(ServerHttpSecurity http) {
  return http
    .authorizeExchange(exchange ->
      exchange.anyExchange().authenticated())     <──┐ All requests
    .build();                                         │ require
}                                                     │ authentication.
```

Spring Security provides several authentication strategies, including HTTP Basic, login form, SAML, and OpenID Connect. For this example, we want to use the login form strategy, which we can enable via the formLogin() method exposed by the ServerHttpSecurity object. We'll go with the default configuration (available via the Spring Security Customizer interface), which includes a login page, provided by the framework out of the box, and an automatic redirect to that page whenever a request is not authenticated:

```
@Bean
SecurityWebFilterChain springSecurityFilterChain(ServerHttpSecurity http) {
  return http
    .authorizeExchange(exchange -> exchange.anyExchange().authenticated())
    .formLogin(Customizer.withDefaults())          ◁─┐  Enables user authentication
    .build();                                          │  via a login form
}
```

Next, annotate the SecurityConfig class with @EnableWebFluxSecurity to enable Spring Security WebFlux support. The final security configuration is shown in the following listing.

Listing 11.2   Requiring authentication for all endpoints via a login form

```
package com.polarbookshop.edgeservice.config;

import org.springframework.context.annotation.Bean;
import org.springframework.security.config.Customizer;
import org.springframework.security.config.annotation.web.reactive.
⇒EnableWebFluxSecurity;
import org.springframework.security.config.web.server.ServerHttpSecurity;
import org.springframework.security.web.server.SecurityWebFilterChain;

@EnableWebFluxSecurity
public class SecurityConfig {

  @Bean
  SecurityWebFilterChain springSecurityFilterChain(
    ServerHttpSecurity http
  ) {
    return http
      .authorizeExchange(exchange ->                  ┌── All requests require
        exchange.anyExchange().authenticated())    ◁─┘   authentication.
      .formLogin(Customizer.withDefaults())        ◁─┐  Enables user authentication
      .build();                                       │  via a login form
  }
}
```

Let's verify that it works correctly. First, start your Redis container, required by Edge Service. Open a Terminal window, navigate to the folder where you keep your Docker Compose file (polar-deployment/docker/docker-compose.yml), and run the following command:

```
$ docker-compose up -d polar-redis
```

Then run the Edge Service application (`./gradlew bootRun`), open a browser window, and head to http://localhost:9000/books. You should be redirected to a login page served by Spring Security, where you can authenticate.

Wait a minute! How can we authenticate without defining a user in the system? By default, Spring Security defines a user account in memory with the username `user` and a password randomly generated and printed out in the application logs. You should look for a log entry like the following:

```
Using generated security password: ee60bdf6-fb82-439a-8ed0-8eb9d47bae08
```

You can authenticate with the predefined user account created by Spring Security. After successfully authenticating, you will be redirected to the `/books` endpoint. Since Catalog Service is down and Edge Service has a fallback method to return an empty list when querying books (implemented in chapter 9), you'll see a blank page. That's expected.

> **NOTE** I recommend you open a new incognito browser window every time you test the application from now on. Since you're going to try out different security scenarios, the incognito mode will prevent you from having issues related to browser caches and cookies from previous sessions.

The crucial point of this test is that a user tried to access a protected endpoint exposed by Edge Service. The application redirected the user to a login page, showed a login form, and asked the user to provide a username and password. Then Edge Service validated the credentials against its internal user database (auto-generated in memory) and, on discovering they were valid, started an authenticated session with the browser. Since HTTP is a stateless protocol, the user session is kept alive through a cookie whose value is provided by the browser with each HTTP request (a *session cookie*). Internally, Edge Service maintains a mapping between the session identifier and user identifier, as shown in figure 11.1.

When you are done testing the application, terminate the process with Ctrl-C. Then navigate to the folder where you keep your Docker Compose file (polar-deployment/docker/docker-compose.yml), and run the following command to stop the Redis container:

```
$ docker-compose down
```

There are a few problems with the previous approach when applied to a cloud native system. In the rest of the chapter, we'll analyze those problems, identify viable solutions for cloud native applications, and use them on top of what we have just implemented.

Authentication flow with login form

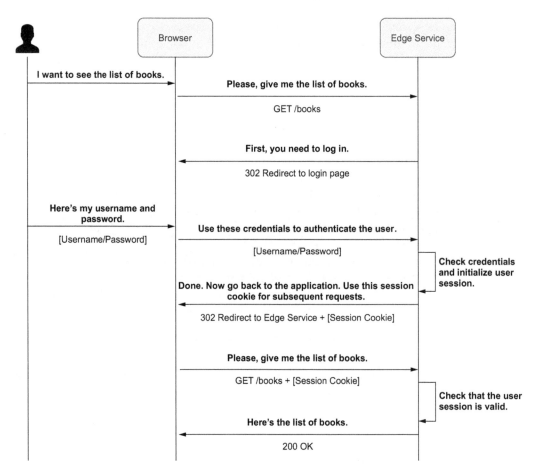

Figure 11.1   After the login step, the user session is kept alive through a session cookie.

11.2   *Managing user accounts with Keycloak*

In the previous section, we added user authentication to Edge Service based on a login form. You tried logging in via a user account that was auto-generated in memory at startup time. That's fine for experimenting with Spring Security the first time, but it's not something you'll want to do in production.

As a minimum requirement, we need persistent storage for user accounts and an option to register new users. There should be a particular focus on storing passwords using a robust encryption algorithm and preventing unauthorized access to the database. Given the criticality of such a feature, it makes sense to delegate it to a dedicated application.

Keycloak (www.keycloak.org) is an open source identity and access management solution developed and maintained by the Red Hat community. It offers a broad set of features, including single sign-on (SSO), social login, user federation, multi-factor authentication, and centralized user management. Keycloak relies on standards like OAuth2, OpenID Connect, and SAML 2.0. For now, we'll use Keycloak to manage user accounts in Polar Bookshop. Later I'll show you how to use its OpenID Connect and OAuth2 features.

> **NOTE** Spring Security provides all the necessary features to implement a user management service. If you'd like to learn more about this subject, you can refer to chapters 3 and 4 of *Spring Security in Action* by Laurențiu Spilcă (Manning, 2020).

You can run Keycloak locally as a standalone Java application or a container. For production, there are a few solutions for running Keycloak on Kubernetes. Keycloak also needs a relational database for persistence. It comes with an embedded H2 database, but you'll want to replace it with an external one in production.

For Polar Bookshop, we'll run Keycloak locally as a Docker container, relying on the embedded H2 database. In production we'll use PostgreSQL. This might seem to contradict the environment parity principle, but since it's a third-party application, it's not your responsibility to test its interaction with a data source.

This section will guide you step-by-step through the Keycloak configuration for the Polar Bookshop use case. First, open your `polar-deployment` repository. Then define a new `polar-keycloak` container in docker/docker-compose.yml.

Listing 11.3 Defining a Keycloak container in Docker Compose

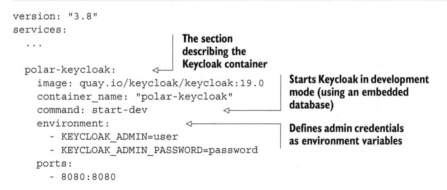

```
version: "3.8"
services:
  ...                          The section
                               describing the
                               Keycloak container
  polar-keycloak:          ◁──┘
    image: quay.io/keycloak/keycloak:19.0      Starts Keycloak in development
    container_name: "polar-keycloak"           mode (using an embedded
    command: start-dev       ◁──────────────   database)
    environment:             ◁──────────────   Defines admin credentials
      - KEYCLOAK_ADMIN=user                     as environment variables
      - KEYCLOAK_ADMIN_PASSWORD=password
    ports:
      - 8080:8080
```

> **NOTE** Later I will provide you with a JSON file you can use to load the entire configuration when starting up the Keycloak container, so you won't need to be concerned about the container's persistence.

You can start a Keycloak container by opening a Terminal window, navigating to the folder where you keep the docker-compose.yml file, and running this command:

```
$ docker-compose up -d polar-keycloak
```

Before we can start managing user accounts, we need to define a security realm. We'll do that next.

11.2.1 Defining a security realm

In Keycloak, any security aspect of an application or a system is defined in the context of a *realm*, a logical domain in which we apply specific security policies. By default, Keycloak comes preconfigured with a *Master* realm, but you'll probably want to create a dedicated one for each product you build. Let's create a new *PolarBookshop* realm to host any security-related aspects of the Polar Bookshop system.

Make sure the Keycloak container you started earlier is still running. Then open a Terminal window, and enter a bash console inside the Keycloak container:

```
$ docker exec -it polar-keycloak bash
```

> **TIP** Keycloak might take several seconds to start up. If you try to access it right after starting the container, you might get an error because it's not yet ready to accept connections. If that happens, wait a few seconds and try again. You can check the Keycloak logs with `docker logs -f polar-keycloak`. After the message "Running the server in development mode" is printed out, Keycloak is ready to be used.

We'll configure Keycloak through its Admin CLI, but you can achieve the same result by using the GUI available at http://localhost:8080. First, navigate to the folder where the Keycloak Admin CLI scripts are located:

```
$ cd /opt/keycloak/bin
```

The Admin CLI is protected by the username and password we defined in Docker Compose for the Keycloak container. We'll need to start an authenticated session before running any other commands:

```
$ ./kcadm.sh config credentials \
    --server http://localhost:8080 \        ← Keycloak runs on
    --realm master \        ←        port 8080 inside
    --user user \        ←          the container.
    --password password        ←
```

The default realm configured in Keycloak

The username we defined in Docker Compose

The password we defined in Docker Compose

> **TIP** You should keep the current Terminal window open until you're done configuring Keycloak. If at any point the authenticated session expires, you can always start a new one by running the previous command.

At this point, you can go ahead and create a new security realm where all the policies associated with Polar Bookshop will be stored:

```
$ ./kcadm.sh create realms -s realm=PolarBookshop -s enabled=true
```

11.2.2 Managing users and roles

We'll need some users to test different authentication scenarios. As anticipated in chapter 2, Polar Bookshop has two types of users: customers and employees.

- *Customers* can browse books and purchase them.
- *Employees* can also add new books to the catalog, modify the existing ones, and delete them.

To manage the different permissions associated with each type of user, let's create two roles: *customer* and *employee*. Later you'll protect application endpoints based on those roles. It's an authorization strategy called *role-based access control* (RBAC).

First, create the two roles in the Polar Bookshop realm from the Keycloak Admin CLI console you have used so far:

```
$ ./kcadm.sh create roles -r PolarBookshop -s name=employee
$ ./kcadm.sh create roles -r PolarBookshop -s name=customer
```

Then create two users. *Isabelle Dahl* will be both an employee and a customer of the bookshop (username: `isabelle`). You can create an account for her as follows:

```
$ ./kcadm.sh create users -r PolarBookshop \
    -s username=isabelle \          ◁──  The username for the
    -s firstName=Isabelle \              new user. It will be
    -s lastName=Dahl \                   used for logging in.
 ▷  -s enabled=true
```

The user should be active.

```
$ ./kcadm.sh add-roles -r PolarBookshop \
    --uusername isabelle \          ◁──  Isabelle is both an
    --rolename employee \                employee and a
    --rolename customer                  customer.
```

Then do the same for *Bjorn Vinterberg* (username: `bjorn`), a customer of the bookshop:

```
$ ./kcadm.sh create users -r PolarBookshop \
    -s username=bjorn \             ◁──  The username for the
    -s firstName=Bjorn \                 new user. It will be
    -s lastName=Vinterberg \             used for logging in.
 ▷  -s enabled=true
```

The user should be active.

```
$ ./kcadm.sh add-roles -r PolarBookshop \
    --uusername bjorn \             ◁──  Bjorn is a
    --rolename customer                  customer.
```

In a real scenario, users would choose a password themselves and preferably enable two-factor authentication. Isabelle and Bjorn are test users, so assigning an explicit password (password) is OK. You can do that from the Keycloak Admin CLI as follows:

```
$ ./kcadm.sh set-password -r PolarBookshop \
    --username isabelle --new-password password
$ ./kcadm.sh set-password -r PolarBookshop \
    --username bjorn --new-password password
```

That's it for user management. You can get out of the bash console inside the Keycloak container with the exit command, but keep Keycloak running.

Next, let's explore how we can improve the authentication strategy in Edge Service.

11.3 Authentication with OpenID Connect, JWT, and Keycloak

At the moment, users must log in via a browser with a username and password. Since Keycloak now manages user accounts, we could go ahead and update Edge Service to check the user credentials with Keycloak itself, rather than using its internal storage. But what happens if we introduce different clients to the Polar Bookshop system, such as mobile applications and IoT devices? How should the users authenticate then? What if the bookshop employees are already registered in the company's Active Directory (AD) and want to log in via SAML? Can we provide a single sign-on (SSO) experience across different applications? Will the users be able to log in via their GitHub or Twitter accounts (*social login*)?

We could think of supporting all those authentication strategies in Edge Service as we get new requirements. However, that is not a scalable approach. A better solution is delegating a dedicated *identity provider* to authenticate users following any supported strategy. Edge Service would then use that service to verify the identity of a user without being concerned about performing the actual authentication step. The dedicated service could let users authenticate in various ways, such as using the credentials registered in the system, through social login, or via SAML to rely on the identity defined in the company's AD.

Using a dedicated service to authenticate users leads to two aspects we need to address for the system to work. First, we need to establish a protocol for Edge Service to delegate user authentication to the identity provider and for the latter to provide information about the authentication result. Second, we need to define a data format that the identity provider can use to securely inform Edge Service about the identity of users after they have been successfully authenticated. This section will address both issues using OpenID Connect and JSON Web Token.

11.3.1 Authenticating users with OpenID Connect

OpenID Connect (OIDC) is a protocol that enables an application (called the *Client*) to verify the identity of a user based on the authentication performed by a trusted party (called an *Authorization Server*) and retrieve the user profile information. The authorization server informs the Client application about the result of the authentication step via an *ID Token*.

OIDC is an identity layer on top of OAuth2, an authorization framework that solves the problem of delegating access using tokens for authorization but doesn't deal with authentication. As you know, authorization can only happen after authentication. That's why I decided to cover OIDC first; OAuth2 will be further explored in the next chapter. This is not the typical way of covering those subjects, but I think it makes sense when designing an access control system like we're doing for Polar Bookshop.

> **NOTE** This book will only cover some essential aspects of OAuth2 and OIDC. If you're interested in learning more about them, Manning has a couple of books in its catalog on the subject: *OAuth 2 in Action* by Justin Richer and Antonio Sanso (Manning, 2017) and *OpenID Connect in Action* by Prabath Siriwardena (Manning, 2022).

When it comes to handling user authentication, we can identify three main actors in the OAuth2 framework that are used by the OIDC protocol:

- *Authorization Server*—The entity responsible for authenticating users and issuing tokens. In Polar Bookshop, this will be Keycloak.
- *User*—Also called the *Resource Owner,* this is the human logging in with the Authorization Server to get authenticated access to the Client application. In Polar Bookshop, it's either a customer or an employee.
- *Client*—The application requiring the user to be authenticated. This can be a mobile application, a browser-based application, a server-side application, or even a smart TV application. In Polar Bookshop, it's Edge Service.

Figure 11.2 shows how the three actors are mapped to the Polar Bookshop architecture.

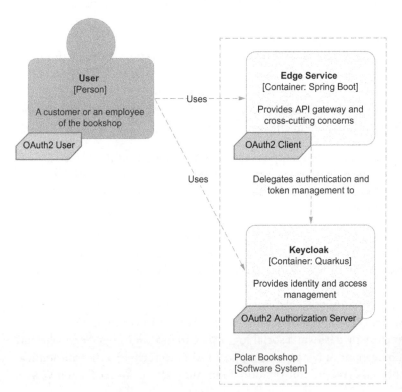

Figure 11.2 How the OIDC/OAuth2 roles are assigned to the entities in the Polar Bookshop architecture for user authentication

NOTE   The roles defined by the OAuth2 framework are also known by different names when used in the context of OpenID Connect. The OAuth2 Authorization Server is also called the *OIDC Provider*. The OAuth2 Client, which relies on the Authorization Server for authentication and token issuing, is also called the *Relying Party* (RP). The OAuth2 User is also called the *End-User*. We'll stick to the OAuth2 naming for consistency, but it's helpful to know the alternative terminology used in OIDC.

In Polar Bookshop, Edge Service will initiate the user login flow, but then it will delegate the actual authentication step to Keycloak via the OIDC protocol (supported out of the box by Spring Security). Keycloak provides several authentication strategies, including traditional login forms, social logins via providers like GitHub or Twitter, and SAML. It also supports two-factor authentication (2FA). In the following sections, we'll use the login form strategy as an example. Since users will interact directly with Keycloak to log in, their credentials will never be exposed to any component of the system except Keycloak, which is one of the benefits of adopting such a solution.

When an unauthenticated user calls a secure endpoint exposed by Edge Service, the following happens:

1 Edge Service (the Client) redirects the browser to Keycloak (the Authorization Server) for authentication.
2 Keycloak authenticates the user (for example, by asking for a username and password via a login form) and then redirects the browser back to Edge Service, together with an *Authorization Code.*
3 Edge Service calls Keycloak to exchange the Authorization Code with an ID Token, containing information about the authenticated user.
4 Edge Service initializes an authenticated user session with the browser based on a session cookie. Internally, Edge Service maintains a mapping between the session identifier and ID Token (the user identity).

NOTE   The authentication flow supported by OIDC is based on the OAuth2 *Authorization Code flow.* The second step might seem redundant, but the Authorization Code is essential for ensuring that only the legitimate Client can exchange it with tokens.

Figure 11.3 describes the essential parts of the authentication flow supported by the OIDC protocol. Even if Spring Security supports that out of the box, and you won't need to implement any of it yourself, it's still beneficial to have an overview of the flow in mind.

When adopting the authentication flow illustrated in figure 11.3, Edge Service is not affected by the specific authentication strategy. We could configure Keycloak to use an Active Directory or perform a social login via GitHub, and Edge Service would not require any changes. It only needs to support OIDC to verify that the authentication happened correctly and get information about the user via an ID Token. What's

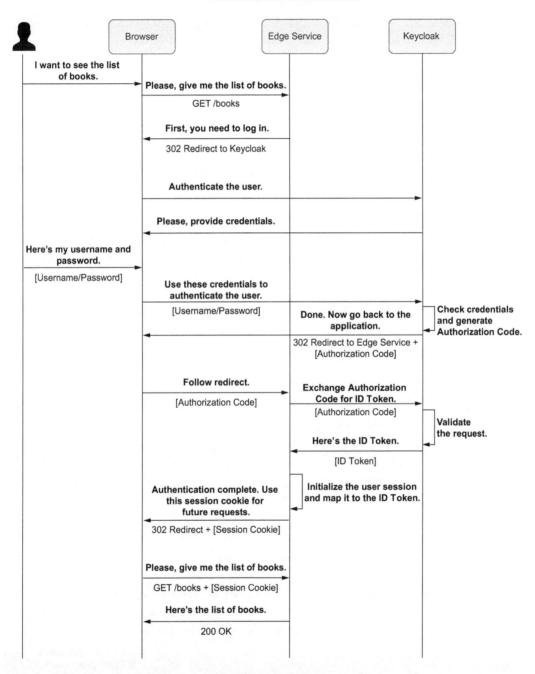

Figure 11.3   The authentication flow supported by the OIDC protocol

an ID Token? It's a *JSON Web Token* (JWT) containing information about the user authentication event. We'll take a closer look at JWTs in the next section.

> **NOTE** Whenever I mention OIDC, I am referring to the OpenID Connect Core 1.0 specification (https://openid.net/specs/openid-connect-core-1_0.html). Whenever I mention OAuth2, unless specified otherwise, I am referring to the OAuth 2.1 specification currently under standardization (https://oauth .net/2.1) and meant to replace the OAuth 2.0 standard described in RFC 6749 (https://tools.ietf.org/html/rfc6749).

11.3.2 *Exchanging user information with JWT*

In distributed systems, including microservices and cloud native applications, the most-used strategy for exchanging information about an authenticated user and their authorization is through tokens.

JSON Web Token (JWT) is an industry-standard for representing *claims* to be transferred between two parties. It's a widely used format for propagating information about an authenticated user and their permissions securely among different parties in a distributed system. A JWT is not used by itself, but it's included in a larger structure, the JSON Web Signature (JWS), which ensures the integrity of the claims by digitally signing the JWT object.

A digitally signed JWT (JWS) is a string composed of three parts encoded in Base64 and separated by a dot (.) character:

```
<header>.<payload>.<signature>
```

> **NOTE** For debugging purposes, you can use the tool available on https:// jwt.io to encode and decode tokens.

As you saw, a digitally signed JWT has three parts:

- *Header*—A JSON object (called *JOSE Header*) containing information about the cryptographic operations performed on the payload. The operations follow the standards from the Javascript Object Signing and Encryption (JOSE) framework. A decoded header looks like this:

```
{
  "alg": "HS256",        ◁──┐ The algorithm used to
  "typ": "JWT"           ◁──┐ sign the token digitally
}                            The type of token
```

- *Payload*—A JSON object (called *Claims Set*) containing the claims conveyed by the token. The JWT specification defines some standard claim names, but you can also define your own. A decoded payload looks like the following:

```
{
  "iss": "https://sso.polarbookshop.com",   ◁──┐ The entity that issued
  "sub": "isabelle",                        ◁──┐ the JWT (the issuer)
                                                The entity that is the subject
                                                of the JWT (the end-user)
}
```

```
  "exp": 1626439022        ◁──┐  When the JWT expires
}                              │  (a timestamp)
```

- *Signature*—The signature of the JWT, ensuring that the claims have not been tampered with. A prerequisite of using a JWS structure is that we trust the entity issuing the token (the *issuer*), and we have a way to check its validity.

When a JWT requires integrity and confidentiality, it's first signed as a JWS and then encrypted with JSON Web Encryption (JWE). In this book, we'll use only JWS.

> **NOTE** If you're interested in learning more about JWT and its related aspects, you can refer to the IETF standard specifications. JSON Web Token (JWT) is documented in RFC 7519 (https://tools.ietf.org/html/rfc7519), JSON Web Signature (JWS) is described in RFC 7515 (https://tools.ietf.org/html/rfc7515), and JSON Web Encryption (JWE) is presented in RFC 7516 (https://tools.ietf.org/html/rfc7516). You might also be interested in JSON Web Algorithms (JWA), which defines the available cryptographic operations for JWTs and is detailed in RFC 7518 (https://tools.ietf.org/html rfc7518).

In the case of Polar Bookshop, Edge Service can delegate the authentication step to Keycloak. After authenticating the user successfully, Keycloak will send a JWT to Edge Service with information about the newly authenticated user (ID Token). Edge Service will validate the JWT through its signature and inspect it to retrieve data (claims) about the user. Finally, it will establish an authenticated session with the user's browser based on a session cookie, whose identifier is mapped to the JWT.

To delegate authentication and retrieve tokens securely, Edge Service must be registered as an OAuth2 Client in Keycloak. Let's see how.

11.3.3 Registering an application in Keycloak

As you learned in the previous sections, an OAuth2 Client is an application that can request user authentication and ultimately receive tokens from an Authorization Server. In the Polar Bookshop architecture, this role is played by Edge Service. When using OIDC/OAuth2, you need to register each OAuth2 Client with the Authorization Server before using it for authenticating users.

Clients can be *public* or *confidential*. We register an application as a public Client if it can't keep a secret. For example, mobile applications would be registered as public Clients. On the other hand, confidential Clients are those that can keep a secret, and they are usually backend applications like Edge Service. The registration process is similar either way. The main difference is that confidential Clients are required to authenticate themselves with the Authorization Server, such as by relying on a shared secret. It's an additional protection layer we can't use for public Clients, since they have no way to store the shared secret securely.

Since Edge Service will be the OAuth2 Client in the Polar Bookshop system, let's register it with Keycloak. We can rely on the Keycloak Admin CLI one more time.

The Client dilemma in OAuth2

The Client role can be assigned either to a frontend or a backend application. The main difference is the level of security of the solution. The Client is the entity that will receive tokens from the Authorization Server. The Client will have to store them somewhere to be used in subsequent requests from the same user. Tokens are sensitive data that should be secured, and there's no better place than a backend application to do that. But it's not always possible.

Here is my rule of thumb. If the frontend is a mobile or desktop application like iOS or Android, that will be the OAuth2 Client, and it will be categorized as a *public* Client. You can use libraries like AppAuth (https://appauth.io) to add support for OIDC/OAuth2 and store the tokens as securely as possible on the device. If the frontend is a web application (like in Polar Bookshop), then a backend service should be the Client. In this case, it would be categorized as a *confidential* Client.

The reason for this distinction is that no matter how much you try to hide the OIDC/OAuth2 tokens in the browser (cookies, local storage, session storage), they will always be at risk of being exposed and misused. "From a security perspective, it is virtually impossible to secure tokens in a frontend web application." That's what application security expert Philippe De Ryck writes,[a] recommending engineers rely on the backend-for-frontend pattern and have a backend application deal with tokens instead.

I recommend basing the interaction between browser and backend on a session cookie (like you'd do for monoliths) and have the backend application be responsible for controlling the authentication flow and using the tokens issued by the Authorization Server, even in the case of SPAs. That is the current best practice recommended by security experts.

---

[a] P. De Ryck, "A Critical Analysis of Refresh Token Rotation in Single-page Applications," *Ping Identity* blog, March 18, 2021, http://mng.bz/QWG6.

Make sure the Keycloak container you started earlier is still running. Then open a Terminal window and enter a bash console inside the Keycloak container:

```
$ docker exec -it polar-keycloak bash
```

Next, navigate to the folder where the Keycloak Admin CLI scripts are located:

```
$ cd /opt/keycloak/bin
```

As you learned earlier, the Admin CLI is protected by the username and password we defined in Docker Compose for the Keycloak container, so we need to start an authenticated session before running any other commands:

```
$ ./kcadm.sh config credentials --server http://localhost:8080 \
    --realm master --user user --password password
```

Finally, register Edge Service as an OAuth2 Client in the `PolarBookshop` realm:

**It must be
enabled.**

**Edge Service is
a confidential
client, not
public.**

```
$ ./kcadm.sh create clients -r PolarBookshop \
    -s clientId=edge-service \
    -s enabled=true \
    -s publicClient=false \
    -s secret=polar-keycloak-secret \
    -s 'redirectUris=["http://localhost:9000",
    ➥ "http://localhost:9000/login/oauth2/code/*"]'
```

**The OAuth2 Client
identifier**

**Since it's a confidential
client, it needs a secret to
authenticate with Keycloak.**

**The application URLs to which Keycloak
is authorized to redirect a request after
a user login or logout**

The valid redirect URLs are the endpoints exposed by the OAuth2 Client application (Edge Service) where Keycloak will redirect authentication requests. Since Keycloak can include sensitive information in a redirect request, we want to limit which applications and endpoints are authorized to receive such information. As you'll learn later, the redirect URL for authentication requests will be `http://localhost:9000/login/oauth2/code/*`, following the default format provided by Spring Security. To support redirects after logout operations, we also need to add `http://localhost:9000` as a valid redirect URL.

That's it for this section. In the source code repository accompanying the book, I included a JSON file you can use to load the entire configuration when starting up the Keycloak container in the future (Chapter11/11-end/polar-deployment/docker/keycloak/realm-config.json). Now that you've familiarized yourself with Keycloak, you can update the container definition to ensure you always have the needed configuration at startup. Copy the JSON file over the same path in your own project, and update the `polar-keycloak` service in your docker-compose.yml file as follows.

> **Listing 11.4   Importing realm configuration in Keycloak container**

```
version: "3.8"
services:
  ...

  polar-keycloak:
    image: quay.io/keycloak/keycloak:19.0
    container_name: "polar-keycloak"
    command: start-dev --import-realm
    volumes:
      - ./keycloak:/opt/keycloak/data/import
    environment:
      - KEYCLOAK_ADMIN=user
      - KEYCLOAK_ADMIN_PASSWORD=password
    ports:
      - 8080:8080
```

**Imports the provided
configuration at
startup time**

**Configures a volume to load
the configuration file into
the container**

> **Why Keycloak**
>
> I decided to use Keycloak since it's a mature, open source solution for running an Authorization Server yourself. After increasing demands from the community, Spring started a new Spring Authorization Server project (https://github.com/spring-projects/spring-authorization-server). Since version 0.2.0, it's been a production-ready solution for setting up an OAuth2 Authorization Server. At the time of writing, the project provides an implementation for the most common OAuth2 features, and it's currently working on extending support for OIDC-specific features. You can follow the progress and contribute to the project on GitHub.
>
> Another option is to use a SaaS solution like Okta (www.okta.com) or Auth0 (https://auth0.com). They are both excellent solutions for getting OIDC/OAuth2 as a managed service, and I encourage you to try them out. For this book, I wanted to use a solution that you could run and reliably reproduce in your local environment without depending on other services that might change over time, making my instructions here invalid.

Before moving on, let's stop any running containers. Open a Terminal window, navigate to the folder where you keep your Docker Compose file (polar-deployment/docker/docker-compose.yml), and run the following command:

```
$ docker-compose down
```

We now have all the pieces for refactoring Edge Service so it can use an authentication strategy relying on OIDC/OAuth2, JWT, and Keycloak. The best part is that it's based on standards and supported by all major languages and frameworks (frontend, backend, mobile, IoT), including Spring Security.

11.4 Authenticating users with Spring Security and OpenID Connect

As mentioned earlier, Spring Security supports several authentication strategies. The current security setup for Edge Service handles user accounts and authentication via a login form provided by the application itself. Now that you've learned about OpenID Connect, we can refactor the application to delegate user authentication to Keycloak via the OIDC protocol.

Support for OAuth2 used to be in a separate project called Spring Security OAuth, which you would use as part of Spring Cloud Security to adopt OAuth2 in a cloud native application. Both of those projects have now been deprecated in favor of the native, more comprehensive support for OAuth2 and OpenID Connect introduced in the main Spring Security project, starting from version 5. This chapter focuses on using the new OIDC/OAuth2 support in Spring Security 5 to authenticate the users of Polar Bookshop.

NOTE If you find yourself working on a project using the deprecated Spring Security OAuth and Spring Cloud Security projects, you might want to check out chapters 12 through 15 of *Spring Security in Action* by Laurenţiu Spilcă (Manning, 2020), where they are explained in great detail.

Using Spring Security and its OAuth2/OIDC support, this section will show you how to do the following for Edge Service:

- Use OpenID Connect to authenticate users.
- Configure user logout.
- Extract information about the authenticated user.

Let's get started!

11.4.1 Adding the new dependencies

First of all, we need to update the dependencies for Edge Service. We can replace the existing Spring Security starter dependency with the more specific OAuth2 Client one, which adds support for OIDC/OAuth2 client features. Furthermore, we can add the Spring Security Test dependency, which provides additional support for testing security scenarios in Spring.

Open the build.gradle file for the Edge Service project (edge-service) and add the new dependencies. Remember to refresh or reimport the Gradle dependencies after the new addition.

Listing 11.5 Adding dependencies for Spring Security OAuth2 Client

```
dependencies {
    ...
    implementation
    ⮕ 'org.springframework.boot:spring-boot-starter-oauth2-client'
    testImplementation 'org.springframework.security:spring-security-test'
}
```

Spring integration with Keycloak

When choosing Keycloak as the Authorization Server, an alternative to the native OpenID Connect/OAuth2 support provided by Spring Security was the Keycloak Spring Adapter. It was a library supplied by the Keycloak project itself to integrate with Spring Boot and Spring Security, but it was retired after the release of Keycloak 17.

If you find yourself working on a project using the Keycloak Spring Adapter, you might want to check out my articles on the subject (www.thomasvitale.com/tag/keycloak) or chapter 9 of *Spring Microservices in Action*, second edition, by John Carnell and Illary Huaylupo Sánchez (Manning, 2021).

11.4.2 Configuring the integration between Spring Security and Keycloak

After adding the relevant dependencies on Spring Security, we need to configure the integration with Keycloak. In the previous section we registered Edge Service in

Keycloak as an OAuth2 Client, defining both a client identifier (`edge-service`) and a shared secret (`polar-keycloak-secret`). Now we'll use that information to tell Spring Security how to interact with Keycloak.

Open the application.yml file in your Edge Service project, and add the following configuration.

Listing 11.6   Configuring Edge Service as an OAuth2 Client

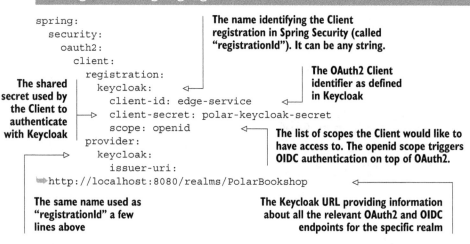

Each Client registration in Spring Security must have an identifier (*registrationId*). In this example, it's `keycloak`. The registration identifier is used to build the URL where Spring Security receives the Authorization Code from Keycloak. The default URL template is /login/oauth2/code/{registrationId}. For Edge Service, the full URL is http://localhost:9000/login/oauth2/code/keycloak, which we already configured in Keycloak as a valid redirect URL.

Scopes are an OAuth2 concept for limiting an application's access to user resources. You can think of them as roles, but for applications instead of users. When we use the OpenID Connect extension on top of OAuth2 to verify the user's identity, we need to include the `openid` scope to inform the Authorization Server and receive an ID Token containing data about the user authentication. The next chapter will explain more about scopes in the context of authorization.

Now that we've defined the integration with Keycloak, let's configure Spring Security to apply the desired security policies.

11.4.3 *Basic Spring Security configuration*

The central place for defining and configuring security policies in Spring Security is a `SecurityWebFilterChain` class. Edge Service is currently configured to require user authentication for all endpoints, and it uses an authentication strategy based on a login form. Let's change that to use OIDC authentication instead.

The `ServerHttpSecurity` object provides two ways of configuring an OAuth2 Client in Spring Security. With `oauth2Login()`, you can configure an application to act as an OAuth2 Client and also authenticate users through OpenID Connect. With `oauth2Client()`, the application will not authenticate users, so it's up to you to define another authentication mechanism. We want to use OIDC authentication, so we'll use `oauth2Login()` and the default configuration. Update the `SecurityConfig` class as follows.

Listing 11.7 Requiring authentication for all endpoints through OIDC

```
@EnableWebFluxSecurity
public class SecurityConfig {

  @Bean
  SecurityWebFilterChain springSecurityFilterChain(
   ServerHttpSecurity http
  ) {
    return http
      .authorizeExchange(exchange ->
        exchange.anyExchange().authenticated())
      .oauth2Login(Customizer.withDefaults())
      .build();
  }
}
```

> **Enables user authentication with OAuth2/OpenID Connect** ← (points to `.oauth2Login(Customizer.withDefaults())`)

Let's verify that this works correctly. First, start the Redis and Keycloak containers. Open a Terminal window, navigate to the folder where you keep your Docker Compose file (polar-deployment/docker/docker-compose.yml), and run the following command:

```
$ docker-compose up -d polar-redis polar-keycloak
```

Then run the Edge Service application (`./gradlew bootRun`), open a browser window, and head to http://localhost:9000. You should be redirected to a login page served by Keycloak, where you can authenticate as one of the users we created previously (figure 11.4).

For example, log in as Isabelle (`isabelle/password`) and pay attention to how Keycloak redirects you back to Edge Service after validating the provided credentials. Since Edge Service doesn't expose any content through the root endpoint, you'll see an error message ("Whitelabel Error Page"). But don't worry! That's where we'll integrate an Angular frontend later. The crucial point of this test is that Edge Service required you to be authenticated before accessing any of its endpoints, and it triggered the OIDC authentication flow.

When you're done trying out the OIDC authentication flow, stop the application with Ctrl-C.

If the authentication is successful, Spring Security will start an authenticated session with the browser and save information about the user. In the next section, you'll see how we can retrieve and use that information.

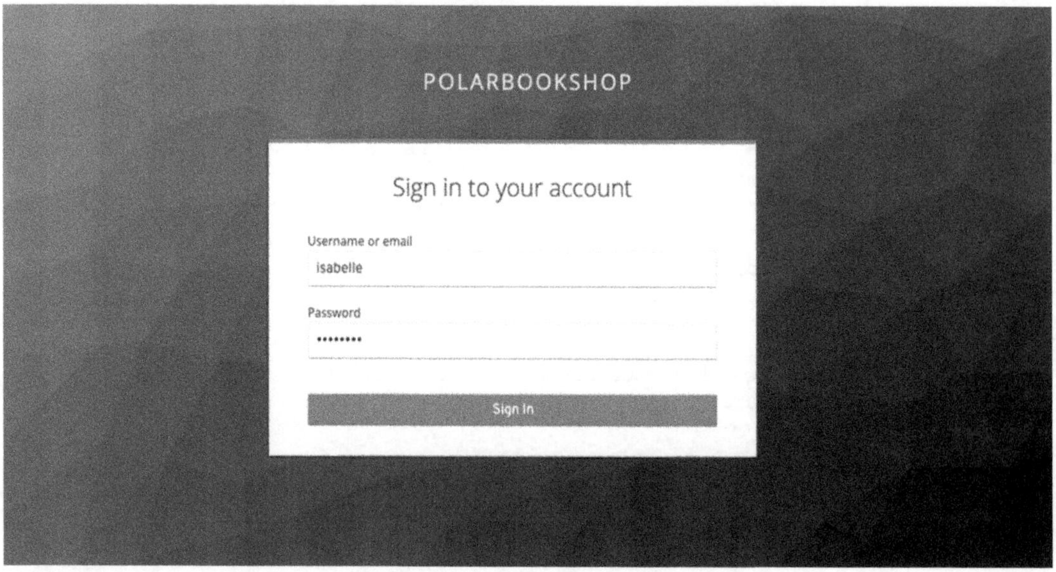

Figure 11.4   The Keycloak login page for the Polar Bookshop realm, shown after Edge Service triggered the OIDC authentication flow

11.4.4 *Inspecting the authenticated user context*

As part of the authentication process, Spring Security defines a context to hold information about the user and map a user session to an ID Token. In this section, you'll learn more about this context, what classes are involved, and how to retrieve the data and expose it through a new /user endpoint in Edge Service.

First, let's define a User model to collect the username, first name, last name, and roles of an authenticated user. That's the same information we provided when registering the two users in Keycloak, and it is the information returned in the ID Token. In a new com.polarbookshop.edgeservice.user package, create a User record as follows.

> **Listing 11.8   Creating the `User` record to hold info about an authenticated user**

```
package com.polarbookshop.edgeservice.user;

import java.util.List;

public record User(          ◁─────┐  Immutable data
  String username,                 │  class holding
  String firstName,                │  user data
  String lastName,
  List<String> roles
){}
```

Independent of the authentication strategy adopted (whether username/password, OpenID Connect/OAuth2, or SAML2), Spring Security keeps the information about an authenticated user (also called the *principal*) in an `Authentication` object. In the case of OIDC, the principal object is of type `OidcUser`, and it's where Spring Security stores the ID Token. In turn, `Authentication` is saved in a `SecurityContext` object.

One way to access the `Authentication` object for the currently logged-in user is extracting it from the related `SecurityContext` retrieved from the `ReactiveSecurity-ContextHolder` (or `SecurityContextHolder` for imperative applications). Figure 11.5 illustrates how all these objects are related to each other.

Security context structure for OIDC authentication in Spring Security

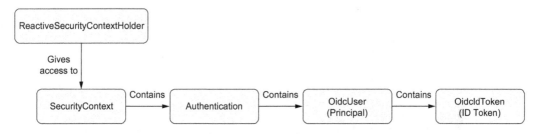

Figure 11.5   The main classes used to store information about the currently authenticated user

You can make that work by doing the following:

1. Create a `UserController` class annotated with `@RestController` in the `com.polarbookshop.edgeservice.user` package.
2. Define a method to handle `GET` requests to a new `/user` endpoint.
3. Return a `User` object for the currently authenticated user, retrieving the necessary information from `OidcUser`. To get the correct data, we can use the call hierarchy shown in figure 11.5.

The resulting method in the `UserController` class will look like this:

```
@GetMapping("user")                                      Gets SecurityContext for the
public Mono<User> getUser() {                            currently authenticated user from
  return ReactiveSecurityContextHolder.getContext()      ReactiveSecurityContextHolder
    .map(SecurityContext::getAuthentication)             <--  Gets Authentication
    .map(authentication ->                                    from SecurityContext
      (OidcUser) authentication.getPrincipal())          <--  Gets the principal from
    .map(oidcUser ->                                           Authentication. For OIDC,
      new User(                                                it's of type OidcUser.
        oidcUser.getPreferredUsername(),
        oidcUser.getGivenName(),
        oidcUser.getFamilyName(),                        Builds a User object using data
        List.of("employee", "customer")                 from OidcUser (extracted from
      )                                                  the ID Token)
  );
}
```

In the next chapter, which focuses on authorization strategies, we'll configure Keycloak to include a custom `roles` claim in the ID Token and use that value to build the `User` object in the `UserController` class. Until then, we'll use a fixed list of values.

For Spring Web MVC and WebFlux controllers, besides using `ReactiveSecurityContextHolder` directly, we can use the annotations `@CurrentSecurityContext` and `@AuthenticationPrincipal` to inject the `SecurityContext` and the principal (in this case, `OidcUser`) respectively.

Let's simplify the implementation of the `getUser()` method by injecting the `OidcUser` object directly as an argument. The final result for the `UserController` class is shown in the following listing.

Listing 11.9   Returning information about the currently authenticated user

```
package com.polarbookshop.edgeservice.user;

import java.util.List;
import reactor.core.publisher.Mono;
import org.springframework.security.core.annotation.
➥AuthenticationPrincipal;
import org.springframework.security.oauth2.core.oidc.user.OidcUser;
import org.springframework.web.bind.annotation.GetMapping;
import org.springframework.web.bind.annotation.RestController;

@RestController
public class UserController {

  @GetMapping("user")
  public Mono<User> getUser(
    @AuthenticationPrincipal OidcUser oidcUser       ⟵  Injects an OidcUser object
  ) {                                                    containing info about the
    var user = new User(                  ⟵             currently authenticated user
      oidcUser.getPreferredUsername(),       Builds a User object
      oidcUser.getGivenName(),               from relevant claims
      oidcUser.getFamilyName(),              contained in OidcUser
      List.of("employee", "customer")
    );
    return Mono.just(user);               ⟵  Wraps the User object in a
  }                                          reactive publisher, since Edge
}                                            Service is a reactive application
```

Ensure that Keycloak and Redis are still running from the previous section, run the Edge Service application (`./gradlew bootRun`), open an incognito browser window, and navigate to http://localhost:9000/user. Spring Security will redirect you to Keycloak, which will prompt you to log in with a username and password. For example, authenticate as Bjorn (`bjorn/password`). After successfully authenticating, you will be redirected back to the `/user` endpoint. The result is the following:

```
{
  "username": "bjorn",
  "firstName": "Bjorn",
  "lastName": "Vinterberg",
```

```
  "roles": [
    "employee",
    "customer"
  ]
}
```

NOTE The `roles` list includes hardcoded values. In the next chapter, we'll change it to return the actual roles assigned to each user in Keycloak.

When you're done trying out the new endpoint, stop the application with Ctrl-C and the containers with `docker-compose down`.

Consider what happened when you tried to access the `/user` endpoint and got redirected to Keycloak. After successfully validating the user's credentials, Keycloak called Edge Service back and sent the ID Token for the newly authenticated user. Then Edge Service stored the token and redirected the browser to the required endpoint, together with a session cookie. From that point on, any communication between the browser and Edge Service will use that session cookie to identify the authenticated context for that user. No token is exposed to the browser.

The ID Token is stored in `OidcUser`, part of `Authentication` and ultimately included in `SecurityContext`. In chapter 9, we used the Spring Session project to make Edge Service store session data in an external data service (Redis), so it could remain stateless and be able to scale out. `SecurityContext` objects are included in the session data and are therefore stored in Redis automatically, making it possible for Edge Service to scale out without any problem.

Another option for retrieving the currently authenticated user (the *principal*) is from the context associated with a specific HTTP request (called the *exchange*). We'll use that option to update the rate limiter configuration. In chapter 9, we implemented rate-limiting with Spring Cloud Gateway and Redis. Currently the rate-limiting is computed based on the total number of requests received every second. We should update it to apply the rate limits to each user independently.

Open the `RateLimiterConfig` class and configure how the username of the currently authenticated principal should be extracted from the request. If no user is defined (that is, the request is unauthenticated, *anonymous*), we use a default key to apply rate-limiting to all unauthenticated requests as a whole.

Listing 11.10 Configuring rate limiting for each user

```
@Configuration
public class RateLimiterConfig {                    Gets the currently
                                                    authenticated user (the
                                                    principal) from the current
  @Bean                                             request (the exchange)
  KeyResolver keyResolver() {                                        Extracts the
    return exchange -> exchange.getPrincipal()      ◁────────        username from
      .map(Principal::getName)                      ◁────────        the principal
      .defaultIfEmpty("anonymous");    ◁────────  If the request is unauthenticated, it
  }                                               uses "anonymous" as the default
}                                                 key to apply rate-limiting.
```

That concludes the basic configuration for authenticating users of Polar Bookshop using OpenID Connect. The following section will cover how logout works in Spring Security and how we can customize it for the OAuth2/OIDC scenario.

11.4.5 *Configuring user logout in Spring Security and Keycloak*

So far, we have addressed the challenges and solutions for authenticating users in a distributed system. Still, we should consider what happens when a user logs out.

In Spring Security, logging out results in all the session data associated with the user being deleted. When OpenID Connect/OAuth2 is used, the tokens stored by Spring Security for that user are also deleted. However, the user will still have an active session in Keycloak. Just as the authentication process involves both Keycloak and Edge Service, completely logging a user out requires propagating the logout request to both components.

By default, a logout performed against an application protected by Spring Security will not affect Keycloak. Fortunately, Spring Security provides an implementation of the "OpenID Connect RP-Initiated Logout" specification, which defines how a logout request should be propagated from an OAuth2 Client (the Relying Party) to the Authorization Server. You'll see how to configure it for Edge Service soon.

> **NOTE**   The OpenID Connect specification includes a few different scenarios for session management and logout. If you'd like to learn more, I recommend you check the official documents for OIDC Session Management (https://openid.net/specs/openid-connect-session-1_0.html), OIDC Front-Channel Logout (https://openid.net/specs/openid-connect-frontchannel-1_0.html), OIDC Back-Channel Logout (https://openid.net/specs/openid -connect-backchannel-1_0.html), and OIDC RP-Initiated Logout (https:// openid.net/specs/openid-connect-rpinitiated-1_0.html).

Spring Security supports logging out by sending a POST request to the /logout endpoint implemented and exposed by the framework by default. We want to enable the RP-Initiated Logout scenario so that when a user logs out of the application, they are also logged out of the Authorization Server. Spring Security has full support for this scenario and provides an OidcClientInitiatedServerLogoutSuccessHandler object you can use to configure how to propagate a logout request to Keycloak.

Let's say the RP-Initiated Logout feature is enabled. In that case, after a user has been successfully logged out of Spring Security, Edge Service will send a logout request to Keycloak through the browser (using a redirect). Next you'll probably want the user to be redirected back to the application after the logout operation has been performed on the Authorization Server as well.

You can configure where the user should be redirected after a logout with the set-PostLogoutRedirectUri() method, which is exposed by the OidcClientInitiated-ServerLogoutSuccessHandler class. You might specify a direct URL, but that will not work well in a cloud environment due to many variables such as hostnames, service names, and protocols (`http` vs. `https`). The Spring Security team knew that, and they added support for placeholders that are resolved dynamically at runtime. Instead of hardcoding a URL value, you can use the `{baseUrl}` placeholder. When you run Edge Service locally, the placeholder will be resolved to `http://localhost:9000`. If you ran it in the cloud behind a proxy with TLS termination and accessible through the DNS name `polarbookshop.com`, it would automatically be replaced with `https://polar-bookshop.com`.

However, the Client configuration in Keycloak requires an exact URL. That's why we added `http://localhost:9000` to the list of valid redirect URLs when we registered Edge Service in Keycloak. In production you'll have to update the list of valid redirect URLs in Keycloak to match the actual URLs used there.

Figure 11.6 illustrates the logout scenario I've just described.

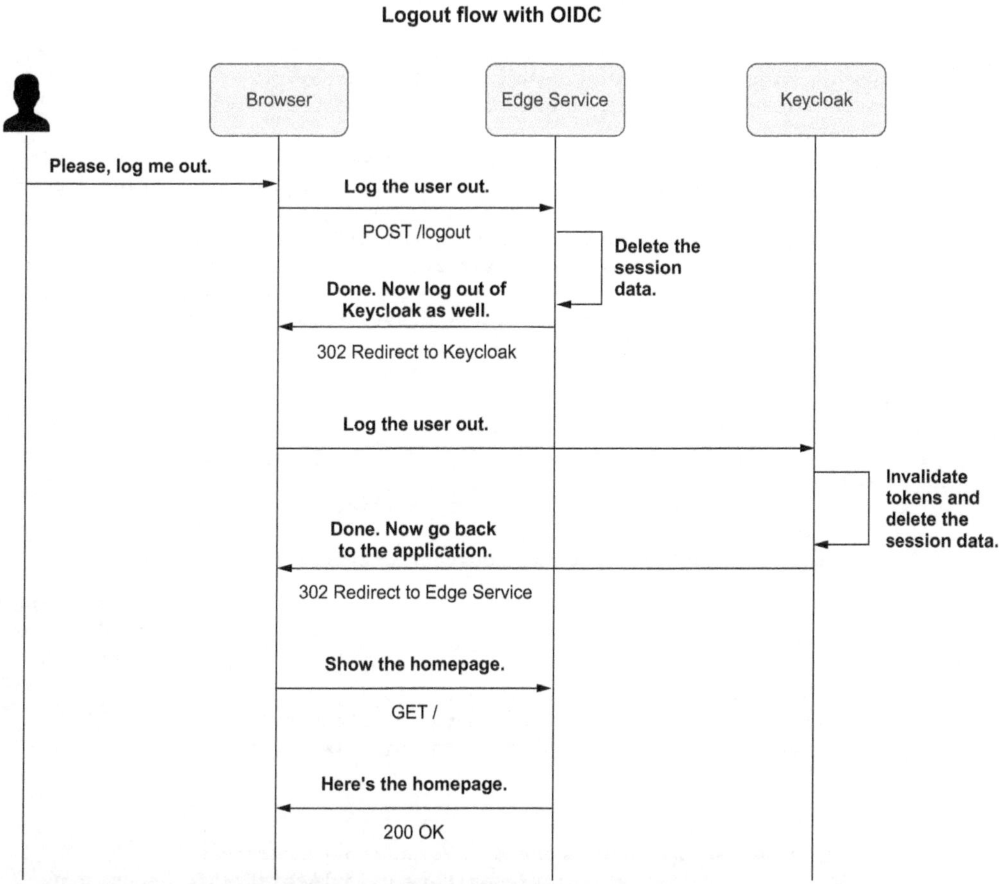

Figure 11.6   When a user logs out, the request is processed by Spring Security first, then forwarded to Keycloak, and the user is finally redirected to the application.

Since the application's logout functionality is already provided by default in Spring Security, you only need to enable and configure the RP-Initiated Logout for Edge Service:

1 In the SecurityConfig class, define an oidcLogoutSuccessHandler() method to build an OidcClientInitiatedServerLogoutSuccessHandler object.

2 Configure the post-logout redirect URL using the setPostLogoutRedirectUri() method.

3 Call the oidcLogoutSuccessHandler() method from the logout() configuration defined in the SecurityWebFilterChain bean.

The resulting configuration in the SecurityConfig class is as follows.

Listing 11.11   Configuring RP-Initiated Logout and redirecting on logout

```
package com.polarbookshop.edgeservice.config;

import org.springframework.context.annotation.Bean;
import org.springframework.security.config.Customizer;
import org.springframework.security.config.annotation.web.reactive.
    EnableWebFluxSecurity;
import org.springframework.security.config.web.server.ServerHttpSecurity;
import org.springframework.security.oauth2.client.oidc.web.server.logout.
    OidcClientInitiatedServerLogoutSuccessHandler;
import org.springframework.security.oauth2.client.registration.
    ReactiveClientRegistrationRepository;
import org.springframework.security.web.server.SecurityWebFilterChain;
import org.springframework.security.web.server.authentication.logout.
    ServerLogoutSuccessHandler;

@EnableWebFluxSecurity
public class SecurityConfig {

  @Bean
  SecurityWebFilterChain springSecurityFilterChain(
    ServerHttpSecurity http,
    ReactiveClientRegistrationRepository clientRegistrationRepository
  ) {
    return http
      .authorizeExchange(exchange ->
        exchange.anyExchange().authenticated())
      .oauth2Login(Customizer.withDefaults())
      .logout(logout -> logout.logoutSuccessHandler(          ◁─┐ Defines a custom
        oidcLogoutSuccessHandler(clientRegistrationRepository)))    handler for the
      .build();                                                     scenario where a
  }                                                                 logout operation is
                                                                    completed successfully
  private ServerLogoutSuccessHandler oidcLogoutSuccessHandler(
    ReactiveClientRegistrationRepository clientRegistrationRepository
  ) {
    var oidcLogoutSuccessHandler =
        new OidcClientInitiatedServerLogoutSuccessHandler(
          clientRegistrationRepository);
```

```
oidcLogoutSuccessHandler
  .setPostLogoutRedirectUri("{baseUrl}");
return oidcLogoutSuccessHandler;
}
}
```

After logging out from the OIDC Provider, Keycloak will redirect the user to the application base URL computed dynamically from Spring (locally, it's http://localhost:9000).

NOTE The `ReactiveClientRegistrationRepository` bean is automatically configured by Spring Boot for storing the information about the clients registered with Keycloak, and it's used by Spring Security for authentication/authorization purposes. In our example, there's only a client: the one we configured earlier in the application.yml file.

I won't ask you to test the logout functionality just yet. The reason will be apparent after we introduce the Angular frontend to the Polar Bookshop system.

The user authentication feature based on OpenID Connect/OAuth2 is now complete, including logout and scalability concerns. If Edge Service used a template engine like Thymeleaf to build the frontend, the work we've done so far would be enough. However, when you're integrating a secured backend application with an SPA like Angular, there are a few more aspects to consider. That will be the focus of the next section.

11.5 Integrating Spring Security with SPAs

The web frontend part of microservice architectures and other distributed systems is often built as one or more single-page applications using frameworks like Angular, React, or Vue. Analyzing how SPAs are created is not in the scope of this book, but it's essential to look at what changes are needed to support such frontend clients.

So far, you have interacted with the services composing the Polar Bookshop system through a Terminal window. In this section, we'll add an Angular application that will be the frontend of the system. It will be served by an NGINX container and be accessible via the gateway provided by Edge Service. Supporting an SPA will require some additional configuration in Spring Security to address concerns like Cross-Origin Request Sharing (CORS) and Cross-Site Request Forgery (CSRF). This section shows how to do that.

11.5.1 Running an Angular application

The Polar Bookshop system will have an Angular application as the frontend. Since this book doesn't cover frontend technologies and patterns, I have prepared one already. We just need to decide how to include it in the Polar Bookshop system.

One option is to let Edge Service serve the SPA static resources. Spring Boot applications serving a frontend usually host the source code in src/main/resources. That's a convenient strategy when using template engines like Thymeleaf, but for SPAs like Angular, I prefer keeping the code in a separate module. SPAs have their own development, build, and release tools, so having a dedicated folder is cleaner and more maintainable. Then you can configure Spring Boot to process the SPA's static resources at build time and include them in the final release.

Another option is to have a dedicated service take care of serving the Angular static resources. That's the strategy we'll use for Polar Bookshop. I have already packaged the Angular application in an NGINX container. NGINX (https://nginx.org) provides HTTP server features, and it's very convenient for serving static resources such as the HTML, CSS, and JavaScript files composing the Angular application.

Let's go ahead and run the Polar Bookshop frontend (polar-ui) in Docker. First, go to your polar-deployment repository, and open your Docker Compose file (docker/docker-compose.yml). Then add the configuration to run polar-ui and expose it through port 9004.

Listing 11.12   Running the Angular application as a container

```yaml
version: "3.8"
services:
  ...

  polar-ui:
    image: "ghcr.io/polarbookshop/polar-ui:v1"      ← The container image I built to package the Angular application
    container_name: "polar-ui"
    ports:
      - 9004:9004      ← NGINX will serve the SPA on port 9004.
    environment:
      - PORT=9004      ← Configures the NGINX server port
```

Like the other applications in the Polar Bookshop system, we don't want the Angular application to be accessible directly from the outside. Instead, we want to make it accessible via the gateway provided by Edge Service. We can do that by adding a new route for Spring Cloud Gateway to forward any requests for static resources to the Polar UI application.

Go to your Edge Service project (edge-service), open the application.yml file, and configure the new route as follows.

Listing 11.13   Configuring a new gateway route for the SPA static resources

```yaml
spring:
  gateway:
    routes:
      - id: spa-route      ← The route ID
        uri: ${SPA_URL:http://localhost:9004}      ← The URI value comes from an environment variable, or else the specified default.
        predicates:
          - Path=/,/*.css,/*.js,/favicon.ico      ← The predicate is a list of paths matching the root endpoint and the SPA static resources.
```

The URI for the Polar UI application is computed using the value from an environment variable (SPA_URL). If it's not defined, the default value written after the first colon (:) symbol will be used.

NOTE When running Edge Service as a container, remember to configure the `SPA_URL` environment variable. On Docker you can use the container name and port as the value, resulting in `http://polar-ui:9004`.

Let's test it out. First, run the Polar UI container together with Redis and Keycloak. Open a Terminal window, navigate to the folder where you keep your Docker Compose file (polar-deployment/docker/docker-compose.yml), and run the following command:

```
$ docker-compose up -d polar-ui polar-redis polar-keycloak
```

Then build the Edge Service project again, and run the application (`./gradlew bootRun`). Finally, open an incognito browser window and navigate to http://localhost:9000.

Spring Security is configured to protect all endpoints and resources, so you'll automatically be redirected to the Keycloak login page. After you authenticate as either Isabelle or Bjorn, you'll be redirected back to the Edge Service root endpoint from which the Angular frontend is served.

For now, there's not much you can do. The authentication flow is triggered by Spring Security when it receives an unauthenticated request, but it won't work if it's an AJAX request due to CORS issues. Furthermore, POST requests (including the logout operation) will fail due to the CSRF protection enabled by Spring Security. In the following sections, I'll show you how to update the Spring Security configuration to overcome those issues.

Before moving on, stop the application with Ctrl-C (but keep the containers running—you'll need them).

11.5.2 *Controlling the authentication flow*

In the previous section, you tried accessing the Edge Service homepage and experienced being automatically redirected to Keycloak to provide a username and password. When the frontend consists of server-rendered pages (such as when using Thymeleaf), that behavior works fine, and it's convenient since it doesn't require any extra configuration. If you're not authenticated yet, or your session has expired, Spring Security will automatically trigger the authentication flow and redirect your browser to Keycloak.

With a single-page application, things work a bit differently. The Angular application is returned by the backend when accessing the root endpoint through a standard HTTP GET request performed by the browser. After that first step, the SPA interacts with the backend through AJAX requests. When the SPA sends an unauthenticated AJAX request to a protected endpoint, you don't want Spring Security to reply with an HTTP 302 response redirecting to Keycloak. Instead, you want it to return a response with an error status like HTTP 401 Unauthorized.

The main reason for not using redirects with SPAs is that you would run into Cross-Origin Request Sharing (CORS) issues. Consider the scenario where an SPA is served from https://client.polarbookshop.com and makes HTTP calls through AJAX to a backend at https://server.polarbookshop.com. The communication is blocked because the two URLs don't have the same origin (the same protocol, domain, and port). That's the standard same-origin policy enforced by all web browsers.

CORS is a mechanism for allowing a server to accept HTTP calls through AJAX from a browser-based client like an SPA, even if the two have different origins. In Polar Bookshop, we serve the Angular frontend via the gateway implemented in Edge Service (same origin). Therefore, there aren't any CORS issues between these two components. However, suppose Spring Security is configured to reply to an unauthenticated AJAX call with a redirect to Keycloak (having a different origin). In that case, the request will be blocked because redirects to different origins are not permitted during AJAX requests.

> **NOTE** To learn more about CORS in Spring Security, you can check out chapter 10 of *Spring Security in Action* by Laurențiu Spilcă (Manning, 2020), where the subject is explained in great detail. For a comprehensive explanation of CORS, see *CORS in Action* by Monsur Hossain (Manning, 2014).

When changing the Spring Security configuration to reply with an HTTP 401 response to unauthenticated requests, it's up to the SPA to handle the error and call the backend to initiate the authentication flow. Redirects are only a problem during AJAX requests. The crucial part here is that the call to the backend to start the user authentication is not an AJAX request sent by Angular. Instead, it's a standard HTTP call sent from the browser, like the following:

```
login(): void {
  window.open('/oauth2/authorization/keycloak', '_self');
}
```

I'd like to stress that the login call is not an AJAX request sent from the Angular Http-Client. Instead, it instructs the browser to call the login URL. Spring Security exposes an /oauth2/authorization/{registrationId} endpoint that you can use to start the authentication flow based on OAuth2/OIDC. Since the client registration identifier for Edge Service is keycloak, the login endpoint will be /oauth2/authorization/keycloak.

To make that possible, we need to define a custom AuthenticationEntryPoint to instruct Spring Security to reply with an HTTP 401 status when an unauthenticated request is received for a protected resource. The framework already provides an Http-StatusServerEntryPoint implementation that perfectly suits this scenario, since it lets you specify which HTTP status to return when a user is required to authenticate.

Listing 11.14 Returning 401 when the user is not authenticated

```
@EnableWebFluxSecurity
public class SecurityConfig {
  ...
```

```
@Bean
SecurityWebFilterChain springSecurityFilterChain(
  ServerHttpSecurity http,
  ReactiveClientRegistrationRepository clientRegistrationRepository
) {
  return http
    .authorizeExchange(exchange -> exchange.anyExchange().authenticated())
    .exceptionHandling(exceptionHandling ->
     exceptionHandling.authenticationEntryPoint(          <
       new HttpStatusServerEntryPoint(HttpStatus.UNAUTHORIZED)))
    .oauth2Login(Customizer.withDefaults())
    .logout(logout -> logout.logoutSuccessHandler(
    oidcLogoutSuccessHandler(clientRegistrationRepository)))
    .build();
}                                    When an exception is thrown because a
}                                      user is not authenticated, it replies
                                          with an HTTP 401 response.
```

At this point, the Angular application can explicitly intercept HTTP 401 responses and trigger the authentication flow. However, since the SPA is now in charge of starting the flow, we need to permit unauthenticated access to its static resources. We would also like to retrieve the books in the catalog without being authenticated, so let's permit GET requests to the /books/** endpoints as well. Go ahead and update the SecurityWebFilterChain bean in the SecurityConfig class as follows.

Listing 11.15 Allowing unauthenticated GET requests to SPA and books

```
@EnableWebFluxSecurity
public class SecurityConfig {
  ...

  @Bean
  SecurityWebFilterChain springSecurityFilterChain(
    ServerHttpSecurity http,
    ReactiveClientRegistrationRepository clientRegistrationRepository
  ) {                                    Allows unauthenticated access
    return http                          to the SPA static resources
      .authorizeExchange(exchange -> exchange
        .pathMatchers("/", "/*.css", "/*.js", "/favicon.ico")
          .permitAll()                         <
        .pathMatchers(HttpMethod.GET, "/books/**")
          .permitAll()            <
        .anyExchange().authenticated()   Allows unauthenticated read
      )                                  access to the books in the catalog
      .exceptionHandling(exceptionHandling -> exceptionHandling
        .authenticationEntryPoint(
        new HttpStatusServerEntryPoint(HttpStatus.UNAUTHORIZED)))
      .oauth2Login(Customizer.withDefaults())
      .logout(logout -> logout.logoutSuccessHandler(
        oidcLogoutSuccessHandler(clientRegistrationRepository)))
      .build();
  }
}
```

Any other request requires user authentication. *(margin note pointing to `.anyExchange().authenticated()`)*

Let's test how Edge Service works now. Ensure that the Polar UI, Redis, and Keycloak containers are still running. Next, build and run the Edge Service application (`./gradlew bootRun`), and then go to http://localhost:9000 from an incognito browser window. The first thing to notice is that you don't get redirected to the login page but are presented with the Angular frontend application immediately. You can start the authentication flow by clicking the Login button in the upper-right menu.

After logging in, the upper-right menu will contain a Logout button, which is only shown if the current user is successfully authenticated. Click the button to log out. It should trigger the logout flow, but it won't work due to CSRF issues. You'll learn how to fix that in the next section. In the meantime, stop the application with Ctrl-C.

11.5.3 *Protecting against Cross-Site Request Forgery*

The interaction between the frontend and backend is based on a session cookie. After the user is successfully authenticated with the OIDC/OAuth2 strategy, Spring will generate a session identifier to match the authenticated context and send it to the browser as a cookie. Any subsequent request to the backend will have to contain the session cookie, from which Spring Security can retrieve the tokens associated with the specific user and validate the request.

However, session cookies are not enough to validate requests, which are vulnerable to Cross-Site Request Forgery (CSRF) attacks. CSRF affects *modifying* HTTP requests like POST, PUT, and DELETE. An attacker could induce users to perform requests they didn't intend by forging a request meant to cause harm. Forged requests could do things like transfer money from your bank account or compromise critical data.

> **WARNING**   Many online tutorials and guides show how to disable the CSRF protection as the first thing when configuring Spring Security. That's dangerous to do without explaining the reasoning or considering the consequences. I recommend keeping the protection enabled unless there's a good reason not to (you'll see one good reason in chapter 12). As a general guideline, browser-facing applications like Edge Service should be protected against CSRF attacks.

Fortunately, Spring Security has built-in protection against such attacks. The protection is based on a so-called CSRF token generated by the framework that's provided to the client at the beginning of the session and required to be sent along with any state-changing requests.

> **NOTE**   To learn more about CSRF protection in Spring Security, you can check out chapter 10 of *Spring Security in Action* by Laurențiu Spilcă (Manning, 2020), where the subject is explained in great detail.

In the previous section, you tried to log out, but the request failed. Since the logout operation is available through a POST request to the /logout endpoint, the application expects to receive the CSRF token generated by Spring Security for that user session. By default, the generated CSRF token is sent to the browser as an HTTP header.

However, Angular applications cannot work with that and expect to receive the token value as a cookie. Spring Security supports this specific requirement, but it's not enabled by default.

You can instruct Spring Security to provide CSRF tokens as cookies through the `csrf()` DSL exposed by `ServerHttpSecurity` and the `CookieServerCsrfToken-Repository` class. For imperative applications, that would be enough. However, for reactive applications like Edge Service, you need to take an extra step to ensure the `CsrfToken` value is actually provided.

In chapter 8, you learned that reactive streams need to be subscribed to in order to activate them. At the moment, `CookieServerCsrfTokenRepository` doesn't ensure a subscription to `CsrfToken`, so you must explicitly provide a workaround in a `Web-Filter` bean. This problem should be solved in future versions of Spring Security (see issue 5766 on GitHub: https://mng.bz/XW89). For now, update the `SecurityConfig` class as follows.

> **Listing 11.16 Configuring CSRF to support a cookie-based strategy for SPAs**

```
@EnableWebFluxSecurity
public class SecurityConfig {
  ...

  @Bean
  SecurityWebFilterChain springSecurityFilterChain(
    ServerHttpSecurity http,
    ReactiveClientRegistrationRepository clientRegistrationRepository
  ) {
    return http
      ...
      .csrf(csrf -> csrf.csrfTokenRepository(         ⟵  Uses a cookie-based strategy
        CookieServerCsrfTokenRepository.withHttpOnlyFalse()))   for exchanging CSRF tokens
      .build();                                              with the Angular frontend
  }

  @Bean                          A filter with the only purpose of subscribing
  WebFilter csrfWebFilter() {  ⟵  to the CsrfToken reactive stream and
    return (exchange, chain) -> {   ensuring its value is extracted correctly
      exchange.getResponse().beforeCommit(() -> Mono.defer(() -> {
        Mono<CsrfToken> csrfToken =
          exchange.getAttribute(CsrfToken.class.getName());
        return csrfToken != null ? csrfToken.then() : Mono.empty();
      }));
      return chain.filter(exchange);
    };
  }
}
```

Let's verify that the logout flow works now. Ensure that the Polar UI, Redis, and Keycloak containers are still up and running. Next, build and run the application (`./gradlew bootRun`), and then go to http://localhost:9000 from an incognito browser window. Start the authentication flow by clicking the Login button from the upper-right menu. Then click the Logout button. Under the hood, Spring Security will now accept your logout request (Angular adds the CSRF token value from the cookie as an HTTP header), terminate your web session, propagate the request to Keycloak, and finally redirect you to the homepage, unauthenticated.

Thanks to this change, you can also perform any POST, PUT, and DELETE requests without receiving a CSRF error. Feel free to explore the Angular application. If you start up Catalog Service and Order Service, you can try adding new books to the catalog, modifying them, or placing an order.

Both Isabelle and Bjorn can perform any action at the moment, which is not what we want, since customers (like Bjorn) shouldn't be allowed to manage the book catalog. The next chapter will cover authorization, and you'll see how to protect each endpoint with different access policies. Before addressing authorization, though, we need to write autotests to cover the new functionality. That's coming up in the next section.

Before moving on, stop the application with Ctrl-C and all the containers with docker-compose down (from polar-deployment/docker).

11.6   *Testing Spring Security and OpenID Connect*

The importance of writing autotests is usually apparent to developers. Still, things can get challenging when it comes to security, and it sometimes ends up not being covered by automated tests because of its complexity. Fortunately, Spring Security provides several utilities to help you include security in your slice and integration tests in a simple way.

In this section, you'll learn how to use the WebTestClient support for Spring Security to test OIDC authentication and CSRF protection. Let's get started.

11.6.1   *Testing OIDC authentication*

In chapter 8, we tested REST controllers exposed by Spring WebFlux by relying on the @SpringWebFlux annotation and WebTestClient. In this chapter, we added a new controller (UserController), so let's write some autotests for it with different security setups.

First of all, open your Edge Service project, create a UserControllerTests class annotated with @WebFluxTest(UserController.class) in src/test/java, and autowire a WebTestClient bean. So far, the setup is similar to what we used in chapter 8: a slice test for the web layer. But we need some extra setup to cover security scenarios, as shown in the following listing.

> **Listing 11.17   Defining a class to test the security policies for UserController**

```
@WebFluxTest(UserController.class)
@Import(SecurityConfig.class)        ◁──┐  Imports the
class UserControllerTests {              │  application's security
                                         │  configuration
```

```
@Autowired
WebTestClient webClient;              A mock bean to skip the interaction with
                                      Keycloak when retrieving information
@MockBean                             about the Client registration
ReactiveClientRegistrationRepository clientRegistrationRepository;
}
```

Since we configured Edge Service to return an HTTP 401 response when a request is unauthenticated, let's verify that happens when calling the /user endpoint without authenticating first:

```
@Test
void whenNotAuthenticatedThen401() {
  webClient
    .get()
    .uri("/user")
    .exchange()
    .expectStatus().isUnauthorized();
}
```

To test the scenario where a user is authenticated, we can use mockOidcLogin(), a configuration object supplied by SecurityMockServerConfigurers to mock an OIDC login, synthesize an ID Token, and mutate the request context in WebTestClient accordingly.

The /user endpoint reads claims from the ID Token through the OidcUser object, so we need to build an ID Token with username, first name, and last name (the roles are hardcoded in the controller for now). The following code shows how to do that:

```
@Test
void whenAuthenticatedThenReturnUser() {                    The expected
  var expectedUser = new User("jon.snow", "Jon", "Snow",    authenticated
    List.of("employee", "customer"));                       user

  webClient
    .mutateWith(configureMockOidcLogin(expectedUser))       Defines an
    .get()                                                  authentication
    .uri("/user")                                           context based on
    .exchange()                                             OIDC and uses
    .expectStatus().is2xxSuccessful()                       the expected user
    .expectBody(User.class)
    .value(user -> assertThat(user).isEqualTo(expectedUser));
}

private SecurityMockServerConfigurers.OidcLoginMutator
  configureMockOidcLogin(User expectedUser) {
  return SecurityMockServerConfigurers.mockOidcLogin().idToken(
    builder -> {                                            Builds a mock
      builder.claim(StandardClaimNames.PREFERRED_USERNAME,  ID Token
        expectedUser.username());
      builder.claim(StandardClaimNames.GIVEN_NAME,
        expectedUser.firstName());
      builder.claim(StandardClaimNames.FAMILY_NAME,
```

Expects a User object with the same information as the currently authenticated user

```
        expectedUser.lastName());
    });
}
```

Finally, run the tests as follows:

```
$ ./gradlew test --tests UserControllerTests
```

The testing utilities supplied by Spring Security cover a wide array of scenarios and integrate well with `WebTestClient`. In the next section, you'll see how to test CSRF protection using a similar approach.

11.6.2 *Testing CSRF*

In Spring Security, CSRF protection applies to all mutating HTTP requests by default (such as `POST`, `PUT`, and `DELETE`). As you saw in previous sections, Edge Service accepts `POST` requests to the `/logout` endpoint to initiate the logout flow, and such requests require a valid CSRF token to be executed. Furthermore, we configured the RP-Initiated Logout feature from OIDC, so a `POST` request to `/logout` will actually result in an HTTP 302 response, redirecting the browser to Keycloak to also log the user out of there.

Create a new `SecurityConfigTests` class and use the same strategy you learned in the previous section to set up a Spring WebFlux test with security support, as shown in the following listing.

Listing 11.18   Defining a class for testing the authentication flow

```
@WebFluxTest
@Import(SecurityConfig.class)        ◁── Imports the application
class SecurityConfigTests {               security configuration

  @Autowired
  WebTestClient webClient;           A mock bean to skip the interaction with
                                     Keycloak when retrieving information
  @MockBean                    ◁──   about the Client registration
  ReactiveClientRegistrationRepository clientRegistrationRepository;
}
```

Then add a test case to check whether the application returns an HTTP 302 response after sending an HTTP `POST` request to the `/logout` with the correct OIDC login and CSRF context.

```
@Test
void whenLogoutAuthenticatedAndWithCsrfTokenThen302() {
  when(clientRegistrationRepository.findByRegistrationId("test"))
    .thenReturn(Mono.just(testClientRegistration()));

  webClient                                        Uses a mock ID Token
    .mutateWith(                                   to authenticate the
    SecurityMockServerConfigurers.mockOidcLogin()) ◁── user
```

```
    .mutateWith(SecurityMockServerConfigurers.csrf())          ◁─────┐  Enhances the
    .post()                                                              request to provide
    .uri("/logout")                              The response is a       the required CSRF
    .exchange()                                  redirect to Keycloak to token
    .expectStatus().isFound();       ◁─────      propagate the logout
}                                                operation.

private ClientRegistration testClientRegistration() {
  return ClientRegistration.withRegistrationId("test")          ◁──────────────────┐
    .authorizationGrantType(AuthorizationGrantType.AUTHORIZATION_CODE)
    .clientId("test")                                                      A mock
    .authorizationUri("https://sso.polarbookshop.com/auth")        ClientRegistration
    .tokenUri("https://sso.polarbookshop.com/token")             used by Spring Security
    .redirectUri("https://polarbookshop.com")                      to get the URLs to
    .build();                                                        contact Keycloak
}
```

Finally, run the tests as follows:

```
$ ./gradlew test --tests SecurityConfigTests
```

As always, you can find more test examples in the source code repository accompanying this book. When it comes to security, unit and integration tests are critical for ensuring the correctness of an application, but they are not enough. Those tests cover the default security configuration, which might be different in production. That's why we also need security-oriented autotests in the acceptance stage of the deployment pipeline (as explained in chapter 3), to test applications deployed in a production-like environment.

Polar Labs

Until now, the only application supposed to be accessed by users directly was Edge Service. All the other Spring Boot applications interact with each other from within the environment where they are deployed.

Service-to-service interactions within the same Docker network or Kubernetes cluster can be configured using the container name or the Service name respectively. For example, Edge Service forwards requests to Polar UI via the `http://polar-ui:9004` URL on Docker (`<container-name>:<container-port>`) and via the `http://polar-ui` URL on Kubernetes (Service name).

Keycloak is different because it's involved in service-to-service interactions (for now, those are just interactions with Edge Service) and also interactions with end users via the web browser. In production, Keycloak will be accessible via a public URL that both applications and users will use, so there will be no problem. How about in local environments?

Since we don't deal with public URLs when working locally, we need to configure things differently. On Docker, we can solve the problem by using the `http://host.docker.internal` special URL configured automatically when installing the software. It resolves to your localhost IP address and can be used both within a Docker network and outside.

(continued)

On Kubernetes, we don't have a generic URL to let Pods within a cluster access your local host. That means Edge Service will interact with Keycloak via its Service name (`http://polar-keycloak`). When Spring Security redirects a user to Keycloak to log in, the browser will return an error because the `http://polar-keycloak` URL cannot be resolved outside the cluster. To make that possible, we can update the local DNS configuration to resolve the `polar-keycloak` hostname to the cluster IP address. Then a dedicated Ingress will make it possible to access Keycloak when requests are directed to the `polar-keycloak` hostname.

If you're on Linux or macOS, you can map the `polar-keycloak` hostname to the minikube local IP address in the /etc/hosts file. On Linux, the IP address is the one returned by the `minikube ip --profile polar` command (as explained in chapter 9). On macOS, it's going to be `127.0.0.1`. Open a Terminal window, and run the following command (make sure you replace the `<ip-address>` placeholder with the cluster IP address, depending on your operating system):

```
$ echo "<ip-address> polar-keycloak" | sudo tee -a /etc/hosts
```

On Windows you must map the `polar-keycloak` hostname to `127.0.0.1` in the hosts file. Open a PowerShell window as an administrator, and run the following command:

```
$ Add-Content C:\Windows\System32\drivers\etc\hosts "127.0.0.1 polar-
    keycloak"
```

I have updated the scripts for deploying all the backing services for Polar Bookshop, including Keycloak and Polar UI. You can get them from the /Chapter11/11-end/polar-deployment/kubernetes/platform/development folder in the code repository accompanying the book (https://github.com/ThomasVitale/cloud-native-spring-in-action) and copy them into the same path in your `polar-deployment` repository. The deployment also includes the configuration of a dedicated Ingress for Keycloak, accepting requests directed to the `polar-keycloak` hostname.

At this point you can run the `./create-cluster.sh` script (polar-deployment/kubernetes/platform/development) to start a minikube cluster and deploy all the backing services for Polar Bookshop. If you're on Linux, you'll be able to access Keycloak directly. If you're on macOS or Windows, remember to run the `minikube tunnel --profile polar` command first. Either way, you can open a browser window and access Keycloak at polar-keycloak/ (include the final slash).

Finally, try running the entire system on Kubernetes after updating the deployment scripts for Edge Service to configure the URLs for Polar UI and Keycloak. You can refer to the Chapter11/11-end folder in the code repository accompanying the book to check the final result (https://github.com/ThomasVitale/cloud-native-spring-in-action).

The next chapter will expand on the subject of security. It will cover how to propagate the authentication context from Edge Service to the downstream applications, and how to configure authorization.

Summary

- Access control systems require identification (who are you?), authentication (can you prove it's really you?), and authorization (what are you allowed to do?).
- A common strategy for implementing authentication and authorization in cloud native applications is based on JWT as the data format, OAuth2 as the authorization framework, and OpenID Connect as the authentication protocol.
- When using OIDC authentication, a Client application initiates the flow and delegates an Authorization Server for the actual authentication. Then the Authorization Server issues an ID Token to the Client.
- The ID Token includes information about the user authentication.
- Keycloak is an identity and access management solution that supports OAuth2 and OpenID Connect and can be used as an Authorization Server.
- Spring Security provides native support for OAuth2 and OpenID Connect, and you can use it to turn Spring Boot applications into OAuth2 Clients.
- In Spring Security, you can configure both authentication and authorization in a `SecurityWebFilterChain` bean. To enable the OIDC authentication flow, you can use the `oauth2Login()` DSL.
- By default, Spring Security exposes a `/logout` endpoint for logging a user out.
- In an OIDC/OAuth2 context, we also need to propagate the logout request to the Authorization Server (such as Keycloak) to log the user out of there. We can do that via the RP-Initiated Logout flow supported by Spring Security via the `OidcClientInitiatedServerLogoutSuccessHandler` class.
- When a secure Spring Boot application is the backend for an SPA, we need to configure CSRF protection through cookies and implement an authentication entry point that returns an HTTP `401` response when a request is not authenticated (as opposed to the default HTTP `302` response redirecting to the Authorization Server automatically).
- The Spring Security Test dependency supplies several convenient utilities for testing security.
- The `WebTestClient` bean can be enhanced by mutating its request context through a particular configuration for OIDC login and CSRF protection.

Security: Authorization and auditing

This chapter covers

- Authorization and roles with Spring Cloud
  Gateway and OAuth2
- Protecting APIs with Spring Security and OAuth2
  (imperative)
- Protecting APIs with Spring Security and OAuth2
  (reactive)
- Protecting and auditing data with Spring Security
  and Spring Data

In the previous chapter, I introduced access control systems for cloud native applications. You saw how to add authentication to Edge Service with Spring Security and OpenID Connect, manage the user session life cycle, and address CORS and CSRF concerns when integrating an Angular frontend with Spring Boot.

By delegating the authentication step to Keycloak, Edge Service is not affected by the specific authentication strategy. For example, we used the login form feature offered by Keycloak, but we could also enable social login via GitHub or rely on an existing Active Directory to authenticate users. Edge Service only needs to support OIDC to verify that the authentication happened correctly and get information about the user via an ID Token.

There are still a few issues we haven't addressed. Polar Bookshop is a distributed system, and after a user authenticates successfully with Keycloak, Edge Service is supposed to interact with Catalog Service and Order Service on behalf of the user. How can we securely propagate the authentication context to the other system applications? This chapter will help you solve that problem using OAuth2 and Access Tokens.

After dealing with authentication, we will address the authorization step. Right now, both customers and employees of Polar Bookshop can perform any action on the system. This chapter will walk you through a few authorization scenarios handled with OAuth2, Spring Security, and Spring Data:

- We'll use a role-based access control (RBAC) strategy to protect the REST endpoints exposed by Spring Boot, depending on whether the user is a customer or an employee of the bookshop.
- We'll configure data auditing to keep track of which user made what changes.
- We'll enforce protection rules for data so that only its owner can access it.

Finally, you'll explore how you can test those changes using Spring Boot, Spring Security, and Testcontainers.

> **NOTE** The source code for the examples in this chapter is available in the Chapter12/12-begin and Chapter12/12-end folders, containing the initial and final states of the project (https://github.com/ThomasVitale/cloud-native -spring-in-action).

12.1 Authorization and roles with Spring Cloud Gateway and OAuth2

In the previous chapter, we added user authentication features to Polar Bookshop. Edge Service is the access point to the system, so it's an excellent candidate for addressing cross-cutting concerns like security. For that reason, we made it responsible for authenticating users. Edge Service initiates the authentication flow but delegates the actual authentication step to Keycloak using the OpenID Connect protocol.

Once a user authenticates successfully with Keycloak, Edge Service receives an ID Token from Keycloak with information about the authentication event and initiates an authenticated session with the user's browser. At the same time, Keycloak also issues an *Access Token*, which is used to grant Edge Service access to downstream applications on behalf of the user as per OAuth2.

OAuth2 is an authorization framework that enables an application (called a *Client*) to obtain limited access to a protected resource provided by another application (called a *Resource Server*) on behalf of a user. When a user authenticates with Edge Service and asks to access their book orders, OAuth2 provides a solution for Edge Service to retrieve orders from Order Service on behalf of that user. This solution relies on a trusted party (called an *Authorization Server*), which issues an *Access Token* to Edge Service and grants access to the user's book orders from Order Service.

You might recognize some of these roles from the OIDC authentication flow we adopted in the previous chapter. As anticipated, OIDC is an identity layer built on top of OAuth2 and relies on the same basic concepts:

- *Authorization Server*—The entity responsible for authenticating users and issuing, refreshing, and revoking Access Tokens. In Polar Bookshop, this is Keycloak.
- *User*—Also called the *Resource Owner*, this is the human logging in with the Authorization Server to get authenticated access to the Client application. It's also the human or service granting a Client access to the protected resources provided by a Resource Server. In Polar Bookshop, it's either a customer or an employee.
- *Client*—The application requiring the user to be authenticated and asking the user for authorization to access protected resources on their behalf. It can be a mobile application, a browser-based application, a server-side application, or even a smart TV application. In Polar Bookshop, it's Edge Service.
- *Resource Server*—This is the application hosting the protected resources a Client wants to access on the user's behalf. In Polar Bookshop, Catalog Service and Order Service are Resource Servers. Dispatcher Service is decoupled from the other applications and won't be accessed on behalf of the user. As a result, it won't participate in the OAuth2 setup.

Figure 12.1 shows how the four actors are mapped into the Polar Bookshop architecture.

Edge Service can access downstream applications on behalf of the user through an Access Token issued by Keycloak during the OIDC authentication phase. In this section, you'll see how to configure Spring Cloud Gateway in Edge Service to use the Access Token whenever a request is routed to Catalog Service and Order Service.

In the previous chapter, we defined two users: Isabelle has both the employee and customer roles, while Bjorn has just the customer role. In this section, you'll also learn how to include that information in both ID Tokens and Access Tokens so Spring Security can read it and set up a role-based access control (RBAC) mechanism.

NOTE   In Polar Bookshop, the OAuth2 Client (Edge Service) and the OAuth2 Resource Servers (Catalog Service and Order Service) belong to the same system, but the same framework can be used when the OAuth2 Client is a third-party application. In fact, that was the original use case for OAuth2 and why it became so popular. Using OAuth2, services like GitHub or Twitter let you give third-party applications limited access to your account. For example, you could authorize a scheduling application to publish tweets on your behalf without exposing your Twitter credentials.

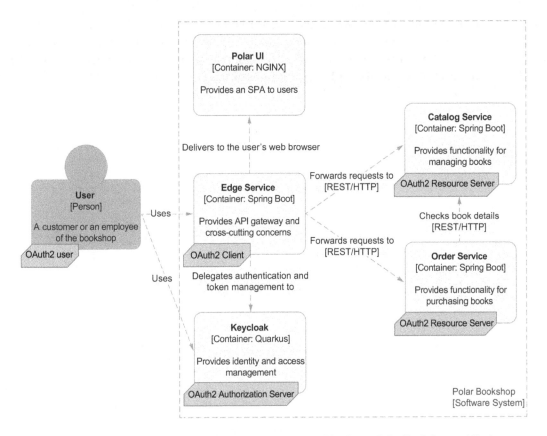

Figure 12.1 How the OIDC/OAuth2 roles are assigned to the entities in the Polar Bookshop architecture

12.1.1 Token relay from Spring Cloud Gateway to other services

After a user successfully authenticates with Keycloak, Edge Service (the OAuth2 Client) receives an ID Token and an Access Token:

- *ID Token*—This represents a successful authentication event and includes information about the authenticated user.
- *Access Token*—This represents the authorization given to the OAuth2 Client to access protected data provided by an OAuth2 Resource Server on the user's behalf.

In Edge Service, Spring Security uses the ID Token to extract information about the authenticated user, set up a context for the current user session, and make the data available through the OidcUser object. That's what you saw in the previous chapter.

The Access Token grants Edge Service authorized access to Catalog Service and Order Service (the OAuth2 Resource Servers) on behalf of the user. After we secure both applications, Edge Service will have to include the Access Token in all requests routed to them as an `Authorization` HTTP header. Unlike ID Tokens, Edge Service doesn't read the Access Token's content because it's not the intended audience. It stores the Access Token received from Keycloak and then includes it as-is in any request to a protected endpoint downstream.

This pattern is called *token relay*, and it's supported by Spring Cloud Gateway as a built-in filter, so you don't need to implement anything yourself. When the filter is enabled, the Access Token is included automatically in all requests sent to one of the downstream applications. Figure 12.2 illustrates how the token relay pattern works.

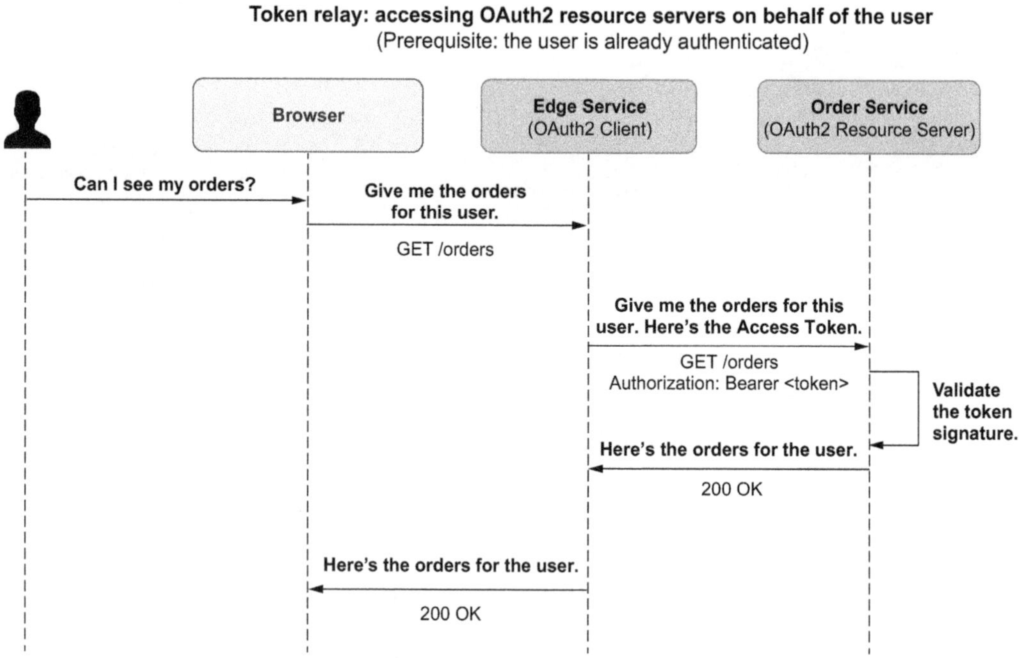

Token relay: accessing OAuth2 resource servers on behalf of the user
(Prerequisite: the user is already authenticated)

Figure 12.2   After a user is authenticated, Edge Service relays the Access Token to Order Service to call its protected endpoints on behalf of the user.

Let's see how we can configure the Access Token relay in Edge Service.

> **NOTE**   An Access Token has a validity period configured in Keycloak, and it should be as short as possible to reduce the exploitation time window in case the token gets leaked. An acceptable length is 5 minutes. When the token expires, the OAuth2 Client can ask the Authorization Server for a new one using a third type of token called a *Refresh Token* (which also has a validity period). The refresh mechanism is handled by Spring Security transparently, and I won't describe it further.

ADOPTING THE TOKEN RELAY PATTERN IN SPRING CLOUD GATEWAY

Spring Cloud Gateway implements the token relay pattern as a filter. In the Edge Service project (edge-service), open the application.yml file and add TokenRelay as a default filter, since we want it applied to all routes.

Listing 12.1 Enabling the token relay pattern in Spring Cloud Gateway

```
spring:
  cloud:
    gateway:                        Enables the propagation
      default-filters:              of the Access Token when
        - SaveSession               calling a downstream
        - TokenRelay      <──┘      service
```

With the filter enabled, Spring Cloud Gateway takes care of propagating the right Access Token as an Authorization header in all outgoing requests to Catalog Service and Order Service. For example:

```
GET /orders
Authorization: Bearer <access_token>
```

> **NOTE** Unlike ID Tokens which are JWTs, the OAuth2 framework doesn't enforce a data format for Access Tokens. They can be of any String-based form. The most popular format is JWT, though, so that's how we'll parse Access Tokens on the consumer side (Catalog Service and Order Service).

By default, Spring Security stores the Access Tokens for the currently authenticated users in memory. When you have multiple instances of Edge Service running (which is always true in a cloud production environment to ensure high availability), you will encounter issues due to the statefulness of the application. Cloud native applications should be stateless. Let's fix that.

STORING ACCESS TOKENS IN REDIS

Spring Security stores Access Tokens in an OAuth2AuthorizedClient object that is accessible through a ServerOAuth2AuthorizedClientRepository bean. The default implementation for that repository adopts an in-memory strategy for persistence. That's what makes Edge Service a stateful application. How can we keep it stateless and scalable?

A simple way to do that is to store OAuth2AuthorizedClient objects in the web session rather than in memory so that Spring Session will pick them up automatically and save them in Redis, just like it does with ID Tokens. Fortunately, the framework already provides an implementation of the ServerOAuth2AuthorizedClientRepository interface to save data in the web session: WebSessionServerOAuth2AuthorizedClient-Repository. Figure 12.3 illustrates how all the mentioned objects are related to each other.

How Spring Security stores Access Tokens in the web session

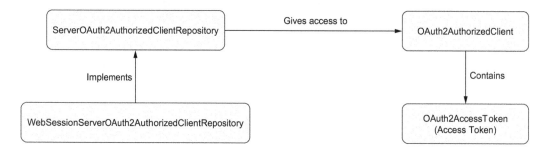

Figure 12.3   The main classes involved in storing an Access Token for the currently authenticated user in Spring Security

In the Edge Service project, open the `SecurityConfig` class and define a bean of type `ServerOAuth2AuthorizedClientRepository` using the implementation that stores Access Tokens in the web session.

Listing 12.2   Saving `OAuth2AuthorizedClient` objects in the web session

```
@EnableWebFluxSecurity
public class SecurityConfig {

  @Bean
  ServerOAuth2AuthorizedClientRepository authorizedClientRepository() {
    return new WebSessionServerOAuth2AuthorizedClientRepository();
  }

  ...
}
```

Defines a repository to store Access Tokens in the web session

> **WARNING**   Access Tokens defined as JWTs should be handled with care. They are *bearer tokens*, meaning that any application can use them in an HTTP request and get access to an OAuth2 Resource Server. Handling the OIDC/OAuth2 flow in the backend rather than in an SPA provides better security because we don't expose any tokens to the browser. However, there might be other risks to manage, so carefully consider the *trust boundaries* of your system.

In the next section you'll see how to enhance ID Tokens and Access Tokens to propagate information about user roles.

12.1.2   *Customizing tokens and propagating user roles*

Both ID Tokens and Access Tokens can include different information about the user, which is formatted as *claims* in the JWT. Claims are simple key/value pairs in JSON format. For example, OpenID Connect defines several standard claims to carry information about the user, like `given_name`, `family_name`, `preferred_username`, and `email`.

Access to such claims is controlled through *scopes*, a mechanism provided by OAuth2 to limit what data an OAuth2 Client can access. You can think of scopes as roles assigned to applications rather than to users. In the previous chapter, we used Spring Security to make Edge Service an OAuth2 Client and configured it with the openid scope. That scope grants Edge Service access to the authenticated user's identity (provided in the sub claim).

Perhaps you have logged in to a third-party website using GitHub or Google (a social login based on OAuth2). If you did, you might have noticed that right after the authentication step, the service prompted you with a second request about what information from your GitHub or Google account you consented to allow the third party to access. That consent functionality is based on scopes, granting the third party (the OAuth2 Client) specific permissions depending on what scopes have been assigned.

Regarding Edge Service, we can decide upfront what scopes it should be granted. This section will show you how to configure a roles claim with the list of roles assigned to the authenticated user. Then you'll use a roles scope to grant Edge Service access to that claim and instruct Keycloak to include it in both ID Tokens and Access Tokens.

Before moving on, you'll need a Keycloak container up and running. Open a Terminal window, navigate to the folder where you keep your Docker Compose file, and run the following command:

```
$ docker-compose up -d polar-keycloak
```

If you haven't followed along, you can refer to Chapter12/12-begin/polar-deployment/docker/docker-compose.yml in the accompanying repository.

> **NOTE** Later I'll provide you with a JSON file you can use to load the entire configuration when starting up the Keycloak container without being concerned with its persistence (as I did in the previous chapter). If you want to follow this second option directly, I still invite you to read through this section, since it provides the essential information you'll need when moving on to the Spring Security part of the chapter.

CONFIGURING ACCESS TO USER ROLES IN KEYCLOAK

Keycloak comes preconfigured with a roles scope you can use to give an application access to the user roles contained in a roles claim. However, the default representation of the roles list is not very convenient to use because it's defined as a nested object. Let's change that.

Once Keycloak is up and running, open a browser window, head to http://localhost:8080, log in to the administration console with the same credentials defined in the Docker Compose file (user/password), and choose the PolarBookshop realm. Then select Client Scopes from the left menu. On the new page (figure 12.4), you'll find a list of all the preconfigured scopes in Keycloak, and you have the option to create

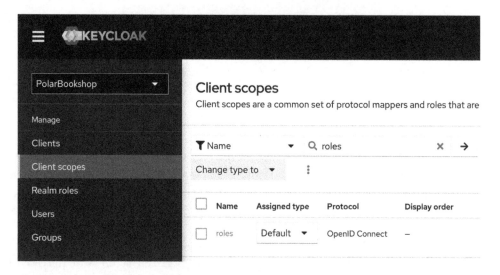

Figure 12.4 Creating and managing client scopes

new ones. In our case, we want to customize the existing `roles` scope, so click on it to open its settings.

In the `roles` scope page, open the Mappers tab. That is where you can define the set of claims to which the given scope provides access (i.e., *mappings*). By default, Keycloak already has some mappers defined to map claims to the `roles` scope. We're interested in the *realm roles* mapper, which maps the user realm roles (including `employee` and `customer`) to a JWT claim. Select that mapper.

The settings page for the *realm roles* mapper provides a few options for customization. We want to change two things:

- The token claim name should be `roles` instead of `realm_access.roles` (so we will remove the nested object).
- The `roles` claim should be included in both ID Token and Access Token, so we must ensure that both options are enabled. We need both because Edge Service reads the claims from the ID Token while Catalog Service and Order Service read the claims from the Access Token. Edge Service is not the intended audience for the Access Token, which is forwarded to downstream applications as-is.

Figure 12.5 shows the final settings. When you're done, click Save.

> **NOTE** In the source code repository accompanying the book, I included a JSON file you can use to load the entire configuration when starting up the Keycloak container in the future, including the latest changes regarding roles (Chapter12/12-end/polar-deployment/docker/keycloak/full-realm-config.json). I recommend updating your `polar-keycloak` container definition in Docker Compose to use this new JSON file.

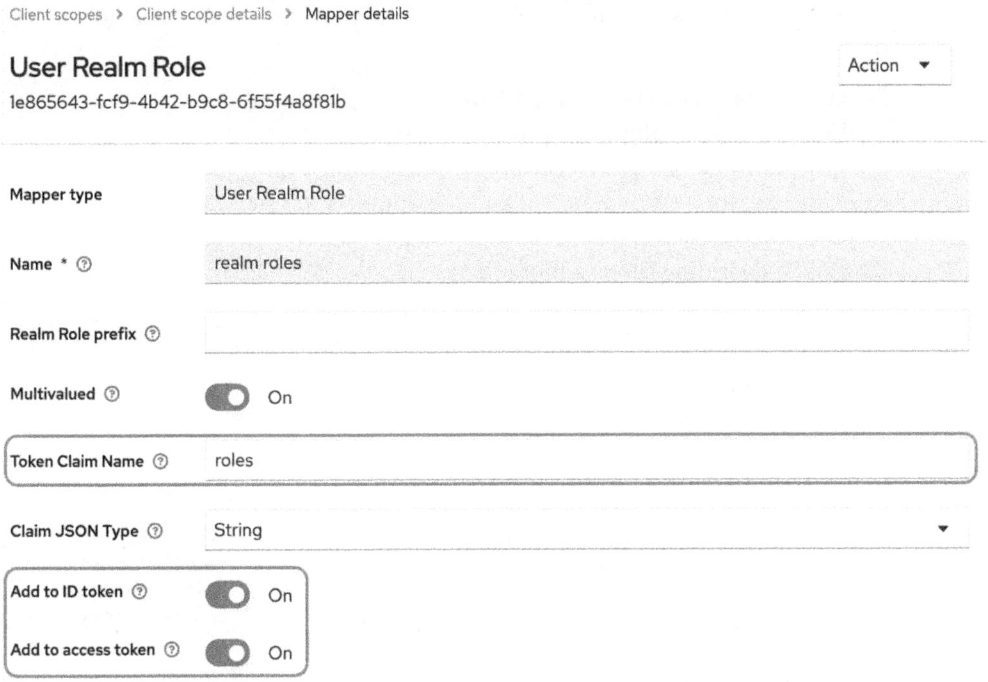

Client scopes > Client scope details > **Mapper details**

User Realm Role

Action ▼

1e865643-fcf9-4b42-b9c8-6f55f4a8f81b

Mapper type	User Realm Role
Name * ⑦	realm roles
Realm Role prefix ⑦	
Multivalued ⑦	🔵 On
Token Claim Name ⑦	roles
Claim JSON Type ⑦	String ▼
Add to ID token ⑦	🔵 On
Add to access token ⑦	🔵 On

Figure 12.5 Configuring the mapper to include the user's realm roles in a `roles` JWT claim

Before moving on to the next section, stop any running containers (`docker-compose down`).

CONFIGURING ACCESS TO USER ROLES IN SPRING SECURITY

Keycloak is now configured to return the authenticated user roles in a `roles` claim included in both the ID Token and Access Token. However, the `roles` claim will only be returned if the OAuth2 Client (Edge Service) asks for the `roles` scope.

In the Edge Service project, open the application.yml file, and update the Client Registration configuration to include the `roles` scope.

Listing 12.3 Assigning the `roles` scope to Edge Service

```
spring:
  security:
    oauth2:
      client:
        registration:
          keycloak:
            client-id: edge-service
            client-secret: polar-keycloak-secret
            scope: openid,roles          ◁──┐   Adds "roles" to the list
        provider:                             │   of scopes so that Edge
          keycloak:                           │   Service can get access
            issuer-uri: http://localhost:8080/realms/PolarBookshop
```

Adds "roles" to the list of scopes so that Edge Service can get access to the user roles

Next you'll see how to extract the roles for the currently authenticated user from the ID Token.

EXTRACTING USER ROLES FROM THE ID TOKEN

In the previous chapter, we hardcoded the list of user roles in the `UserController` class of the Edge Service project because we didn't have them in the ID Token yet. Now that we do, let's refactor the implementation to fetch the roles for the currently authenticated user from the `OidcUser` class, which gives us access to the claims in the ID Token, including the brand-new `roles` claim.

Listing 12.4   Extracting the user roles list from the ID Token via `OidcUser`

```
@RestController
public class UserController {

  @GetMapping("user")
  public Mono<User> getUser(@AuthenticationPrincipal OidcUser oidcUser) {
    var user = new User(
      oidcUser.getPreferredUsername(),
      oidcUser.getGivenName(),
      oidcUser.getFamilyName(),
      oidcUser.getClaimAsStringList("roles")       ← Gets the "roles"
    );                                               claim and extracts it
    return Mono.just(user);                          as a list of strings
  }
}
```

Finally, remember to update the test setup in `UserControllerTests` so that the mock ID Token contains a `roles` claim.

Listing 12.5   Adding `roles` list to the mock ID Token

```
@WebFluxTest(UserController.class)
@Import(SecurityConfig.class)
class UserControllerTests {

  ...

  private SecurityMockServerConfigurers.OidcLoginMutator
    configureMockOidcLogin(User expectedUser)
  {
    return mockOidcLogin().idToken(builder -> {
      builder.claim(StandardClaimNames.PREFERRED_USERNAME,
        expectedUser.username());
      builder.claim(StandardClaimNames.GIVEN_NAME,
        expectedUser.firstName());
      builder.claim(StandardClaimNames.FAMILY_NAME,
        expectedUser.lastName());
      builder.claim("roles", expectedUser.roles());     ← Adds a "roles"
    });                                                    claim to the
  }                                                        mock ID Token
}
```

You can verify that the changes are correct by running the following command:

```
$ ./gradlew test --tests UserControllerTests
```

> **NOTE**   The `roles` claim configured in Keycloak will include our custom roles
> (`employee` and `customer`) together with a few extra roles managed and assigned
> by Keycloak itself.

So far, we've configured Keycloak to include the user roles in the tokens and updated
Edge Service to relay the Access Token to the applications downstream. We're now ready
to start securing Catalog Service and Order Service with Spring Security and OAuth2.

12.2   Protecting APIs with Spring Security and OAuth2 (imperative)

When a user accesses the Polar Bookshop application, Edge Service initiates the
OpenID Connect authentication flow through Keycloak and ultimately receives an
Access Token granting it access to downstream services on behalf of that user.

In this section and the next one, you'll see how to secure Catalog Service and
Order Service by requiring a valid Access Token to access their protected endpoints.
In the OAuth2 authorization framework, they play the role of OAuth2 Resource Servers: the applications hosting protected data that a user can access through a third
party (Edge Service, in our example).

OAuth2 Resource Servers don't deal with user authentication. They receive an
Access Token in the `Authorization` header of each HTTP request. Then they verify
the signature and authorize the request according to the content of the token. We
have already configured Edge Service to send over an Access Token when routing a
request downstream. Now you'll see how to use that token on the receiver side. This
section will guide you through securing Catalog Service, built on the imperative
Spring stack. The next section will show you how to achieve the same result in Order
Service, built on the reactive Spring stack.

12.2.1   Securing Spring Boot as an OAuth2 Resource Server

The first step in securing a Spring Boot application leveraging OAuth2 is to add a
dependency on the dedicated Spring Boot starter that includes Spring Security and
OAuth2 support for Resource Servers.

In the Catalog Service project (catalog-service), open the build.gradle file, and add
the new dependency. Remember to refresh or reimport the Gradle dependencies
after the new addition.

Listing 12.6   Adding dependency for Spring Security OAuth2 Resource Server

```
dependencies {
    ...
    implementation 'org.springframework.boot:
    ➥ spring-boot-starter-oauth2-resource-server'
}
```

Next, let's configure the integration between Spring Security and Keycloak.

CONFIGURING THE INTEGRATION BETWEEN SPRING SECURITY AND KEYCLOAK

Spring Security supports protecting endpoints using two data formats for the Access Token: JWT and opaque tokens. We'll work with Access Tokens defined as JWTs, similar to what we did for ID Tokens. With Access Tokens, Keycloak grants Edge Service access to downstream applications on behalf of the user. When the Access Token is a JWT, we can also include relevant information as claims about the authenticated user and propagate this context to Catalog Service and Order Service with ease. In contrast, opaque tokens would require the application downstream to contact Keycloak every time to fetch the information associated with the token.

Configuring Spring Security to integrate with Keycloak as an OAuth2 Resource Server is more straightforward than the OAuth2 Client scenario. When working with JWTs, the application will contact Keycloak mainly to fetch the public keys necessary to verify the token's signature. Using the `issuer-uri` property, similar to what we did for Edge Service, we'll let the application auto-discover the Keycloak endpoint where it can find the public keys.

The default behavior is for the application to fetch the public keys lazily upon the first received HTTP request rather than at startup, both for performance and coupling reasons (you don't need Keycloak up and running when starting the application). OAuth2 Authorization Servers provide their public keys using the JSON Web Key (JWK) format. The collection of public keys is called a *JWK Set*. The endpoint where Keycloak exposes its public keys is called the *JWK Set URI*. Spring Security will automatically rotate the public keys whenever Keycloak makes new ones available.

For each incoming request containing an Access Token in the `Authorization` header, Spring Security will automatically validate the token's signature using the public keys provided by Keycloak and decode its claims via a `JwtDecoder` object, which is auto-configured behind the scenes.

In the Catalog Service project (catalog-service), open the application.yml file, and add the following configuration.

Listing 12.7   Configuring Catalog Service as an OAuth2 Resource Server

```
spring:
  security:
    oauth2:
      resourceserver:
        jwt:
          issuer-uri:
⮕http://localhost:8080/realms/PolarBookshop
```

OAuth2 doesn't enforce a data format for Access Tokens, so we must be explicit about our choice. In this case, we want to use JWT.

The Keycloak URL providing information about all the relevant OAuth2 endpoints for the specific realm

---

NOTE   Explaining the cryptographic algorithm used to sign the Access Token is out of scope for this book. If you'd like to learn more about cryptography, you might want to look up *Real-World Cryptography* by David Wong (Manning, 2021).

The integration between Catalog Service and Keycloak is now established. Next you'll define some basic security policies to protect the application endpoints.

DEFINING SECURITY POLICIES FOR JWT AUTHENTICATION

For the Catalog Service application, we want to enforce the following security policies:

- `GET` requests to fetch books should be allowed without authentication.
- All other requests should require authentication.
- The application should be configured as an OAuth2 Resource Server and use JWT authentication.
- The flow for handling JWT authentication should be stateless.

Let's expand on the last policy. Edge Service triggers the user authentication flow and leverages the web session to store data like ID Tokens and Access Tokens that would otherwise get lost at the end of each HTTP request, forcing a user to authenticate at each request. To make it possible for the application to scale, we used Spring Session to store the web session data in Redis and keep the application stateless.

Unlike Edge Service, Catalog Service only needs an Access Token to authenticate a request. Since the token is always provided in each HTTP request to a protected endpoint, Catalog Service doesn't need to store any data between requests. We call this strategy *stateless authentication* or *token-based authentication*. We use JWTs as Access Tokens, so we can also refer to it as *JWT authentication.*

Now on to the code. In the Catalog Service project, create a new `SecurityConfig` class in the `com.polarbookshop.catalogservice.config` package. Similar to what we did for Edge Service, we can use the DSL provided by `HttpSecurity` to build a `SecurityFilterChain` configured with the required security policies.

Listing 12.8 Configuring security policies and JWT authentication

```
@EnableWebSecurity                          ◁──  Enables Spring
public class SecurityConfig {                    MVC support for
                                                 Spring Security

  @Bean
  SecurityFilterChain filterChain(HttpSecurity http) throws Exception {
    return http
      .authorizeHttpRequests(authorize -> authorize          Allows users to fetch
        .mvcMatchers(HttpMethod.GET, "/", "/books/**")       greetings and books
          .permitAll()                              ◁──      without being
        .anyRequest().authenticated()                        authenticated
      )
      .oauth2ResourceServer(                                 Enables OAuth2 Resource
        OAuth2ResourceServerConfigurer::jwt        ◁──       Server support using the
      )                                                      default configuration based
      .sessionManagement(sessionManagement ->                on JWT (JWT authentication)
        sessionManagement
          .sessionCreationPolicy(SessionCreationPolicy.STATELESS))
```

Any other request requires authentication. (pointing to `.anyRequest().authenticated()`)

(arrow pointing to `.sessionManagement`)

Each request must include an Access Token, so there's no need to keep a user session alive between requests. We want it to be stateless.

```
        .csrf(AbstractHttpConfigurer::disable)    ◁────────────────┐
        .build();
    }                             Since the authentication strategy is stateless
}                                 and doesn't involve a browser-based client, we
                                       can safely disable the CSRF protection.
```

Let's check if it works. First, the Polar UI, Keycloak, Redis, and PostgreSQL containers should be started. Open a Terminal window, navigate to the folder where you keep your Docker Compose configuration (polar-deployment/docker) and run the following:

```
$ docker-compose up -d polar-ui polar-keycloak polar-redis polar-postgres
```

Then run both Edge Service and Catalog Service (./gradlew bootRun from each project). Finally, open a browser window, and go to http://localhost:9000.

Ensure you can see the list of books in the catalog without being authenticated, but not add, update, or delete them. Then log in as Isabelle (isabelle/password). She is an employee of the bookshop, so she should be allowed to modify the books in the catalog. Next, log in as Bjorn (bjorn/password). He is a customer, so he shouldn't be able to change anything in the catalog.

Under the hood, the Angular application fetches the user roles from the /user endpoint exposed by Edge Service and uses them to block pieces of functionality. That improves the user experience, but it's not secure. The actual endpoints exposed by Catalog Service don't take roles into account. We need to enforce role-based authorization. That's the topic of the next section.

12.2.2 *Role-based access control with Spring Security and JWT*

So far, when talking about authorization, we referred to granting an OAuth2 Client (Edge Service) access to an OAuth2 Resource Server (like Catalog Service) on behalf of the user. Now we'll move from application authorization to user authorization. What can an authenticated user do in the system?

Spring Security associates each authenticated user with a list of GrantedAuthority objects that model the authorities the user has been granted. Granted authorities can be used to represent fine-grained permissions, roles, or even scopes and come from different sources depending on the authentication strategy. The authorities are available through the Authentication object representing the authenticated user and stored in the SecurityContext.

Since Catalog Service is configured as an OAuth2 Resource Server and uses JWT authentication, Spring Security extracts the list of scopes from the scopes claim of the Access Token and uses them as granted authorities for the given user automatically. Each GrantedAuthority object built in this way will be named with the SCOPE_ prefix and the scope value.

The default behavior is acceptable in many scenarios where scopes are used to model permissions, but it doesn't fit our case where we rely on user roles to know which privileges each user has. We want to set up a role-based access control (RBAC) strategy using the user roles provided in the `roles` claim of the Access Token (see figure 12.6). In this section, I'll show you how to define a custom converter for the Access Token to build a list of `GrantedAuthority` objects using the values in the `roles` claim and the `ROLE_` prefix. Then we'll use those authorities to define authorization rules for the endpoints of Catalog Service.

Conversion of user roles from JWT to GrantedAuthority objects

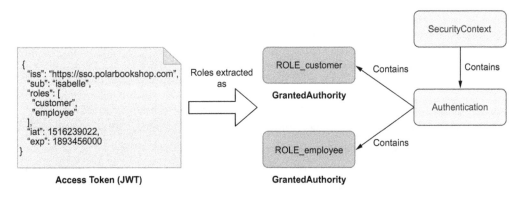

Figure 12.6   How the user roles listed in the Access Token (JWT) are converted into `GrantedAuthority` **objects used by Spring Security for RBAC**

> **NOTE**   You might be wondering why we're using the `SCOPE_` or `ROLE_` prefix. Since granted authorities can be used to represent different items (roles, scopes, permissions), Spring Security uses prefixes to group them. We'll rely on this default naming convention for the Polar Bookshop example, but it's possible to use different prefixes or even no prefixes at all. For more information, refer to the Spring Security documentation (https://spring.io/projects/spring-security).

EXTRACTING USER ROLES FROM THE ACCESS TOKEN

Spring Security provides a `JwtAuthenticationConverter` class we can use to define a custom strategy to extract information from a JWT. In our case, the JWT is an Access Token, and we want to configure how to build `GrantedAuthority` objects from the values in the `roles` claim. In the Catalog Service project (catalog-service), open the `SecurityConfig` class and define a new `JwtAuthenticationConverter` bean.

Listing 12.9   Mapping the roles from the JWT to granted authorities

```
@EnableWebSecurity
public class SecurityConfig {

    ...

    @Bean
    public JwtAuthenticationConverter jwtAuthenticationConverter() {
```

```
      var jwtGrantedAuthoritiesConverter =
        new JwtGrantedAuthoritiesConverter();        ◁──┐   Defines a converter to map claims
      jwtGrantedAuthoritiesConverter                         to GrantedAuthority objects
        .setAuthorityPrefix("ROLE_");           ◁────────┐   Applies the "ROLE_"
      jwtGrantedAuthoritiesConverter                          prefix to each user role
        .setAuthoritiesClaimName("roles");    ◁──────┐
                                                            Extracts the list of roles
      var jwtAuthenticationConverter =                     from the roles claim
   ▷    new JwtAuthenticationConverter();
      jwtAuthenticationConverter
        .setJwtGrantedAuthoritiesConverter(jwtGrantedAuthoritiesConverter);
      return jwtAuthenticationConverter;
    }
  }
```

**Defines a strategy to convert a JWT. We'll only
customize how to build granted authorities out of it.**

With this bean in place, Spring Security will associate a list of `GrantedAuthority` objects with each authenticated user, and we can use them to define authorization policies.

DEFINING AUTHORIZATION POLICIES BASED ON USER ROLES

The Catalog Service endpoints should be protected according to the following policies:

- All `GET` requests sent to the `/`, `/books` or `/books/{isbn}` endpoints should be allowed, even without authentication.
- Any other request should require both user authentication and the `employee` role.

Spring Security provides an expression-based DSL for defining authorization policies. The most generic one is `hasAuthority("ROLE_employee")`, which you can use to check for any type of authority. In our case, authorities are roles, so we can use the most descriptive `hasRole("employee")` and drop the prefix (which is added by Spring Security under the hood).

> **Listing 12.10 Applying RBAC to limit write access to users with the `employee` role**

```
@EnableWebSecurity                          Any other request requires not only authentication
public class SecurityConfig {                  but also the employee role (which is the same as
                                                     the ROLE_employee authority).
  @Bean
  SecurityFilterChain filterChain(HttpSecurity http) throws Exception {
    return http
      .authorizeHttpRequests(authorize -> authorize
        .mvcMatchers(HttpMethod.GET, "/", "/books/**")
        .permitAll()
        .anyRequest().hasRole("employee")                      ◁───────────────┘
      )
      .oauth2ResourceServer(OAuth2ResourceServerConfigurer::jwt)
      .sessionManagement(sessionManagement -> sessionManagement
        .sessionCreationPolicy(SessionCreationPolicy.STATELESS))
      .csrf(AbstractHttpConfigurer::disable)
      .build();
  }
```

**Allows users to
fetch greetings
and books
without being
authenticated**

```
    . . .
}
```

Now you can rebuild and run Catalog Service (`./gradlew bootRun`) and go through the same flows as before. This time Catalog Service will ensure that only the bookshop employees are allowed to add, update, and delete books.

Finally, stop the running applications (Ctrl-C) and containers (`docker-compose down`).

> **NOTE** To learn more about the authorization architecture in Spring Security and the different strategies available for access control, you can refer to chapters 7 and 8 in *Spring Security in Action* by Laurențiu Spilcă (Manning, 2020), where they are explained in great detail.

Next I'll guide you through some techniques for testing security in an imperative Spring Boot application configured as an OAuth2 Resource Server.

12.2.3 Testing OAuth2 with Spring Security and Testcontainers

When it comes to security, writing autotests is usually challenging. Fortunately, Spring Security provides us with convenient utilities to verify the security setup in slice tests.

This section will show you how to write slice tests for the web slice using mock Access Tokens and full integration tests relying on an actual Keycloak container run via Testcontainers.

Before starting, we need to add new dependencies on Spring Security Test and Testcontainers Keycloak. Open the build.gradle file for the Catalog Service project (catalog-service), and update it as follows. Remember to refresh or reimport the Gradle dependencies after the new addition.

Listing 12.11 Adding dependencies to test Spring Security and Keycloak

```
ext {
  . . .
  set('testKeycloakVersion', "2.3.0")        ◁──  The version of
}                                                  Testcontainers
                                                   Keycloak

dependencies {
  . . .
  testImplementation 'org.springframework.security:spring-security-test'
  testImplementation 'org.testcontainers:junit-jupiter'
  testImplementation "com.github.dasniko:
➥   testcontainers-keycloak:${testKeycloakVersion}"   ◁──  Provides Keycloak
}                                                           testing utilities on
                                                            top of Testcontainers
```

TESTING SECURED REST CONTROLLERS WITH @WEBMVCTEST AND SPRING SECURITY

First, let's update the `BookControllerMvcTests` class to cover the new scenarios, depending on the user authentication and authorization. For example, we could write test cases for `DELETE` operations in these situations:

- The user is authenticated and has the `employee` role.
- The user is authenticated but doesn't have the `employee` role.
- The user is not authenticated.

Delete operations are only allowed to the bookshop employees, so only the first request will return a successful answer.

As part of the OAuth2 Access Token validation, Spring Security relies on the public keys provided by Keycloak to verify the JWT signature. Internally, the framework configures a `JwtDecoder` bean to decode and verify a JWT using those keys. In the context of a web slice test, we can provide a mock `JwtDecoder` bean so that Spring Security skips the interaction with Keycloak (which we'll validate later in a full integration test).

Listing 12.12 Verifying security policies at the web layer with slice tests

```
@WebMvcTest(BookController.class)
@Import(SecurityConfig.class)            ◁──┐  Imports the
class BookControllerMvcTests {               │  application's security
                                             │  configuration
  @Autowired
  MockMvc mockMvc;

  @MockBean
  JwtDecoder jwtDecoder;         ◁──┐  Mocks the JwtDecoder so that the application
                                     │  doesn't try to call Keycloak and get the public
  ...                                │  keys for decoding the Access Token

  @Test
  void whenDeleteBookWithEmployeeRoleThenShouldReturn204()
    throws Exception
  {                                          Mutates the HTTP request with a mock
    var isbn = "7373731394";                 JWT-formatted Access Token for a user
    mockMvc                            ◁──┘  with the "employee" role
      .perform(MockMvcRequestBuilders.delete("/books/" + isbn)
        .with(SecurityMockMvcRequestPostProcessors.jwt()
          .authorities(new SimpleGrantedAuthority("ROLE_employee"))))
      .andExpect(MockMvcResultMatchers.status().isNoContent());
  }


  @Test
  void whenDeleteBookWithCustomerRoleThenShouldReturn403()
    throws Exception
  {                                          Mutates the HTTP request with a mock
    var isbn = "7373731394";                 JWT-formatted Access Token for a user
    mockMvc                            ◁──┘  with the "customer" role
      .perform(MockMvcRequestBuilders.delete("/books/" + isbn)
        .with(SecurityMockMvcRequestPostProcessors.jwt()
          .authorities(new SimpleGrantedAuthority("ROLE_customer"))))
      .andExpect(MockMvcResultMatchers.status().isForbidden());
  }


  @Test
  void whenDeleteBookNotAuthenticatedThenShouldReturn401()
```

```
    throws Exception
  {
    var isbn = "7373731394";
    mockMvc
      .perform(MockMvcRequestBuilders.delete("/books/" + isbn))
      .andExpect(MockMvcResultMatchers.status().isUnauthorized());
  }
}
```

Open a Terminal window, navigate to the Catalog Service root folder, and run the newly added tests as follows:

```
$ ./gradlew test --tests BookControllerMvcTests
```

Feel free to add more web slice autotests to cover GET, POST, and PUT requests. For inspiration, you can refer to the source code accompanying the book (Chapter12/12-end/catalog-service).

INTEGRATION TESTS WITH @SPRINGBOOTTEST, SPRING SECURITY, AND TESTCONTAINERS

The integration tests we wrote in the previous chapters will not work anymore for two reasons. First, all POST, PUT, and DELETE requests will fail because we are not providing any valid OAuth2 Access Token. Even if we were, there is no Keycloak up and running, required by Spring Security to fetch the public keys used to validate the Access Tokens.

You can verify the failure by running the following command from the Catalog Service root folder:

```
$ ./gradlew test --tests CatalogServiceApplicationTests
```

We have already seen how to use Testcontainers to write integration tests against data services like a PostgreSQL database, making our tests more reliable and ensuring environment parity. In this section we'll do the same for Keycloak.

Let's start by configuring a Keycloak container via Testcontainers. Open the Catalog-ServiceApplicationTests class and add the following setup.

> **Listing 12.13 Setup for a Keycloak test container**

```
@SpringBootTest(webEnvironment = SpringBootTest.WebEnvironment.RANDOM_PORT)
@ActiveProfiles("integration")
@Testcontainers                              ◁─── Activates automatic
class CatalogServiceApplicationTests {            startup and cleanup
                                                  of test containers
  @Autowired
  private WebTestClient webTestClient;       Defines a Keycloak
                                             container for testing
  @Container                           ◁───┘
  private static final KeycloakContainer keycloakContainer =
    new KeycloakContainer("quay.io/keycloak/keycloak:19.0")
      .withRealmImportFile("test-realm-config.json");
```

```
@DynamicPropertySource
static void dynamicProperties(DynamicPropertyRegistry registry) {
  registry.add("spring.security.oauth2.resourceserver.jwt.issuer-uri",
    () -> keycloakContainer.getAuthServerUrl() + "realms/PolarBookshop");
}
...
}
```

Overwrites the Keycloak Issuer URI configuration to point to the test Keycloak instance

The Keycloak test container is initialized via a configuration file I included in the code repository accompanying this book (Chapter12/12-end/catalog-service/src/test/resources/test-realm-config.json). Go ahead and copy it over to the src/test/resources folder of your Catalog Service project (catalog-service).

In production, we would call Catalog Service via Edge Service, which is responsible for authenticating users and relaying Access Tokens to the downstream applications. We now want to test Catalog Service in isolation and verify different authorization scenarios. Therefore, we need to generate some Access Tokens first, so that we can use them to call the Catalog Service endpoints under testing.

The Keycloak configuration I provided in the JSON file includes the definition of a test Client (polar-test) that we can use to authenticate users via a username and password directly, instead of going through the browser-based flow we implemented in Edge Service. In OAuth2, such a flow is called a *Password Grant*, and it's not recommended for production use. In the following section, we'll use it just for testing purposes.

Let's set up CatalogServiceApplicationTests to authenticate with Keycloak as Isabelle and Bjorn so that we can obtain the Access Tokens we need to call the Catalog Service's protected endpoints. Keep in mind that Isabelle is both a customer and employee, whereas Bjorn is only a customer.

Listing 12.14   Setup for obtaining test Access Tokens

```
@SpringBootTest(webEnvironment = SpringBootTest.WebEnvironment.RANDOM_PORT)
@ActiveProfiles("integration")
@Testcontainers
class CatalogServiceApplicationTests {
  private static KeycloakToken bjornTokens;
  private static KeycloakToken isabelleTokens;
  ...

  @BeforeAll
  static void generateAccessTokens() {
    WebClient webClient = WebClient.builder()
      .baseUrl(keycloakContainer.getAuthServerUrl()
        + "realms/PolarBookshop/protocol/openid-connect/token")
      .defaultHeader(HttpHeaders.CONTENT_TYPE,
        MediaType.APPLICATION_FORM_URLENCODED_VALUE)
      .build();

    isabelleTokens = authenticateWith(
      "isabelle", "password", webClient);
```

A WebClient used to call Keycloak

Authenticates as Isabelle and obtains an Access Token

```
          bjornTokens = authenticateWith(            ⊲─┐   Authenticates as Bjorn
            "bjorn", "password", webClient);            │   and obtains an Access
      }                                                 │   Token

      private static KeycloakToken authenticateWith(
        String username, String password, WebClient webClient
      ) {                                                   Uses the Password Grant
        return webClient                                    flow to authenticate with
          .post()                                           Keycloak directly
          .body(                                 ⊲─┘
            BodyInserters.fromFormData("grant_type", "password")
            .with("client_id", "polar-test")
            .with("username", username)
            .with("password", password)
          )
          .retrieve()                            Blocks until a result is available.
          .bodyToMono(KeycloakToken.class)       This is how we use WebClient
          .block();                       ⊲─┘    imperatively rather than reactively.
      }
                                                    Instructs Jackson to use
                                                    this constructor when
      private record KeycloakToken(String accessToken) {   deserializing JSON into
        @JsonCreator                              ⊲─┐       KeycloakToken objects
        private KeycloakToken(
          @JsonProperty("access_token") final String accessToken
        ) {
          this.accessToken = accessToken;
        }
      }
  }
```

Finally, we can update the test cases in `CatalogServiceApplicationTests` to cover several authentication and authorization scenarios. For example, we could write test cases for `POST` operations in these situations:

- The user is authenticated and has the `employee` role (extending the existing test case).
- The user is authenticated but doesn't have the `employee` role (new test case).
- The user is not authenticated (new test case).

NOTE In the context of an OAuth2 Resource Server, authentication means token authentication. In this case, it happens by providing an Access Token in the `Authorization` header of each HTTP request.

Create operations are only allowed to the bookshop employees, so only the first request will return a successful answer.

Listing 12.15 Verifying security scenarios in integration tests

```
@Test
void whenPostRequestThenBookCreated() {
  var expectedBook = Book.of("1231231231", "Title", "Author",
    9.90, "Polarsophia");
```

Sends a request to add a book to
the catalog as an authenticated
employee user (Isabelle)

```
webTestClient.post().uri("/books")
  .headers(headers ->
    headers.setBearerAuth(isabelleTokens.accessToken()))
  .bodyValue(expectedBook)
  .exchange()
  .expectStatus().isCreated()
  .expectBody(Book.class).value(actualBook -> {
    assertThat(actualBook).isNotNull();
    assertThat(actualBook.isbn()).isEqualTo(expectedBook.isbn());
  });
}
```

The book has been
successfully created (201).

```
@Test
void whenPostRequestUnauthorizedThen403() {
  var expectedBook = Book.of("1231231231", "Title", "Author",
    9.90, "Polarsophia");

  webTestClient.post().uri("/books")
    .headers(headers ->
      headers.setBearerAuth(bjornTokens.accessToken()))
    .bodyValue(expectedBook)
    .exchange()
    .expectStatus().isForbidden();
}
```

Sends a request to add a book to
the catalog as an authenticated
customer user (Bjorn)

The book has not been created
because the user doesn't have the
correct authorization, no
"employee" role (403).

```
@Test
void whenPostRequestUnauthenticatedThen401() {
  var expectedBook = Book.of("1231231231", "Title", "Author",
    9.90, "Polarsophia");

  webTestClient.post().uri("/books")
    .bodyValue(expectedBook)
    .exchange()
    .expectStatus().isUnauthorized();
}
```

Sends a request to add a
book to the catalog as an
unauthenticated user

The book has not been created because
the user is not authenticated (401).

Open a Terminal window, navigate to the Catalog Service root folder, and run the newly added tests as follows:

```
$ ./gradlew test --tests CatalogServiceApplicationTests
```

There are still tests failing. Go ahead and update them by including the right Access Token (Isabelle's or Bjorn's) in any POST, PUT, or DELETE request, as you learned in the previous example. When you're done, rerun the tests and verify that they are all successful. For inspiration, you can refer to the source code accompanying this book (Chapter12/12-end/catalog-service).

12.3 Protecting APIs with Spring Security and OAuth2 (reactive)

Securing reactive Spring Boot applications like Order Service is similar to what we did for Catalog Service. Spring Security provides intuitive and consistent abstractions across the two stacks, which makes it easy to move from one stack to the other.

In this section, I'll guide you through configuring Order Service as an OAuth2 Resource Server, enabling JWT authentication, and defining security policies for the web endpoints.

12.3.1 Securing Spring Boot as an OAuth2 Resource Server

The Spring Boot starter dependency that includes Spring Security and OAuth2 support for Resource Servers is the same for both imperative and reactive applications. In the Order Service project (order-service), open the build.gradle file, and add the new dependency. Remember to refresh or reimport the Gradle dependencies after the new addition.

Listing 12.16 **Adding dependency for Spring Security OAuth2 Resource Server**

```
dependencies {
  ...
  implementation 'org.springframework.boot:
  ➥ spring-boot-starter-oauth2-resource-server'
}
```

Next we'll configure the integration between Spring Security and Keycloak.

CONFIGURING THE INTEGRATION BETWEEN SPRING SECURITY AND KEYCLOAK

The strategy for integrating Spring Security with Keycloak will be similar to what we did in Catalog Service. Open the Order Service project (order-service), and update the application.yml file with the following configuration.

Listing 12.17 **Configuring Order Service as an OAuth2 Resource Server**

```
spring:
  security:
    oauth2:
      resourceserver:
        jwt:           ◀──┐  OAuth2 doesn't enforce a data
          issuer-uri:      │  format for Access Tokens, so
➥http://localhost:8080/realms/PolarBookshop
```

> OAuth2 doesn't enforce a data format for Access Tokens, so we must be explicit about our choice. In this case, we want to use JWT.

> The Keycloak URL providing information about all the relevant OAuth2 endpoints for the specific realm

The integration between Order Service and Keycloak is now established. Next we'll define the necessary security policies to protect the application endpoints.

DEFINING SECURITY POLICIES FOR JWT AUTHENTICATION

For the Order Service application, we want to enforce the following security policies:

- All requests should require authentication.
- The application should be configured as an OAuth2 Resource Server and use JWT authentication.
- The flow for handling JWT authentication should be stateless.

There are two main differences here from what we did in Catalog Service:

- The reactive syntax is slightly different from its imperative counterpart, especially the part for enforcing JWT authentication (stateless).
- We're not extracting user roles from the Access Token because the endpoints don't have special requirements depending on user roles.

In the Order Service project, create a SecurityConfig class in a new com.polarbook-shop.orderservice.config package. Then use the DSL provided by ServerHttp-Security to build a SecurityWebFilterChain configured with the required security policies.

Listing 12.18   Configuring security policies and JWT authentication for Order Service

```
@EnableWebFluxSecurity                          Enables Spring WebFlux
public class SecurityConfig {                    support for Spring
                                                 Security
    @Bean
    SecurityWebFilterChain filterChain(ServerHttpSecurity http) {
        return http
            .authorizeExchange(exchange -> exchange          Enables OAuth2 Resource Server
                .anyExchange().authenticated()               support using the default configuration
            )                                                based on JWT (JWT authentication)
            .oauth2ResourceServer(
                ServerHttpSecurity.OAuth2ResourceServerSpec::jwt)
            .requestCache(requestCacheSpec ->
                requestCacheSpec.requestCache(NoOpServerRequestCache.getInstance()))
            .csrf(ServerHttpSecurity.CsrfSpec::disable)
            .build();
    }
}
```

All requests require authentication.

Enables OAuth2 Resource Server support using the default configuration based on JWT (JWT authentication)

Since the authentication strategy is stateless and doesn't involve a browser-based client, we can safely disable the CSRF protection.

Each request must include an Access Token, so there's no need to keep a session cache alive between requests. We want it to be stateless.

Let's check if this works. First, we need to run the backing services (Polar UI, Keycloak, Redis, RabbitMQ, and PostgreSQL). Open a Terminal window, navigate to the folder where you keep your Docker Compose configuration (polar-deployment/docker) and run the following:

```
$ docker-compose up -d polar-ui polar-keycloak polar-redis \
    polar-rabbitmq polar-postgres
```

Then run Edge Service, Catalog Service, and Order Service on the JVM (`./gradlew bootRun` from each project). Finally, open a browser window, and go to http://localhost:9000.

Since Order Service doesn't have particular requirements depending on the user's role, you can log in with either Isabelle (`isabelle/password`) or Bjorn (`bjorn/password`). Then pick a book from the catalog, and submit an order for it. Since you're authenticated, you're allowed to create an order. When you're done, you can visit the Orders page to check all the submitted orders.

"Wait a second! What do you mean, all the submitted orders?" I'm glad you asked. At the moment, each person can see the orders submitted by all users. Don't worry! Later in the chapter, we'll fix that.

Before we do, though, we need to discuss how to test the new Order Service security policies. Stop the running applications (Ctrl-C) and containers (`docker-compose down`). The next section will show you how to test security in a reactive application.

12.3.2 Testing OAuth2 with Spring Security and Testcontainers

Testing secured reactive Spring Boot applications is similar to testing imperative applications. Before starting, we need to add new dependencies on Spring Security Test and Testcontainers Keycloak. The dependency adding JUnit5 support for Testcontainers is already there. Open the build.gradle file and update it as follows. Remember to refresh and reimport the Gradle dependencies after the new addition.

> **Listing 12.19   Adding dependencies to test Spring Security and Keycloak**

```
ext {
    ...
    set('testKeycloakVersion', "2.3.0")        ⟵  The version of
}                                                  Testcontainers
                                                   Keycloak

dependencies {
    ...
    testImplementation 'org.springframework.security:spring-security-test'
    testImplementation 'org.testcontainers:junit-jupiter'
    testImplementation "com.github.dasniko:
    ⮩  testcontainers-keycloak:${testKeycloakVersion}"   ⟵  Provides Keycloak
}                                                             testing utilities on top
                                                              of Testcontainers
```

We can implement full integration tests using `@SpringBootTest` and Testcontainers Keycloak. Since the setup is the same as for Catalog Service, I won't cover those tests here, but you can find them in the repository accompanying the book (Chapter12/12-end/order-service/src/test). Make sure you update those integration tests, or the application build will fail.

In this section, we'll test the web slice of a reactive application when the endpoints are secured, much like we did for Catalog Service.

TESTING SECURED REST CONTROLLERS WITH @WEBFLUXTEST AND SPRING SECURITY

We have already written autotests in OrderControllerWebFluxTests for the web slice using @WebFluxTest. Let's see now how to update them to take security into account.

As part of the OAuth2 Access Token validation, Spring Security relies on the public keys provided by Keycloak to verify the JWT signature. Internally, the framework configures a ReactiveJwtDecoder bean to decode and verify a JWT using those keys. In the context of a web slice test, we can provide a mock ReactiveJwtDecoder bean so that Spring Security skips the interaction with Keycloak (which will be validated by full integration tests).

Listing 12.20   Verifying security policies at the web layer with slice tests

```
@WebFluxTest(OrderController.class)
@Import(SecurityConfig.class)          ◁──┐ Imports the
class OrderControllerWebFluxTests {       │ application security
                                          │ configuration
  @Autowired
  WebTestClient webClient;

  @MockBean
  OrderService orderService;                   Mocks the ReactiveJwtDecoder so
                                               that the application doesn't try to
  @MockBean                                    call Keycloak and get the public
  ReactiveJwtDecoder reactiveJwtDecoder;  ◁──┘ key for decoding the Access Token

  @Test
  void whenBookNotAvailableThenRejectOrder() {
    var orderRequest = new OrderRequest("1234567890", 3);
    var expectedOrder = OrderService.buildRejectedOrder(
     orderRequest.isbn(), orderRequest.quantity());
    given(orderService.submitOrder(
     orderRequest.isbn(), orderRequest.quantity()))
        .willReturn(Mono.just(expectedOrder));
                                                    Mutates the HTTP request
    webClient                                       with a mock, JWT-formatted
      .mutateWith(SecurityMockServerConfigurers     Access Token for a user with
        .mockJwt()                            ◁──┘  the "customer" role
        .authorities(new SimpleGrantedAuthority("ROLE_customer")))
      .post()
      .uri("/orders/")
      .bodyValue(orderRequest)
      .exchange()
      .expectStatus().is2xxSuccessful()
      .expectBody(Order.class).value(actualOrder -> {
        assertThat(actualOrder).isNotNull();
        assertThat(actualOrder.status()).isEqualTo(OrderStatus.REJECTED);
      });
  }
}
```

Open a Terminal window, navigate to the Order Service root folder, and run the newly added tests as follows:

```
$ ./gradlew test --tests OrderControllerWebFluxTests
```

As always, you can find more test examples in the source code repository accompanying this book (Chapter12/12-end/order-service).

12.4   Protecting and auditing data with Spring Security and Spring Data

So far, we've looked at securing the APIs exposed by Spring Boot applications and handling concerns like authentication and authorization. What about data? Once you have Spring Security in place, you can also secure the business and data layers.

Regarding the business logic, you can enable the method security feature to check for user authentication or authorization directly on business methods, leveraging annotations like `@PreAuthorize`. In the Polar Bookshop system, the business layer is not complex enough to require additional security policies, so I won't describe that.

> **NOTE**   To learn more about how to use method authentication and authorization, refer to chapter 8 of *Spring Security in Action* by Laurenţiu Spilcă (Manning, 2020), where those topics are explained in great detail.

On the other hand, the data layer requires some extra work to address two main concerns:

- How can we tell which users created what data? Who changed it last?
- How can we ensure that each user can only access their own book orders?

This section will address both concerns. First I'll explain how to enable auditing for users' actions on data in both Catalog Service and Order Service. Then I'll walk you through the changes required by Order Service to keep the data private.

12.4.1   Auditing data with Spring Security and Spring Data JDBC

Let's start by considering Catalog Service, where the data layer is implemented with Spring Data JDBC. In chapter 5, you learned how to enable JDBC data auditing, and you configured it to save both the creation date and last modified date for each data entity. Building on top of that, we can now extend the audit scope to include the usernames of the person who created the entity and the person who modified it last.

First we need to tell Spring Data where to get the information about the currently authenticated user. In the previous chapter, you learned that Spring Security stores information about authenticated users in an `Authentication` object, which is stored in a `SecurityContext` object available through the `SecurityContextHolder`. We can use that object hierarchy to specify how to extract the principal for Spring Data.

DEFINING AN AUDITOR TO CAPTURE WHO CREATED OR UPDATED A JDBC DATA ENTITY

In the Catalog Service project (catalog-service), open the `DataConfig` class. That's where we used the `@EnableJdbcAuditing` annotation to enable data auditing. Now, we'll also define an `AuditorAware` bean that should return the principal—the currently authenticated user.

Listing 12.21   Configuring user auditing in Spring Data JDBC

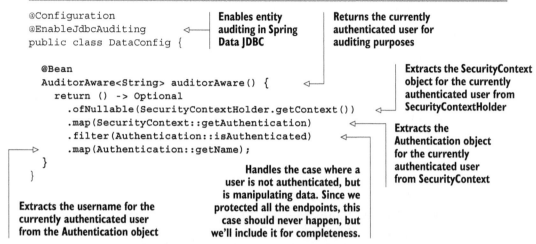

```
@Configuration
@EnableJdbcAuditing
public class DataConfig {

  @Bean
  AuditorAware<String> auditorAware() {
    return () -> Optional
      .ofNullable(SecurityContextHolder.getContext())
      .map(SecurityContext::getAuthentication)
      .filter(Authentication::isAuthenticated)
      .map(Authentication::getName);
  }
}
```

Enables entity auditing in Spring Data JDBC

Returns the currently authenticated user for auditing purposes

Extracts the SecurityContext object for the currently authenticated user from SecurityContextHolder

Extracts the Authentication object for the currently authenticated user from SecurityContext

Handles the case where a user is not authenticated, but is manipulating data. Since we protected all the endpoints, this case should never happen, but we'll include it for completeness.

Extracts the username for the currently authenticated user from the Authentication object

ADDING AUDIT METADATA FOR USERS WHO CREATED OR UPDATED A JDBC DATA ENTITY

When an `AuditorAware` bean is defined and auditing is enabled, Spring Data will use it to extract the principal. In our case, it's the username of the currently authenticated user, represented as a `String`. Then we can use `@CreatedBy` and `@LastModifiedBy` to annotate two new fields in the `Book` record. They will be populated by Spring Data automatically whenever a create or update operation is performed on the entity.

Listing 12.22   Fields to capture user audit metadata in a JDBC entity

```
public record Book (
  ...
  @CreatedBy                      Who created
  String createdBy,               the entity

  @LastModifiedBy                 Who modified the
  String lastModifiedBy,          entity the last time
){
  public static Book of(String isbn, String title, String author,
    Double price, String publisher
  ) {
    return new Book(null, isbn, title, author, price, publisher,
      null, null, null, null, 0);
  }
}
```

After adding the new fields, we need to update a few classes using the `Book` all-args constructor, which now requires passing values for `createdBy` and `lastModifiedBy`.

The `BookService` class contains the logic for updating books. Open it and change the `editBookDetails()` method to ensure the audit metadata is correctly passed along when calling the data layer.

Listing 12.23 Including the existing audit metadata when updating a book

```
@Service
public class BookService {
  ...

  public Book editBookDetails(String isbn, Book book) {
    return bookRepository.findByIsbn(isbn)
      .map(existingBook -> {
        var bookToUpdate = new Book(
          existingBook.id(),
          existingBook.isbn(),
          book.title(),
          book.author(),
          book.price(),
          book.publisher(),
          existingBook.createdDate(),
          existingBook.lastModifiedDate(),
          existingBook.createdBy(),           ◁──┐  Who created
          existingBook.lastModifiedBy(),      ◁───   the entity
          existingBook.version());                 └  Who updated
        return bookRepository.save(bookToUpdate);     the entity last
      })
      .orElseGet(() -> addBookToCatalog(book));
  }
}
```

I'll leave it to you to update the autotests in a similar way. You can also extend the tests in `BookJsonTests` to verify the serialization and deserialization of the new fields. As a reference, you can check Chapter12/12-end/catalog-service in the code repository accompanying this book. Make sure you update the tests that use the `Book()` constructor, or else the application build will fail.

WRITING A FLYWAY MIGRATION TO ADD THE NEW AUDIT METADATA TO THE SCHEMA

Since we changed the entity model, we need to update the database schema accordingly. Let's assume that Catalog Service is already in production, so we need a Flyway migration to update the schema in the next release. In chapter 5, we introduced Flyway to add version control to our databases. Each change to a schema must be registered as a migration, ensuring robust schema evolution and reproducibility.

Any change to a database schema should also be backward compatible to support common deployment strategies for cloud native applications, like rolling upgrades, blue/green deployments, or canary releases (a subject we'll cover in chapter 15). In this case, we need to add new columns to the `book` table. As long as we don't make them mandatory, the change will be backward compatible. After we change the schema, any running instance of the previous release of Catalog Service will continue to work without errors, simply ignoring the new columns.

In the src/main/resources/db/migration folder for the Catalog Service project, create a new `V3__Add_user_audit.sql` migration script to add two new columns to the `book` table. Ensure you type two underscores after the version number.

Listing 12.24   Adding new audit metadata to the `book` table

```
ALTER TABLE book                                 Add a column to hold the username
  ADD COLUMN created_by varchar(255);      ◁─┘   of who created the row.
ALTER TABLE book                                 Add a column to hold the username
  ADD COLUMN last_modified_by varchar(255);  ◁─┤ of who last updated the row.
```

During the application's startup, Flyway will automatically go through all the migration scripts and apply those not yet applied.

The tradeoff of enforcing backward-compatible changes is that we now have to treat as optional two fields that we need to have always filled in, and that may possibly fail validation if they're not. That is a common problem that can be solved over two subsequent releases of the application:

1 In the first release, you add the new columns as optional and implement a data migration to fill in the new columns for all the existing data. For Catalog Service, you could use a conventional value to represent that we don't know who created or updated the entity, such as unknown or anonymous.

2 In the second release, you can create a new migration to update the schema safely and make the new columns required.

I'll leave that up to you if you'd like to do that. If you're interested in implementing data migrations, I recommend that you check out Flyway's official documentation (https://flywaydb.org).

In the next section, you'll see how to test user-related auditing in Spring Data JDBC.

12.4.2 *Testing data auditing with Spring Data and @WithMockUser*

When we test security at the data layer, we're not interested in which authentication strategy has been adopted. The only thing we need is to know whether the operation is performed in the context of an authenticated request.

The Spring Security Test project provides us with a handy @WithMockUser annotation we can use on test cases to make them run in an authenticated context. You can also add information about the mock user. Since we're testing auditing, we want to define at least a username that can be used as the principal.

Let's extend the BookRepositoryJdbcTests class with new test cases covering data auditing for users.

Listing 12.25   Testing data auditing when users are authenticated or not

```
@DataJdbcTest
@Import(DataConfig.class)
@AutoConfigureTestDatabase(replace = AutoConfigureTestDatabase.Replace.NONE)
@ActiveProfiles("integration")
class BookRepositoryJdbcTests {

    ...
```

```
@Test
void whenCreateBookNotAuthenticatedThenNoAuditMetadata() {
  var bookToCreate = Book.of("1232343456", "Title",
    "Author", 12.90, "Polarsophia");
  var createdBook = bookRepository.save(bookToCreate);

  assertThat(createdBook.createdBy()).isNull();
  assertThat(createdBook.lastModifiedBy()).isNull();
}

@Test
@WithMockUser("john")
void whenCreateBookAuthenticatedThenAuditMetadata() {
  var bookToCreate = Book.of("1232343457", "Title",
    "Author", 12.90, "Polarsophia");
  var createdBook = bookRepository.save(bookToCreate);

  assertThat(createdBook.createdBy())
    .isEqualTo("john");
  assertThat(createdBook.lastModifiedBy())
    .isEqualTo("john");
}
}
```

This test case is executed in an unauthenticated context.

No audit data when there is no authenticated user

This test case is executed in an authenticated context for the user "john."

Audit data when there is an authenticated user

Open a Terminal window, navigate to the Catalog Service root folder, and run the newly added tests as follows:

```
$ ./gradlew test --tests BookRepositoryJdbcTests
```

If you experience any failures, it might be because you haven't updated the test cases where the Book() constructor is used. We have added new fields to the domain model, so remember to update those test cases as well.

12.4.3 Protecting user data with Spring Security and Spring Data R2DBC

Similar to what we did in Catalog Service, this section will show you how to add data auditing for users in Order Service. Thanks to the abstractions provided by Spring Data and Spring Security, the implementation will not be much different, even though we're using Spring Data R2DBC and reactive Spring.

Besides data auditing, Order Service has one additional critical requirement. Users should be able to access only their own orders. We need to ensure the privacy of all that data. This section will also walk you through the changes necessary to accomplish that result.

DEFINING AN AUDITOR TO CAPTURE WHO CREATED OR UPDATED AN R2DBC DATA ENTITY

Even in this case, we need to tell Spring Data where to get the information about the currently authenticated user. Since it's a reactive application, this time we'll get the SecurityContext object for the principal from the ReactiveSecurityContextHolder.

In the Order Service project (order-service), open the `DataConfig` class and add a `ReactiveAuditorAware` bean to return the username of the currently authenticated user.

Listing 12.26   Configuring user auditing in Spring Data R2DBC

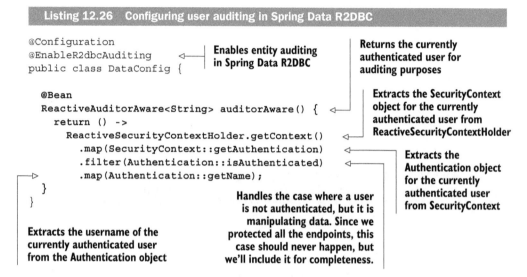

```
@Configuration
@EnableR2dbcAuditing                          Enables entity auditing
public class DataConfig {                     in Spring Data R2DBC

  @Bean
  ReactiveAuditorAware<String> auditorAware() {
    return () ->
      ReactiveSecurityContextHolder.getContext()
        .map(SecurityContext::getAuthentication)
        .filter(Authentication::isAuthenticated)
        .map(Authentication::getName);
  }
}
```

Returns the currently authenticated user for auditing purposes

Extracts the SecurityContext object for the currently authenticated user from ReactiveSecurityContextHolder

Extracts the Authentication object for the currently authenticated user from SecurityContext

Handles the case where a user is not authenticated, but it is manipulating data. Since we protected all the endpoints, this case should never happen, but we'll include it for completeness.

Extracts the username of the currently authenticated user from the Authentication object

ADDING AUDIT METADATA FOR USERS WHO CREATED OR UPDATED AN R2DBC DATA ENTITY

When a `ReactiveAuditorAware` bean is defined and auditing is enabled, Spring Data will use it to extract the username of the currently authenticated user represented as a `String`. Even in this case, we can use `@CreatedBy` and `@LastModifiedBy` to annotate two new fields in the `Order` record. They will be populated by Spring Data automatically whenever a create or update operation is performed on the entity.

Listing 12.27   Fields to capture user audit metadata in an R2DBC entity

```
@Table("orders")
public record Order (
  ...
                          Who created
  @CreatedBy              the entity
  String createdBy,

                          Who modified
  @LastModifiedBy         the entity the
  String lastModifiedBy,  last time

) {
  public static Order of(String bookIsbn, String bookName,
    Double bookPrice, Integer quantity, OrderStatus status
  ) {
    return new Order(null, bookIsbn, bookName, bookPrice, quantity, status,
      null, null, null, null, 0);
  }
}
```

After adding the new fields, we need to update a few classes using the `Order` all-args constructor, which now requires you to pass values for `createdBy` and `lastModifiedBy`.

The `OrderService` class contains the logic for updating dispatched orders. Open it and change the `buildDispatchedOrder()` method to ensure the audit metadata is correctly passed along when calling the data layer.

Listing 12.28 Including the existing audit metadata when updating an order

```
@Service
public class OrderService {

  ...

  private Order buildDispatchedOrder(Order existingOrder) {
    return new Order(
      existingOrder.id(),
      existingOrder.bookIsbn(),
      existingOrder.bookName(),
      existingOrder.bookPrice(),
      existingOrder.quantity(),
      OrderStatus.DISPATCHED,
      existingOrder.createdDate(),
      existingOrder.lastModifiedDate(),
      existingOrder.createdBy(),            ⊲──┐ Who created
      existingOrder.lastModifiedBy(),       ⊲─┐  the entity
      existingOrder.version()                 │ Who last
    );                                        │ updated
  }                                           │ the entity
}
```

I'll leave it to you to update the autotests in a similar way. You can also extend the tests in `OrderJsonTests` to verify the serialization of the new fields. As a reference, you can check Chapter12/12-end/order-service in the code repository accompanying this book. Ensure that you update the tests using the `Order()` constructor, or the application build will fail.

WRITING A FLYWAY MIGRATION TO ADD THE NEW AUDIT METADATA TO THE SCHEMA

Similar to what we did for Catalog Service, we need to write a migration to update the database schema with the two new fields hosting the usernames of who created an entity and who modified it last.

In the src/main/resources/db/migration folder for the Order Service project, create a new V2__Add_user_audit.sql migration script to add two new columns to the orders table. Ensure you type two underscores after the version number.

Listing 12.29 Adding new audit metadata to the `orders` table

```
ALTER TABLE orders
  ADD COLUMN created_by varchar(255);          ⊲──┐ Add a column for the username
ALTER TABLE orders                                  of who created the row.
  ADD COLUMN last_modified_by varchar(255);    ⊲──┐ Add a column for the username
                                                    of who last updated the row.
```

ENSURING USER DATA PRIVACY

There's one last requirement we haven't covered yet: ensuring that order data is only accessed by the users who created the orders. No user should be able to see the orders from another person.

There are a few different solutions for implementing this requirement in Spring. We'll follow these steps:

1 Add a custom query to OrderRepository to filter orders based on the user who created them.
2 Update OrderService to use the new query instead of the default findAll().
3 Update OrderController to extract the username of the currently authenticated user from the security context and pass it to OrderService when asking for orders.

WARNING   We'll rely on a specific solution that ensures each user can only access their own orders via the /orders endpoint. However, this won't prevent developers from using the other methods exposed by OrderRepository in the future and leaking private data. If you'd like to know how to improve this solution, refer to chapter 17 of *Spring Security in Action* by Laurențiu Spilcă (Manning, 2020).

Let's start with OrderRepository. Using the conventions you learned in chapter 5, define a method to find all orders created by the specified user. Spring Data will generate an implementation for it at runtime.

Listing 12.30   Defining a method returning orders created by a user

```
public interface OrderRepository
  extends ReactiveCrudRepository<Order,Long>         Custom method to query
{                                                    only the orders created
  Flux<Order> findAllByCreatedBy(String userId);  ◁┘ by the given user
}
```

Next we need to update the getAllOrders() method in OrderService to accept a username as input and use the new query method provided by OrderRepository.

Listing 12.31   Returning orders only for the specified user

```
@Service
public class OrderService {                          When requesting all
  private final OrderRepository orderRepository;      orders, the response
                                                      includes only those
  public Flux<Order> getAllOrders(String userId) {  ◁┘ belonging to the given
    return orderRepository.findAllByCreatedBy(userId);  user.
  }

  ...
}
```

Finally, let's update the `getAllOrders()` method in `OrderController`. As you learned in the previous chapter, you can autowire an object representing the currently authenticated user through the `@AuthenticationPrincipal` annotation. In Edge Service, the object was of type `OidcUser` because it's based on OpenID Connect authentication. Since Order Service is configured with JWT authentication, the principal will be of type `Jwt`. We can use the JWT (an Access Token) to read the `sub` claim containing the username for which the Access Token was generated (the subject).

Listing 12.32 Getting the username and returning only orders created by them

```
@RestController
@RequestMapping("orders")
public class OrderController {
  private final OrderService orderService;

  @GetMapping                               Autowires the JWT
  public Flux<Order> getAllOrders(          representing the currently
    @AuthenticationPrincipal Jwt jwt    <── authenticated user
  ) {
    return orderService.getAllOrders(jwt.getSubject());   <── Extracts the subject
  }                                                            of the JWT and uses
                                                               it as the user
  ...                                                          identifier
}
```

That's it for Order Service. In the next section, you'll write some autotests to verify the data auditing and protection requirements.

12.4.4 Testing data auditing and protection with @WithMockUser and Spring Data R2DBC

In the previous section we configured data auditing for users and enforced a policy to return only the orders for the currently authenticated user. This section will show you how to test the data auditing as a slice test. To verify the data protection requirement, you can refer to the repository accompanying the book and check how it's been covered by the integration tests in the `OrderServiceApplicationTests` class (Chapter12/12-end/order-service/src/test/java).

Data auditing is applied at the repository level. We can extend the `OrderRepositoryR2dbcTests` class with extra test cases covering the scenario where the user is authenticated and when it is not.

Similar to what we did in Catalog Service, we can use the `@WithMockUser` annotation from Spring Security to execute a test method in an authenticated context, relying on a mock user representation.

Listing 12.33 Testing data auditing when users are authenticated or not

```
@DataR2dbcTest
@Import(DataConfig.class)
@Testcontainers
```

```
class OrderRepositoryR2dbcTests {
  ...

  @Test
  void whenCreateOrderNotAuthenticatedThenNoAuditMetadata() {
    var rejectedOrder = OrderService.buildRejectedOrder( "1234567890", 3);
    StepVerifier.create(orderRepository.save(rejectedOrder))
      .expectNextMatches(order -> Objects.isNull(order.createdBy()) &&
        Objects.isNull(order.lastModifiedBy()))
      .verifyComplete();
  }

  @Test
  @WithMockUser("marlena")
  void whenCreateOrderAuthenticatedThenAuditMetadata() {
    var rejectedOrder = OrderService.buildRejectedOrder( "1234567890", 3);
    StepVerifier.create(orderRepository.save(rejectedOrder))
      .expectNextMatches(order -> order.createdBy().equals("marlena") &&
        order.lastModifiedBy().equals("marlena"))
      .verifyComplete();
  }
}
```

When the user is not authenticated, no audit metadata is saved.

When the user is authenticated, the information about who created or updated the entity is correctly included in the data.

Open a Terminal window, navigate to the Catalog Service root folder, and run the newly added tests as follows:

```
$ ./gradlew test --tests OrderRepositoryR2dbcTests
```

If you experience any failures, it might be because you haven't updated the test cases where the `Order()` constructor is used. We have added new fields to the domain model, so remember to update those test cases as well.

That concludes our discussion of authentication, authorization, and auditing for both imperative and reactive cloud native applications using Spring Boot, Spring Security, Spring Data, and Keycloak.

Polar Labs

Feel free to apply what you have learned in the previous chapters and update Catalog Service and Order Service for deployment.

1 Update the Docker Compose definitions for both applications to configure the Keycloak URL. You can use the container name (`polar-keycloak:8080`), which gets resolved by the built-in Docker DNS.

2 Update the Kubernetes manifests for both applications to configure the Keycloak URL. You can use the Keycloak Service name (`polar-keycloak`) as the URL, since all interactions happen within the cluster.

You can refer to the Chapter12/12-end folder in the code repository accompanying the book to check the final results (https://github.com/ThomasVitale/cloud-native -spring-in-action). You can deploy the backing services from the manifests available in

the Chapter12/12-end/polar-deployment/kubernetes/platform/development folder
with `kubectl apply -f services` or the entire cluster with `./create-cluster.sh`.

Summary

- In an OIDC/OAuth2 setup, the Client (Edge Service) is granted access to a Resource Server (Catalog Service and Order Service) on behalf of the user through an Access Token.
- Spring Cloud Gateway provides a `TokenRelay` filter to add the Access Token to any request routed downstream automatically.
- Following the JWT format, ID Tokens and Access Tokens can propagate relevant information as claims about the authenticated user. For example, you can add a `roles` claim and configure Spring Security with authorization policies depending on the user role.
- Spring Boot applications can be configured as OAuth2 Resource Servers using Spring Security.
- In an OAuth2 Resource Server, the strategy for authenticating users is entirely based on a valid Access Token provided in the `Authorization` header of each request. We call it JWT authentication.
- In an OAuth2 Resource Server, security policies are still enforced through a `SecurityFilterChain` (imperative) or `SecurityWebFilterChain` (reactive) bean.
- Spring Security represents permissions, roles, and scopes as `GrantedAuthority` objects.
- You can provide a custom `JwtAuthenticationConverter` bean to define how to extract granted authorities from a JWT, for example, using the `roles` claim.
- Granted authorities can be used to adopt an RBAC strategy and protect endpoints, depending on the user role.
- The Spring Data libraries support auditing to track who created an entity and who updated it last. You can enable this feature in both Spring Data JDBC and Spring Data R2DBC by configuring an `AuditorAware` (or `ReactiveAuditorAware`) bean to return the username of the currently authenticated user.
- When data auditing is enabled, you can use the `@CreatedBy` and `@LastModifiedBy` annotations to automatically inject the right values when a create or update operation occurs.
- Testing security is challenging, but Spring Security provides convenient utilities to make that easier, including expressions that mutate HTTP requests to include a JWT Access Token (`.with(jwt())` or `.mutateWith(mockJwt())`) or to run a test case in a specific security context for a given user (`@WithMockUser`).
- Testcontainers can help write full integration tests by using an actual Keycloak container to verify the interactions with Spring Security.

Part 4

Cloud native production

It's been an incredible journey so far. Chapter after chapter, we have gone through patterns, principles, and best practices for working with cloud native applications, and we've built a bookshop system using Spring Boot and Kubernetes. It's time to prepare for production. Part 4 guides you through the last few steps to make your cloud native applications production-ready, addressing concerns like observability, configuration management, secrets management, and deployment strategies. It also covers serverless and native images.

Chapter 13 describes how to make your cloud native applications observable using Spring Boot Actuator, OpenTelemetry, and the Grafana observability stack. You'll learn how to configure Spring Boot applications to produce relevant telemetry data, such as logs, health, metrics, traces, and more. Chapter 14 covers advanced configuration and secrets management strategies, including Kubernetes-native options like ConfigMaps, Secrets, and Kustomize. Chapter 15 guides you through the final steps of your cloud native journey and teaches you how to configure Spring Boot for production. You'll then set up continuous deployment for your applications and deploy them to a Kubernetes cluster in the public cloud, adopting a GitOps strategy. Finally, chapter 16 covers serverless architectures and functions with Spring Native and Spring Cloud Function. You'll also learn about Knative and its powerful features that provide a superior developer experience on top of Kubernetes.

Observability and monitoring

This chapter covers

- Logging with Spring Boot, Loki, and Fluent Bit
- Using health probes with Spring Boot Actuator and Kubernetes
- Producing metrics with Spring Boot Actuator, Prometheus, and Grafana
- Configuring distributed tracing with OpenTelemetry and Tempo
- Managing applications with Spring Boot Actuator

In the previous chapters, you learned about several patterns and technologies you can use to build secure, scalable, and resilient applications. However, we still lack visibility into the Polar Bookshop system, especially when something goes wrong. Before going to production, we should ensure our applications are observable and that the deployment platform provides all the tools needed to monitor and gain insights into the system.

Monitoring involves checking the telemetry available for the application and defining alerts for known failure states. *Observability* goes beyond that and aims at reaching a state where we can ask arbitrary questions about the system without

447

knowing the question in advance. The product team should ensure their applications expose relevant information; and the platform team should provide an infrastructure for consuming that information and asking questions about their operations.

As you'll remember from chapter 1, *observability* is one of the properties of cloud native applications. Observability is a measure of how well we can infer the internal state of an application from its outputs. In chapter 2, you learned about the 15-Factor methodology, which contains two factors that help build observable applications. Factor 14 suggests treating your applications as space probes and reasoning about what kind of telemetry you'd need to monitor and control your applications remotely, such as logs, metrics, and traces. Factor 6 recommends treating logs as a stream of events rather than dealing with log files.

In this chapter, you'll learn how to ensure your Spring Boot applications expose relevant information to infer their internal states, such as logs, health probes, metrics, traces, and additional valuable data regarding schema migrations and builds. I'll also show you how to use the Grafana open source observability stack to validate the changes you'll make to your applications. However, I won't go into too many details, because that's something the platform team deploys and operates.

> **NOTE** The source code for the examples in this chapter is available in the Chapter13/13-begin and Chapter13/13-end folders, which contain the initial and final states of the project (https://github.com/ThomasVitale/cloud-native -spring-in-action).

13.1 *Logging with Spring Boot, Loki, and Fluent Bit*

Logs (or *event logs*) are discrete records of something that happened over time in a software application. They are composed of a timestamp necessary to answer the question "when did the event happen?" and some information providing details about the event and its context, which lets us answer questions like "what happened at this time?", "which thread was processing the event?", or "which user/tenant was in the context?"

During troubleshooting and debugging tasks, logs are among the essential tools we can use to reconstruct what happened at a specific point in time in a single application instance. They're usually categorized according to the type or severity of the event, such as *trace, debug, info, warn,* and *error.* It's a flexible mechanism that lets us log only the most severe events in production while still giving us the chance to change the log level temporarily during debugging.

The format of a log record can vary, going from simple plain text to a more organized collection of key/value pairs to fully structured records produced in a JSON format.

Traditionally we've configured logs to be printed out in files located on the host machine, which has resulted in applications dealing with filename conventions, file rotation, and file sizes. In the cloud we follow the 15-Factor methodology, which recommends treating logs as events streamed to the standard output. Cloud native applications stream logs and are not concerned with how they are processed or stored.

This section will teach you how to add and configure logs in Spring Boot applications. Then I'll explain how logs are collected and aggregated in a cloud native infrastructure. Finally, you'll run Fluent Bit for log collection, run Loki for log aggregation, and use Grafana to query the logs produced by your Spring Boot applications.

13.1.1 Logging with Spring Boot

Spring Boot comes with built-in support and auto-configuration for the most common logging frameworks, including Logback, Log4J2, Commons Logging, and Java Util Logging. By default, Logback is used (https://logback.qos.ch), but you can easily replace it with another library thanks to the abstraction provided by the Simple Logging Facade for Java (SLF4J).

Using the interfaces from SLF4J (www.slf4j.org), you have the freedom to change the logging library without changing your Java code. Furthermore, cloud native applications should treat logs as events and stream them to the standard output. That's precisely what Spring Boot does out of the box. Convenient, right?

CONFIGURING LOGGING IN SPRING BOOT

Event logs are categorized by level with decreasing details and increasing importance: trace, debug, info, warn, error. By default, Spring Boot logs everything from the *info* level up.

A *logger* is a class that produces log events. You can set logger levels through configuration properties, with options to apply global configurations or to target specific packages or classes. For example, in chapter 9 we set a *debug* logger to get more details about the circuit breakers implemented with Resilience4J (in the application.yml file in the Edge Service project):

```
logging:
  level:
    io.github.resilience4j: debug    ◁── Sets a debug logger
                                         for the Resilience4J
                                         library
```

You might need to configure multiple loggers at the same time. In that case, you can collect them in a *log group* and apply the configuration to the group directly. Spring Boot provides two predefined log groups, `web` and `sql`, but you can also define your own. For example, to better analyze the behavior of the circuit breakers defined in the Edge Service application, you could define a log group and configure a log level for both Resilience4J and Spring Cloud Circuit Breaker.

In the Edge Service project (edge-service), you can configure the new log group in the application.yml file as follows.

> **Listing 13.1 Configuring a group to control the circuit breaker logs**

```
logging:
  group:
    circuitbreaker: io.github.resilience4j,       ◁── Collects multiple loggers
↪org.springframework.cloud.circuitbreaker            into a group to apply the
                                                     same configuration
```

```
level:
    circuitbreaker: info
```
⟵ **Sets an "info" logger for both Resilience4J and Spring Cloud Circuit Breaker, which is easy to change if you need to debug the circuit breakers**

By default, each event log provides essential information, including the date and time of the occurrence, the log level, the process identifier (PID), the name of the thread from which the event was triggered, the logger name, and the log message. If you check the application logs from a Terminal that supports ANSI, the log messages will also be colored to improve readability (figure 13.1). The logging format can be customized using the `logging.pattern` configuration property group.

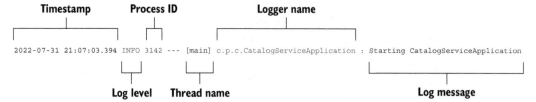

Figure 13.1   Event logs include a timestamp, contextual information, and a message about what happened.

> **NOTE**   Spring Boot provides extensive options for configuring logging to files. Since that's not useful for cloud native applications, I won't cover it in this book. If you're interested in the subject, see the official documentation to learn more about log files (http://spring.io/projects/spring-boot).

ADDING LOGS TO SPRING BOOT APPLICATIONS

Besides configuring loggers for the frameworks and libraries used in your project, you should define event logs in your code whenever applicable. How much logging is enough? It depends on the context. In general, I reckon that it's better to have too much logging than too little. I've seen many deployments that just contain changes to add more logging, while it's pretty rare to see the opposite.

Thanks to the SLF4J façade, the syntax for defining new event logs in Java is the same no matter which logging library you use: a `Logger` instance created from a `LoggerFactory`. Let's see how it works by adding new log messages to the web controller in Catalog Service.

In the Catalog Service project (catalog-service), go to the `BookController` class, define a `Logger` instance from SLF4J, and add messages to be printed out whenever a client calls the application's REST API.

Listing 13.2   Defining log events using SL4FJ

```
package com.polarbookshop.catalogservice.web;

import org.slf4j.Logger;
import org.slf4j.LoggerFactory;
...


@RestController
@RequestMapping("books")
public class BookController {
  private static final Logger log =
    LoggerFactory.getLogger(BookController.class);
  private final BookService bookService;

  @GetMapping
  public Iterable<Book> get() {
    log.info(
      "Fetching the list of books in the catalog"
    );
    return bookService.viewBookList();
  }
}


  ...
}
```

Defines a logger for the BookController class

Logs the given message at the "info" level

NOTE Go ahead and define new loggers and log events for all the applications composing the Polar Bookshop system wherever it makes sense. As a reference, you can look at the source code repository accompanying this book (Chapter13/13-end).

> **The Mapped Diagnostic Context (MDC)**
>
> You'll likely need to add common information to your log messages, such as the identifier of the currently authenticated user, the tenant for the current context, or the request URI. You could directly add that information to your log message, as you did in the previous listing, and it would work, but the data would not be structured. Instead, I prefer working with structured data.
>
> SLF4J and common logging libraries, like Logback and Log4J2, support adding structured information depending on the request context (authentication, tenant, thread) through a tool named Mapped Diagnostic Context (MDC). If you'd like to know more about MDC, I recommend checking the official documentation for the specific logging library you're using.

Now that our applications log messages as an event stream, we need to collect and store them in a central place that we can query. The following section will provide a solution to accomplish that.

13.1.2 *Managing logs with Loki, Fluent Bit, and Grafana*

When you move to distributed systems like microservices and complex environments like the cloud, managing logs becomes challenging and requires a different solution than in more traditional applications. If something goes wrong, where can we find data about the failure? Traditional applications would rely on log files stored on the host machine. Cloud native applications are deployed in dynamic environments, are replicated, and have different life spans. We need to collect the logs from all applications running in the environment and send them to a central component where they can be aggregated, stored, and searched.

There are plenty of options for managing logs in the cloud. Cloud providers have their own offerings, like Azure Monitor Logs and Google Cloud Logging. There are also many enterprise solutions available on the market, such as Honeycomb, Humio, New Relic, Datadog, and Elastic.

For Polar Bookshop, we'll use a solution based on the Grafana observability stack (https://grafana.com). It's composed of open source technologies, and you can run it yourself in any environment. It's also available as a managed service (Grafana Cloud) offered by Grafana Labs.

The components of the Grafana stack we'll use for managing logs are Loki for log storage and search, Fluent Bit for log collection and aggregation, and Grafana for log data visualization and querying.

> **NOTE** Which technology you use for managing logs is a platform choice and shouldn't impact the applications at all. For example, you should be able to replace the Grafana stack with Humio without making any changes to the Polar Bookshop applications.

We need a *log collector* to fetch log messages from the standard output of all the running applications. Using the Grafana stack, you're free to choose a log collector from among several options. For the Polar Bookshop system, we'll use Fluent Bit, an open source and CNCF-graduated project that "enables you to collect logs and metrics from multiple sources, enrich them with filters, and distribute them to any defined destination" (https://fluentbit.io). Fluent Bit is a subproject of Fluentd, "an open source data collector for unified logging layer" (www.fluentd.org).

Fluent Bit will collect logs from all running containers and forward them to Loki, which will store them and make them searchable. Loki is "a log aggregation system designed to store and query logs from all your applications and infrastructure" (https://grafana.com/oss/loki).

Finally, Grafana will use Loki as a data source and provide log visualization features. Grafana "allows you to query, visualize, alert on and understand" your telemetry, no matter where it is stored (https://grafana.com/oss/grafana). Figure 13.2 illustrates this logging architecture.

Let's start by running Grafana, Loki, and Fluent Bit as containers. In your Polar Deployment project (polar-deployment), update the Docker Compose configuration

Logging architecture using the Grafana stack

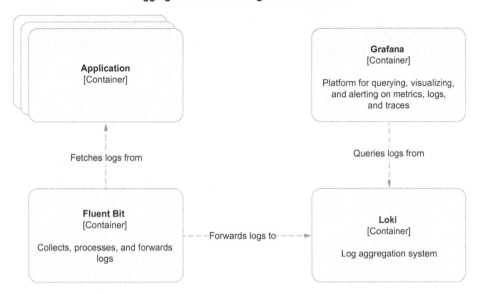

Figure 13.2 Logging architecture for cloud native applications based on the Grafana stack

(docker/docker-compose.yml) to include the new services. They are configured through files I have included in the source code repository accompanying this book (Chapter13/13-end/polar-deployment/docker/observability). Copy the observability folder over the same path in your own project.

Listing 13.3 Defining containers for Grafana, Loki, and Fluent Bit

```
version: "3.8"
services:
  ...

  grafana:
    image: grafana/grafana:9.1.2
    container_name: grafana
    depends_on:
      - loki
    ports:
      - "3000:3000"
    environment:
      - GF_SECURITY_ADMIN_USER=user
      - GF_SECURITY_ADMIN_PASSWORD=password
    volumes:
      - ./observability/grafana/datasource.yml:/etc/grafana/provisioning/
➥datasources/datasource.yml
      - ./observability/grafana/dashboards:/etc/grafana/provisioning/
➥dashboards
      - ./observability/grafana/grafana.ini:/etc/grafana/grafana.ini
```

Username and password to access Grafana ◁

Volumes are used to load configuration for data sources and dashboards. ◁

```
loki:
  image: grafana/loki:2.6.1
  container_name: loki
  depends_on:
    - fluent-bit
  ports:
    - "3100:3100"

fluent-bit:
  image: grafana/fluent-bit-plugin-loki:2.6.1-amd64
  container_name: fluent-bit
  ports:
    - "24224:24224"
  environment:
    - LOKI_URL=http://loki:3100/loki/api/v1/push        ◄──
  volumes:                                              ◄──
    - ./observability/fluent-bit/fluent-bit.conf:/fluent-bit/etc/
⮩fluent-bit.conf
```

Defines the Loki URL used to forward log messages

Volumes are used to load configuration for collecting and delivering logs.

Next, start all three containers with the following command:

```
$ docker-compose up -d grafana
```

Thanks to the dependencies defined in Docker Compose between containers, starting Grafana will also run Loki and Fluent Bit.

Fluent Bit can be configured to collect logs from different sources. For Polar Bookshop we'll rely on the Fluentd driver available in Docker to collect logs automatically from running containers. The Docker platform itself listens to the log events from each container and routes them to the specified service. In Docker, a logging driver can be configured directly on a container. For example, update the Catalog Service configuration in Docker Compose to use the Fluentd logging driver, which will send the logs over to the Fluent Bit container.

Listing 13.4   Using Fluentd driver to route container logs to Fluent Bit

```
version: "3.8"
services:
  ...

  catalog-service:
    depends_on:
      - fluent-bit        ◄──
      - polar-keycloak
      - polar-postgres
    image: "catalog-service"
    container_name: "catalog-service"
    ports:
      - 9001:9001
      - 8001:8001
    environment:
      - BPL_JVM_THREAD_COUNT=50
      - BPL_DEBUG_ENABLED=true
```

Ensures the Fluent Bit container is started before Catalog Service

```
          - BPL_DEBUG_PORT=8001
          - SPRING_CLOUD_CONFIG_URI=http://config-service:8888
          - SPRING_DATASOURCE_URL=
⇒jdbc:postgresql://polar-postgres:5432/polardb_catalog
          - SPRING_PROFILES_ACTIVE=testdata
          - SPRING_SECURITY_OAUTH2_RESOURCESERVER_JWT_ISSUER_URI=
⇒http://host.docker.internal:8080/realms/PolarBookshop
      logging:
        driver: fluentd          ◁——|  Which logging
        options:                       driver to use
          fluentd-address: 127.0.0.1:24224   ◁——|  The address of the Fluent
                                                   Bit instance where the
   Section to configure the                        logs should be routed
   container logging driver
```

Next, package Catalog Service as a container image (`./gradlew bootBuildImage`), and run the application container as follows:

```
$ docker-compose up -d catalog-service
```

Thanks to the dependencies defined in Docker Compose between containers, Keycloak and PostgreSQL will automatically be started as well.

Now we're ready to test the logging setup. First, send a few requests to Catalog Service to trigger the generation of some log messages:

```
$ http :9001/books
```

Next, open a browser window, head to Grafana (http://localhost:3000), and use the credentials configured in Docker Compose to log in (user/password). Then select the Explore page from the left menu, choose Loki as the data source, choose Last 1 Hour from the time drop-down menu, and run the following query to search for all the logs produced by the `catalog-service` container:

```
{container_name="/catalog-service"}
```

The result should be similar to what you can see in figure 13.3, showing the logs from application startup as well as the custom log messages you added to the `BookController` class.

When you're done testing the logging setup, stop all containers with `docker-compose down`.

> **NOTE** Following the same approach, update the Docker Compose configuration for all the other Spring Boot applications in the Polar Bookshop system to use the Fluentd logging driver and rely on Fluent Bit for collecting logs. As a reference, you can look at the source code repository accompanying this book (Chapter13/13-end/polar-deployment/docker).

Logs provide some information about how an application behaves, but they're not enough to infer its internal state. The next section will cover how you can make applications expose more data about their health status.

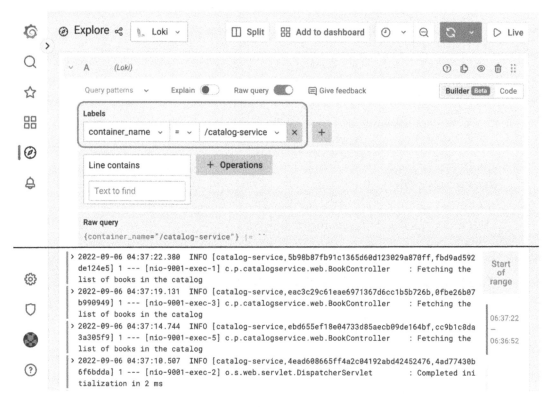

Figure 13.3   In Grafana, you can browse and search log messages aggregated and stored by Loki.

13.2   *Health probes with Spring Boot Actuator and Kubernetes*

Once an application is deployed, how can we tell if it's healthy? Is it capable of handling new requests? Did it enter a faulty state? Cloud native applications should provide information about their health so that monitoring tools and deployment platforms can detect when there's something wrong and act accordingly. We need dedicated health endpoints to check on the status of the application and any components or services it might use.

The deployment platform can periodically invoke health endpoints exposed by applications. A monitoring tool could trigger an alert or a notification when an application instance is unhealthy. In the case of Kubernetes, the platform will check the health endpoints and automatically replace the faulty instance or temporarily stop sending traffic to it until it's ready to handle new requests again.

For Spring Boot applications, you can leverage the Actuator library to expose information about their health through a /actuator/health HTTP endpoint, including details about the application's status and the components in use, like databases, event brokers, and config servers.

Spring Boot Actuator is a useful library, providing many endpoints for monitoring and managing Spring Boot applications. Such endpoints can be exposed through HTTP or JMX, but either way we must protect them from unauthorized access. We'll limit ourselves to using the HTTP endpoints, so we can use Spring Security to define access policies like those for any other endpoint we've worked with so far.

This section will cover configuring health endpoints in Spring Boot applications using Actuator. You'll then see how you can define liveness and readiness probes so Kubernetes can use its self-healing functionality.

13.2.1   Defining health probes for Spring Boot applications using Actuator

First of all, open the build.gradle file in the Catalog Service project (catalog-service), and ensure that it contains a dependency on Spring Boot Actuator (we used it in chapter 4 for refreshing configuration at runtime).

Listing 13.5   Adding dependency for Spring Boot Actuator in Catalog Service

```
dependencies {
    ...
    implementation 'org.springframework.boot:spring-boot-starter-actuator'
}
```

There are a few viable solutions for protecting the Spring Boot Actuator endpoints. For example, you could enable HTTP Basic authentication just for the Actuator endpoints, while all the others will keep using OpenID Connect and OAuth2. For simplicity, in the Polar Bookshop system, we'll keep the Actuator endpoints unauthenticated from inside the Kubernetes cluster and block any access to them from the outside (as you'll see in chapter 15).

WARNING   In a real production scenario, I would recommend protecting access to the Actuator endpoints even from within the cluster.

Go to the `SecurityConfig` class of your Catalog Service project and update the Spring Security configuration to allow unauthenticated access to the Spring Boot Actuator endpoints.

Listing 13.6   Allowing unauthenticated access to the Actuator endpoints

```
@EnableWebSecurity                                          Allows unauthenticated access
public class SecurityConfig {                                to any Spring Boot Actuator
                                                                           endpoint
    @Bean
    SecurityFilterChain filterChain(HttpSecurity http) throws Exception {
        return http
            .authorizeHttpRequests(authorize -> authorize
                .mvcMatchers("/actuator/**").permitAll()           ◁──
                .mvcMatchers(HttpMethod.GET, "/", "/books/**").permitAll()
                .anyRequest().hasRole("employee")
            )
```

```
    .oauth2ResourceServer(OAuth2ResourceServerConfigurer::jwt)
    .sessionManagement(sessionManagement -> sessionManagement
      .sessionCreationPolicy(SessionCreationPolicy.STATELESS))
    .csrf(AbstractHttpConfigurer::disable)
    .build();
  }
}
```

Finally, open the application.yml file in your Catalog Service project (catalog-service), and configure Actuator to expose the health HTTP endpoint. If you followed the examples in chapter 4, you might have an existing configuration for the `refresh` endpoint. In that case, go ahead and replace it with the `health` endpoint.

> **Listing 13.7   Exposing the `health` Actuator endpoint**

```
management:
  endpoints:
    web:                          Exposes the
      exposure:                   /actuator/health
        include: health    ◁──┘   endpoint via HTTP
```

Let's check the result. First we need to run all the backing services used by Catalog Service: Config Service, Keycloak, and PostgreSQL. We'll run them as containers. Package Config Service as a container image (`./gradlew bootBuildImage`). Then open a Terminal window, navigate to the folder where you keep your Docker Compose file (polar-deployment/docker), and run the following command:

```
$ docker-compose up -d config-service polar-postgres polar-keycloak
```

After ensuring that all the containers are ready, run Catalog Service on the JVM (`./gradlew bootRun`), open a Terminal window, and send an HTTP GET request to the health endpoint:

```
$ http :9001/actuator/health
```

The endpoint will return the overall health status for the Catalog Service application, which can be one of UP, OUT_OF_SERVICE, DOWN, or UNKNOWN. When the health status is UP, the endpoint returns a 200 OK response. If it's not, it produces a 503 Service Unavailable response.

```
{
  "status": "UP"
}
```

By default, Spring Boot Actuator only returns the overall health status. Through application properties, however, you can make it provide more specific information regarding several components by the application. To better protect access to this kind of information, you can enable showing health details and components always (always) or only when the request is authorized (when_authorized). Since we're not protecting the Actuator endpoints at the application level, let's make the extra information always available.

Listing 13.8 Configuring the `health` endpoint to expose more information

```
management:
  endpoints:
    web:
      exposure:
        include: health
  endpoint:
    health:
      show-details: always
      show-components: always
```

Always shows details about the application's health

Always shows information about the components used by the application

---

Once again, rerun Catalog Service (`./gradlew bootRun`), and send an HTTP GET request to http://localhost:9001/actuator/health. This time, the resulting JSON object contains more detailed information about the application's health. Here's a partial result as an example.

```
{
  "components": {
    "clientConfigServer": {
      "details": {
        "propertySources": [
          "configserver:https://github.com/PolarBookshop/
config-repo/catalog-service.yml",
          "configClient"
        ]
      },
      "status": "UP"
    },
    "db": {
      "details": {
        "database": "PostgreSQL",
        "validationQuery": "isValid()"
      },
      "status": "UP"
    },
    ...
  },
  "status": "UP"
}
```

Detailed health information about components and features used by the application

Overall application health status

The generic health endpoint provided by Spring Boot Actuator is useful for monitoring and configuring alerts or notifications, since it contains details regarding both the application and the integration with its backing services. In the next section, you'll see how to expose more specific information that's used by a deployment platform like Kubernetes to manage containers.

Before moving on, stop the application process (Ctrl-C), but keep all the current containers running. You'll need them soon!

13.2.2 *Configuring health probes in Spring Boot and Kubernetes*

Besides showing detailed information about the application's health, Spring Boot Actuator automatically detects when the application runs on a Kubernetes environment and enables the *health probes* to return liveness (/actuator/health/liveness) and readiness (/actuator/health/readiness) states, as illustrated in figure 13.4:

- *Liveness state*—When an application is not live, this means it has entered a faulty internal state from which it won't recover. By default, Kubernetes will try restarting it to fix the problem.
- *Readiness state*—When an application is not ready, this means it can't process new requests, either because it's still initializing all its components (during the startup phase) or because it's overloaded. Kubernetes will stop forwarding requests to that instance until it's ready to accept new requests again.

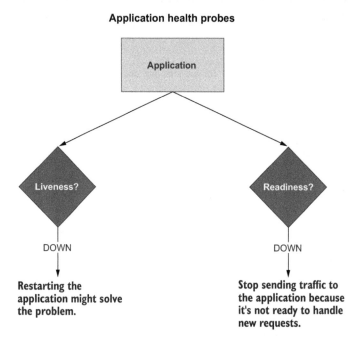

Figure 13.4   Kubernetes uses liveness and readiness probes to accomplish its self-healing features in case of failures.

CUSTOMIZING LIVENESS AND READINESS PROBES

To extend support for the health probes in any environment, you can configure Spring Boot Actuator through the dedicated properties. Open the Catalog Service project (catalog-service), and update the application.yml file as follows.

> Listing 13.9   Enabling liveness and readiness probes in any environment

```
management:
  endpoints:
```

```
web:
  exposure:
    include: health
endpoint:
  health:
    show-details: always
    show-components: always        Enables support
    probes:                        for the health
      enabled: true          ⟵──┘  probes
```

Let's check the result. All the backing services for Catalog Service should be up and running on Docker from the previous section. If not, go back and follow the instructions to start them all (`docker-compose up -d config-service polar-postgres polar-keycloak`). Then run Catalog Service on the JVM (`./gradlew bootRun`), and invoke the endpoint for the liveness probe:

```
$ http :9001/actuator/health/liveness
{
  "status": "UP"
}
```

The liveness state of a Spring Boot application indicates whether it's in a correct or broken internal state. If the Spring application context has started successfully, the internal state is valid. It doesn't depend on any external components. Otherwise, it will cause cascading failures, since Kubernetes will try to restart the broken instances.

   Finally, check the result for the readiness probe endpoint:

```
$ http :9001/actuator/health/readiness
{
  "status": "UP"
}
```

The readiness state of a Spring Boot application indicates whether it's ready to accept traffic and process new requests. During the startup phase or graceful shutdown, the application is not ready and will refuse any requests. It might also become temporarily not ready if, at some point, it's overloaded. When it's not ready, Kubernetes will not send any traffic to the application instance.

   When you're done testing the health endpoints, stop the application (Ctrl-C) and the containers (`docker-compose down`).

NOTE   Go ahead and add Spring Boot Actuator to all the applications composing the Polar Bookshop system. In Order Service and Edge Service, remember to configure unauthenticated access to the Actuator endpoints in the `SecurityConfig` class, as we did for Catalog Service. In Dispatcher Service you'll also need to add a dependency on Spring WebFlux (`org.springframe-work.boot:spring-boot-starter-webflux`) because Actuator needs a web server configured to serve its endpoints over HTTP. Then configure the health endpoints for all the applications, as you learned in this section. As a reference, you can look at the source code repository accompanying this book (Chapter13/13-end).

By default, the readiness probe in Spring Boot doesn't depend on any external components. You can decide whether any external systems should be included in the readiness probe.

For example, Catalog Service is an external system for Order Service. Should you include it in the readiness probe? Since Order Service adopts resilience patterns to deal with the scenario where Catalog Service is unavailable, you should keep Catalog Service out of the readiness probe. When it's not available, Order Service will keep working correctly, but with graceful functionality degradation.

Let's consider another example. Edge Service depends on Redis for storing and retrieving web session data. Should you include it in the readiness probe? Since Edge Service can't process any new requests without accessing Redis, including Redis in the readiness probe might be a good idea. Spring Boot Actuator will consider both the internal state of the application and the integration with Redis to determine whether the application is ready to accept new requests.

In the Edge Service project (edge-service), open the application.yml file, and define which indicators to use in the readiness probe: the application standard readiness state and the Redis health status. I'll assume you have already added Spring Boot Actuator to Edge Service and configured the health endpoints as described earlier.

> **Listing 13.10   Including Redis in the computation of the readiness state**

```
management:
  endpoints:
    web:
      exposure:
        include: health
  endpoint:
    health:
      show-details: always
      show-components: always
      probes:
        enabled: true
      group:                              ◁─┐  The readiness probe will combine
        readiness:                           │  the application's readiness state
          include: readinessState,redis   ◁─┘  and Redis's availability.
```

CONFIGURING LIVENESS AND READINESS PROBES IN KUBERNETES

Kubernetes relies on the health probes (liveness and readiness) to accomplish its tasks as a container orchestrator. For example, when the desired state of an application is to have three replicas, Kubernetes ensures there are always three application instances running. If any of them doesn't return a 200 response from the liveness probe, Kubernetes will restart it. When starting or upgrading an application instance, we'd like the process to happen without downtime for the user. Therefore, Kubernetes will not enable an instance in the load balancer until it's ready to accept new requests (when Kubernetes gets a 200 response from the readiness probe).

Since liveness and readiness information is application-specific, Kubernetes needs the application itself to declare how to retrieve that information. Relying on Actuator, Spring Boot applications provide liveness and readiness probes as HTTP endpoints. Let's see how we can configure Kubernetes to use those endpoints for the health probes.

In your Catalog Service project (catalog-service), open the Deployment manifest (k8s/deployment.yml), and update it with configuration for liveness and readiness probes as follows.

Listing 13.11   Configuring liveness and readiness probes for Catalog Service

```
apiVersion: apps/v1
kind: Deployment
metadata:
  name: catalog-service
  ...
spec:
  ...
  template:
    ...
    spec:
      containers:
        - name: catalog-service
          image: catalog-service
          ...
          livenessProbe:
            httpGet:
              path: /actuator/health/liveness
              port: 9001
            initialDelaySeconds: 10
            periodSeconds: 5
          readinessProbe:
            httpGet:
              path: /actuator/health/readiness
              port: 9001
            initialDelaySeconds: 5
            periodSeconds: 15
```

Annotations:
- Configuration for the liveness probe → `livenessProbe:`
- Uses an HTTP GET request to get the liveness state → `httpGet:`
- The endpoint to call for the liveness state → `path: /actuator/health/liveness`
- The port to use to fetch the liveness state → `port: 9001`
- An initial delay before starting checking the liveness state → `initialDelaySeconds: 10`
- The frequency for checking the liveness state → `periodSeconds: 5`
- Configuration for the readiness probe → `readinessProbe:`

Both probes can be configured so that Kubernetes will start using them after an initial delay (initialDelaySeconds), and you can also define the frequency with which to invoke them (periodSeconds). The initial delay should consider that the application will take a few seconds to start, and it will depend on the available computational resources. The polling period should not be too long, to reduce the time between the application instance entering a faulty state and the platform taking action to self-heal.

> **WARNING** If you run these examples on resource-constrained environments, you might need to adjust the initial delay and the polling frequency to allow the application more time to start and get ready to accept requests. You might

need to do the same when running these examples on Apple Silicon computers until ARM64 support is part of Paketo Buildpacks (you can follow the updates here: https://github.com/paketo-buildpacks/stacks/issues/51). That's because AMD64 container images are run on the Apple Silicon computers (ARM64) through a compatibility layer based on Rosetta, which impacts application startup time.

Go ahead and configure the liveness and readiness probes in the Deployment manifests for all the applications composing the Polar Bookshop system. As a reference, you can look at the source code repository accompanying this book (Chapter13/13-end).

On top of event logs, health information improves the information we can infer about the application's internal state, but it's not enough to achieve complete visibility. The following section will introduce the concept of metrics and how we can configure them in Spring Boot.

13.3 *Metrics and monitoring with Spring Boot Actuator, Prometheus, and Grafana*

To properly monitor, manage, and troubleshoot an application running in production, we need to be able to answer questions like "how much CPU and RAM is the application consuming?", "how many threads are used over time?", and "what's the rate of failing requests?" Event logs and health probes can't help us answer those questions. We need something more. We need more data.

Metrics are numeric data about the application, measured and aggregated in regular time intervals. We use metrics to track the occurrence of an event (such as an HTTP request being received), count items (such as the number of allocated JVM threads), measure the time taken to perform a task (such as the latency of a database query), or get the current value of a resource (such as current CPU and RAM consumption). This is all valuable information for understanding why an application behaves in a certain way. You can monitor metrics and set alerts or notifications for them.

Spring Boot Actuator collects application metrics out of the box by leveraging the Micrometer library (https://micrometer.io). Micrometer contains instrumentation code for collecting valuable metrics from common components in a JVM-based application. It provides a vendor-neutral façade so that you can export the metrics collected from Micrometer using different formats, such as Prometheus/Open Metrics, Humio, Datadog, and VMware Tanzu Observability. Just as SLF4J provides a vendor-neutral façade for logging libraries, Micrometer does the same for metrics exporters.

On top of the default Micrometer instrumentation libraries that are configured by Spring Boot, you can import additional instrumentation to collect metrics from specific libraries like Resilience4J or even define your own without vendor lock-in.

The most common format for exporting metrics is the one used by Prometheus, which is "an open-source systems monitoring and alerting toolkit" (https://prometheus.io). Just as Loki aggregates and stores event logs, Prometheus does the same with metrics.

In this section you'll see how to configure metrics in Spring Boot. Then you'll use Prometheus to aggregate metrics and Grafana to visualize them in dashboards.

13.3.1 *Configuring metrics with Spring Boot Actuator and Micrometer*

Spring Boot Actuator auto-configures Micrometer out of the box to collect metrics about a Java application. One way of exposing such metrics is by enabling the /actuator/metrics HTTP endpoint implemented by Actuator. Let's see how to do that.

In your Catalog Service project (catalog-service), update the application.yml file to expose the metrics endpoint via HTTP.

Listing 13.12 Exposing the `metrics` Actuator endpoint

```
management:
  endpoints:
    web:
      exposure:
        include: health, metrics
```

Exposes both health and metrics endpoints

Ensure the backing services required by Catalog Service are up and running with the following command:

```
$ docker-compose up -d polar-keycloak polar-postgres
```

Then run the application (./gradlew bootRun), and call the /actuator/metrics endpoint:

```
$ http :9001/actuator/metrics
```

The result is a collection of metrics you can further explore by adding the name of a metric to the endpoint (for example, /actuator/metrics/jvm.memory.used).

Micrometer provides the instrumentation to generate those metrics, but you might want to export them in a different format. After deciding which monitoring solution you'd like to use to collect and store the metrics, you'll need to add a specific dependency on that tool. In the Grafana observability stack, that tool is Prometheus.

In the Catalog Service project (catalog-service), update the build.gradle file with a dependency on the Micrometer library that provides integration with Prometheus. Remember to refresh or reimport the Gradle dependencies after the new addition.

Listing 13.13 Adding dependency for Micrometer Prometheus

```
dependencies {
  ...
  runtimeOnly 'io.micrometer:micrometer-registry-prometheus'
}
```

Then update the application.yml file to expose the prometheus Actuator endpoint via HTTP. You can also remove the more generic metrics endpoint, since we're not going to use it anymore.

Listing 13.14   Exposing the `prometheus` Actuator endpoint

```
management:
  endpoints:
    web:                              Exposes both health
      exposure:                       and prometheus
        include: health, prometheus ◁─┘ endpoints
```

The default strategy used by Prometheus is pull-based, meaning that a Prometheus instance scrapes (*pulls*) metrics in regular time intervals from the application via a dedicated endpoint, which is `/actuator/prometheus` in the Spring Boot scenario. Rerun the application (`./gradlew bootRun`), and call the Prometheus endpoint to check the result:

```
$ http :9001/actuator/prometheus
```

The result is the same collection of metrics you got from the `metrics` endpoint, but this time they are exported using a format understood by Prometheus. The following snippet shows an extract of the complete response, highlighting metrics related to the current number of threads:

```
# HELP jvm_threads_states_threads The current number of threads
# TYPE jvm_threads_states_threads gauge
jvm_threads_states_threads{state="terminated",} 0.0
jvm_threads_states_threads{state="blocked",} 0.0
jvm_threads_states_threads{state="waiting",} 13.0
jvm_threads_states_threads{state="timed-waiting",} 7.0
jvm_threads_states_threads{state="new",} 0.0
jvm_threads_states_threads{state="runnable",} 11.0
```

This format is based on plain text and is called *Prometheus exposition format*. Given the wide adoption of Prometheus for generating and exporting metrics, this format has been polished and standardized in OpenMetrics (https://openmetrics.io), a CNCF-incubating project. Spring Boot supports both the original Prometheus format (the default behavior) and OpenMetrics, depending on the `Accept` header of the HTTP request. If you'd like to get metrics according to the OpenMetrics format, you need to ask for it explicitly:

```
$ http :9001/actuator/prometheus \
    'Accept:application/openmetrics-text; version=1.0.0; charset=utf-8'
```

When you're done analyzing the Prometheus metrics, stop the application (Ctrl-C) and all the containers (`docker-compose down`).

> **NOTE** You might encounter scenarios where you need to collect metrics from ephemeral applications or batch jobs that don't run long enough to be pulled. In that case, Spring Boot lets you adopt a push-based strategy so that the application itself sends metrics to the Prometheus server. The official documentation explains how to configure such behavior (http://spring.io/ projects/spring-boot).

Spring Boot Actuator relies on the Micrometer instrumentation and provides auto-configuration to generate metrics for various technologies you might use in your applications: JVM, loggers, Spring MVC, Spring WebFlux, RestTemplate, WebClient, data sources, Hibernate, Spring Data, RabbitMQ, and more.

When Spring Cloud Gateway is in the classpath, as in the case of Edge Service, additional metrics are exported regarding the gateway routes. Some libraries, like Resilience4J, contribute dedicated Micrometer instrumentation through specific dependencies to register additional metrics.

Open the build.gradle file in the Edge Service project (edge-service), and add the following dependency to include Micrometer instrumentation for Resilience4J. Remember to refresh or reimport the Gradle dependencies after the new addition.

Listing 13.15   Adding dependency for Micrometer Resilience4J

```
dependencies {
  ...
  runtimeOnly 'io.github.resilience4j:resilience4j-micrometer'
}
```

Now that we've configured Spring Boot to expose metrics, let's see how we can configure Prometheus to scrape them and Grafana to visualize them.

13.3.2 *Monitoring metrics with Prometheus and Grafana*

Like Loki, Prometheus collects and stores metrics. It even provides a GUI to visualize them and to define alarms, but we'll use Grafana for that since it's a more comprehensive tool.

Metrics are stored as time-series data, containing the timestamp when they were registered and, optionally, labels. In Prometheus, labels are key/value pairs that add more information to the metric being recorded. For example, a metric registering the number of threads used by the application could be enhanced with labels qualifying the state of the threads (such as blocked, waiting, or idle). Labels help aggregate and query metrics.

Micrometer provides the concept of *tags*, which are equivalent to Prometheus's *labels*. In Spring Boot you can leverage configuration properties to define common labels for all the metrics produced by an application. For example, it's useful to add an `application` label that tags each metric with the name of the application that produces it.

Open the Catalog Service project (catalog-service), go to the application.yml file, and define a Micrometer tag with the application's name, which will result in a label that's applied to all metrics. Since the application name is already defined in the `spring.application.name` property, let's reuse that instead of duplicating the value.

Listing 13.16   Tagging all metrics with the application name

```
management:
  endpoints:
    web:
```

```
    exposure:
      include: health, prometheus
  endpoint:
    health:
      show-details: always
      show-components: always          Adds a Micrometer
      probes:                          common tag with the
        enabled: true                  application name. This
  metrics:                             results in a Prometheus
    tags:                              label being applied to all
      application: ${spring.application.name}  ◁──  metrics.
```

With this change, all metrics will have an `application` label with the application name, which is very useful when querying metrics and building dashboards to visualize them in Grafana:

```
jvm_threads_states_threads{application="catalog-service",
➡state="waiting",} 13.0
```

You have already encountered Grafana when working with logs. Just as you browsed logs using Loki as a data source for Grafana, you can query metrics using Prometheus as a data source. Furthermore, you can use the metrics stored by Prometheus to define dashboards, graphically visualize data, and set alarms or notifications when certain metrics return known critical values. For example, when the rate of failing HTTP requests per minute goes above a certain threshold, you might want to get an alarm or a notification so you can act on it. Figure 13.5 illustrates the monitoring architecture.

In your Polar Deployment project (polar-deployment), update the Docker Compose configuration (docker/docker-compose.yml) to include Prometheus. Grafana is already

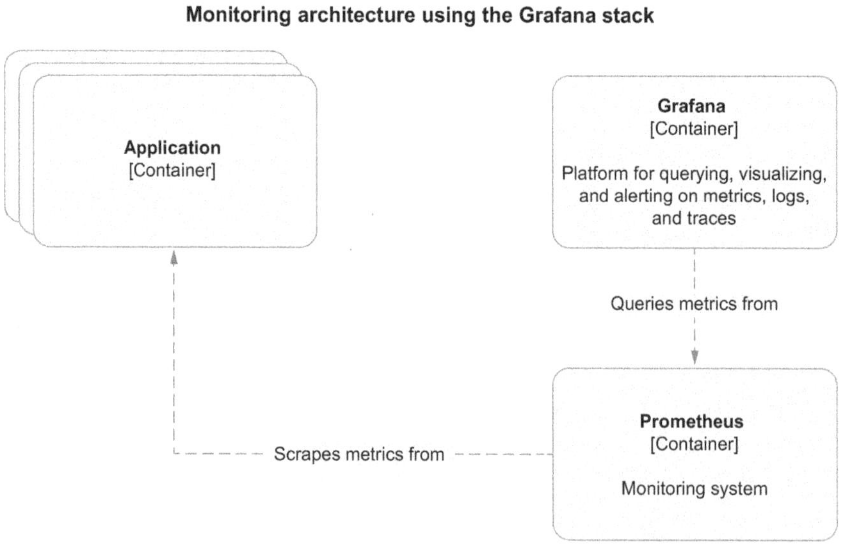

Monitoring architecture using the Grafana stack

Figure 13.5 Monitoring architecture for cloud native applications based on the Grafana stack

configured to use Prometheus as a data source in the configuration files you imported into your project earlier from Chapter13/13-end/polar-deployment/docker/observability.

Listing 13.17 Defining Prometheus container for collecting metrics

```
version: "3.8"
services:
  ...

  grafana:
    image: grafana/grafana:9.1.2
    container_name: grafana
    depends_on:
      - loki                    Ensures Prometheus
      - prometheus         ◁─── is started before
      ...                        Grafana

  prometheus:
    image: prom/prometheus:v2.38.0
    container_name: prometheus
    ports:                          Volumes are used to
      - "9090:9090"                 load configuration for
    volumes:                    ◁── Prometheus scraping.
      - ./observability/prometheus/prometheus.yml:/etc/prometheus/
      ↪ prometheus.yml
```

Unlike Loki, we don't need a dedicated component to collect metrics from the applications. The Prometheus Server container can both collect and store metrics.

Next, open a Terminal window, navigate to the folder where you keep your Docker Compose file (polar-deployment/docker), and run the complete monitoring stack with the following command:

```
$ docker-compose up -d grafana
```

The Prometheus container is configured to poll metrics every 2 seconds from all the Spring Boot applications in Polar Bookshop when they run as containers. Package Catalog Service as a container image (./gradlew bootBuildImage), and run it from Docker Compose:

```
$ docker-compose up -d catalog-service
```

Send a few requests to Catalog Service (http:9001/books), and then open a browser window and go to Grafana at http://localhost:3000 (user/password). In the Explore section, you can query metrics like you browsed logs. Choose Prometheus as the data source, select Last 5 Minutes from the time drop-down menu, and query the metrics related to the JVM memory used by the application as follows (figure 13.6):

```
jvm_memory_used_bytes{application="catalog-service"}
```

The metrics data can be used to draw dashboards for monitoring different application aspects. Select Dashboards > Manage from the left menu, and explore the dashboards I have included in Grafana, grouped within the Application folder.

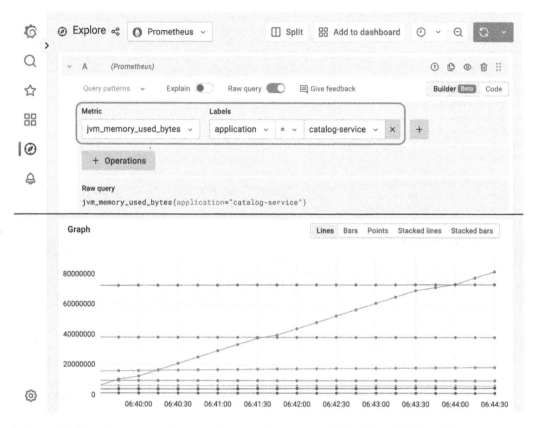

Figure 13.6   In Grafana, you can browse and query metrics aggregated and stored by Prometheus.

For example, open the JVM Dashboard (figure 13.7). It visualizes different metrics regarding the JVM where Spring Boot applications run, such as CPU usage, heap memory, non-heap memory, garbage collections, and threads.

On the Dashboards page, explore the other dashboards I have configured to get more visibility into the Polar Bookshop applications. Each dashboard is enhanced with additional information on its goal and how to use it.

When you're done checking the application metrics in Grafana, stop all the containers (docker-compose down).

13.3.3 *Configuring Prometheus metrics in Kubernetes*

When running applications in Kubernetes, we can use dedicated annotations to mark which containers the Prometheus server should scrape and inform it about the HTTP endpoint and port number to call.

You'll have the chance to test this setup later in the book, where we'll deploy the full Grafana observability stack in a production Kubernetes cluster. For now, let's prepare the Deployment manifests for all of the Spring Boot applications in Polar

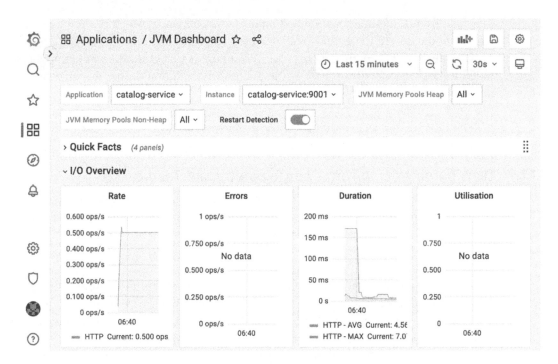

Figure 13.7   In Grafana, dashboards can be used to visualize Prometheus metrics.

Bookshop. For example, the following listing shows how to change the Catalog Service manifest (catalog-service/k8s/deployment.yml).

Listing 13.18   Annotating Catalog Service for Prometheus metrics scraping

```
apiVersion: apps/v1
kind: Deployment
metadata:
  name: catalog-service
  labels:
    app: catalog-service
spec:
  replicas: 1
  selector:
    matchLabels:
      app: catalog-service
  template:
    metadata:
      labels:
        app: catalog-service
      annotations:
        prometheus.io/scrape: "true"
        prometheus.io/path: /actuator/prometheus
        prometheus.io/port: "9001"
  ...
```

Signals that Prometheus should scrape containers in this Pod

Identifies the HTTP endpoint that exposes Prometheus metrics

Specifies the port number where the metrics endpoint is available

Annotations in Kubernetes manifests should be of type `String`, which is why quotes are needed in the case of values that could be mistakenly parsed as numbers or Boolean.

Go ahead and configure metrics and Prometheus for all the remaining applications in the Polar Bookshop system, including the configuration for the Kubernetes manifests. As a reference, you can look at the source code repository accompanying this book (Chapter13/13-end).

The next section will cover another type of telemetry we need in order to monitor applications and make them observable: traces.

13.4   *Distributed tracing with OpenTelemetry and Tempo*

Event logs, health probes, and metrics provide a wide variety of valuable data for inferring the internal state of an application. However, none of them consider that cloud native applications are distributed systems. A user request is likely to be processed by multiple applications, but so far we have no way to correlate data across application boundaries.

A simple way to solve that problem could be to generate an identifier for each request at the edge of the system (a *correlation ID*), use it in event logs, and pass it over to the other services involved. By using that correlation ID, we could fetch all log messages related to a particular transaction from multiple applications.

If we follow that idea further, we'll get to *distributed tracing*, a technique for tracking requests as they flow through a distributed system, letting us localize where errors occur and troubleshoot performance issues. There are three main concepts in distributed tracing:

- A *trace* represents the activities associated with a request or a transaction, identified uniquely by a *trace ID*. It's composed of one or more spans across one or more services.
- Each step of the request processing is called a *span*, characterized by start and end timestamps and identified uniquely by the pair trace ID and *span ID*.
- *Tags* are metadata that provide additional information regarding the span context, such as the request URI, the username of the currently logged-in user, or the tenant identifier.

Let's consider an example. In Polar Bookshop, you can fetch books through the gateway (Edge Service), and the request is then forwarded to Catalog Service. The trace related to handling such a request would involve these two applications and at least three spans:

- The first span is the step performed by Edge Service to accept the initial HTTP request.
- The second span is the step performed by Edge Service to route the request to Catalog Service.
- The third span is the step performed by Catalog Service to handle the routed request.

There are multiple choices related to distributed tracing systems. First, we must choose the format and protocol we'll use to generate and propagate traces. For this we'll use OpenTelemetry (also called *OTel*), a CNCF-incubating project that is quickly becoming the de facto standard for distributed tracing and aims at unifying the collection of telemetry data (https://opentelemetry.io).

Next we need to choose whether to use OpenTelemetry directly (with the OpenTelemetry Java instrumentation) or rely on a façade that instruments the code in a vendor-neutral way and integrates with different distributed tracing systems (such as Spring Cloud Sleuth). We'll go with the first option.

Once the applications are instrumented for distributed tracing, we'll need a tool to collect and store traces. In the Grafana observability stack, the distributed tracing backend of choice is Tempo, a project that "lets you scale tracing as far as possible with minimal operational cost and less complexity than ever before" (https://grafana.com/oss/tempo). Unlike the way we used Prometheus, Tempo follows a push-based strategy where the application itself pushes data to the distributed tracing backend.

This section will show you how to complete the Grafana observability setup with Tempo and use it to collect and store traces. Then I'll show you how to use the OpenTelemetry Java instrumentation in your Spring Boot applications to generate and send traces to Tempo. Finally, you'll learn how to query traces from Grafana.

OpenTelemetry, Spring Cloud Sleuth, and Micrometer Tracing

A few standards have emerged for implementing distributed tracing and defining guidelines for generating and propagating traces and spans. OpenZipkin is the more mature project (https://zipkin.io). OpenTracing and OpenCensus are more recent projects that have tried to standardize ways of instrumenting application code to support distributed tracing. They are both deprecated now, since they joined forces to work on OpenTelemetry: the ultimate framework to "instrument, generate, collect, and export telemetry data (metrics, logs, and traces)." Tempo supports all those options.

Spring Cloud Sleuth (https://spring.io/projects/spring-cloud-sleuth) is a project that provides auto-configuration for distributed tracing in Spring Boot applications. It takes care of instrumenting commonly used libraries in Spring applications and provides an abstraction layer on top of specific distributed tracing libraries. OpenZipkin is the default choice.

In this book, I decided to show you how to use the OpenTelemetry Java instrumentation directly for two main reasons. First, support for OpenTelemetry in Spring Cloud Sleuth is still experimental and not ready for production at the time of writing (https://github.com/spring-projects-experimental/spring-cloud-sleuth-otel).

Second, Spring Cloud Sleuth will not be developed further once Spring Framework 6 and Spring Boot 3 are released. The Spring project donated the Sleuth core framework to Micrometer and created a new Micrometer Tracing subproject aiming to provide a vendor-neutral façade for traces, similar to what Micrometer already does for metrics. Micrometer Tracing will provide support for OpenZipkin and OpenTelemetry. Based on Micrometer Tracing, code instrumentation will become a core aspect of all Spring libraries as part of the Spring Observability initiative.

13.4.1 *Managing traces with Tempo and Grafana*

A distributed tracing backend is responsible for aggregating, storing, and making traces searchable. Tempo is the solution in the Grafana observability stack. Figure 13.8 illustrates the tracing architecture.

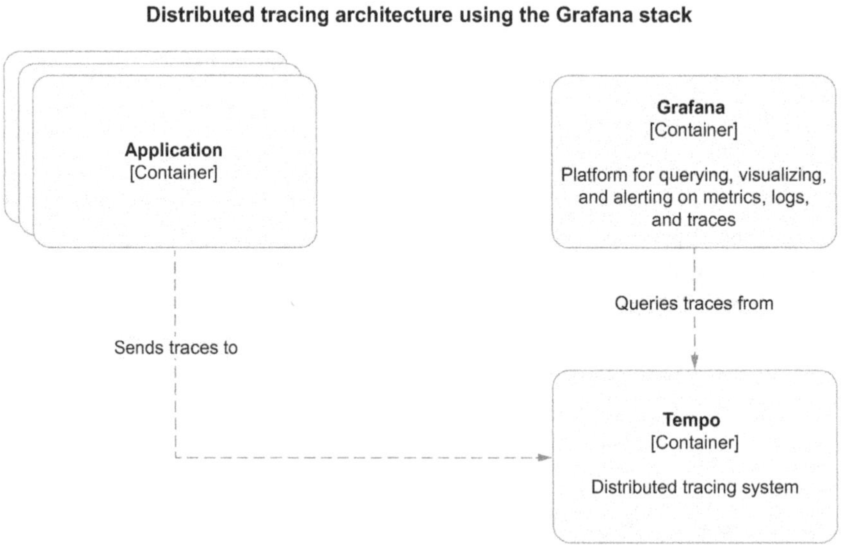

Distributed tracing architecture using the Grafana stack

Figure 13.8 Distributed tracing architecture for cloud native applications based on the Grafana stack

> **NOTE** Most vendors support OpenTelemetry, so you can easily swap your distributed tracing backend without changing anything in your applications. For example, instead of Tempo, you could send traces to other platforms like Honeycomb, Lightstep, or VMware Tanzu Observability.

First, let's update the Docker Compose file for Polar Bookshop to include Tempo (polar-deployment/docker/docker-compose.yml). Grafana is already configured to use Tempo as a data source in the configuration files you imported earlier into your project from Chapter13/13-end/polar-deployment/docker/observability.

Listing 13.19   Defining a Tempo container for collecting and storing traces

```
version: "3.8"
services:
  ...

  grafana:
    image: grafana/grafana:9.1.2
    container_name: grafana
    depends_on:
```

```
        - loki
        - prometheus          Ensures Tempo is
        - tempo          ◁───  started before
        ...                    Grafana

    tempo:
      image: grafana/tempo:1.5.0
      container_name: tempo
      command: -config.file /etc/tempo-config.yml      ◁───  Loads the custom
      ports:                                                 configuration during
        - "4317:4317"                                        the startup phase
      volumes:
        - ./observability/tempo/tempo.yml:/etc/tempo-config.yml
```

**Volumes are used to load
configuration for Tempo.**

**Port to accept traces using the
OpenTelemetry protocol over gRPC**

Next let's run the full Grafana observability stack on Docker. Open a Terminal window, navigate to the folder where you keep your Docker Compose file, and run the following command:

```
$ docker-compose up -d grafana
```

Tempo is now ready to accept OpenTelemetry traces over gRPC on port 4317. In the next section, you'll see how to update a Spring Boot application to generate traces and send them over to Tempo.

13.4.2 Configuring tracing in Spring Boot with OpenTelemetry

The OpenTelemetry project includes instrumentation that generates traces and spans for the most common Java libraries, including Spring, Tomcat, Netty, Reactor, JDBC, Hibernate, and Logback. The OpenTelemetry Java Agent is a JAR artifact provided by the project that can be attached to any Java application. It injects the necessary bytecode dynamically to capture traces and spans from all those libraries, and it exports them in different formats without you having to change your Java source code.

Java agents are often provided to the application at runtime from the outside. For better dependency management capabilities, in this case, I prefer using Gradle (or Maven) to include the agent JAR file in the final application artifact. Let's see how.

Open your Catalog Service project (catalog-service). Then add a dependency on the OpenTelemetry Java Agent in your build.gradle file. Remember to refresh or reimport the Gradle dependencies after the new addition.

> **Listing 13.20 Adding dependency for OpenTelemetry Java Agent in Catalog Service**

```
ext {
  ...
  set('otelVersion', "1.17.0")      ◁───  The OpenTelemetry
}                                          version
```

```
dependencies {
  ...
  runtimeOnly "io.opentelemetry.javaagent:
  ➥ opentelemetry-javaagent:${otelVersion}"
}
```

The OpenTelemetry agent instrumenting the Java code dynamically via bytecode

Besides instrumenting the Java code to capture traces, the OpenTelemetry Java Agent also integrates with SLF4J (and its implementation). It provides trace and span identifiers as contextual information that can be injected into log messages through the MDC abstraction provided by SLF4J. That makes it extremely simple to navigate from log messages to traces and vice versa, achieving better visibility into the application than querying the telemetry in isolation.

Let's expand on the default log format used by Spring Boot and add the following contextual information:

- Application name (value from the `spring.application.name` property we configured for all applications)
- Trace identifier (value from the `trace_id` field populated by the OpenTelemetry agent, when enabled)
- Span identifier (value from the `span_id` field populated by the OpenTelemetry agent, when enabled)

In your Catalog Service project, open the application.yml file, and add the three new pieces of information next to the log level (represented by %5p) following the Logback syntax. This is the same format used by Spring Cloud Sleuth.

Listing 13.21   Adding contextual information to logs, next to the level field

Includes application name, trace ID, and span ID next to the log level (%5p)

```
logging:
  pattern:
    level: "%5p [${spring.application.name},%X{trace_id},%X{span_id}]"
```

Next, open a Terminal window, navigate to the Catalog Service root folder, and run `./gradlew bootBuildImage` to package the application as a container image.

The final step is configuring and enabling the OpenTelemetry Java Agent. For simplicity, we'll enable OpenTelemetry only when running applications in containers and rely on environment variables to configure it.

We need three pieces of configuration to successfully enable tracing:

- *Instruct the JVM to load the OpenTelemetry Java agent.* We can do that via the `JAVA_TOOL_OPTIONS` standard environment variable supported by OpenJDK to provide additional configuration to the JVM.
- *Use the application name to tag and categorize traces.* We'll use the `OTEL_SERVICE_NAME` environment variable supported by the OpenTelemetry Java agent.
- *Define the URL of the distributed tracing backend.* In our case, it's Tempo on port 4317, and it can be configured via the `OTEL_EXPORTER_OTLP_ENDPOINT` environment

variable supported by the OpenTelemetry Java agent. By default, traces are sent over gRPC.

Go to your Polar Deployment project (polar-deployment), and open the Docker Compose file (docker/docker-compose.yml). Then add the necessary configuration to Catalog Service to support tracing.

Listing 13.22   Defining OpenTelemetry for the Catalog Service container

```
version: "3.8"
services:
  ...

  catalog-service:
    depends_on:
      - fluent-bit
      - polar-keycloak          Ensures Tempo
      - polar-postgres          is started before
      - tempo                   Catalog Service
    image: "catalog-service"
    container_name: "catalog-service"
    ports:                  Instructs the JVM to run the OpenTelemetry Java
      - 9001:9001           agent from the path where Cloud Native Buildpacks
      - 8001:8001                     placed the application dependencies
    environment:
      - JAVA_TOOL_OPTIONS=-javaagent:/workspace/BOOT-INF/lib/
        opentelemetry-javaagent-1.17.0.jar
      - OTEL_SERVICE_NAME=catalog-service
      - OTEL_EXPORTER_OTLP_ENDPOINT=http://tempo:4317
      - OTEL_METRICS_EXPORTER=none
    ...                                     The URL of the distributed
                                            tracing backend supporting the
The name of the application, used to tag    OpenTelemetry protocol (OTLP)
the traces produced by Catalog Service
```

Finally, from the same folder, run Catalog Service as a container:

```
$ docker-compose up -d catalog-service
```

Once the application is up and running, send a few requests to trigger the generation of some logs and traces about your HTTP requests:

```
$ http :9001/books
```

Then check the logs from the container (`docker logs catalog-service`). You'll see that each log message now has a new section containing the application name and, when available, the trace and span identifiers:

```
[catalog-service,d9e61c8cf853fe7fdf953422c5ff567a,eef9e08caea9e32a]
```

Distributed tracing helps us follow a request through multiple services, so we need another application to test whether it works correctly. Go ahead and make the same changes to Edge Service to support OpenTelemetry. Then run the application as a container from your Docker Compose file:

```
$ docker-compose up -d edge-service
```

Once again, send a few requests to trigger the generation of some logs and traces about your HTTP requests. This time you should go through the gateway:

```
$ http :9000/books
```

Using the trace ID logged by Catalog Service, we can retrieve (*correlate*) all the steps involved in processing the HTTP request to the /books endpoint started in Edge Service. Being able to navigate from logs to traces (and the other way around) is extremely useful for getting more visibility into all the steps involved in processing a request throughout a distributed system. Let's see how it works in the Grafana stack.

Open a browser window, go to Grafana (http://localhost:3000), and log in with the credentials configured in Docker Compose (user/password). On the Explore page, check the logs for Catalog Service ({container_name="/catalog-service"}), much like we did earlier. Next, click on the most recent log message to get more details. You'll see a Tempo button next to the trace identifier associated with that log message. If you click that, Grafana redirects you to the related trace using data from Tempo, all in the same view (figure 13.9).

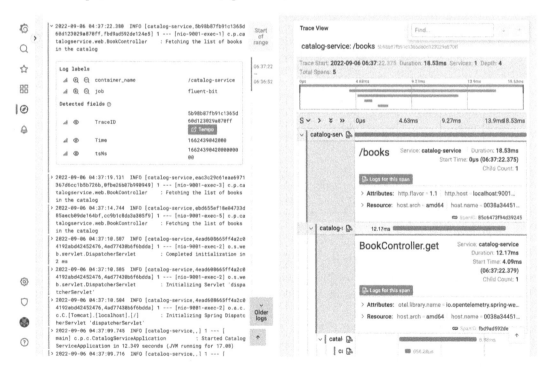

Figure 13.9   In Grafana, you can navigate from logs (Loki) to traces (Tempo) using the trace ID included in the logs.

When you're done inspecting logs and traces, stop all the containers (docker-compose down). Before moving on, go ahead and configure OpenTelemetry for all the remaining applications in the Polar Bookshop system. As a reference, you can look at the source code repository accompanying this book (Chapter13/13-end).

So far, we have worked with the three main types of telemetry data: logs, metrics, and traces. We also enabled health endpoints to provide additional information regarding application status. The following section will cover how you can retrieve even more information from the applications and achieve better visibility into their operations.

13.5   Application management and monitoring with Spring Boot Actuator

In the previous sections, I've shown you the primary telemetry data that all cloud native applications should provide to achieve better observability. This final section will be dedicated to some specific information you can retrieve from applications to further enhance what you can infer about their operations.

Spring Boot Actuator provides many features to make your applications production-ready. You have already learned about health and metrics endpoints, but there are more. Table 13.1 lists some of the most useful management and monitoring endpoints implemented by Actuator. This section will show you how to use some of them.

Table 13.1   Some of the most useful management and monitoring endpoints exposed by Spring Boot Actuator.

Endpoint	Description
/beans	Shows a list of all the Spring beans managed by the application
/configprops	Shows a list of all the @ConfigurationProperties-annotated beans
/env	Shows a list of all the properties available to the Spring Environment
/flyway	Lists all the migrations run by Flyway and their statuses
/health	Shows information about the application's health
/heapdump	Returns a heap dump file
/info	Shows arbitrary application information
/loggers	Shows the configuration of all the loggers in the application and allows you to modify them
/metrics	Returns metrics about the application
/mappings	Lists all the paths defined in web controllers
/prometheus	Returns metrics about the application either in Prometheus or OpenMetrics format
/sessions	Lists all the active sessions managed by Spring Session and allows you to delete them
/threaddump	Returns a thread dump in JSON format

13.5.1 *Monitoring Flyway migrations in Spring Boot*

In chapters 5 and 8, you saw how to version-control your database schemas using Flyway migrations and integrate them with Spring Boot, both in imperative and reactive stacks. Flyway keeps the history of all the migrations run on the application in a dedicated table in the database. It would be convenient to extract such information and monitor it, so you could be alerted if any migration should fail.

Spring Boot Actuator provides a dedicated endpoint (/actuator/flyway) to display information about all the migrations run by Flyway, including their status, date, type, and version. As you learned in the previous sections, you can enable new HTTP endpoints to be implemented by Actuator through the `management.endpoints.web` `.exposure.include` property. Let's see that in action.

> **NOTE** If you use Liquibase instead of Flyway, Spring Boot Actuator provides an /actuator/liquibase endpoint.

Open the Catalog Service project (catalog-service), go to the application.yml file, and configure the Flyway endpoint to be exposed over HTTP by Spring Boot Actuator.

> **Listing 13.23 Exposing the `flyway` Actuator endpoint**

```yaml
management:
  endpoints:
    web:
      exposure:
        include: flyway, health, prometheus
```
Adds flyway to the list of Actuator endpoints exposed over HTTP

Then run the backing services required by Catalog Service as a container. From your Docker Compose file, execute the following command:

```
$ docker-compose up -d polar-keycloak polar-postgres
```

Next, run Catalog Service (./gradlew bootRun), and call the Flyway endpoint:

```
$ http :9001/actuator/flyway
```

The result is a JSON file containing the list of all migrations run by Flyway and their details. The following snippet shows an extract of the complete response:

```json
{
  "contexts": {
    "catalog-service": {
      "flywayBeans": {
        "flyway": {
          "migrations": [
            {
              "checksum": -567578088,
              "description": "Initial schema",
              "executionTime": 66,
              "installedBy": "user",
```

The checksum of the migration script, used to ensure the file has not been changed

Description of the migration

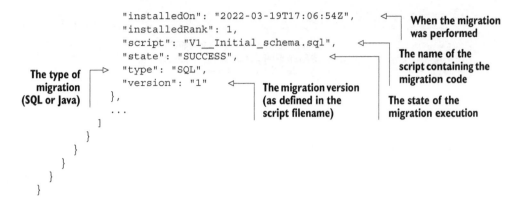

```
            "installedOn": "2022-03-19T17:06:54Z",      ◁──┐  When the migration
            "installedRank": 1,                             │  was performed
            "script": "V1__Initial_schema.sql",    ◁──────┘
            "state": "SUCCESS",                    ◁─────────┐ The name of the
 The type of      "type": "SQL",                              script containing the
  migration       "version": "1"    ◁──────┐                  migration code
 (SQL or Java)  },                          │  The migration version
            ...                             │  (as defined in the     The state of the
          ]                                 │  script filename)       migration execution
        }
      }
    }
  }
}
```

13.5.2 Exposing application information

Among all the endpoints implemented by Spring Boot Actuator, /actuator/info is the most peculiar one, since it doesn't return any data. Instead, it's up to you to define what data you consider useful.

One way to contribute data for the endpoint is through configuration properties. For example, go to your Catalog Service project (catalog-service), open the application.yml file, and add the following property to include the name of the system of which Catalog Service is part. You'll also need to enable the info endpoint to be exposed through HTTP (similar to what we did with the other endpoints) and enable the env contributor responsible for parsing all the properties with the info. prefix.

Listing 13.24   Exposing and configuring the `info` Actuator endpoint

```
info:
    system: Polar Bookshop    ◁──┐  Any property starting
                                   │  with the "info." prefix
management:                        │  will be returned by
    endpoints:                     │  the info endpoint.
        web:
            exposure:                                        Adds info to the list of
                include: flyway, health, info, prometheus  ◁─┘  Actuator endpoints to
    info:                                                    be exposed over HTTP
        env:                         Enables environmental info
            enabled: true    ◁─────  fetched from "info." properties
```

You can also include information that's generated automatically by Gradle or Maven regarding the application build or the last Git commit. Let's see how we can add details about the application's build configuration. In your Catalog Service project, go to the build.gradle file and configure the springBoot task to generate build information that will be parsed into a BuildProperties object and included in the result from the info endpoint.

Listing 13.25   Configuring Spring Boot to include build information

```
springBoot {
  buildInfo()            ◁──┤   Stores build information in a META-
}                             INF/build-info.properties file parsed
                              by a BuildProperties object.
```

Let's test it out. Rerun Catalog Service (`./gradlew bootRun`). Then invoke the info endpoint:

```
$ http :9001/actuator/info
```

The result will be a JSON object containing build information and the custom `info`
`.system` property we defined explicitly:

```
{
  "build": {
    "artifact": "catalog-service",
    "group": "com.polarbookshop",
    "name": "catalog-service",
    "time": "2021-08-06T12:56:25.035Z",
    "version": "0.0.1-SNAPSHOT"
  },
  "system": "Polar Bookshop"
}
```

You can expose additional information about the operating system and the Java version in use. Both can be enabled via configuration properties. Let's update the appli-
cation.yml file for the Catalog Service project as follows.

Listing 13.26   Adding Java and OS details to the `info` Actuator endpoint

```
management:
  ...
  info:
    env:
      enabled: true        Enables Java information
    java:                   in the info endpoint
      enabled: true   ◁──
    os:                     Enables OS information
      enabled: true   ◁──  in the info endpoint
```

Let's test it out. Rerun Catalog Service (`./gradlew bootRun`). Then invoke the info
endpoint:

```
$ http :9001/actuator/info
```

The result now includes additional information about the Java version and operating
system in use, which will be different depending on where you run the application:

```
{
  ...
```

```
"java": {
  "version": "17.0.3",
  "vendor": {
    "name": "Eclipse Adoptium",
    "version": "Temurin-17.0.3+7"
  },
  "runtime": {
    "name": "OpenJDK Runtime Environment",
    "version": "17.0.3+7"
  },
  "jvm": {
    "name": "OpenJDK 64-Bit Server VM",
    "vendor": "Eclipse Adoptium",
    "version": "17.0.3+7"
  }
},
"os": {
  "name": "Mac OS X",
  "version": "12.3.1",
  "arch": "aarch64"
}
}
```

13.5.3 Generating and analyzing heap dumps

Among the most annoying errors to debug in Java applications, memory leaks are probably the first that come to mind. Monitoring tools should alert you when a memory leak pattern is detected, usually inferred if the JVM heap usage metric keeps increasing over time. If you don't catch the memory leak in advance, the application will throw the dreaded `OutOfMemoryError` error and crash.

Once you suspect an application might suffer from a memory leak, you must find out which objects are held in memory and block the garbage collection. There are different ways to proceed with finding problematic objects. For example, you could enable the Java Flight Recorder or attach a profiler like jProfiler to the running application. Another way is to take a snapshot of all the Java objects in the JVM heap memory (a *heap dump*), and analyze it with a specialized tool to find the root cause of the memory leak.

Spring Boot Actuator provides a convenient endpoint (`/actuator/heapdump`) that you can call to generate a heap dump. Let's see that in action. Go to your Catalog Service project (catalog-service), open the application.yml file, and configure Actuator to expose the `heapdump` endpoint.

Listing 13.27　Exposing the `heapdump` Actuator endpoint

```
management:
  endpoints:
    web:
      exposure:
        include: flyway, health, heapdump, info, prometheus
```
Adds heapdump to the list of Actuator endpoints to be exposed over HTTP

Next, build and run Catalog Service (`./gradlew bootRun`). Finally, invoke the `heapdump` endpoint:

```
$ http --download :9001/actuator/heapdump
```

The command will save a heapdump.bin file in the current directory. You can then open it in a dedicated tool for heap analysis like VisualVM (https://visualvm.github.io) or JDK Mission Control (https://adoptopenjdk.net/jmc.html). Figure 13.10 shows an example of heap analysis in VisualVM.

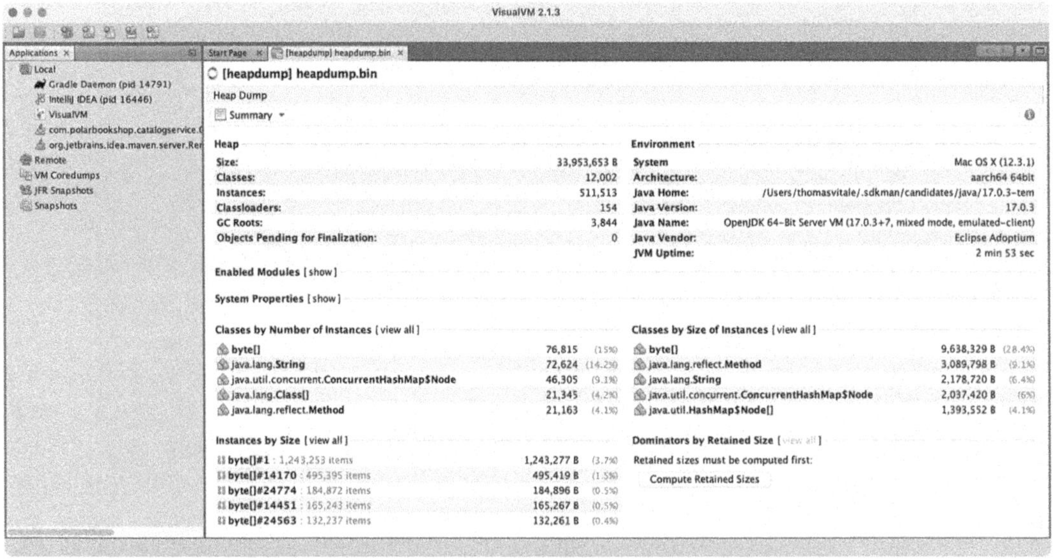

Figure 13.10 VisualVM provides tools to analyze a Java application's heap dump.

Finally, stop the application process (Ctrl-C) and all containers (`docker-compose down`).

I encourage you to check out the Spring Boot Actuator official documentation, try out all the supported endpoints, and make the applications of the Polar Bookshop system more observable. For inspiration, refer to the source code repository accompanying the book to see which endpoints I have enabled on each application (Chapter13/13-end). They're powerful tools that you'll likely find helpful and convenient in real-world applications running in production.

Summary

- Observability is a property of cloud native applications that measures how well we can infer the internal state of an application from its outputs.
- Monitoring is about controlling known faulty states. Observability goes beyond that and permits us to ask questions about the unknown.
- Logs (or event logs) are discrete records of something that happened over time in a software application.

- Spring Boot supports logging through SLF4J, which provides a façade over the most common logging libraries.
- By default, logs are printed through the standard output as recommended by the 15-Factor methodology.
- Using the Grafana observability stack, Fluent Bit collects logs produced by all applications and forwards them to Loki, which stores them and makes them searchable. Then you can use Grafana to navigate the logs.
- Applications should expose health endpoints to check their status.
- Spring Boot Actuator exposes an overall health endpoint showing the status of the application and all the components or services it might use. It also provides specialized endpoints to be used as liveness and readiness probes by Kubernetes.
- When the liveness probe is down, it means the application has entered an unrecoverable faulty state, so Kubernetes will try to restart it.
- When the readiness probe is down, the application is not ready to handle requests, so Kubernetes will stop any traffic directed to that instance.
- Metrics are numeric data about the application, measured at regular time intervals.
- Spring Boot Actuator leverages the Micrometer façade to instrument the Java code, generate metrics, and expose them through a dedicated endpoint.
- When the Prometheus client is on the classpath, Spring Boot can expose metrics in the Prometheus or OpenMetrics format.
- Using the Grafana observability stack, Prometheus aggregates and stores metrics from all applications. Then you can use Grafana to query metrics, design dashboards, and set alerts.
- Distributed tracing, a technique for tracking requests as they flow through a distributed system, lets us localize where errors occur in a distributed system and troubleshoot performance issues.
- Traces are characterized by a trace ID and are composed of multiple spans, representing steps in a transaction.
- The OpenTelemetry project includes APIs and instrumentation that generates traces and spans for the most common Java libraries.
- The OpenTelemetry Java Agent is a JAR artifact provided by the project that can be attached to any Java application. It injects the necessary bytecode dynamically to capture traces and spans from all those libraries and export them in different formats without having to change your Java source code explicitly.
- Using the Grafana observability stack, Tempo aggregates and stores metrics from all applications. Then you can use Grafana to query traces and correlate them with logs.
- Spring Boot Actuator provides management and monitoring endpoints to fulfill any requirements you might have to make your applications production-ready.

Configuration and secrets management

Releasing applications to production involves two important aspects: an executable artifact and its configuration. The executable artifact could be a JAR file or a container image. The previous chapters covered several principles, patterns, and tools for building applications that are loosely coupled, resilient, scalable, secure, and observable. You saw how to package applications as executable JAR artifacts or container images. I also guided you through the implementation of the commit stage of a deployment pipeline, which ultimately produces a release candidate.

The other aspect of being ready for production is configuration. Chapter 4 introduced the importance of externalized configuration for cloud native applications and covered several techniques for configuring Spring Boot applications. This chapter will continue that discussion in preparation for deploying an entire cloud native system to a Kubernetes production environment.

First I'll describe a few options for configuring Spring Boot applications on Kubernetes and describe what's missing for using Spring Cloud Config in production.

Then you'll learn how to use ConfigMaps and Secrets, a native mechanism for handling configuration on Kubernetes. As part of the discussion, you'll get to know Spring Cloud Kubernetes and its primary use cases. Finally, I'll expand on configuration and secrets management for production workloads on Kubernetes, and you'll learn how to implement that using Kustomize.

NOTE   The source code for the examples in this chapter is available in the Chapter14/14-begin and Chapter14/14-end folders, containing the initial and final states of the project (https://github.com/ThomasVitale/cloud-native -spring-in-action).

14.1   Configuring applications on Kubernetes

According to the 15-Factor methodology, configuration is anything that changes between deployment environments. We started working with configuration in chapter 4 and since then have used different configuration strategies:

- *Property files packaged with the application*—These can act as specifications of what configuration data the application supports, and they are useful for defining sensible default values, mainly oriented to the development environment.
- *Environment variables*—These are supported by any operating system, so they are great for portability. They're useful for defining configuration data depending on the infrastructure or platform where the application is deployed, such as active profiles, hostnames, service names, and port numbers. We used them in Docker and Kubernetes.
- *Configuration service*—This provides configuration data persistence, auditing, and accountability. It's useful for defining configuration data specific to the application, such as feature flags, thread pools, connection pools, timeouts, and URLs for third-party services. We adopted this strategy with Spring Cloud Config.

Those three strategies are generic enough that we can use them to configure applications for any cloud environment and service model (CaaS, PaaS, FaaS). When it comes to Kubernetes, there's an additional configuration strategy that is provided natively by the platform: ConfigMaps and Secrets.

These are a very convenient way to define configuration data that depends on the infrastructure and platform where the application is deployed: service names (defined by Kubernetes `Service` objects), credentials and certificates for accessing other services running on the platform, graceful shutdown, logging, and monitoring. You could use ConfigMaps and Secrets to complement or completely replace what a configuration service does. Which you choose depends on the context. In any case, Spring Boot provides native support for all those options.

For the Polar Bookshop system, we'll use ConfigMaps and Secrets instead of the Config Service to configure applications in Kubernetes environments. Still, all the work we've done so far on Config Service would make including it in the overall deployment of Polar Bookshop on Kubernetes straightforward. In this section, I'll share some final considerations for making Config Service production-ready, in case you'd like to expand on the examples and include it in the final deployment in production.

14.1.1 *Securing the configuration server with Spring Security*

In previous chapters, we spent quite some time ensuring a high-security level for the Spring Boot applications in Polar Bookshop. However, Config Service was not one of them, and it's still unprotected. Even if it's a config server, it's still a Spring Boot application at its heart. As such, we can secure it using any of the strategies provided by Spring Security.

Config Service is accessed over HTTP by the other Spring Boot applications in the architecture. Before using it in production, we must ensure that only authenticated and authorized parties can retrieve configuration data. One option would be to use the OAuth2 Client credentials flow to secure the interactions between Config Service and applications based on an Access Token. It's an OAuth2 flow specific for protecting service-to-service interactions.

Assuming that applications will communicate over HTTPS, the *HTTP Basic* authentication strategy would be another viable option. When using this strategy, applications can be configured with the username and password via the properties exposed by Spring Cloud Config Client: `spring.cloud.config.username` and `spring.cloud.config.password`. For more information, refer to the official documentation for Spring Security (https://spring.io/projects/spring-security) and Spring Cloud Config (https://spring.io/projects/spring-cloud-config).

14.1.2 *Refreshing configuration at runtime with Spring Cloud Bus*

Imagine you have deployed your Spring Boot applications in a cloud environment like Kubernetes. During the startup phase, each application loaded its configuration from an external config server, but at some point you decide to make changes in the config repo. How can you make the applications aware of the configuration changes and have them reload it?

In chapter 4, you learned that you could trigger a configuration refresh operation by sending a `POST` request to the `/actuator/refresh` endpoint provided by Spring Boot Actuator. A request to that endpoint results in a `RefreshScopeRefreshedEvent` event inside the application context. All beans marked with `@ConfigurationProperties` or `@RefreshScope` listen to that event and get reloaded when it happens.

You tried the refresh mechanism on Catalog Service, and it worked fine, since it was just one application, and not even replicated. How about in production? Considering the distribution and scale of cloud native applications, sending an HTTP request to all the instances of each application might be a problem. Automation is a crucial part of any cloud native strategy, so we need a way to trigger a `RefreshScopeRefreshedEvent` event in all of them in one shot. There are a few viable solutions. Using Spring Cloud Bus is one of them.

Spring Cloud Bus (https://spring.io/projects/spring-cloud-bus) establishes a convenient communication channel for broadcasting events among all the application instances linked to it. It provides an implementation for AMQP brokers (like RabbitMQ) and Kafka, relying on the Spring Cloud Stream project you learned about in chapter 10.

Any configuration change consists of pushing a commit to the config repo. It would be convenient to set up some automation to make Config Service refresh the configuration when a new commit is pushed to the repository, completely removing the need for manual intervention. Spring Cloud Config provides a Monitor library that makes that possible. It exposes a /monitor endpoint that can trigger a configuration change event in Config Service, which then would send it over the Bus to all the listening applications. It also accepts arguments describing which files have been changed and supports receiving push notifications from the most common code repository providers like GitHub, GitLab, and Bitbucket. You can set up a webhook in those services to automatically send a POST request to Config Service after each new push to the config repo.

Spring Cloud Bus solves the problem of broadcasting a configuration change event to all connected applications. With Spring Cloud Config Monitor, we can further automate the refresh and make it happen after a configuration change is pushed to the repository backing the config server. This solution is illustrated in figure 14.1.

Refreshing configuration at runtime with Spring Cloud Bus and Spring Cloud Config Monitor

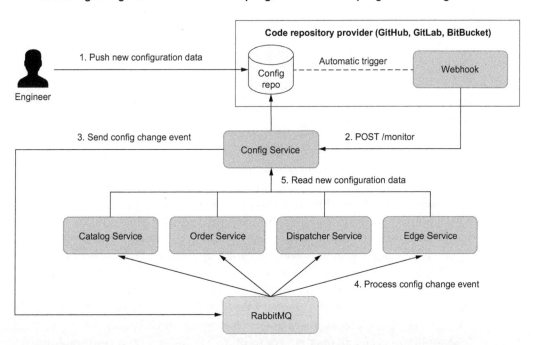

Figure 14.1 **Broadcasting configuration changes through Spring Cloud Bus after the Config Service receives push notifications on every config repo change.**

NOTE You can rely on Spring Cloud Bus to broadcast configuration changes even when you use other options like Consul (with Spring Cloud Consul), Azure Key Vault (Spring Cloud Azure), AWS Parameter Store or AWS Secrets Manager (Spring Cloud AWS), or Google Cloud Secret Manager (Spring Cloud GCP). Unlike Spring Cloud Config, they don't have built-in push notification capabilities, so you need to trigger a configuration change or implement your monitor functionality manually.

14.1.3 *Managing secrets with Spring Cloud Config*

Managing secrets is a critical task for any software system, and it's dangerous when mistakes are made. So far, we have included passwords either in property files or environment variables, but they were unencrypted in both cases. One of the consequences of not encrypting them is that we can't version-control them safely. We would like to keep everything under version control and use Git repositories as the single sources of truth, which is one of the principles behind the GitOps strategy I'll cover in chapter 15.

The Spring Cloud Config project is well-equipped with features to handle configuration for cloud native applications, including secrets management. The main goal is to include secrets in the property files and put them under version control, which can only be done if they are encrypted.

Spring Cloud Config Server supports encryption and decryption and exposes two dedicated endpoints: /encrypt and /decrypt. Encryption can be based on a symmetric key or asymmetric key pair.

When using a symmetric key, Spring Cloud Config Server decrypts secrets locally and sends them decrypted to the client applications. In production, all communications between applications will happen over HTTPS, so the response sent from Config Service will be encrypted even if the configuration property is not, making this approach secure enough for real-world usage.

You also have the option to send property values encrypted and let the applications themselves decrypt them, but that will require you to configure the symmetric key for all applications. You should also consider that decryption is not a cheap operation to perform.

Spring Cloud Config also supports encryption and decryption through asymmetric keys. This option provides more robust security than the symmetric alternative but it also increases complexity and maintenance costs due to key management tasks. In that case, you might want to consider relying on a dedicated secrets management solution. For example, you can use one of those offered by cloud providers and rely on the Spring Boot integration implemented by Spring Cloud, such as Azure Key Vault (Spring Cloud Azure), AWS Parameter Store or AWS Secrets Manager (Spring Cloud AWS), or Google Cloud Secret Manager (Spring Cloud GCP).

Should you prefer an open source solution, HashiCorp Vault (www.vaultproject.io) might be a good fit for you. It's a tool you can use to manage all your credentials, tokens, and certificates, both from a CLI and from a convenient GUI. You can integrate it directly with your Spring Boot applications using the Spring Vault project or add it as an additional backend for Spring Cloud Config Server.

For more information about secrets management in Spring, check out the official documentation for Spring Vault (https://spring.io/projects/spring-vault) and Spring Cloud Config (https://spring.io/projects/spring-cloud-config).

14.1.4 *Disabling Spring Cloud Config*

The next section will introduce a different way of configuring Spring Boot applications based on the native functionality provided by Kubernetes through ConfigMaps and Secrets. That's what we're going to use in production.

Even if we're not going to use Config Service anymore in the rest of the book, we'll keep all the work we have done with it so far. However, to make things easier, we'll turn the Spring Cloud Config Client integration off by default.

Open your Catalog Service project (catalog-service), and update the application.yml file to stop importing configuration data from Config Service and disable the Spring Cloud Config Client integration. Everything else will stay the same. Whenever you want to use Spring Cloud Config again, you can enable it with ease (for example, when running the applications on Docker).

Listing 14.1 Disabling Spring Cloud Config in Catalog Service

```
spring:                    Stops importing
  config:                  configuration data
    import: ""        ◁───┘ from Config Service
  cloud:
    config:
      enabled: false              ◁────  Disables the Spring
      uri: http://localhost:8888        Cloud Config Client
      request-connect-timeout: 5000     integration
      request-read-timeout: 5000
      fail-fast: false
      retry:
        max-attempts: 6
        initial-interval: 1000
        max-interval: 2000
        multiplier: 1.1
```

In the next section, you'll use ConfigMaps and Secrets to configure Spring Boot applications instead of the Config Service.

14.2 *Using ConfigMaps and Secrets in Kubernetes*

The 15-Factor methodology recommends keeping code, configuration, and credentials always separate. Kubernetes fully embraces that principle and defines two APIs to handle configuration and credentials independently: ConfigMaps and Secrets. This section will introduce this new configuration strategy, which is provided natively by Kubernetes.

Spring Boot provides native and flexible support for both ConfigMaps and Secrets. I'll show you how to work with ConfigMaps and their relationships with environment variables, which are still a valid configuration option in Kubernetes. You'll see that Secrets are not really secret, and you'll learn what to do to make them really so. Finally, I'll go through a few options for dealing with configuration changes and propagating them to applications.

Before moving on further, let's set the scene and start a local Kubernetes cluster. Go to your Polar Deployment project (polar-deployment), navigate to the kubernetes/ platform/development folder, and run the following command to start a minikube cluster and deploy the backing services used by Polar Bookshop:

```
$ ./create-cluster.sh
```

> **NOTE** If you haven't followed along with the examples implemented in the previous chapters, you can refer to the repository accompanying the book (https://github.com/ThomasVitale/cloud-native-spring-in-action) and use the projects in Chapter14/14-begin as a starting point.

The command will take a few minutes to complete. When it's finished, you can verify that all the backing services are ready and available with the following command:

```
$ kubectl get deploy

NAME              READY   UP-TO-DATE   AVAILABLE   AGE
polar-keycloak    1/1     1            1           3m94s
polar-postgres    1/1     1            1           3m94s
polar-rabbitmq    1/1     1            1           3m94s
polar-redis       1/1     1            1           3m94s
polar-ui          1/1     1            1           3m94s
```

Let's start by introducing ConfigMaps.

14.2.1 Configuring Spring Boot with ConfigMaps

In chapter 7, we used environment variables to pass hardcoded configuration to containers running in Kubernetes, but they lack maintainability and structure. ConfigMaps let you store configuration data in a structured, maintainable way. They can be version-controlled together with the rest of your Kubernetes deployment manifests and have the same nice properties of a dedicated configuration repository, including data persistence, auditing, and accountability.

A *ConfigMap* is "an API object used to store non-confidential data in key-value pairs. Pods can consume ConfigMaps as environment variables, command-line arguments, or as configuration files in a volume" (https://kubernetes.io/docs/concepts/configuration/configmap).

You can build a ConfigMap starting with a literal key/value pair string, with a file (for example, .properties or .yml), or even with a binary object. When working with

Spring Boot applications, the most straightforward way to build a ConfigMap is to start with a property file.

Let's look at an example. In the previous chapters, we configured Catalog Service via environment variables. For better maintainability and structure, let's store some of those values in a ConfigMap.

Open the Catalog Service project (catalog-service), and create a new config-map.yml file in the k8s folder. We'll use it to apply the following configuration, which will overwrite the default values included in the application.yml file packaged with the application:

- Configure a custom greeting.
- Configure the URL for the PostgreSQL data source.
- Configure the URL for Keycloak.

Listing 14.2 Defining a ConfigMap to configure Catalog Service

The API version for ConfigMap objects

The type of object to create

The name of the ConfigMap

A set of labels attached to the ConfigMap

A key/value pair where the key is the name of a YAML configuration file and the value is its content

Section containing the configuration data

```
apiVersion: v1
kind: ConfigMap
metadata:
  name: catalog-config
  labels:
    app: catalog-service
data:
  application.yml: |
    polar:
      greeting: Welcome to the book catalog from Kubernetes!
    spring:
      datasource:
        url: jdbc:postgresql://polar-postgres/polardb_catalog
      security:
        oauth2:
          resourceserver:
            jwt:
              issuer-uri: http://polar-keycloak/realms/PolarBookshop
```

Like the other Kubernetes objects we have worked with so far, manifests for Config-Maps can be applied to a cluster using the Kubernetes CLI. Open a Terminal window, navigate to your Catalog Service project (catalog-service), and run the following command:

```
$ kubectl apply -f k8s/configmap.yml
```

You can verify that the ConfigMap has been created correctly with this command:

```
$ kubectl get cm -l app=catalog-service

NAME            DATA   AGE
catalog-config  1      7s
```

The values stored in a ConfigMap can be used to configure containers running in a few different ways:

- Use a ConfigMap as a configuration data source to pass command-line arguments to the container.
- Use a ConfigMap as a configuration data source to populate environment variables for the container.
- Mount a ConfigMap as a volume in the container.

As you learned in chapter 4 and practiced since then, Spring Boot supports externalized configuration in many ways, including via command-line arguments and environment variables. Passing configuration data as command-line arguments or environment variables to containers has its drawbacks, even if it is stored in a ConfigMap. For example, whenever you add a property to a ConfigMap, you must update the Deployment manifest. When a ConfigMap is changed, the Pod is not informed about it and must be re-created to read the new configuration. Both those issues are solved by mounting ConfigMaps as volumes.

When a ConfigMap is mounted as a volume to a container, it generates two possible outcomes (figure 14.2):

- If the ConfigMap includes an *embedded property file*, mounting it as a volume results in the property file being created in the mounted path. Spring Boot automatically finds and includes any property files located in a `/config` folder either in the same root as the application executable or in a subdirectory, so it's the perfect path for mounting a ConfigMap. You can also specify additional locations to search for property files via the `spring.config.additional-location=<path>` configuration property.
- If the ConfigMap includes *key/value pairs*, mounting it as a volume results in a *config tree* being created in the mounted path. For each key/value pair, a file is

Mounting ConfigMaps as volumes to Spring Boot applications

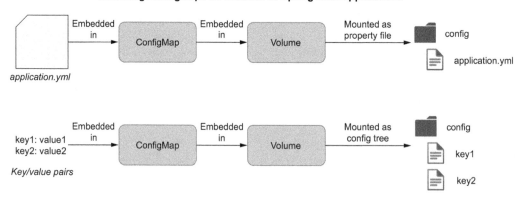

Figure 14.2   ConfigMaps mounted as volumes can be consumed by Spring Boot as property files or as config trees.

created, named like the key and containing the value. Spring Boot supports reading configuration properties from a config tree. You can specify where the config tree should be loaded from via the `spring.config.import=config-tree:<path>` property.

When configuring Spring Boot applications, the first option is the most convenient, since it uses the same property file format used for the default configuration inside the application. Let's see how we can mount the ConfigMap created earlier into the Catalog Service container.

Open the Catalog Service project (catalog-service), and go to the deployment.yml file in the k8s folder. We need to apply three changes:

- Remove the environment variables for the values we declared in the ConfigMap.
- Declare a volume generated from the `catalog-config` ConfigMap.
- Specify a volume mount for the `catalog-service` container to load the Config-Map as an application.yml file from /workspace/config. The /workspace folder is created and used by Cloud Native Buildpacks to host the application executables, so Spring Boot will automatically look for a /config folder in the same path and load any property files contained within. There's no need to configure additional locations.

Listing 14.3 Mounting a ConfigMap as a volume to the application container

```
apiVersion: apps/v1
kind: Deployment
metadata:
  name: catalog-service
  labels:
    app: catalog-service
spec:
  ...
  template:
    ...
    spec:
      containers:
        - name: catalog-service
          image: catalog-service
          imagePullPolicy: IfNotPresent        ◁── JVM threads and Spring
          ...                                       profile are still configured
          env:                                      via environment variables.
            - name: BPL_JVM_THREAD_COUNT
              value: "50"
            - name: SPRING_PROFILES_ACTIVE
              value: testdata
          ...                                       Mounts the ConfigMap
          volumeMounts:                       ◁──  in the container as a
            - name: catalog-config-volume          volume
              mountPath: /workspace/config    ◁──  Spring Boot will automatically
      volumes:                                     find and include property files
        - name: catalog-config-volume         ◁──  from this folder.
                                                    The name of the volume
```

Defines volumes for the Pod →

```
configMap:                    ◁─────┐
    name: catalog-config            │   The ConfigMap
                                    │   from which to
                                    │   create a volume
```

We previously applied the ConfigMap to the cluster. Let's do the same for the Deployment and Service manifests so that we can verify whether Catalog Service is correctly reading configuration data from the ConfigMap.

First, we must package the application as a container image and load it into the cluster. Open a Terminal window, navigate to the root folder of your Catalog Service project (catalog-service), and run the following commands:

```
$ ./gradlew bootBuildImage
$ minikube image load catalog-service --profile polar
```

Now we're ready to deploy the application in the local cluster by applying the Deployment and Service manifests:

```
$ kubectl apply -f k8s/deployment.yml -f k8s/service.yml
```

You can verify when Catalog Service is available and ready to accept requests with this command:

```
$ kubectl get deploy -l app=catalog-service

NAME              READY   UP-TO-DATE   AVAILABLE   AGE
catalog-service   1/1     1            1           21s
```

Internally, Kubernetes uses the liveness and readiness probes we configured in the previous chapter to infer the application's health.

Next, forward traffic from your local machine to the Kubernetes cluster by running the following command:

```
$ kubectl port-forward service/catalog-service 9001:80
Forwarding from 127.0.0.1:9001 -> 9001
Forwarding from [::1]:9001 -> 9001
```

> **NOTE** The process started by the kubectl port-forward command will keep running until you explicitly stop it with Ctrl-C.

Now you can call Catalog Service from your local machine on port 9001, and the request will be forwarded to the Service object inside the Kubernetes cluster. Open a new Terminal window, and call the root endpoint exposed by the application to verify that the polar.greeting value specified in the ConfigMap is used instead of the default one:

```
$ http :9001/
Welcome to the book catalog from Kubernetes!
```

Try also retrieving the books from the catalog to verify that the PostgreSQL URL specified in the ConfigMap is used correctly:

```
$ http :9001/books
```

When you're done testing the application, stop the port-forward process (Ctrl-C) and delete the Kubernetes objects created so far. Open a Terminal window, navigate to your Catalog Service project (catalog-service), and run the following command, but keep the cluster running, since we're going to use it again soon:

```
$ kubectl delete -f k8s
```

ConfigMaps are convenient for providing configuration data to applications running on Kubernetes. But what if we had to pass sensitive data? In the next section, you'll see how to use Secrets in Kubernetes.

14.2.2 *Storing sensitive information with Secrets (or not)*

The most critical part of configuring applications is managing secret information like passwords, certificates, tokens, and keys. Kubernetes provides a Secret object to hold such data and pass it to containers.

A *Secret* is an API object used to store and manage sensitive information, such as passwords, OAuth tokens, and ssh keys. Pods can consume Secrets as environment variables or configuration files in a volume (https://kubernetes.io/docs/concepts/configuration/secret).

What makes this object *secret* is the process used to manage it. By themselves, Secrets are just like ConfigMaps. The only difference is that data in a Secret is usually Base64-encoded, a technical choice made to support binary files. Any Base64-encoded object can be decoded in a very straightforward way. It's a common mistake to think that Base64 is a kind of encryption. If you remember only one thing about Secrets, make it the following: *Secrets are not secret!*

The configuration we have been using to run Polar Bookshop on a local Kubernetes cluster relies on the same default credentials used in development, so we won't need Secrets yet. We'll start using them in the next chapter when deploying applications in production. For now, I want to show you how to create Secrets. Then I'll go through some options you have for ensuring that they are adequately protected.

One way of creating a Secret is using the Kubernetes CLI with an imperative approach. Open a Terminal window and generate a `test-credentials` Secret object for some fictitious test credentials (`user`/`password`).

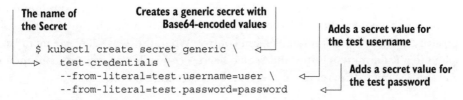

We can verify that the Secret has been created successfully with the following command:

```
$ kubectl get secret test-credentials

NAME               TYPE      DATA    AGE
test-credentials   Opaque    2       73s
```

We can also retrieve the internal representation of the Secret in the familiar YAML format with the following command:

```
$ kubectl get secret test-credentials -o yaml
```

```
apiVersion: v1              ◁———┐  The API version for
kind: Secret                    │  Secret objects
metadata:
  name: test-credentials    ◁———┐
type: Opaque                    │  The name of
data:                       ◁   │  the Secret
  test.username: dXNlcg==       │
  test.password: cGFzc3dvcmQ=   │  Section containing the secret data
                                   with Base64-encoded values
```

The type of
object to create

Note that I rearranged the preceding YAML to increase its readability and omitted additional fields that are not relevant to our discussion.

I want to repeat this: Secrets are not secret! I can decode the value stored in the test-credentials Secret with a simple command:

```
$ echo 'cGFzc3dvcmQ=' | base64 --decode
password
```

Like ConfigMaps, Secrets can be passed to a container as environment variables or through a volume mount. In the second case, you can mount them as property files or config trees. For example, the test-credentials Secret would be mounted as a config tree because it's composed of key/value pairs rather than a file.

Since Secrets are not encrypted, we can't include them in a version control system. It's up to the platform engineers to ensure that Secrets are adequately protected. For example, Kubernetes could be configured to store Secrets in its internal *etcd* storage encrypted. That would help ensure security at rest, but it doesn't solve the problem of managing them in a version control system.

Bitnami introduced a project called *Sealed Secrets* (https://github.com/bitnami-labs/sealed-secrets), aimed at encrypting Secrets and putting them under version control. First you would generate an encrypted SealedSecret object, starting from literal values, similar to what we did for the plain Secret. Then you would include that in your repository and safely put it under version control. When the SealedSecret manifest is applied to a Kubernetes cluster, the Sealed Secrets controller decrypts its content and generates a standard Secret object that can be used within a Pod.

What if your secrets are stored in a dedicated backend like HashiCorp Vault or Azure Key Vault? In that case, you can use a project like *External Secrets* (https://github.com/external-secrets/kubernetes-external-secrets). As you can guess from its name, this project lets you generate a Secret from an external source. The `External-Secret` object would be safe to store in your repository and put under version control. When the `ExternalSecret` manifest is applied to a Kubernetes cluster, the External Secrets controller fetches the value from the configured external source and generates a standard Secret object that can be used within a Pod.

> **NOTE** If you're interested in learning more about how to secure Kubernetes Secrets, you can check out chapter 7 of *GitOps and Kubernetes* by Billy Yuen, Alexander Matyushentsev, Todd Ekenstam, and Jesse Suen (Manning, 2021) and *Kubernetes Secrets Management* by Alex Soto Bueno and Andrew Block (Manning, 2022). I won't provide more information here, since this is usually a task for the platform team, not developers.

When we start using ConfigMaps and Secrets, we must decide which policy to use to update configuration data and how to make applications use the new values. That's the topic of the next section.

14.2.3   *Refreshing configuration at runtime with Spring Cloud Kubernetes*

When using an external configuration service, you'll probably want a mechanism to reload the applications when configuration changes. For example, when using Spring Cloud Config, we can implement such a mechanism with Spring Cloud Bus.

In Kubernetes, we need a different approach. When you update a ConfigMap or a Secret, Kubernetes takes care of providing containers with the new versions when they're mounted as volumes. If you use environment variables, they will not be replaced with the new values. That's why we usually prefer the volume solution.

The updated ConfigMaps or Secrets are provided to the Pod when they're mounted as volumes, but it's up to the specific application to refresh the configuration. By default, Spring Boot applications read configuration data only at startup time. There are three main options for refreshing configuration when it's provided through ConfigMaps and Secrets:

- *Rolling restart*—Changing a ConfigMap or a Secret can be followed by a rolling restart of all the Pods affected, making the applications reload all the configuration data. With this option, Kubernetes Pods would remain immutable.
- *Spring Cloud Kubernetes Configuration Watcher*—Spring Cloud Kubernetes provides a Kubernetes controller called Configuration Watcher that monitors ConfigMaps and Secrets mounted as volumes to Spring Boot applications. Leveraging the Spring Boot Actuator's `/actuator/refresh` endpoint or Spring Cloud Bus, when any of the ConfigMaps or Secrets is updated, the Configuration Watcher will trigger a configuration refresh for the affected applications.

- *Spring Cloud Kubernetes Config Server*—Spring Cloud Kubernetes provides a configuration server with support for using ConfigMaps and Secrets as one of the configuration data source options for Spring Cloud Config. You could use such a server to load configuration from both a Git repository and Kubernetes objects, with the possibility of using the same configuration refresh mechanism for both.

For Polar Bookshop, we'll use the first option and rely on Kustomize to trigger a restart of the applications whenever a new change is applied to a ConfigMap or a Secret. I'll describe that strategy further in the next section of the chapter. Here we'll focus on the features offered by Spring Cloud Kubernetes and its subprojects.

Spring Cloud Kubernetes (https://spring.io/projects/spring-cloud-kubernetes) is an exciting project that provides Spring Boot integration with the Kubernetes API. Its original goal was to make it easier to transition from a microservices architecture based on Spring Cloud to Kubernetes. It provides an implementation for standard Spring Cloud interfaces used for service discovery and load balancing to integrate with Kubernetes, and it adds support for loading configuration from ConfigMaps and Secrets.

If you work on a greenfield project, you don't need Spring Cloud Kubernetes. Kubernetes provides service discovery and load balancing natively, as you experienced in chapter 7. Furthermore, Spring Boot supports configuration via ConfigMaps and Secrets natively, so there's no need for Spring Cloud Kubernetes, even in this case.

When migrating a brownfield project to Kubernetes, and it uses libraries like Spring Cloud Netflix Eureka for service discovery and Spring Cloud Netflix Ribbon or Spring Cloud Load Balancer for load balancing, you might use Spring Cloud Kubernetes for a smoother transition. However, I would recommend refactoring your code to leverage the native service discovery and load-balancing features from Kubernetes rather than adding Spring Cloud Kubernetes to your project.

The main reason why I recommend not using Spring Cloud Kubernetes in standard applications is that it requires access to the Kubernetes API Server to manage Pods, Services, ConfigMaps, and Secrets. Besides the security concerns related to granting applications access to the Kubernetes internal objects, it would also couple the applications to Kubernetes unnecessarily and affect the maintainability of the solution.

When does it make sense to use Spring Cloud Kubernetes? As one example, Spring Cloud Gateway could be enhanced with Spring Cloud Kubernetes to get more control over service discovery and load balancing, including automatic registration of new routes based on Services metadata and the choice of load-balancing strategy. In this case, you could rely on the Spring Cloud Kubernetes Discovery Server component, limiting the need for Kubernetes API access to the discovery server.

Spring Cloud Kubernetes really shines when it comes to implementing Kubernetes controller applications to accomplish administrative tasks within the cluster. For example, you could implement a controller that monitors when ConfigMaps or Secrets change and then triggers a configuration refresh on the application using them. As a matter of fact, the Spring team used Spring Cloud Kubernetes to build a controller that does precisely that: the Configuration Watcher.

> **NOTE** Spring Cloud Kubernetes Configuration Watcher is available as a container image on Docker Hub. If you'd like to know more about how it works and how to deploy it, you can refer to the official documentation (https://spring.io/projects/spring-cloud-kubernetes).

Besides the Configuration Watcher, Spring Cloud Kubernetes provides other convenient off-the-shelf applications for addressing common concerns of distributed systems in Kubernetes. One of them is a configuration server built on top of Spring Cloud Config and extending its functionality to support reading configuration data from ConfigMaps and Secrets. It's called Spring Cloud Kubernetes Config Server.

You can use this application directly (the container image is published on Docker Hub) and deploy it on Kubernetes following the instructions provided in the official documentation (https://spring.io/projects/spring-cloud-kubernetes).

As an alternative, you can use its source code on GitHub as a foundation to build your own Kubernetes-aware configuration server. For example, as I explained earlier in this chapter, you might want to protect it via HTTP Basic authentication. In that case, you could use your experience working with Spring Cloud Config and build an enhanced version of Config Service for Polar Bookshop on top of Spring Cloud Kubernetes Config Server.

In the next section, I will introduce Kustomize for managing deployment configurations in Kubernetes.

14.3 Configuration management with Kustomize

Kubernetes provides many useful features for running cloud native applications. Still, it requires writing several YAML manifests, which are sometimes redundant and not easy to manage in a real-world scenario. After collecting the multiple manifests needed to deploy an application, we are faced with additional challenges. How can we change the values in a ConfigMap depending on the environment? How can we change the container image version? What about Secrets and volumes? Is it possible to update the health probe's configuration?

Many tools have been introduced in the last few years to improve how we configure and deploy workloads in Kubernetes. For the Polar Bookshop system, we would like a tool that lets us handle multiple Kubernetes manifests as a single entity and customize parts of the configuration depending on the environment where the application is deployed.

Kustomize (https://kustomize.io) is a declarative tool that helps configure deployments for different environments via a layering approach. It produces standard Kubernetes manifests, and it's built natively in the Kubernetes CLI (kubectl), so you don't need to install anything else.

> **NOTE** Other popular options for managing deployment configuration in Kubernetes are ytt from the Carvel suite (https://carvel.dev/ytt) and Helm (https://helm.sh).

This section will show you the key features offered by Kustomize. First you'll see how to *compose* related Kubernetes manifests and handle them as a single unit. Then I'll show you how Kustomize can generate a ConfigMap for you from a property file. Finally, I'll guide you through a series of customizations that we'll apply to the base manifests before deploying workloads in a staging environment. The next chapter will expand on that and cover the production scenario.

Before moving on, make sure you still have your local minikube cluster up and running and that the Polar Bookshop backing services have been deployed correctly. If you don't, run `./create-cluster.sh` from polar-deployment/kubernetes/platform/ development.

> **NOTE** The platform services are exposed only within the cluster. If you want to access any of them from your local machine, you can use the port-forward-ing feature you learned about in chapter 7. You can either leverage the GUI provided by Octant or use the CLI (`kubectl port-forward service/polar-postgres 5432:5432`).

Now that we have all the backing services available, let's see how we can manage and configure a Spring Boot application using Kustomize.

14.3.1 *Using Kustomize to manage and configure Spring Boot applications*

So far, we've been deploying applications to Kubernetes by applying multiple Kubernetes manifests. For example, deploying Catalog Service requires applying the Config-Map, Deployment, and Service manifests to the cluster. When using Kustomize, the first step is composing related manifests together so that we can handle them as a single unit. Kustomize does that via a `Kustomization` resource. In the end, we want to let Kustomize manage, process, and generate Kubernetes manifests for us.

Let's see how it works. Open your Catalog Service project (catalog-service) and create a kustomization.yml file inside the k8s folder. It will be the entry point for Kustomize.

We'll first instruct Kustomize about which Kubernetes manifests it should use as a foundation for future customizations. For now, we'll use the existing Deployment and Service manifests.

Listing 14.4   Defining the base Kubernetes manifests for Kustomize

```
apiVersion: kustomize.config.k8s.io/v1beta1          ◁──┐  The API version
kind: Kustomization          ◁──┐  The kind of resource       for Kustomize
                                  defined by the manifest
resources:          ◁──
  - deployment.yml          ┌── Kubernetes manifests that Kustomize
  - service.yml             └── should manage and process
```

You might be wondering why we didn't include the ConfigMap. I'm glad you asked! We could have included the configmap.yml file we created earlier in the chapter, but Kustomize offers a better way. Instead of referencing a ConfigMap directly, we can provide a property file and let Kustomize use it to generate a ConfigMap. Let's see how it works.

For starters, let's move the body of the ConfigMap we created previously (configmap.yml) to a new application.yml file within the k8s folder.

Listing 14.5 Configuration properties provided via a ConfigMap

```
polar:
  greeting: Welcome to the book catalog from Kubernetes!
spring:
  datasource:
    url: jdbc:postgresql://polar-postgres/polardb_catalog
  security:
    oauth2:
      resourceserver:
        jwt:
          issuer-uri: http://polar-keycloak/realms/PolarBookshop
```

Then delete the configmap.yml file. We won't need it anymore. Finally, update the kustomization.yml file to generate a `catalog-config` ConfigMap starting from the application.yml file we just created.

Listing 14.6 Getting Kustomize to generate a ConfigMap from a property file

```
apiVersion: kustomize.config.k8s.io/v1beta1
kind: Kustomization

resources:                           The section containing
  - deployment.yml                   information to generate
  - service.yml                      ConfigMaps

configMapGenerator:     ◁────        Uses a property file
  - name: catalog-config             as the source for a
    files:              ◁────        ConfigMap
      - application.yml
    options:                         Defines the labels to
      labels:           ◁────        assign to the generated
        app: catalog-service         ConfigMap
```

NOTE In a similar way, Kustomize can also generate Secrets starting with literal values or files.

Let's pause for a moment and verify that what we have done so far works correctly. Your local cluster should already have your Catalog Service container image from before. If that's not the case, build the container image (`./gradlew bootBuildImage`), and load it into minikube (`minikube image load catalog-service --profile polar`).

Next, open a Terminal window, navigate to your Catalog Service project (catalog-service), and deploy the application using the familiar Kubernetes CLI. When applying standard Kubernetes manifests, we use the -f flag. When applying a Kustomization, we use the -k flag:

```
$ kubectl apply -k k8s
```

The final result should be the same as we got earlier when applying the Kubernetes manifests directly, but this time Kustomize handled everything via a Kustomization resource.

To complete the verification, use the port-forwarding strategy to expose the Catalog Service application to your local machine (kubectl port-forward service/catalog-service 9001:80). Then open a new Terminal window, and ensure that the root endpoint returns the message configured via the ConfigMap generated by Kustomize:

```
$ http :9001/
Welcome to the book catalog from Kubernetes!
```

ConfigMaps and Secrets generated by Kustomize are named with a unique suffix (a *hash*) when they're deployed. You can verify the actual name assigned to the catalog-config ConfigMap with the following command:

```
$ kubectl get cm -l app=catalog-service

NAME                       DATA   AGE
catalog-config-btcmff5d78  1      7m58s
```

Every time you update the input to the generators, Kustomize creates a new manifest with a different hash, which triggers a *rolling restart* of the containers where the updated ConfigMaps or Secrets are mounted as volumes. That is a highly convenient way to achieve an automated configuration refresh without implementing or configuring any additional components.

Let's verify that it's true. First, update the value for the polar.greeting property in the application.yml file used by Kustomize to generate the ConfigMap.

Listing 14.7   Updating the configuration input to the ConfigMap generator

```
polar:
  greeting: Welcome to the book catalog from a development
  ➥ Kubernetes environment!
...
```

Then apply the Kustomization again (kubectl apply -k k8s). Kustomize will generate a new ConfigMap with a different suffix hash, triggering a rolling restart of all the Catalog Service instances. In this case there's only one instance running. In production there will be more. The fact that the instances are restarted one at a time means that the update happens with zero downtime, which is what we aim for in the cloud. The Catalog Service root endpoint should now return the new message:

```
$ http :9001/
Welcome to the book catalog from a development Kubernetes environment!
```

If you're curious, you could compare this result with what would happen when updating a ConfigMap without Kustomize. Kubernetes would update the volume mounted to the Catalog Service container, but the application would not be restarted and would still return the old value.

> **NOTE** Depending on your requirements, you might need to avoid a rolling restart and have the applications reload their configuration at runtime. In that case, you can disable the hash suffix strategy with the `disableName-SuffixHash: true` generator option and perhaps rely on something like Spring Cloud Kubernetes Configuration Watcher to notify the applications whenever a ConfigMap or Secret is changed.

When you're done experimenting with the Kustomize setup, you can stop the port-forwarding process (Ctrl-C) and undeploy Catalog Service (`kubectl delete -k k8s`).

Since we moved from plain Kubernetes manifests to Kustomize, we still need to update a couple of things. In chapter 7, we used Tilt to achieve a better development workflow when working locally on Kubernetes. Tilt supports Kustomize, so we can configure it to deploy applications via a `Kustomization` resource rather than via plain Kubernetes manifests. Go ahead and update the Tiltfile in your Catalog Service project as follows.

Listing 14.8 Configuring Tilt to deploy Catalog Service using Kustomize

```
custom_build(
    ref = 'catalog-service',
    command = './gradlew bootBuildImage --imageName $EXPECTED_REF',
    deps = ['build.gradle', 'src']
)                                        Runs the application from
                                         the Kustomization located
k8s_yaml(kustomize('k8s'))          ◁─── in the k8s folder

k8s_resource('catalog-service', port_forwards=['9001'])
```

Finally, we need to update the manifest validation step in the commit stage workflow for Catalog Service, or it will fail the next time we push changes to GitHub. In your Catalog Service project, open the commit-stage.yml file (`.github/workflows`) and update it as follows.

Listing 14.9 Using Kubeval to validate the manifests generated by Kustomize

```
name: Commit Stage
on: push
...
```

```
jobs:
  build:
    name: Build and Test
    ...
    steps:
      ...
      - name: Validate Kubernetes manifests
        uses: stefanprodan/kube-tools@v1
        with:
          kubectl: 1.24.3
          kubeval: 0.16.1
          command: |
            kustomize build k8s | kubeval --strict -
```

> **Uses Kustomize to generate the manifests and then validates them with Kubeval**

So far, the most significant benefit we got from Kustomize is the automatic rolling restart of applications when a ConfigMap or Secret is updated. In the next section, you'll learn more about Kustomize and explore its powerful features for managing different Kubernetes configurations depending on the deployment environment.

14.3.2 Managing Kubernetes configuration for multiple environments with Kustomize

During development we followed the 15-Factor methodology and externalized the configuration for each aspect of an application that could change between deployments in different environments. You saw how to use property files, environment variables, configuration services, and ConfigMaps. I also showed you how to use Spring profiles to customize the application configuration based on the deployment environment. Now we need to take a step further and define a strategy to customize the entire deployment configuration depending on where we deploy an application.

In the previous section, you learned how to compose and process Kubernetes manifests together via a `Kustomization` resource. For each environment, we can specify *patches* to apply changes or additional configurations on top of those basic manifests. All the customization steps you'll see in this section will be applied without changing anything in the application source code but using the same release artifacts produced earlier. That's quite a powerful concept and one of the main features of cloud native applications.

The Kustomize approach to configuration customization is based on the concepts of *bases* and *overlays*. The k8s folder we created in the Catalog Service project can be considered a *base*: a directory with a kustomization.yml file that combines Kubernetes manifests and customizations. An *overlay* is another directory with a kustomization.yml file. What makes it special is that it defines customizations in relation to one or more bases and combines them. Starting from the same base, you can specify an overlay for each deployment environment (such as development, test, staging, and production).

As shown in figure 14.3, each `Kustomization` includes a kustomization.yml file. The one acting as the *base* composes together several Kubernetes resources like Deployments, Services, and ConfigMaps. Also, it's not aware of the overlays, so it's

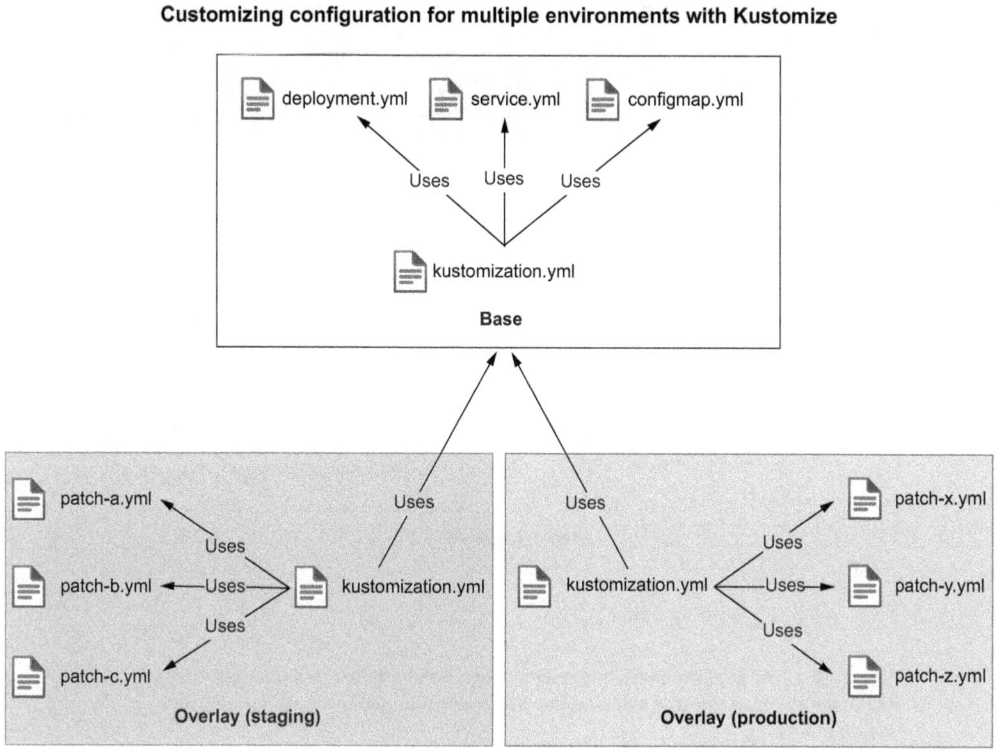

Customizing configuration for multiple environments with Kustomize

Figure 14.3 Kustomize bases can be used as the foundation for further customizations (overlays) depending on the deployment environment.

completely independent of them. The *overlays* use one or more *bases* as a foundation and provide additional configuration via patches.

Bases and overlays can be defined either in the same repository or different ones. For the Polar Bookshop system, we'll use the k8s folder in each application project as a base and define overlays in the `polar-deployment` repository. Similar to what you learned in chapter 3 about application codebases, you can decide whether to keep your deployment configuration in the same repository as your application or not. I decided to go for a separate repository for a few reasons:

- It makes it possible to control the deployment of all the system components from a single place.
- It allows focused version-control, auditing, and compliance checks before deploying anything to production.
- It fits the GitOps approach, where delivery and deployment tasks are decoupled.

As an example, figure 14.4 shows how the Kustomize manifests could be structured in the case of Catalog Service, having bases and overlays in two separate repositories.

Customizing Catalog Service for multiple environments with Kustomize

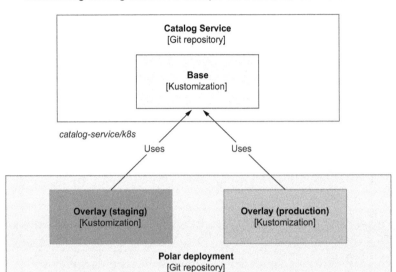

polar-deployment/applications/catalog-service

Figure 14.4   Kustomize bases and overlays can be stored in the same repository or two separate ones. Overlays can be used to customize deployments for different environments.

Another decision to make is whether to keep the base Kubernetes manifests together with the application source code or move them to the deployment repository. I decided to go with the first approach for the Polar Bookshop example, similar to what we did with the default configuration properties. One of the benefits is that it makes it simple to run each application on a local Kubernetes cluster during development, either directly or using Tilt. Depending on your requirements, you might decide to use one approach or the other. Both are valid and used in real-world scenarios.

Patches vs. templates

Kustomize's approach to customizing configuration is based on applying patches. It's quite the opposite of how Helm works (https://helm.sh). Helm requires you to template every part of a manifest that you would like to change (resulting in non-valid YAML). After that, you can provide different values for those templates in each environment. If a field is not templated, you can't customize its value. For that reason, it's not rare to use Helm and Kustomize in sequence, overcoming each other's shortcomings. Both approaches have pros and cons.

In this book I decided to use Kustomize because it's natively available in the Kubernetes CLI, it works with valid YAML files, and it's purely declarative. Helm is more powerful and can also handle complex application rollouts and upgrades that Kubernetes doesn't support natively. On the other hand, it has a steep learning curve, its templating solution has a few drawbacks, and it's not declarative.

Another option is ytt from the Carvel suite (https://carvel.dev/ytt). It provides a superior experience, with support for both patches and templates, it works with valid YAML files, and its templating strategy is more robust. It takes a bit more effort to get familiar with ytt than Kustomize, but it's worth the effort. Because it treats YAML as a first-class citizen, ytt can be used to configure and customize any YAML file, even outside Kubernetes. Do you use GitHub Actions workflows? Ansible playbooks? Jenkins pipelines? You can use ytt in all those scenarios.

Let's consider Catalog Service. We already have the base deployment configuration composed with Kustomize. It's located within the project repository in a dedicated folder (catalog-service/k8s). Now let's define an overlay to customize the deployment for staging.

14.3.3 Defining a configuration overlay for staging

In the previous sections, we used Kustomize to manage the configuration of Catalog Service in a local development environment. Those manifests will represent the *base* for multiple customizations applied for each environment as *overlays*. Since we'll define overlays in the `polar-deployment` repository while the base is in the `catalog-service` repository, all the Catalog Service manifests must be available in the main remote branch. If you haven't done so yet, push all the changes applied to your Catalog Service project so far to the remote repository on GitHub.

> **NOTE** As I explained in chapter 2, I expect you have created a different repository on GitHub for each project in the Polar Bookshop system. In this chapter we're working only with the `polar-deployment` and `catalog-service` repositories, but you should have also created repositories for `edge-service`, `order-service`, and `dispatcher-service`.

As anticipated, we'll store any configuration overlay in the `polar-deployment` repository. In this section and the following ones, we'll define an overlay for the staging environment. The next chapter will cover production.

Go ahead and create a new kubernetes/applications folder in your `polar-deployment` repository. We'll use it to keep the customizations for all the applications in the Polar Bookshop system. In the newly created path, add a catalog-service folder that will contain any overlay for customizing the deployment of Catalog Service in different environments. In particular, we'll want to prepare the deployment in staging, so create a "staging" folder for Catalog Service.

Any customization (base or overlay) requires a kustomization.yml file. Let's create one for the staging overlay of Catalog Service (polar-deployment/kubernetes/applications/catalog-service/staging). The first thing to configure is a reference to the base manifests.

If you've followed along, you should have your Catalog Service source code tracked in a `catalog-service` repository on GitHub. A reference to a remote base needs to point to the folder containing the kustomization.yml file, which is k8s in our case. Also, we should refer to a specific tag or digest for the version we want to deploy. We'll talk about release strategies and versioning in the next chapter, so we'll simply point to the `main` branch for now. The final URL should be something like `github .com/<your_github_username>/catalog-service/k8s?ref=main`. For example, in my case, it would be `github.com/polarbookshop/catalog-service/k8s?ref=main`.

Listing 14.10   Defining an overlay for staging on top of a remote base

```
apiVersion: kustomize.config.k8s.io/v1beta1
kind: Kustomization                              Uses the manifests in your Catalog
                                                 Service repo on GitHub as the base
resources:                              ◁─────┘  for further customizations
  - github.com/<your_github_username>/catalog-service/k8s?ref=main
```

NOTE   I'll assume that all the GitHub repositories you created for Polar Book-shop are publicly accessible. If that's not the case, you can go to the specific repository page on GitHub and access the Settings section for that repository. Then scroll to the bottom of the settings page, and make the package public by clicking the Change Visibility button.

We could now deploy Catalog Service from the staging overlay using the Kubernetes CLI, but the result wouldn't be different than using the base directly. Let's start applying some customizations specifically for staging deployments.

14.3.4 *Customizing environment variables*

The first customization we could apply is an environment variable to activate the `staging` Spring profile for Catalog Service. Most customizations can be applied via patches following a merge strategy. Much like Git merges changes from different branches, Kustomize produces final Kubernetes manifests with changes coming from different `Kustomization` files (one or more bases and an overlay).

A best practice when defining Kustomize patches is to keep them small and focused. To customize environment variables, create a patch-env.yml file within the staging overlay for Catalog Service (kubernetes/applications/catalog-service/staging). We need to specify some contextual information so Kustomize can figure out where to apply the patch and how to merge the changes. When the patch is for customizing a container, Kustomize requires us to specify the kind and name of the Kubernetes resource (that is, `Deployment`) and the name of the container. This customization option is called a *strategic merge patch*.

Listing 14.11   A patch for customizing environment variables

```
apiVersion: apps/v1
kind: Deployment
```

```
metadata:
  name: catalog-service
spec:
  template:
    spec:
      containers:
        - name: catalog-service
          env:
            - name: SPRING_PROFILES_ACTIVE        Defines which Spring
              value: prod                         profiles should be
                                                  activated
```

Next we need to instruct Kustomize to apply the patch. In the kustomization.yml file for the staging overlay of Catalog Service, list the patch-env.yml file as follows.

Listing 14.12   Getting Kustomize to apply the patch for environment variables

```
apiVersion: kustomize.config.k8s.io/v1beta1
kind: Kustomization

resources:
  - github.com/<your_github_username>/catalog-service/k8s?ref=main

patchesStrategicMerge:              Section containing the list of patches to
  - patch-env.yml                   apply to the base manifests according
                                    to the strategic merge strategy
   The patch for customizing the
 environment variables passed to
    the Catalog Service container
```

You can use this same approach to customize many aspects of a Deployment, such as the number of replicas, liveness probe, readiness probe, graceful shutdown timeout, environment variables, volumes, and more. In the next section, I'll show you how to customize ConfigMaps.

14.3.5   Customizing ConfigMaps

The base Kustomization for Catalog Service instructs Kustomize to generate a catalog-config ConfigMap starting from an application.yml file. To customize the values in that ConfigMap, we have two main options: replace the entire ConfigMap or overwrite only the values that should be different in staging. In this second case, we could generally rely on some advanced Kustomize patching strategy to overwrite specific values in the ConfigMap.

When working with Spring Boot, we can take advantage of the power of Spring profiles. Instead of updating values in the existing ConfigMap, we can add an application-staging.yml file, which we know takes precedence over application.yml when the staging profile is active. The final result will be a ConfigMap containing both files.

First, let's create an application-staging.yml file within the staging overlay for Catalog Service. We'll use this property file to define a different value for the polar .greeting property. Since we'll use the same minikube cluster from earlier as the staging environment, URLs to backing services and credentials will be the same as in the development environment. In a real-world scenario, this stage would involve more customizations.

Listing 14.13   Staging-specific configuration for Catalog Service

```
polar:
  greeting: Welcome to the book catalog from a staging
➥Kubernetes environment!
```

Next we can rely on the ConfigMap Generator provided by Kustomize to combine the application-staging.yml file (defined in the staging overlay) with the application.yml file (defined in the base `Kustomization`) within the same `catalog-config` ConfigMap. Go ahead and update the kustomization.yml file for the staging overlay as follows.

Listing 14.14   Merging property files within the same ConfigMap

```
apiVersion: kustomize.config.k8s.io/v1beta1
kind: Kustomization

resources:
  - github.com/<your_github_username>/catalog-service/k8s?ref=main

patchesStrategicMerge:              Merges this ConfigMap
  - patch-env.yml                   with the one defined in
                                    the base Kustomization

configMapGenerator:
  - behavior: merge    ◄──┘         The additional property
    files:                          file added to the
      - application-staging.yml  ◄── ConfigMap
    name: catalog-config  ◄──┐
                            └── The same ConfigMap name used
                                in the base Kustomization
```

That's it for ConfigMaps. The following section will cover how you can configure which image name and version to deploy.

14.3.6 *Customizing image name and version*

The base Deployment manifest defined in the Catalog Service repository (catalog-service/k8s/deployment.yml) is configured to use a local container image and doesn't specify a version number (which means the `latest` tag is used). That's convenient in the development phase, but it doesn't work for other deployment environments.

If you followed along, you should have your Catalog Service source code tracked in a `catalog-service` repository on GitHub and a `ghcr.io/<your_github_username>/catalog-service:latest` container image published to GitHub Container Registry (as per the Commit Stage workflow). The next chapter will cover release strategies and versioning. Until then, we'll still use the `latest` tag. Regarding the image name, though, it's time to start pulling container images from the registry rather than using the local ones.

NOTE Images published to GitHub Container Registry will have the same visibility as the related GitHub code repository. I'll assume that all the images we build for Polar Bookshop are publicly accessible via the GitHub Container Registry. If that's not the case, you can go to the specific repository page on GitHub and access the Packages section for that repository. Then select Package Settings from the sidebar menu, scroll to the bottom of the settings page, and make the package public by clicking the Change Visibility button.

Similar to what we've done for environment variables, we could use a patch to change the image that's used by the Catalog Service Deployment resource. Since it's a very common customization and would need to be changed every time we deliver a new version of our applications, however, Kustomize provides a more convenient way to declare which image name and version we want to use for each container. Furthermore, we can either update the kustomization.yml file directly or rely on the Kustomize CLI (installed as part of the Kubernetes CLI). Let's try the latter.

Open a Terminal window, navigate to the staging overlay for Catalog Service (kubernetes/applications/catalog-service/staging), and run the following command to define which image and version to use for the `catalog-service` container. Remember to replace `<your_github_username>` with your GitHub username in lowercase:

```
$ kustomize edit set image \
    catalog-service=ghcr.io/<your_github_username>/catalog-service:latest
```

This command will automatically update the kustomization.yml file with the new configuration, as you can see in the following listing.

Listing 14.15   Configuring the image name and version for the container

```
apiVersion: kustomize.config.k8s.io/v1beta1
kind: Kustomization

resources:
  - github.com/<your_github_username>/catalog-service/k8s?ref=main

patchesStrategicMerge:
  - patch-env.yml

configMapGenerator:
  - behavior: merge
    files:
      - application-staging.yml        The name of the              The new image name
    name: catalog-config               container as defined        for the container (with
                                       in the Deployment           your GitHub username
images:                                manifest                    in lowercase)
  - name: catalog-service      ◁──
    newName: ghcr.io/<your_github_username>/catalog-service       ◁──
    newTag: latest      ◁──
                             The new tag for
                             the container
```

In the next section, I'll show you how to configure the number of replicas to deploy.

14.3.7 *Customizing the number of replicas*

Cloud native applications should be highly available, and Catalog Service is not. So far we've been deploying a single application instance. What happens if it crashes or becomes momentarily unavailable due to a high workload? We would not be able to use the application anymore. Not very resilient, is it? Among other things, a staging environment is a good target for performance and availability tests. At a minimum, we should have two instances running. Kustomize provides a convenient way to update the number of replicas for a given Pod.

Open the kustomization.yml file in the staging overlay for Catalog Service (kubernetes/ applications/catalog-service/staging) and configure two replicas for the application.

Listing 14.16   Configuring replicas for the Catalog Service container

```
apiVersion: kustomize.config.k8s.io/v1beta1
kind: Kustomization

resources:
  - github.com/<your_github_username>/catalog-service/k8s?ref=main

patchesStrategicMerge:
  - patch-env.yml

configMapGenerator:
  - behavior: merge
    files:
      - application-staging.yml
    name: catalog-config

images:
  - name: catalog-service
    newName: ghcr.io/<your_github_username>/catalog-service
    newTag: latest
```

The name of the Deployment for which to define the number of replicas

The number of replicas

```
replicas:
  - name: catalog-service
    count: 2
```

It's finally time to deploy Catalog Service and test the configuration provided by the staging overlay. For simplicity, we'll use the same minikube local cluster we have been using so far as the staging environment. If you still have your minikube cluster up and running from before, you're good to go. Otherwise, you can start it by running ./create-cluster.sh from polar-deployment/kubernetes/platform/development. The script will spin up a Kubernetes cluster and deploy the backing services required by Polar Bookshop.

Then open a Terminal window, navigate to the staging overlay folder for Catalog Service (applications/catalog-service/staging), and run the following command to deploy the application via Kustomize:

```
$ kubectl apply -k .
```

You can monitor the operation's result via the Kubernetes CLI (kubectl get pod -1 app=catalog-service) or the Octant GUI (refer to chapter 7 for more information). Once the applications are available and ready, we can check the application logs using the CLI:

```
$ kubectl logs deployment/catalog-service
```

One of the first Spring Boot log events will tell you that the staging profile is enabled, just like we configured in the staging overlay via a patch.

The application is not exposed outside the cluster, but you can use the port-forwarding functionality to forward traffic from your local environment on port 9001 to the Service running in the cluster on port 80:

```
$ kubectl port-forward service/catalog-service 9001:80
```

Next, open a new Terminal window and call the application's root endpoint:

```
$ http :9001
Welcome to the book catalog from a staging Kubernetes environment!
```

The result is the customized message we defined in the application-staging.yml file for the polar.greeting property. That's exactly what we were expecting.

> **NOTE** It's worth noticing that if you send a GET request to :9001/books, you'll get an empty list. In staging, we haven't enabled the testdata profile controlling the generation of books at startup time. We want that only in a development or test environment.

The last customization we applied to the staging overlay was the number of replicas to deploy. Let's verify that with the following command:

```
$ kubectl get pod -1 app=catalog-service
```

```
NAME                                READY  STATUS   RESTARTS  AGE
catalog-service-6c5fc7b955-9kvgf    1/1    Running  0         3m94s
catalog-service-6c5fc7b955-n7rgl    1/1    Running  0         3m94s
```

Kubernetes is designed to ensure the availability of each application. If enough resources are available, it will try to deploy the two replicas on two different nodes. If one node crashes, the application will still be available on the other one. At the same time, Kubernetes takes care of deploying the second instance somewhere else to ensure there are always two replicas up and running. You can check which node each Pod has been allocated on with kubectl get pod -o wide. In our case, the minikube cluster has only one node, so both instances will be deployed together.

If you're curious, you can also try to update the application-staging.yml file, apply the Kustomization to the cluster again (kubectl apply -k .), and see how the Catalog Service Pods are restarted one after the other (*rolling restarts*) to load the new

ConfigMap with zero downtime. To visualize the sequence of events, you can either use Octant or launch this command on a separate Terminal window before applying the `Kustomization`: `kubectl get pods -l app=catalog-service --watch`.

When you're done testing the application, you can terminate the port-forwarding process with Ctrl-C and delete the cluster with `./destroy-cluster.sh` from polar-deployment/kubernetes/platform/development.

Now that you've learned the fundamentals of configuring and deploying Spring Boot applications in Kustomize, it's time to go to production. That's what the next chapter is all about.

Polar Labs

Feel free to apply what you've learned in this chapter to all the applications in the Polar Bookshop system. You'll need these updated applications in the next chapter, where we'll deploy everything in production.

1 Disable the Spring Cloud Config client.
2 Define a base Kustomization manifest, and update Tilt and the commit stage workflow.
3 Use Kustomize to generate a ConfigMap.
4 Configure a staging overlay.

You can refer to the Chapter14/14-end folder in the code repository accompanying the book to check the final result (https://github.com/ThomasVitale/cloud-native -spring-in-action).

Summary

- A configuration server built with Spring Cloud Config Server can be protected with any of the features offered by Spring Security. For example, you can require a client to use HTTP Basic authentication to access the configuration endpoints exposed by the server.
- Configuration data in a Spring Boot application can be reloaded by calling the `/actuator/refresh` endpoint exposed by Spring Boot Actuator.
- To propagate the config refresh operation to other applications in the system, you can use Spring Cloud Bus.
- Spring Cloud Config Server offers a Monitor module that exposes a `/monitor` endpoint that code repository providers can call through a webhook whenever a new change is pushed to the configuration repository. The result is that all the applications affected by the configuration change will be triggered by Spring Cloud Bus to reload the configuration. The whole process happens automatically.
- Managing secrets is a critical task of any software system, and it is dangerous when mistakes are made.

- Spring Cloud Config offers encryption and decryption features for handling secrets safely in the configuration repository, using either symmetric or asymmetric keys.
- You can also use secrets management solutions offered by cloud providers like Azure, AWS, and Google Cloud and leverage the integration with Spring Boot provided by Spring Cloud Azure, Spring Cloud AWS, and Spring Cloud GCP.
- HashiCorp Vault is another option. You can either use it to configure all Spring Boot applications directly through the Spring Vault project or make it a backend for Spring Cloud Config Server.
- When Spring Boot applications are deployed to a Kubernetes cluster, you can also configure them through ConfigMaps (for non-sensitive configuration data) and Secrets (for sensitive configuration data).
- You can use ConfigMaps and Secrets as a source of values for environment variables or mount them as volumes to the container. The latter approach is the preferred one and is supported by Spring Boot natively.
- Secrets are not secret. The data contained within them is not encrypted by default, so you shouldn't put them under version control and include them in your repository.
- The platform team is responsible for protecting secrets, such as by using the Sealed Secrets project to encrypt secrets and make it possible to put them under version control.
- Managing several Kubernetes manifests to deploy an application is not very intuitive. Kustomize provides a convenient way to manage, deploy, configure, and upgrade an application in Kubernetes.
- Among other things, Kustomize provides generators to build ConfigMaps and Secrets, and a way to trigger a rolling restart whenever they are updated.
- The Kustomize approach to configuration customization is based on the concepts of bases and overlays.
- Overlays are built on top of base manifests, and any customization is applied via patches. You saw how to define patches for customizing environment variables, ConfigMaps, container images, and replicas.

Continuous delivery and GitOps

This chapter covers

- Understanding continuous delivery and release management
- Configuring Spring Boot for production with Kustomize
- Deploying in production with GitOps and Kubernetes

Chapter after chapter, we have gone through patterns, principles, and best practices for working with cloud native applications, and we've built a bookshop system using Spring Boot and Kubernetes. It's time to deploy Polar Bookshop to production.

I expect you have the projects of the Polar Bookshop system in separate Git repositories stored on GitHub. If you haven't followed along in the previous chapters, you can refer to the Chapter15/15-begin folder in the source code accompanying the book, and use it as a foundation to define those repositories.

This chapter will guide you through some final aspects of preparing applications for production. First I'll discuss versioning strategies for release candidates and how to design the acceptance stage of a deployment pipeline. Then you'll see how to configure Spring Boot applications for production and deploy them on a Kubernetes cluster in a public cloud. Next, I'll show you how to complete the deployment pipeline by implementing the production stage. Finally, you'll use Argo CD to implement continuous deployment based on the GitOps principles.

> **NOTE** The source code for the examples in this chapter is available in the Chapter15/15-begin and Chapter15/15-end folders, containing the initial and final states of the project (https://github.com/ThomasVitale/cloud-native -spring-in-action).

15.1 Deployment pipeline: Acceptance stage

Continuous delivery is one of the fundamental practices we have identified that can support us in our journey to achieve the cloud native goals: speed, resilience, scale, and cost optimization. It's a holistic approach for delivering high-quality software quickly, reliably, and safely. The main idea behind continuous delivery is that an application is always in a releasable state. The primary pattern for adopting continuous delivery is the deployment pipeline, which goes from code commit to releasable software. It should be automated as much as possible and represent the only path to production.

Chapter 3 explained that a deployment pipeline can be composed of three key stages: commit stage, acceptance stage, and production stage. Throughout the book, we have automated the commit stage as a workflow in GitHub Actions. After a developer commits new code to the mainline, this stage goes through build, unit tests, integration tests, static code analysis, and packaging. At the end of this stage, an executable application artifact is published to an artifact repository. That is a *release candidate.*

This section will cover how we can version release candidates for continuous delivery. Then you'll learn more about the acceptance stage, its purpose, and its outcome. Finally, I'll show you how to implement a minimal workflow in GitHub Actions for the acceptance stage. At the end of this stage, the release candidate will be ready to be deployed to production.

15.1.1 Versioning release candidates for continuous delivery

The output of the commit stage of the deployment pipeline is a release candidate. That's the deployable artifact for an application. In our case, it's a container image. All the subsequent steps in the pipeline will evaluate the quality of that container image through different tests. If no issue is found, the release candidate is ultimately deployed to production and released to users.

A release candidate is stored in an artifact repository. If it's a JAR, it would be stored in a Maven repository. In our case, it's a container image and will be stored in a container registry. In particular, we'll use GitHub Container Registry.

Each release candidate must be uniquely identified. So far, we have used the implicit latest tag for all container image versions. Also, we ignored the 0.0.1-SNAPSHOT version configured in each Spring Boot project by default in Gradle. How should we version release candidates?

A popular strategy is *semantic versioning* (https://semver.org). It consists of identifiers in the form of <major>.<minor>.<patch>. Optionally, you can also add a hyphen at the end, followed by a string, marking a pre-release. By default, a Spring Boot project generated from Spring Initializr (https://start.spring.io) is initialized with version 0.0.1-SNAPSHOT, which identifies a snapshot release. A variation of this strategy is *calendar versioning* (https://calver.org), which combines the concepts of semantic versioning with date and time.

Both those strategies are broadly used for open source projects and software released as products to customers, because they provide implicit information about what a new release contains. For example, we expect a new major version to contain new functionality and API changes incompatible with the previous major version. On the other hand, we would expect a patch to have a limited scope and guarantee backward compatibility.

> **NOTE** If you're working on software projects for which semantic versioning makes sense, I recommend checking out JReleaser, a release automation tool. "Its goal is to simplify creating releases and publishing artifacts to multiple package managers while providing customizable options" (https://jreleaser.org).

Semantic versioning will require some form of manual step to assign a version number based on the content of the release artifact: Does it contain breaking changes? Does it only contain bug fixes? When we have a number, it's still not clear what's included in the new release artifact, so we need to use Git tags and define a mapping between Git commit identifiers and version numbers.

Things get even more challenging for snapshot artifacts. Let's consider a Spring Boot project as an example. By default, we start with version 0.0.1-SNAPSHOT. Until we're ready to cut the 0.0.1 release, every time we push new changes to the main branch, the commit stage will be triggered, and a new release candidate will be published with the number 0.0.1-SNAPSHOT. All release candidates will have the same number until version 0.0.1 is released. This approach doesn't ensure traceability of changes. Which commits are included in release candidate 0.0.1-SNAPSHOT? We can't tell. Furthermore, it's affected by the same unreliability as using latest. Any time we retrieve the artifact, it might be different from the last time.

When it comes to continuous delivery, using an approach like semantic versioning is not ideal for uniquely identifying release candidates. When we follow the principles of continuous integration, we'll have many release candidates built daily. And every release candidate can potentially be promoted to production. Will we have to update the semantic version for each new code commit, with a different approach based on its content (major, minor, patch)? The path from code commit to production should be automated as much as possible, trying to eliminate manual intervention. If we go with continuous deployment, even the promotion to production will happen automatically. What should we do?

One solution would be using the Git commit hash to version release candidates—that would be automated, traceable, and reliable, and you wouldn't need Git tags. You could use the commit hash as is (for example, `486105e261cb346b87920aaa4ea6dce6eebd6223`) or use it as the base for generating a more human-friendly number. For example, you could prefix it with a timestamp or with an increasing sequence number, with the goal of making it possible to tell which release candidate is the newest (for example, `20220731210356-486105e261cb346b87920aaa4ea6dce6eebd6223`).

Still, semantic versioning and similar strategies have their place in continuous delivery. They can be used as *display names* in addition to the unique identifier, as Dave Farley suggests in his book *Continuous Delivery Pipelines* (2021). That would be a way to provide users with information about the release candidate while still making it possible to benefit from continuous delivery.

For Polar Bookshop, we'll adopt a simple solution and use the Git commit hash directly to identify our release candidates. Therefore, we'll ignore the version number configured in the Gradle project (which could instead be used as the display version name). For example, a release candidate for Catalog Service would be `ghcr.io/<your_github_username>/catalog-service:<commit-hash>`.

Now that we have a strategy, let's see how we can implement it for Catalog Service. Go to your Catalog Service project (catalog-service), and open the commit-stage.yml file within the .github/workflows folder. We previously defined a `VERSION` environment variable to hold the release candidate's unique identifier. At the moment, it's statically set to `latest`. Let's replace that with `${{ github.sha }}`, which will be dynamically resolved to the current Git commit hash by GitHub Actions. For convenience, we'll also add the `latest` tag to the newest release candidate, which is useful for local development scenarios.

Listing 15.1 Using the Git commit hash to version release candidates

```
name: Commit Stage
on: push

env:
  REGISTRY: ghcr.io
  IMAGE_NAME: polarbookshop/catalog-service
  VERSION: ${{ github.sha }}          ◁─────────┐
                                                 │
build:                                           │
  name: Build and Test                           │
  ...                                   Publishes a release candidate
                                        with a version equal to the
package:                                Git commit hash
  name: Package and Publish                      │
  ...                                            │
  steps:                                         │
    ...                                          │
    - name: Publish container image  ◁───────────┘
```

```
    run: docker push \
            ${{ env.REGISTRY }}/${{ env.IMAGE_NAME }}:${{ env.VERSION }}
  - name: Publish container image (latest)
    run: |
      docker tag \
        ${{ env.REGISTRY }}/${{ env.IMAGE_NAME }}:${{ env.VERSION }} \
        ${{ env.REGISTRY }}/${{ env.IMAGE_NAME }}:latest
      docker push ${{ env.REGISTRY }}/${{ env.IMAGE_NAME }}:latest
```

**Adds the "latest" tag to the
newest release candidate**

After updating the workflow, commit your changes and push them to GitHub. That
will trigger the execution of the commit stage workflow (figure 15.1). The outcome
will be a container image published to GitHub Container Registry, versioned with the
current Git commit hash and the additional latest tag.

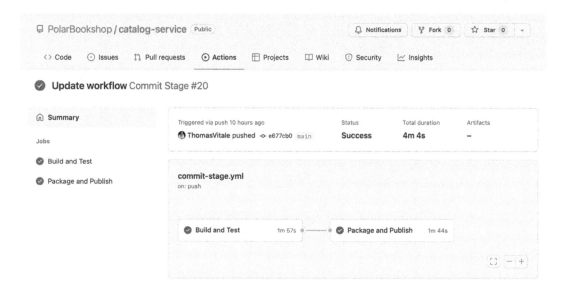

Figure 15.1   The commit stage goes from code commit to release candidate published to an artifact repository.

Once the pipeline is executed successfully, you'll be able to see the newly published
container image from your catalog-service repository main page on GitHub. In the
sidebar you'll find a Packages section with a "catalog-service" item. Click that, and
you'll be directed to the container repository for Catalog Service (figure 15.2). When
using the GitHub Container Registry, container images are stored next to the source
code, which is very convenient.

At this point, the container image (our release candidate) is uniquely identified
and ready to go through the acceptance stage. That's the topic of the next section.

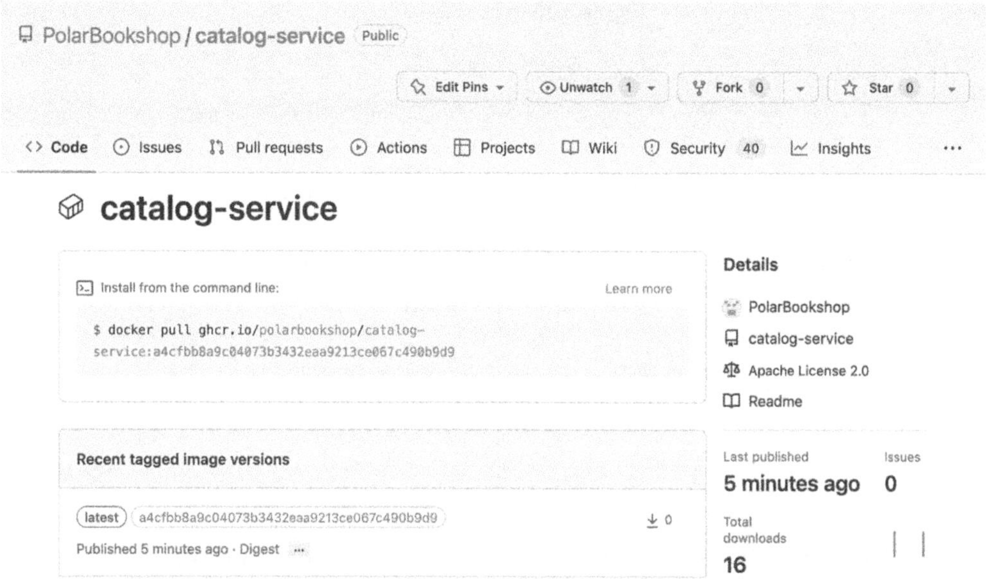

🖵 PolarBookshop / **catalog-service** `Public`

    ⚡ Edit Pins ▾   ⊙ Unwatch `1` ▾   ⑂ Fork `0` ▾   ☆ Star `0` ▾

‹› **Code** ⊙ Issues ⑂ Pull requests ▷ Actions ⊞ Projects ▯ Wiki ⊙ Security `40` ⬩ Insights   **⋯**

⬡ **catalog-service**

▣ Install from the command line: Learn more

```
$ docker pull ghcr.io/polarbookshop/catalog-
  service:a4cfbb8a9c04073b3432eaa9213ce067c490b9d9
```

Details

🎭 PolarBookshop

🖵 catalog-service

⚖ Apache License 2.0

▭ Readme

Recent tagged image versions

(latest) a4cfbb8a9c04073b3432eaa9213ce067c490b9d9   ⤓ 0

Published 5 minutes ago · Digest **⋯**

Last published   Issues
5 minutes ago   **0**

Total
downloads | |
16

Figure 15.2   In our case, release candidates are container images published to GitHub Container Registry.

15.1.2 *Understanding the acceptance stage of the deployment pipeline*

The acceptance stage of the deployment pipeline is triggered whenever a new release candidate is published to the artifact repository at the end of the commit stage. It consists of deploying the application to a production-like environment and running additional tests to increase the confidence in its releasability. The tests that run in the acceptance stage are usually slow, but we should strive to keep the whole deployment pipeline's execution under one hour.

In chapter 3, you learned about the software test classification provided by the *Agile Testing Quadrants* (figure 15.3). The quadrants classify software tests based on whether they are technology or business facing, and whether they support development teams or are used to critique the project.

In the commit stage, we mainly focus on the first quadrant, including unit and integration tests. They are technology-facing tests that support the team, ensuring they build the *software right*. On the other hand, the acceptance stage focuses on the second and fourth quadrants and tries to eliminate the need for manual regression testing. This stage includes functional and non-functional acceptance tests.

The *functional acceptance tests* are business-facing tests that support development teams, ensuring they are building the *right software*. They take on the user perspective and are usually implemented via *executable specifications* using a high-level domain-specific language (DSL), which is then translated into a lower-level programming language. For example, you could use Cucumber (https://cucumber.io) to write scenarios like "browse the book catalog" or "place a book order" in human-friendly plain text. Those scenarios can then be executed and verified using a programming language like Java.

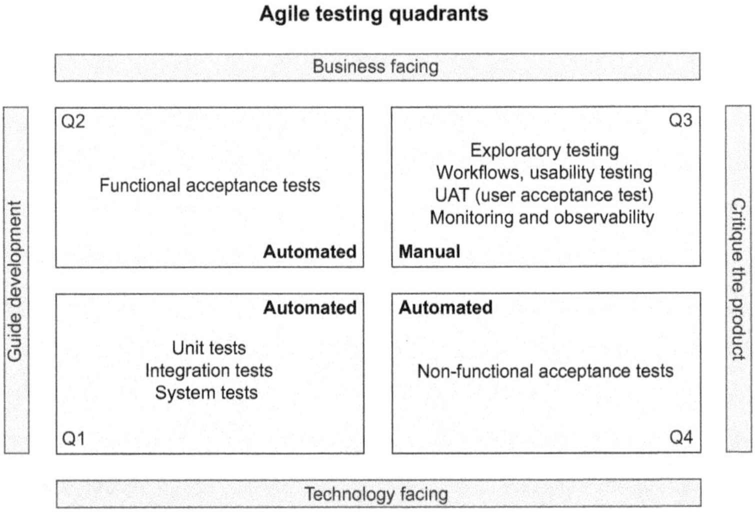

Agile testing quadrants

Figure 15.3 **The Agile Testing Quadrants are a taxonomy helpful for planning a software testing strategy.**

In the acceptance stage, we can also verify the *quality attributes* of a release candidate via *non-functional acceptance tests*. For example, we could run performance and load tests using a tool like Gatling (https://gatling.io), security and compliance tests, and resilience tests. In this last case, we could embrace *chaos engineering*, a discipline made popular by Netflix and consisting of making certain parts of the system fail to verify how the rest will react and how resilient the system is to failures. For Java applications, you can look at Chaos Monkey for Spring Boot (https://codecentric.github.io/chaos-monkey-spring-boot).

> **NOTE** How about the third quadrant? Following the continuous delivery principles, we strive not to include manual tests in the deployment pipeline. Yet we usually need them. They are particularly important for software products aimed at end users like web and mobile applications. Therefore, we run them on the side in the form of *exploratory testing* and *usability testing*, so that we ensure more freedom for testers and fewer constraints on the pace and timing required by continuous integration and the deployment pipeline.

An essential feature of the acceptance stage is that all tests are run against a production-like environment to ensure the best reliability. The deployment would follow the same procedure and scripts as production and could be tested via dedicated system tests (first quadrant).

If a release candidate passes all the tests in the acceptance stage, that means it's in a *releasable* state and can be delivered and deployed to production. Figure 15.4 illustrates inputs and outputs for the commit and acceptance stages in a deployment pipeline.

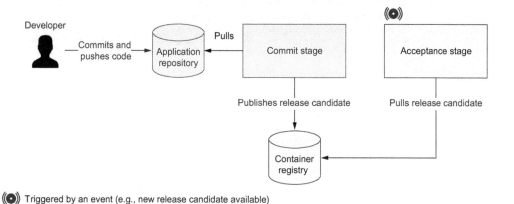

Triggered by an event (e.g., new release candidate available)

Figure 15.4   The commit stage goes from code commit to a release candidate, which then goes through the acceptance stage. If it passes all the tests, it's ready for production.

15.1.3 Implementing the acceptance stage with GitHub Actions

In this section, you'll see how to implement the skeleton of a workflow for the acceptance stage using GitHub Actions. Throughout the book we've focused on unit and integration tests, which we run in the commit stage. For the acceptance stage, we would need to write functional and non-functional acceptance tests. That's out of scope for this book, but I still want to show you some principles for designing the workflow using Catalog Service as an example.

Open your Catalog Service project (catalog-service), and create a new acceptance-stage.yml file within the .github/workflows folder. The acceptance stage is triggered whenever a new release candidate is published to the artifact repository. One option for defining such a trigger is listening for the events published by GitHub whenever the commit stage workflow has completed a run.

Listing 15.2   Triggering the acceptance stage after the commit stage is done

```
name: Acceptance Stage          ◁────┤  The name of
on:                                   │  the workflow
  workflow_run:              ◁────
    workflows: ['Commit Stage']      ┐  This workflow is triggered
    types: [completed]               │  when the Commit Stage
    branches: main                   │  workflow completes a run.
```

This workflow runs only on the main branch. (label pointing to `branches: main`)

However, that's not enough. Following the continuous integration principles, developers commit often during the day and repeatedly trigger the commit stage. Since the commit stage is much faster than the acceptance stage, we risk creating a bottleneck. When an acceptance stage run has completed, we are not interested in verifying all the release candidates that have queued up in the meantime. We are only interested in the newest one, so the others can be discarded. GitHub Actions provides a mechanism for handling this scenario via concurrency controls.

Listing 15.3   Configuring concurrency for the workflow execution

```
name: Acceptance Stage
on:
  workflow_run:
    workflows: ['Commit Stage']
    types: [completed]
    branches: main
concurrency: acceptance
```

Ensures that only one
workflow runs at a time

Next, you would define several jobs to run in parallel against a production-like environment, accomplishing functional and non-functional acceptance tests. For our example, we'll simply print a message, since we haven't implemented the autotests for this stage.

Listing 15.4   Running functional and non-functional acceptance tests

```
name: Acceptance Stage
on:
  workflow_run:
    workflows: ['Commit Stage']
    types: [completed]
    branches: main
concurrency: acceptance

jobs:
  functional:
    name: Functional Acceptance Tests
    if: ${{ github.event.workflow_run.conclusion == 'success' }}
    runs-on: ubuntu-22.04
    steps:
      - run: echo "Running functional acceptance tests"
  performance:
    name: Performance Tests
    if: ${{ github.event.workflow_run.conclusion == 'success' }}
    runs-on: ubuntu-22.04
    steps:
      - run: echo "Running performance tests"
  security:
    name: Security Tests
    if: ${{ github.event.workflow_run.conclusion == 'success' }}
    runs-on: ubuntu-22.04
    steps:
      - run: echo "Running security tests"
```

The job runs
only if the
commit stage
completed
successfully.

NOTE   The acceptance tests could be run against a staging environment that closely resembles production. The application could be deployed using the staging overlay we configured in the previous chapter.

At this point, push your changes to your GitHub `catalog-service` repository, and have a look at how GitHub first runs the commit stage workflow (triggered by your code commit) and then the acceptance stage workflow (triggered by the commit stage workflow completing successfully). Figure 15.5 shows the result of the acceptance stage workflow's execution.

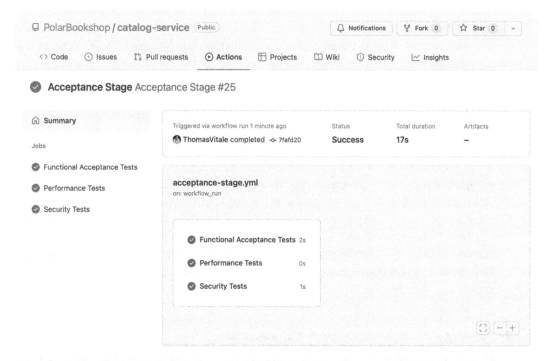

Figure 15.5 The commit stage goes from code commit to a release candidate, which then goes through the acceptance stage. If it passes all the tests, it's ready for production.

Deploying to production requires a combination of a release candidate and its configuration. Now that we've validated that a release candidate is ready for production, it's time to customize its configuration.

15.2   *Configuring Spring Boot for production*

We're getting closer and closer to deploying cloud native applications to a Kubernetes cluster in production. So far we have worked with local clusters using minikube. We now need a full-fledged Kubernetes cluster for our production environment. Before you continue reading this section, follow the instructions in appendix B (sections B.1 through B.6) to initialize a Kubernetes cluster on the DigitalOcean public cloud. You'll also find some tips if you want to use a different cloud provider.

Once you have a Kubernetes cluster up and running in the cloud, you can continue reading this section, which will cover the additional configuration we need to provide our Spring Boot applications with before deploying them to the production environment.

In the previous chapter, you learned about Kustomize and the overlay technique for managing customizations for different deployment environments on top of a common base. You also tried your hand at customizing the Catalog Service deployment for a staging environment. In this section we'll do something similar for production. Extending what you saw in chapter 14, I'll show you how to customize volume mounts for ConfigMaps and Secrets. Also, you'll see how to configure the CPU and memory for containers running in Kubernetes, and you'll learn more about how the Paketo Buildpacks manage resources for the Java Virtual Machine (JVM) within each container.

15.2.1   *Defining a configuration overlay for production*

First we need to define a new overlay to customize the deployment of Catalog Service for a production environment. As you'll probably remember from the previous chapter, the Kustomization base for Catalog Service is stored in the catalog-service repository. We keep the overlays in the polar-deployment repository.

Go ahead and create a new "production" folder within kubernetes/applications/ catalog-service (in the polar-deployment repository). We'll use it to store all customizations related to the production environment. Any base or overlay requires a kustomization.yml file, so let's create one for the production overlay. Remember, in the following listing, to replace <your_github_username> with your GitHub username in lowercase. Also, replace <release_sha> with the unique identifier associated with your latest release candidate for Catalog Service. You can retrieve that version from the Packages section of your catalog-service GitHub repository main page.

> **Listing 15.5   Defining an overlay for production on top of a remote base**

```
apiVersion: kustomize.config.k8s.io/v1beta1
kind: Kustomization
```

```
resources:
  - github.com/<your_github_username>/catalog-service/k8s?ref=<release_sha>
```

**The git commit hash (sha) identifying
your latest release candidate**

> **NOTE**   I'll assume that all the GitHub repositories you created for Polar Book-
> shop are publicly accessible. If that's not the case, you can go to the specific
> repository page on GitHub and access the Settings section for that repository.
> Scroll to the bottom of the settings page, and make the package public by
> clicking the Change Visibility button.

CUSTOMIZING ENVIRONMENT VARIABLES

The first customization we'll apply is an environment variable to activate the `prod`
Spring profile for Catalog Service. Following the same approach as in the previous
chapter, create a patch-env.yml file within the production overlay for Catalog Service
(kubernetes/applications/catalog-service/production).

Listing 15.6   A patch for customizing environment variables in a container

```
apiVersion: apps/v1
kind: Deployment
metadata:
  name: catalog-service
spec:
  template:
    spec:
      containers:
        - name: catalog-service
          env:
            - name: SPRING_PROFILES_ACTIVE       Defines which Spring
              value: prod                        profiles should be
                                                 activated
```

Next, we need to instruct Kustomize to apply the patch. In the kustomization.yml file
for the production overlay of Catalog Service, list the patch-env.yml file as follows.

Listing 15.7   Getting Kustomize to apply the patch for environment variables

```
apiVersion: kustomize.config.k8s.io/v1beta1
kind: Kustomization

resources:
  - github.com/<your_github_username>/catalog-service/k8s?ref=<release_sha>

patchesStrategicMerge:          Section containing the list of
  - patch-env.yml               patches to apply, according to
                                the strategic merge strategy
```

**The patch for customizing the
environment variables passed
to the Catalog Service container**

CUSTOMIZING SECRETS AND VOLUMES

In the previous chapter, you learned how to define ConfigMaps and Secrets, and you saw how to mount them as volumes to Spring Boot containers. In the base `Kustomization` we have no Secrets configured, since we are relying on the same default values from development. In production we need to pass different URLs and credentials to make it possible for Catalog Service to access the PostgreSQL database and Keycloak.

When you set up the production environment on DigitalOcean earlier, you also created a Secret with the credentials to access the PostgreSQL database (`polar-postgres-catalog-credentials`) and another for Keycloak (`keycloak-issuer-resourceserver-secret`). Now we can mount them as volumes to the Catalog Service container, similar to what we did with ConfigMaps in chapter 14. We'll do that in a dedicated patch.

Create a patch-volumes.yml file within the production overlay for Catalog Service (kubernetes/applications/catalog-service/production), and configure the patch as shown in listing 15.8. When Kustomize applies this patch to the base deployment manifests, it will merge the ConfigMap volume defined in the base with the Secret volumes defined in the patch.

Listing 15.8 Mounting Secrets as volumes to the Catalog Service container

```
apiVersion: apps/v1
kind: Deployment
metadata:
  name: catalog-service
spec:
  template:
    spec:
      containers:
        - name: catalog-service
          volumeMounts:
            - name: postgres-credentials-volume
              mountPath: /workspace/secrets/postgres          ◁  Mounts the volume
            - name: keycloak-issuer-resourceserver-secret-volume    with the Secret
              mountPath: /workspace/secrets/keycloak          ◁    containing the
      volumes:                                                      PostgreSQL
        - name: postgres-credentials-volume                         credentials
          secret:                                            Mounts the volume with
            secretName: polar-postgres-catalog-credentials  the Secret containing the
        - name: keycloak-issuer-resourceserver-secret-volume  Keycloak issuer URL
          secret:                                                 ◁
            secretName: keycloak-issuer-resourceserver-secret
```

Defines a volume from the Secret containing the PostgreSQL credentials

Defines a volume from the Secret containing the Keycloak issuer URL

Then, just like you learned in the previous section, we need to reference the patch in the kustomization.yml file for the production overlay.

Listing 15.9   Getting Kustomize to apply the patch for mounting Secrets

```
apiVersion: kustomize.config.k8s.io/v1beta1
kind: Kustomization

resources:
  - github.com/<your_github_username>/catalog-service/k8s?ref=<release_sha>

patchesStrategicMerge:
  - patch-env.yml
  - patch-volumes.yml       Defines a patch for mounting
                            Secrets as volumes
```

Currently, the Secrets are configured to be provided to the container, but Spring Boot is not aware of them yet. In the next section I'll show you how to instruct Spring Boot to load those Secrets as config trees.

CUSTOMIZING CONFIGMAPS

The base `Kustomization` for Catalog Service instructs Kustomize to generate a `catalog-config` ConfigMap starting with an application.yml file. As you learned in the previous chapter, we can ask Kustomize to add an additional file to that same ConfigMap, application-prod.yml, which we know takes precedence over the base application.yml file. That's how we're going to customize the application configuration for production.

First, create an application-prod.yml file within the production overlay for Catalog Service (kubernetes/applications/catalog-service/production). We'll use this property file to configure a custom greeting. We also need to instruct Spring Boot to load the Secrets as config trees, using the `spring.config.import` property. For more information on config trees, refer to chapter 14.

Listing 15.10   Production-specific configuration for Catalog Service

```
polar:
  greeting: Welcome to our book catalog from a production
⟿Kubernetes environment!
spring:
  config:                              Imports configuration from the
    import: configtree:/workspace/secrets/*/   path where volumes with Secrets are
                                       mounted. Make sure you include the
                                       final slash, or the import will fail.
```

Next, we can rely on the ConfigMap Generator provided by Kustomize to combine the application-prod.yml file (defined in the production overlay) with the application.yml file (defined in the base `Kustomization`), within the same `catalog-config` ConfigMap. Go ahead and update the kustomization.yml file for the production overlay as follows.

Listing 15.11   Merging property files within the same ConfigMap

```
apiVersion: kustomize.config.k8s.io/v1beta1
kind: Kustomization
```

```
resources:
  - github.com/<your_github_username>/catalog-service/k8s?ref=<release_sha>

patchesStrategicMerge:
  - patch-env.yml
  - patch-volumes.yml                    Merges this ConfigMap
                                         with the one defined in
                                         the base Kustomization
configMapGenerator:
  - behavior: merge      ◄──────
    files:                           The additional property file
      - application-prod.yml  ◄──    added to the ConfigMap
    name: catalog-config     ◄──
                                     The same ConfigMap name used
                                     in the base Kustomization
```

CUSTOMIZING IMAGE NAME AND VERSION

The next step is updating the image name and version, following the same procedure we used in the previous chapter. This time we'll be able to use a proper version number for the container image (our release candidate).

First, make sure you have the `kustomize` CLI installed on your computer. You can refer to the instructions at https://kustomize.io. If you're on macOS or Linux, you can install `kustomize` with the following command: `brew install kustomize`.

Then open a Terminal window, navigate to the production overlay for Catalog Service (kubernetes/applications/catalog-service/production), and run the following command to define which image and version to use for the `catalog-service` container. Remember to replace `<your_github_username>` with your GitHub username in lowercase. Also, replace `<sha>` with the unique identifier associated with your latest release candidate for Catalog Service. You can retrieve that version from the Packages section of your `catalog-service` GitHub repository main page:

```
$ kustomize edit set image \
    catalog-service=ghcr.io/<your_github_username>/catalog-service:<sha>
```

This command will automatically update the kustomization.yml file with the new configuration, as you can see in the following listing.

> **Listing 15.12 Configuring the image name and version for the container**

```
apiVersion: kustomize.config.k8s.io/v1beta1
kind: Kustomization

resources:
  - github.com/<your_github_username>/catalog-service/k8s?ref=<release_sha>

patchesStrategicMerge:
  - patch-env.yml
  - patch-volumes.yml

configMapGenerator:
  - behavior: merge
    files:
```

```
        - application-prod.yml
      name: catalog-config
```

```
images:
  - name: catalog-service
    newName:
    ⮑ ghcr.io/<your_github_username>/catalog-service
    newTag: <release_sha>
```

The name of the container as defined in the Deployment manifest

The new image name for the container (with your GitHub username in lowercase)

The new tag for the container (with your release candidate's unique identifier)

NOTE Images published to GitHub Container Registry will have the same visibility as the related GitHub code repository. I'll assume that all the images you build for Polar Bookshop are publicly accessible via the GitHub Container Registry. If that's not the case, you can go to the specific repository page on GitHub and access the Packages section for that repository. Then select Package Settings from the sidebar menu, scroll to the bottom of the settings page, and make the package public by clicking the Change Visibility button.

Currently we use the release candidate's unique identifier in two places: the URL for the remote base and the image tag. Whenever a new release candidate is promoted to production, we need to remember to update both of them. Even better, we should automate the update. I'll describe that later when we implement the production stage of the deployment pipeline.

CUSTOMIZING THE NUMBER OF REPLICAS

Cloud native applications are supposed to be highly available, but only one instance of Catalog Service is deployed by default. Similar to what we did for the staging environment, let's customize the number of replicas for the application.

Open the kustomization.yml file within the production overlay for Catalog Service (kubernetes/applications/catalog-service/production) and define two replicas for the catalog-service container.

Listing 15.13 Configuring the number of replicas for the container

```
apiVersion: kustomize.config.k8s.io/v1beta1
kind: Kustomization

resources:
  - github.com/<your_github_username>/catalog-service/k8s?ref=<release_sha>

patchesStrategicMerge:
  - patch-env.yml
  - patch-volumes.yml

configMapGenerator:
  - behavior: merge
    files:
      - application-prod.yml
    name: catalog-config
```

```
images:
  - name: catalog-service
    newName: ghcr.io/<your_github_username>/catalog-service
    newTag: <release_sha>

replicas:
  - name: catalog-service
    count: 2
```

The name of the Deployment you're defining the number of replicas for

The number of replicas

NOTE   In a real scenario, you would probably want Kubernetes to dynamically scale applications in and out depending on the current workload, rather than providing a fixed number. Dynamic scaling is a pivotal feature of any cloud platform. In Kubernetes, it's implemented by a dedicated component called Horizontal Pod Autoscaler based on well-defined metrics, such as the CPU consumption per container. For more information, refer to the Kubernetes documentation (https://kubernetes.io/docs).

The next section will cover configuring CPU and memory for Spring Boot containers running in Kubernetes.

15.2.2 *Configuring CPU and memory for Spring Boot containers*

When dealing with containerized applications, it's best to assign *resource limits* explicitly. In chapter 1 you learned that containers are isolated contexts leveraging Linux features, like namespaces and cgroups, to partition and limit resources among processes. However, suppose you don't specify any resource limits. In that case, each container will have access to the whole CPU set and memory available on the host machine, with the risk of some of them taking up more resources than they should and causing other containers to crash due to a lack of resources.

For JVM-based applications like Spring Boot, defining CPU and memory limits is even more critical because they will be used to properly size items like JVM thread pools, heap memory, and non-heap memory. Configuring those values has always been a challenge for Java developers, and it's critical since they directly affect application performance. Fortunately, if you use the Paketo implementation of Cloud Native Buildpacks included in Spring Boot, you don't need to worry about that. When you packaged the Catalog Service application with Paketo in chapter 6, a *Java Memory Calculator* component was included automatically. When you run the containerized application, that component will configure the JVM memory based on the resource limits assigned to the container. If you don't specify any limits, the results will be unpredictable, which is not what you want.

There's also an economic aspect to consider. If you run your applications in a public cloud, you're usually charged based on how many resources you consume. Consequently, you'll probably want to be in control of how much CPU and memory each of your containers can use to avoid nasty surprises when the bill arrives.

When it comes to orchestrators like Kubernetes, there's another critical issue related to resources that you should consider. Kubernetes schedules Pods to be deployed in any of the cluster nodes. But what if a Pod is assigned to a node that has insufficient resources to run the container correctly? The solution is to declare the minimum CPU and memory a container needs to operate (*resource requests*). Kubernetes will use that information to deploy a Pod to a specific node only if it can guarantee the container will get at least the requested resources.

Resource requests and limits are defined per container. You can specify both requests and limits in a Deployment manifest. We haven't defined any limits in the base manifests for Catalog Service because we've been operating in a local environment and we didn't want to constrain it too much in terms of resource requirements. However, production workloads should always contain resource configurations. Let's look at how we can do that for the production deployment of Catalog Service.

ASSIGNING RESOURCE REQUESTS AND LIMITS TO A CONTAINER

It shouldn't be a surprise that we'll use a patch to apply CPU and memory configurations to Catalog Service. Create a patch-resources.yml file within the production overlay for Catalog Service (kubernetes/applications/catalog-service/production), and define both requests and limits for the container resources. Even though we're considering a production scenario, we'll use low values to optimize the resource usage in your cluster and avoid incurring additional costs. In a real-world scenario, you might want to analyze more carefully which requests and limits would be appropriate for your use case.

Listing 15.14 Configuring resource requests and limits for the container

Next, open the kustomization.yml file in the production overlay for Catalog Service, and configure Kustomize to apply the patch.

Listing 15.15 Applying the patch for defining resource requests and limits

```
apiVersion: kustomize.config.k8s.io/v1beta1
kind: Kustomization
```

```
resources:
  - github.com/<your_github_username>/catalog-service/k8s?ref=<release_sha>

patchesStrategicMerge:
  - patch-env.yml
  - patch-resources.yml          ◁──┐  Configures resource
  - patch-volumes.yml               └  requests and limits

configMapGenerator:
  - behavior: merge
    files:
      - application-prod.yml
    name: catalog-config

images:
  - name: catalog-service
    newName: ghcr.io/<your_github_username>/catalog-service
    newTag: <release_sha>

replicas:
  - name: catalog-service
    count: 2
```

In listing 15.14, the memory request and limit are the same, but that's not true for the CPU. The following section will explain the reasoning behind those choices.

OPTIMIZING CPU AND MEMORY FOR SPRING BOOT APPLICATIONS

The amount of CPU available to a container directly affects the startup time of a JVM-based application like Spring Boot. In fact, the JVM leverages as much CPU as available to run the initialization tasks concurrently and reduce the startup time. After the startup phase, the application will use much lower CPU resources.

A common strategy is to define the CPU request (`resources.requests.cpu`) with the amount the application will use under normal conditions, so that it's always guaranteed to have the resources required to operate correctly. Then, depending on the system, you may decide to specify a higher CPU limit or omit it entirely (`resources.limits.cpu`) to optimize performance at startup so that the application can use as much CPU as available on the node at that moment.

CPU is a *compressible resource*, meaning that a container can consume as much of it as is available. When it hits the limit (either because of `resources.limits.cpu` or because there's no more CPU available on the node), the operating system starts throttling the container process, which keeps running but with possibly lower performance. Since it's compressible, not specifying a CPU limit can be a valid option sometimes to gain a performance boost. Still, you'll probably want to consider the specific scenario and evaluate the consequences of such a decision.

Unlike CPU, *memory* is a *non-compressible resource*. If a container hits the limit (either because of `resources.limits.memory` or because there's no more memory available on the node), a JVM-based application will throw the dreadful `OutOfMemoryError`, and the operating system will terminate the container process with an `OOMKilled`

(OutOfMemory killed) status. There is no throttling. Setting the correct memory value is, therefore, particularly important. There's no shortcut to inferring the proper configuration; you must monitor the application running under normal conditions. That's true for both CPU and memory.

Once you find a suitable value for how much memory your application needs, I recommend you use it both as a request (`resources.requests.memory`) and as a limit (`resources.limits.memory`). The reason for that is deeply connected to how the JVM works, and particularly how the JVM heap memory behaves. Growing and shrinking the container memory dynamically will affect the application's performance, since the heap memory is dynamically allocated based on the memory available to the container. Using the same value for the request and the limit ensures that a fixed amount of memory is always guaranteed, resulting in better JVM performance. Furthermore, it allows the Java Memory Calculator provided by the Paketo Buildpacks to configure the JVM memory in the most efficient way.

I've mentioned the Java Memory Calculator a few times now. The following section will expand on the subject.

Configuring resources for the JVM

The Paketo Buildpacks used by the Spring Boot plugin for Gradle/Maven provide a Java Memory Calculator component when building container images for Java applications. This component implements an algorithm that has been refined and improved over the years, thanks to the Pivotal (now VMware Tanzu) experience with running containerized Java workloads in the cloud.

In a production scenario, the default configuration is a good starting point for most applications. However, it can be too resource-demanding for local development or demos. One way to make the JVM consume fewer resources is to lower the default 250 JVM thread count for imperative applications. For that reason, we've been using the `BPL_JVM_THREAD_COUNT` environment variable to configure a low number of threads for the two Servlet-based applications in Polar Bookshop: Catalog Service and Config Service. Reactive applications are already configured with fewer threads, since they are much more resource-efficient than their imperative counterparts. For that reason, we haven't customized the thread count for Edge Service, Order Service, or Dispatcher Service.

> **NOTE** The Paketo team is working on extending the Java Memory Calculator to provide a low-profile mode, which will be helpful when working locally or on low-volume applications. In the future, it will be possible to control the memory configuration mode via a flag rather than having to tweak the individual parameters. You can find more information about this feature on the GitHub project for Paketo Buildpacks (http://mng.bz/5Q87).

The JVM has two main memory areas: heap and non-heap. The Calculator focuses on computing values for the different non-heap memory parts according to a specific formula. The remaining memory resources are assigned to the heap. If the default configuration is not good enough, you can customize it as you prefer. For example, I experienced some memory issues with an imperative application handling session management with Redis. It required more direct memory than was configured by default. In that case, I used the standard `-XX:MaxDirectMemorySize=50M` JVM setting via the `JAVA_TOOL_OPTIONS` environment variable and increased the maximum size for the direct memory from 10 MB to 50 MB. If you customize the size of a specific memory region, the Calculator will adjust the allocation of the remaining areas accordingly.

> **NOTE** Memory handling in the JVM is a fascinating topic that would require its own book to fully cover. Therefore, I won't go into details regarding how to configure it.

Since we are configuring deployments for production, let's update the thread count for Catalog Service using a more suitable number like `100`. In a real-world scenario, I would recommend starting with the default value of `250` as a baseline. For Polar Bookshop, I'm trying to compromise between showing what an actual production deployment would look like and minimizing the resources you need to consume (and perhaps pay for) on a public cloud platform.

We can update the thread count for Catalog Service in the patch we defined earlier to customize environment variables. Open the patch-env.yml file in the production overlay for Catalog Service (kubernetes/applications/catalog-service/production), and update the JVM thread count as follows.

Listing 15.16   Number of JVM threads used by the Java Memory Calculator

```
apiVersion: apps/v1
kind: Deployment
metadata:
  name: catalog-service
spec:
  template:
    spec:
      containers:
        - name: catalog-service
          env:
            - name: BPL_JVM_THREAD_COUNT        ◁──┐  The number of threads
              value: "100"                           considered in the
            - name: SPRING_PROFILES_ACTIVE          memory calculation
              value: prod
```

That was the last configuration change we needed to make before deploying the application in production. We'll do that next.

15.2.3 *Deploying Spring Boot in production*

Our end goal is to automate the full process from code commit to production. Before looking into the production stage of the deployment pipeline, let's verify that the customizations we've defined so far are correct by deploying Catalog Service in production manually.

As you learned in the previous chapter, we can use the Kubernetes CLI to deploy applications on Kubernetes from a `Kustomization` overlay. Open a Terminal window, navigate to the production overlay folder for Catalog Service (polar-deployment/ kubernetes/applications/catalog-service/production), and run the following command to deploy the application via Kustomize:

```
$ kubectl apply -k .
```

You can follow their progress and see when the two application instances are ready to accept requests by running this command:

```
$ kubectl get pods -l app=catalog-service --watch
```

For additional information on the deployment, you can keep using the Kubernetes CLI or rely on Octant, a tool that lets you visualize your Kubernetes workloads via a convenient GUI. As explained in chapter 7, you can start Octant with the command `octant`. Furthermore, the application logs might be interesting for verifying that Catalog Service is running correctly:

```
$ kubectl logs deployment/catalog-service
```

The application is not exposed outside the cluster yet (for that, we need Edge Service), but you can use the port-forwarding functionality to forward traffic from your local environment on port 9001 to the Service running in the cluster on port 80:

```
$ kubectl port-forward service/catalog-service 9001:80
```

> **NOTE** The process started by the `kubectl port-forward` command will keep running until you explicitly stop it with Ctrl-C.

Now you can call Catalog Service from your local machine on port 9001, and the request will be forwarded to the Service object inside the Kubernetes cluster. Open a new Terminal window and call the root endpoint exposed by the application to verify that the `polar.greeting` value specified in the ConfigMap for the `prod` Spring profile is used instead of the default one:

```
$ http :9001/
Welcome to our book catalog from a production Kubernetes environment!
```

Congratulations! You are officially in production! When you're done, you can terminate the port-forwarding with Ctrl-C. Finally, delete the deployment by running the following command from the production overlay folder for Catalog Service:

```
$ kubectl delete -k .
```

Kubernetes provides the infrastructure for implementing different types of deployment strategies. When we update our application manifests with a new release version and apply them to the cluster, Kubernetes performs a *rolling update*. This strategy consists in incrementally updating Pod instances with new ones and guarantees zero downtime for the user. You saw that in action in the previous chapter.

By default, Kubernetes adopts the rolling update strategy, but there are other techniques that you can employ based on the standard Kubernetes resources or you can rely on a tool like Knative. For example, you might want to use *blue/green deployments*, consisting of deploying the new version of the software in a second production environment. By doing that, you can test one last time that everything runs correctly. When the environment is ready, you move the traffic from the first (*blue*) to the second (*green*) production environment.[1]

Another deployment technique is the *canary release*. It's similar to the blue/green deployment, but the traffic from the blue to the green environment is moved gradually over time. The goal is to roll out the change to a small subset of users first, perform some verifications, and then do the same for more and more users until everyone is using the new version.[2] Both blue/green deployments and canary releases provide a straightforward way to roll back changes.

NOTE   If you're interested in learning more about deployment and release strategies on Kubernetes, I recommend reading chapter 5 of *Continuous Delivery for Kubernetes* by Mauricio Salatino, published by Manning (https://livebook .manning.com/book/continuous-delivery-for-kubernetes/chapter-5).

Currently, every time you commit changes, a new release candidate is ultimately published and approved if it passes successfully through the commit and acceptance stages. Then you need to copy the version number of the new release candidate and paste it into the Kubernetes manifests before you can update the application in production manually. In the next section, you'll see how to automate that process by implementing the final part of the deployment pipeline: the production stage.

15.3   *Deployment pipeline: Production stage*

We started implementing a deployment pipeline back in chapter 3, and we have come a long way since then. We've automated all the steps from code commit up to having a release candidate ready for production. There are still two operations that we have performed manually so far: updating the production scripts with the new application version, and deploying it to Kubernetes.

In this section, we'll start looking at the final part of a deployment pipeline, the production stage, and I'll show you how to implement it as a workflow in GitHub Actions.

---

[1] See M. Fowler, "BlueGreenDeployment," *MartinFowler.com*, March 1, 2010, http://mng.bz/WxOl.
[2] See D. Sato, "CanaryRelease," *MartinFowler.com*, June 25, 2014, http://mng.bz/8Mz5.

15.3.1   Understanding the production stage of the deployment pipeline

After a release candidate has gone through the commit and acceptance stages, we are confident enough to deploy it to production. The production stage can be triggered manually or automatically, depending on whether you'd like to achieve *continuous deployment*.

Continuous delivery is "a software development discipline where you build software in such a way that the software can be released to production at any time."[3] The key part is understanding that the software *can* be released to production, but it doesn't *have to.* That's a common source of confusion between continuous delivery and continuous deployment. If you also want to take the newest release candidate and deploy it to production automatically, then you would have *continuous deployment.*

The production stage consists of two main steps:

1 Update the deployment scripts (in our case, the Kubernetes manifests) with the new release version.
2 Deploy the application to the production environment.

NOTE   An optional third step would be to run some final automated tests to verify that the deployment was successful. Perhaps you could reuse the same system tests that you will have included in the acceptance stage to verify the deployment in a staging environment.

The next section will show you how to implement the first step of the production stage using GitHub Actions, and we'll discuss some implementation strategies for the second step. We'll aim to automate the whole path from code commit to production and achieve continuous deployment.

15.3.2   Implementing the production stage with GitHub Actions

Compared to the previous stages, implementing the production stage of a deployment pipeline can differ a lot depending on several factors. Let's start by focusing on the first step of the production stage.

At the end of the acceptance stage, we have a release candidate that's proven to be ready for production. After that, we need to update the Kubernetes manifests in our production overlay with the new release version. When we're keeping both the application source code and deployment scripts in the same repository, the production stage could be listening to a specific event published by GitHub whenever the acceptance stage completes successfully, much like how we configured the flow between the commit and acceptance stages.

In our case, we are keeping the deployment scripts in a separate repository, which means that whenever the acceptance stage workflow completes its execution in the application repository, we need to notify the production stage workflow in the

---

[3] See M. Fowler, "ContinuousDelivery," *MartinFowler.com*, May 30, 2013, http://mng.bz/7yXV.

deployment repository. GitHub Actions provides the option of implementing this notification process via a custom event. Let's see how it works.

Open your Catalog Service project (catalog-service), and go to the acceptance-stage.yml file within the .github/workflows folder. After all the acceptance tests have run successfully, we have to define a final step that will send a notification to the polar-deployment repository and ask it to update the Catalog Service production manifests with the new release version. That will be the trigger for the production stage, which we'll implement in a moment.

Listing 15.17 Triggering the production stage in the deployment repository

```
name: Acceptance Stage
on:
  workflow_run:
    workflows: ['Commit Stage']
    types: [completed]
    branches: main
concurrency: acceptance                    Defines relevant data as
                                           environment variables
env:
  OWNER: <your_github_username>
  REGISTRY: ghcr.io
  APP_REPO: catalog-service
  DEPLOY_REPO: polar-deployment
  VERSION: ${{ github.sha }}

jobs:
  functional:
    ...                                    Runs only when all
  performance:                             functional and non-
    ...                                    functional acceptance
  security:                                tests are completed
    ...                                    successfully
  deliver:                                                    An action to send
    name: Deliver release candidate to production             an event to another
    needs: [ functional, performance, security ]             repository and
    runs-on: ubuntu-22.04                                    trigger a workflow
    steps:
      - name: Deliver application to production               A token to grant the
        uses: peter-evans/repository-dispatch@v2             action permission
        with:                                                to send events to
          token: ${{ secrets.DISPATCH_TOKEN }}               another repository
          repository:
            ${{ env.OWNER }}/${{ env.DEPLOY_REPO }}          The repository
          event-type: app_delivery                           to notify
          client-payload: '{
            "app_image":
              "${{ env.REGISTRY }}/${{ env.OWNER }}/${{ env.APP_REPO }}",
            "app_name": "${{ env.APP_REPO }}",
            "app_version": "${{ env.VERSION }}"
          }'
```

A name to identify the event (this is up to you)

The payload of the message sent to the other repository. Add any information that the other repository might need to perform its operations.

With this new step, if no error is found during the execution of the acceptance tests, a notification is sent to the `polar-deployment` repository to trigger an update for Catalog Service.

By default, GitHub Actions doesn't allow you to trigger workflows located in other repositories, even if they both belong to you or your organization. Therefore, we need to provide the `repository-dispatch` action with an access token that grants it such permissions. The token can be a personal access token (PAT), a GitHub tool that we used in chapter 6.

Go to your GitHub account, navigate to Settings > Developer Settings > Personal Access Token, and choose Generate New Token. Input a meaningful name, and assign it the `workflow` scope to give the token permissions to trigger workflows in other repositories (figure 15.6). Finally, generate the token and copy its value. GitHub will show you the token value only once. Make sure you save it since you'll need it soon.

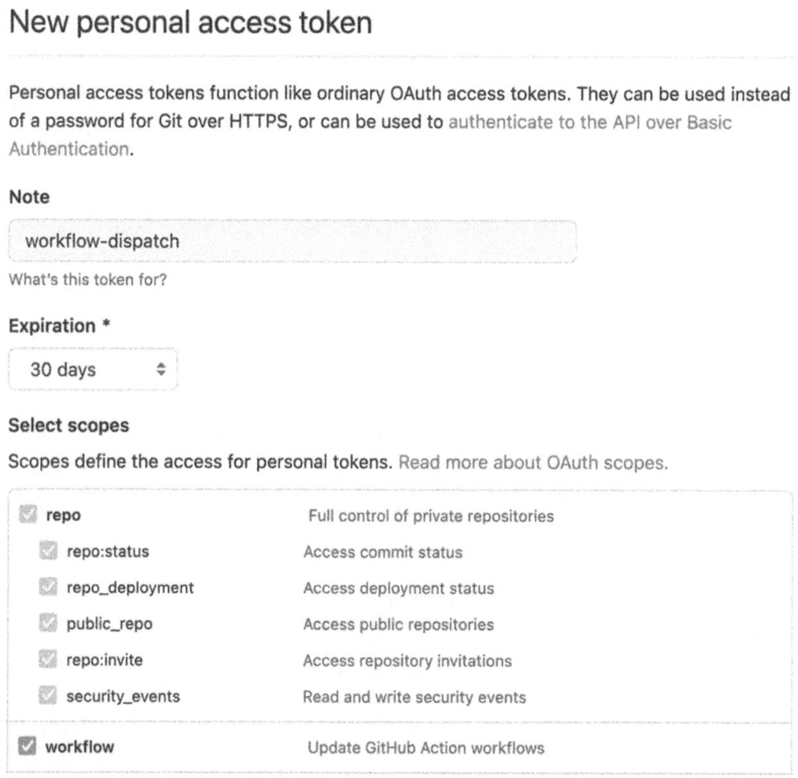

New personal access token

Personal access tokens function like ordinary OAuth access tokens. They can be used instead of a password for Git over HTTPS, or can be used to authenticate to the API over Basic Authentication.

Note

> workflow-dispatch

What's this token for?

Expiration *

> 30 days   ⇕

Select scopes

Scopes define the access for personal tokens. Read more about OAuth scopes.

☑ **repo**	Full control of private repositories
☑ repo:status	Access commit status
☑ repo_deployment	Access deployment status
☑ public_repo	Access public repositories
☑ repo:invite	Access repository invitations
☑ security_events	Read and write security events
☑ **workflow**	Update GitHub Action workflows

Figure 15.6   A personal access token (PAT) granting permissions to trigger workflows in other repositories

Next, go to your Catalog Service repository on GitHub, navigate to the Settings tab, and then select Secrets > Actions. On that page, choose New Repository Secret, name it DISPATCH_TOKEN (the same name we used in listing 15.17), and input the value of the PAT you generated earlier. Using the Secrets feature provided by GitHub, we can provide the PAT securely to the acceptance stage workflow.

> **WARNING**   As explained in chapter 3, when using actions from the GitHub marketplace, you should handle them like any other third-party application and manage the security risks accordingly. In the acceptance stage, we provide an access token to a third-party action with permissions to manipulate repositories and workflows. You shouldn't do that light-heartedly. In this case, I trusted the author of the action and decided to trust the action with the token.

Don't commit your changes to the catalog-service repository yet. We'll do that later. At this point, we have implemented the trigger for the production stage, but we haven't initialized the final stage yet. Let's move on to the Polar Deployment repository and do that.

Open your Polar Deployment project (polar-deployment), and create a production-stage.yml file within a new .github/workflows folder. The production stage is triggered whenever the acceptance stage from an application repository dispatches an app_delivery event. The event itself contains contextual information about the application name, image, and version for the newest release candidate. Since the application-specific information is parameterized, we can use this workflow for all the applications of the Polar Bookshop system, not only Catalog Service.

The first job of the production stage is updating the production Kubernetes manifests with the new release version. This job will consist of three steps:

1 Check out the polar-deployment source code.
2 Update the production Kustomization with the new version for the given application.
3 Commit the changes to the polar-deployment repository.

We can implement those three steps as follows.

Listing 15.18 Updating the image version upon a new application delivery

```
name: Production Stage

on:
  repository_dispatch:          ◁──┐  Executes the workflow only
    types: [app_delivery]            when a new app_delivery
                                     event is received, dispatched
                                     from another repository

jobs:
  update:
    name: Update application version
    runs-on: ubuntu-22.04            Saves the event payload
    permissions:                     data as environment
      contents: write                variables for convenience
    env:                      ◁──────┘
      APP_IMAGE: ${{ github.event.client_payload.app_image }}
      APP_NAME: ${{ github.event.client_payload.app_name }}
      APP_VERSION: ${{ github.event.client_payload.app_version }}
```

```
                         steps:
Checks out                 - name: Checkout source code
the repository               uses: actions/checkout@v3
                           - name: Update image version
                             run: |                              Navigates to the
                               cd \                              production overlay for
                                 kubernetes/applications/${{ env.APP_NAME }}/production
Updates the image
name and version         └─▷ kustomize edit set image \
via Kustomize for              ${{ env.APP_NAME }}=${{ env.APP_IMAGE }}:${{ env.APP_VERSION }}
the given application         sed -i 's/ref=[\w+]/${{ env.APP_VERSION }}/' \
                  ┌─────────▷ kustomization.yml
                  │        - name: Commit updated manifests
                             uses: stefanzweifel/git-auto-commit-action@v4      ◁─
                             with:                                           ◁─
                               commit_message: "Update ${{ env.APP_NAME }}
              ➥to version ${{ env.APP_VERSION }}"
                               branch: main
```

Checks out the repository

Navigates to the production overlay for the given application

Updates the image name and version via Kustomize for the given application

Updates the tag used by Kustomize to access the correct base manifests stored in the application repository

Details about the commit operation

An action to commit and push the changes applied to the current repository from the previous step

That's all we need for now. Commit and push the changes to your remote polar-deployment on GitHub. Then go back to your Catalog Service project, commit your previous changes to the acceptance stage, and push them to your remote catalog-service on GitHub.

The new commit to the catalog-service repository will trigger the deployment pipeline. First, the commit stage will produce a container image (our release candidate) and publish it to GitHub Container Registry. Then the acceptance stage will fictitiously run further tests on the application and finally send a notification (a custom app_delivery event) to the polar-deployment repository. The event triggers the production stage, which will update the production Kubernetes manifests for Catalog Service and commit the changes to the polar-deployment repository. Figure 15.7 illustrates the inputs and outputs for the three stages of the deployment pipeline.

Go to your GitHub projects and follow the execution of the three stages. In the end, you'll find a new commit in your polar-deployment repository, which was submitted by GitHub Actions and contains a change to the Catalog Service production overlay so it uses the newest release version.

Perfect! We just got rid of the first of the two remaining manual steps: updating the deployment scripts with the newest release version. We still have to apply the Kubernetes manifests to the cluster manually, using the Kubernetes CLI. The second step of the production stage will take care of automating the application deployment whenever a new version is promoted to production. That's the topic of the next section.

Deployment pipeline: From code commit to ready for production deployment

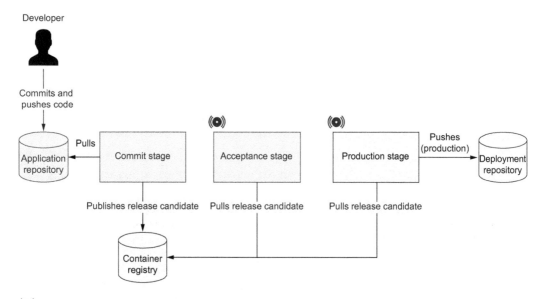

Figure 15.7 The commit stage goes from code commit to a release candidate, which goes through the acceptance stage. If it passes all the tests, the production stage updates the deployment manifests.

Polar Labs

It's time to apply what you learned in this section to Edge Service, Dispatcher Service, and Order Service.

1 Generate a PAT with a `workflow` scope for each application. It's a security best practice not to reuse tokens for multiple purposes.

2 For each application, save the PAT as a Secret from the GitHub repository page.

3 Update the acceptance stage workflow with a final step that sends a notification to the production stage with information about the newest release candidate.

4 Push your changes to GitHub, ensure the workflow is completed successfully, and check that the production stage workflow in the `polar-deployment` repository is triggered correctly.

Edge Service is the only application available through the public internet, and it requires an additional patch to configure the Ingress to block requests to the Actuator endpoints from outside the cluster. You can get the additional patch from the applications/edge-service/production folder, within Chapter15/15-end/polar-deployment.

For simplicity, we accept that the Actuator endpoints are available without authentication from within the cluster. Internal applications like Catalog Service are not affected, since their Actuator endpoints are not accessible through Spring Cloud Gateway. On the other hand, the Edge Service ones are currently accessible via the public internet.

That's not safe in a production environment. A simple way of fixing that is configuring the Ingress to block any request to the /actuator/** endpoints from outside the cluster. They will all still be available from within the cluster so that the health probes can work. We are using an NGINX-based Ingress Controller, so we can use its configuration language to express a *deny rule* for the Actuator endpoints.

In the source code repository accompanying the book, you can check the final results in the Chapter15/15-end folder (https://github.com/ThomasVitale/cloud-native-spring -in-action).

15.4 Continuous deployment with GitOps

Traditionally, continuous deployment is implemented by adding a further step to the production stage of the deployment pipeline. This additional step would authenticate with the target platform (such as a virtual machine or a Kubernetes cluster) and deploy the new version of the application. In recent years, a different approach has become more and more popular: GitOps. The term was coined by Alexis Richardson, CEO and founder of Weaveworks (www.weave.works).

GitOps is a set of practices for operating and managing software systems, enabling continuous delivery and deployment while ensuring agility and reliability. Compared to the traditional approach, GitOps favors decoupling between delivery and deployment. Instead of having the pipeline *pushing* deployments to the platform, it's the platform itself *pulling* the desired state from a source repository and performing deployments. In the first case, the deployment step is implemented within the production stage workflow. In the second case, which will be our focus, the deployment is still theoretically considered part of the production stage, but the implementation differs.

GitOps doesn't enforce specific technologies, but it's best implemented with Git and Kubernetes. That will be our focus.

The GitOps Working Group, part of the CNCF, defines GitOps in terms of four principles (https://opengitops.dev):

1 *Declarative*—"A system managed by GitOps must have its desired state expressed declaratively."
   – Working with Kubernetes, we can express the desired state via YAML files (manifests).
   – Kubernetes manifests declare what we want to achieve, not how. The platform is responsible for finding a way to achieve the desired state.
2 *Versioned and immutable*—"Desired state is stored in a way that enforces immutability, versioning and retains a complete version history."
   – Git is the preferred choice for ensuring the desired state is versioned and the whole history retained. That makes it possible, among other things, to roll back to a previous state with ease.
   – The desired state stored in Git is immutable and represents the single source of truth.

3 *Pulled automatically*—"Software agents automatically pull the desired state declarations from the source."
   – Examples of software agents (*GitOps agents*) are Flux (https://fluxcd.io), Argo CD (https://argoproj.github.io/cd), and kapp-controller (https://carvel.dev/kapp-controller).
   – Rather than granting CI/CD tools like GitHub Actions full access to the cluster or running commands manually, we grant the GitOps agent access to a source like Git so that it pulls changes automatically.
4 *Continuously reconciled*—"Software agents continuously observe actual system state and attempt to apply the desired state."
   – Kubernetes is composed of controllers that keep observing the system and ensuring the actual state of the cluster matches the desired state.
   – On top of that, GitOps ensures that it's the right desired state to be considered in the cluster. Whenever a change is detected in the Git source, the agent steps up and reconciles the desired state with the cluster.

Figure 15.8 illustrates the result of applying the GitOps principles.

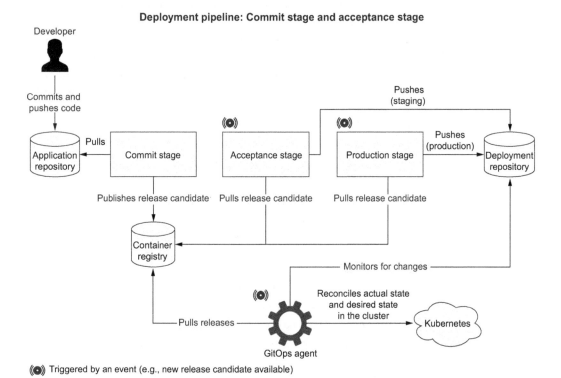

Figure 15.8 Every time the production stage workflow updates the deployment repository, the GitOps controller reconciles the desired and actual states.

If you consider the four principles, you'll notice that we've applied the first two already. We expressed the desired state for our applications declaratively using Kubernetes manifests and Kustomize. And we stored the desired state in a Git repository on GitHub (`polar-deployment`), making it versioned and immutable. We are still missing a software agent that automatically pulls the desired state declarations from the Git source and continuously reconciles them inside the Kubernetes cluster, therefore achieving continuous deployment.

We'll start by installing Argo CD (https://argo-cd.readthedocs.io), a GitOps software agent. Then we'll configure it to complete the final step of the deployment pipeline and let it monitor our `polar-deployment` repository. Whenever there's a change in the application manifests, Argo CD will apply the changes to our production Kubernetes cluster.

15.4.1 Implementing GitOps with Argo CD

Let's start by installing the Argo CD CLI. Refer to the project website for installation instructions (https://argo-cd.readthedocs.io). If you are on macOS or Linux, you can use Homebrew as follows:

```
$ brew install argocd
```

We'll use the CLI to instruct Argo CD about which Git repository to monitor, and we'll configure it to apply changes to the cluster to achieve continuous deployment automatically. But first we need to deploy Argo CD to the production Kubernetes cluster.

> **NOTE** I'll assume your Kubernetes CLI is still configured to access the production cluster on DigitalOcean. You can check that with `kubectl config current-context`. If you need to change the context, you can run `kubectl config use-context <context-name>`. A list of all the contexts available can be retrieved from `kubectl config get-contexts`.

Open a Terminal window, go to your Polar Deployment project (polar-deployment), and navigate to the kubernetes/platform/production/argocd folder. You should have copied that folder over to your repository when you set up the production cluster. If that's not the case, please do so now from the source code repository accompanying this book (Chapter15/15-end/polar-deployment/platform/production/argocd).

Then run the following script to install Argo CD into the production cluster. Feel free to open the file and look at the instructions before running it:

```
$ ./deploy.sh
```

> **TIP** You might need to make the script executable first, with the command `chmod +x deploy.sh`.

The deployment of Argo CD consists of several components, including a convenient web interface where you can visualize and control all the deployments controlled by Argo CD. For now, we'll use the CLI. During the installation, Argo CD will have autogenerated a password for the admin account (the username is admin). Run the following command to fetch the password value (it will take a few seconds before the value is available):

```
$ kubectl -n argocd get secret argocd-initial-admin-secret \
    -o jsonpath="{.data.password}" | base64 -d; echo
```

Next, let's identify the external IP address assigned to Argo CD server:

```
$ kubectl -n argocd get service argocd-server

NAME            TYPE           CLUSTER-IP     EXTERNAL-IP
argocd-server   LoadBalancer   10.245.16.74   <external-ip>
```

The platform might take a few minutes to provision a load balancer for Argo CD. During the provisioning, the EXTERNAL-IP column will show a <pending> status. Wait and try again until an IP address is shown. Note it down, because we're going to use it soon.

Since the Argo CD server is now exposed via a public load balancer, we can use the external IP address to access its services. For this example, we'll use the CLI, but you can achieve the same results by opening <argocd-external-ip> (the IP address assigned to your Argo CD server) in a browser window. Either way, you'll have to log in with the auto-generated admin account. The username is admin, and the password is the one you fetched earlier. Be aware that you might get a warning, since you are not using HTTPS:

```
$ argocd login <argocd-external-ip>
```

It's now time to see continuous deployment in action with GitOps. I'll assume you have been through all the previous sections of this chapter. At this point, the commit stage of your Catalog Service repository on GitHub (catalog-service) should have built a container image, the acceptance stage should have triggered the Polar Deployment repository on GitHub (polar-deployment), and the production stage should have updated the production overlay for Catalog Service with the newest release version (polar-deployment/kubernetes/applications/catalog-service/production). Now we'll configure Argo CD to monitor the production overlay for Catalog Service and synchronize it with the production cluster whenever it detects a change in the repository. In other words, Argo CD will continuously deploy new versions of Catalog Service as made available by the deployment pipeline.

The Git repository to monitor for changes. Insert your GitHub username.

Creates a catalog-service application in Argo CD

The folder to monitor for changes within the configured repository

```
$ argocd app create catalog-service \
    --repo \
      https://github.com/<your_github_username>/polar-deployment.git \
    --path kubernetes/applications/catalog-service/production \
```

```
--dest-server https://kubernetes.default.svc \           ◄─────
--dest-namespace default \              ◄────────────────
--sync-policy auto \        ◄──────────────────
--auto-prune
```

**Configures Argo CD to
delete old resources
after a synchronization
automatically**

**Configures Argo CD to
automatically reconcile
the desired state in the
Git repo with the actual
state in the cluster**

**The Kubernetes cluster where the
application should be deployed.
We are using the default cluster
configured in the kubectl context.**

**The namespace where the
application should be deployed. We
are using the "default" namespace.**

You can verify the status of the continuous deployment of Catalog Service with the following command (I have filtered the results for the sake of clarity):

```
$ argocd app get catalog-service

GROUP   KIND        NAMESPACE   NAME                        STATUS   HEALTH
        ConfigMap   default     catalog-config-6d5dkt7577   Synced
        Service     default     catalog-service             Synced   Healthy
apps    Deployment  default     catalog-service             Synced   Healthy
```

Argo CD has automatically applied the production overlay for Catalog Service (polar-deployment/kubernetes/applications/catalog-service/production) to the cluster.

Once all the resources listed by the previous command have the Synced status, we can verify that the application is running correctly. The application is not exposed outside the cluster yet, but you can use the port-forwarding functionality to forward traffic from your local environment on port 9001 to the Service running in the cluster on port 80:

```
$ kubectl port-forward service/catalog-service 9001:80
```

Next, call the root point exposed by the application. We expect to get the value we configured for the polar.greeting property in the Catalog Service production overlay.

```
$ http :9001/
Welcome to our book catalog from a production Kubernetes environment!
```

Perfect! In one step we automated not only the first deployment but also any future updates. Argo CD will detect any change in the production overlay for Catalog Service and apply the new manifests to the cluster immediately. There could be a new release version to deploy, but it could also be a change to the production overlay. For example, let's try configuring a different value for the polar.greeting property.

Open your Polar Deployment project (polar-deployment), go to the production overlay for Catalog service (kubernetes/applications/catalog-service/production), and update the value of the polar.greeting property in the application-prod.yml file.

Listing 15.19   Updating the production-specific configuration for the app

```
polar:
  greeting: Welcome to our production book catalog
  ➥ synchronized with Argo CD!
```

```
spring:
  config:
    import: configtree:/workspace/secrets/*/
```

Then commit and push the changes to your remote `polar-deployment` repository on GitHub. By default, Argo CD checks the Git repository for changes every three minutes. It will notice the change and apply the `Kustomization` again, resulting in a new ConfigMap being generated by Kustomize and a rolling restart of the Pods to refresh the configuration. Once the deployment in the cluster is in sync with the desired state in the Git repo (you can check this with `argocd app get catalog-service`), call the root endpoint exposed by Catalog Service again. We'll expect to get the value we have just updated. If you get a network error, it might be that the port-forwarding process was interrupted. Run `kubectl port-forward service/catalog-service 9001:80` again to fix it:

```
$ http :9001/
Welcome to our production book catalog synchronized with Argo CD!
```

Great! We have finally achieved continuous deployment! Pause for a minute and celebrate with a beverage of your choice. You deserve it!

Polar Labs

It's time to apply what you learned in this section to Edge Service, Dispatcher Service, and Order Service.

1   Using the Argo CD CLI, register each of the remaining applications as we did for Catalog Service. Remember to authenticate to Argo CD first, as explained earlier.
2   For each application, verify that Argo CD has synchronized the desired state from the `polar-deployment` repository with the actual state in the cluster.

In the case of problems with Argo CD, you can use the `argocd app get catalog-service` command to verify the synchronization status or directly use the web interface available at `<argocd-external-ip>`. For troubleshooting Kubernetes resources, you can take advantage of Octant or use one of the techniques explained in the last section of chapter 7.

15.4.2   *Putting it all together*

If you followed along and completed all the Polar Labs, you'll now have the whole Polar Bookshop system up and running in a production Kubernetes cluster in the public cloud. That's a huge accomplishment! In this section, we'll give it a try and refine a few last points. Figure 15.9 shows the status of the applications from the Argo CD GUI, accessible via the `<argocd-external-ip>` address discovered earlier.

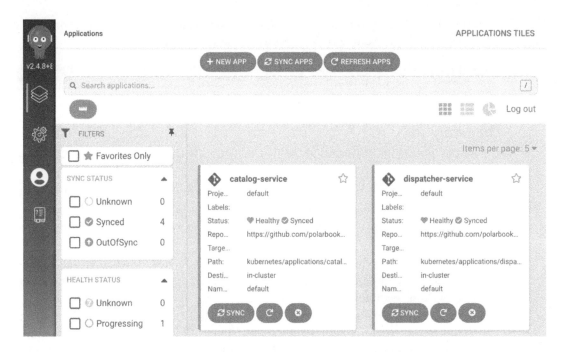

Figure 15.9 The Argo CD GUI shows an overview of all the applications managed via a GitOps flow.

So far, we have worked with Catalog Service, an internal application that is not exposed outside the cluster. For that reason, we relied on the port-forwarding functionality to test it out. Now that the whole system is deployed, we can access the applications as intended: via the Edge Service. The platform automatically configures a load balancer with an external IP address whenever we deploy an Ingress resource. Let's discover the external IP address for the Ingress sitting in front of Edge Service:

```
$ kubectl get ingress

NAME            CLASS    HOSTS    ADDRESS           PORTS   AGE
polar-ingress   nginx    *        <ip-address>      80      31m
```

Using the Ingress external IP address, you can use Polar Bookshop from the public internet. Open a browser window and navigate to <ip-address>.

Try logging in as Isabelle. Feel free to add some books and browse the catalog. Then log out and log in again, this time as Bjorn. Verify that you can't create or edit books, but you can place orders.

When you are done testing the application using the two accounts, log out and ensure that you can't access the Actuator endpoints by visiting <ip-address>/actuator/health, for example. NGINX, the technology that powers the Ingress Controller, will reply with a 403 response.

NOTE If you'd like to provision the Grafana observability stack, refer to the instructions in the source code repository accompanying the book.

Great job! When you're done using the production cluster, follow the last section of appendix B to delete all the cloud resources from DigitalOcean. That's fundamental to avoid incurring unexpected costs.

Summary

- The idea behind continuous delivery is that an application is always in a releasable state.
- When the delivery pipeline completes its execution, you'll obtain an artifact (the container image) you can use to deploy the application in production.
- When it comes to continuous delivery, each release candidate should be uniquely identifiable.
- Using the Git commit hash, you can ensure uniqueness, traceability, and automation. Semantic versioning can be used as the *display name* communicated to users and customers.
- At the end of the commit stage, a release candidate is delivered to the artifact repository. Next, the acceptance stage deploys the application in a production-like environment and runs functional and non-functional tests. If they all succeed, the release candidate is ready for production.
- The Kustomize approach to configuration customization is based on the concepts of bases and overlays. Overlays are built on top of base manifests and customized via patches.
- You saw how to define patches for customizing environment variables, Secrets mounted as volumes, CPU and memory resources, ConfigMaps, and Ingress.
- The final part of a deployment pipeline is the production stage, where the deployment manifests are updated with the newest release version and ultimately deployed.
- Deployment can be push-based or pull-based.
- GitOps is a set of practices for operating and managing software systems.
- GitOps is based on four principles according to which a system deployment should be declarative, versioned and immutable, pulled automatically, and continuously reconciled.
- Argo CD is a software agent running in a cluster that automatically pulls the desired state from a source repository and applies it to the cluster whenever the two states diverge. That's how we implemented continuous deployment.

Serverless, GraalVM, and Knative

16

> **This chapter covers**
>
> - Producing native images with Spring Native and GraalVM
> - Building serverless applications with Spring Cloud Function
> - Deploying serverless applications with Knative and Kubernetes

In the previous chapter, you completed a long journey from development to production. You've built cloud native applications using Spring and deployed them on a Kubernetes cluster in a public cloud. This final chapter aims to provide you with some additional tools to get even more out of your cloud native applications.

One significant benefit of cloud infrastructures is that you can increase or reduce resources on demand and pay only for what you use. Java applications have traditionally been very resource-intensive, resulting in higher CPU and memory consumption than other stacks like Go. Not anymore. Using GraalVM and Spring Native, you can compile your Spring Boot applications to native executables, which are more performant and efficient than their JVM counterparts. The first part of this chapter will guide you through taking advantage of this new technology.

The second part of the chapter will expand on serverless architectures. Compared to CaaS and PaaS infrastructures, serverless architectures move most operational tasks to the platform and let developers focus on the applications. Some applications are naturally event-driven and aren't always busy processing requests. Or they might have sudden peaks that require more computational resources. Serverless platforms provide fully managed auto-scaling features and can scale application instances to zero so that you don't have to pay anything if there's nothing to process. You'll learn more about the serverless model, and you'll build a serverless application using Spring Native and Spring Cloud Function. Finally, you'll see how to deploy applications using Knative, a Kubernetes-based serverless platform.

> **NOTE**   The source code for the examples in this chapter is available in the Chapter16/16-begin and Chapter16/16-end folders, containing the initial and final states of the project (https://github.com/ThomasVitale/cloud-native -spring-in-action).

16.1 *Native images with Spring Native and GraalVM*

One of the reasons why Java applications became widely popular was the common platform (the Java Runtime Environment, or JRE), allowing developers to "write them once, run them everywhere," no matter the operating system. That comes from the way applications are compiled. Rather than compiling the application code directly into machine code (the code understood by operating systems), the Java compiler produces bytecode that a dedicated component (the Java Virtual Machine, or JVM) runs. During execution, the JRE interprets the bytecode into machine code dynamically, allowing the same application executable to run on any machine and OS where a JVM is available. This is called a *just-in-time (JIT) compilation.*

Applications running on the JVM are subject to startup and footprint costs. The startup phase used to be quite long for traditional applications, for which it could even take several minutes. Standard cloud native applications have a much faster startup phase: a few seconds rather than a few minutes. This is good enough for most scenarios, but it can become a serious issue for serverless workloads that are required to start almost instantaneously.

Standard Java applications also have a higher footprint cost than other stacks like Go. Cloud services are usually based on a pay-per-use model, so reducing CPU and memory footprint means cutting down costs. This section will show you how to address this issue using GraalVM and Spring Native.

16.1.1 *Understanding GraalVM and native images*

So far, you've used the JVM and tools provided by OpenJDK, which comes in many distributions, such as Eclipse Adoptium (previously known as AdoptOpenJDK), BellSoft Liberica JDK, and Microsoft OpenJDK. GraalVM is a newer distribution from Oracle based on OpenJDK and is "designed to accelerate the execution of applications written in Java and other JVM languages" (www.graalvm.org).

By replacing a standard OpenJDK distribution with GraalVM as the runtime environment for your Java applications, you can increase their performance and efficiency, thanks to a new optimized technology for performing JIT compilation (the GraalVM compiler). GraalVM also provides runtimes to execute code written in other languages like JavaScript, Python, and R. You can even write polyglot applications, including Python scripts in your Java code, for example.

GraalVM offers two primary operational modes. The *JVM Runtime* mode lets you run your Java applications like any other OpenJDK distribution while improving performance and efficiency thanks to the GraalVM compiler. What makes GraalVM so innovative and popular in the serverless context is the *Native Image* mode. Rather than compiling your Java code into bytecode and relying on a JVM to interpret it and convert it to machine code, GraalVM offers a new technology (the Native Image builder) that compiles Java applications directly into machine code, obtaining a *native executable* or *native image* that contains the whole machine code necessary for its execution.

Java applications compiled as native images have faster startup times, optimized memory consumption, and instant peak performance compared to the JVM options. GraalVM builds them by changing the way applications are compiled. Instead of a JIT-compiler optimizing and producing machine code at runtime, the *Native Image* mode is based on *Ahead-Of-Time (AOT) compilation*. Starting from the main() method, all classes and methods that are reachable during the application's execution are statically analyzed at build time and compiled into a standalone binary executable, including any dependencies and libraries. Such an executable doesn't run on a JVM but directly on the machine, just like C or C++ applications.

When using native images, much of the work that used to be performed at runtime by the JVM is now done at build time. As a result, building an application into a native executable takes longer and requires more computational resources than the JVM option. The GraalVM AOT compiler does not support some Java features out of the box. For example, reflection, dynamic proxies, serialization, and dynamic class loading require extra configuration to help the AOT compiler understand how to analyze them statically.

How can we adapt existing Java applications to run as native images? How much configuration is required to support frameworks and libraries? How can we provide the necessary configuration for the AOT compiler? That's where Spring Native enters the scene.

16.1.2 Introducing GraalVM support for Spring Boot with Spring Native

Spring Native is a new project introduced to support compiling Spring Boot applications with GraalVM. The main goal of Spring Native is to make it possible to compile any Spring application into a native executable using GraalVM without any code changes. To achieve that goal, the project provides an AOT infrastructure (invoked from a dedicated Gradle/Maven plugin) that contributes all the required configurations for GraalVM to AOT-compile Spring classes. The project is one of the latest additions to the Spring portfolio and it's currently in beta. At the time of writing, most Spring libraries are supported, as well as common libraries like Hibernate, Lombok, and gRPC.

For Spring libraries not yet supported, or for your own code, Spring Native offers helpful tools for configuring the GraalVM compiler. For example, if you use reflection or dynamic proxies in your code, GraalVM will require a dedicated configuration to know how to AOT-compile it. Spring Native offers convenient annotations like `@Native-Hints` and `@TypedHint` to instruct the GraalVM compiler directly from your Java code, taking advantage of the IDE auto-completion features and type checks.

> **NOTE** Spring Native will come out of the beta phase and become part of the core Spring libraries starting with Spring Framework 6 and Spring Boot 3, which are expected to be released in December 2022.

In this section, we'll explore the features of Spring Native by building Quote Service, a web application that exposes an API to fetch quotes from books.

BOOTSTRAPPING A NEW PROJECT WITH SPRING NATIVE AND SPRING REACTIVE WEB

You can initialize the Quote Service project from Spring Initializr (https://start .spring.io), store the result in a new `quote-service` Git repository, and push it to GitHub. The parameters for the initialization are shown in figure 16.1.

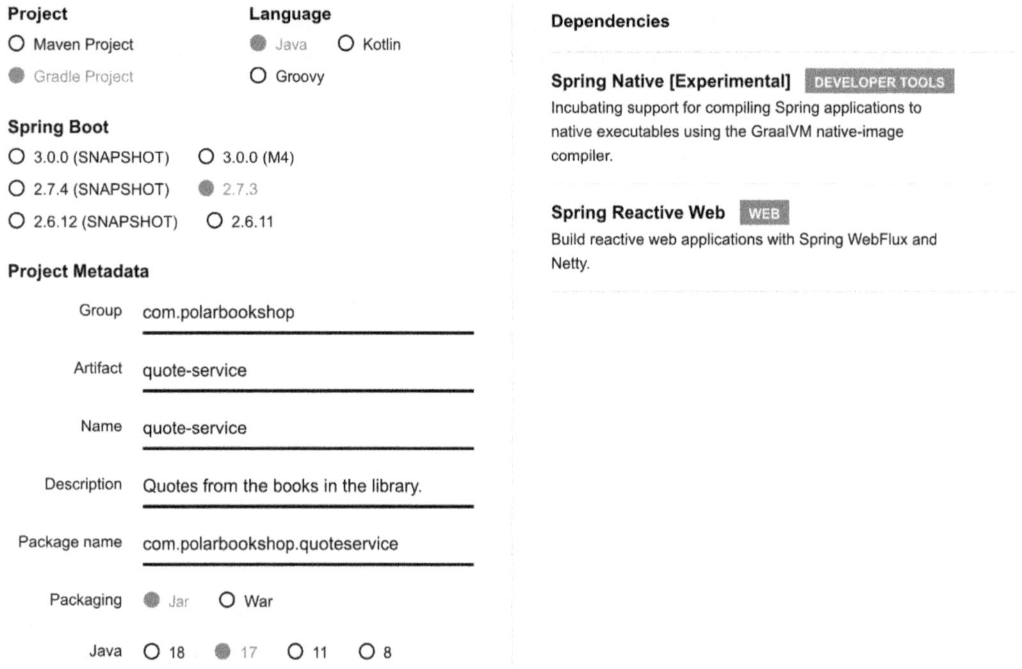

Project
- ○ Maven Project
- ● Gradle Project

Language
- ● Java   ○ Kotlin
- ○ Groovy

Spring Boot
- ○ 3.0.0 (SNAPSHOT)   ○ 3.0.0 (M4)
- ○ 2.7.4 (SNAPSHOT)   ● 2.7.3
- ○ 2.6.12 (SNAPSHOT)   ○ 2.6.11

Project Metadata

Group	com.polarbookshop
Artifact	quote-service
Name	quote-service
Description	Quotes from the books in the library.
Package name	com.polarbookshop.quoteservice
Packaging	● Jar ○ War
Java	○ 18 ● 17 ○ 11 ○ 8

Dependencies

Spring Native [Experimental] `DEVELOPER TOOLS`
Incubating support for compiling Spring applications to native executables using the GraalVM native-image compiler.

Spring Reactive Web `WEB`
Build reactive web applications with Spring WebFlux and Netty.

Figure 16.1   The parameters for initializing the Quote Service project

The project contains the following main dependencies:

- *Spring Reactive Web* provides the necessary libraries for building reactive web applications with Spring WebFlux, and it includes Netty as the default embedded server.
- *Spring Native* supports compiling Spring applications to native executables using the GraalVM native-image compiler.

The resulting `dependencies` section of the build.gradle file is as follows:

```
dependencies {
  implementation 'org.springframework.boot:spring-boot-starter-webflux'
  testImplementation 'org.springframework.boot:spring-boot-starter-test'
  testImplementation 'io.projectreactor:reactor-test'
}
```

At this point, you might ask: where is the Spring Native dependency? There isn't one. Where is Spring Native? The answer can be found in the `plugins` sections of the build.gradle file:

```
plugins {
    id 'org.springframework.boot' version '2.7.3'
    id 'io.spring.dependency-management' version '1.0.13.RELEASE'
    id 'java'
    id 'org.springframework.experimental.aot' version '0.12.1'   ◁── Spring AOT plugin provided by Spring Native
}
```

When you add Spring Native to a project, you'll get the Spring AOT plugin, which provides the required configuration for GraalVM to compile the Spring classes as well as convenient functionality for building native executables from Gradle (or Maven).

   If you bootstrap a new project from Spring Initializr, you'll also get additional information in the HELP.md file about how to use Spring Native. Should you select any unsupported dependencies, you'll find a message warning you about it. For example, Spring Cloud Stream is not fully supported at the time of writing. If you initialize a project with Spring Native and Spring Cloud Stream, the HELP.md file will show you a message like the following:

> The following dependency is not known to work with Spring Native: `'Cloud Stream'`. As a result, your application may not work as expected.

> **NOTE** You can follow which Spring libraries are supported in the Spring Native official documentation (https://docs.spring.io/spring-native/docs/current/reference/htmlsingle).

Next, let's implement the business logic for Quote Service.

IMPLEMENTING THE BUSINESS LOGIC

Quote Service will return random book quotes through a REST API. First, create a new com.polarbookshop.quoteservice.domain package and define a `Quote` record to model the domain entity.

Listing 16.1   Defining a domain entity for representing book quotes

```
public record Quote (
  String content,
  String author,
  Genre genre
){}
```

Quotes are categorized by the genre of the book from which they are extracted. Add a Genre enum to model this classification.

Listing 16.2   Defining an enumeration to represent book genres

```
public enum Genre {
  ADVENTURE,
  FANTASY,
  SCIENCE_FICTION
}
```

Finally, implement the business logic to retrieve book quotes in a new QuoteService class. Quotes will be defined and stored in a static in-memory list.

Listing 16.3   The business logic to query book quotes

```
@Service
public class QuoteService {
  private static final Random random = new Random();
  private static final List<Quote> quotes = List.of(        ⬅──  Stores a list of
    new Quote("Content A", "Abigail", Genre.ADVENTURE),            quotes in memory
    new Quote("Content B", "Beatrix", Genre.ADVENTURE),
    new Quote("Content C", "Casper", Genre.FANTASY),
    new Quote("Content D", "Dobby", Genre.FANTASY),
    new Quote("Content E", "Eileen", Genre.SCIENCE_FICTION),
    new Quote("Content F", "Flora", Genre.SCIENCE_FICTION)
  );

  public Flux<Quote> getAllQuotes() {
    return Flux.fromIterable(quotes);        ⬅──  Returns all quotes as a
  }                                                reactive data stream

  public Mono<Quote> getRandomQuote() {
    return Mono.just(quotes.get(random.nextInt(quotes.size() - 1)));
  }

  public Mono<Quote> getRandomQuoteByGenre(Genre genre) {
    var quotesForGenre = quotes.stream()
      .filter(q -> q.genre().equals(genre))
      .toList();
    return Mono.just(quotesForGenre.get(
      random.nextInt(quotesForGenre.size() - 1)));
  }
}
```

NOTE   Since the focus of this example is the native-image compilation with GraalVM and Spring Native, we'll keep it simple and skip the persistence layer. Feel free to expand it on your own. For example, you could add Spring Data R2DBC and Spring Security, both supported by Spring Native.

That's it for the business logic. Next we'll expose the functionality through an HTTP API.

IMPLEMENTING THE WEB CONTROLLER

Create a new com.polarbookshop.quoteservice.web package and add a Quote-Controller class to expose three endpoints for the following:

- Return all the quotes
- Return a random quote
- Return a random quote for a given genre

Listing 16.4 Defining handlers for HTTP endpoints

```
@RestController
public class QuoteController {
  private final QuoteService quoteService;

  public QuoteController(QuoteService quoteService) {
    this.quoteService = quoteService;
  }

  @GetMapping("/quotes")
  public Flux<Quote> getAllQuotes() {
    return quoteService.getAllQuotes();
  }

  @GetMapping("/quotes/random")
  public Mono<Quote> getRandomQuote() {
    return quoteService.getRandomQuote();
  }

  @GetMapping("/quotes/random/{genre}")
  public Mono<Quote> getRandomQuote(@PathVariable Genre genre) {
    return quoteService.getRandomQuoteByGenre(genre);
  }
}
```

Then configure the embedded Netty server to listen to port 9101, and define the application name. Open the application.yml file and add the following configuration.

Listing 16.5 Configuring the Netty server port and the application name

```
server:
  port: 9101

spring:
  application:
    name: quote-service
```

Finally, let's write some integration tests using the same techniques you learned in chapter 8.

WRITING INTEGRATION TESTS

When we bootstrapped the project from Spring Initializr, we got an autogenerated QuoteServiceApplicationTests class. Let's update it with a few integration tests to check the REST API exposed by Quote Service.

Listing 16.6   Integration tests for Quote Service

```
@SpringBootTest(webEnvironment = SpringBootTest.WebEnvironment.RANDOM_PORT)
class QuoteServiceApplicationTests {

  @Autowired
  WebTestClient webTestClient;

  @Test
  void whenAllQuotesThenReturn() {
    webTestClient.get().uri("/quotes")
      .exchange()
      .expectStatus().is2xxSuccessful()
      .expectBodyList(Quote.class);
  }

  @Test
  void whenRandomQuoteThenReturn() {
    webTestClient.get().uri("/quotes/random")
      .exchange()
      .expectStatus().is2xxSuccessful()
      .expectBody(Quote.class);
  }

  @Test
  void whenRandomQuoteByGenreThenReturn() {
    webTestClient.get().uri("/quotes/random/FANTASY")
      .exchange()
      .expectStatus().is2xxSuccessful()
      .expectBody(Quote.class)
      .value(quote -> assertThat(quote.genre()).isEqualTo(Genre.FANTASY));
  }
}
```

That's it for the implementation. Next we'll execute the auto-tests and run the application on the JVM.

RUNNING AND TESTING ON THE JVM

So far, Quote Service is a standard Spring Boot application, no different from any other applications we built in the previous chapters. For example, we can run the autotests with Gradle and ensure that it behaves correctly. Open a Terminal window, navigate to the project's root folder, and execute the following command:

```
$ ./gradlew test
```

We can also run it on the JVM or package it as a JAR artifact. From the same Terminal window, execute the following command to run the application:

```
$ ./gradlew bootRun
```

Feel free to verify that the application works correctly by calling the endpoints exposed by Quote Service:

```
$ http :9101/quotes
$ http :9101/quotes/random
$ http :9101/quotes/random/FANTASY
```

When you're done testing the application, stop the process with Ctrl-C.

How can we compile it to a native executable and take advantage of instant startup time, instant peak performance, and reduced memory consumption? That's the topic of the next section.

16.1.3   Compiling Spring Boot applications as native images

There are two ways to compile your Spring Boot applications into native executables. The first option uses GraalVM explicitly and produces an OS-specific executable that runs directly on a machine. The second option relies on Cloud Native Buildpacks to containerize the native executable and run it on a container runtime like Docker. We'll use both.

COMPILING NATIVE EXECUTABLES WITH GRAALVM

The first option requires the GraalVM runtime to be available on your machine. You can install it directly from the website (www.graalvm.org) or use a tool like sdkman. You can find instructions on how to install sdkman in section A.1 of appendix A.

For the examples in this chapter, I'll be using the latest GraalVM 22.1 distribution available at the time of writing, based on OpenJDK 17. Using sdkman, you can install GraalVM as follows:

```
$ sdk install java 22.2.r17-grl
```

At the end of the installation procedure, sdkman will ask whether you want to make that distribution the default one. I recommend you say no, since we're going to be explicit whenever we need to use GraalVM instead of the standard OpenJDK.

Then open a Terminal window, navigate to your Quote Service project (quote-service), configure the shell to use GraalVM, and install the `native-image` GraalVM component as follows:

```
$ sdk use java 22.2.r17-grl      ◁──┐  Configures the current shell to
$ gu install native-image    ◁──┐   └── use the specified Java runtime
                                 │
                                 └── Uses the gu utility provided by GraalVM
                                     to install the native-image component
```

When you initialized the Quote Service project, the GraalVM Gradle/Maven official plugin was included automatically. That's the one providing the functionality to compile applications using the GraalVM Native Image mode.

> **NOTE**   The following Gradle tasks require that GraalVM is the current Java runtime. When using sdkman, you can do that by running `sdk use java 22.2.r17-grl` in the Terminal window where you want to use GraalVM.

Take into account that the compilation step for GraalVM apps is more prolonged, taking several minutes depending on the computational resources available on your machine. That is one of the drawbacks of working with native images. Also, since Spring Native is still in an experimental phase, you might get several debug logs and warnings, but that should be fine if the process completes successfully.

From the same Terminal window where you switched to GraalVM as the current Java runtime, run the following command to compile the application to a native image:

```
$ ./gradlew nativeCompile
```

A standalone binary is the result of the command. Since it's a native executable, it will be different on macOS, Linux, and Windows. You can run it on your machine natively, without the need for a JVM. In the case of Gradle, the native executable is generated in the build/native/nativeCompile folder. Go ahead and run it.

```
$ build/native/nativeCompile/quote-service
```

The first thing to notice is the startup time, usually less than 100 ms with Spring Native. It's an impressive improvement compared to the JVM option, which takes a few seconds. The best part of this is that we didn't have to write any code to make that happen! Let's send a request to ensure that the application is running correctly:

```
$ http :9101/quotes/random
```

When you're done testing the application, stop the process with Ctrl-C.

You can also run the autotests as native executables to make them even more reliable, since they will use the actual runtime environment used in production. However, the compilation step still takes longer than when running on the JVM:

```
$ ./gradlew nativeTest
```

Finally, you can run a Spring Boot application as a native image directly from Gradle/Maven:

```
$ ./gradlew nativeRun
```

Remember to stop the application process with Ctrl-C before moving to the next section, which will show you another option for compiling your Spring Boot applications to native executables. It won't require having GraalVM installed on your computer, and it will produce a containerized native executable using Cloud Native Buildpacks.

CONTAINERIZING NATIVE IMAGES WITH BUILDPACKS

The second option for compiling Spring Boot applications to native executables relies on Cloud Native Buildpacks. Similar to how we packaged Spring Boot applications as container images in chapter 6, we can use Buildpacks to build a container image from the application native executable compiled by GraalVM. This approach benefits from not requiring GraalVM to be installed on your machine.

Spring Initializr didn't just include the Spring AOT plugin when you bootstrapped the Quote Service project; it also provided additional configuration for the Buildpacks integration available in Spring Boot. If you check the build.gradle file again, you can see that the bootBuildImage task is configured to produce a containerized native image through the BP_NATIVE_IMAGE environment variable. While you're there, configure the image name and the container registry authentication as we did for the other Polar Bookshop applications.

Listing 16.7   Configuration for containerizing Quote Service

```
tasks.named('bootBuildImage') {
  builder = 'paketobuildpacks/builder:tiny'     ◁── Uses the "tiny" version of Paketo
                                                     Buildpacks to minimize the
                                                     container image size
  environment = ['BP_NATIVE_IMAGE': 'true']     ◁── Enables GraalVM
  imageName = "${project.name}"                      support and produces a
                                                     containerized native image
  docker {
   publishRegistry {
     username = project.findProperty("registryUsername")
     password = project.findProperty("registryToken")
     url = project.findProperty("registryUrl")
   }
  }
}
```

NOTE   As you probably noticed when running the native image compilation process on your machine, it takes not only time but also more computational resources than usual. When using Buildpacks, make sure you have at least 16 GB of RAM on your computer. If you use Docker Desktop, configure the Docker virtual machine with at least 8 GB of RAM. On Windows, it's recommended that you use Docker Desktop on WSL2 rather than Hyper-V. For more recommendations about the setup, refer to the Spring Native documentation (https://docs.spring.io/spring-native/docs/current/reference/htmlsingle).

The command to use Buildpacks and produce a containerized native image is the same that you'd use for JVM images. Open a Terminal window, navigate to your Quote Service project (quote-service), and run the following command:

```
$ ./gradlew bootBuildImage
```

When it's done, try running the resulting container image:

```
$ docker run --rm -p 9101:9101 quote-service
```

The startup time should again be less than 100 ms. Go ahead and send a few requests to test whether the application is working correctly:

```
$ http :9101/quotes/random
```

When you're done testing the application, stop the container process with Ctrl-C.

16.2 *Serverless applications with Spring Cloud Function*

As introduced in chapter 1, serverless is a further abstraction layer on top of virtual machines and containers, moving even more responsibilities from product teams to the platform. Following the serverless computing model, developers focus on implementing the business logic for their applications. Using an orchestrator like Kubernetes still requires infrastructure provisioning, capacity planning, and scaling. In contrast, a serverless platform takes care of setting up the underlying infrastructure needed by the applications to run, including virtual machines, containers, and dynamic scaling.

Serverless applications typically only run when there is an event to handle, such as an HTTP request (*request-driven*) or a message (*event-driven*). The event can be external or produced by another function. For example, whenever a message is added to a queue, a function might be triggered, process the message, and then exit the execution. When there is nothing to process, the platform shuts down all the resources involved with the function, so you can really pay for your actual usage.

In the other cloud native topologies like CaaS or PaaS, there is always a server involved running 24/7. Compared to traditional systems, you get the advantage of dynamic scalability, reducing the number of resources provisioned at any given time. Still, there is always something up and running that has a cost. In the serverless model, however, resources are provisioned only when necessary. If there is nothing to process, everything is shut down. That's what we call *scaling to zero*, and it's one of the main features offered by serverless platforms.

A consequence of scaling applications to zero is that when eventually there's a request to handle, a new application instance is started, and it must be ready to process the request very quickly. Standard JVM applications are not suitable for serverless applications, since it's hard to achieve a startup time lower than a few seconds. That's why GraalVM native images became popular. Their instant startup time and reduced memory consumption make them perfect for the serverless model. The *instant startup time* is required for scaling. The *reduced memory consumption* helps reduce costs, which is one of the goals of serverless and cloud native in general.

Besides cost optimization, serverless technologies also move some extra responsibility from the application to the platform. That might be an advantage, since it allows developers to focus exclusively on the business logic. But it's also essential to consider what degree of control you would like to have and how you will deal with vendor lock-in. Each serverless platform has its own features and APIs. Once you start writing functions for a specific platform, you can't move them easily to another, as you would do with containers. You might compromise to gain responsibility and scope and lose on control and portability more than with any other approach. That's why *Knative* became popular quickly: it's built on Kubernetes, which means that you can easily move your serverless workloads between platforms and vendors.

This section will guide you through developing and deploying a serverless application. You'll use Spring Native to compile it to a GraalVM native image and use Spring

Cloud Function to implement the business logic as functions, which is an excellent choice, since serverless applications are event-driven.

16.2.1   Building serverless applications with Spring Cloud Function

You have already worked with Spring Cloud Function in chapter 10. As you learned there, it's a project aimed at promoting business logic implementation via functions based on the standard interfaces introduced by Java 8: `Supplier`, `Function`, and `Consumer`.

Spring Cloud Function is very flexible. You have already seen how it integrates transparently with external messaging systems like RabbitMQ and Kafka, a handy feature for building serverless applications that are triggered by messages. In this section I'd like to show you one more feature offered by Spring Cloud Function that lets you expose functions as endpoints triggered by HTTP requests and CloudEvents, which is a specification standardizing the format and distribution of events in cloud architectures.

We'll use the same requirements as those for the Quote Service application we built earlier, but this time we'll implement the business logic as functions and let the framework deal with exposing them as HTTP endpoints.

BOOTSTRAPPING A NEW PROJECT WITH SPRING NATIVE AND SPRING CLOUD FUNCTION

You can initialize the Quote Function project from Spring Initializr (https://start .spring.io), store the result in a new `quote-function` Git repository, and push it to GitHub. The parameters for the initialization are shown in figure 16.2.

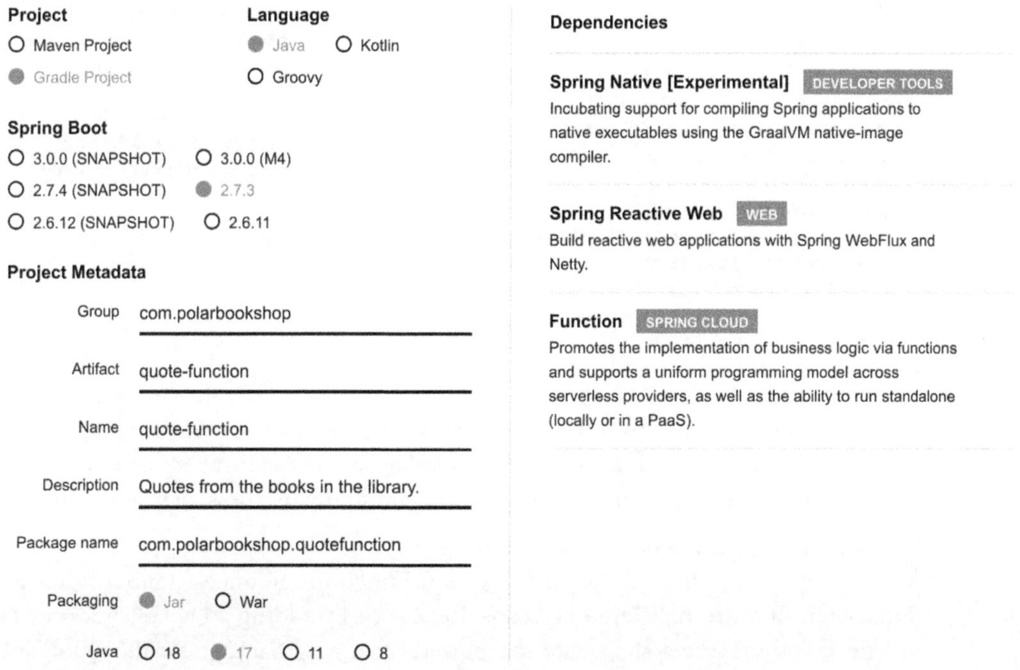

Project
- O Maven Project
- ● Gradle Project

Language
- ● Java   O Kotlin
- O Groovy

Spring Boot
- O 3.0.0 (SNAPSHOT)   O 3.0.0 (M4)
- O 2.7.4 (SNAPSHOT)   ● 2.7.3
- O 2.6.12 (SNAPSHOT)   O 2.6.11

Project Metadata

Group   com.polarbookshop

Artifact   quote-function

Name   quote-function

Description   Quotes from the books in the library.

Package name   com.polarbookshop.quotefunction

Packaging   ● Jar   O War

Java   O 18   ● 17   O 11   O 8

Dependencies

Spring Native [Experimental]   `DEVELOPER TOOLS`
Incubating support for compiling Spring applications to native executables using the GraalVM native-image compiler.

Spring Reactive Web   `WEB`
Build reactive web applications with Spring WebFlux and Netty.

Function   `SPRING CLOUD`
Promotes the implementation of business logic via functions and supports a uniform programming model across serverless providers, as well as the ability to run standalone (locally or in a PaaS).

Figure 16.2   The parameters for initializing the Quote Function project

The project contains the following dependencies:

- *Spring Reactive Web* provides the necessary libraries for building reactive web applications with Spring WebFlux, and it includes Netty as the default embedded server.
- *Spring Cloud Function* provides the necessary libraries to support business logic implementation via functions, export them via several communication channels, and integrate them with serverless platforms.
- *Spring Native* supports compiling Spring applications to native executables using the GraalVM native-image compiler.

The resulting dependencies section of the build.gradle file looks like the following.

```
dependencies {
  implementation 'org.springframework.boot:spring-boot-starter-webflux'
  implementation
  'org.springframework.cloud:spring-cloud-starter-function-web'
  testImplementation 'org.springframework.boot:spring-boot-starter-test'
  testImplementation 'io.projectreactor:reactor-test'
}
```

Then you can update the Cloud Native Buildpacks configuration in build.gradle much like we did for Quote Service.

Listing 16.8   Configuration for containerizing Quote Function

```
tasks.named('bootBuildImage') {
  builder = 'paketobuildpacks/builder:tiny'     ◁——  Uses the "tiny" version of
  environment = ['BP_NATIVE_IMAGE': 'true']     ◁——  Paketo Buildpacks to minimize
  imageName = "${project.name}"                       the container image size

  docker {                                            Enables the GraalVM
   publishRegistry {                                  support and produces a
     username = project.findProperty("registryUsername")    containerized native image
     password = project.findProperty("registryToken")
     url = project.findProperty("registryUrl")
   }
  }
}
```

Next, copy all the classes from the com.polarbookshop.quoteservice.domain package in Quote Service to a new com.polarbookshop.quotefunction.domain package in Quote Function. In the next section we'll implement the business logic as functions.

IMPLEMENTING THE BUSINESS LOGIC AS FUNCTIONS

As you learned in chapter 10, Spring Cloud Function enhances standard Java functions when they are registered as beans. Let's start by adding a QuoteFunctions class in a new com.polarbookshop.quotefunction.functions package for the Quote Function project.

The application should expose similar functionality to Quote Service:

- Returning all the quotes can be expressed as a `Supplier`, since it takes no input.
- Returning a random quote can also be expressed as a `Supplier`, since it takes no input.
- Returning a random quote for a given genre can be expressed as a `Function`, since it has both input and output.
- Logging a quote to standard output can be expressed as a `Consumer`, since it has input but no output.

Listing 16.9 Implementing the business logic as functions

```
                                    ┌─ Functions are declared as beans
                                    │  in a Spring configuration class.
@Configuration              ◁──────┘
public class QuoteFunctions {
  private static final Logger log =
    LoggerFactory.getLogger(QuoteFunctions.class);   ◁──┐ A logger used by
                                                        │ the functions
  @Bean
  Supplier<Flux<Quote>> allQuotes(QuoteService quoteService) {
    return () -> {
      log.info("Getting all quotes");
      return Flux.fromIterable(quoteService.getAllQuotes())
        .delaySequence(Duration.ofSeconds(1));   ◁──┐ Quotes are streamed one
    };                                                │ at a time with a 1-second
  }                                                   │ pause between them.
                          ┌─ A supplier producing
                          │  a random quote
  @Bean               ◁──┘
  Supplier<Quote> randomQuote(QuoteService quoteService) {
    return () -> {
      log.info("Getting random quote");
      return quoteService.getRandomQuote();
    };
  }
                          ┌─ A function logging the quote
                          │  received as the input
  @Bean               ◁──┘
  Consumer<Quote> logQuote() {
    return quote -> log.info("Quote: '{}' by {}",
      quote.content(), quote.author());
  }
}
```

A supplier producing all the quotes *(annotation pointing to `allQuotes`)*

Spring Cloud Function will automatically expose all the registered functions as HTTP endpoints when the Spring web dependencies are on the classpath. Each endpoint uses the same name as the function. In general, suppliers can be invoked through GET requests and functions and consumers as POST requests.

Quote Function contains the Spring Reactive Web dependency, so Netty will be the server to handle HTTP requests. Let's make it listen to port 9102 and configure the application name. Open the application.yml file, and add the following configuration.

Listing 16.10   Configuring the Netty server port and application name

```
server:
  port: 9102

spring:
  application:
    name: quote-function
```

Then run the Quote Function application (`./gradlew bootRun`) and open a Terminal window. For starters, you can test the two suppliers by sending GET requests:

```
$ http :9102/allQuotes
$ http :9102/randomQuote
```

To get a random quote by genre, you need to provide a genre string in the body of a POST request:

```
$ echo 'FANTASY' | http :9102/genreQuote
```

When only one function is registered as a bean, Spring Cloud Function will automatically expose it through the root endpoint. In the case of multiple functions, you can choose the function through the `spring.cloud.function.definition` configuration property.

For example, we could expose the `allQuotes` function through the root endpoint. In the Quote Function project, open the application.yml file and update it as follows.

Listing 16.11   Defining the main function managed by Spring Cloud Function

```
server:
  port: 9102

spring:
  application:
    name: quote-function
  cloud:
    function:
      definition: allQuotes
```

Re-run the application and send a GET request to the root endpoint. Since the `allQuotes` function is a `Supplier` returning a `Flux` of `Quote`, you can leverage the streaming capabilities of Project Reactor and ask the application to return the quotes as they become available. That is done automatically when the `Accept:text/event-stream` header is used (for example, `curl -H 'Accept:text/event-stream' local-host:9102`). When using the `httpie` utility, you'll also need to use the `--stream` argument to enable data streaming:

```
$ http :9102 Accept:text/event-stream --stream
```

Similar to what you did in chapter 10, you can build a pipeline by combining functions. When functions are exposed as HTTP endpoints, you can use the comma (`,`) character to compose functions on the fly. For example, you could combine the genreQuote function with logQuote as follows:

```
$ echo 'FANTASY' | http :9102/genreQuote,logQuote
```

Since logQuote is a consumer, the HTTP response has a 202 status with no body. If you check the application logs, you'll see that the random quote by genre has been printed out instead.

Spring Cloud Function integrates with several communication channels. You have seen how you can expose functions through exchanges and queues leveraging Spring Cloud Stream and how to expose them as HTTP endpoints. The framework also supports RSocket, which is a binary reactive protocol, and CloudEvents, a specification standardizing the format and distribution of events in cloud architectures (https://cloudevents.io).

CloudEvents can be consumed over HTTP, messaging channels like AMPQ (RabbitMQ), and RSocket. They ensure a standard way of describing events, thus making them portable across a wide variety of technologies, including applications, messaging systems, build tools, and platforms.

Since Quote Function is already configured to expose functions as HTTP endpoints, you can make it consume CloudEvents without changing any code. Ensure the application is up and running, and then send an HTTP request with the additional headers defined by the CloudEvents specification:

```
$ echo 'FANTASY' | http :9102/genreQuote \          The CloudEvents
    ce-specversion:1.0 \          ⟵          specification version
    ce-type:quote \     ⟵——— The type of event (domain-specific)
    ce-id:394       ⟵
                        │  The ID of the event
```

When you're done testing the application, stop the process with Ctrl-C.

> **NOTE** You can refer to the Spring Cloud Function official documentation for more details on how HTTP, CloudEvents, and RSocket are supported (https://spring.io/projects/spring-cloud-function).

16.2.2 Deployment pipeline: Build and publish

Following the continuous delivery principles and techniques explained throughout the book, we can implement a deployment pipeline for Quote Service and Quote Function. Since the release candidate for those projects is a container image, most of the operations will be the same as for standard JVM applications.

When working locally, it's convenient to run and test serverless applications on the JVM rather than using GraalVM due to the shorter build time and the less resource-demanding process. However, to achieve better quality and catch errors earlier, we should run and verify the applications in native mode as early in the delivery process as possible. The commit stage is where we compile and test our applications, so it might be a good place to add those additional steps.

In your Quote Function project (quote-function), add a new .github/workflows folder, and create a commit-stage.yml file. As a starting point, you can copy the implementation of the commit stage from one of the other applications we built in the previous chapters, such as Catalog Service. The commit stage workflow we have used so far is composed of two jobs: "Build & Test" and "Package and Publish." We'll reuse the implementation from the other applications, but we'll add an intermediate job responsible for testing the native mode.

Listing 16.12   A job to build and test the application in native mode

```
name: Commit Stage
on: push

env:                                     Uses the GitHub          The name of the image.
  REGISTRY: ghcr.io            ◁──       Container Registry       Remember to add your
                                                                  GitHub username, all
  IMAGE_NAME: <your_github_username>/quote-function   ◁──        in lowercase.
  VERSION: ${{ github.sha }}    ◁──┐
                                   For simplicity, any
                                   new image will be
jobs:                              tagged as "latest."
  build:
    name: Build and Test
    ...
                              The job unique
  native:                     identifier           A human-friendly
    name: Build and Test (Native)  ◁──             name for the job
    runs-on: ubuntu-22.04     ◁──┐
    permissions:                 The type of
      contents: read             machine where
    steps:                       the job will run
      - name: Checkout source code
        uses: actions/checkout@v3   ◁──    Checks out the current Git
      - name: Set up GraalVM                repository (quote-function)
        uses: graalvm/setup-graalvm@v1   ◁──
        with:                                Installs and configures
          version: '22.1.0'                  GraalVM with Java 17 and
          java-version: '17'                 the native image component
          components: 'native-image'
          github-token: ${{ secrets.GITHUB_TOKEN }}
      - name: Build, unit tests and integration tests (native)
        run: |
          chmod +x gradlew              Compiles the application as
          ./gradlew nativeBuild  ◁──    a native executable and runs
                                        unit and integration tests
  package:
    name: Package and Publish
    if: ${{ github.ref == 'refs/heads/main' }}    The "Package and Publish" job
    needs: [ build, native ]   ◁──               runs only if both of the previous
    ...                                          jobs complete successfully.
```

The permissions granted to the job ←

Permission to check out the current Git repository ←

NOTE   In the source code repository accompanying the book, you can check the final result in the Chapter16/16-end/quote-function folder.

When you're done, commit all your changes and push them to your GitHub `quote-function` repository to trigger the commit stage workflow. We're going to use the container image published by that workflow later in the chapter, so make sure it runs successfully.

You'll notice that the commit stage execution for Quote Function takes quite a bit longer than for the other applications throughout the book. In chapter 3 I wrote that the commit stage is supposed to be fast, possibly under five minutes, to provide developers with fast feedback about their changes and allow them to move on to the next task, in the spirit of continuous integration. The additional steps using GraalVM that we have just added might slow down the workflow too much. In that case, you might consider moving this check to the acceptance stage, where we allow the overall process to take longer.

The following section will cover some options for deploying serverless applications implemented with Spring Cloud Function.

16.2.3 *Deploying serverless applications on the cloud*

Applications using Spring Cloud Function can be deployed in a few different ways. First of all, since they're still Spring Boot applications, you can package them as JAR artifacts or container images and deploy them on servers or container runtimes like Docker or Kubernetes, respectively, just like you did in the previous chapters.

Then, when Spring Native is included, you also have the option to compile them to native images and run them on servers or container runtimes. Thanks to instant startup time and reduced memory consumption, you can also seamlessly deploy such applications on serverless platforms. The next section covers how to use Knative to run your serverless workloads on Kubernetes.

Spring Cloud Function also supports deploying applications on vendor-specific FaaS platforms like AWS Lambda, Azure Functions, and Google Cloud Functions. Once you choose a platform, you can add the related adapter provided by the framework to accomplish the integration. Each adapter works in a slightly different way, depending on the specific platform and the configuration required to integrate the functions with the underlying infrastructure. The adapters provided by Spring Cloud Function don't require any changes to your business logic, but they might need some additional code to configure the integration.

When you use one of those adapters, you must choose which function to integrate with the platform. If there's only one function registered as a bean, that's the one used. If there are more (like in Quote Function), you need to use the `spring.cloud` `.function.definition` property to declare which function the FaaS platform will manage.

> **NOTE** You can refer to the Spring Cloud Function official documentation for more details on the Spring Cloud Function adapters for AWS Lambda, Azure Functions, and Google Cloud Functions (https://spring.io/projects/spring -cloud-function).

The following section will cover deploying a serverless application like Quote Function on a Kubernetes-based platform using Knative.

16.3   *Deploying serverless applications with Knative*

In the previous sections, you learned about Spring Native and how to use it with Spring Cloud Function to build serverless applications. This section will guide you through deploying Quote Function to a serverless platform on top of Kubernetes, using the Knative project.

Knative is a "Kubernetes-based platform to deploy and manage modern serverless workloads" (https://knative.dev). It's a CNCF project that you can use to deploy standard containerized workloads and event-driven applications. The project offers a superior user experience to developers and higher abstractions that make it simpler to deploy applications on Kubernetes.

You can decide to run your own Knative platform on top of a Kubernetes cluster or choose a managed service offered by a cloud provider, such as VMware Tanzu Application Platform, Google Cloud Run, or Red Hat OpenShift Serverless. Since they are all based on open source software and standards, you could migrate from Google Cloud Run to VMware Tanzu Application Platform without changing your application code and with minimal changes to your deployment pipeline.

The Knative project consists of two main components: Serving and Eventing.

- *Knative Serving* is for running serverless workloads on Kubernetes. It takes care of autoscaling, networking, revisions, and deployment strategies while letting engineers focus on the application business logic.
- *Knative Eventing* provides management for integrating applications with event sources and sinks based on the CloudEvents specification, abstracting backends like RabbitMQ or Kafka.

Our focus will be on using Knative Serving to run serverless workloads while avoiding vendor lock-in.

> **NOTE**   Originally, Knative consisted of a third component called "Build" that subsequently became a standalone product, renamed Tekton (https://tekton.dev) and donated to the Continuous Delivery Foundation (https://cd.foundation). Tekton is a Kubernetes-native framework for building deployment pipelines that support continuous delivery. For example, you could use Tekton instead of GitHub Actions.

This section will show you how to set up a local development environment comprising both Kubernetes and Knative. Then I'll introduce Knative manifests, which you can use to declare the desired state for serverless applications, and I'll show you how to apply them to a Kubernetes cluster.

16.3.1 Setting up a local Knative platform

Since Knative runs on top of Kubernetes, we first need a cluster. Let's create one with minikube following the same approach we've used throughout the book. Open a Terminal window and run the following command:

```
$ minikube start --profile knative
```

Next, we can install Knative. For simplicity, I have collected the necessary commands in a script that you'll find in the source code repository accompanying the book. From the Chapter16/16-end/polar-deployment/kubernetes/development folder, copy the install-knative.sh file to the same path in your Polar Deployment repository (polar-deployment).

Then open a Terminal window, navigate to the folder where you just copied the script, and run the following command to install Knative on your local Kubernetes cluster:

```
$ ./install-knative.sh
```

Feel free to open the file and look at the instructions before running it. You can find more information about installing Knative on the project website (https://knative .dev/docs/install).

> **NOTE** On macOS and Linux, you might need to make the script executable via the chmod +x install-knative.sh command.

The Knative project provides a convenient CLI tool that you can use to interact with Knative resources in a Kubernetes cluster. You can find instructions on how to install it in section A.4 of appendix A. In the next section I'll show you how to deploy Quote Function using the Knative CLI.

16.3.2 Deploying applications with the Knative CLI

Knative provides a few different options for deploying applications. In production, we'll want to stick to a declarative configuration as we did for standard Kubernetes deployments and rely on a GitOps flow to reconcile the desired state (in a Git repository) and actual state (in the Kubernetes cluster).

When experimenting or working locally, we can also take advantage of the Knative CLI to deploy applications in an imperative way. From a Terminal window, run the following command to deploy Quote Function. The container image is the one published by the commit stage workflow we defined before. Remember to replace <your_github_username> with your GitHub username in lowercase:

```
$ kn service create quote-function \
    --image ghcr.io/<your_github_username>/quote-function \
    --port 9102
```

You can refer to figure 16.3 for a description of the command.

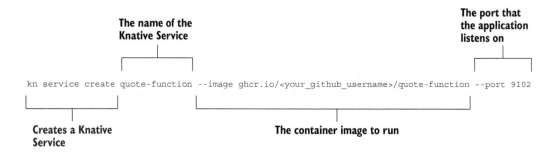

Figure 16.3   The Knative command for creating a Service from a container image. Knative will take care of creating all the resources necessary to deploy the applications on Kubernetes.

The command will initialize a new `quote-function` service in the `default` namespace on Kubernetes. It will return the public URL through which the application is exposed, in a message like the following:

```
Creating service 'quote-function' in namespace 'default':

  0.045s The Route is still working to reflect the latest desired
  ➥specification.
  0.096s Configuration "quote-function" is waiting for a Revision
  ➥to become ready.
  3.337s ...
  3.377s Ingress has not yet been reconciled.
  3.480s Waiting for load balancer to be ready
  3.660s Ready to serve.

Service 'quote-function' created to latest revision 'quote-function-00001'
➥is available at URL:
http://quote-function.default.127.0.0.1.sslip.io
```

Let's test it out! First we need to open a tunnel to the cluster with minikube. The first time you run this command, you might be asked to input your machine password to authorize the tunneling to the cluster:

```
$ minikube tunnel --profile knative
```

Then open a new Terminal window and call the application at the root endpoint to fetch the complete list of quotes. The URL to call is the same one returned by the previous command (`http://quote-function.default.127.0.0.1.sslip.io`), which is in the format `<service-name>.<namespace>.<domain>`:

```
$ http http://quote-function.default.127.0.0.1.sslip.io
```

Since we are working locally, I configured Knative to use sslip.io, a DNS service that "when queried with a hostname with an embedded IP address, returns that IP address." For example, the `127.0.0.1.sslip.io` hostname would be resolved to the `127.0.0.1` IP address. Since we opened a tunnel to the cluster, requests to `127.0.0.1` will be handled by the cluster, where Knative will route them to the right service.

Knative takes care of scaling the application without any further configuration. For each request, it determines whether more instances are required. When an instance stays idle for a specific time period (30 seconds, by default), Knative will shut it down. If no request is received for more than 30 seconds, Knative will scale the application to zero, meaning there will be no instances of Quote Function running.

When a new request is eventually received, Knative starts a new instance and uses it to handle the request. Thanks to Spring Native, the startup time of Quote Function is almost instantaneous, so users and clients won't have to deal with long wait times, as would be the case with standard JVM applications. This powerful feature lets you optimize costs and pay only for what you use and need.

Using an open source platform like Knative has the advantage of letting you migrate your applications to another cloud provider without any code changes. But that's not all! You can even use the same deployment pipeline as-is, or with minor modifications. The next section will show you how to define Knative Services in a declarative way via YAML manifests, which is the recommended approach for production scenarios.

Before moving on, make sure you have deleted the Quote Function instance you created previously:

```
$ kn service delete quote-function
```

16.3.3 Deploying applications with the Knative manifests

Kubernetes is an extensible system. Besides using built-in objects like Deployments and Pods, we can define our own objects via Custom Resource Definitions (CRDs). That is the strategy used by many tools built on top of Kubernetes, including Knative.

One of the benefits of using Knative is a better developer experience and the possibility to declare the desired state for our applications in a more straightforward and less verbose way. Rather than dealing with Deployments, Services, and Ingresses, we can work with a single type of resource: the Knative Service.

> **NOTE** Throughout the book, I talked about applications as *services*. Knative offers a way to model an application in a single resource declaration: the Knative Service. At first, the naming might not be very clear, since there is already a Kubernetes built-in Service type. In reality, the Knative choice is very intuitive because it maps one-to-one the architectural concept with the deployment concept.

Let's see what Knative Services look like. Open your Quote Function project (quote-function), and create a new "knative" folder. Then, define a new kservice.yml file inside to declare the desired state of the Knative Service for Quote Function. Remember to replace <your_github_username> with your GitHub username in lowercase.

Listing 16.13   Knative Service manifest for Quote Function

```
apiVersion: serving.knative.dev/v1              ◁──┐ The API version for
kind: Service                        ◁──┐           Knative Serving
metadata:                               │ The type of   objects
  name: quote-function      ┌──▷        │ object to create
spec:                       │
  template:                 │       The name of
    spec:                   │       the container
      containers:           │                         The image used to run
        - name: quote-function      ◁──┐              the container. Remember to
          image:                        ◁──┐          insert your GitHub username.
⇒ghcr.io/<your_github_username>/quote-function
          ports:
            - containerPort: 9102      ◁──┐
          resources:        ◁──┐             The port exposed
            requests:          │             by the container
              cpu: '0.1'
              memory: '128Mi'      CPU and memory
            limits:              configuration for
              cpu: '2'           the container
              memory: '512Mi'
```

The name of the Service ▷ (label for `name: quote-function`)

Like any other Kubernetes resource, you can apply a Knative Service manifest to a cluster with `kubectl apply -f <manifest-file>` or through an automated flow like we did with Argo CD in the previous chapter. For this example, we'll use the Kubernetes CLI.

Open a Terminal window, navigate to your Quote Function project (quote-function), and run the following command to deploy Quote Function from the Knative Service manifest:

```
$ kubectl apply -f knative/kservice.yml
```

Using the Kubernetes CLI, you can get information about all the created Knative Services and their URLs by running the following command (the result displayed is partial, to fit on the page):

```
$ kubectl get ksvc

NAME             URL                                               READY
quote-function   http://quote-function.default.127.0.0.1.sslip.io   True
```

Let's verify that the application is correctly deployed by sending an HTTP request to its root endpoint. If the tunnel you opened earlier is not active anymore, run `minikube tunnel --profile knative` before calling the application:

```
$ http http://quote-function.default.127.0.0.1.sslip.io
```

Knative provides an abstraction on top of Kubernetes. However, it still runs Deployments, ReplicaSets, Pods, Services, and Ingresses under the hood. This means you can use all the techniques you learned in the previous chapters. For example, you can configure Quote Function through ConfigMaps and Secrets:

```
$ kubectl get pod

NAME                                                     READY   STATUS
pod/quote-function-00001-deployment-c6978b588-11f9w      2/2     Running
```

If you wait for 30 seconds and then check for the running Pods in your local Kubernetes cluster, you'll see there are none, because Knative scaled the application to zero due to inactivity:

```
$ kubectl get pod
No resources found in default namespace.
```

Now try sending a new request to the application on `http http://quote-function .default.127.0.0.1.sslip.io`. Knative will immediately spin up a new Pod for Quote Function to answer the request:

```
$ kubectl get pod

NAME                                                 READY   STATUS
quote-function-00001-deployment-c6978b588-f49x8      2/2     Running
```

When you're done testing the application, you can remove it with `kubectl delete -f knative/kservice.yml`. Finally, you can stop and delete the local cluster with the following command:

```
$ minikube stop --profile knative
$ minikube delete --profile knative
```

The Knative Service resource represents an application service in its entirety. Thanks to this abstraction, we no longer need to deal directly with Deployments, Services, and Ingresses. Knative takes care of all that. It creates and manages them under the hood while freeing us from dealing with those lower-level resources provided by Kubernetes. By default, Knative can even expose an application outside the cluster without the need to configure an Ingress resource, providing you directly with a URL to call the application.

Thanks to its features focused on developer experience and productivity, Knative can be used to run and manage any kind of workload on Kubernetes, limiting its scale-to-zero functionality only to the applications that provide support for it (for example, using Spring Native). We could easily run the entire Polar Bookshop system on Knative. We could use the `autoscaling.knative.dev/minScale` annotation to mark the applications we don't want to be scaled to zero:

```
apiVersion: serving.knative.dev/v1
kind: Service
metadata:
  name: catalog-service
  annotations:
    autoscaling.knative.dev/minScale: "1"
...
```

Ensures this Service is never scaled to zero

Knative offers such a great developer experience that it's becoming the de facto abstraction when deploying workloads on Kubernetes, not only for serverless but also for more standard containerized applications. Whenever I provision a new Kubernetes cluster, Knative is the first thing I install. It's also a foundational part of platforms like Tanzu Community Edition, Tanzu Application Platform, Red Hat OpenShift, and Google Cloud Run.

NOTE Tanzu Community Edition (https://tanzucommunityedition.io) is a Kubernetes platform that provides a great developer experience on top of Knative. It's open source and free to use.

Another great feature offered by Knative is an intuitive and developer-friendly option for adopting deployment strategies like blue/green deployments, canary deployments, or A/B deployments, all via the same Knative Service resource. Implementing those strategies in plain Kubernetes would require a lot of manual work. Instead, Knative supports them out of the box.

NOTE To get more information about serverless applications and Knative, you can refer to the official documentation (https://knative.dev). Also, I recommend checking out a couple of books from the Manning catalog on this subject: *Knative in Action* by Jacques Chester (Manning, 2021; https://www.manning.com/books/knative-in-action) and *Continuous Delivery for Kubernetes* by Mauricio Salatino (www.manning.com/books/continuous-delivery-for-kubernetes).

Polar Labs

Feel free to apply what you learned in the last sections to Quote Service.

1 Define a commit stage workflow, including the steps for compiling and testing the application as a native executable.
2 Push your changes to GitHub, and ensure that the workflow completes successfully and publishes a container image for your application.
3 Deploy Quote Service on Kubernetes via the Knative CLI.
4 Deploy Quote Service on Kubernetes via the Kubernetes CLI from a Knative Service manifest.

You can refer to the Chapter16/16-end folder in the code repository accompanying the book to check the final result (https://github.com/ThomasVitale/cloud-native-spring-in-action).

Summary

- By replacing a standard OpenJDK distribution with GraalVM as the runtime environment for your Java applications, you can increase their performance and efficiency, thanks to a new optimized technology for performing JIT compilation (the GraalVM compiler).

- What makes GraalVM so innovative and popular in the serverless context is the Native Image mode.

- Rather than compiling your Java code into bytecode and relying on a JVM to interpret it and convert it to machine code at runtime, GraalVM offers a new technology (the Native Image builder) to compile Java applications directly into machine code, obtaining a native executable or native image.

- Java applications compiled as native images have faster startup times, optimized memory consumption, and instant peak performance, unlike the JVM options.

- The main goal of Spring Native is to make it possible to compile any Spring application into a native executable using GraalVM without any code changes.

- Spring Native provides an AOT infrastructure (invoked from a dedicated Gradle/Maven plugin) for contributing all the required configurations for GraalVM to AOT-compile Spring classes.

- There are two ways to compile your Spring Boot applications into native executables. The first option produces an OS-specific executable and runs the application directly on a machine. The second option relies on Buildpacks to containerize the native executable and run it on a container runtime like Docker.

- Serverless is a further abstraction layer on top of virtual machines and containers, which moves even more responsibility from product teams to the platform.

- Following the serverless computing model, developers focus on implementing the business logic for their applications.

- Serverless applications are triggered by an incoming request or a specific event. We call such applications request-driven or event-driven.

- Applications using Spring Cloud Function can be deployed in a few different ways.

- When Spring Native is included, you can also compile applications to native images and run them on servers or container runtimes. Thanks to instant startup time and reduced memory consumption, you can seamlessly deploy such applications on Knative.

- Knative is a "Kubernetes-based platform to deploy and manage modern serverless workloads" (https://knative.dev). You can use it to deploy standard containerized workloads and event-driven applications.

- The Knative project offers a superior user experience to developers and higher abstractions that make it simpler to deploy applications on Kubernetes.

- Knative offers such a great developer experience that it's becoming the de facto abstraction when deploying workloads on Kubernetes, not only for serverless but also for more standard containerized applications.

appendix A
Setting up your
development environment

> **This appendix covers**
> - Setting up Java
> - Setting up Docker
> - Setting up Kubernetes
> - Setting up other tools

In this appendix, you'll find instructions for setting up your development environment and installing the tools we'll use throughout the book to build, manage, and deploy cloud native applications.

A.1 Java

All the examples in this book are based on Java 17, the latest long-term release of Java at the time of writing. You can install any of the OpenJDK 17 distributions. I'll be using Eclipse Temurin from the Adoptium project (https://adoptium.net), previously known as AdoptOpenJDK, but feel free to choose another one.

Managing different Java versions and distributions on your machine might be painful. I recommend using a tool like sdkman (https://sdkman.io) to install, update, and switch between different JDKs easily. On macOS and Linux, you can install sdkman as follows:

```
$ curl -s "https://get.sdkman.io" | bash
```

Refer to the official documentation for installation instructions for Windows.

Once it's installed, check all the available OpenJDK distributions and versions by running the following command:

```
$ sdk list java
```

Then choose a distribution and install it. For example, I can install the latest 17 version of Eclipse Temurin available at the moment of writing as follows:

```
$ sdk install java 17.0.3-tem
```

By the time you read this section, newer versions might be available, so please check the list returned from the `list` command to identify the latest one.

At the end of the installation procedure, sdkman will ask whether you want to make that distribution the default one. I recommend you say yes to ensure that you have access to Java 17 from all the projects you build throughout the book. You can always change the default version with the following command:

```
$ sdk default java 17.0.3-tem
```

Let's now verify the OpenJDK installation:

```
$ java --version
openjdk 17.0.3 2022-04-19
OpenJDK Runtime Environment Temurin-17.0.3+7 (build 17.0.3+7)
OpenJDK 64-Bit Server VM Temurin-17.0.3+7 (build 17.0.3+7, mixed mode)
```

You also have the option to change the Java version only within the context of the current shell:

```
$ sdk use java 17.0.3-tem
```

Finally, if you want to check which version of Java is configured in the current shell, you can do that as follows:

```
$ sdk current java
Using java version 17.0.3-tem
```

A.2   Docker

The Open Container Initiative (OCI), a Linux Foundation project, defines industry standards for working with containers (https://opencontainers.org). In particular, the OCI Image Specification defines how to build container images, the OCI Runtime Specification defines how to run those container images, and the OCI Distribution

Specification defines how to distribute them. The tool we use throughout the book to work with containers is Docker, which is compliant with the OCI specifications.

On the Docker website (www.docker.com), you can find instructions for setting up Docker in your local environment. I'll be using the latest versions available at the time of writing: Docker 20.10 and Docker Desktop 4.11.

- On Linux, you can install the Docker open source platform directly. It's also known as Docker Community Edition (Docker CE).
- On macOS and Windows, you have the option to use Docker Desktop, a commercial product built on top of Docker that makes it possible to run Linux containers from those operating systems. At the time of writing, Docker Desktop is free for personal use, education, non-commercial open source projects, and small businesses. Please read the Docker Subscription Service Agreement carefully before installing the software, and make sure you are compliant with it (www.docker.com/legal).

Docker Desktop provides support for both ARM64 and AMD64 architectures, meaning that you can run all the examples in this book on the new Apple computers with Apple Silicon processors.

If you work on Windows, Docker Desktop provides two types of setup: Hyper-V or WSL2. I recommend you choose the latter, since it offers better performance, and it's more stable.

Docker comes preconfigured to download OCI images from Docker Hub, a container registry hosting images for many popular open source projects, like Ubuntu, PostgreSQL, and Redis. It's free to use, but it's subjected to strict rate-limiting policies if you use it anonymously. Therefore, I recommend you create a free account on the Docker website (www.docker.com).

After creating an account, open a Terminal window and authenticate with Docker Hub (make sure your Docker Engine is running). Since it's the default container registry, you don't need to specify its URL:

```
$ docker login
```

When asked, insert your username and password.

Using the Docker CLI, you can now interact with Docker Hub to download images (*pull*) or upload your own (*push*). For example, try pulling the official Ubuntu image from Docker Hub:

```
$ docker pull ubuntu:22.04
```

Throughout the book, you'll learn more about using Docker. Until then, if you would like to experiment with containers, I'll leave you a list of useful commands for controlling the container life cycle (table A.1).

Table A.1 Useful Docker CLI commands for managing images and containers

Docker CLI command	What it does
`docker images`	Shows all images
`docker ps`	Shows the running containers
`docker ps -a`	Shows all containers created, started, and stopped
`docker run <image>`	Runs a container from the given image
`docker start <name>`	Starts an existing container
`docker stop <name>`	Stops a running container
`docker logs <name>`	Shows the logs from a given container
`docker rm <name>`	Removes a stopped container
`docker rmi <image>`	Removes an image

All the containers we build throughout the book are OCI-compliant and will work with any other OCI container runtime, such as Podman (https://podman.io). Should you decide to use a platform other than Docker, be aware that some tools we use for local development and integration testing might require additional configuration to work correctly.

A.3 Kubernetes

There are a few ways to install Kubernetes in your local environment. These are some of the most commonly used options:

- *minikube* (https://minikube.sigs.k8s.io) lets you run a local Kubernetes cluster on any operating system. It's maintained by the Kubernetes community.
- *kind* (https://kind.sigs.k8s.io) lets you run local Kubernetes clusters as Docker containers. It was primarily developed to test Kubernetes itself, but you can also use it for local development with Kubernetes. It's maintained by the Kubernetes community.
- *k3d* (https://k3d.io) lets you run local Kubernetes clusters based on k3s, a minimal distribution of Kubernetes implemented by Rancher Labs. It's maintained by the Rancher community.

Feel free to choose the tool that best fits your needs. I'll be using minikube throughout the book because of its stability and compatibility with all operating systems and architectures, including the new Apple Silicon computers. You should have at least two CPUs and 4 GB of free memory to use minikube to run all the examples in the book.

You can find the installation guide on the project's website (https://minikube.sigs .k8s.io). I'll be using the latest versions available at the time of writing: Kubernetes 1.24 and minikube 1.26. On macOS you can install minikube with Homebrew as follows:

```
$ brew install minikube
```

Running a local Kubernetes cluster with minikube requires a container runtime or a virtual machine manager. Since we are already using Docker, that's what we're going to use. Under the hood, any minikube cluster will run as a Docker container.

After installing minikube, you can start a new local Kubernetes cluster using the Docker driver. The first time you run this command, it will take a few minutes to download all the components needed to run the cluster:

```
$ minikube start --driver=docker
```

I recommend making Docker the default driver for minikube by running the following command:

```
$ minikube config set driver docker
```

To interact with the newly created Kubernetes cluster, you need to install kubectl, the Kubernetes CLI. Installation instructions are available on the official website (https://kubernetes.io/docs/tasks/tools). On macOS and Linux, you can install it with Homebrew as follows:

```
$ brew install kubectl
```

Then you can verify that the minikube cluster is started correctly and check that a node is running in your local cluster:

```
$ kubectl get nodes
NAME       STATUS   ROLES                  AGE     VERSION
minikube   Ready    control-plane,master   2m20s   v1.24.3
```

I recommend stopping minikube whenever you don't need it to free up resources in your local environment:

```
$ minikube stop
```

Throughout the book you'll learn more about using Kubernetes and minikube. Until then, if you would like to experiment with Kubernetes resources, I'll leave you with some useful commands (table A.2).

Table A.2 Useful Kubernetes CLI commands for managing Pods, Deployments, and Services

Kubernetes CLI command	What it does
kubectl get deployment	Shows all Deployments
kubectl get pod	Shows all Pods
kubectl get svc	Shows all Services
kubectl logs <pod_id>	Shows the logs for the given Pod
kubectl delete deployment <name>	Deletes the given Deployment

Table A.2 *(continued)*   **Useful Kubernetes CLI commands for managing Pods, Deployments, and Services**

Kubernetes CLI command	What it does
`kubectl delete pod <name>`	Deletes the given Pod
`kubectl delete svc <service>`	Deletes the given Service
`kubectl port-forward svc <service> <host-port>:<cluster-port>`	Forwards traffic from your local machine to within the cluster

A.4   Other tools

This section will present a series of helpful tools used throughout the book for performing specific tasks, such as security vulnerability scanning or HTTP interactions.

A.4.1   HTTPie

HTTPie is a convenient "command-line HTTP and API testing client" (https://httpie .org). It's designed for humans and offers a superior user experience. Refer to the official documentation for installation instructions and more information on the tool.

On macOS and Linux, you can install it with Homebrew as follows:

```
$ brew install httpie
```

As part of the installation, you'll get two tools you can use from your Terminal window: `http` and `https`. For example, you can send a GET request as follows:

```
$ http pie.dev/get
```

A.4.2   Grype

In the context of supply chain security, we use Grype to scan Java codebases and container images for vulnerabilities (https://github.com/anchore/grype). The scanning happens locally on the machine where you run it, meaning that none of your files or artifacts are sent to an external service. That makes it a good fit for more regulated environments or air-gapped scenarios. Refer to the official documentation for more information.

On macOS and Linux, you can install it with Homebrew as follows:

```
$ brew tap anchore/grype
$ brew install grype
```

The tool is not available for Windows yet. If you are a Windows user, I recommend taking advantage of the Windows Subsystem for Linux 2 (WSL2) and installing Grype there. For more information on WSL2, you can refer to the official documentation (https://docs.microsoft.com/en-us/windows/wsl/).

A.4.3   Tilt

Tilt (https://tilt.dev) aims at providing a good developer experience when working on Kubernetes. It's an open source tool that offers features for building, deploying, and managing containerized workloads in your local environment. Refer to the official documentation for installation instructions (https://docs.tilt.dev/install.html).

On macOS and Linux, you can install it with Homebrew as follows:

```
$ brew install tilt-dev/tap/tilt
```

A.4.4   Octant

Octant (https://octant.dev) is an "open source developer-centric web interface for Kubernetes that lets you inspect a Kubernetes cluster and its applications." Refer to the official documentation for installation instructions (https://reference.octant.dev).

On macOS and Linux, you can install it with Homebrew as follows:

```
$ brew install octant
```

A.4.5   Kubeval

Kubeval (www.kubeval.com) is a convenient tool when you need to "validate one or more Kubernetes configuration files." We'll use it in a deployment pipeline to ensure that all our Kubernetes manifests are properly formatted and compliant with the Kubernetes API. Refer to the official documentation for installation instructions (www.kubeval.com/installation/).

On macOS and Linux, you can install it with Homebrew as follows:

```
$ brew tap instrumenta/instrumenta
$ brew install kubeval
```

A.4.6   Knative CLI

Knative is a "Kubernetes-based platform to deploy and manage modern serverless workloads" (https://knative.dev). The project provides a convenient CLI tool you can use to interact with Knative resources in a Kubernetes cluster. Refer to the official documentation for installation instructions (https://knative.dev/docs/install/quickstart-install).

On macOS and Linux, you can install it with Homebrew as follows:

```
$ brew install kn
```

appendix B
Kubernetes in production
with DigitalOcean

This appendix covers

- Running a Kubernetes cluster on DigitalOcean
- Running a PostgreSQL database on DigitalOcean
- Running Redis on DigitalOcean
- Running RabbitMQ using a Kubernetes Operator
- Running Keycloak using a Helm chart

Kubernetes is the de facto standard for deploying and managing containerized workloads. We've been relying on a local Kubernetes cluster to deploy applications and services in the Polar Bookshop system throughout the book. For production, we need something else.

All major cloud providers offer a managed Kubernetes service. In this appendix, you'll see how to use DigitalOcean to spin up a Kubernetes cluster. We'll also rely on other managed services provided by the platform, including PostgreSQL and Redis. Finally, this appendix will guide you through the deployment of RabbitMQ and Keycloak directly in Kubernetes.

Before moving on, you need to ensure that you have a DigitalOcean account. When you sign up, DigitalOcean offers a 60-day free trial with a $100 credit that is more than enough to go through the examples in chapter 15. Follow the instructions

on the official website to create an account and start a free trial (https://try.digitalocean
.com/freetrialoffer).

> **NOTE** The source code repository accompanying this book contains additional instructions for setting up a Kubernetes cluster on a few different cloud platforms, in case you'd like to use something other than DigitalOcean.

There are two main options for interacting with the DigitalOcean platform. The first one is through the web portal (https://cloud.digitalocean.com), which is very convenient for exploring the available services and their features. The second option is via doctl, the DigitalOcean CLI. That's what we're going to use in the following sections.

You can find instructions for installing doctl on the official website (https://docs
.digitalocean.com/reference/doctl/how-to/install). If you're on macOS or Linux, you can easily install it using Homebrew:

```
$ brew install doctl
```

You can follow the subsequent instructions on the same doctl page to generate an API token and grant doctl access to your DigitalOcean account.

> **NOTE** In a real production scenario, you would automate the platform management tasks using a tool like Terraform or Crossplane. That is usually the responsibility of the platform team, not of application developers, so I won't add extra complexity here by introducing yet another tool. Instead we'll use the DigitalOcean CLI directly. If you're interested in Terraform, Manning has a book in its catalog on the subject: *Terraform in Action* by Scott Winkler (Manning, 2021; https://www.manning.com/books/terraform-in-action). For Crossplane, I recommend reading chapter 4 of *Continuous Delivery for Kubernetes* by Mauricio Salatino (https://livebook.manning.com/book/continuous-delivery
-for-kubernetes/chapter-4).

B.1   *Running a Kubernetes cluster on DigitalOcean*

The first resource we need to create on DigitalOcean is a Kubernetes cluster. You could rely on the IaaS capabilities offered by the platform and install a Kubernetes cluster manually on top of virtual machines. Instead, we'll move up the abstraction staircase and go for a solution managed by the platform. When we use DigitalOcean Kubernetes (https://docs.digitalocean.com/products/kubernetes), the platform will take care of many infrastructural concerns, so that we developers can focus more on application development.

You can straightforwardly create a new Kubernetes cluster using doctl. I promised that we would deploy Polar Bookshop in a real production environment, and that's what we'll do, although I won't ask you to size and configure the cluster as I would in a real scenario.

For starters, setting up a Kubernetes cluster is not a developer's responsibility—it's a job for the platform team. Second, it would require more in-depth coverage of Kubernetes than is provided by this book to fully understand the configuration. Third, I don't want you to incur extra costs on DigitalOcean for using a lot of computational resources and services. Cost optimization is a cloud property that applies to real applications. However, it might become expensive if you're trying things out or running demo applications. Please keep an eye on your DigitalOcean account to monitor when your free trial and $100 credit expire.

Each cloud resource can be created in a data center hosted in a specific geographical region. For better performance, I recommend you choose one near to you. I'll use "Amsterdam 3" (ams3), but you can get the complete list of regions with the following command:

```
$ doctl k8s options regions
```

Let's go ahead and initialize a Kubernetes cluster using DigitalOcean Kubernetes (DOKS). It will be composed of three worker nodes, for which you can decide the technical specifications. You can choose between different options in terms of CPU, memory, and architecture. I'll use nodes with 2 vCPU and 4 GB of memory:

```
$ doctl k8s cluster create polar-cluster \                    Defines the name of
    --node-pool "name=basicnp;size=s-2vcpu-4gb;count=3;label=type=basic;" \    the cluster to create
    --region <your_region>
```

The data center region of your choice, such as "ams3"

Provides the requested specifications for the worker nodes

> **NOTE** If you'd like to know more about the different compute options and their prices, you can use the `doctl compute size list` command.

The cluster provisioning will take a few minutes. In the end, it will print out the unique ID assigned to the cluster. Take note, since you'll need it later. You can fetch the cluster ID at any time by running the following command (I have filtered the results for the sake of clarity):

```
$ doctl k8s cluster list

ID            Name            Region    Status    Node Pools
<cluster-id>  polar-cluster   ams3      running   basicnp
```

At the end of the cluster provisioning, doctl will also configure the context for your Kubernetes CLI so that you can interact with the cluster running on DigitalOcean from your computer, similar to what you've done so far with your local cluster. You can verify the current context for kubectl by running the following command:

```
$ kubectl config current-context
```

> **NOTE** If you want to change the context, you can run `kubectl config use-context <context-name>`.

Once the cluster is provisioned, you can get information about the worker nodes as follows:

```
$ kubectl get nodes

NAME       STATUS   ROLES    AGE     VERSION
<node-1>   Ready    <none>   2m34s   v1.24.3
<node-2>   Ready    <none>   2m36s   v1.24.3
<node-3>   Ready    <none>   2m26s   v1.24.3
```

Do you remember the Octant dashboard you used to visualize the workloads on your local Kubernetes cluster? You can now use it to get information about the cluster on DigitalOcean as well. Open a Terminal window and start Octant with the following command:

```
$ octant
```

Octant will open in your browser and show data from your current Kubernetes context, which should be the cluster on DigitalOcean. From the upper-right menu, you can switch between contexts from the drop-down box, as shown in figure B.1.

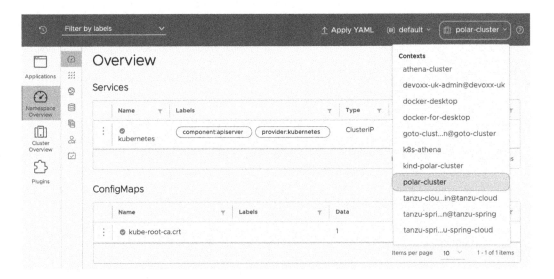

Figure B.1   Octant lets you visualize workloads from different Kubernetes clusters by switching contexts.

As I mentioned in chapter 9, Kubernetes doesn't come packaged with an Ingress Controller; it's up to you to install one. Since we'll rely on an Ingress resource to allow traffic from the public internet to the cluster, we need to install an Ingress Controller. Let's install the same one we used locally: ingress-nginx.

In your `polar-deployment` repository, create a new kubernetes/platform/production folder, and copy over the content from the Chapter15/15-end/polar-deployment/kubernetes/platform/production folder in the source code repository accompanying the book.

Then open a Terminal window, navigate to the kubernetes/platform/production/ingress-nginx folder in your polar-deployment project, and run the following command to deploy ingress-nginx to your production Kubernetes cluster:

```
$ ./deploy.sh
```

Feel free to open the file and look at the instructions before running it.

> **NOTE**   You might need to make the script executable first with the command `chmod +x deploy.sh`.

In the next section, you'll see how to initialize a PostgreSQL database on DigitalOcean.

B.2   *Running a PostgreSQL database on DigitalOcean*

In most of the book, you've been running PostgreSQL database instances as containers, both in Docker and in your local Kubernetes cluster. In production, we'd like to take advantage of the platform and use a managed PostgreSQL service provided by DigitalOcean (https://docs.digitalocean.com/products/databases/postgresql).

The applications we developed throughout the book are cloud native and follow the 15-Factor methodology. As such, they treat backing services as attached resources that can be swapped without changing anything in the application code. Furthermore, we followed the environment parity principle and used a real PostgreSQL database both for development and testing, and it's the same database we want to use in production.

Moving from a PostgreSQL container running in your local environment to a managed service with high availability, scalability, and resilience is a matter of changing the values of a few configuration properties for Spring Boot. How great is that?

First, create a new PostgreSQL server named `polar-postgres`, as shown in the following code snippet. We'll use PostgreSQL 14, which is the same version we used for development and testing. Remember to replace `<your_region>` with the geographical region you'd like to use. It should be the same as the region you used for the Kubernetes cluster. In my case, it's `ams3`:

```
$ doctl databases create polar-db \
    --engine pg \
    --region <your_region> \
    --version 14
```

The database server provisioning will take several minutes. You can verify the installation status with the following command (I have filtered the result for the sake of clarity):

```
$ doctl databases list

ID                   Name         Engine    Version    Region    Status
<polar-db-id>        polar-db     pg        14         ams3      online
```

When the database is `online`, your database server is ready. Take note of the database server ID. You'll need it later.

To mitigate unnecessary attack vectors, you can configure a firewall so that the PostgreSQL server is only accessible from the Kubernetes cluster created previously. Remember that I asked you to take notes of the resource IDs for PostgreSQL and Kubernetes? Use them in the following command to configure the firewall and secure access to the database server:

```
$ doctl databases firewalls append <postgres_id> --rule k8s:<cluster_id>
```

Next, let's create two databases to be used by Catalog Service (`polardb_catalog`) and Order Service (`polardb_order`). Remember to replace `<postgres_id>` with your PostgreSQL resource ID:

```
$ doctl databases db create <postgres_id> polardb_catalog
$ doctl databases db create <postgres_id> polardb_order
```

Finally, let's retrieve the details for connecting to PostgreSQL. Remember to replace `<postgres_id>` with your PostgreSQL resource ID:

```
$ doctl databases connection <postgres_id> --format Host,Port,User,Password

Host          Port          User          Password
<db-host>     <db-port>     <db-user>     <db-password>
```

Before concluding this section, let's create some Secrets in the Kubernetes cluster with the PostgreSQL credentials required by the two applications. In a real-world scenario, we should create dedicated users for the two applications and grant limited privileges. For simplicity, we'll use the admin account for both.

First, create a Secret for Catalog Service using the information returned by the previous `doctl` command:

```
$ kubectl create secret generic polar-postgres-catalog-credentials \
    --from-literal=spring.datasource.url=
➥jdbc:postgresql://<postgres_host>:<postgres_port>/polardb_catalog \
    --from-literal=spring.datasource.username=<postgres_username> \
    --from-literal=spring.datasource.password=<postgres_password>
```

Similarly, create a Secret for Order Service. Pay attention to the slightly different syntax required by Spring Data R2DBC for the URL:

```
$ kubectl create secret generic polar-postgres-order-credentials \
    --from-literal="spring.flyway.url=
➥jdbc:postgresql://<postgres_host>:<postgres_port>/polardb_order" \
```

```
    --from-literal="spring.r2dbc.url=
➥r2dbc:postgresql://<postgres_host>:<postgres_port>/polardb_order?
➥ssl=true&sslMode=require" \
    --from-literal=spring.r2dbc.username=<postgres_username> \
    --from-literal=spring.r2dbc.password=<postgres_password>
```

That's it for PostgreSQL. In the next section, you'll see how to initialize Redis using DigitalOcean.

B.3   Running Redis on DigitalOcean

In most of the book, you've been running Redis instances as containers, both in Docker and in your local Kubernetes cluster. In production we'd like to take advantage of the platform and use a managed Redis service provided by DigitalOcean (https://docs.digitalocean.com/products/databases/redis/).

Once again, since we followed the 15-Factor methodology, we can swap the Redis backing service used by Edge Service without changing anything in the application code. We'll only need to change a few configuration properties for Spring Boot.

First, create a new Redis server named polar-redis as shown in the following code snippet. We'll use Redis 7, which is the same version we used for development and testing. Remember to replace <your_region> with the geographical region you'd like to use. It should be the same region you used for the Kubernetes cluster. In my case, it's ams3:

```
$ doctl databases create polar-redis \
    --engine redis \
    --region <your_region> \
    --version 7
```

The Redis server provisioning will take several minutes. You can verify the installation status with the following command (I have filtered the result for the sake of clarity):

```
$ doctl databases list
```

ID	Name	Engine	Version	Region	Status
<redis-db-id>	polar-redis	redis	7	ams3	creating

When the server is online, your Redis server is ready. Take note of the Redis resource ID. You'll need it later.

To mitigate unnecessary attack vectors, we can configure a firewall so that the Redis server is only accessible from the Kubernetes cluster created previously. Remember that I asked you to take notes of the resource IDs for Redis and Kubernetes? Use them in the following command to configure the firewall and secure access to the Redis server:

```
$ doctl databases firewalls append <redis_id> --rule k8s:<cluster_id>
```

Finally, let's retrieve the details for connecting to Redis. Remember to replace `<redis_id>` with your Redis resource ID:

```
$ doctl databases connection <redis_id> --format Host,Port,User,Password

Host            Port            User            Password
<redis-host>    <redis-port>    <redis-user>    <redis-password>
```

Before concluding this section, let's create a Secret in the Kubernetes cluster with the Redis credentials required by Edge Service. In a real-world scenario, we should create a dedicated user for the application and grant limited privileges. For simplicity, we'll use the default account. Populate the Secret with the information returned by the previous `doctl` command:

```
$ kubectl create secret generic polar-redis-credentials \
    --from-literal=spring.redis.host=<redis_host> \
    --from-literal=spring.redis.port=<redis_port> \
    --from-literal=spring.redis.username=<redis_username> \
    --from-literal=spring.redis.password=<redis_password> \
    --from-literal=spring.redis.ssl=true
```

That's it for Redis. The following section will cover how to deploy RabbitMQ using a Kubernetes Operator.

B.4   *Running RabbitMQ using a Kubernetes Operator*

In the previous sections, we initialized and configured PostgreSQL and Redis servers that are offered and managed by the platform. We can't do the same for RabbitMQ because DigitalOcean doesn't have a RabbitMQ offering, similar to other cloud providers like Azure or GCP.

A popular and convenient way of deploying and managing services like RabbitMQ in a Kubernetes cluster is to use the *operator* pattern. Operators are "software extensions to Kubernetes that make use of custom resources to manage applications and their components" (https://kubernetes.io/docs/concepts/extend-kubernetes/operator).

Think about RabbitMQ. To use it in production, you'll need to configure it for high availability and resilience. Depending on the workload, you might want to scale it dynamically. When a new version of the software is available, you'll need a reliable way of upgrading the service and migrating existing constructs and data. You could perform all those tasks manually. Or you could use an Operator to capture all those operational requirements and instruct Kubernetes to take care of them automatically. In practice, an Operator is an application that runs on Kubernetes and interacts with its API to accomplish its functionality.

The RabbitMQ project provides an official Operator to run the event broker on a Kubernetes cluster (www.rabbitmq.com). I have already configured all the necessary resources to use the RabbitMQ Kubernetes Operator and prepared a script to deploy it.

Open a Terminal window, go to your Polar Deployment project (polar-deployment), and navigate to the kubernetes/platform/production/rabbitmq folder. You should have copied that folder over to your repository when configuring the Kubernetes cluster. If that's not the case, please do so now from the source code repository accompanying this book (Chapter15/15-end/polar-deployment/platform/production/rabbitmq).

Then run the following command to deploy RabbitMQ to your production Kubernetes cluster:

```
$ ./deploy.sh
```

Feel free to open the file and look at the instructions before running it.

> **NOTE** You might need to make the script executable first with the command
> chmod +x deploy.sh.

The script will output details about all the operations performed to deploy RabbitMQ. Finally, it will create a `polar-rabbitmq-credentials` Secret with the credentials that Order Service and Dispatcher Service will need to access RabbitMQ. You can verify that the Secret has been successfully created as follows:

```
$ kubectl get secrets polar-rabbitmq-credentials
```

The RabbitMQ broker is deployed in a dedicated `rabbitmq-system` namespace. Applications can interact with it at `polar-rabbitmq.rabbitmq-system.svc.cluster.local` on port 5672.

That's it for RabbitMQ. In the next section, you'll see how to deploy a Keycloak server to a production Kubernetes cluster.

B.5   Running Keycloak using a Helm chart

As with RabbitMQ, DigitalOcean doesn't provide a managed Keycloak service. The Keycloak project is working on an Operator, but it's still in beta at the time of writing, so we'll deploy it using a different approach: Helm charts.

Think of Helm as a package manager. To install software on your computer, you would use one of the operating system package managers, like apt (Ubuntu), Homebrew (macOS), or Chocolatey (Windows). In Kubernetes you can similarly use Helm, but they're called *charts* instead of *packages*.

Go ahead and install Helm on your computer. You can find the instructions on the official website (https://helm.sh). If you are on macOS or Linux, you can install Helm with Homebrew:

```
$ brew install helm
```

I have already configured all the necessary resources to use the Keycloak Helm chart provided by Bitnami (https://bitnami.com), and I've prepared a script to deploy it.

Open a Terminal window, go to your Polar Deployment project (polar-deployment), and navigate to the kubernetes/platform/production/keycloak folder. You should have copied that folder over to your repository when configuring the Kubernetes cluster. If that's not the case, please do so now from the source code repository accompanying this book (Chapter15/15-end/polar-deployment/platform/production/keycloak).

Then run the following command to deploy Keycloak to your production Kubernetes cluster:

```
$ ./deploy.sh
```

Feel free to open the file and look at the instructions before running it.

> **NOTE** You might need to make the script executable first with the command chmod +x deploy.sh.

The script will output details about all the operations performed to deploy Keycloak and print the admin username and password you can use to access the Keycloak Admin Console. Feel free to change the password after your first login. Note the credentials down, since you might need them later. The deployment can take several minutes to complete, so it's a good time to take a break and drink a beverage of your choice as a reward for everything you have accomplished so far. Good job!

Finally, the script will create a polar-keycloak-client-credentials Secret with the Client secret that Edge Service will need to authenticate with Keycloak. You can verify that the Secret has been successfully created as follows. The value is generated randomly by the script:

```
$ kubectl get secrets polar-keycloak-client-credentials
```

> **NOTE** The Keycloak Helm chart spins up a PostgreSQL instance inside the cluster and uses it to persist the data used by Keycloak. We could have integrated it with the PostgreSQL service managed by DigitalOcean, but the configuration on the Keycloak side would have been quite complicated. If you'd like to use an external PostgreSQL database, you can refer to the Keycloak Helm chart documentation (https://bitnami.com/stack/keycloak/helm).

The Keycloak server is deployed in a dedicated keycloak-system namespace. Applications can interact with it at polar-keycloak.keycloak-system.svc.cluster.local on port 8080 from within the cluster. It's also exposed outside the cluster via a public IP address. You can find the external IP address with the following command:

```
$ kubectl get service polar-keycloak -n keycloak-system
```

NAME	TYPE	CLUSTER-IP	EXTERNAL-IP
polar-keycloak	LoadBalancer	10.245.191.181	<external-ip>

The platform might take a few minutes to provision a load balancer. During the provisioning, the EXTERNAL-IP column will show a <pending> status. Wait and try again until an IP address is shown. Note it down, since we're going to use it in multiple scenarios.

Since Keycloak is exposed via a public load balancer, you can use the external IP address to access the Admin Console. Open a browser window, navigate to http://<external-ip>/admin, and log in with the credentials returned by the previous deployment script.

Now that you have a public DNS name for Keycloak, you can define a couple of Secrets to configure the Keycloak integration in Edge Service (OAuth2 Client), Catalog Service, and Order Service (OAuth2 Resource Servers). Open a Terminal window, navigate to the kubernetes/platform/production/keycloak folder in your polar-deployment project, and run the following command to create the Secrets that the applications will use to integrate with Keycloak. Feel free to open the file and look at the instructions before running it. Remember to replace <external-ip> with the external IP address assigned to your Keycloak server:

```
$ ./create-secrets.sh http://<external-ip>/realms/PolarBookshop
```

That's it for Keycloak. The following section will show you how to deploy Polar UI to the production cluster.

B.6   Running Polar UI

Polar UI is a single-page application built with Angular and served by NGINX. As you saw in chapter 11, I have already prepared a container image you can use to deploy this application, since frontend development is out of scope for this book.

Open a Terminal window, go to your Polar Deployment project (polar-deployment), and navigate to the kubernetes/platform/production/polar-ui folder. You should have copied that folder over to your repository when configuring the Kubernetes cluster. If that's not the case, please do so now from the source code repository accompanying this book (Chapter15/15-end/polar-deployment/platform/production/polar-ui).

Then run the following command to deploy Polar UI to your production Kubernetes cluster. Feel free to open the file and look at the instructions before running it:

```
$ ./deploy.sh
```

> **NOTE**   You might need to make the script executable first with the command chmod +x deploy.sh.

Now that you have Polar UI and all the main platform services up and running, you can proceed with reading chapter 15 and complete the configuration of all the Spring Boot applications in Polar Bookshop for production deployment.

B.7   *Deleting all cloud resources*

When you're done experimenting with the Polar Bookshop project, follow the instructions in this section to delete all the cloud resources created on DigitalOcean. That's fundamental to avoid incurring unexpected costs.

First, delete the Kubernetes cluster:

```
$ doctl k8s cluster delete polar-cluster
```

Next, delete the PostgreSQL and Redis databases. You'll need to know their IDs first, so run this command to extract that information:

```
$ doctl databases list

ID               Name         Engine   Version   Region   Status
<polar-db-id>    polar-db     pg       14        ams3     online
<redis-db-id>    polar-redis  redis    7         ams3     creating
```

Then go ahead and delete both of them using the resource identifiers returned by the previous command:

```
$ doctl databases delete <polar-db-id>
$ doctl databases delete <redis-db-id>
```

Finally, open a browser window, navigate to the DigitalOcean web interface (https:// cloud.digitalocean.com), and go through the different categories of cloud resources in your account to verify that there's no outstanding services. If there are, delete them. There could be load balancers or persistent volumes created as a side effect of creating a cluster or a database, and that may not have been deleted by the previous commands.

index

RELATED MANNING TITLES

Spring in Action, Sixth Edition
by Craig Walls

ISBN 9781617297571
520 pages, $59.99
January 2022

Kubernetes for Developers
by William Denniss

ISBN 9781617297175
265 pages (estimated), $49.99
Spring 2023 (estimated)

*Java Persistence with Spring Data
and Hibernate*
by Cătălin Tudose

ISBN 9781617299186
562 pages (estimated), $59.99
December 2022 (estimated)

*Amazon Web Services in Action,
Third Edition*
by Andreas Wittig and Michael Wittig

ISBN 9781633439160
500 pages (estimated), $59.99
Spring 2023 (estimated)

For ordering information go to www.manning.com